Comparative Perspectives
on History and Historians

Bryce Lyon, mid-1960s. Photo courtesy of the Lyon family.

Medieval Institute Publications is a program of
The Medieval Institute, College of Arts and Sciences

 WESTERN MICHIGAN UNIVERSITY

Comparative Perspectives on History and Historians

Essays in Memory of Bryce Lyon (1920–2007)

Edited by David Nicholas, Bernard S. Bachrach,
and James M. Murray

MEDIEVAL INSTITUTE PUBLICATIONS
Western Michigan University
Kalamazoo

Library of Congress Cataloging-in-Publication Data

Comparative perspectives on history and historians : essays in memory of Bryce
Lyon (1920-2007) / edited by David Nicholas, Bernard S. Bachrach, and James
M. Murray.
   p. cm.
 Includes bibliographical references and index.
 ISBN 978-1-58044-168-1 (clothbound : alk. paper)
 1. Middle Ages--Historiography. 2. Civilization, Medieval. 3. Economic
history--Medieval, 500-1500. 4. Constitutional history, Medieval. 5. Law,
Medieval. 6. Pirenne, Henri, 1862-1935. I. Lyon, Bryce Dale, 1920- II.
Nicholas, David, 1939- III. Bachrach, Bernard S., 1939- IV. Murray, James M.,
1954-
 D116.C54 2012
 940.1072--dc23

                    2012006071

Contents

Bryce Lyon: In Memoriam

David Nicholas, Bernard S. Bachrach, and James M. Murray

B RYCE LYON DIED in Hanover, New Hampshire, on May 24, 2007. Born on
April 22, 1920 in Bellevue, Ohio, he graduated from Baldwin-Wallace College
in 1942. After two years of service with the United States Air Force as a crypto-
graphic security officer, he matriculated at Cornell University, where he received a
PhD in 1949. He was Assistant Professor of History at the University of Colorado
at Boulder (1949–51) and at Harvard University (1951–56), Associate Professor
at the University of Illinois (1956–59), and Professor of History at the University
of California at Berkeley (1959–65). He occupied the Barnaby C. and Mary
Critchfield Keeney Professorship of History at Brown University from 1965 until
his retirement in 1986, an occasion celebrated belatedly by the publication of
fifteen papers by former students and professional friends under the title *Law,
Custom, and the Social Fabric in Medieval Europe: Essays in Honor of Bryce Lyon*
(Medieval Institute Publications, 1990). He received honorary degrees of Doctor
of Pedagogy from Baldwin-Wallace College in 1971 and of Doctor Honoris
Causa in de Letteren en Wijsbegeerte from the University of Ghent in 1988. A
fellow of the Medieval Academy of America since 1972, he was also a Fellow of
the American Academy of Arts and Sciences, the Royal Historical Society, and
Associate Member of the Royal Academy of Sciences of Belgium. In 2005 he
established the Bryce and Mary Lyon Prize at the Belgian Royal Commission of
History (Brussels) to recognize the researcher under age thirty whose work was
included in the commission's collections during the previous year.

Continuing his research and writing into an extraordinarily active retirement, Bryce Lyon was the author of five scholarly monographs, five volumes

Reprinted from *Speculum* 84 (2009): 834–36, with the permission of the Medieval Academy of
America.

of edited original records, five short works of general and pedagogical interest, coauthor of three textbooks, and author of fifty-two articles and several introductions to reprinted or newly translated monographs. Although his publications encompassed topics from mentalities to military logistics, he was primarily interested in institutional history and in the linked histories of England and the Low Countries. Lyon's doctoral thesis concerned the use of the money fief by the English kings. So many of these were given to Low Country princes in the interest of furthering English diplomacy in that region that the natural next step was to expand his study to the Continent. This research produced *From Fief to Indenture: The Transition from Feudal to Non-feudal Contract in Western Europe* (Harvard University Press, 1957), a work whose conclusions have never been questioned seriously. Although Lyon always insisted that feudalism was a useful historical construct, his work perhaps subconsciously undercut its premise in showing fundamental alterations toward contractual forms that in no sense could be considered "feudal." Feudal relations also provided him with insight into the diplomacy of the English Crown with the Low Countries that eventuated in several other books and articles.

Lyon's *A Constitutional and Legal History of Medieval England* (Harper and Row, 1960; W. W. Norton, 1980) was a landmark. Conceived in the tradition of F. W. Maitland, whose work Lyon greatly admired, it signaled a turn of English constitutional scholars away from political theory and toward public administration. Lyon was ever-practical, and for him the interesting features of government were those that made it work and brought it in to the lives of subjects. Yet *A Constitutional and Legal History* was also a turning point in his intellectual orientation. *From Fief to Indenture* had turned his attention to the Low Countries, and most of what he wrote on English history and diplomacy thereafter also concerned the Netherlands. The Low Countries, particularly Flanders, became the dominant strain in Lyon's work and historical thought between the publication of *A Constitutional and Legal History* and the articles that he wrote in retirement. Lyon's mentor at Cornell, Carl Stephenson, had studied with Henri Pirenne at the University of Ghent and introduced him to the scholarship and theories of his revered master. As Lyon became acquainted with Pirenne's successors at the University of Ghent, notably F. L. Ganshof and Hans Van Werveke, and in turn their successors and his own contemporaries, R. C. Van Caenegem and Adriaan Verhulst, he came to see Flanders as a paradigm of the transition from an essentially agricultural to an urban, commercial, and capitalistic economic environment. Realizing the importance of the Carolingian period as the genesis of changes that had an impact for centuries afterward, he and his wife, Mary, published translations of several of Ganshof's most important essays in *Frankish Institutions under Charlemagne* (Brown University Press, 1967).

Lyon's fascination with comparative history on both the local and regional scale produced a major collaborative work with Verhulst: *Medieval Finance: A Comparative Study of Financial Institutions in Northwestern Europe* (Brown University Press, 1967). It also led him to promote works of Pirenne's contemporaries that were less known in the English-speaking world. Lyon had reservations about the collective mentalities approach of the Annales school of history that Marc Bloch had largely founded, and he considered Bloch's *Feudal Society* imprecise and not his best work. Yet he admired Bloch's local studies and supervised a translation of his *French Rural History: An Essay on Its Basic Characteristics* (University of California Press, 1966). Lyon's approach to comparative history was always firmly institutional but in the broad sense of that term: the most accurate expressions of a group's identity are the governmental institutions that it creates to regulate interpersonal relations and the economic institutions that provide the framework within which people make their livings and obtain goods and services. He was somewhat impatient with theory until his last years, when he published works on Johan Huizinga and Bloch that were more interdisciplinary and concerned with the history of ideas and the nature of history.

Lyon's study of Pirenne's environment and his undisguised admiration of the scholarship and intellectual vitality of his great contemporaries produced editions of Pirenne's correspondence with Bloch and Karl Lamprecht and a major article on Maurice Prou's ties with Pirenne. His affinity for Pirenne's grand syntheses and his workaholic personality culminated in *Henri Pirenne: A Biographical and Intellectual Study* (E. Story-Scientia, 1974). Yet for all his admiration of Pirenne, Lyon's mind-set was quite different and original. While Pirenne's work concentrated on the cities and emphasized systems and saw the historical process in terms of great caesuras, Lyon's focused more on political institutions and on comparison and continuity, similarities across different times and places. While Pirenne's "grand ideas" involved the towns as a catalyst of economic and material advance, Lyon's leitmotiv was constitutionalism.

Lyon's edition of *The Wardrobe Book of William de Norwell, 12 July 1338 to 27 May 1340* (Commission royale d'histoire, 1983) was unquestionably his most important contribution after the Pirenne biography. Building on a partial transcription begun by Henry S. Lucas, Lyon and his wife began work in the early 1960s, while his focus was still as much English constitutional as Low Country history, although it was published much later. The record itself is invaluable for the history of English diplomacy and logistics in the early stages of the Hundred Years' War, and Lyon's masterly introduction, really a short monograph, is of independent value as the most detailed description of the evolution and function of any department of medieval household government. Many of his late works show a growing interest in military history that stemmed from his work with the Wardrobe records. Only three years before his demise he published a comparative edition, *The Wardrobe Book of 1296–1297: A Financial and Logistical Record of Edward I's 1297 Autumn Campaign in Flanders against Philip IV of France* (Commission royale d'histoire, 2004). One signer of this memoir remembers working in 1963 with photocopies of this document in Lyon's paleography seminar. Only death could stop his mind or stanch his energy.

Bryce Lyon's name was not the first on the title page of *The Wardrobe Book of William de Norwell*. On 6 June 1944 he married Mary Elizabeth Lewis, a classics major whom he had met when both were undergraduates at Baldwin-Wallace. Thus began a beautiful personal and professional partnership that was sadly terminated by Mary's death on 24 June 2002. A privately outspoken woman who preferred to remain in her husband's shadow publicly, she was an invaluable sounding board, critic, and helpmate. They were rarely apart geographically and never emotionally. She eventually yielded to his insistence that her name be included with his on several articles beginning in 1965 and most importantly the edition of the Wardrobe Account. Bryce's pride in and respect for Mary were apparent to anyone who ever met him. It is impossible to conceive of his career without the encouragement and intellectual stimulation that she provided. Both their children (Geoffrey, an attorney with Judicial Watch, and Jacqueline, a radiation oncologist) survive them.

Bryce Lyon was not an easy man to know well. He was devoted to inquiry and spared no effort in pursuit of scholarship. Possessed of a vigorous, clear prose style, he loved to write. He was driven to achieve, and he expected no less of his students. He conveyed to them an interest in broad questions of human history, an intellectual curiosity to ascertain why exact contemporaries might structure their lives and political frameworks completely differently. He read widely and fostered links with disciplines related to history, particularly art history. Yet he always understood that theories encompassing a myriad of cases are only as valid as the individual examples from which the broad picture was extrapolated. His students have written both micro- and macro-historical studies, on topics ranging from feudalism to comparative urbanization to early medieval military practice to attitudes toward pain in the Middle Ages. Their intellectual linchpin is the scholarship, pedagogy, dynamism, and integrity of Bryce Lyon.

Bryce Lyon: A Personal Memoir

R. C. Van Caenegem

W HEN I WAS INVITED as Bryce Lyon's very old friend to contribute something personal to this Denkschrift, I gladly accepted: not only in order to take part in an homage to an eminent medievalist but also because it led me to reflect on the many years I admired his work and enjoyed his company and entertaining letters.

Bryce Lyon as a Medievalist

Bryce Lyon was a true medievalist. He had a great feeling for and a profound knowledge of the dramas and achievements of Europe's past, which in many ways was also that of his own fatherland. Bryce was an *érudit*, familiar with the published and unpublished sources and equipped with the techniques and the languages—Latin, German, French, Dutch—that gave him access to international scholarship. His interest in the *ipsissima verba* of medieval people led him to publish, with the help of his devoted wife, Mary, several editions of medieval texts in the series of the Belgian Koninklijke Commissie voor Geschiedenis (Commission royale d'histoire), which will be discussed by Professor Prevenier. Bryce's knowledge of every aspect of the medieval world—political, economic, and cultural—led him to publish general textbooks of great merit. His original contributions concerned constitutional and feudal law. His work on the money fief and his analysis of the evolution from fief to indenture being "the transition from feudal to non-feudal contract in Western Europe"[1] signaled a legal historian in the prestigious tradition of the *Staats- und Rechtsgeschichte*.

---

[1] Lyon, *From Fief to Indenture*.

He always took care, however, to see the technicalities of the law in their wider historical context and was critical of historians who failed to do so. I refer here to the concluding words of his review of S. F. C. Milsom's *Legal Framework of English Feudalism*, where he writes that Milsom "fails to make the connections so essential between the world of courts and law and that of social, economic and political man," so that "cases, procedures, and remedies seem suspended in the sky with no ties to historical reality."[2] In this perspective I also refer to Bryce's foreword to F. L. Ganshof's *Frankish Institutions under Charlemagne:*[3] in a dozen pages that are striking by their wide sweep, eloquence, and elegant style, he placed Ganshof's technical pages on political, military, and administrative institutions against the background of the historic and the mythical figure of Charlemagne.

Bryce realized the importance of constitutional law for the peaceful development of society. In this field he published several inspiring articles on points of detail and one comprehensive book devoted to medieval England. It is not surprising that Bryce could not resist studying that primordial constitutional text, the Magna Carta Libertatum of 1215. In 1951 he published a thoughtful article posing the question of why modern lawyers, starting with Sir Edward Coke and reaching a climax with the Victorians, persistently read much more into the Great Charter than the text and the reality of 1215 warranted, even after "certain iconoclastic historians" had exposed the myth of Magna Carta.[4] He showed that political expediency is to blame. Coke, as Bryce put it, "was not always attempting to find the truth in the sources. Why should he? He was using them in his fight with James I and Charles I. It was Coke . . . against the defenders of the royal prerogative." History the *ancilla* of politics! Somewhat in the same vein, in his article on Henry II, Bryce looked at another Victorian construct.[5] Here he portrays the "father of the common law" not as "an institution" but as a typical fighting and hunting man of his class and century. The article also explained Bryce's fascination with the Middle Ages "because of the recognition that in the medieval past lay the secrets to national institutions and culture and, above all, the secret to Western civilisation."

Bryce was not only the author of learned articles destined for his fellow scholars. He was also a teacher, who wrote textbooks for his students.[6] The fruits of his interest in English legal history were summarized in his *Constitutional and Legal History of Medieval England*, which betrayed his mastery of the subject and his pedagogical gift for clarity and selection of the main lines of development. His

[2] Lyon, "Emancipation of Land Law," p. 787.
[3] Ganshof, *Frankish Institutions.*
[4] Lyon, "Lawyer and Magna Carta," p. 18.
[5] Lyon, "Henry II."
[6] Lyon and Stephenson, *Medieval History.*

edition and revision of Carl Stephenson's textbook had an even wider scope, as it dealt with Europe from the second to the sixteenth century. Among many other virtues this book betrays the broad view and the healthy skepticism of the authors concerning historical periodization. I cannot refrain from quoting the concluding remarks, where the authors rightly point out the relative value of the traditional caesura around AD 1500: "Without serious distortion of the truth the Protestant Revolution might be called a chapter in the history of medieval religion, the opening of the New World a chapter in the history of medieval commerce."[7]

Bryce Lyon as Historian of Historiography

Bryce was fascinated by the lives and thought-processes of leading historians, some of whose correspondence he carefully edited. His main contribution to *Gelehrtengeschichte*, however, was his biography of Henri Pirenne, published in 1974 after ten years of assiduous research.[8] This massive book was based on Pirenne's publications, but also on extensive unprinted materials, such as lecture notes and letters, conserved in various archives, libraries, and private collections in Belgium and elsewhere. As a detailed chronological account of the historian's life and academic achievement it has never been replaced. It was a remarkable achievement for a twentieth-century American scholar to familiarize himself so thoroughly with the personality and social environment of an *érudit* whose roots lay in nineteenth-century Europe and with his very complex native country. For years to come people will turn to this book to find out how university professors—at that time influential citizens—lived and worked: a precious contribution to social history.

Biography is a genre with many pitfalls. Some authors delight their readers with facetious debunking stories, such as in Lytton Strachey's *Eminent Victorians*. More often the biographer identifies himself so much with his admirable subject that the danger of hagiography lurks around the corner. Bryce Lyon's book is not uncritical. In his remarks on Pirenne's *Mahomet et Charlemagne* he admitted that Pirenne "obviously overemphasized Merovingian economic activity" and "may have underemphasized Carolingian economic activity."[9] He also spoke of Pirenne's "overemphasis regarding the continuity of Roman institutions" and wrote that his thesis "generalizes at times upon evidence too scant and cryptic."[10] Bryce also admitted that Pirenne wrote from a pro-Belgian political perspective, which "occasionally blurred his vision of Belgian history, causing him to force some points, gloss over others, and stretch still others."[11]

[7] Lyon and Stephenson, *Medieval History*, p. 575.
[8] Lyon, *Henri Pirenne*.
[9] Lyon, *Henri Pirenne*, p. 452.
[10] Lyon, "Reply," p. 21.
[11] Lyon, "Reply," p. 14.

Nonetheless, Bryce greatly admired his subject and felt personally very close to him. It was therefore not surprising that when the late professor Jan Dhondt in 1966 "assailed" Pirenne, Bryce published the reply I just quoted in unusually sharp tones. Lyon's Pirenne story is more descriptive than analytical and presents no profound philosophical insights, which is in character with the realistic close-to-the-sources attitude of both Pirenne and his biographer. It nevertheless must rank as one of the American medievalist's main contributions to medieval studies.

Perhaps reflecting his own dynamism and positive attitude to life, Bryce Lyon stressed Pirenne's optimism and self-confidence. But for all his successes, the great medievalist was in many ways a tragic figure. In addition to his personal tragedies—the loss of three sons and a beloved pupil—Pirenne suffered painful political and ideological disappointments. His nineteenth-century belief in progress and European peace was rudely shattered by the First World War, as was his admiration for Germany, where he had made good friends and where his *Geschichte Belgiens* was published. He witnessed the decline of the Liberal Party, whose staunch supporter his father had been, and its descent to third place, behind the Catholic and the Socialist Parties. As a scion of the affluent bourgeois elite, he had no sympathy for the democratic mass-parties after 1918, let alone for Fascism and Nazism, which he observed with dismay. The decline of France and the French language in the wider world was another disillusionment he had to endure, as was the onslaught on the French-dominated unitary kingdom of Belgium, in which he passionately believed. Some readers of Bryce Lyon's biography of Pirenne will feel that this aspect of the latter's life was underexposed.

The same can be said of the paradoxes in the great historian's life. Was it not paradoxical that the author of *Les anciennes démocraties des Pays-Bas* and sincere admirer of medieval urban democracy had so little sympathy for the democratic currents in his own time? Another paradox was that Pirenne, who had extolled the glories of the Flemish past and by so doing inspired the nineteenth-century Flemish movement, opposed the introduction of the cultural language of Flanders, which it shared with Holland, in the University of Ghent. Pirenne understood the Flemish complaints, as Bryce Lyon clearly demonstrates, and yet "he strongly opposed the movement to make Ghent into an exclusively Flemish university."[12] Pirenne's biographer fails to explain this amazing attitude, as it was obviously unjust and undemocratic to deny Flemish youth the right to study in their own language in their own country.

That Pirenne opposed German general von Bissing's Flemish university was understandable enough, and his attitude was shared by the vast majority of the Flemish population, who rejected a measure imposed by a foreign invader

[12] Lyon, *Henri Pirenne*, pp. 78–79, 284.

(they must have paraphrased Homer and said "timeo Germanos et dona feren-
tes"). Even when the freely elected Belgian parliament was about to establish the
Dutch-language University of Ghent, Pirenne still objected. As Bryce put it, in
1926 he knew that "it was inevitable that the Belgian parliament would soon pass
legislation transforming Ghent into a Flemish university with all instruction to
be in Dutch" and Bryce added that Pirenne "believed that such a linguistic regime
was arbitrary and detrimental to the best educational and cultural interests of
Ghent and Belgium." Pirenne preferred a bilingual university in Ghent, but this
was politically unacceptable, for there would have been separate classes for the old
bourgeois elite and the ordinary people. It also would have been discriminatory,
as it was obvious that "the university of Liège, for example, would never become
bilingual."

Did Pirenne not see that Belgian unity, to which he was so attached, could
not survive while anti-Flemish discrimination and the nineteenth-century power
structures were maintained? Did he not realize that teaching in Dutch would not
prevent the staff of the university publishing their scholarly work in internation-
ally known languages? Pirenne, as Bryce put it, "simply could not fathom why
the Flemish were prepared to cut off a distinguished university community from
the international language of French and the great culture associated with it." It
was the medium, so Pirenne felt, which "remained the universal language of cul-
tured men," and yet the Flemings preferred to speak their own language! These
are some of the questions that Bryce could have probed into more deeply, and it
would have been interesting to know what he himself thought of it all, but in his
book he tended to mirror the opinions and sentiments of his subject, even though
he acknowledged "the long discrimination of the Walloons against the Flemish
and the record of French political, cultural, social and economic domination and
exploitation."[13]

Bryce Lyon as a Friend of Belgium

Bryce the historian was interested in Belgian history and worked in the archives
there. He had a good command of French and a reading knowledge of Dutch.
One of his earliest articles concerned aspects of English and Belgian law.[14] It was,
of course, above all his fascination with Henri Pirenne that linked him to Belgium,
but he also made numerous and lasting friendships there ever since his first stay
in 1951–52. I mention Carlos Wyffels, whom he first met in 1952 and to whom
he devoted a moving memoir in *Speculum*, and the Pirenne family. He was also
on terms of friendship with Professor François-Louis Ganshof, whom he invited,

---

[13] Lyon, *Henri Pirenne*, pp. 349, 340, 239, 213.
[14] Lyon, "Fact and Fiction."

with his wife, to Berkeley, where they enjoyed numerous lively talks. Bryce and Mary invited the Ganshofs to tea at the Auberge du Pêcheur in Deurle, where in 1973 they spent an enchanting month of September, walking and bicycling. Bryce kept some 145 letters from Ganshof spanning a period from the early 1950s to about 1980. Bryce and Mary were also friendly with Professor Marcel Storme and his wife, in whose house in Ghent they lived for some time. They were wonderful hosts to my wife and me and our three children in their charming house in East Alstead (New Hampshire), where we stayed together with their other Belgian friends, Dr. Henri Van Houtte and his wife and their three children. Bryce and Mary knew how to spoil their friends! Bryce's life-long collaboration with the Royal Historical Commission in Brussels constituted, of course, another link with Belgium, as did his friendship with its secretary, Jean-Luc De Paepe.

Bryce had close links with the Faculty of Letters of the University of Ghent, where he gave some brilliant guest lectures and where he made many friends, such as Professors Walter Prevenier, Ludo Milis, and Marc Boone and particularly Professor Adriaan Verhulst, with whom he wrote a comparative study on the financial institutions of northwestern Europe in the Middle Ages.[15] It was on the proposal of that faculty that Bryce was given an honorary doctorate by the University of Ghent, on which occasion Professor Verhulst had the pleasure of pronouncing Bryce's *laudatio*. Bryce was a great fan of the Maatschappij voor Geschiedenis en Oudheidkunde te Gent, the local Ghent Historical Society, in whose *Handelingen* he wrote and which he supported financially with generous contributions.

The most exciting moment in Bryce and Mary's long love affair with Belgium was their private audience with King Baudouin, who took great interest in Bryce's biography of Henri Pirenne, who had been his father's teacher. Bryce and Mary traveled widely in Europe. Besides Belgium they very much liked Italy and particularly France, where they made boat trips on canals and where Bryce made a special study of the *villages perchés* in Provence. They loved conversations with ordinary French people, but also had an admiring eye for the great cathedrals. Thus, after I told him about a conference in Toulouse where I gave a paper, Bryce wrote about that city: "I viewed it first in 1952 and then some years later with Mary. I sat and sat looking at that magnificent Romanesque cathedral with its superb barrel vaults."[16]

Bryce the Critical Patriot

Bryce loved his fatherland even though, on a bad day, he spoke of it as "my crass, materialistic country"[17] and could be critical of its government. As a young man

---

[15] Lyon and Verhulst, *Medieval Finance*.

[16] Letter of Bryce Lyon to the author, August 18, 2005.

[17] Letter of Bryce Lyon to the author, May 2, 2005.

he served in the US forces in the Pacific against Japan and in 1963, at the time of the Cuba crisis, when he and Mary were living in Brussels, he was constantly in touch with the American embassy and ready to fly home if something dramatic should happen and he was called up. My wife and I vividly remember the occasion, since on that particular evening we were dining with them in the Belgian capital. Bryce knew and admired the US Constitution and explained its idiosyncrasies with great patience and clarity to his European colleagues. He made illuminating comparisons between the checks and balances in the American and some medieval constitutions, which also knew the tug of war between head of state and parliament.

Bryce as a Warm Human Being

Bryce Lyon had an extrovert character and a most engaging personality. He made friends wherever he went and added personal to scholarly contacts. When he worked in the archives in Ghent he and Dr. Carlos Wyffels went to the pub for a pint and a talk. Bryce inspired confidence because he combined efficiency with friendliness, which is why he got on so well with the Pirenne family, especially Count Jacques Pirenne, and was given the voluminous correspondence of the great historian to peruse at leisure.

Bryce also was tenacious in tracing documents and had the luck he deserved. I remember him telling me of the discovery of some eight hundred letters of Henri Pirenne to Maurice Prou which were hidden behind rows of books in the Municipal Library of Sens, even though the librarian maintained there was nothing there of the famous professor in the École des Chartes. Bryce, always helped and encouraged by Mary, was not discouraged and eventually discovered what he was looking for.

Bryce's letters were full of irony. On October 21, 2006, for example, he wrote: "I am told that von Ranke was still at his desk at the age of 90. I'll wager he was mostly napping." His interest in scholarship continued unabated until the end, but he was sadly affected by Mary's death in 2002. On August 18, 2005, complaining that life in solitude was becoming monotonous, he said: "I surely am no St. Jerome who loved his cave for a year."[18]

Bryce was a wonderful family man, devoted to his learned and warmhearted wife, Mary, and to his two children, Geoffrey, who became a successful lawyer in Washington, and Jackie, the medical doctor who lovingly looked after her parents during their illnesses.

---

[18] Letters of Bryce Lyon to the author.

Bibliography

Ganshof, François L. *Frankish Institutions under Charlemagne.* Trans. Bryce Lyon and Mary Lyon, with an introduction by Bryce Lyon. Providence, RI: Brown University Press, 1968.

Lyon, Bryce. *A Constitutional and Legal History of Medieval England.* 2nd ed. New York: W. W. Norton, 1980.

————. "The Emancipation of Land Law from Feudal Custom." *Yale Law Journal* 82 (1977): 782–87.

————. "Fact and Fiction in English and Belgian Constitutional Law." *Mediaevalia et Humanistica* 10 (1956): 82–101.

————. *From Fief to Indenture: The Transition from Feudal to Non-feudal Contract in Western Europe.* Cambridge, MA: Harvard University Press, 1957.

————. *Henri Pirenne: A Biographical and Intellectual Study.* Ghent: E. Story-Scientia, 1974.

————. "Henry II: A Non-Victorian Interpretation." In *Documenting the Past: Essays in Medieval History Presented to George Peddy Cuttino,* ed. J. S. Hamilton and Patricia J. Bradley, pp. 22–31. Woodbridge: Boydell and Brewer, 1989.

————. "The Lawyer and Magna Carta." *Rocky Mountain Law Review* 23 (1951): 416–33.

————. "A Reply to Jan Dhondt's Critique of Henri Pirenne." *Handelingen der Maatschappij voor Geschiedenis en Oudheidkunde te Gent,* n.s., 29 (1975): 1–25.

Lyon, Bryce, and Carl Stephenson. *Mediaeval History: Europe from the Second to the Sixteenth Century.* 4th ed. New York: Harper and Row, 1962.

Lyon, Bryce D., and Adriaan Verhulst. *Medieval Finance: A Comparison of Financial Institutions in Northwestern Europe.* Rijksuniversiteit te Gent: Werken uitgegeven door de Faculteit van de Letteren en Wijsbegeerte 143. Bruges: De Tempel; Providence, RI: Brown University Press, 1967.

Bryce Lyon and the Royal Historical Commission of Belgium

Walter Prevenier

M Y TASK for this commemoration of Professor Bryce D. Lyon is to report, as a former general secretary, on the role of this American scholar in the Royal Historical Commission of Belgium (Koninklijke Commissie voor Geschiedenis, Commission royale d'histoire), of which he was one of the most prominent correspondents. If there is any single explanation for the ambition of Bryce Lyon as a magnificent and expert editor of medieval texts, it is marriage. Bryce's spouse, Mary Lyon, was a scholar in classical studies and as such the perfect companion for his conviction of the usefulness of critical text editions. His second source of inspiration was professor Carl Stephenson.[1] Bryce Lyon was a student of Stephenson at Cornell University, who influenced his young graduate student at least in three ways. As a former student of Pirenne in Ghent, in 1924–25, Stephenson introduced Lyon to Pirenne's writings and his manner of seminar teaching.[2] Secondly, he immersed his student in the study of medieval financial history. Finally, Stephenson told Bryce that he had experienced Pirenne in Ghent not only as a master of broad synthesis, but also as an outstanding erudite, fascinated by the importance of critical text edition as a first and crucial step to real knowledge of the past.[3]

I had the good luck to sit several times in the front row to observe Bryce Lyon's various talents. Just like Raoul Van Caenegem I saw him in action as a guest teacher for our Ghent students: his warm and sonorous voice, his emphasis of the

---

[1] On the link with Carl Stephenson, see Lyon, *Henri Pirenne*, pp. xiii–xiv, 300, 338.

[2] I refer to a few studies on Pirenne published since Lyon's biography: Despy and Verhulst, *La fortune*; Bierlaire and Kupper, *Henri Pirenne*; Violante, *La fine*; Schöttler, "Henri Pirenne"; Boone, "Henri Pirenne"; Prevenier, "Henri Pirenne."

[3] On the impact of Pirenne on his American students and scholars, see Boyce, "Legacy."

13

essential lines, his love for sensitive one-liners, all of that was close to the habits of the Pirenne that Ganshof and my other Ghent teachers so often pictured.[4] As a secretary of the Royal Commission of History I also saw the other side of the coin, also very Pirennean: Lyon as a scrupulous text editor, wrestling with the many questions that critical editions pose. Bryce had a perfect understanding of the underlying philosophy behind the sophisticated edition rules of the Belgian commission, so that in the heated discussions of technical remarks by the four readers of the commission, he most often won. He had a strong ally in Mary Lyon, for whom, as a philologist, Latin had no secrets. My favorite memories include the many meetings that my wife and I enjoyed from the late 1970s until recently with the Lyons in Brussels, Ghent, and Sint-Martens-Latem, and even more our encounters in marvelous American places, such as Providence, Hilton Head, and Hanover, New Hampshire, which were always filled with wonderful anecdotes about common friends. These brief encounters were always extremely cheerful: the Lyons were perfect hosts, with a great sense for the enjoyable *choses de la vie*, filled with wines, literature, art, and history. But I also recall that I never escaped their incredible professionalism. None of the otherwise very social evenings could end without forcing me to give my opinion on how to streamline the next index, how to justify in the forthcoming text edition the solution of an abbreviation of an unknown family or place name.

Bryce's first sojourns in Belgium in 1951–52 were linked to his research on the transition from feudal to non-feudal contracts in England and the Low Countries during the late Middle Ages.[5] This topic greatly interested Jean de Sturler, professor at the University of Brussels and a member of the Royal Commission of History.[6] De Sturler invited Bryce to publish his first text edition in the *Bulletin* of the commission in 1955, an account of the Exchequer of King Edward I, which reveals some crucial links between England and Brabant.[7] During the successive Belgian stays Lyon's earlier fascination for Pirenne got a new incentive through his friendship with François L. Ganshof of the University of Ghent, Hans Van Werveke, and later with the younger generation of Ghent medievalists. It led to systematic archival research for Lyon's authoritative biography on Pirenne of 1974.[8] That project became the genesis for most of his text editions through the Belgian commission. First, in 1966 he published the correspondence of Henri Pirenne with Karl Lamprecht.[9] An even more impressive

---

[4] Ganshof, "Pirenne."

[5] Published as Lyon, *From Fief to Indenture.*

[6] See the statement in the edition of Lyon et al., *Wardrobe Book of William de Norwell*, p. viii.

[7] Lyon, "Un compte de l'échiquier."

[8] Lyon, *Henri Pirenne.* Note also Lyon, "Henri Pirenne: *Connu* or *inconnu?*"

[9] Lyon, "Letters." In 1972 Hans Van Werveke edited a few more letters: Van Werveke, "Karl Lamprecht et Henri Pirenne."

edition is a book of the letters to Pirenne from Marc Bloch and Lucien Febvre, between 1921 and 1935, when Pirenne died, that includes a long and penetrating introduction.[10] The Bloch-Febvre letters brought an excellent and original view on the early history of the influential French review *Annales: Économies, sociétés, civilisations* and a significant insight into the way historians of the early twentieth century communicated and influenced each other. The third publication, of the scholarly notes of Pirenne as a war prisoner in Germany from 1916 to 1918, was no less spectacular.[11] These notes revealed many unknown facets of Pirenne's personality, particularly his early fascination with sociology and anthropology. They also formed some of Pirenne's early reflections on issues treated in two later, major works, *Mahomet et Charlemagne* and *Histoire de l'Europe*.[12] One more text edition of the Lyons on Pirenne, but not published by the Belgian Commission, is Pirenne's war diary covering 1914–18.[13]

Bryce's other early interest, the financial records of the English kings, never waned after the first publication in 1955. Bryce and Mary Lyon published two editions of account books of the English Wardrobe. The first was the record of William de Norwell, royal keeper of the Wardrobe, which details English military logistics in the Low Countries from 1338 to 1340.[14] Its fascinating information includes military expenses, wages, horses, and ships, as well as gifts (money and jewels) to and from Continental allies, merchants, and bankers. Bryce's introduction relates the historical *fortuna*, the Pirennean *hasard*, leading to the edition: in 1951–52, while working in the Belgian archives, Bryce had the good fortune to meet Henry S. Lucas, a specialist in the history of the Netherlands, who told him what a wonderful source this Wardrobe Book was. When Lucas died in 1961, he had transcribed half of the 362 folios of the manuscript. After a talk with Jean de Sturler and a visit to Lucas's widow, who gave them the unfinished transcription, Bryce and Mary were invited by de Sturler to publish it through the Belgian commission. A second Wardrobe Book edition concerned the campaign of King Edward I in Flanders against King Philip IV of France in 1297.[15] It is a goldmine of military information on the nine thousand soldiers and the 273 ships in the operation, but no less for diplomatic activities and the purchase of political support on the Continent. Later Bryce and Mary edited another much shorter account, by the clerk Robert de Segre, of the campaign of the English

---

[10] Lyon, *Birth of Annales*.

[11] Lyon, "Réflexions d'un solitaire."

[12] Soon after he returned from Germany Pirenne published his first article on these "reflexions": Pirenne, "Mahomet et Charlemagne."

[13] Lyon, *Journal de Guerre*.

[14] Lyon et al., *Wardrobe Book of William de Norwell*.

[15] Lyon, *Wardrobe Book of 1296–1297*.

army against the French King in Flanders and Brabant in 1297. It gives fascinating information on the residence of the English king at the courts of the count of Flanders in Ghent and Bruges and on the salaries of Flemish workers hired by the royal army.[16]

Over the years the Lyons developed exceptional friendships with the Royal Commission of History and several of its members, especially Carlos Wyffels, with whom Bryce discovered good Belgian beers and many archival treasures;[17] Raoul Van Caenegem, who wrote a poignant memoir on Bryce as a member of the Royal Flemish Academy of Belgium;[18] and Adriaan Verhulst, with whom he wrote an erudite comparative study on financial institutions in England and the Low Countries.[19] In 2007 the commission initiated a new type of text editions, memoirs and testimonials on important people. Bryce Lyon opened the series with his personal memories of François-Louis Ganshof.[20] Altogether Bryce was an assiduous collaborator of the commission for fifty-two years.

In his capacity as text editor Bryce Lyon entrusted the commission with an endowment to be used for a yearly award, but of course without any suggestion on the name of the prize. In its session of June 26, 2004, the commission accepted this proposal and created a prize for young text editors, agreeing unanimously to call it the Bryce and Mary Lyon Prize.[21] The prize is given every two years, for the first time in December 2005.[22] The prize is intended to encourage the publication of scientific texts. It is awarded to the youngest author, aged thirty at most, whose works were published in the two previous years in either the *Bulletin* or another of the commission's collections. Although the republic of letters is universal and knows no frontiers, the prize will certainly keep the memory alive of the remarkable familiarity with Belgium of two marvelously erudite scholars: Bryce and Mary Lyon.

Bibliography

Bierlaire, Franz, and Jean-Louis Kupper, eds. *Henri Pirenne de la cité de Liège à la ville de Gand: Actes du colloque organisé à l'Université de Liège le 13 décembre 1985*. Liège: Université de Liège, 1987.

---

[16] Lyon, "Account."

[17] Lyon et al., "Carlos Wyffels."

[18] Van Caenegem, "Bryce Lyon."

[19] Lyon and Verhulst, *Medieval Finance*.

[20] Lyon, "François Louis Ganshof."

[21] "Séance du samedi 26 juin 2004," *Bulletin de la Commission royale d'histoire* 171 (2005): 402–3.

[22] See comments and names of the laureates of the Bryce and Mary Lyon Prize on the website of the Royal Historical Commission: http://www.kcgeschiedenis.be/en/prixAnnuels/lyon_en.html [accessed May 2011].

Boone, Marc. "Henri Pirenne (1862–1935), Godfather van de Gentse historische school?" *Handelingen der Maatschappij voor Geschiedenis en Oudheidkunde te Gent, Nieuwe reeks* 60 (2006): 3–19.

Boyce, Gray C. "The Legacy of Henri Pirenne." *Byzantion* 15 (1940–41): 449–64.

Despy, Georges, and Adriaan Verhulst, eds. *La fortune historiographique des thèses d'Henri Pirenne.* Brussels: Institut des hautes études de Belgique, 1986.

Ganshof, François L. "Pirenne (Henri)." *Biographie nationale* 30 (1958): 671–723.

Lyon, Bryce D. "François Louis Ganshof: Medieval Historian and Friend." *Bulletin de la Commission royale d'histoire* 173 (2007): 5–14.

———. *From Fief to Indenture: The Transition from Feudal to Non-feudal Contract in Western Europe.* Cambridge, MA: Harvard University Press, 1957.

———. *Henri Pirenne: A Biographical and Intellectual Study.* Ghent: E. Story-Scientia, 1974.

———. "Henri Pirenne: *Connu* or *inconnu?*" *Revue belge de philologie et d'histoire* 81 (2003): 1231–41.

———. "The Letters of Henri Pirenne to Karl Lamprecht (1894–1915)." *Bulletin de la Commission royale d'histoire* 132 (1966): 161–231.

———. "Un compte de l'échiquier relatif aux relations d'Edouard Ier d'Angleterre avec le duc Jean II de Brabant." *Bulletin de la Commission royale d'histoire* 120 (1955): 1–27.

Lyon, Bryce D., and Mary Lyon. "An Account of the Provisions Received by Robert de Segre, Clerk of Edward I of England, in Flanders and Brabant in the Autumn of 1297." *Bulletin de la Commission royale d'histoire* 169 (2003): 37–50.

———. *The Birth of Annales History: The Letters of Lucien Febvre and Marc Bloch to Henri Pirenne (1921–1935).* Brussels: Palais des Académies, 1991.

———, eds. *The Journal de Guerre of Henri Pirenne.* Amsterdam: North-Holland, 1976.

———, eds. *The Wardrobe Book of 1296–1297: A Financial and Logistical Record of Edward I's 1297 Autumn Campaign in Flanders against Philip IV of France.* Brussels: Palais des Académies, 2004.

Lyon, Bryce D., Mary Lyon, and Jean-Henri Pirenne. "Réflexions d'un solitaire, by Henri Pirenne." *Bulletin de la Commission royale d'histoire* 160 (1994): 143–312.

Lyon, Bryce, Raoul Van Caenegem, and Walter Prevenier, "Carlos Wyffels." *Speculum* 79 (2004): 893–95.

Lyon, Bryce D., and Adriaan Verhulst. *Medieval Finance: A Comparison of Financial Institutions in Northwestern Europe.* Rijksuniversiteit te Gent: Werken uitgegeven door de Faculteit van de Letteren en Wijsbegeerte 143. Bruges: De Tempel; Providence, RI: Brown University Press, 1967.

Lyon, Mary, Bryce Lyon, and Henry S. Lucas, eds., with the collaboration of Jean de Sturler. *The Wardrobe Book of William de Norwell, 12 July 1338 to 27 May 1340.* Brussels: Palais des Académies, 1983.

Pirenne, Henri. "Mahomet et Charlemagne." *Revue belge de philologie et d'histoire* 1 (1921): 77–86.

Prevenier, Walter. "Henri Pirenne (1862–1935)." In *Europa-Historiker: Ein biographisches Handbuch,* ed. Heinz Duchhardt et al., 3 vols. (Göttingen: Vandenhoeck & Ruprecht, 2007), 2:147–67.

———, "Henri Pirenne (1862–1935)." In *New Historical Writing in Twentieth-Century France: French Historians, 1900–2000,* ed. Philip Daileader and Philip Whalen, pp. 486–500. Oxford: Wiley-Blackwell, 2010.

Schöttler, Peter. "Henri Pirenne, historien européen entre la France et l'Allemagne." *Revue belge de philologie et d'histoire* 76 (1998): 875–83.

Van Caenegem, Raoul. "Bryce Lyon (22 april 1920–24 mei 2007)." *Jaarboek 2007: Koninklijke Vlaamse Academie van België voor Wetenschappen en Kunsten* (Brussels: Paleis der Academiën, 2008), pp. 166–67.

Van Werveke, Hans. "Karl Lamprecht et Henri Pirenne." *Bulletin de la Commission royale d'histoire* 138 (1972): 39–60.

Violante, Cinzio. *La fine della 'grande illusione': Uno storico europeo tra guerra e dopoguerra, Henri Pirenne (1914–1923)*. Bologna: Società editrici il Mulino, 1997.

Books and Articles of Bryce Lyon

1951

"The Lawyer and Magna Carta." *Rocky Mountain Law Review* 23:416–33.
"The Money Fief under the English Kings, 1066–1485." *English Historical Review* 66:161–93.

1953

"Le fief-rente aux Pays-Bas: Sa terminologie et son aspect financier." *Revue du Nord* 35:221–32.

1954

"The Feudal Antecedent of the Indenture System." *Speculum* 29:503–11.
"The Fief-Rente in the Low Countries: An Evaluation." *Revue belge de philologie et d'histoire* 32:422–65.
Stephenson, Carl. *Medieval Institutions: Selected Essays*, ed. Bryce Lyon. Ithaca, NY: Cornell University Press.

1955

"Un compte de l'échiquier relative aux relations d'Edouard Ier d'Angleterre avec le duc Jean II de Brabant." *Bulletin de la Commission royale d'histoire* 120:1–27.

1956

"Fact and Fiction in English and Belgian Constitutional Law." *Medievalia et Humanistica* 10:82–101.
Introduction to *Medieval Feudalism*, by Carl Stephenson, pp. i–xii. Ithaca, NY: Cornell University Press.

1957

From Fief to Indenture: The Transition from Feudal to Non-feudal Contract in Western Europe. Cambridge, MA: Harvard University Press.
"Medieval Real Estate Developments and Freedom." *American Historical Review* 63:47–61.

19

1959

The Middle Ages in Recent Historical Thought. Washington: Service Center for Teachers of History 23. Washington, DC: Service Center for Teachers of History.

1960

A Constitutional and Legal History of Medieval England. New York: Harper and Row.

[With C. G. Starr, C. E. Nowell, R. P. Stearns, and T. S. Hamerow]. "The Middle Ages in the West." In *A History of the World,* 1:344–610. 2 vols. Chicago: Rand McNally.

1961

"Medieval Constitutionalism: A Balance of Power." In *Album Helen Maud Cam,* pp. 157–83. Studies Presented to the International Commission for the History of Representative and Parliamentary Institutions 24. Louvain: Publications universitaires de Louvain.

1962

[With Carl Stephenson]. *Mediaeval History: Europe from the Second to the Sixteenth Century.* 4th ed. New York: Harper and Row.

1963

"The Feudalism of Marc Bloch." *Tijdschrift voor Geschiedenis* 76:275–83.

"From Hengist and Horsa to Edward of Caernarvon: Recent Writing on English History." *Tijdschrift voor Geschiedenis* 76:377–422. Reprinted with supplementary note in *Changing Views on British History: Essays on Historical Writing since 1939,* ed. Elizabeth Chapin Furber, pp. 1–57. Cambridge, MA: Harvard University Press, 1966.

"Once Again the Chronology of Labor Services." *Le Moyen Âge* 69:615–30.

1964

The High Middle Ages: Sources in Western Civilization. New York: Free Press.

1965

[With Mary Lyon]. "Maurice Prou, ami de Henri Pirenne." *Le Moyen Âge* 71:71–107.

1966

The Correspondence of Henri Pirenne with Karl Lamprecht (1894–1915), ed. Bryce Lyon. Brussels: Palais des Académies.

Foreword to *French Rural History: An Essay on Its Basic Characteristics,* by Marc Bloch, pp. i–xii. Berkeley and Los Angeles: University of California Press.

Introduction to *Domesday Book and Beyond,* by Frederic William Maitland, pp. iv–x. New York: W. W. Norton.

1967

[With Adriaan Verhulst]. *Medieval Finance: A Comparison of Financial Institutions in Northwestern Europe.* Rijksuniversiteit te Gent: Werken uitgegeven door de Faculteit van de Letteren en Wijsbegeerte 143. Bruges: De Tempel; Providence, RI: Brown University Press.

1968

Introduction to *Frankish Institutions under Charlemagne,* by François L. Ganshof, pp. i–xvi. Trans. Bryce and Mary Lyon. Providence, RI: Brown University Press; repr. New York: W. W. Norton, 1970.

1969

"Was There a Renaissance in the Twelfth Century?" In *The Renaissance of the Twelfth Century,* ed. S. Scher, pp. 1–9. Providence: Museum of Art, Rhode Island School of Design.

"What Made a Medieval King Constitutional?" In *Essays in Medieval History Presented to Bertie Wilkinson*, ed. T. A. Sandquist and Michael R. Powicke, pp. 157–75. Toronto: University of Toronto Press.

[With H. H. Rowen and T. S. Hamerow]. "Ancient and Medieval Worlds." In *History of the Western World*, 1:1–355. 3 vols. Chicago: Rand McNally; 2nd ed., 1974.

1971
The Origins of the Middle Ages: Pirenne's Challenge to Gibbon. New York: W. W. Norton.

1974
Henri Pirenne: A Biographical and Intellectual Study. Ghent: E. Story-Scientia.

"Nieuwe Biografie van Henri Pirenne: Interview met Prof. Lyon." *Spiegel Historiael: Maandblad voor Geschiedenis en Archeologie* 9:532–37.

"Toespraken bij de Voorstelling van het Boek van Prof. Bryce Lyon over H. Pirenne." *Studia historica Gandensia* 170:147–62.

1975
"A Reply to Jan Dhondt's Critique of Henri Pirenne." *Handelingen der Maatschappij voor Geschiedenis en Oudheidkunde te Gent*, n.s., 29:1–25.

1976
"L'oeuvre de Henri Pirenne après vingt-cinq ans." *Le Moyen Âge* 66:437–93. Reprinted in *The Pirenne Thesis*, ed. A. F. Havighurst, pp. 183–90. 3rd ed. Lexington, MA: D. C. Heath, 1976.

"Review Article: Edward IV." *Journal of British Studies* 16:178–86.

[Edited, with Mary Lyon]. *The "Journal de Guerre" of Henri Pirenne.* Amsterdam: North Holland.

1977
"The Emancipation of Land Law from Feudal Custom." *Yale Law Journal* 86:782–87.

1978
Introduction to *Essays on Medieval Civilization*, ed. Richard Eugene Sullivan, Bede Karl Lackner, and Kenneth Roy Philp, pp. xi–xvi. Walter Prescott Webb Memorial Lectures 12. Austin: University of Texas Press.

Studies of West European Medieval Institutions. Collected Studies Series 78. London: Variorum.

1980
A Constitutional and Legal History of Medieval England. 2nd ed. New York: W. W. Norton.

Emergence of the Common Law and Parliament. St. Louis: Forum Press.

"Henri Pirenne and the Origins of *Annales* History." *Annals of Scholarship: Metastudies of the Humanities and Social Sciences* 1:69–84.

1981
"Historical Research in Belgium and Its Meaning on an International Level." In *Belgium and Europe: Proceedings of the International Francqui-Colloquium, Brussels-Ghent, 12–14 November 1980*, ed. G. Verbeke, pp. 185–97. Brussels: Koninklijke Academie voor Wetenschappen, Letteren en Schone Kunsten van België.

1983
"Continent of Castles and Cathedrals." In *Peoples and Places of the Past: The National Geographic Illustrated Cultural Atlas of the Ancient World*, pp. 161–93. Washington, DC: National Geographic Society.

[Edited, with Mary Lyon and Henry S. Lucas, with the collaboration of Jean de Sturler]. *The Wardrobe Book of William de Norwell, 12 July 1338 to 27 May 1340.* Brussels: Palais des Académies.

1984
"Change or Continuity: Writing since 1965 on English History before Edward of Caernarvon." In *Recent Views on British History: Essays on Historical Writing since 1966,* ed. Richard Schlatter, pp. 1–34. New Brunswick, NJ: Rutgers University Press.

1985
"Il dibattito accademico intorno a Mohammed e Carlomagno di H. Pirenne." In *Maometto e Carlomagno,* pp. 9–23. Milan: Jaca Book.
"Marc Bloch: Did He Repudiate *Annales* History?" *Journal of Medieval History* 11:181–91.
"Was Johan Huizinga Interdisciplinary?" *Handelingen der Maatschappij voor Geschiedenis en Oudheidkunde te Gent* 39:181–88.

1987
"Henri Pirenne and Johan Huizinga in Search of Historical Truth: Two Different Approaches." In *Papers from the Second Interdisciplinary Conference on Netherlandic Studies Held at Georgetown University,* ed. William H. Fletcher, pp. 3–16. Papers in Netherlandic Studies 2. Lanham, MD: University Press of America.
"Marc Bloch: Historian." *French Historical Studies* 15:195–207.
"The Role of Cavalry in Medieval Warfare: Horses, Horses All Around and Not a One to Use." *Mededelingen van de Koninklijke Academie voor Wetenschappen, Letteren en Schone Kunsten van België* 49:75–90.

1989
"Henry II: A Non-Victorian Interpretation." In *Documenting the Past: Essays in Medieval History Presented to George Peddy Cuttino,* ed. J. S. Hamilton and Patricia J. Bradley, pp. 21–31. Woodbridge: Boydell and Brewer.
"Past and Present: The Loss of Historical Memory." Lecture, Beall-Russell Lectures in the Humanities, Baylor University, Waco, TX.

1990
"The Achievements of Marc Bloch." *French Historical Studies* 16:923–27.

1991
[Edited, with Mary Lyon]. *The Birth of Annales History: The Letters of Lucien Febvre and Marc Bloch to Henri Pirenne (1921–1935).* Brussels: Palais des Académies.

1992
"Does Historical Reality Influence Historical Methodology?" *Mededelingen van de Koninklijke Academie voor Wetenschappen, Letteren en Schone Kunsten van België* 54:109–22.
"The Influence of Emile Durkheim on Marc Bloch and Jules Romains." *Mededelingen van de Koninklijke Academie voor Wetenschappen, Letteren en Schone Kunsten van België* 54:125–46.

1994
"What Role Did Communes Have in the Feudal System?" *Revue belge de philologie et d'histoire* 72:241–53.
[Edited, with Mary Lyon and J. H. Pirenne]. *Réflexions d'un solitaire by Henri Pirenne.* Brussels: Palais des Académies.

1995

"Henri Pirenne (1862–1935)." In *Medieval Scholarship: Biographical Studies on the Formation of a Discipline*, ed. Helen Damico and Joseph B. Zavadil. Vol. 1, *History*, pp. 153–58. New York: Garland.

"The Dividends from War in the Low Countries (1338–1340)." In *Peasants and Townsmen in Medieval Europe: Studia in Honorem Adriaan Verhulst*, pp. 693–705. Ghent: Snoeck-Ducaju & Zoon.

1997

"Henri Pirenne's *Réflexions d'un solitaire* and His Re-evaluation of History." *Journal of Medieval History* 23:285–99.

"The Infrastructure and Purpose of an English Medieval Fleet in the First Phase of the Hundred Years' War (1338–1340)." *Handelingen der Maatschappij voor Geschiedenis en Oudheidkunde te Gent* 51:61–76.

"What Were Edward III's Priorities: The Pleasures of Sports or Charity?" *Revue d'histoire écclésiastique* 92:1236–34.

1998

"Coup d'oeil sur l'infrastructure de la chasse au Moyen Âge." *Le Moyen Âge* 104:211–26.

"The War of 1914 and Henri Pirenne's Revision of His Methodology." In *De Lectuur van het Verleden: Liber amicorum in Honour of Professor Reginald de Schryver*, pp. 505–14. Leuven: Leuven University Press.

1999

"Communication during Medieval Warfare: The Campaign of Edward III of England in the Low Countries (1338–1340)." *Handelingen der Maatschappij voor Geschiedenis en Oudheidkunde te Gent* 53:61–75.

"Guillaume Des Marez and Henri Pirenne: A Remarkable Rapport." *Revue belge de philologie et d'histoire* 77:1051–78.

2001

"The Logistics for Edward I's Ill-Fated Campaign in Flanders (1297–1298)." *Handelingen der Maatschappij voor Geschiedenis en Oudheidkunde te Gent* 55:77–91.

2003

"Henri Pirenne: *Connu* or *inconnu?*" *Revue belge de philologie et d'histoire* 81:1231–41.

"An Account of the Provisions Received by Robert de Segre, Clerk of Edward I of England, in Flanders and Brabant in the Autumn of 1297." *Bulletin de la Commission royale d'histoire* 169:37–49.

"What Were the Expenses of the Kings Edward I and Edward III When Absent from Their Realms?" *Journal of Medieval History* 29:331–45.

2004

[Edited, with †Mary Lyon]. *The Wardrobe Book of 1296–1297: A Financial and Logistical Record of Edward I's 1297 Campaign in Flanders against Philip IV of France*. Brussels: Palais des Académies.

Part 1

The Legacy of Henri Pirenne

Continuity in Late Antique Gaul:
A Demographic and Economic Perspective

Bernard S. Bachrach

AN IMPORTANT PART of Bryce Lyon's impressive career always will be associated with the work of Henri Pirenne and particularly with his argument that the so-called barbarian invasions did not destroy the later Roman economy in the West.[1] As Lyon emphasized, Pirenne and his contemporary Alfons Dopsch maintained that in various of Rome's successor states, especially in Gaul where both men focused their work in regard to the early Middle Ages, the economy remained comparable to what had existed prior to the dissolution of imperial authority in the West.[2] Pirenne, of course, parted company with Dopsch and maintained that continuity was destroyed by the Muslim conquest of much of the Mediterranean littoral during the late seventh and early eighth centuries.[3]

In response to Pirenne and Dopsch, modern scholars quickly embraced the view that throughout the West of the later Roman Empire and the early Middle Ages, now called "late antiquity" by many scholars, the economy suffered massive decline due in large part to the barbarian invasions.[4] In 1951 Robert Lopez asserted, as though it were a noncontroversial fact, "the Roman economy collapsed in the fifth century."[5] By the 1970s most specialists in medieval economic history had rejected the views of both Dopsch and Pirenne. As Renée Doehaerd summed up the state of the question, a "scarcity of goods" was "the essential characteristic of the [economy of the] West between the fifth and

---

[1] Lyon, *Origins*, pp. 57–75; Lyon, *Henri Pirenne*, pp. 435–38.

[2] Pirenne, *Mohammed and Charlemagne*, pp. 9–11, and Dopsch, *Economic and Social Foundations*.

[3] Lyon, *Origins*, pp. 57–75.

[4] Goffart, *Barbarian Tides*. Concerning late antiquity, see Marcone, "Late Antiquity," and Ando, "Decline."

[5] Lopez, "Dollar," p. 18.

ninth centuries."[6] Georges Duby, whose authority went virtually unchallenged among medievalists for some thirty years in the French- and English-speaking worlds, echoed these views throughout the 1970s and 1980s.[7] He found strong support from Robert Fossier, his colleague at the Collège de France.[8]

This model remains dominant today among many influential medievalists. For example, Paul Fouracre, editor of the first volume of the *New Cambridge Medieval History*, observed recently: "[T]here is a consensus among historians and archaeologists" that "there was a deep and lasting economic recession in Europe between at least the fourth and eighth centuries AD."[9] A prominent archaeologist, Bryan Ward-Perkins, has characterized the general view of a decline in economic conditions as being calculated from "a high point sometime in the Roman period sinking to a low sometime between 400–700."[10] Michael McCormick has observed: "The overall economic trend of the Roman world from c. 200 to c. 700 was downward."[11]

By contrast, some specialists in the history of the later Roman Empire now defend Pirenne's thesis. For example, C. R. Whittaker has observed that it "is still—despite some dissent—largely supported by modern research."[12] S. J. B. Barnish notes that "[o]n the whole, recent archaeology has tended to confirm Pirenne's picture of a lively Mediterranean commerce in the 5th and 6th centuries."[13] Jeremy Knight emphasizes that "the economic unity of the Mediterranean world into the seventh century is now supported by much archaeological evidence still below ground when Pirenne wrote."[14] The failure of some medieval historians to keep abreast of the relevant literature is summarized by Christine Delaplace: "Some historians are able to remain ignorant of innovative works when the period being studied is not that of their special interest."[15]

Many scholars argue that the supposedly abysmal level of the economy during the late antique era is to be explained by drastic demographic decline.[16] Doehaerd characterized the state of the question: "The existence of a low population

---

[6] Doehaerd, *Early Middle Ages*, p. 22.

[7] Duby, *Early Growth*.

[8] Fossier, "Les tendences"; and McCormick, "Origins of the European Economy," p. 263n1.

[9] Fouracre, "Space," p. 367.

[10] Ward-Perkins, "Specialized Production," p. 362.

[11] McCormick, *Origins*, p. 30. Wood, "North-Western Provinces," p. 499; and Liebeschuetz, *Decline*, p. 10.

[12] Whittaker, "Late Roman Trade," p. 162.

[13] Barnish, "Transformation," p. 396.

[14] Knight, *End of Antiquity*, p. 166.

[15] Delaplace, "Débats et problèmes," pp. 16–17; also Loseby, "Marseille"; Loseby, "Marseille and Pirenne"; and Banaji, *Agrarian Change*, p. 265.

[16] For lists, see Lyon, *Origins*, pp. 36–38, 48–54; and Lewit, *Agricultural Production*, pp. 1–11.

index between the fifth and the eleventh centuries is based on the *hypothesis* of a contraction of the population under the Roman Empire, beginning in the second century AD and becoming more pronounced during the following centuries."[17] This consensus permeates the scholarly literature.[18] McCormick claims there is widespread agreement among medievalists that economic problems were driven by an unrelenting pattern of significant demographic decline.[19] Ward-Perkins recently observed, "It is generally assumed that the population of the west, or at least of most of its provinces, declined under the later empire (in the third and fourth century), and then fell markedly in the immediately post-Roman centuries (the fifth to seventh)."[20]

It should be emphasized that despite strong belief concerning both demographic and economic decline in the late antique West, scholars agree that there is no corpus of statistical data upon which to base quantitative judgments. A. H. M. Jones, for example, believed that there was a general decline in the population of the later Roman Empire through the end of the sixth century. Nevertheless, he recognized that one could not assert that this supposed decline was "certain," because "our information is so vague, and the facts and figures are so sparse." He observed, "if it [the population] did decline" as he believed, "it is impossible to calculate how much it declined."[21] He summarily dismissed the notion of a labor shortage.[22]

Some Methodological Observations: The Written Sources

In light of a dearth of statistical data regarding the late antique economy and population in the West, it has been traditional for historians to manipulate, following one or another rhetorical strategy, various types of qualitative information, both written and material, as surrogates to support their interpretations.[23] The search by historians, in contrast to archaeologists, for evidence of population decline and economic failure has led most to rely on written sources such as the works of Gregory of Tours, whose oeuvre provides a considerable percentage of the surviving narrative texts for Gaul in the sixth century.[24]

---

[17] Doehaerd, *Early Middle Ages*, p. 22 (my emphasis); and Riché, "Problèmes."

[18] Russell, *Late Ancient*, pp. 106–8, 119; Herlihy, "Demography"; Reuter, *Germany*, p. 94; and Deyperot, *Richesse*, p. 9.

[19] McCormick, *Origins*, p. 30.

[20] Ward-Perkins, "Land," p. 323; Liebeschuetz, *Decline*, p. 393; and Wickham, *Framing*, p. 12.

[21] Jones, *Later Roman Empire*, p. 1040: also Salmon, *Population*, pp. 114–79; Whittaker, "Agri Deserti," p. 200n113; and Scheidel, "Progress," p. 67n272.

[22] Jones, *Later Roman Empire*, p. 1042.

[23] Done brilliantly by McCormick, *Origins*.

[24] Goffart, *Narrators*, pp. 112–234.

During the past thirty years our understanding of the aims and biases of writers such as Gregory, which had a seriously distorting effect in regard to information concerning the economy, has become much more sophisticated.[25] Many long-held views, based on Gregory's *Ten Books of History* and the corpus of Merovingian hagiographical works to which the prolific bishop of Tours also contributed, are thus being reevaluated. Scholars can no longer treat the information provided by such authors at face value or as "plain text." This has been shown especially in regard to economic matters.[26] In general, we must heed warnings such as that of Neil Christie: "[O]ne needs to beware throughout of authors' biases . . . and of the constant desire to exaggerate narratives in terms of numbers, brutality, or misery, whether for poetical and dramatic effect or from diplomatic and political motives."[27]

To this list of abuses by late antique authors we must add those attributable to a religious bias. This is the case with Gregory of Tours and many of his fellow clerics of the Merovingian era. The dearth of positive information in the narrative sources regarding economic success in general and commerce in particular is now widely attributed to the distaste shared by ecclesiastics for those engaged in commerce and their profession. Christian writers attached considerable importance to teaching the lesson of the omnipresence of divine retribution.[28] In addition to providing exaggerated, inaccurate, and even fabricated information regarding war, famine, and disease to demonstrate how God-sent disasters punished malefactors in the wake of behavior that was either un-Christian or anti-Christian, apocalyptic motives often were at work to demonstrate that "the end of days" was near.[29]

Material Sources

Most archaeological evidence provides a no more secure basis for drawing quantitative conclusions than do the narrative sources. Philip Grierson's observation— "It has been said that the spade cannot lie, but it owes this merit in part to the fact that it cannot speak"—is as true today as when he wrote in 1959.[30] During the past two decades, for example, the number of archaeological excavations in northern France has increased exponentially.[31] Yet, despite a vast volume of

---

[25] Goffart, *Narrators*; Breukelaar, *Historiography*; and Heinzelmann, *Gregory*.

[26] McCormick, *Origins*, pp. 12–15; and Goffart, *Narrators*, p. 190.

[27] Christie, "Barren Fields," p. 255. He thus rejects the contrary approach, for example of Heather, *Fall*, p. xiii.

[28] Goffart, *Narrators*, pp. 187–91.

[29] Rouche, "Grégoire," pp. 41–57.

[30] Grierson, "Commerce," p. 129.

[31] Peytremann, *Archéologie*, 1:13; Davis and McCormick, "Early Middle Ages," p. 5.

publication, no statistical information has been unearthed to demonstrate the downward direction of the demographic curve in late antique Gaul. As Ward-Perkins recently put it, "The archaeological evidence available at present ... cannot prove dramatic demographic decline."[32]

Urban Archaeology

In regard to the cities of Merovingian Gaul, Paul-Albert Février observed: "The archaeological study of most towns has yet to be carried out, and it is possible to count on the fingers of one hand the localities for which, in this area of antiquity, firm and extensive documentation is available."[33] Although Février penned these lines a generation ago, very little work in urban archaeology permits generalizations concerning a downward turn of the demographic curve or an economic crash in any particular part of the hexagon, much less the region as a whole.[34] By contrast, there are good reasons to believe that many of the urban centers of Gaul maintained significant population densities and continued the production of various types of goods and services.[35]

The problems associated with sustaining negative conclusions regarding the maintenance of urban population levels are only rooted in part in an insufficiency of excavation. In some places prior to World War II excavators, looking for high classical remains, are known to have shoveled off late antique strata without giving them proper attention.[36] In other places, it was not abuse by treasure hunters but the needs of the city's inhabitants that caused the massive destruction of "evidence." For example, the people of Marseilles during the later Middle Ages traditionally leveled the sites where they intended to carry out new construction to a base which now we know was at about 800 AD. As a result, information embedded in several centuries of strata, which normally would have been available to archaeologists, was eliminated.[37]

Many archaeologists bent upon demonstrating population decline are not unaware of the fragility of their conclusions. A generation ago, scholars were beginning to digest the bits and pieces of information that had been made available as a result of World War II bombing and subsequent reconstruction. At the

---

[32] Ward-Perkins, "Land," p. 324n17.

[33] Février, "Towns," p. 317.

[34] Cf. Liebeschuetz, *Decline.*

[35] Ward-Perkins, "Urban Continuity?," pp. 4–17; Bachrach, "Metz," pp. 363–81; and Samson, "Populous."

[36] Hodges and Whitehouse, *Mohammed,* p. 12; and Bouard and Fournier, "Country," pp. 169, 175.

[37] Hesnard et al., *Parcours des villes,* pp. 126, 142; Biarne, "Marseilles," pp. 121–33; Horden and Purcell, *Corrupting Sea,* pp. 165–66. Ganshof, "Les bureaux," pp. 125–33; Ganshof, "Notes"; and Zerner, "Enfants."

height of this period Edith Wightman warned: "Archaeological evidence is by its nature incomplete and always increasing: conclusions drawn from it are temporary halting-points and generalizations from the particular are always hazardous."[38] Three decades later an increasing number of archaeological excavations in Gaul's late antique cities has led Peter Wells to conclude that urban population decline "may have been the exception rather than the rule."[39]

The slowly growing archaeological record has rendered declarations about "ghost towns" or the "survival of ruins"[40] untenable. Rather, if any conclusion is to be drawn, following Wells, there is increasing information from throughout the hexagon regarding urban population growth, which overcomes earlier negative conclusions based upon what previously had not yet been found, that is, an argument from silence.[41] This growth in material information is perhaps most important in regard to the *urbes* of the middle and lower Rhineland, often characterized as the region most abused by the so-called barbarian invasions.[42] New studies in this area, however, support the view that there was noteworthy continuity from the later Roman Empire through the Carolingian period in terms of the size of urban populations and urban physical structures.[43]

It is important to emphasize that even scholars who posit severe urban decline during the late antique era finally have given up the dubious claim that the fortification of the area of Gaul's late antique *urbes* can be used as evidence for the diminution of the population. As Ramsey MacMullen has observed: "From this fact [the creation of fortress cities] it was once inferred that the subsequent urban population could all fit inside the walls and was therefore permanently reduced by a quarter, a half, or three-quarters at different sites: but the inference, having been tested as much as possible is now generally doubted and the existence of very substantial suburbs is sometimes demonstrable."[44] The continued use of the basic street grid is important in this context.[45] As Walter Scheidel put it: "Smaller cities need not be less populous, only more compact."[46]

---

[38] Wightman, "Towns," p. 304.

[39] Wells, *Barbarians*, p. 73.

[40] Schütte, "Continuity," pp. 168–69; Aten, "Römische"; Trier, "Köln"; and Bachrach, "Metz." Cf. Steuer, "Stadtarchäologie," p. 59; and Halsall, "Towns," p. 248.

[41] Gauthiez, "La réoccupation," and Gauthier, "Rouen," pp. 1–20. Cf. Hodges, *Towns*, pp. 77–78, 106.

[42] Liebeschuetz, *Decline*, p. 86; and cf. Gissinger, *Reseraches*, p. 22.

[43] Staab, *Untersuchungen*, and Bernhard, "Die Merowingerzeit," pp. 9–14.

[44] McMullen, *Corruption*, p. 21.

[45] Ward-Perkins, *Classical Antiquity*, p. 180; and Ward-Perkins, "Towns," p. 20.

[46] Scheidel, "Progress," p. 65.

Rural Archaeology

On the basis of so-called field surveys archaeologists were accustomed to argue for a progressive and rapid decline in the number and size of rural sites in late antique Gaul. It is now clear that "evidence" produced in this way is fundamentally misleading. The field survey technique relies on so-called samples of ceramic shards turned up through plowing done by farmers in the normal course of their agricultural efforts and subsequently gathered by field walkers.[47] Despite much posturing to the contrary, these "surface scatters" are in no sense statistically valid samples.[48] They are merely elements of a fuzzy set. The shards provide no basis for determining the statistical characteristics of the whole corpus of presumed sites from which they emanated.[49]

Field surveys have numerous additional flaws.[50] In terms of chronology, for example, it is obvious that the uppermost strata in any field that has been under the plow for generations if not centuries are far more likely to have seen the disappearance over time of greater quantities of shards, prior to any modern survey, as compared to the strata below them. Despite the fact that many of the upper strata at any field are likely to have been compromised, it has not been uncommon for some archaeologists to use bits and pieces of pottery, or their absence, to draw firm conclusions regarding the abandonment of a particular site at a particular time.[51]

Even if the strata provided reliable data, the dating of pottery shards often is problematic. This is especially important in regard to the northeast of Gaul, where rural population decline is supposed to be most dramatic. There often has been a lack of methodological rigor in distinguishing between a supposed fifth- and sixth-century site or even a seventh-century site on the basis of bits and pieces of ceramic detritus picked up in plowed fields of the Moselle region. For example, since archaeologists assumed that 400 is roughly the date when things Roman came to an end in the region, Gallo-Roman "Argonne" pottery until recently was given a pro forma terminal date of ca. 400. This is an excellent example of the type of circular reasoning often found in archaeological dating geared to sustaining particular historical conclusions such as "catastrophic" rural decline which some scholars suppose brought about the fall of the Roman Empire.[52] More to the point, however, it has now been established that Argonne ware was manufactured and used throughout the fifth and

---

[47] Van Ossel and Ouzoulias, "Rural Settlement," p. 134.

[48] Christie, "Barren Fields?," p. 275.

[49] Cf. Barker and Lloyd's introduction to *Roman Landscapes*, pp. 1–9; and Vallat, "Survey," pp. 10–17, critiqued by Scheidel, "Progress," p. 65.

[50] Bowden and Lavan, "Late Antique," pp. xxi–xxiii; and Cherry, "Vox Populi," pp. 561–82.

[51] Christie, "Barren Fields?," pp. 274–75.

[52] Cheyette, "Disappearance," pp. 131–35.

sixth centuries and likely beyond. Thus there must be a reexamination of the chronology of all sites previously determined by Argonne-dates.[53]

Agreement is now growing that the results of field-walking surveys, unsupported by extensive excavations, are at best untrustworthy. J. H. W. G. Liebeschuetz, whose own bias is toward economic and demographic decline, nevertheless admits, "[I]t is evident that the results of field surveys not supported by excavation are to a significant degree misleading."[54] Christi has observed that "surface survey alone cannot provide coherent guides to underlying structural sequences."[55] Ward-Perkins considers the numbers produced by field walking for the disappearance of settlements "self-evidently nonsense" and concludes "there must have been people living in these areas, and we just cannot find them."[56]

For some historians field-walking information, though seriously flawed, was given a great deal more weight than it deserved because of the traditional treatment of the few mentions of *agri deserti* in the *Codex Theodosianus* and the *Codex Justianianus*.[57] In recent years, scholars have concluded that edicts mentioning *agri deserti* were dealing with a fiscal accounting scheme that was relevant to neither the quantity of land under cultivation nor the magnitude of crop production. Most *agri deserti* were not lands that lacked either the people to work them or the production of crops.[58] Whatever broader conclusions may be drawn regarding recent work, the edicts regarding *agri deserti* were neither *acta* that had empire-wide juridical warrant, nor did any of this legislation focus specifically on Gaul in the fifth century.[59]

Demographic Theory

It is clear that information culled from field walking about the nature of the demographic curve in late antique Gaul is highly suspect, when not seriously misleading. It is further evident that legislation dealing with *agri deserti* cannot be relied upon to demonstrate rural population decline in Gaul. It seems reasonable, therefore, that we revisit the essentials of demographic theory that are implicit in all discussions of population growth and decline. Traditionally, demographers

---

[53] Feller and Poplineau, "Ateliers," pp. 173–80; Verdel, "Archéologie," pp. 353–61; Collot, "Fouilles," pp. 5–32; and Bayard, "La fin," pp. 223–33.

[54] Liebeschuetz, *Decline*, pp. 389–90.

[55] Christie, "Landscapes," p. 8.

[56] Ward-Perkins, "Land," pp. 324–25; and Van Ossel and Ouzoulias, "Rural Settlement," p. 135; cf. Cheyette, "Disappearance"; and Hodges, *Goodbye*, p. 180.

[57] Whittaker, "*Agri deserti*," pp. 137–43.

[58] Whittaker, "*Agri Deserti*," pp. 137–65; Scheidel, "Progress," p. 67n272; Grey, "Revisiting," pp. 362–76, and Durand and Leveau, "Farming," p. 179.

[59] Whittaker, "*Agri Deserti*," pp. 137–65.

identify three key variables as fundamental to population decline in the preindustrial West: endemic patterns of disease, for example, plague; cyclical episodes
of famine occurring at close intervals; and both the direct and indirect effects
of long-term and widespread military conflict. In the absence of these negative
variables at significant levels, either individually or in some combination, the only
brake on population growth recognized by demographers treating the preindustrial West is a lack of arable land needed to feed an ever-increasing population.[60]

During the Merovingian period Gaul saw no widespread famines, much
less regular cycles of food shortage that were dramatic in nature and involved
large areas.[61] There were no devastating long-term and/or widespread military
conflicts.[62] Finally and most importantly, the so-called Justinianic plague, which
did strike Gaul, was not endemic within the confines of the hexagon. It appeared
rarely, at wide temporal intervals and in so few places that population recovery
was rapid.[63] Thus, for example, the port city of Marseilles, which was struck more
frequently than any other locality in Gaul during the sixth century, saw both population growth and economic development during this period.[64] In this context
it is important that the Merovingians understood the use of a *cordon sanitaire*,
which was deployed to keep supposed plague carriers out of more or less densely
populated cities.[65]

It is important to recognize the inability of scholars to identify serious
insults to the population in the archaeological record of Merovingian Gaul. No
less important, however, is the absence of compelling evidence in the written
sources. Authors such as Gregory of Tours and his fellow clerics were wont to
focus on and to exaggerate instances of disease, famine, and war. Thus, from a theoretical perspective, their failure to provide information, even obviously corrupt
information, regarding serious shocks to the population permits the inference that
the demographic curve in the *regnum Francorum* was trending upward.[66] Empty
land both within and beyond the hexagon as well as extensive assartable forests
were available to provide arable for an increasing population.[67]

---

[60] Livi-Bacchi, *Population*, pp. 1–5; and McCleary, *Malthusian Population*.

[61] Matthisen, "Nature"; Stathakopoulos, *Famine*; and Deyperot, *Richesse*, p. 7.

[62] Bachrach, *Merovingian Military*; and Bachrach, *Anatomy*. Samson, "Merovingian." Cf. Halsall,
Warfare, pp. 231–33.

[63] Bachrach, "Plague." Cf. McCormick, "Rats."

[64] Bachrach, "Plague," pp. 55–56; Ganshof, "Bureaux," pp. 125–33; Ganshof, "Notes"; and Zerner,
"Enfants."

[65] McCormick, "Molecular History," p. 311; McCormick, "Bateaux," pp. 52–65; and Bachrach,
"Plague," pp. 53–54.

[66] Cf. Cheyette, "Disappearance."

[67] Doehaerd, *Early Middle Ages*, pp. 24–25; Higounet, "Les forêts," pp. 343–98; and Wickham,
"European Forests."

Population Growth: Empirical Information

Fortunately, scholars no longer have to rely on misleading field surveys. There has been a vast increase in the number of excavations of rural sites in northern France in recent years.[68] Large-scale or mega-studies of excavations have made clear that conclusions based upon field walking in Gaul now must be abandoned. Thus Paul Van Ossel and Pierre Ouzoulias have observed that "it became overwhelmingly obvious that 'theories' based on the material picked up by field walking could not be reconciled with the rapidly increasing corpus of information developed as a result of excavation."[69] Once common characterizations based on field walking such as "depopulation of the countryside," "general abandonment of rural settlement," "the profound impoverishment of the countryside," a "return to the subsistence economy," and "autarchy" are no longer valid.[70]

It is important that a growing body of scholarship based on archaeological excavations, in combination with the written sources, supports the view that agriculture was in a growth phase. As Banaji recently put it, "The general implication of the later Roman expansion of settlement is a demographic upswing."[71] This is crucial because it is widely agreed that roughly 90 percent of the population of late antique Gaul lived in the countryside and that these people were engaged in agriculture or related enterprises.[72] Thus, in terms of ascertaining general demographic patterns, the focus must be on the rural population, which if increasing, as now is frequently suggested, could provide surpluses to feed and clothe an increased number of people living in the *urbes* and their *suburbia*.

As early as 1991 Tamara Lewit's pioneering mega-study of excavated sites in Gaul not only undermined the already suspect conclusions drawn from field surveys but affirmed that the countryside was flourishing.[73] In the second edition of this work, published in 2004, which has been sustained by a great deal more excavation, she reiterated her conclusions:

> In sum, the archaeological evidence presented here shows that the later empire was far from being a period of agricultural decline and crisis. Rural occupation was at its maximum level or close to it, except in a few specific regions, and in some regions the level of occupation exceeds that of the high empire. Farms continued to prosper, and even to expand, and very few suffered decline or were spontaneously abandoned in any region.[74]

---

[68] Peytremann, *Archéologie*, 1:13.

[69] Van Ossel and Ouzoulias, "Rural Settlement," pp. 134–35.

[70] Van Ossel and Ouzoulias, "Rural Settlement," p. 133.

[71] Banaji, *Agrarian Change*, p. 20.

[72] Wickham, *Framing*, p. 12; Cheyette, "Disappearance," p. 128n3; and Devroey, "Economy," p. 98.

[73] Lewit, *Agricultural Production*, pp. v–xxi; and Lenz, "Late Roman."

[74] Lewit, *Agricultural Production*, p. 33.

Independently of Lewit, Patrick Périn has drawn fundamentally similar conclusions.[75]

Support for the notion of an increasing rural population in sixth-century Gaul is also provided by Edith Peytremann's mega-study of 308 excavated sites from northern France. This work provides a wide variety of information regarding rural settlements from the fourth to the twelfth century.[76] Of primary interest here is the chronology of new settlement sites. According to the information provided in the studies aggregated by Peytremann, four new foundations were established sometime between the fifth and sixth centuries, fifty-nine sites were settled in the course of the sixth century, and another twenty-nine sites likely were founded in the sixth century. Thus far archaeologists have identified a total of ninety-two new settlements made in this region during the first Merovingian century.[77]

At least one prominent scholar has treated this catalogue, at least implicitly, as though it were a random sample of all sites, known and unknown, excavated or as yet to be excavated, that had been established in this region between the fourth and twelfth centuries.[78] Although of course these data constitute a fuzzy set, subject to the limitations regarding so-called samples of this type discussed above, some observations regarding the numbers aggregated by Peytremann may have heuristic value. The information provided suggests that almost 30 percent of all excavated sites in this region were established during the first century of Merovingian rule. Nineteen sites were settled either during the fourth century or earlier and another twenty-four were established in the fifth century. Thus only eighty-one new settlements represented in Peytremann's catalogue were made during the five centuries between ca. 600 and ca. 1100, an average of about sixteen per century. This contrasts significantly with the establishment of approximately one new foundation per year in the same region during the first Merovingian century.[79]

Two points need to be made regarding these excavated sites. First, all were "failures," for they ceased to exist by ca. 1100 at the latest. We have no corpus of information indicating how many late antique settlements succeeded (survived until the present). For obvious reasons these sites cannot be excavated as fully as abandoned villages. Nevertheless, archaeologists are generally agreed that many late antique villages lie beneath the many thousands of contemporary villages and larger agglomerations of habitation in the north of France.[80]

---

[75] Périn, "Origin," pp. 255–78, and Lewit and Chavarría, "Archaeological Research."

[76] Peytremann, *Archéologie*, 1:14–16.

[77] Here I follow the information aggregated by Cheyette, "Disappearance," p. 141, from Peytremann's research.

[78] Cheyette, "Disappearance," p. 141.

[79] Peytremann, *Archéologie*, 1:18–20.

[80] Hamerow, *Early Medieval*, p. 54; Zadora-Rio, "Le habitat," pp. 5–8; and Périn, "Origin," pp. 266–75.

There is surrogate data to demonstrate a Merovingian past. As Patrick Périn has pointed out, Merovingian "cemeteries are found almost systematically in proximity to modern villages and hamlets." As Périn concludes, this is a prima facie indicator that early villages lie beneath these modern centers of habitation.[81]

Secondly, it cannot be concluded prima facie that all the new sites identified by Peytremann were the result of demographic growth. In the densely populated Seine valley, for example, need for additional arable is evidenced both in the documentary and archaeological records during the Merovingian era, and land reclamation projects were undertaken in the Paris region.[82] Lacking other more obvious causes, such as the establishment of new settlements on hilltops for protection from enemy attacks and/or the abandonment of settlements in militarily vulnerable river valleys, neither of which occurred, overpopulation in already existing settlements certainly cannot be ignored as a reason for the establishment of new settlements.

Between the later third and later sixth centuries, the cooling trend manifested in the Dunkirk II Transgression caused considerable material destruction and the withdrawal of elements of the population from northern coastal areas.[83] Numerous Roman sites such as Aardenburg, Oudenburg, and Bruges were flooded.[84] By the later sixth century this climatic phase was coming to an end, and new settlements in northern Gaul were being made as the process of warming and drying out progressed, and storm surges and flooding became less frequent.[85] Of particular importance is population growth and economic development in Frisia and its environs in the later sixth and seventh centuries.[86] These resulted in surplus production and played a key role in the development of the so-called emporia phenomenon.[87] Quentovic was founded ca. 600 and Duurstede only a short time later.[88]

In the south there is also evidence of population growth in both Aquitaine and Burgundy. Some excavations demonstrate a doubling of the population in the century between ca. 550 and ca. 650.[89] This burial evidence is supported by

---

[81] Périn, "Origin," p. 268; cf. Cheyette, "Disappearance," pp. 129–30.

[82] Verhulst, *Carolingian*, pp. 13, 41; Schwarz, "Village Populations"; Zerner, "La population"; Theuws, "Landed Property."

[83] Durand and Leveau, "Farming," p. 182.

[84] Verhulst, *Rise*, pp. 15–20.

[85] TeBrake, *Medieval Frontier*, pp. 107–10; and Siegmund, "Social Relations."

[86] Slicher van Bath, "Economic," pp. 97–105; Heidinga, *Medieval Settlement*, pp. 12–20, 52, 55, 87–88, 162–63, 168–73; Halbertsma, "Frisian Kingdom"; and Besteman, "North Holland."

[87] Clarke and Ambrosiani, *Towns*, pp. 5–45.

[88] Verhulst, *Rise*, p. 20; and Es, "Dorestad Centered."

[89] Verhulst, *Carolingian*, p. 26.

settlement excavations in the valley of the lower Rhône. It is now clear that a significantly greater number of new settlement sites for the fifth and sixth centuries have been identified than for the third and fourth centuries.[90] As in the region of Paris, where land reclamation has been noted, there is evidence for a similar phenomenon from the Burgundian region. In the south, detailed regulations were established in regard to assarting as a response to contemporary practices that were regarded as requiring new legal controls.[91]

On a broader canvas, a massive inventory of Provençal *villae* has demonstrated conclusively that they were "well occupied in the fourth and fifth centuries."[92] Neither these southern *villae* nor those in the north can be shown simply to have disappeared en masse during the early Merovingian era.[93] Rather, they were gradually replaced as part of a widespread cultural shift.[94] As Wickham observed, "The end of the villa as a settlement type ... is not a marker of economic and political crisis."[95] These changes resulted in the creation of highly productive agricultural estates, due in large part to the introduction and development of the bipartite type of organization, which gradually replaced the villa system in Gaul beginning in the early fifth century.[96]

Scholars also have uncovered considerable information indicating population growth further east. Some sites in southwest Germany under Merovingian rule have been shown to have had a population toward the latter part of the seventh century that was 400 percent larger than in Roman times.[97] In the more northerly parts of these borderlands, scholars have identified considerable increase in the number of so-called Germanic settlements in the Rhineland and its environs between ca. 400 and ca. 700.[98] Data from excavations throughout the city of Cologne, especially in the "Hay Market," make it clear that there was continuous significant settlement from the later Roman era through both the Merovingian and Carolingian periods.[99] These conclusions are supported by a wider sample of evidence from Cologne-area cemeteries, indicating an increase of some 60 percent in the size of the population

---

[90] Trémont, "Habitat"; and Lewit, *Agricultural Production*, p. xx; cf. Cheyette, "Disappearance."

[91] Innes, "Land," pp. 42, 46, 59, 63, 72, 73.

[92] Carru et al., "Les villae," p. 491.

[93] Lewit, "'Vanishing villas.'"

[94] Lewit, "'Vanishing villas,'" and Van Ossel and Ouzoulias, "Rural Settlement," pp. 145–49.

[95] Wickham, *Framing*, p. 481.

[96] Saris, "Origins"; Ganshof, "Manorial Organization," pp. 29–31; and Van Ossel, *Établissements*, p. 183.

[97] Verhulst, *Carolingian*, p. 26.

[98] Randsborg, *First Millennium*, pp. 67–69.

[99] Schütte, "Continuity," pp. 168–69; Aten, "Römische"; Trier, "Köln."

during approximately one hundred years between the mid-sixth and the mid-seventh centuries.[100]

Colonization

Overpopulation, which limits economic opportunity at home, is often identified by scholars as an important stimulus to explain immigration from rich settled and secure agricultural areas to largely uninhabited sites, often on the frontier. Substantial population growth has been noted on the borders of the *regnum Francorum* and beyond. This seems to have been the result of people moving eastward from various parts of the hexagon. In the southeast, for example, Bavaria, which only sometimes was under direct Frankish control, would evidently witness substantial colonization and land reorganization.[101] The same is true of Franconia, parts of Hesse, and Thuringia, regions along the eastern frontiers of what traditionally has been regarded as Frankish territory.[102]

Additional archaeological work, dealing with pollen analysis and land clearance, provides support for these growth patterns. For example, with regard to "German" territory, evidence from "the Rhön and Eifel show a clear increase in grain pollen from the seventh century onwards." This pattern of extension of the arable into fields in which wheat was grown is sustained by written sources.[103] East of the Rhine, for example, the Kassel area on the Fulda River not only had been settled from the west beginning in the later seventh century, but this area is regarded by modern scholars to have been fully occupied if not overcrowded by the mid-eighth century.[104] Similarly, the region around Würzburg had become crowded by the last quarter of the seventh century or perhaps even earlier,[105] and immigrants were moving north into the area where the monastery of Fulda later was established.[106]

New Ecclesiastical Construction

New construction on a large scale is prima facie evidence for the availability of surplus human and material resources. In addition, some construction, such as the building of larger numbers of houses and perhaps of bigger houses, unlike the building of new fortifications, may be taken as an indication of the need to

---

[100] Verhulst, *Carolingian*, p. 26.
[101] Bowlus, *Franks*, pp. 33–45.
[102] Franz, "Bevölkerungsgeschichte"; Bosl, *Franken*, pp. 13–14; Parsons, "Sites"; and Nitz, "Church."
[103] Verhulst, *Carolingian*, pp. 26–27.
[104] Gensen, *Althessens*, pp. 16–38.
[105] Wood, *Missionary Life*, pp. 160–61.
[106] Parsons, "Sites."

accommodate population increases and perhaps economic growth.[107] Constantine's Edict of Milan in 313 resulted in the construction of massive numbers of churches throughout the Roman Empire, including Gaul. This process, which continued through the Merovingian period, not only saw the construction of great cathedrals but also thousands of churches in *urbes, castra, castella*, and *vici*, as well as throughout the countryside in villages, on rural estates, and as part of monastic centers.[108] Of special importance is the construction of massive cathedral complexes of two or more churches and church houses, which became commonplace in the *urbes* of Gaul from the mid-fifth century onward.[109] The immense quantity of surplus human and material resources required to sustain this ongoing construction is obvious. In addition, large numbers of clergy and their support staffs, which did not produce agricultural surpluses, were required by the church to undertake its religious and educational work.[110]

Numerous monasteries for both men and women were built throughout Gaul in addition to the construction of churches of various sizes and types. As of thirty-five years ago, scholars were able to identify 215 urban monasteries flourishing in sixth-century Gaul. During the seventh century 330 new urban monasteries were built, an increase in excess of 150 percent. A disproportionate number of the 215 identified from the sixth century were located further south, and a disproportionate number of the 330 constructed in the seventh century were located in the more northerly parts of the hexagon. The jejune sources surviving from the sixth century and the even more limited number of sources surviving from the seventh century likely have resulted in an undercount of the total number of urban monasteries in general, and in regard to those founded in the seventh century in particular.[111]

The indices that traditionally are regarded as evidence for the direction of the demographic curve, such as surplus human and material resources, point upward for the Merovingian era. In addition, scholars are unable to identify serious depressants on the population, such as famine, war, and disease, either in the archaeological or written records of Merovingian Gaul. By contrast, the archaeological and written evidence, taken together, demonstrate the establishment of significant numbers of new settlements within the hexagon and colonization beyond the frontiers. These should be considered indicators of population growth until a more convincing

---

[107] Hvass, "Eine Dorfsiedlung."

[108] Février et al., *Topographie*; Brühl, *Palatium*; Vieillard-Troiekournoff, *Monuments*, pp. 84–95; Février, "*Vetera et Nova*"; Harries, "Christianity," pp. 87–88; Jones, "Church Finance"; and Verhulst, *Rise*, pp. 1–23.

[109] Piva, "Metz."

[110] Sotinel, "Le personnel," and Berlière, "Le nombre."

[111] Atsma, "Les monastères."

explanation can be fashioned. We also find the construction of massive numbers of churches and large numbers of monasteries, which are indices of an increasing population in need of religious support, if not of an increasing population in general. These investments in building are indicators of surpluses in both manpower and material resources. In short, a process of population growth would seem to have been in train for a period of more than two and a half centuries between the accession of Clovis to the Merovingian throne in 481 and the deposition of Childeric III in 751.[112]

Conclusion

Present research, both archaeological information not available to Pirenne and Dopsch as well as a more critical evaluation of the narrative sources, has lent support to the view that the barbarian invasions did not destroy the later Roman economy in Gaul. If, in fact, the population of Gaul followed traditional premodern demographic patterns fundamental to subsistence economies in the West and was increasing, it would have been highly unlikely for the aggregate production of goods and services to have declined seriously. Approximately the same order of magnitude of population requires approximately the same quantities of food, clothing, shelter, and tools over a period of some three centuries even to sustain relative demographic stasis. An increasing population requires the production of greater quantities of goods and services. It seems reasonable to suggest that since the Merovingian period likely saw an increase in population because there were no significant or sustained assaults on the demographic curve, it also likely saw economic growth, an increase in the production of goods and services.

Abbreviations

BAR   British Archaeological Reports
CAH   Cameron, Avril, Bryan Ward-Perkins, and Michael Whitby, eds. *Late Antiquity: Empire and Successors, A.D. 425–600.* Vol. 14 of *The Cambridge Ancient History.* 2nd ed. Cambridge: Cambridge University Press, 2000.
Campagnes   Ouzoulias, Pierre, et al., eds. *Les campagnes de la Gaule à la fin de l'Antiquité.* Antibes: APCDA, 2001.
European Towns Barley, M. W., ed. *European Towns: Their Archaeology and Early History.* London: Academic Press, 1977.
JLA   *Journal of Late Antiquity*
JRA   *Journal of Roman Archaeology*
JRS   *Journal of Roman Studies*

---

[112] Coale and Demeny, *Life Tables,* pp. 5–41; Parkin, *Demography,* pp. 79–90; Scheidel, "Progress," pp. 17–19.

SSCI   Settimane di studio del Centro italiano di studi sull'alto medioevo
                (Spoleto: Centro italiano di studi sull'alto medioevo, 1953–)
TRHS   *Transactions of the Royal Historical Society*

Bibliography

Ando, Clifford. "Decline, Fall, and Transformation," *JLA* 1, no. 1 (2008): 20–30.

Aten, N. "Römische bis neuzeitliche Befunde der Ausgrabung auf dem Heumarkt in Köln." *Kölner Jahrbuch* 34 (2001): 623–700.

Atsma, Hartmut. "Les monastères urbains du nord de la Gaule." *Revue d'histoire de l'église de France* 62 (1976): 163–87.

Bachrach, Bernard S. *The Anatomy of a Little War: A Diplomatic and Military History of the Gundovald Affair: 568–586.* Boulder: Westview, 1994.

———. "Fifth Century Metz: Later Roman Christian *Urbs* or Ghost Town?" *Antiquité Tardive* 10 (2002): 363–81.

———. *Merovingian Military Organization 481–751.* Minneapolis: University of Minnesota Press, 1972.

———. "Plague, Population and Economy in Merovingian Gaul." *Journal of the Australian Early Medieval Association* 3 (2007): 29–56.

Banaji, Jairus. *Agrarian Change in Late Antiquity: Gold, Labour, and Aristocratic Dominance.* 2nd ed. Oxford: Oxford University Press, 2007.

Barker, Graeme, and John Lloyd, eds. *Roman Landscapes.* Rome: British School, 1991.

Barley, M. W. ed. *European Towns: Their Archaeology and Early History.* London: Academic Press, 1977.

Barnish, S. J. B. "The Transformation of Classical Cities and the Pirenne Debate." *JRA* 2 (1989): 385–400.

Bayard, Dedier. "La fin de la domination romaine dans le nord de la Gaule: L'apport de la sigillée d'Argonne." In *L'armée romaine et les barbares du III\<sup\> au VII\<sup\> siècle*, ed. Françoise Vallet and Michel Kazanski, pp. 223–33. Paris: CNRS, 1993.

Berlière, Ursmer, "Le nombre des moines dans les anciens monastères." *Revue Bénédictine* 41 (1929): 231–61; 42 (1930): 19–42.

Bernhard, H., "Die Merowingerzeit in der Pfalz. Bemerkungen zum Übergang von der Spätantike zum frühen Mittelalter und zum Stand der Erforschung." *Mitteilungen des Historischen Vereins der Pfalz* 95 (1997): 9–14.

Besteman, J. C. "North Holland AD 400–1200: Turning Tide or Tide Turned?" In *Medieval Archaeology in the Netherlands: Studies Presented to H. H. van Regteren Altena*, ed. J.C. Besteman, J. M. Bos, and H. A. Heidinga, pp. 91–120. Assen/Maastricht: Van Gorcum, 1990.

Biarne, Jacques. "Marseilles." In *Provinces écclesiastiques de Vienne et d'Arles (Viennensis et alpes Graiae et Poeninae)*, ed. Jacques Biarne et al., pp. 121–33. Paris: De Boccard, 1986.

Bosl, Karl. *Franken um 800: Structuranalyse einer fränkischen Königsprovinz.* 2nd ed. Munich: Beck, 1969.

Bouard, Michel de, and Gabriel Fournier. "Country and Regional Surveys of France." In *European Towns*, pp. 169–84.

Bowden, William, and Luke Lavan. "The Late Antique Countryside: An Introduction." In *Recent Research*, ed. Bowden, Lavan, and Machado, pp. xvii–xxvi.

Bowden, William, Luke Lavan, and Carlos Machado, eds. *Recent Research on the Late Antique Countryside.* Leiden: Brill, 2004.

Bowlus, Charles. *Franks, Moravians, and Magyars: The Struggle for the Middle Danube, 778–907.* Philadelphia: University of Pennsylvania Press, 1995.

Breukelaar, Adriaan H. B. *Historiography and Episcopal Authority in Sixth-Century Gaul: The Histories of Gregory of Tours Interpreted in Their Historical Context.* Göttingen: Vandenhoeck & Ruprecht, 1994.

Brühl, Carlrichard. *Palatium und Civitas: Studien zur Profantopographie spätantiker Civitates vom 3. bis zum 13 Jahrhundert.* 2 vols. Cologne: Böhlau, 1975–90.

Carru, Dominique, Fabienne Gateau, Philippe Leveau, and Nadège Renaud. "Les villae en Provence aux IVᵉ et Vᵉ siècles: Apports et limites des inventaries archéologues." In *Campagnes*, pp. 475–501.

Cherry, J. F. "Vox Populi: Landscape Archaeology in Mediterranean Europe." *JRA* 1 (2002): 561–82.

Cheyette, Fredric. "The Disappearance of the Ancient Landscape and the Climatic Anomaly of the Early Middle Ages: A Question to Be Pursued." *Early Medieval Europe* 16 (2008): 127–65.

Christie, Neil. "Barren Fields? Landscapes and Settlements in Late Roman and Post-Roman Italy." In *Human Landscapes in Classical Antiquity: Environment and Culture*, ed. Graham Shipley and John Salmon, pp. 254–83. London: Routledge, 1996.

———, ed. *Landscapes of Change: Rural Evolutions in Late Antiquity and the Early Middle Ages.* Aldershot: Ashgate, 2004.

Clarke, Helen, and Björn Ambrosiani. *Towns in the Viking Age.* 2nd ed. London: University of Leicester Press, 1995.

Coale, Ansley, and Paul Demeny. *Regional Model Life Tables and Stable Populations.* Princeton, NJ: Princeton University Press, 1966.

Collot, G. "Fouilles archéologiques sur le chantier de l'École des Arts Appliqués." *Annuaire de la Société d'histoire et d'archéologie de la Lorraine*, 67–68 (1967–68): 5–32.

Davis, Jennifer R., and Michael McCormick. "The Early Middle Ages: Europe's Long Morning." In *The Long Morning of Medieval Europe: New Directions in Early Medieval Studies*, ed. Jennifer R. Davis and Michael McCormick, pp. 1–18. Aldershot: Ashgate, 2008.

Delaplace, Christine. "Débats et problèmes." In *Campagnes*, pp. 15–20.

Depeyrot, Georges. *Richesse et Société chez les Merovingiens et Carolingiens.* Paris: Hespérides, 1994.

Doehaerd, Renée. *The Early Middle Ages in the West: Economy and Society.* Trans. W. G. Deakin. Amsterdam: North Holland, 1978.

Dopsch, Alfons. *The Economic and Social Foundations of European Civilization.* Abridged by Erna Patzelt and trans. M. G. Beard and N. Marshall. London: Routledge, 1937.

Durand, Aline, and Philippe Leveau. "Farming in Mediterranean France and Rural Settlement in the Late Roman and Early Medieval Periods: The Contribution from Archaeology and Environmental Sciences in the Last Twenty Years." In *The Making of Feudal Agricultures?*, ed. Miquel Barceló and François Sigaut, pp. 177–253. Leiden: Brill, 2004.

Feller, M., and G. Poplineau, with the collaboration of Sabine Baccega. "Ateliers de céremiques gallo-romaine d'Argonne: Préalables méthodologiques." *Les cahiers lorrains* (1988): 173–80.

Février, Paul-Albert. "Towns in the Western Mediterranean." In *European Towns*, pp. 315–42.

———. "*Vetera et Nova*: Le poids du passé, les germes de l'avenir, IIIe–VIe siècle." In *Histoire de la France urbaine*. Vol. 1, *La ville antique des origines au IXe siècle*, ed. Georges Duby, pp. 399–493. Paris: Éditions du Seuil, 1981.

Février, Paul-Albert, et al., eds. *Topographie chrétienne des cites de la Gaule des origines au milieu du VIIIe siècle*. 13 vols. Paris: De Boccard, 1975–2007.

Fossier, Robert. "Les tendences de l'économie: stagnation ou croissance?" In SSCI 27, 1:261–74. 1981.

Fouracre, Paul, "Space, Culture and Kingdoms in Early Medieval Europe." In *The Medieval World*, ed. Peter Linehan and Janet L. Nelson, pp. 366–80. London: Routledge, 2001.

Franz, L. "Zur Bevölkerungsgeschichte des frühen Mittelalters." *Deutsches Archiv für Landes- und Volksforschung* 2 (1938): 404–16.

Ganshof, F. L. "Les bureaux de tonlieu de Marseille et de Fos: contribution à l'histoire des institutions de la monarchie franque." In *Études historiques à la mémoire de Noël Didier*, pp. 125–33. Paris: Montchrestien, 1960.

———. "Manorial Organization in the Low Countries in the Seventh, Eighth, and Ninth Centuries." *TRHS*, 4th ser., 31 (1949): 29–59.

———. "Notes sur les ports de Provence du VIIIe au Xe siècle." *Revue historique* 183 (1938): 28–37.

Gauthier, Nancy. "Rouen pendant le haute Moyen Âge (650–850)." In *La Neustrie: Les Pays au Nord de la Loire de 650 à 850*, ed. Hartmut Atsma, pp. 1–20. Sigmaringen: Thorbecke, 1989.

Gauthiez, Bernard. "La réoccupation plantifée de la Cité de Rouen au Haut Moyen Âge." In *Medieval Art, Architecture and Archaeology at Rouen*, ed. J. Stratford, pp. 12–19. London: British Archaeological Association, 1986.

Gensen, Rolf. *Althessens Frühzeit: Frühgeschichtliche Fundstätten und Funde in Nordhessen*. Wiesbaden: Landesamtes Hessen, 1977.

Gissinger, Bastien. *Recherches sur le site fortifieé de Strasbourg durant l'Antiquité tardive: Le castrum d'Argentoratum*. Oxford: BAR, 2002.

Goffart, Walter. *Barbarian Tides: The Migration Age and the Later Roman Empire*. Philadelphia: University of Pennsylvania Press, 2006.

———. *The Narrators of Barbarian History (550–800): Jordanes, Gregory of Tours, Bede, and Paul the Deacon*. Princeton, NJ: Princeton University Press, 1988.

Grey, Cam. "Revisiting the 'Problem' of *agri deserti* in the Late Roman Empire." *JRA*, 20 (2007): 362–76.

Grierson, Philip. "Commerce in the Dark Ages: A Critique of the Evidence." *TRHS*, 5th ser., 9 (1958): 123–40.

Halbertsma, H. "The Frisian Kingdom." *Berichten van de Rijksdienst voor het Oudheidkundig Bodemonderzoek*, 15–16 (1965–66): 69–108.

Halsall, Guy. "Towns, Societies and Ideas: The Not-so-Strange Case of Late Roman and Early Merovingian Metz." In *Towns in Transition: Urban Evolution in Late Antiquity and the Early Middle Ages*, ed. Neil Christie and Simon T. Loseby, pp. 235–61. Aldershot: Ashgate, 1996.

———. *Warfare and Society in the Barbarian West, 450–900*. London: Routledge, 2003.

Hamerow, H. *Early Medieval Settlements: The Archaeology of Rural Communities in North-west Europe, A.D. 400–800.* Oxford: Oxford University Press, 2002.

Harries, Jill. "Christianity and the City in Late Roman Gaul." In *The City in Late Antiquity,* ed. John Rich, pp. 77–98. London: Routledge, 1992.

Heather, Peter. *The Fall of the Roman Empire: A New History of Rome and the Barbarians.* Oxford: Oxford University Press, 2005.

Heidinga, H. A., *Medieval Settlement and Economy North of the Lower Rhine: Archeology and History of Kootwijk and the Veluwe (the Netherlands).* Assen: Van Gorcum, 1987.

Heinzelmann, Martin. *Gregory of Tours: History and Society in the Sixth Century.* Trans. C. Carroll. Cambridge: Cambridge University Press, 2001.

Herlihy, David. "Demography." In *Dictionary of the Middle Ages,* ed. J. R. Strayer, 4:139–48. 13 vols. New York: Scribner, 1982–89.

Hesnard, Antoinette et al. *Parcours des villes: Marseilles 10 ans d'archéologie, 2600 ans d'histoire.* Aix-en-Provence: Édosid, 1999.

Higounet, Charles. "Les forêts de l'Europe occidentale du Vᵉ au XIᵉ siècle." SSCI 13, 1:343–98. 1966.

Hodges, Richard. *Towns and Trade in the Age of Charlemagne.* London: Duckworth, 2000.

———. *Goodbye to the Vikings? Re-reading Early Medieval Archaeology.* London: Duckworth, 2006.

Hodges, Richard, and David Whitehouse. *Mohammed, Charlemagne & the Origins of Europe.* Ithaca, NY: Cornell University Press, 1983.

Horden, Peregrine, and Nicholas Purcell. *The Corrupting Sea: A Study of Mediterranean History.* Oxford: Blackwell, 2000.

Hvass, S. "Eine Dorfsiedlung während des 1. Jts. n. Chr. in Mitteljütland, Dänemark." *Bericht der Römisch-Germanischen Kommission* 67 (1986): 529–42.

Innis, Matthew. "Land, Freedom and the Making of the Medieval West." *TRHS,* 6th ser., 16 (2006): 39–74.

Jones, A. H. M. "Church Finance in the Fifth and Sixth Centuries." *Journal of Theological Studies,* n.s. 11 (1960): 84–94.

———. *The Later Roman Empire, 284–602: A Social, Economic and Administrative Survey.* 2 vols. Norman: University of Oklahoma Press, 1964.

Knight, Jeremy K. *The End of Antiquity: Archaeology, Society and Religion, AD 235–700.* Stroud: Tempus, 1999.

Lenz, Karl Heinz. "Late Roman Rural Settlement in the Southern Part of the Province of Germania Secunda in Comparision with other Regions of the Roman Rhineland." In *Campagnes,* pp. 113–46.

Lewit, Tamara. *Agricultural Production in the Roman Economy, A.D. 200–400.* 2nd ed. Oxford: BAR, 2004.

———. "'Vanishing villas': What Happened to Élite Rural Habitation in the West in the 5th–6th c.?" *JRA* 16 (2003): 260–74.

Lewit, Tamara, and Alexandra Chavarría. "Archaeological Research on the Late Antique Countryside: A Bibliographic Essay." In *Recent Research,* ed. Bowden, Lavan, and Machado, pp. 3–51.

Liebeschuetz, J. H. W. G. *Decline and Fall of the Roman City.* Oxford: Oxford University Press, 2001.

Livi-Bacchi, Massimo. *The Population of Europe: A History.* Trans. C. De Nardi Ipsen and C. Ipsen. Oxford: Blackwell, 2000.

Lopez, Robert. "The Dollar of the Middle Ages." *Journal of Economic History* 11 (1951): 209–34.

Loseby, Simon T. "Marseille: A Late Antique Success Story?" *JRS* 82 (1992): 165–85.

———. "Marseille and the Pirenne Thesis, I: Gregory of Tours, the Merovingian Kings, and 'Un Grand Port.'" In *The Sixth Century: Production, Distribution and Demand*, ed. Richard Hodges and William Bowden, pp. 203–29. Leiden: Brill, 1998.

Lyon, Bryce D. *Henri Pirenne: A Biographical and Intellectual Study.* Ghent: E. Story-Scientia, 1974.

———. *The Origins of the Middle Ages: Pirenne's Challenge to Gibbon.* New York: W. W. Norton, 1972.

MacMullen, Ramsey. *Corruption and the Decline of Rome.* New Haven, CT: Yale University Press, 1988.

Marcone, Arnaldo. "A Long Late Antiquity? Considerations on a Controversial Periodization: The Rise and Function of the Concept 'Late Antiquity.'" *JLA* 1, no. 1 (2008): 4–19.

Matthisen, Ralph. "'Nature or Nurture?': Some Perspectives on the Gallic Famine of ca. A.D. 470." *Ancient World* 24 (1993): 91–105.

McCleary, G. F. *The Malthusian Population Theory.* London: Faber & Faber, 1953.

McCormick, Michael. "Bateaux de vie, bateaux de mort: maladie, commerce, transports annonaires et le passage économique du Bas-empire au Moyen Âge." In SSCI 45, 1:52–65. 1998.

———. "Origins of the European Economy: A Debate with Michael McCormick." *Early Medieval Europe* 12 (2003): 259–306.

———. *Origins of the Western Economy: Communications and Commerce, A.D. 300–900.* Cambridge: Cambridge University Press, 2001.

———. "Rats, Communications, and Plague: Toward an Ecological History." *Journal of Interdisciplinary History* 34 (2003): 1–25.

———. "Toward a Molecular History of the Justinianic Pandemic." In *Plague and the End of Antiquity: The Pandemic of 541–750*, ed. Lester K. Little, pp. 290–312. Cambridge: Cambridge University Press, 2007.

Nitz, Hans-Jürgen, "The Church as Colonist: The Benedictine Abbey of Lorsch and Planned Waldhufen Colonization in the Odenwald." *Journal of Historical Geography* 9 (1983): 105–26.

Ouzoulias, Pierre, et al., eds. *Les campagnes de la Gaule à la fin de l'Antiquité.* Antibes: APCDA, 2001.

Parkin, Tim G. *Demography and Roman Society.* Baltimore: Johns Hopkins University Press, 1992.

Parsons, David. "Sites and Monuments of the Anglo-Saxon Mission in Central Germany." *Archaeological Journal* 140 (1983): 280–321.

Périn, Patrick. "The Origin of the Village in Early Medieval Gaul." In *Landscapes of Change: Rural Evolutions in Late Antiquity and the Early Middle Ages*, ed. Neil Christie, pp. 225–78. Aldershot: Ashgate, 2004.

Peytremann, Edith. *Archéologie de l'habitat rural dans le nord de la France du IVe au XIIe siècle.* 2 vols. Saint-Germain-en-Laye: AFAM, 2003.

Pirenne, Henri. *Mohammed and Charlemagne.* Trans. Bernard Mial. New York: Meridian, 1957.

Piva, Paolo. "Metz: Un Gruppo Episcopale Alla Svolta Dei Tempi (Secoli IV–IX)." *Antiquité Tardive* 8 (2000): 337–52.

Randsborg, Klaus. *The First Millennium AD in Europe and the Mediterranean: An Archaeological Essay.* Cambridge: Cambridge University Press, 1991.

Reuter, Timothy. *Germany in the Early Middle Ages: 800–1056.* London: Longman, 1991.

Riché, Pierre. "Problèmes de démographie historique du Haut Moyen Âge (Vᵉ–VIIIᵉ siècles)." *Annales de démographie historique* 3 (1966): 37–55.

Rouche, Michel. "Grégoire le Grand face à la situation économique de son temps." In *Grégoire le Grand*, ed. Jacques Fontaine, Robert Gillet, and Stan Pellistrandi, pp. 41–57. Paris: CNRS, 1986.

Russell, J. C. *Late Ancient and Medieval Population.* Philadelphia: American Philosophical Society, 1985.

Samson, Ross. "The Merovingian Nobleman's Home: Castle or Villa." *Journal of Medieval History* 13 (1987): 287–315.

———. "Populous Dark-Age Towns: The Finleyesque Approach." *Journal of European Archaeology* 2 (1994): 97–129.

Saris, Peter. "The Origins of the Manorial Economy: New Insights from Late Antiquity." *English Historical Review* 119 (2004): 280–311.

Scheidel, Walter. "Progress and Problems in Roman Demography." In *Debating Roman Demography*, ed. Walter Scheidel, pp. 1–81. Leiden: Brill, 2001.

Schütte, Svenn. "Continuity Problems and Authority Structures in Cologne." In *After Empire: Towards an Ethnology of Europe's Barbarians*, ed. Georgio Ausenda, pp. 170–75. Woodbridge: Boydell, 1995.

Schwarz, G. M. "Village Populations according to the Polyptyque of the Abbey of St. Bertin." *Journal of Medieval History* 11 (1985): 31–41.

Siegmund, Frank. "Social Relations among the Old Saxons." In *The Continental Saxons from the Migration Period to the Tenth Century: An Ethnographic Perspective*, ed. D. H. Green and Frank Siegmund, pp. 77–95. Woodbridge: Boydell, 2003.

Slater, T. R. *Towns in Decline, AD 100–1600.* Aldershot: Ashgate, 2000.

Slicher van Bath, B. H. "The Economic and Social Conditions in the Frisian Districts from 900 to 1500." *A.A.G. Bijdragen* 13 (1965): 97–133.

Sotinel, Claire. "Le personnel épiscopal: Enquête sur la puissance de l'évêque et la cité." In *L'évêque dans la cité du IVᵉ au Vᵉ siècle: Image et autorité*, ed. Éric Rebillard and Claire Sotinel, pp. 105–26. Rome: École française, 1998.

Staab, Franz. *Untersuchungen zur Gesellschaft am Mittelrhein in der Karolingerzeit.* Geschichtliche Landeskunde 11. Wiesbaden: F. Steiner, 1975.

Stathakopoulos, Dionysios. *Famine and Pestilence in the Late Roman and Early Byzantine Empire: A Systematic Survey of Subsistence Crises and Epidemics.* Aldershot: Ashgate, 2004.

Steuer, Heiko. "Stadtarchäologie in Köln." In *Stadtkernforschung*, ed. Helmut Jäger, pp. 61–102. Cologne: Böhlau, 1987.

TeBrake, William H. *Medieval Frontier: Culture and Ecology in Rijnland.* College Station: Texas A&M Press, 1985.

Theuws, Frans. "Landed Property and Manorial Organisation in Northern Austrasia: Some Considerations and a Case Study." In *Images of the Past: Studies of Ancient Societies in Northwestern Europe*, ed. N. Roymans and Frans Theuws, pp. 340–47. Amsterdam: Instituut voor Pre- en Protohistorische Archeologie, 1991.

Toubert, Pierre. "The Carolingian Moment." In *A History of the Family*, ed. André Burguière et al. Trans. S. H. Tenison, R. Morris, and A. Wilson, pp. 379–406. Cambridge, MA: Harvard University Press, 1996.

Trémont, F. "Habitat et peuplement en Provence à la fin de l'Antiquité." In *Campagnes*, pp. 275–301.

Trier, Marcus. "Köln im frühen Mittelalter: Zur Stadt des 5. bis 10. Jahrhunderts aufgrund archäologischer Quellen." In *Europa im 10. Jahrhundert Archäologie einer Aufbruchszeit*, ed. Joachim Henning, pp. 301–10. Mainz: P. von Zabern, 2002.

Vallat, Jean-Pierre. "Survey Archaeology and Rural History—A Difficult but Productive Relationship." In *Roman Landscapes*, ed. Barker and Lloyd, pp. 10–17.

Van Es, W. A. "Dorestad Centered." In *Medieval Archaeology in the Netherlands: Studies Presented to H. H. van Regteren Altena*, ed. J. C. Besteman, J. M. Bos, and H. A. Heidinga, pp. 151–82. Assen: Van Gorcum, 1990.

Van Ossel, Paul. *Établissements ruraux de l'Antiquité tardive dans le Nord de la Gaule, Gallia.* Supplément 51. Paris: Éditions du centre national de recherché scientifique, 1992.

Van Ossel, Paul, and Pierre Ouzoulias. "Rural Settlement Economy in the Later Empire: An Overview and Assessment." Trans. R. Bruce Hitchner. *JRA* 13 (2000): 133–60.

Verdel, E. "Archéologie urbaine à Metz, Fouille de sauvetage de l'espace Serpenois à Metz." *Les cahiers lorrains* 4 (1986): 353–61.

Verhulst, Adriaan. *The Carolingian Economy.* Cambridge: Cambridge University Press, 2002.

———. *The Rise of Cities in North-West Europe.* Cambridge: Cambridge University Press, 1999.

Vieillard-Troiekournoff, May. *Les monuments religieus de la Gaul d'apré les oeuvres de Grégoire de Tours.* Paris: Honoré Champion, 1976.

Ward-Perkins, Bryan. *From Classical Antiquity to the Middle Ages: Urban Public Building in Northern and Central Italy, AD 300–830.* Oxford: Oxford University Press, 1984.

———. "Land, Labour and Settlement." In *CAH*, pp. 1315–45.

———. "Specialized Production and Exchange." In *CAH*, pp. 346–91.

———. "The Towns of Northern Italy: Rebirth or Renewal?" In *The Rebirth of Towns in the West, AD 700–1050*, ed. R. Hodges and B. Hobley, 16–27. London: Academic Press, 1988.

Wells, Peter S. *Barbarians to Angels: The Dark Ages Reconsidered.* New York: W. W. Norton, 2008.

Whittaker, C. R. "Agri Deserti." In *Studies in Roman Property*, ed. M. I. Finley, pp. 137–65, 194–200. London: Cambridge University Press, 1976. Reprinted in C. R. Whittaker, *Land, City and Trade in the Roman Empire.* Aldershot: Ashgate, 1993.

———. "Late Roman Trade and Traders." In *Trade in the Ancient Economy*, ed. P. Garnsey, K. Hopkins and C. R. Whittaker, pp. 163–80. Berkeley and Los Angeles: University of California Press, 1983.

Wickham, Chris. "European Forests in the Early Middle Ages: Landscape and Land Clearance." In SSCI 37, 2:479–545. 1990.

———. *Framing the Early Middle Ages: Europe and the Mediterranean, 400–800.* Oxford: Oxford University Press, 2005.

Wightman, Edith. "The Towns of Gaul with Special Reference to the North-East." In *European Towns*, pp. 303–14.

Wood, Ian. *The Missionary Life: Saints and the Evangelisation of Europe, 400–1050.* London: Longman, 2001.

————. "The North-Western Provinces." In *CAH*, pp. 497–524.

Zadora-Rio, E. "Le habitat rural au Moyen Âge." *Les nouvelles de l'archéologie* 92 (2003): 5–33.

Zerner, Monique. "Enfants et jeunes au IXᵉ siècle: La démographie du polyptyque de Marseilles, 813–814." *Provence historique* 36 (1981): 355–80.

————. "La population de Villeneuve-Saint-Georges et de Nogent-sur-Mane au IXᵉ siècle d'après le polyptyque de Saint-Germain-des-Prés." *Annales de la faculté des lettres de sciences humaines de Nice* 37 (1979): 17–24.

Henri Pirenne at Work:
Editing Galbert of Bruges

Jeff Rider

H ENRI PIRENNE'S EDITION of Galbert of Bruges's *De multro, traditione, et occisione gloriosi Karoli comitis Flandriarum*, published in 1891, is not his greatest or most influential work, but it nonetheless played an important role in his career and was his most important work at the time it was published.[1] As Bryce Lyon wrote in his biography of Pirenne, "his reputation was furthered by an edition of Galbert of Bruges' account of the murder of Count Charles the Good of Flanders. … [T]his study revealed his gift for work on key historical problems. By choosing to edit Galbert, who was a well-placed witness to many of the dramatic events he described, Pirenne made available the finest narrative account of twelfth-century Flemish feudal, institutional, and communal history. … No more valuable text on medieval communal history exists."[2] Pirenne's friend Maurice Prou, one of the editors of the series in which the edition appeared, wrote to him not long after the publication of the edition that "[v]otre Galbert a parfaitement réussi. On en

I would like to thank Professor Michel de Waha, Françoise Jurion, the staff of the archives of the Université libre de Bruxelles, especially Françoise Delloye, and the staff of the Bibliothèque municipale de Sens, especially the conservateur en chef Michèle Degrave, for all their help during my trips to the Pirenne archives in Brussels and the Prou archives in Sens. I also owe a special debt of gratitude to Professor Sara McDougall, who took the time to provide me with some desperately needed materials at the last minute. The research for this essay was made possible by a grant from the Thomas and Catharine McMahon Memorial Fund of Wesleyan University.

[1] Galbert of Bruges, *Histoire du meurtre*. For a bibliography of Pirenne's publications, see Ganshof et al., "Bibliographie."

[2] Lyon, *Henri Pirenne*, pp. 94–96. In his entry on Pirenne in the *Biographie nationale* F. L. Ganshof wrote that "l'excellente édition de cette source de qualité et de portée exceptionnelles qu'est l'*Histoire du meurtre de Charles le Bon, comte de Flandre*, par Galbert de Bruges" was the first of the two editions "hors de pair" published by Pirenne ("Pirenne," col. 685).

parle beaucoup. Tout le monde le trouve excellent, très bien fait, et à juste titre." Pirenne was, in fact, somewhat anxious about the reception of the edition, and Prou assured him again a little over a week later that "[v]otre édition de Galbert a établi ici votre réputation," and wrote yet again several months later that "[c]omme je sais que l'estime des Français vous est précieuse, je puis vous assurer que votre Galbert vous l'a acquise."[3] The edition also played a significant role in Pirenne's nomination to the Commission royale d'histoire, which occurred soon after its publication. Writing in July 1891 to inform Pirenne of this honor, Napoléon de Pauw noted that "[v]otre dernière et excellente publication sur Galbertus n'a pas été étrangère à cette désignation. Je l'avais lu comme un roman et vos notes judicieuses en facilitent admirablement l'intelligence."[4]

The foundation of Pirenne's edition of Galbert's chronicle was in some sense laid in 1883–84, when he spent nine months in Paris taking courses at the École des Chartes and the École pratique des hautes études, where he studied with Arthur Giry and Marcel Thévenin, among others, and became friends with his fellow students Maurice Prou and Abel Lefranc.[5] The relationships and friendships that Pirenne formed that year, especially those with Giry, Prou, and Lefranc, were maintained actively in the following years, and it was out of them that the edition of Galbert's chronicle grew.

The immediate origin of the edition appears to have been a visit Pirenne made to Paris in late April 1890 and a meeting he had with Giry and Prou at that time. A new series of editions of primary sources, the "Collection de textes pour servir à l'étude et à l'enseignement de l'histoire," had been founded in January 1885 "par l'initiative d'un certain nombre de membres de l'Institut, de l'Université, de l'Ecole des Chartes et de l'Ecole des Hautes-Etudes." The purpose of the collection, as its title suggests, was to provide reasonably inexpensive texts of primary sources that could be purchased by students as well as teachers and scholars and used in courses. It was directed by an editorial committee made up of Arthur Giry, Régis Jaliffer, Charles-Victor Langlois, Ernest Lavisse, Henry Lemonnier, Achille Luchaire, Maurice Prou, Marcel Thévenin, and Antoine Thomas. The first volume in the collection, *Les cinq livres de ses histoires* of Raoul Glaber, edited by Prou, was published in 1886.[6] The collection was thus still reasonably young when

[3] Letter from Prou to Pirenne, from Nanterre, Sept. 24, 1891 (Pirenne, Papiers personnels, sér. 1, vol. 01/01/002: Correspondences II: 1885–91; subsequent references to this volume are cited as vol. 01/01/002); Prou, Paris, Oct. 3, 1891 (vol. 01/01/002); letter from Prou to Pirenne, from Paris, Jan. 3, 1892 (Pirenne, Papiers personnels, sér. 1, vol. 01/01/003: Correspondances III: 1892–94; subsequent references to this volume are cited as vol. 01/01/003).

[4] Letter from Pauw to Pirenne, from Ghent, July 9, 1891 (Pirenne, Papiers personnels, sér. 3, vol. 01/03/001; subsequent references to this volume are cited as vol. 01/03/001).

[5] Lyon, *Henri Pirenne*, pp. 46–58; Lyon, "Maurice Prou," pp. 71–72, 77–80.

[6] Alphonse Picard Editeur, *Extrait du Catalogue général* (vol. 01/03/001) [brochure].

Pirenne visited Paris in spring 1890 (only nine volumes had appeared by then), and its editors were eager to have new proposals and new texts to print, especially narrative texts. In a letter to Pirenne written on January 4, 1892, for example, Giry announced the publication of the eleventh volume of the collection, noting that "C'est un recueil de documents sur l'administration financière de la France aux XVe & XVIe siècles. Je l'ai trouvé fort intéressant. Mais," he continued, "ce qui nous manque le plus ce sont les chroniqueurs—cherchez nous de bons éditeurs."[7]

As I noted above, the idea for the edition of Galbert's chronicle seems to have arisen at a meeting between Pirenne, Prou, and Giry during a visit Pirenne made to Paris in late April 1890. Galbert's name and text are never mentioned in Pirenne's correspondence before that visit, but soon after his departure from Paris, Prou wrote to him:

> Je vous écris aujourd'hui de la part du Comité de publication des textes historiques, qui a tenu hier séance. Je viens vous rappeler la promesse que vous nous avez faite à Giry et à moi de nous envoyer une édition de chronique. Le nom de votre chroniqueur m'a encore échappé. Veuillez donc m'écrire une lettre que je puisse lire, en partie au moins, au comité indiquant l'époque où vivait ce chroniqueur, les raisons pour lesquelles il serait intéressant de le publier, *l'époque* à laquelle vous nous livrerez le manuscrit, le nombre de feuilles—approximatif—que le texte et la préface occuperont. Vous serez bien aimable si vous vous mettez promptement à cette besogne. Je compte donc sur une bonne réponse de vous.[8]

Giry wrote to him similarly three days later: "Prou a dû vous écrire au nom de notre Comité de publication de la Collection de textes pour vous prier de nous donner quelques indications sur la Chronique dont nous avons parlé et que vous nous offriez de publier. Si elle offre un intérêt historique un peu général & si elle n'est pas trop longue, nous serions très heureux de vous éditer."[9]

It thus appears that Pirenne's "proposal" to Prou and Giry had been rather spontaneous and informal. Had it occurred during a friendly lunch or dinner? Had Giry or Prou told Pirenne how much they wanted new texts, especially chronicles, to publish in their series and asked him if he might possibly have something to contribute? Had Pirenne, hearing them tell of their need, said that he thought he might have something for them? The passages from Prou's and Giry's letters suggest either that Pirenne's proposal had been somewhat short on details or that Prou and Giry could not remember clearly what they had discussed. What they seem to have retained above all was that their friend had offered to edit a new text for their collection and that in their delight at the prospect of a new volume, they

---

[7] Giry, Paris, Jan. 4, 1892 (vol. 01/01/003).
[8] Prou, Paris, May 9, 1890 (vol. 01/03/001).
[9] Giry, Paris, May 12, 1890 (vol. 01/03/001).

mentioned Pirenne's proposal to the editorial committee at its next meeting without knowing or remembering much about what it was he intended to edit, except that it was a chronicle! The recurrence of the word in the passages cited above makes it clear that this is what really caught their attention in whatever Pirenne proposed. When he did send the more detailed proposal that Prou had requested in his letter of May 9 shortly thereafter, Prou responded: "Pour un homme pressé, je ne le suis guère à vous répondre et à vous remercier. Dieu sait cependant si nous avons reçu M. Giry et moi, votre proposition avec plaisir."[10] Galbert's chronicle was exactly the kind of text they wanted for the series.

On his side, Pirenne probably proposed an edition of Galbert's chronicle for a number of reasons. First, it would be a book-length publication in a series edited by a number of prominent scholars that would display his erudition.[11] In order to understand how important this might have been to Pirenne at the time, we need to remember that he was only twenty-seven years of age when he proposed the edition, had been a professor for only five years, was in only his fourth year as a professor at Ghent, and his major (i.e., book-length) publications at this point consisted of his 72-page *Sedulius de Liège, suivi de Sedulli Carmina Inedita*, a "Travail présenté au cours d'histoire de M. le professeur Kurth, à l'Université de Liège" and published in 1882 when he was nineteen, and his 119-page *Histoire de la constitution de la ville de Dinant au Moyen-Âge* published in 1889 in the newly established publication series of the Faculty of Letters of the University of Ghent.[12] An edition of Galbert's chronicle for the collection would be his most important book-length work to date and the first to be published outside of Belgium.

Secondly, he would get paid for this publication. As Lyon's biography shows, money had been important in the family in which Pirenne had grown up. His father had kept him on a strict allowance when he was studying in Paris and had expected him to keep and send him detailed accounts of his expenditures.[13] Pirenne's interest in the financial side of the publication of the Galbert edition is evident from his correspondence. Replying, evidently, to a query from Pirenne, Prou first informed him in a letter dated June 14, 1890, that he would be paid thirty francs per printed folio.[14] Two weeks later he repeated this in a second letter whose wording suggests that Pirenne had written something in the interim that made Prou feel that his friend was somewhat disappointed with the compensation: "Je crois vous avoir répondu pour la rétribution, 30 frcs par feuille; à côté de

---

[10] Prou, Paris, May 20, 1890 (vol. 01/03/001).

[11] In his biographical notice on Pirenne Ganshof places the edition among Pirenne's "travaux d'érudition" ("Pirenne," col. 685).

[12] Pirenne, *Sedulius de Liège*; Pirenne, *Histoire de la constitution*.

[13] Lyon, *Henri Pirenne*, pp. 46–49, 53–55, 57.

[14] Prou, Paris, June 14, 1890 (vol. 01/03/001).

ce que donnent beaucoup d'éditeurs, *rien*, c'est pas mal."[15] Pirenne evidently then wrote to the publisher, Alphonse Picard, sometime within the next month and asked him to confirm this amount and to tell him when he would be paid, to which Picard replied: "Oui c'est bien 30 francs par feuille qui sont alloués à l'auteur pour la remise du manuscrit—je crois que nous ne pourrons le publier que l'année prochaine c'est à dire l'année scolaire."[16] Prou wrote him again in November, reiterating that "[p]our la rétribution de votre Galbert, vous avez droit à 30 francs par feuille d'impression et à 10 exemplaires. Il est claire que ces 10 exemplaires ne sont pas destinés à la presse ni aux membres du Comité qui sont souscripteurs. C'est pour vos amis."[17] He was eventually paid 480 francs, about 5.5 percent of the anticipated sales, for his work.[18]

These first two reasons for Pirenne's proposal to edit a text for the collection would, of course, have held good for any chronicle Pirenne proposed to edit. He perhaps suggested Galbert's chronicle in particular for two further reasons. First, it is a striking and original narrative—Pauw, as noted above, wrote that he had read it as if it were a novel[19]—and it dealt with subjects of primary interest to Pirenne. In his preface to Lyon's biography of Pirenne, Ganshof identified three major poles in Pirenne's work: the history of Belgium, the history of the town in the Middle Ages, and the economic and social history of the Middle Ages, and Galbert's chronicle is a potentially important source for all of these subjects.[20] Pirenne's next major work, which he in fact seems to have interrupted in order to work on the edition of Galbert's chronicle, was on "L'origine des constitutions urbaines au Moyen Âge,"[21] and he also published articles in the next several years on "La chancellerie

---

[15] Prou, Nanterre, June 27, 1890 (vol. 01/03/001).

[16] Picard, Paris, July 10, 1890 (vol. 01/03/001).

[17] Prou, Paris, Nov. 30, 1890, returned and resent Dec. 3, 1890 (vol. 01/03/001).

[18] Picard, Paris, June 8, 1891 (vol. 01/03/001).

[19] Compare the remarks of Köpke in the introduction to his 1856 publication of Galbert's work: "Sic condidit librum, etsi ipse spe metuque et tristitia vehementer erat commotus, quo lectoris animum non minus teneat quam commoveat" ("Vita Karolis," p. 534); and the remarks of Wauters in his entry on Galbert in the *Biographie nationale*, published several years before Pirenne's edition: "Bien supérieur à Gautier, son contemporain, dont la latinité est meilleure, il est comme lui exact, et plus concis, plus animé, plus attachant. Le 'martyre du comte Charles de Flandre', *Passio Karoli comitis Flandriae*, constitue certainement la meilleure page d'histoire que son époque ait laissée" ("Gualbert," col. 393).

[20] Ganshof, preface to Lyon, *Henri Pirenne*, pp. ix–x.

[21] Pirenne, "L'origine." Toward the end of a letter to Pirenne of June 27, 1890, Prou wrote: "je dois vous laisser aux communes flamandes et pour l'instant à Galbert" (Prou, Nanterre, June 27, 1890 [vol. 01/03/001]). Shortly after the publication of the edition, Pirenne wrote to Prou that "[j]e vais me mettre, à partir de demain, à la confection d'un travail sur les origines constitutionnelles des villes flamandes" (Letter from Pirenne to Prou, from Ghent, Aug. 9, 1891 [Sens, Bibliothèque municipale, Fonds Maurice Prou; subsequent references to this archive are cited as Sens]). It thus seems that Pirenne had begun work on, or at least projected, this 109-page article before he began work on the edition of Galbert's chronicle and that he returned to it immediately after the latter's publication.

et les notaires des comtes de Flandre avant le XIIIᵉ siècle," and "Villes, marchés et marchands au Moyen Âge."[22] Given his interests at the time, Galbert's chronicle was a natural and important source for Pirenne to study and edit.

Finally, Pirenne also thought that he could complete and publish the edition very quickly without much work. Prou, as we have seen, wrote to Pirenne on May 9, 1890, to remind him of "la promesse que vous nous avez faite à Giry et à moi de nous envoyer une édition de chronique," and to ask him to send them as quickly as possible a proposal that could be presented to the editorial committee of the collection. Pirenne evidently responded immediately, and Prou wrote again on May 20, 1890, in a letter whose beginning I have already cited:

> Mon bien cher ami,
> Pour un homme pressé, je ne le suis guère à vous répondre et à vous remercier. Dieu sait cependant si nous avons reçu M. Giry et moi, votre proposition avec plaisir. Je ne puis vous donner cependant une réponse ferme, définitive, officielle. Mais je suis sûr que le comité accueillera Galbert, *Passio Karoli Comitis* avec empressement. Seulement nous ne pouvons convoquer le Comité avant le 15 juin à cause des fêtes universitaires de Montpellier qui appellent la plupart d'entre nous. . . . Quoiqu'il en soit, vous pouvez préparer vos notes. Pour ce qui est du texte, croyez-vous utile de demander une permission aux *Monumenta*? Ne serait-il pas mieux—c'est l'avis de Giry et le mien—que vous dressiez un texte, puisqu'il n'y a qu'un ms. Si vous empruntez des corrections aux Monumenta, vous les noterez. Car, puisqu'il n'y a qu'un ms., ce n'est rien de le collationner; et ça vaudrait mieux. Réfléchissez à cela. Je pense que le Comité partagera sur ce point notre opinion. Avez-vous quelque objection à faire? Vous me répondrez quand nous avons officiellement inscrit votre publication sur notre programme. Vous savez que dès que nous aurons votre ms., nous le remettrons à l'imprimeur. Si l'on commence à l'imprimer en juillet, je pense que ça pourra être terminé en novembre, pour la rentrée.[23]

It is clear from this letter that Pirenne proposed initially simply to reprint the text of the chronicle that had been published by R. Köpke in the Monumenta Germaniae Historica in 1856,[24] to which he would add a series of historical notes,[25] and that he and Prou thought he could finish work on the edition within a couple of months.

---

[22] Pirenne, "La chancellerie"; Pirenne, "Villes."

[23] Prou, Paris, May 20, 1890 (vol. 01/03/001).

[24] Galbert of Bruges, "Passio Karoli comitis."

[25] See also the letter from Prou to Pirenne dated May 24, 1890, in which Prou referred to the "pas mal de remarques et de notes nouvelles," which Pirenne intended to add to the text (Prou, Paris, May 24, 1890 [vol. 01/03/001]).

Köpke's edition of Galbert's work in the Monumenta, which Pirenne proposed initially simply to reprint, was somewhat curious. Galbert's chronicle had first been published in 1668 by the Bollandists, who wrote that they had consulted four manuscripts.[26] The Bollandists' text had then been reprinted by Jacob Langebek in his *Scriptores rerum Danicorum medii aevi* in 1776.[27] The manuscripts used by the Bollandists were all lost by the time Köpke undertook an edition of the chronicle for the Monumenta, and although he had identified two other surviving manuscripts—one in Arras and one in Paris—he wrote in the introduction to his edition that he had not, for unknown reasons, been able to consult them. "Nobis nihil relictum est," therefore, he wrote, "quam quod paucis mendis remotis editionem ex Actis Sanctorum repeteremus, capitibus libri more nostro institutis."[28]

As Pirenne discovered in the course of his work on his own edition, however, Köpke "malheureusement, par une négligence inexplicable chez un érudit de sa valeur, . . . n'a pas eu recours au texte original des *Acta Sanctorum*, et s'est servi de la réimpression de Langebek [which Pirenne qualifies as "peu correcte"]. Les nombreuses fautes typographiques de cette dernière ont ainsi passé dans l'édition de Köpke. Cette édition ne présente donc pas un texte meilleur que celui des précédentes."[29]

Pirenne seems to have accepted quickly Prou and Giry's suggestion that he publish a new, or at least a revised, text of the chronicle rather than simply reprinting Köpke's text, and, immediately after receiving Prou's letter of May 20, he seems to have started looking into the possibility of having the two manuscripts mentioned by Köpke sent to him in Ghent.[30] On May 24, Prou wrote to Pirenne to inform him what he had been able to discover with respect to sending the Paris manuscript to Ghent: it would be "long, long et difficile" to have the manuscript sent directly to Pirenne, but "rien ne sera[it] plus facile" than to have it sent to the library of the University of Ghent if the librarian would promise that

---

[26] Galbert of Bruges, "Alia vita."

[27] Galbert of Bruges, "Vita Caroli comitis."

[28] Köpke, "Vita Karolis comitis," p. 536.

[29] Pirenne, "Préface," in Galbert of Bruges, *Histoire du meurtre de Charles le Bon*, pp. xxii–xxiii.

[30] Since, as Prou's letter makes clear, Pirenne knew Galbert's work principally through the Monumenta—only Köpke entitles the work the "Passio Karoli comitis"—and since Köpke referred to two surviving manuscripts, Prou's references to a single manuscript are confusing. It seems either that Pirenne was working from memory when he sent Prou and Giry his proposal and did not remember that Köpke had mentioned two manuscripts, or that he had written to Prou to ask for help in gaining access to the *one* manuscript in Paris, and Prou had misunderstood him to mean that there was only one surviving manuscript in all. I should perhaps note in passing that it took only a day for a letter to travel between Paris and Ghent in the 1880s–90s: when Prou sent a letter from Paris it was in Pirenne's hands the next day and, if Pirenne replied immediately, Prou could have an answer to his letter in two days.

it would not leave the library.[31] This was fine with Pirenne and the manuscript left Paris on June 2 and arrived at the university library in Ghent on June 6.[32]

Pirenne also wrote to the public library of Arras some time in late May to ask if the manuscript mentioned by Köpke was, indeed, still there and if it could be sent to him in Ghent. The librarian replied on May 30:

> Le manuscrit dont vous me parlez se trouve effectivement à la bibliothèque d'Arras; il a pour titre: "Galbertus Brudgensis, de mulctro, traditione et occisione Caroli comitis Flandriarum." L'écriture est du XVIe siècle, sans indication du manuscrit sur lequel a été faite cette copie. C'est un in folio de 70 feuillets. Je dois seulement ajouter, Monsieur, qu'aucun des 1200 manuscrits de la bibliothèque n'est jamais envoyé hors de France (le règlement est formel sur ce point).

Pirenne, he concluded, would have to consult the manuscript in Arras or at the Bibliothèque nationale in Paris.[33] Pirenne was not happy with this response and asked both Prou and Giry to see if they could somehow arrange for the Arras manuscript to be sent to him, but to no avail.[34] Since he had not yet had a definitive response from the editorial committee of the collection to his proposal to edit Galbert's chronicle, he wrote a letter to Prou on June 27 to explain his situation and ask his advice:

> Mon cher ami,
> Excusez mon importunité mais ne recevant pas la réponse définitive du comité, je voudrais avoir votre avis sur ce que j'ai à faire maintenant. Voici la situation. Les cours sont terminés ici et les examens ne commencent que le 8 juillet. Je suis donc absolument libre jusqu'à cette date. Je pourrais par conséquent aller consulter à Arras le 2e ms. de Galbert. Mais vous comprenez que je voudrais avant de partir pouvoir être assuré que mon déplacement ne sera pas inutile. D'autre part, si je ne vais pas à Arras maintenant, je ne pourrai plus m'y rendre qu'au mois d'août, à cause des examens, d'où retard pour l'édition de Galbert, si le comité est toujours d'avis de l'entreprendre.[35]

He concluded by asking Prou to write as soon as he had any word from the editorial committee. Prou had, in fact, written him that same day to inform him that the editorial committee had met the previous evening and that his proposal had

---

[31] Prou, Paris, May 24, 1890 (vol. 01/03/001).

[32] Card from Ghent library, June 6, 1890 (vol. 01/03/001); Martinet [?], secrétaire à la Direction de la Bibliothèque nationale, Paris, June 18, 1890 (vol. 01/03/001).

[33] Wicquos, librarian of Arras, Arras, May 30, 1890 (vol. 01/03/001).

[34] Prou, Paris, June 14, 1890 (vol. 01/03/001); Giry, Paris, June 28, 1890 (vol. 01/03/001).

[35] Pirenne, Ghent, June 27, 1890 (Sens).

been well received and definitively accepted.[36] Pirenne wrote back the next day to say that, reassured, he would leave the following Tuesday (July 1) for Arras.[37] He wrote to Prou again on July 9 to say that he had just returned from Arras and, having discovered that the manuscript there contained no important variants, he had written to Picard to ask how long the printing process would take and when the book might best appear.[38]

Pirenne also took pains in the latter part of July to discover other surviving manuscripts of Galbert's chronicle. Having perhaps learned that a manuscript of Walter of Thérouanne's *Life of Charles, Count of Flanders* existed in the library of St. Martin of Tournai in the seventeenth century,[39] Pirenne wrote to both the public library and the episcopal library there to ask if they had a manuscript of the work, which they did not.[40] He also wrote to Oswald Holder-Egger to ask if there were any indications as to other manuscripts in the archives of the Monumenta Germaniae Historica, and likewise received a negative response.[41] When he received Holder-Egger's letter in early August, therefore, Pirenne must have felt that the first part of his work on the edition—identifying and collating the surviving manuscripts of the chronicle—was done. The Paris manuscript had arrived in Ghent on June 6 and, as his letter to Prou of July 9 shows, he had finished collating it by the time he left for Arras on July 1. He had finished collating the Arras manuscript by July 9,[42] had identified no new manuscripts, and his other sources were all printed and available to him in Ghent.[43]

---

[36] Prou, Nanterre, June 27, 1890 (vol. 01/03/001).

[37] Pirenne, Ghent, June 28, 1890 (Sens).

[38] Pirenne, Ghent, July 9, 1890 (Sens).

[39] Perhaps in Sanders, *Bibliotheca belgica manuscripta*, 1:114, no. 13.

[40] Bibliothèque publique of Tournai, July 10, 1890 (vol. 01/03/001); Canon Vos, episcopal archivist, Tournai, July 17, 1890 (vol. 01/03/001).

[41] Holder-Egger, Berlin, Aug. 5, 1890 (vol. 01/03/001).

[42] Pirenne, Ghent, July 9, 1890 (Sens): "Je viens de revenir d'Arras où j'ai collationné le ms. de Galbert. Il ne m'a rien fourni de neuf. Il est absolument identique, sauf quelques variantes orthographiques sans importance à celui de Paris."

[43] Holder-Egger had informed him of the existence of an incomplete sixteenth-century French translation of the chronicle in the Königlichen öffentlichen Bibliothek in Hannover (Holder-Egger, Berlin, Aug. 5, 1890 [vol. 01/03/001]), of which Pirenne evidently acquired a copy which he collated at some point with the Latin text (see Pirenne, "Préface," in Galbert of Bruges, *Histoire du meurtre de Charles le Bon*, p. xxi), but it is not clear when he did so. Perhaps it was after November 25, when he received a card from the Königlichen öffentlichen Bibliothek with information about the French translation (Bibliothecae regiae Hannoveranae, Nov. 25, 1890 [vol. 01/03/001]). Pirenne's other potential sources for the text (see Pirenne, "Préface," to Galbert de Bruges, *Histoire du meurtre de Charles le Bon*, pp. xxi–xxiii) were the excerpts printed by André Duchesne in his *Histoire généalogique des maisons de Guines, d'Ardres, de Gand et de Coucy* (1631); the edition of the chronicle in the *Acta Sanctorum* (1668); the reprint of this edition by Langebek in the *Scriptores rerum Danicorum medii aevi* (1776);

This first period of Pirenne's work on the edition—from when it was first discussed in mid-April until the end of July 1890, and especially from June 6, when the Paris manuscript arrived in Ghent, until Pirenne's return from Arras shortly before July 9—was characterized by a certain negligence. Given, for example, that Pirenne made some efforts to discover other surviving manuscripts of the chronicle, it is surprising that he did not discover the Bruges manuscript (Bruges, Openbare Bibliotheek, HS 570), which would have permitted him to review and evaluate the Bollandists' work more thoroughly and accurately. This manuscript had belonged to Charles-Louis Carton (1802–63), a canon of the cathedral of Bruges, who had published between 1843 and 1847 a series of notes and studies on the people and events surrounding the assassination of Charles the Good, notably in the *Biographie des hommes remarquables de la Flandre occidentale*. The manuscript had been put up for sale in 1866 and had been acquired by the public library of Bruges before 1882, when it was catalogued in the second supplement to the *Catalogue des livres de la Bibliothèque publique de la ville de Bruges*.[44] It is curious that Pirenne did not look for any new manuscripts in Bruges, where he would have found this one in the published catalogue of the library.

Pirenne's transcription of the Paris and Arras manuscripts, moreover, at least as it is revealed in the notes to his edition, was somewhat careless and inaccurate. A comparison of the notes to his edition and those to mine[45] shows the large number of variant readings in the Paris and Arras manuscripts that he failed to note, or at least did not include in his notes. In the second line from the bottom of page 4, for example, his text reads "cautis," the reading of the Bollandists' edition,[46] and he notes no variants, whereas both the Paris and Arras manuscripts[47] in fact read "cautos," which was also one of the corrections to the edition suggested by Paul Thomas.[48] One also finds numerous examples of inaccuracies in

---

excerpts from the Bollandists' edition printed in the *Recueil des historiens des Gaules et de la France* (Galbert of Bruges, "Ex alia ejusdem B Caroli vita"; 1786); and Köpke's reprint of Langebek's reprint in the Monumenta (1856), but, as we will see, he in fact seems to have worked primarily with Köpke's reprint.

[44] Claeys, *Catalogue des livres de la Bibliothèque publique*, p. 4, no. 570. See also *Catalogue des livres, manuscrits et documents originaux*, p. 120, no. 1849.

[45] Galbert of Bruges, *De multro*.

[46] This edition—Galbert of Bruges, "Alia vita [B. Caroli boni comitis Flandriae], auctore Galberto notario," ed. Godefroid Henschen and Daniel Van Papenbroeck, in *Acta Sanctorum*, March, 3 vols. (Antwerp: Joannes Meursius, 1668), 1:179–219—will be cited hereafter as E.

[47] These manuscripts—Arras, Bibliothèque municipale, MS 115 and Paris, BnF, MS Baluze 43—will be cited hereafter as *A* and *P*, respectively.

[48] Thomas, "Notes." One can find other examples of such omissions on p. 12, l. 16, where Pirenne gives the reading of E ("unus"), without noting that *A* and *P* both read "unde"; p. 14, l. 26, where he gives the reading of E ("justae"), without noting that *A* and *P* both read "juste"; p. 3, n. c., where he fails to note that *P* also reads "filius itaque"; p. 4, l. 15, where he gives the reading of E ("rhetorices") but

the transcription of *A* and *P*. On page 1 of the edition, for example, Pirenne notes that "comes" is missing in *A* when it is not (n. c), and that "ac" is an emendation suggested by Köpke when, in fact, Köpke's edition, reproducing a change made by Langebek, reads "et," and "ac" is found in E, *A* and *P* (n. e).[49]

These omissions and inaccuracies, this negligence, can be attributed to various causes. First, as we have seen, Pirenne had originally intended simply to reprint Köpke's text, even though he knew, through Köpke's introduction, of surviving manuscripts in Paris and Arras. He thus seems to have felt initially that the justification for the new edition in the collection was not the opportunity to provide a better text, but the opportunity to enrich the reader's comprehension of the existing text through the addition to it of new historical notes.[50] He was a historian rather than a philologist and was more interested in what the text had to tell scholars about medieval social, economic, and urban history than he was in it as a work of literature or historiography. His introduction to the edition, in fact, disparages Galbert as a writer and thinker, although it does praise him for his qualities as a witness. Textual details, especially when it was a question of

---

fails to note that *A* and *P* both read "rhetoricae"; p. 4, l. 19/20, where he gives the reading of E ("prestiterat") without noting that *A* and *P* both read "praestiterant"; p. 5, l. 16, where he gives the reading of E ("injurias") without noting that *A* reads "injuries" and *P* "imuries"; p. 5, l. 21, where he gives the reading of E ("omne") without noting that *A* and *P* both read "omnem"; p. 5, l. 22, where he gives the reading of E ("poterat") without noting that *A* and *P* both read "poterant"; p. 5, l. 4, where he gives the reading of E ("carnes") without noting that *A* and *P* both read "canes" (!); p. 5, l. 4, where he gives the reading of E ("comederunt") without noting that *A* and *P* both read "comederent"; p. 5, l. 6, where he gives the reading of E and *P* ("sibi") without noting that *A* reads "ibi"; p. 5, l. 7, where he gives the reading of E ("semiperfecto") without noting that *A* reads "semperfecto" and *P* "semper fecto"; p. 8, l. 18, where he gives the reading of E ("ut") without noting that *A* and *P* both read "et"; and so on.

[49] Other inaccuracies of this kind may be found on p. 5, n. c, where Pirenne attributes the reading "penetravit" to both *A* and *P*, when *A* actually reads "peretravit"; p. 6, n. b, where he attributes the reading "Scaldum" only to E when both E and *A* have that reading; p. 6, n. d, where he attributes "dum" only to *A*, whereas both *A* and *P* have that reading; p. 8, n. b, where he attributes "et postulantes et observantes" only to *P*, whereas both *A* and *P* have that reading; p. 8, n. c, where he attributes "ac" only to *A*, whereas both *A* and *P* have it; p. 10, n. b, where he attributes a fictional reading to *P* and fails to note the actual variant shared by *A* and *P*; p. 14, n. f, where he notes that *A* and *P* omit the word "tractare," whereas both in fact have it (they do, however, omit the next word, "et," an omission Pirenne fails to note, which suggests this is a printer's error he failed to correct); p. 18, nn. c and g, where he attributes omissions to E that are actually omissions in *P* (n. c) and in *A* and *P* (n. g); and so on.

[50] On November 10, just after sending the manuscript of the text and notes to Giry, Pirenne wrote to Prou: "Je crains d'avoir donné peut-être un peu beaucoup de notes mais il m'a paru qu'un texte d'histoire passionnant comme celui-ci devrait avoir une annotation plus copieuse que celle qui convient aux sources d'intérêt plus général. Du moment qu'on entre dans le détail, il faut être complet. D'ailleurs une annotation copieuse rendra des services. Tout le monde ne connaît pas l'histoire de Flandre au commencement du XIIe s. et il faut cependant en avoir une connaissance assez exacte pour comprendre Galbert. D'où encore une fois la nécessité de notes assez nombreuses" (Pirenne, Ghent, Nov. 10, 1890 [Sens]).

something like an *ac* or an *et*, probably just did not seem significant to Pirenne. He had quickly accepted Prou and Giry's suggestion that he prepare a new text, or at least revise the existing one, but he had not, himself, seen the need for doing so initially, and this sense that the existing text was sufficient for his purposes probably influenced the time and attention he devoted to the establishment of his own text. Pirenne, moreover, recognized in himself a certain inattention to textual details. In a letter to Prou in October 1890, as he was finishing the main part of his work on the edition, he acknowledged that he had mis-cited a source in his article on the Battle of Courtrai[51] and lamented his "malheureuse manie de négliger les détails. Il me semble que je suis incapable de citer correctement un livre et de corriger une épreuve. Voilà n'est-ce pas une bien mauvaise note pour un éditeur de textes. Mais je me surveillerai et j'espère que mon Galbert sera présentable."[52]

Secondly, it is evident throughout Pirenne's correspondence with respect to the edition that both Pirenne and the editors of the collection were in a hurry to get the book published. We have seen how eager the editors of the collection were to bring out new texts, and when Prou first wrote on May 9 to ask for a formal proposal, the very next day after the meeting of the editorial committee at which he first mentioned Pirenne's offer to edit a text for them, he did not fail to add: "Vous serez bien aimable si vous vous mettez promptement à cette besogne."[53] His subsequent letter, dated May 20, is preoccupied with time and haste. He begins it by referring to himself as a "homme pressé" and goes on to say that he is sure the editorial committee will accept Pirenne's proposal "avec empressement." He concludes the section of the letter devoted to the edition by writing: "Vous savez que dès que nous aurons votre ms., nous le remettrons à l'imprimeur. Si l'on commence à l'imprimer en juillet, je pense que ça pourra être terminé en novembre, pour la rentrée."[54] On June 28, Giry wrote that he was pleased to inform Pirenne "que nous avons adopté à l'unanimité votre projet de publier dans notre collection de textes la *Passio* Karoli comitis de Galbert de Bruges—Vous pouvez donc mettre la dernière main à l'établissement de votre texte & nous envoyer votre manuscrit aussitôt qu'il sera prêt. . . . Nous pourrons vous mettre à l'impression aussitôt que vous serez prêt."[55] The notes of haste in another letter from Giry a couple of weeks later echo those in Prou's of May 20:

> Mon cher ami,
> Je m'empresse de répondre à votre lettre pour vous dire de m'adresser vote manuscrit le plus tôt possible—mais sans pouvoir vous fixer de terme.

---

[51] Pirenne, "La version flamande."
[52] Pirenne, Ghent, Oct. 27, 1890 (Sens).
[53] Prou, Paris, May 9, 1890 (vol. 01/03/001).
[54] Prou, Paris, May 20, 1890 (vol. 01/03/001).
[55] Giry, Paris, June 28, 1890 (vol. 01/03/001).

Nos publications sont en retard & nous avons hâte de nous mettre au courant. Naturellement en août ou septembre cela n'avancerait pas les choses; mais à partir d'octobre nous serons rentrés à Paris & disposés à vous imprimer. Plus vous nous enverrez votre manuscrit tôt & plus rapidement on vous l'imprimera. Nous voudrions que le fascicule soit distribué dans les premiers mois de 91—en mars au plus tôt.[56]

Pirenne evidently shared their sense that the edition could and should be done quickly and could be finished by the end of his summer vacation (fall courses began October 16 at the University of Ghent in 1890). And at the end of July, he wrote to Prou to say, "Mon travail [on the edition] est très avancé. Le tout pourra être envoyé à M. Picard au mois d'octobre, s'il hâte l'impression le brochure pourra donc encore paraître cette année."[57] It was this haste, one presumes, that led him to spend a maximum of three or four days collating *A*—the more important of the two at his disposal—without ever going back and reviewing his work, and that likewise led to a certain degree of negligence in the collation of *P*.

Armed with whatever printed sources he took with him and what seem to have been hastily made and faulty transcriptions of *A* and *P*, Pirenne did the bulk of the work on the edition—establishing the text, preparing the textual and historical notes—during his vacation in Verviers in August and September. He wrote to Prou from there on September 15 that "[j]'achève mon édition de Galbert et je prépare mes cours pour la rentrée,"[58] and wrote again from Ghent on October 27 to say:

Le texte est pour le moment entièrement constitué et les notes y sont mises. Je n'ai plus qu'à rédiger le préface, mais je ne m'y mettrai que quand l'impression du texte sera commencée. J'attends donc maintenant le bon plaisir de l'imprimeur. Dès que j'apprendrai qu'il peut commencer j'enverrai mon texte à M. Giry. . . . Vous voyez que je n'ai pas chômé pendant les vacances. Maintenant que mon Galbert est prêt j'espère qu'il ne tardera pas à paraître. Vous me feriez grand plaisir si vous voyez un de ces jours M. Picard, de lui demander quand il pourra commencer l'impression.[59]

The final text that Pirenne established during this period was, unfortunately, flawed by the negligence noted above in the transcription of *A* and *P* which, in addition to the simple omissions and errors it introduced into the text and textual notes, had the unhappy effect of preventing him from understanding the relation

---

[56] Giry, Paris, July 15, 1890 (vol. 01/03/001).
[57] Pirenne, Ghent, July 30, 1890 (Sens).
[58] Pirenne, Verviers, Sept. 15, 1890 (Sens).
[59] Pirenne, Ghent, Oct. 27, 1890 (Sens).

between *A* and *P*. He realized that they are "étroitement apparentés" and "dérivent d'un même original," but the errors in his collation of the two manuscripts led him to believe that they descended independently from a common original: "On serait tenté de croire que l'un de ces manuscrits n'est qu'une copie de l'autre si A ne contenait pas certains mots qui manquent dans P, et réciproquement."[60] This is not true—*A* has no independent omissions, while *P* has several—and there are a sufficient number of other indications, which were evidently not apparent to Pirenne from his collation of the manuscripts, to show that *P* descends indirectly from *A*. Pirenne's inattentive reading of the manuscripts thus prevented him from realizing that *P* has no independent value as a witness to the text (except for the passages on the leaves that were cut out of *A* and sold by an unscrupulous librarian in 1816) and thus from realizing the importance of *A* for the establishment of the text.[61]

Pirenne's final text was further flawed by mistakes in his transcription or reading of E (which was, in principle, his base text for the new edition),[62] although there were fewer mistakes in his transcription of E than in that of his manuscript sources.[63]

What is perhaps more serious is that in practice Pirenne often seems to have consulted the Bollandists' text in Köpke's reprint of Langebek's faulty reprint of the Bollandists' edition rather than in the Bollandists' edition itself—even though, as we have seen, he himself takes Köpke to task in his preface for the "négligence inexplicable" he showed in reprinting Langebek's reprint of the Bollandists' edition rather than reprinting the original edition. See, for example, page 16, note e, where Pirenne writes that "illam" is omitted by E, when it is not, although it is omitted in Langebek's reprint[64] of E and thus

---

[60] Pirenne, "Préface," in Galbert of Bruges, *Histoire du meurtre de Charles le Bon*, p. xx. See also what he wrote to Prou after returning from collating *A*: the manuscript "ne m'a rien fourni de neuf. Il est absolument identique, sauf quelques variantes orthographiques sans importance à celui de Paris" (Pirenne, Ghent, July 9, 1890 [Sens]).

[61] For a discussion of *A* and *P* and the relation between them, see Rider, "Introduction," in Galbert of Bruges, *De multro, traditione, et occisione gloriosi Karoli comitis Flandriarum*, pp. xxix–xxxv.

[62] "Il n'existe, en réalité, jusqu'ici qu'une seule édition originale de Galbert: celle des Bollandistes. Grâce aux manuscrits d'Arras et de Paris, j'ai pu rétablir dans la présente édition, plus d'un passage corrompu. . . . J'ai indiqué les variantes des manuscrits par rapport à l'édition des Bollandistes" (Pirenne, "Préface," in Galbert of Bruges, *Histoire du meurtre de Charles le Bon*, pp. xxiii–xxiv).

[63] On p. 5, l. 25, for example, he gives the reading of *A* and *P* ("sic"), but fails to note that E reads "ita"; on p. 6, l. 3, he gives the reading of *A* and *P* ("et"), but fails to note that E reads "etiam"; on p. 7, l. 4, he gives the reading of *A* and *P* ("eo"), but fails to note that E reads "hoc"; on p. 16, l. 23, he gives the reading of *P* ("justitia"), but fails to note that E and *A* read "justitiae"; on p. 17, l. 8, he gives the reading of *P* ("conscensa"), but fails to note that E reads "concessa" (and *A* reads "conscescia"); and so on.

[64] This edition—Galbert of Bruges, "Vita Caroli Comitis Flandriae, Auctore Galberto notario," ed. Jacob Langebek, in *Scriptores rerum Danicorum medii aevi* (1776; repr. Nendeln, Liechtenstein: Kraus Reprint, 1969), 4:112–92—will be cited hereafter as L.

in Köpke's reprint[65] of L: Pirenne must here have been looking at K when he writes this note rather than E. He makes similar mistakes elsewhere, with the result that some of the "nombreuses fautes typographiques" of Langebek's edition that "[avaient] passé dans l'édition de Köpke" thus also made their way into Pirenne's edition thanks to the same "négligence inexplicable" he pointed out in Köpke's work.[66]

It thus seems in the end that Pirenne in fact did by and large what he had originally planned to do. Rather than taking E as his base text and correcting it with readings from *A* and *P* (or taking *A* as his base text and correcting it with readings from E and *P*), he used K as his base text, collating it, negligently, with E and restoring some—but far from all—of E's readings that had been corrupted in L and taken over by K, and then further corrected the partially corrected text of K with readings from his faulty transcription of *A* and *P*, sometimes attributing the variant readings of one of his sources to another source.[67] Pirenne's final

---

[65] This edition—Galbert of Bruges, "Passio Karoli comitis auctore Galberto," ed. R. Köpke, in Monumenta Germaniae Historica, Scriptores, 12 (Hannover: Hahn, 1856), pp. 561–619—will be cited hereafter as K.

[66] On p. 19, n. d, he notes that E reads "et," when that is actually a reading found only in L and K; on p. 19, n. e, he notes that E reads "versi," when that is actually a reading found only in L and K; on p. 20, n. a, l. 15, his notes suggest that E reads "in" and *A* and *P* read "ad," whereas in fact E, *A* and *P* all read "ad" and only L and K read "in"; on p. 26, n. b, l. 4, his note suggests that E reads "januas" and *A* and *P* read "januis," whereas in fact E, *A* and *P* all read "januis" and only L and K read "januas"; on p. 27, n. c, l. 10/11, he notes that "sacerdotibus" is omitted by E, when it is not, although it is omitted by L and K; on p. 29, n. b, l. 29, his note suggests that E reads "discursantes" and *A* and *P* read "discursitantes," whereas in fact E, *A* and *P* all read "discursitantes" and only L and K read "discursantes"; on p. 34, n. a, l. 2, his note suggests that E reads "fugerent" and *A* and *P* read "fugerunt," whereas in fact E, *A* and *P* all read "fugerunt" and only L and K read "fugerent"; on p. 37, n. a, l. 9, his note suggests that E reads "conciliaret" and *A* and *P* read "reconciliaret," whereas in fact E, *A* and *P* all read "reconciliaret" and only L and K read "conciliaret"; on p. 65, l. 31, he prints "vocati" without noting any variants, whereas "vocati" is actually a reading found only in L and K, and E, *A* and *P* all read "vexati"; on p. 73, l. 12, he prints "obsessos et obsidentes" without noting any variants, whereas "et" is in fact K's resolution of L's "&," and E, *A* and *P* all read "ac"; and on p. 84, l. 8/9, he prints "convenerunt" without noting any variants, whereas "convenerunt" is found only in L and K, and E, *A* and *P* all read "convenerant."

[67] There are two other indications that Pirenne in fact used K rather than E as his base text, although it is clear that he also collated, negligently, E with K. First, he noted that the orthography of his text "est celle du texte de Köpke" (Pirenne, "Préface," in Galbert of Bruges, *Histoire du meurtre de Charles le Bon*, p. xxiv) even though the orthography of Köpke's text is an editorially "restored" twelfth-century spelling with no support from the Bollandists' edition or any of the surviving manuscripts. Second, in a letter of July 9, 1891, Pauw asked Pirenne if he would please return volumes 12 (the volume containing Köpke's reprint) and 25 of the Monumenta to the university library so that he could consult them (Pauw, Ghent, July 9, 1891 [vol. 01/03/001]). It is also interesting to note that at the very end of his work on the edition in April 1891, Pirenne compared his edition to that of Köpke rather than to that of the Bollandists, even though the latter, as he had recently written in the preface to his edition (Mar. 1891), was the "seule édition originale de Galbert": "J'ai presque terminé Galbert. . . . Maintenant que

text, in sum, contains a few passages omitted in the Bollandists' edition, provides more information about the textual tradition than theirs, and may here and there be closer to what Galbert wrote, but it provides an incomplete and flawed image of the textual tradition, and many of its readings need to be corrected (because they are unnecessary and unmotivated "improvements" made by the Bollandists or errors introduced by Langebek). Fortunately, the extant versions of the text agree on roughly 95 percent of the text, so no editor can go too far wrong.

Yet some of Pirenne's mistaken readings have had substantial and unhappy consequences for our comprehension of Galbert's work. We find an example in chapter 121. The sudden death of William Clito on July 27 or 28, 1128, and Thierry of Alsace's subsequent acquisition of the county led Galbert to a long reflection, added some time after the events. It consists of a single manuscript chapter (modern chapters [120], 15; [121], 43), although this is obscured by the editorial chapter divisions of Köpke, which Pirenne adopted. This reflection takes up and resolves in turn three problems that William's death and Thierry's accession posed for Galbert.[68]

The second problem that Galbert takes up in the course of this final reflection begins with a scholastic "Queratur ergo":

> It may be asked why, therefore, when God wished to restore the peace of the fatherland through the death of one of the two, He ordained that Count William should die, who had the more just claim [*justiorem causam*] to rule the land, and why it was not rather Count Thierry who died, who seemed unjustly substituted [*qui injuste superpositus videbatur*]; or by what justice [*qua justitia*] God granted the countship to the one who violently [*violenter*] seized the office. If, therefore, neither of them received the countship in the correct way [*bene*], by right [*jure*] both of them should have been removed.[69]

Galbert's response to this question was that the violent substitution of Thierry for William, while it might at first appear unjust, was in fact the just correction of William's unjust election as count, which had been flawed in two ways. First, the electors had ignored the letters Thierry had sent to Flanders before William's election claiming the county for himself, and they had chosen a candidate whose

---

c'est terminé je ne suis plus content de mon travail. Il me semble que je le ferais beaucoup mieux si je le recommençerais [*sic*]. C'est d'ailleurs toujours ainsi avec moi. Je pars enthousiaste et j'arrive au but dégouté de ce que j'ai fait. Enfin mon édition vaudra toujours mieux que celle de Köpke, mais ce n'est pas beaucoup dire" (Pirenne, Ghent, Apr. 26, 1891 [Sens]).

[68] For a more developed discussion of this final reflection, see Rider, *God's Scribe*, pp. 178–82.

[69] Galbert of Bruges, *De multro*, [121], 1/7; Galbert of Bruges, *Murder*, pp. 310–11 (translation modified).

hereditary claim was weaker than Thierry's. William's election was also flawed because the king of France had influenced the election unduly and "unjustly . . . sold" (*injuste . . . vendita*) the county, which William had purchased with a monetary relief. Given Galbert's ideas about the "canonical" election of the count by the clergy and people, this amounted to a secular version of simony. William's election had not, therefore, been "free." It had been "a great wrong" which God himself had "righted" since "no human power could or would" do so.[70]

Galbert then states his solution to the problem he posed in the *quaestio*, beginning with an equally scholastic "Igitur":

> Therefore, after so many arguments, we assert that the more just claim [*justiorem causam*] belonged to Count Thierry, who is not justly said to have been substituted [*non juste dicitur superpositus*] for Count William; that dead count, rather, was most unjustly substituted [*injustissime superpositus est*] for Thierry and, in return for a relief, forcibly made count through the king's power. And so God by right [*jure*] preserved the life of Count Thierry in accordance with old justice [*antiqua justitia*],[71] and restored him to his heritage, and removed the other one from the countship by death.[72]

Galbert thus concludes, with a vocabulary that deliberately recalls the way the *quaestio* was first posed, that although Thierry may have *seemed* (*videbatur*) to have usurped the county unjustly and violently from William because the latter had been recognized as count before Thierry and thus had for this reason the prior and more just claim, Thierry had in fact claimed the county before William and had a better right to it. If the citizens of Flanders had acted justly and rightly in spring 1127, they would have elected Thierry. When they did not do so, God had had to set things right, but had done so only after they had suffered for a while the consequences of their negligence and sloth. The shift of "the more just claim" (*justiorem causam*) from William in the first passage to Thierry in the second, and that from the appearance that Thierry was "unjustly substituted" (*injuste superpositus*) for William in the first passage to the assertion in the second that he is not justly said to have been substituted (*non juste dicitur superpositus*) for William, who was rather most unjustly substituted (*injustissime superpositus est*) for him, are typical of Galbert's subtlety and style and a clear sign that he is refuting and correcting

---

[70] Galbert of Bruges, *De multro*, [121], 14, 28/30; Galbert of Bruges, *Murder*, p. 311.

[71] The injustice done to Thierry, when his claim to the county in spring 1127 was ignored, preceded the injustice done to William when Thierry was set up in his place by some of the citizens of Flanders and was thus an "old(er)" injustice. When God removed William and elevated Thierry to the countship, therefore, he was correcting the older of the two injustices, was restoring the older justice that had been the first one to be upset.

[72] Galbert of Bruges, *De multro*, [121], 14/21; Galbert of Bruges, *Murder*, p. 311 (translation modified).

in the latter passage the assertion of the injustice of Thierry's claim in the earlier passage. He has discovered the divine justice hidden behind the veil of event.

In his edition, Pirenne replaced the *juste* of the second clause (*qui non juste dicitur superpositus consuli Willelmo*) with *injuste*, a reading he found in E and K, even though he noted that both manuscripts he consulted, *A* and *P*, read *juste*. If one reads *injuste* with the Bollandists, Köpke, and Pirenne, one has to translate the core of this sentence something like "we assert that the more just claim belonged to Count Thierry, who is not unjustly [*non injuste*] said to have been substituted for Count William; that dead count, rather, was most unjustly [*injustissime*] substituted for Thierry." According to Bollandists', Köpke's and Pirenne's text, that is, Galbert is here suggesting that Thierry is justly ("not unjustly") said to have usurped the county from William, but that William had already usurped the county "most unjustly" from Thierry in the first place: both had been put in office by dubious means, even though Thierry's claim to the county was better than William's. This is tortuous and leaves Galbert in the same place he started from, faced with the paradox that had led him to pose his question in the first place: "If, therefore, neither of them received the countship in the correct way, by right both of them should have been removed."[73]

Like *A* and *P*, *B* reads *juste*.[74] This is also the preferable reading for stylistic reasons (that is, this reading is more in accord with Galbert's style) and makes better sense. Köpke, who consulted no manuscripts and simply reprinted the Bollandists' text, was in no position to correct their reading of "injuste," but Pirenne, who had consulted both *A* and *P*, was in such a position. So why did he prefer what seems in every way an inferior reading first found in E (which may have been an emendation on the part of the Bollandists) and reprinted by Köpke to a superior reading in both of his manuscripts? His reasoning will, of course, never be known to us, but in general, I think one might suggest that his decision was based on a number of factors including the haste with which he was working, the fact that he used Köpke's reprint as his base text, a respect for the Bollandists' and Köpke's editorial skills that was occasionally unreasonable and obsequious, a lack of sensitivity to the text, and a lack of respect for the scribes of his manuscripts and for Galbert as a thinker and author. Pirenne attributed to Galbert a "versatilité politique" and a "naïveté complète" that blinded him to Galbert's sophistication.[75] The reading *non juste* is but one of many examples that show that Galbert was a subtle author capable of constructing

[73] Ross ingeniously made better sense of Pirenne's text by somewhat freely associating the "non" with "dicitur" and "injuste" with "superpositus" and translating the whole as: "who cannot be called unjustly substituted for Count William; on the contrary that dead count was most unjustly substituted for Thierry" (Galbert of Bruges, *Murder*, p. 311). She thus corrects Pirenne's text in her translation and arrives at more or less the same meaning as one gets from "non juste" in a roundabout way.

[74] This manuscript—Bruges, Openbare Bibliotheek, HS 570—will be cited hereafter as *B*.

[75] Pirenne, "Préface," to Galbert of Bruges, *Histoire du meurtre de Charles le Bon*, pp. xii, xiii.

a complex argument in several parts over a considerable stretch of text; the reading *non injuste* turns him into a muddled thinker incapable of rhetorical subtlety and its adoption by the Bollandists and Pirenne says much about their opinion of him.

Pirenne's relatively low opinion of Galbert as a thinker and writer led him to make a series of textual choices like this one, and these choices, in conjunction with what he wrote about Galbert in the introduction to his edition, have had an unhappy influence on the reading and interpretation of Galbert's text ever since.[76] The ongoing force of this influence, increased by the prestige Pirenne earned later in life, can perhaps be gauged by Professor Van Caenegem's remark in his review of my edition that "dans le chapitre 121, p. 168, la leçon correcte de Pirenne *qui non injuste dicitur superpositus* est remplacé par *qui non juste dicitur superpositus* dans Rider, ce qui n'a pas de sens."[77]

The already heavy pressure to publish the edition as soon as possible increased dramatically in the autumn of 1890, when Picard, the publisher, and the editors of the collection learned that Suger's *Life of Louis VI the Fat* would be on the reading list for the *agrégation* that academic year. They thought that teachers and students would want to study Galbert's text, which provides a great deal of detailed information about Louis VI's interventions in Flanders in 1127–28, alongside Suger's *Life*. "Il y a là," Giry wrote to Pirenne on November 3, "une occasion de vente que l'éditeur ne veut pas perdre & nous devons faire le possible pour l'aider."[78] In July, as we have seen, Giry had written to Pirenne that "[n]ous voudrions que le fascicule soit distribué dans les premiers mois de 91—en mars au plus tôt,"[79] but in light of this new development he now wrote to Pirenne, "Si vous ne nous faites pas attendre pour la préface & la table on pourra mettre le volume en vente vers la fin de janvier ce que nous désirerions beaucoup."[80] Giry also complained in this same letter about the length of Pirenne's historical notes and suggested that some of them be reduced. This was a complaint repeated by both Giry and Prou in the coming months—they were afraid that the lengthy notes would increase the volume's length, and thus its price, to the point where students would not be able to afford it; but Pirenne stood up for his notes and seems in the end to have gotten to keep most of them.[81]

---

[76] See Rider, *God's Scribe*, pp. 3–9, and Rider and Murray, "Introduction," pp. 7–10, for a discussion of Pirenne's ideas about Galbert and their influence on subsequent scholarship.

[77] Van Caenegem, review of Jeff Rider, *God's Scribe*, p. 419.

[78] Giry, Paris, Nov. 3, 1890 (vol. 01/03/001).

[79] Giry, Paris, July 15, 1890 (vol. 01/03/001).

[80] Giry, Paris, Nov. 3, 1890 (vol. 01/03/001).

[81] See Giry, Paris, Nov. 3, 1890 (vol. 01/03/001); Pirenne, Ghent, Nov. 10, 1890 (Sens); Prou, Paris, Dec. 31, 1890 (vol. 01/03/001); Giry, Paris, Jan. 20, 1891 (vol. 01/03/001); Giry, Paris, Mar. 9, 1891 (vol. 01/03/001).

From November 1890 until May 1891, a month before the edition's appearance, Pirenne received a steady stream of increasingly insistent letters from Giry, Prou, the publisher Picard, and the printer Protat urging him to finish the work as quickly as possible.[82] Pirenne did his best, occasionally protesting that the speed with which he was having to work was leading him to overlook certain errors in need of correction.[83] Giry received the first part of the text and notes from Pirenne on November 3 and sent a sample printed text to him on November 6.[84] Pirenne sent the rest of the text and notes to Giry on November 10 and wrote in a letter to Prou that "[l]'impression va marcher me semble-t-il avec une rapidité foudroyante."[85]

Publication of the edition, however, was delayed for another seven months for a couple of reasons. First, Pirenne had decided in late October that he wanted to include in the volume a series of contemporary Latin poems on Charles's death and a map of early twelfth-century Bruges.[86] Giry, who was in charge of the publication for the collection, did not say no, so Pirenne sent him the text of the poems on November 30.[87] Giry and other members of the editorial committee did have some reservations about the desirability of publishing them, however,[88] and it was not until mid-February that they finally agreed to do so.[89] The committee agreed quickly, on the other hand, to include the map of Bruges,[90] and it was decided that Pirenne would have it prepared under his direction in Ghent. He did not send it to Giry until April 1891, however, and when the publisher looked it over, he decided it would have to be redone; the new map was not ready until mid-May.[91]

Work on the text and notes continued while the inclusion of the poems was under discussion and the map in preparation. Giry wrote to Pirenne on December

---

[82] See, for example, Prou, Paris, Oct. 28, 1890 (vol. 01/03/001); Picard, Paris, Nov. 2, 1890 (vol. 01/03/001); Prou, Paris, Dec. 31, 1890 (vol. 01/03/001); Protat, Mâcon, Jan. 17, 1891 (vol. 01/03/001); Giry, Paris, Jan. 19, 1891 (vol. 01/03/001); Giry, Paris, Feb. 24, 1891 (vol. 01/03/001); Picard, Paris, Apr. 23, 1891 (vol. 01/03/001); Picard, Paris, May 19, 1891 (vol. 01/03/001).

[83] For example, "Mon Galbert avance ferme. Je suppose que l'on doit être satisfait de la rapidité que je mets à corriger les épreuves. Je voudrais bien aller moins vite, car je laisse échapper çà et là quelques détails que je devrais corriger dans un erratum" (Pirenne, Ghent, Feb. 15, 1891 [Sens]).

[84] Giry, Paris, Nov. 3, 1890 (vol. 01/03/001); Giry, Paris, Nov. 6, 1890 (vol. 01/03/001).

[85] Pirenne, Ghent, Nov. 10, 1890 (Sens).

[86] See Pirenne, Ghent, Oct. 27, 1890 (Sens); Giry, Paris, Nov. 3, 1890 (vol. 01/03/001); Giry, Paris, Nov. 16, 1890 (vol. 01/03/001).

[87] Pirenne, Ghent, Nov. 30, 1890 (Sens).

[88] Prou, Paris, Nov. 30, 1890, returned and resent Dec. 3, 1890 (vol. 01/03/001); Giry, Paris, Dec. 4, 1890 (vol. 01/03/001); Prou, Paris, Jan. 9, 1891(vol. 01/01/002).

[89] Pirenne, Ghent, Feb. 15, 1891 (Sens); Giry, Paris, Feb. 24, 1891 (vol. 01/03/001).

[90] Giry, Paris, Nov. 16, 1890 (vol. 01/03/001); Prou, Paris, Nov. 30, 1890, returned and resent Dec. 3 1890 (vol. 01/03/001); Giry, Paris, Dec. 4, 1890 (vol. 01/03/001).

[91] Giry, Paris, Apr. 27, 1891 (vol. 01/03/001); Giry, Paris, May 17, 1891 (vol. 01/03/001).

4 to say that half the manuscript was at the printer's but that it no longer seemed realistic to think that the volume could appear by the end of January.[92] The printer Protat wrote on December 6 to say that the proofs of the first folio (pp. 1–16 of the printed edition) would be ready the following week.[93] Pirenne evidently received them shortly thereafter, corrected them, and sent them to Giry to look over; Prou saw them at Giry's apartment shortly before December 31.[94]

At the end of December, however, Pirenne received potentially disastrous news: a thirteenth-century manuscript preserved in the library of Middelburg in the Netherlands perhaps contained a copy of Galbert's chronicle. Pirenne arranged to have the manuscript sent to him in Ghent, and the text in question turned out to be a copy of Walter of Thérouanne's *Life of Charles, Count of Flanders* rather than Galbert's work, but Pirenne was not sure of this until sometime in late January or early February and he had, of course, to put a hold on his correction of the proofs until he had seen the manuscript.[95]

Pirenne's correction of the proofs was sometimes problematic,[96] but the first four folios of the edition (pp. 1–64) were proofed and ready by the first week of February, when Giry showed them to the editorial committee.[97] By March 9 everything was ready except for the preface and the genealogical table.[98] Giry wrote on April 10 to say that he had received the preface and sent it to the printer around April 1. He wrote again the same day to ask Pirenne to redo and augment his summary of the contents of the chronicle (pp. xxvii–xl of the printed edition).[99]

[92] Giry, Paris, Dec. 4, 1890 (vol. 01/03/001).

[93] Protat, Mâcon, Dec. 6, 1890 (vol. 01/03/001).

[94] Giry, Paris, Dec. 22, 1890 (vol. 01/03/001); Prou, Paris, Dec. 31, 1890 (vol. 01/03/001).

[95] The episcopal or municipal archivist [?] of Bruges, Bruges, Dec. 29, 1890 (vol. 01/03/001); Pirenne, Ghent, Dec. 31, 1890 (Sens); the episcopal or municipal archivist [?] of Bruges, Bruges, Jan. 1, 1891 (vol. 01/03/001); R. Vanden Bergh, university librarian, Jan. 3, 1890 (vol. 01/03/001); Prou, Paris, Jan. 9, 1891 (vol. 01/01/002); Prou, Paris, Feb. 6, 1891 (vol. 01/01/002).

[96] Giry, Paris, Dec. 22, 1890 (vol. 01/03/001); Giry, Paris, Jan. 20, 1891 (vol. 01/03/001); Giry, Paris, letter, Apr. 10, 1891 (vol. 01/03/001).

[97] Prou, Paris, Feb. 6, 1891 (vol. 01/01/002).

[98] Giry, Paris, Mar. 9, 1891 (vol. 01/03/001).

[99] Giry, Paris, postcard and letter, Apr. 10, 1891 (vol. 01/03/001). It is interesting to note that it was in fact Giry, in this letter of April 10, who suggested to Pirenne that the passages he had found in the manuscripts that were not in the Bollandists' edition may have been deliberately suppressed by the Bollandists: "Il me semble en lisant vos épreuves que les passages inédits que vous avez retrouvés avaient un caractère commun: ils sont hostiles à l'église de Bruges. On s'expliquerait dès lors leur suppression—mais de qui pensez-vous qu'elle pourrait être le fait: d'un copiste brugeois ou peut-être du bollandiste éditeur? Ne croyez-vous pas qu'il y aurait lieu de dire un mot à ce sujet?" Pirenne indeed added a note to this effect to his edition ("Ces passages [missing from E] renfermant des attaques très violents contre le clergé, il est probable que les Bollandistes se seront fait scrupule de les insérer dans leur édition"; "Préface," in Galbert of Bruges, *Histoire du meurtre de Charles le Bon*, pp. xxivn1), which launched an extended polemic with the Bollandists in 1892 (on which see Lyon, *Henri Pirenne*, pp.

Giry wrote again on April 27 that he had sent the corrected proofs of the preface, genealogical table, and summary to Protat. "Nous touchons donc," he wrote, "à la fin." All that remained to be done was the map and the index.[100]

In early May, however, the count of Limburg-Stirum informed Pirenne that he had discovered in his library a modern copy of Galbert's work that had belonged to Canon Carton and offered to make it available to Pirenne if he wanted to see it.[101] Pirenne wrote to Prou on May 10 that "[j]e corrige les dernières pages de Galbert. Dans huit jours j'espère tout sera fini. Ce jour là je me donnerai une petite fête, car cette correction d'épreuves devient à la fin une supplice. On vient de trouver ici à Gand un nouveau manuscrit que j'ai chez moi. Heureusement il ne change rien au texte. J'ai pu le signaler encore et le décris dans la préface."[102] This addition to the preface (pp. xxv–xxvi of the printed addition) nonetheless required adding a new page to the preface and thus a new proof,[103] and it was not until June 8 that Picard wrote to Pirenne to tell him that he had received the first copies of the book from the printer.[104]

Much of this story will seem familiar to most of those reading this. It is the story of a young professor eager to publish, wanting to publish as much as possible as quickly as possible, unwilling to let an opportunity to publish slip by, trying to juggle his familial and professional obligations, concentrating on the part of the work that he deems most interesting and worthwhile, taking the shortcuts he thinks possible.[105] It is, thus, not surprising that Pirenne's text was not as good as it might have been. Indeed, his remark with respect to Köpke's edition—that it "ne présente donc pas un texte meilleur que celui des précédentes"—could with

---

94–95). The Pirenne archives at the Université libre de Bruxelles contain extensive correspondence relating to this polemic, including drafts of Pirenne's reply to the Bollandists.

[100] Giry, Paris, Apr. 27, 1891 (vol. 01/03/001).

[101] Limburg-Stirum, n.p., n.d. (vol. 01/03/001).

[102] Pirenne, Ghent, May 10, 1891 (Sens).

[103] Giry, Paris, May 17, 1891 (vol. 01/03/001).

[104] Picard, Paris, June 8, 1891 (vol. 01/03/001). Protat printed 900 copies: 880 were sent to Picard for sale; the other 20 were "pour les dépôts légaux, nos archives, les planches gâtées en brochage" (Protat, Mâcon, Jan. 17, 1891 [vol. 01/03/001]).

[105] We have probably all heard—and perhaps made—comments similar to those Pirenne made to Prou in March 1888: "Je compte faire paraitre d'ici à quelques mois une étude sur la constitution de Dinant au Moyen-Age. Voilà trois ans que ce malheureux travail dort dans mes tiroirs et que je n'ai pas le temps de le rédiger tant mes cours me donnent de besogne. Le métier de professeur serait le plus beau de tous les métiers si l'on n'avait pas à faire de cours" (Pirenne, Ghent, Mar. 25, 1888 [Sens]); or those he made in February 1890 when he announced to Prou that he would be able to come to Paris around Easter: "car à Pâques . . . nous avons des vacances de trois semaines et je serai libre comme l'air. Ma femme, pendant ce temps sera à Verviers chez mes parents avec son [!] bébé et, libre d'impedimenta, je pourrai donc—enfin!—partir pour Paris" (Pirenne, Ghent, Feb. 16, 1890 [Sens]).

justice be made of the text his edition as well, or at best one could agree with his own estimation that his text "vau[t] toujours mieux que celle de Köpke, mais ce n'est pas beaucoup dire." His achievement was thus not that of an editor but that of a historian. He recognized the importance and potential of a source, brought it to the attention of a wider audience of scholars and students, and significantly enhanced their understanding and appreciation of it.

Bibliography

Archival and Manuscript Sources

Henri Pirenne. Papiers personnels. Séries 1, La correspondance générale d'Henri Pirenne. 32 vols. Archives de l'Université libre de Bruxelles.

Henri Pirenne. Papiers personnels. Séries 3, Les manuscrits et les différentes éditions annotées des ouvrages et articles d'Henri Pirenne ainsi que la correspondance y afférente. 47 vols. Archives de l'Université libre de Bruxelles.

Arras, Bibliothèque municipale, MS 115.
Bruges, Openbare Bibliotheek, HS 570.
Paris, Bibliothèque nationale de France, MS Baluze 43.
Sens, Bibliothèque municipale, Fonds Maurice Prou.

Published Sources and Literature

Catalogue des livres, manuscrits et documents originaux, formant la bibliothèque de feu Monsieur Charles-Louis Carton. Ghent: Van der Meersch, 1866.

Claeys, Gustave. *Catalogue des livres de la Bibliothèque publique de la ville de Bruges: Deuxième supplément.* Bruges: Bogaert, 1882.

Duchesne, André. *Histoire généalogique des maisons de Guines, d'Ardres, de Gand et de Coucy.* Paris: Cramoisy, 1631.

Galbert of Bruges. "Alia vita [B. Caroli boni comitis Flandriae], auctore Galberto notario." In *Acta Sanctorum*, March, ed. Godefroid Henschen and Daniel Van Papenbroeck, 1:179–219. 3 vols. Antwerp: Joannes Meursius, 1668.

———— (Galbertus notarius Brugensis). "Ex alia ejusdem B. Caroli vita, auctore Galberto Brugensi notario, coaevo." In *Recueil des historiens des Gaules et de la France.* Vol. 13, *Contenant la suite des monumens des trois règnes, de Philippe I, de Louis VI dit le Gros, et de Louis VII surnommé le Jeune, depuis l'an MLX jusqu'en MCLXXX*, pp. 347–92. Paris: Libraires Associés, 1786.

————. *Histoire du meurtre de Charles le Bon, comte de Flandre (1127–28).* Ed. Henri Pirenne. Collection de textes pour servir à l'étude et l'enseignement de l'histoire 10. Paris: Picard, 1891.

————. *De multro, traditione, et occisione gloriosi Karoli comitis Flandriarum.* Ed. Jeff Rider. Corpus Christianorum Continuatio Medievalis 131. Turnhout: Brepols, 1994.

————. *The Murder of Charles the Good, Count of Flanders.* Trans. James Bruce Ross. Records of Civilization, Sources and Studies 61. Rev. ed. New York: Columbia University Press, 2005.

————. "Passio Karoli comitis auctore Galberto." Ed. R. Köpke. In Monumenta Germaniae Historica, Scriptores 12, pp. 561–619. Hannover: Hahn, 1856.

———. "Vita Caroli comitis Flandriae, auctore Galberto notario." Ed. Jacob Langebek. In *Scriptores rerum Danicorum medii aevi*, 4:112–92. 1776. Reprinted Nendeln, Liechtenstein: Kraus Reprint, 1969.

Ganshof, F. L. "Pirenne *(Henri)*." In *Biographie nationale publiée par l'Académie royale des sciences, des lettres et des beaux-arts de Belgique*, vol. 30, cols. 671–723. Brussels, Établissements Emile Bruylant, 1958.

Ganshof, F. L., et al. "Bibliographie des travaux historiques d'Henri Pirenne." In *Henri Pirenne: Hommages et souvenirs*, ed. Jules Duesberg, 1:145–64. 2 vols. Brussels: Nouvelle société d'éditions, 1938.

Köpke, R. "Vita Karolis comitis Flandriae." In Monumenta Germaniae Historica, Scriptores 12, pp. 531–37. Hannover: Hahn, 1856.

Lyon, Bryce. *Henri Pirenne: A Biographical and Intellectual Study*. Ghent: E. Story-Scientia, 1974.

———. "Maurice Prou, ami de Henri Pirenne." *Le Moyen Âge* 71 (1965): 71–107.

Pirenne, Henri. "La chancellerie et les notaires des comtes de Flandre avant le XIIIᵉ siècle." In *Mélanges Julien Havet: Receuil de travaux d'érudition dédiés à la mémoire de Julien Havet*, pp. 733–48. Paris: E. Leroux, 1895.

———. *Histoire de la constitution de la ville de Dinant au Moyen-Âge*. Recueil de travaux publiés par la faculté de philosophie et lettres 2. Ghent: Clemm (H. Engelcke), 1889.

———. "L'origine des constitutions urbaines au Moyen Âge." *Revue historique* 53 (1893): 52–83; 57 (1895): 57–98, 293–327.

———. *Sedulius de Liège, suivi de Sedulli Carmina Inedita*. Bulletin de la classe des lettres et des sciences morales et politiques de l'Académie royale de Belgique 33, no. 4 (1881). Brussels: Hayez, 1882.

———. "La version flamande et la version française de la bataille de Courtrai." *Bulletin de la Commission royale d'histoire*, 4th ser., 17 (1890): 11–50.

———. "Villes, marchés et marchands au Moyen Âge." *Revue historique* 67 (1898): 59–70.

Rider, Jeff. *God's Scribe: The Historiographical Art of Galbert of Bruges*. Washington, DC: Catholic University of America Press, 2001.

Rider, Jeff, and Alan V. Murray. "Introduction." In *Galbert of Bruges and the Historiography of Medieval Flanders*, ed. Jeff Rider and Alan V. Murray, pp. 1–10. Washington, DC: Catholic University of America Press, 2009.

Sanders, Antoon (Antonius Sanderus). *Bibliotheca belgica manuscripta*. 2 vols. Lille: Le Clercq, 1641–44.

Thomas, Paul. "Notes sur Galbert de Bruges." In *Mélanges d'histoire offerts à Henri Pirenne*, 2:515–17. 2 vols. Brussels: Vromant, 1926.

Van Caenegem, R. C. Review of Jeff Rider, *God's Scribe: The Historiographical Art of Galbert of Bruges*. *Cahiers de civilisation médiévale* 41 (1998): 418–19.

Wauters, Alphonse. "Gualbert." In *Biographie nationale, publiée par l'Académie royale des sciences, des lettres et des beaux-arts de Belgique*, vol. 8, cols. 392–94. Brussels: Bruylant-Christophe, 1884–85.

The Urban Typologies of Henri Pirenne and Max Weber: Was There a "Medieval" City?

David Nicholas

Henri Pirenne and Max Weber were almost exact contemporaries: Pirenne was two years older and outlived Weber by fifteen years. They evidently never met, although they were both at the University of Berlin in 1884–85, but Weber thought Pirenne uninformed about economic history, while Pirenne disagreed publicly with Weber's views of the origins of capitalism.[1]

Although Weber was trained as a historian of medieval commercial techniques and the Roman agrarian economy,[2] his academic appointments were in economics. He took a historical-behavioral rather than a model-driven or mathematical approach to the economy. While Weber made the medieval city part of a larger type,[3] Pirenne's work was limited to the cities of medieval northern Europe. Most historians now use a "bundle" of criteria to define town or city, differing in the relative importance that they assign to each,[4] but Weber may have been the only scholar of his generation who realized that the city was too complex to fit a single explanation. Pirenne's monocausal theories achieved wide currency through the force of his personality, his career in Belgium, and the early English translations of his works.[5] The vigor with which Pirenne defended his theses contributed to a sharp decline in his reputation after his death. While few historians were paying much attention to Weber when Pirenne died, Weber's standing, not only among historians but more generally among social scientists, is now higher than

---

[1] Swedberg, *Max Weber*, p. 7; Lyon, *Henri Pirenne*, pp. 199, 222–23.

[2] Van Caenegem, "History and Experiment," p. 1.

[3] Gerth and Mills, introduction to Weber, *Essays in Sociology*, pp. 32–39, 46–50; Swedberg, *Max Weber*, p. 8.

[4] Hodges, *Dark Age Economics*, p. 21.

[5] Van Caenegem, "Henri Pirenne," p. 167; Lyon, *Henri Pirenne,* pp. 124–27, 277–308.

Pirenne's. Yet Pirenne and Weber developed strikingly complementary concepts of an urban type peculiar to the European Middle Ages that remain generally satisfactory, although Pirenne's ideas require more adaptation than Weber's to the imperatives of logic and modern scholarship.

The major works of both Pirenne and Weber have been translated into English. While English, French, and German have different words for town and village, only English and in one specific context French distinguishes city from town. Weber and Pirenne had to use compounds: *Großstadt* for Weber, *grande ville* for Pirenne. But they rarely did so. The issue is not serious for Weber; although he uses *Stadt* for both cities and towns, his context makes his meaning clear. But translations have distorted Pirenne's views. French *cité* means the fortified part of a pre-urban nucleus, most often the Roman ruin that housed a bishopric. On the rare occasions when Pirenne used *cité*, he meant that, not the entire urban settlement. I have found only one place where Pirenne speaks of "grandes cités du Moyen Âge" in a context where in his other work he invariably used *ville*.[6] Pirenne's English translators generally rendered his *ville* as "town," but occasionally as "city."[7] Insofar as his native language permitted, Pirenne tried not to blur the distinction between town and city, but trying to deduce his notion of the medieval city requires analyzing his words in terms in which he was not thinking. When this caution is heeded, Pirenne's conceptual framework becomes much more sophisticated than one would gather by reading his works in English.

Our problem is thus threefold: what were the common points and differences in Weber's and Pirenne's views of medieval urbanization as a type? is it permissible based on their approaches and conclusions to distinguish a medieval town from the medieval city? and how has that typology held up under the scrutiny of recent research? This paper will not dispute Weber's high standing but will rehabilitate Pirenne's to a degree; for in infrequently cited passages Pirenne nuanced some of his more extreme positions.

---

[6] Pirenne, "L'origine des constitutions," p. 21.

[7] For example, Pirenne's most famous short work is *Medieval Cities*, which is *Les villes du Moyen Âge* in French. Chapter 3 of the French text has a heading "Les cités et les bourgs," which the English translator makes "City Origins." But Pirenne then goes on to discuss the question of whether "cities" originated in the rural environment of the ninth century and says that "the answer depends on the meaning given to the word 'city.'" In each of these cases *except the heading* where the translator uses "city," Pirenne used "ville." He used "cités" for the episcopal complexes around which *bourgs* developed, not city in the modern sense. In *Les villes du Moyen Âge* he used "cité" as the French equivalent of *civitas* for the city of antiquity; Pirenne thus used "town" for a place having typically a suburb and a *cité*. In *Les villes du Moyen Âge* Pirenne used "la formation des villes et la bourgeoisie" and in the text always used "ville" for the medieval town/city. Other examples abound. Pirenne, *Medieval Cities*, pp. 130, 180; Pirenne, *Les villes du Moyen Âge*, pp. 333, 335, 374, 402.

Defining the "Medieval" City

Weber spoke of the desirability of comparing "the developmental stages of the ancient polis with those of the medieval city" but admitted the methodological pitfalls of doing so.[8] In other contexts he occasionally used the term *medieval city* without defining it.[9] His notion of the peculiarly "medieval" city thus must be deduced from what he said about it in the context of his broader expositions on Western urbanization.

Although Pirenne admitted that medieval cities can be "classified according to certain general types," in most of his work he emphasized their diversity.[10] Yet in a late work he gave a definition: "[T]he medieval town in the true sense of the word only existed in places where urban law, *i.e.* a law established for a population essentially devoted to commerce and industry, became developed to a point when the town became a clearly defined legal person. . . . [A] medieval town was a community under the aegis of a fortified enclosure, living by the exercise of commerce and industry, and enjoying exceptional judicial and administrative rights which constituted it a privileged body." In each case where *town* occurs in the English version, Pirenne's French version used *ville*,[11] which could refer to either city or town. This is a less exclusively economic definition than Pirenne suggested in his other work. Although he was writing about the northern cities, this definition is general enough to include those of Italy. Pirenne thus thought that "all (*toutes*) medieval *villes* were enclosed," and the wall was "an attribute by which towns were distinguished from villages."[12] Weber took a similar view, describing the medieval city as "the fusion of fortress and market." Weber noted that the city had a denser population than other types of settlement and a more defined space than most towns and all villages.[13]

Weber saw the occidental city as the "catalyst of a 'trend toward rationality' that distinguished Western European institutions from the 'patriarchal and 'charismatic' regimes of other parts of the world."[14] He admitted broad similarities: non-Western cities were political capitals, markets (he saw the medieval city as more a demand market than Pirenne did), fortresses, with some farmland, and a powerful lord. But only in the West in the High Middle Ages was the city also an autonomous union of citizens, equal before the special law that governed the city, with its own organs of government. For both Pirenne and Weber the populations

---

[8] Weber, *Agrarian Sociology*, p. 305; Schluchter, *Rationalism*, p. 282.

[9] Weber, *General Economic History*, p. 335; Weber, *City*, p. 197.

[10] Pirenne, *Medieval Cities*, p. 133; Pirenne, "L'origine des constitutions," p. 32.

[11] Pirenne, "Northern Towns,"p. 523; Pirenne, *Les villes et les institutions*, 1:7; 2:118.

[12] Pirenne, "L'origine des constitutions,"pp. 80–81.

[13] Weber, *City*, pp. 65, 77; see also Pirenne, *Medieval Cities*, p. 150.

[14] Nicholas, *Urban Europe*, p. 1.

of the medieval cities were legally free, and Weber distinguished them thereby from those of antiquity, who in his formulation were slaves.[15]

From Ancient to Medieval City

While noting that the ancient city and the medieval city of Italy and southern France had much in common, including domination by landed elites, Weber did not claim directly that there was topographical or institutional continuity between them, but he saw transition, not rupture in continuity. He did not extend this idea to the north, thereby evading a question that has damaged Pirenne's reputation. Weber divided the "medieval city" into two "sub-forms," which he variously defined in geographical and chronological terms. Pirenne saw commercial continuity in both north and south, and some continued habitation in late Roman *civitates*, followed by a sharp decline in both from the mid-seventh century. Pirenne saw the trade that produced the medieval city originating in Italy but said little about the structures of the Italian cities. Like all their contemporaries, Weber and Pirenne saw a starker difference between the medieval cities of southern Europe and the north than do most modern scholars.[16]

Weber considered the northern European city to be more peculiarly "Western" than that of the south. From the late eleventh century in Italy and slightly later in the north movements of municipal independence culminated in "patrician cities," and the personal urban community became a "spatial community."[17] The merchants as well as the landed "patricians" who were the urban elites of antiquity and early medieval southern Europe more often had significant agricultural property than did those of the north.[18] Venice provides his example of a closed patriciate; his section on medieval patriciates of the north has few examples (the chief one was the small planned town of Freiburg-im-Breisgau), but he has a section on "contrasts with the medieval city"[19] in which he sees differences between the ancient and medieval patrician cities in the extent to which that of antiquity was based on extended families and militia duty, characteristics generally absent from the medieval city until it became the "plebeian city." He contrasts this situation to "the dominance of peaceful economic interests in the medieval city," for the medieval city was more an economic creation, while that of antiquity was political-military.[20] Although Pirenne also used the term *patrician*,

---

[15] His points of reference were fifth-century BC Athens and the Roman Republic, not the city of the late empire. Weber, *City*, p. 91; Abramowski, *Geschichtsbild*, pp. 98, 102.

[16] Weber, *City*, p. 197; Weber, *General Economic History*, pp. 323–24.

[17] Abramowski, *Geschichtsbild*, p. 88.

[18] Weber, *City*, pp. 71, 121–56.

[19] Weber, *City*, pp. 149–51.

[20] Weber, *City*, pp. 208–12 (pp. 212–13).

he meant the thirteenth-century town rulers and claimed that, in contrast to the landowning Roman patricians, the medieval "patricians" with rare exceptions were merchants.[21] Later research has suggested that the early medieval cities of the north had stronger Roman antecedents than either Weber or Pirenne thought.[22]

Weber spoke of "the blurring of the lines between noble and merchant,"[23] particularly during the period of the "plebeian" city, when the cities were governed by occupational guilds that the older families had to join, in Weber's view, if they wanted to participate in city government. Weber did not note that some of those guilds were not craft-based, and his examples include the Italian *popolo*, which he saw (more starkly than scholars now do) as middle and lower class.[24] The "plebeian city" in the north amounted to the guild-based regimes that took power (or more often shared it with the older lineages) between about 1275 and 1330. As types the patrician city has analogies with the ancient and early medieval cities, while the plebeian city seems to be late medieval and modern, because it was based on occupational guilds, which did not have political power in the cities of antiquity. Weber called the medieval guilds "the first organization of free labor."[25]

Weber also thought that the "establishment of democracy" distinguished the medieval from the ancient city and, like Pirenne, associated democracy with the craft guild regimes of the late Middle Ages, although neither meant "democracy" in a contemporary sense.[26] From around 1370 many cities apportioned seats on their councils by guilds and groups of guilds, in effect guaranteeing seats to them. As this happened, town policy was controlled by great wholesalers who dominated the nominally "artisan" guilds, including members of some old patrician lineages who joined a guild in order to participate in politics. The wealthier guildsmen bought rural land, developed an exaggerated consciousness of ancestry, and generally tried to imitate the older elites. Weber and Pirenne both realized this in broad outline, although Weber was more aware that the newly rich could be just as tenacious in ancestor worship as those of more rooted pedigree. Weber understood that the older urban elite families were never excluded completely from government. Both show a family basis to the medieval city, both before and after 1370, that was substantially accurate.[27] On balance, taking the northern European city as the "medieval city," while the contemporary Italian cities were

[21] Pirenne, *Early Democracies*, p. 110.

[22] Nicholas, *Growth of the Medieval City*, pp. 33–35.

[23] Weber, *City*, p. 153.

[24] Nicholas, *Growth of the Medieval City*, pp. 262–71.

[25] Weber, *City*, pp. 157–95; Weber, *General Economic History*, p. 137; Abramowski, *Geschichtsbild*, pp. 108–9.

[26] Abramowski, *Geschichtsbild*, p. 106.

[27] Nicholas, *Urban Europe*, p. 99; Weber, *City*, pp. 121–95; Nicholas, *Later Medieval City*, pp. 141–55.

continuations of an ancient city type, the medieval burgher was much more an "economic man" than his Italian or ancient counterpart.[28]

Market, Domain, Freedom, and City

Weber and Pirenne held similar views of the extent to which the medieval city evolved from antecedents in the rural economy and the territorial state, but neither represents the modern consensus. Pirenne denied all connections. When faced with hard evidence, such as the presence of serfs in town elites, he simply said that they were relics that quickly passed.[29] Weber saw no agrarian and peasant aspects of the medieval city, although its Mediterranean version was ruled by nobles who divided residence between town and countryside. In the medieval north the urban and peasant-feudal worlds were distinct.[30]

Pirenne's refusal to admit that a place on the site of a later city could have been its antecedent except in topography[31] is the most egregious example of his view of history as a series of revolutions, not gradual evolution.[32] Thus, while most scholars agree that charters regulated or confirmed the legality of activities that people were already doing, Pirenne seems to have thought that it gave them permission to do things that they never would have thought of otherwise.

The evolution of site into city occurred at two levels. The northern medieval city of "old Europe" (Pirenne did not discuss the colonial towns of the German east) took a specific topographical form: a fortification such as a princely stronghold, an abbey, or a Roman ruin that most commonly served as a bishopric, and suburbs where in Pirenne's view "wandering merchants" settled. The city was thus binuclear initially, but additional sectors developed as successive suburbs were incorporated within the walls. The development of site-based trade was slow in creating suburbs that were large enough to wall. The earliest town walls in Flanders and the Meuse valley are from the late eleventh century. Except for the tenth-century *Rheinvorstadt* of Cologne, the others start in the twelfth century.[33] Weber essentially agreed with Pirenne's position.[34] Modern scholars generally agree that a topographic division of the mature city into fortress and trading settlement(s) was a characteristic of medieval urbanization in the north[35] but reject Pirenne's

---

[28] Abramowski, *Geschichtsbild*, pp. 106–7.

[29] Pirenne, *Economic and Social History*, p. 183.

[30] Abramowski, *Geschichtsbild*, pp. 99–100.

[31] Pirenne, *Medieval Cities*, p. 141.

[32] Bachrach and Nicholas, *Law*, p. xiii; cf. Lyon, *Henri Pirenne*, p. 440.

[33] Verhulst, *Rise of Cities*, p. 115.

[34] Weber, *City*, p. 67.

[35] Nicholas, *Growth of the Medieval City*, pp. 92–104.

corollary that the fortress was economically passive except for the demand for luxuries.[36] While Pirenne thought that fortifications existed first, as wandering merchants sought the protection of their walls, this is generally true of only cities that developed around bishoprics and monasteries. Some castles were built where there was already a trading settlement.[37]

Since not all inhabitants of the medieval city were wandering merchants, Pirenne had to explain the occupations and legal status of other residents of the pre-urban nuclei. He rejected the idea that the "servitors" of the abbeys who acted as their agents on markets were the ancestors of the merchant class of the towns, because they were not professional merchants, a group whose transience had caused them to be placed under royal protection by Charlemagne. Pirenne thus excluded considerable buying and selling from his definition of merchant.[38] Although he saw economic change causing the breakthrough to medieval urbanization, he denied that local market law could have been the catalyst; for while all towns have markets, not all markets are towns. Pirenne further was concerned almost entirely with external demand for the goods and services that were supplied by the townspeople. Weber defined the city as a primarily commercial rather than agricultural settlement, but he realized that this could fit smaller settlements and thus added a requirement that there be both site-specific supply and demand. For a place to be urban it had to provide "regular rather than occasional exchange of goods,"[39] which evokes Pirenne's distinction between the professional merchant of the mature city and the occasional merchant of the early Middle Ages.

Pirenne's requirement that urban merchants be both full-time and free threw him into the position of arguing that serfs could not be townspeople or merchants.[40] *Ministerials* are often defined as "serf knights," but the word was also used for servants of bishops and others who became the lords of towns. They bought and sold goods for their masters and handled other specialized duties in their lords' households, such as minting. Pirenne admitted that "a few serfs" lived in the towns but were "not members of the city population."[41] He argued that towns were different in kind from rural villages, deriving neither their law nor their elites from them. Yet virtually all modern scholars concede that *ministerials* were an important, arguably the most important, part of the early urban elites, particularly in the Rhineland, where their descendants' lineages continued powerful into the fourteenth and even fifteenth century.

[36] Pirenne, "L'origine des constitutions," p. 33.
[37] Verhulst, *Rise of Cities*, pp. 68–69, 111, 116–17.
[38] Pirenne, "Stages," p. 499; Pirenne, *Medieval Cities*, p. 109.
[39] Weber, *City*, p. 66.
[40] Pirenne, "L'origine des constitutions," p. 54; Pirenne, "Northern Towns," p. 509.
[41] Pirenne, *Medieval Cities*, p. 194.

Interestingly, Pirenne was correct that freedom of movement was characteristic of the townspeople; he was wrong in equating this with legal freedom. Not only were the *ministerials* in the elites, but the "ordinary" subjects of the early town lords, the *censuales*, were not bound to the soil. The property and standing of the *censuales* were enhanced as trade developed around their lords' markets. Lists of inhabitants furthermore often list *ministeriales* among *liberi;* thus if we use the modern idea of freedom, most "ordinary" inhabitants of the cities were free while their elites were unfree but enjoyed a higher social condition. Some texts call the same person both *ministerialis* and *civis*, although Pirenne insisted that serfs could not be citizens.[42] Pirenne did not deny that the bishops had councils consisting of both *ministeriales* and *burgenses* during the period before the breakthrough to genuine urbanization, but during the "urban revolution" of the eleventh and twelfth century this changed and "the last vestiges of domainial law disappeared."[43]

A critical point of Pirenne's analysis that is now generally rejected is his assertion that after the merchants of the eleventh and twelfth centuries made money through long-distance trade, they lost interest in risk-taking and invested in land, both in the town and outside. He attributes the presence of separate groups of *viri hereditarii* in the thirteenth-cities to the increasing demand for land, as population increase made rents more profitable.[44] Modern scholarship places land investment at the beginning of the urbanization process, not as something that merchants later considered a safe investment. The early elites consisted of landholders in the original territory of their cities, and even in such places as Cologne and Arras they only expanded into long-distance trade and money lending in the late twelfth and thirteenth centuries.[45]

Thus, contrary to Pirenne's view, most inhabitants of the late eleventh- and early twelfth-century towns were dependents of the town lords, not wandering merchants. Since the lords' dependents in the places that were developing urban characteristics, who by this time were more craftsmen than agriculturalists, were the population base of the new cities, the merchants were of two types: 1) natives who accumulated money and expanded into long-distance trade; and 2) a smaller group of non-native immigrants. At Arras in 1024 outsiders tried to become *homines* of the abbot of Saint-Vaast in order to gain toll exemption.[46]

---

[42] Schulz, *Freiheit des Bürgers*, pp. 69–77, 131–70.
[43] Pirenne, "L'origine des constitutions," pp. 6–7.
[44] Pirenne, "Stages," p. 506.
[45] Nicholas, *Growth of the Medieval City*, pp. 125–29, and literature cited.
[46] Verhulst, *Rise of Cities*, pp. 119–21.

Long-Distance Trade and the Breakthrough to Urbanization

Pirenne, Weber, and most of their critics and disciples alike have agreed that the transition to genuine urbanization occurred during the eleventh and twelfth centuries. Pirenne argued that long-distance trade caused the breakthrough, then was followed by the elaboration of a separate urban law, but he did not deny that long-distance trade occurred before the development of cities. He maintained that Roman trading patterns persisted into the seventh century and that the Carolingian period was a nadir in long-distance trade. Recent scholarship rejects this; for evidence, much of it archaeological and unavailable to Pirenne, has shown a growth in long-distance trade even before the period of Charlemagne.[47] How important this trade was in relation to the rise of indigenous markets for food and other consumer goods is debatable. The North Sea emporia of Quenvovic and Duurstedel and English Hamwih were part of a network that focused largely—not exclusively, since they had some artisans—on royal courts and gift giving.[48] They yielded from the late eighth century to permanent settlements that were more complex and provided non-princely demand and eventually supply markets in and around the environs of the sites that were becoming towns. Thus in the late Carolingian period the northern trade was growing and was increasingly based on economic regionalism, central places, and trade in craft goods. In the tenth century the evidence for trade expands tremendously, but recent studies suggest that it was conducted in permanent settlements in locally based crafts and merchandising. Long-distance trade declined but would resume in the eleventh century.[49]

An important aspect of the change from emporia to urbanization was the monetization of economic relationships. The growth of trade under the Carolingians has been attributed to the flow of silver originating in the Abbasid caliphate and moving west. Curiously, Pirenne seemed less concerned than Weber with the impact of the money supply on transforming trade.[50] Modern scholars have attributed the eventual urban revolution in large measure to a rapid increase in the amount of precious metal and money, which facilitated deducing equivalent values of dissimilar goods.[51]

---

[47] McCormick, *Origins*, pp. 639–69. While building an impressive case for the volume and sophistication of long-distance trade before and during the Carolingian period, McCormick does not link this to urbanization and notes that his analysis does not include the tenth century, when trade became more site based; cf. McCormick, "Complexity," p. 315.

[48] Hodges, *Anglo-Saxon Achievement*, pp. 54–55, 83–86, 119–42; Verhulst, *Rise of Cities*, pp. 43–46.

[49] Hodges, *Dark Age Economics*, pp. 101, 183; Hodges, *Anglo-Saxon Achievement*, pp. 155–59; more generally Nicholas, *Growth of the Medieval City*, pp. 64–81.

[50] Weber, *Theory*, pp. 32–33, 64, 182.

[51] Spufford, *Money and Its Use*, pp. 55–131.

Central Places and Wandering Merchants

Pirenne argued that places that became cities had advantages of site that attracted wandering merchants to settle in their suburbs. Weber saw the logical contradiction of attributing the origin of a site-based urban class or group to wanderers and accordingly said that the town is characterized by the *resident* trader, although he admitted that wandering merchants existed and eventually settled and worked their way into the local urban elites.[52] Weber rejected Pirenne's idea that a true town—or at least a city—depended on long-distance commerce, for he realized that a mass market for goods and services presupposed not only local demand but also diversification and industrial production, which Pirenne did not see as important until the late twelfth century. He understood further that no city could feed itself and that the medieval city was thus a farm market, a fact that Pirenne admitted but did not emphasize.[53]

Leaving the "wandering merchant" aside, what was "long-distance" trade? While towns typically developed centrally within a region that produced food that was sold and consumed on the urban market, and in return bought crafts made in the town, cities more often developed on economic frontiers, at the border between areas of supply and demand of goods.[54] The larger the city and more diversified the demand on its market, the wider its range of attraction. While some cities were gateways, acting as conduits of goods coming from outside the immediate region and then reconsigned to the interior markets of the region, most developed as central places. To use the Low Countries as an economic region, Bruges was a gateway, while Ghent was a central place.

The term *central place* comes from geographical theory, with which Pirenne was understandably unfamiliar. The details of central place are not relevant for this discussion,[55] but improvements in transportation and communication, particularly when the major cities were expanding rapidly in the late twelfth and thirteenth centuries, made the cities' range of attraction increasingly broad and overlapping. Initially the economic region that gave birth to a town could be defined largely in terms of the area required to feed it, since the early towns were markets for the food surpluses produced on the domains of their lords and others. As they evolved into cities, this area of attraction grew, as they had to import grain from large distances.

Much more than geographical centrality is necessary for a "central place." Elements such as transaction costs, competition for resources, and ease of communication are important. Political considerations play a role. By the eleventh

[52] Weber, *General Economic History*, pp. 215, 323–24.
[53] Weber, *City*, pp. 66–67; Pirenne, *Economic and Social History*, pp. 172–75.
[54] Nicholas, "Structures," pp. 523–25.
[55] See the discussion in Nicholas, *Urban Europe*, pp. 33–45.

century the English kings were trying to require that major commercial transactions be conducted on named markets, often the chief town of a county. More famous are the "staples" enjoyed by some late medieval cities, such as that of Ghent on grain going downstream on the Scheldt and Leie Rivers, that of Bruges on commerce in the Zwin, and that of Dordrecht on goods coming down the Waal. These monopoly privileges were granted by princes, and at least the Continental examples clearly extended the economic range of cities and promoted their central place functions, although many of them applied only to trade coming toward the city from a single direction.[56]

Still, if "long-distance" means a merchant who dealt in goods that are unavailable within the region of which the city was a central place, this was a much smaller area in the early twelfth century than in the late thirteenth. While a merchant who brought goods from twenty miles away might be considered "long-distance" at the beginning of our period, the range was much greater by 1300. English law in the thirteenth century treatise enforced the principle that a new market should not be founded within 6⅔ miles (about 10 km) of an existing one, to avoid competition with the sales monopoly of the lord of the earlier market.[57] Including time spent at the market site, this would be difficult but possible in a single day. The area would have been smaller in the late eleventh century, the period when Pirenne and Weber agreed that genuine cities were forming. Thus we may call a place whose merchants ventured twenty to twenty-five miles (three to four days en route and back) a "town," while a "city" acting as a regional central place would serve a still larger area.

Urban populations are composed of "basic" and "nonbasic" producers. The sources of income of basic producers come from outside the town. Nonbasic producers' income is generated *in situ*, selling goods and providing services to residents of the town. Thus a merchant who imported grain was a basic producer, while a baker was nonbasic. Clearly these categories must be conceived broadly (the same weaver might produce luxuries for a court clientele and coarser cloth for the local market). The more occupationally differentiated a place was, the more nonbasic producers would be needed to provide for even its local needs. A city was distinguished from a town not only by its geographical range but also by the fact that its craftsmen produced exportable goods, which meant specialized items from a skilled labor force, since no one in a distant market would buy something that had built-in transaction costs when something of comparable quality was available locally.[58] Although craft suburbs were developing around the larger towns in the

[56] Nicholas, *Growth of the Medieval City*, pp. 88, 96, 135–40, 182–84, 302–6; Nicholas, *Later Medieval City*, pp. 36–37, 40–44.

[57] Masschaele, *Peasants, Merchants, and Markets*, p. 62.

[58] Nicholas, *Urban Europe*, pp. 33, 38–39.

twelfth century, only from the late twelfth century is there much evidence that their products were being exported over a great distance. This change is accompanied by a two- to fourfold growth in population, mainly of industrial artisans, in some towns in the thirteenth century.[59]

Diversity of goods was thus key. A regional market would sell basic crafts and import food and distribute farmers' produce through an area broader than their native village markets. A major city obtained food and industrial raw materials from a wide area. This complexity of operations involved the presence of crafts marketable over a great distance, both utilitarian and specialty (the latter because someone such as a goldsmith would be too specialized to be site-bound in markets except in a major city, often with demand from a court). This in turn meant demand for imports from a greater distance, and a population too large to be fed by its immediate environs. Thus the characteristic of the medieval city, as opposed to the medieval town, is involvement in long-distance trade, as Pirenne said.

Most medieval cities, even those of Flanders, originated as local markets and were large before they developed exportable industry. Pirenne understood that the difference between the large and small towns was in the extent to which trade was complicated and industrial operations, even domestic, more complex and thus subject to regulation in the larger place. He thus saw two urban social groups "side by side with the craftsmen-*entrepreneurs* living by the local market, an entirely different group, which worked for export. Instead of producing only for the limited clientele of the town and its environs, these were the purveyors of the wholesale merchants, carrying on international commerce." The first group got their raw materials from the great merchants and in some contexts became "mere wage-earners." Thus Pirenne recognized that the towns had a local base, and that much of the business of the townsmen was in provisioning other townsmen.[60] The first suburb, generally developing if not walled by 1150, was typically commercial and included the major markets of the eventual city. The later suburbs, developing between about 1150 and 1300, more often had mainly craft populations. This corresponds to the city having something to sell outside its immediate environs, while the town was more site-bound.

Weber too built a typology that distinguished between a type of medieval *Stadt* that existed as a local market and one based on long-distance trade. He recognized that utilitarian goods are the most conducive to marketing, luxuries the least because demand is less. Exportable crafts thus followed trade but were an important component in differentiating city from town. Weber and his followers distinguished between "consumer and producer city," corresponding to cities made

---

[59] Nicholas, *Growth of the Medieval City*, pp. 171–201.
[60] Pirenne, *Economic and Social History*, pp. 176–77, 185.

up largely of "nonbasic" as opposed to "basic" producers. But even in its early stages this was too schematic, as Weber realized, for the city created its own demand as it grew and became more occupationally differentiated.[61]

If we use a flexible concept of the economic region and understand that long-distance merchants not only sold the city's products over a wide area but also imported items of high value, long-distance trade was clearly a presupposition of the evolution of town into city. Long-distance merchants were not always in municipal government, but they were part of the city elites. Importers always had greater prestige in their cities than did manufacturers, even those who produced for export.[62] A merchant who brought high-quality wool to Flanders from northern England was a more substantial figure, as was the merchant who brought needed grain from northern France, than the merchant who imported utilitarian items. The city differs from the town in that while a few long-distance merchants worked in towns, the demand market of the medieval city was so large, differentiated, and sophisticated that long-distance merchants were numerous and rich enough to form a significant part (not all) of its still site-based ruling elite. The artisan regimes of the late Middle Ages in the city (not the town) were really merchant-dominated, with some crafts.

This analysis validates long-distance trade as a characteristic distinguishing city from town, but it breaks with Pirenne in arguing that most long-distance traders were site-based from the beginning, not wanderers. Local crafts provided them with something that could be exchanged outside the town's immediate environs for food and industrial raw materials. Further, the development of a network of cities that became central places through dominating long-distance trade meant that merchants of towns need only have recourse to merchants of the central city to gain access to wider markets. The economy of a place that at its time of origin fit the paradigm of a city based on long-distance trade in Pirenne's formulation would, if it did not expand, decline into a town. Unfortunately Pirenne reversed this process. He argued that cities based on long-distance trade came first; then new towns were founded as their satellites: "Their production is determined by the needs of their population and that of the environs which extend two or three leagues around their walls and, in exchange for the manufactured articles which the city furnishes to them, attend to the food supply of the urban inhabitants." He distinguished these from a second type of medieval town. To the locally based town economy (*Stadtwirtschaft*), which tended to be narrowly focused and protectionist, he apposed the medieval city that was based on long-distance trade, and he divided these into two: exporters of industrial goods made from local raw

---

[61] Weber, *Theory*, p. 183; Weber, *City*, pp. 67–68.
[62] Nicholas, *Later Medieval City*, pp. 217–27.

materials, and coastal emporia. They had capitalistic economies; the locally based *Stadtwirtschaften* did not.[63]

These different economic structures corresponded for Pirenne to two types of urban constitution in the north, the original and derived; but he argued that the original form was of the city based on long-distance trade, while the derived type was that characterized by the grant of bourgeois privileges that were based on those of the larger cities. He distinguishes between the Flemish type and other towns "whose members gained a livelihood from local industry and commerce, and chiefly consisted of artisans engaged in tasks indispensable to the daily life of the commune and the surrounding country, together with a few property owners of a semi-rural character. . . . The towns with merely local economic relations are not examples of the earliest municipal development. Nearly all of them ought to be considered as of secondary origin, as villages [French: *villages*] or towns endowed with municipal privileges [French: *bourgs dotés de franchises municipales*] and raised to the position of civic communities [French: *et érigés en communes bourgeoises*] on the model of the great trading centres [French: *grandes agglomerations marchandes*]."[64]

Urban Law and the Inviolability of Rights

Legal and institutional considerations were more important for Weber than for Pirenne. Weber distinguished three types of government: traditional, charismatic, and rational. The rational form operated under laws.[65] Weber noted "that the city is not peculiar to the West, but the urban community is." "Urban community" included "at least partial autonomy and autocephaly, thus also an administration by authorities in the election of whom the burghers participated."[66] Urban privileges, as given to the sworn association of the town and later extended to its territory, could not be violated by princes without due process, and the city had an independent magistracy with judicial and eventually legislative power over the citizens, and the right to defend itself. Clearly, there were great differences in the degree of urban autonomy. Town lords retained rights of oversight and confirmation, particularly of the choice of new members of the city council. Weber distinguished between "objective" law and the "subjective" right of individuals and between public and private law developing in the medieval city. Thus he saw the medieval city as a legal forerunner of the modern bureaucratic state, which he distinguished from the patrimonial state of the Middle Ages.[67]

---

[63] Pirenne, "Stages," pp. 507–8.

[64] Pirenne, *Early Democracies*, pp. 100–101 (Pirenne, *Anciennes démocraties*, 1:210).

[65] Van Caenegem, *Max Weber*, pp. 1–27.

[66] Nicholas, *Urban Europe*, p. 92; Weber, *City*, pp. 80–81.

[67] Abramowski, *Geschichtsbild*, pp. 91–94; Lachmann, *Capitalists*, p. 45.

Weber thought that competition among businesses, cities, and states fostered rationality, and he accordingly felt that the dense urbanization of Europe and the accompanying plethora of (mainly) small states produced a more rational system than what resulted in either patriarchal or charismatic regimes. The legal rights of corporate entities such as cities that could not be overridden by the imperatives of the central or territorial state was critical in creating a self-perpetuating dialectic between rationality and irrationality.[68] Weber did not think that the antagonisms of "classes" or between rich and poor provided "the medieval city with its historical peculiarities." Instead, it was the distinct place that the medieval city assumed within the larger territorial legal and political organization.[69] The laws of modern cities must conform to those of the surrounding territorial state, but there was no such obligation in the Middle Ages. The privileges of the medieval cities, at least outside England and France, made them largely independent of princes. Nothing of this sort existed outside Europe, and it fostered exchange between relatively independent economic units. The medieval city was ended when the rights of individual cities were ended by the bearers of modern state power.[70]

Weber noted that the urban community was sometimes formalized in a contract with the town lord, as in the town plantations in the east. A charter issued by the lord generally confirmed the gains made by the townsmen.[71] Pirenne too recognized that the medieval cities had their own laws, but his focus on the town as legally distinguished from the rural environs misled him into insisting that urban law could not have evolved from the customs of rural principalities or estates. Pirenne thought that urban law had to be enshrined in a charter, given by or extracted from a town lord, and was unaware of evidence that many cities had governments before they obtained charters. The early urban governments were usually courts rather than councils, often staffed hereditarily, that judged cases involving their burgesses. London had such a tribunal even in the tenth century, and they became general in the eleventh. The early town courts were staffed by *ministerials* of the town lord and did not have legislative powers. Pirenne admitted this point, which meant that the same persons (*scabini*) were serving both the urban community and the town lord, evidently without realizing that it destroyed his claim that urban government had no ties with those of territorial lords:[72] "It

---

[68] Nicholas, *Urban Europe*, pp. 1–2.

[69] Weber, *City*, p. 197.

[70] Weber, *General Economic History*, pp. 132–33.

[71] Weber, *City*, pp. 107–8.

[72] "The mediaeval city . . . constituted a legal unit distinct from the surrounding country. Its gates once passed, a man escaped from territorial law and came under an exceptional jurisdiction. Between countryman and the burgher there was neither community of interest nor community of civil status" (Pirenne, "Northern Towns," pp. 521–22).

formed a legal island, a real 'immunity.'"[73] But the fact that the first urban court was often of *scabini*, who were officials of the town lord, did not make it less urban. Pirenne, who maintained in his most conspicuous work that the towns were a revolutionary phenomenon that was totally divorced from the surrounding countryside, is thus caught in a logical contradiction.[74] Although they were not always judged by one of their own number, the fact of being subordinated to the same law made the citizens a community.[75] The eleventh-century town charters did not give the citizens the right to participate in local government. Those of the twelfth century did, although a rotating council with legislative powers was unusual.[76]

Both Weber and Pirenne considered the movements for urban independence revolutionary.[77] Thus they attached considerable importance to the "communal" movements that—whether or not in the specific form of a "commune" or sworn association[78]—gave at least some *de facto* and often *de jure* autonomy of law and administration to the medieval city. The town as a sworn corporation of citizens was the common characteristic everywhere. The early citizen community was "democratic" in the sense that all were equal before the (urban) law, enjoyed the same legal status and privileges, and were subject in principle to the same obligations.[79]

Weber made the *coniuratio* the revolutionary onset of the burghers' movement of independence. Most of his examples of *coniurationes* are Italian. He thus saw the early Italian urban elites as more revolutionary than in the north, where older aldermanic families persisted in the councils of the towns. Some regimes mixed representatives of the oath community with old families, as in the Low Countries, with *jurés*. While in Italy the urban nobles dominated the sworn associations, the rich merchants did so in the north, where there was no urban nobility on the Italian scale. Weber distinguished between the northern French *coniurationes*, which were "oath-bound confederations for peace without other corporate attributes," and city associations in England and Germany, which were legal corporations.[80]

Weber realized that the market presupposed mutual economic advantages to all parties to a contract, which could only be realized if the serf had freedom of movement and could accumulate property that he might exchange for money or goods or for legal emancipation. The medieval citizen-city reduced inequalities

---

[73] Pirenne, *Early Democracies*, p. 36.

[74] Pirenne, *Early Democracies*, p. 47.

[75] Weber, *City*, pp. 95, 105.

[76] Nicholas, *Growth of the Medieval City*, pp. 141–46.

[77] "The urbanites therefore usurped the right to violate lordly law. This was the major revolutionary innovation of medieval occidental cities in contrast to all others" (Weber, *City*, p. 94).

[78] See discussion in Nicholas, *Growth of the Medieval City*, pp. 146–62.

[79] Pirenne, *Early Democracies*, pp. 51–53.

[80] Weber, *City*, pp. 108–9, 115; Abramowski, *Geschichtsbild*, pp. 89–90.

based on birth and became a place where unfree persons could rise into the freedom of a common urban law. The legal maxim "town air makes a man free" did not appear simultaneously everywhere. Indeed, it became common only in the late twelfth century, just before the city council became the standard expression of urban corporate particularity.[81]

Weber paid particular attention to the development of the city area as an autonomous jurisdiction, as the liberties that initially applied personally to townspeople came to be extended to the territory that the cities occupied, and thus territoriality of law was a further criterion of the city that only later was extended to territorial states.[82] Pirenne admitted that he could not explain how this happened, because he did not think it possible that serfs who lived in cities could be subject to a town law that by definition applied only to free persons.[83] Weber was clearer, seeing a peculiarity of the Western city as the urban community of citizens with some degree of self-determination and a specific law, meaning a fundamental charter against which subsequent refinements such as statutes would be measured.[84]

For both Weber and Pirenne the transition to the *Ratsverfaßung* during the decades around 1200 was the beginning of genuine urbanization. In most cities of "old Europe" a council drawn specifically from the citizen community (which included the town lord's officials) either replaced his council or functioned alongside it. The councils normally rotated annually in the north, more frequently in Italy. City councils had the right to legislate within the principles provided by the urban charter. Although there was considerable variety, urban law more than rural facilitated both acquisition and alienation of property. The definition of "movable" property was extended. After 1200 written instruments were increasingly used as evidence in courts and were employed for commercial transactions. Market regulation was the area where the city government's competence reached its fullest development. Often acting through occupational guilds, town councils legislated on debt and credit issues.[85] Interestingly, internal market and industrial regulation was the area of their legal competence that was least altered as the cities became incorporated into territorial states.[86]

The Medieval City and the Birth of Commercial Capitalism

The idea of capitalism is a modern construct, and Pirenne, Weber, and countless others have debated about what if any form of it existed in the Middle Ages. Yet

[81] Abramowski, *Geschichtsbild*, p. 91; Nicholas, *Growth of the Medieval City*, pp. 156–57.

[82] Nicholas, *Growth of the Medieval City*, pp. 146, 150–54.

[83] Pirenne, "L'origine des constitutions," pp. 64–65.

[84] Weber, *City*, pp. 80–89.

[85] Nicholas, "Urban Revolution"; Weber, *City*, p. 156.

[86] Weber, *City*, pp. 186–90.

the economic legislation of city councils created the legal framework for "commercial capitalism," which involves the use of money to make money. It is also an arrangement in which "fixed capital" (land and buildings) is less important than liquid capital, given that most industrial technology was simple. The economy was highly differentiated and largely locally regulated, although this was changing with some intervention of princely governments in the late Middle Ages. There was little mass production of crafts, as producers at this level could not anticipate demand in distant markets. Most wealth was generated by trade rather than industry, but this does not mean that industrial production was insignificant, but rather that finding markets for it meant establishing an infrastructure that was created by the network of cities.[87] Thus both the medieval city and the medieval urban network were prerequisites of the development of commercial capitalism. The regulations that created commercial capitalism in this sense were perhaps the most characteristic historic function of the medieval city. While Pirenne held positions about the development of the medieval city as a type that have not been sustained by modern research, although some of them can be validated by phrasing them differently, his notion of capitalism was less rigid than Weber's and can apply to the medieval city. Pirenne looked for capitalism in economic behavior and recognized that medieval capitalism did not have to be the same as modern in order to be capitalism. Unfortunately, again showing his predilection for revolution over evolution, he also argued that it was not an antecedent of modern capitalism, which he saw developing from independent roots.[88]

This is close to some of what Weber said, but he does not seem to have considered "commercial capitalism" to be truly capitalistic, for he distinguished modern capitalism from medieval by "the rational capitalistic organization of (formally) free labour," although he admitted that free wage labor and industry existed in the Middle Ages. He conceded that pursuit of profit through acquisition of money and/or goods by maximizing market and exchange actions that can be quantified in monetary terms did not begin with the modern period. He distinguished between political capitalism (including imperialism and the economic opportunities that it provided) and what he variously termed economic, "modern industrial," or "bourgeois" capitalism. His argument loses credibility by his inclusion of the English merchant adventurers, the Hanse, and the activities of the

---

[87] Nicholas, *Urban Europe*, pp. 2–3; Nicholas, "Lords."

[88] "I believe that, for each period into which our economic history may be divided, there is a distinct and separate class of capitalists. In other words, the group of capitalists of a given epoch does not spring from the capitalist group of the preceding epoch. At every change in economic organization we find a breach of continuity. . .There are as many classes of capitalists as there are epochs in economic history. . . . All the essential features of capitalists—individual enterprise, advances on credit, commercial profits, speculation, etc.—are to be found from the twelfth century on" (Pirenne, "Stages," pp. 493–96).

Italian merchant companies under the heading of "adventure capitalism," which is basically raiding for treasure or "booty capitalism." Profit coming from state privileges, such as tax farming and loans to states, he considered "fiscal capitalism."[89]

Weber and Pirenne thus agreed that even if a form of capitalism existed in the Middle Ages, it was different from modern capitalism and had no influence on it. Modern capitalism had an industrial base and a firmer organization of markets and companies than medieval. In *Protestant Ethic* Weber did not claim that capitalism was not present in medieval Europe, but rather that a "spirit" of capitalism was lacking as a mental attitude. He did not deny that people liked to make money in the Middle Ages, but only that it did not become a moral imperative, with ethical value placed on human effort and gain. Weber was more interested in the intellectual origins of the idea that gain was good, which he considered the great caesura, rather than the practice of gain.[90]

Pirenne considered the legislation of the late medieval guild regimes in the city contrary to the free trade that he identified with the capitalism of the thirteenth-century patricians. Weber saw the guilds as anticapitalistic in that they tried to prevent members from monopolizing, accumulating too much capital or hiring too many workers. But since they promoted a high level of occupational specialization, they encouraged competition at this level.[91] Yet legislation by city councils that was intended to foster high quality of crafts, including quality control, consumer protection, security of contract, and a stable coinage was clearly designed to further at least that city's own trade beyond the walls, however much it may be protectionist of native goods and services.[92] While Weber saw early modern capitalism, spurred by Calvinist theology, as increasing incentives to gain, Pirenne made the modern state, and specifically its ideology of mercantilism, the agent that snuffed out late medieval capitalism;[93] yet what the medieval city councils were doing for their local economies was essentially what mercantilism attempted at a territorial level.

The medieval city was perhaps the most sophisticated incorporation of the Western city as Weber understood the term. "It was of central importance for the emergence of the medieval city" that when economic change propelled the cities toward independence "they were not prevented . . . by the presence of magical or

---

[89] Weber, *Protestant Ethic*, pp. 17–19, 21, 24; Weber, *General Economic History*, pp. 275–77; Gerth and Mills, introduction to Weber, *Essays in Sociology*, pp. 66–69. See also the discussion in Lachmann, *Capitalists*, p. 45.

[90] Weber, *Protestant Ethic*, pp. 24, 47, 52.

[91] Weber, *General Economic History*, p. 138.

[92] Nicholas, *Later Medieval City*, pp. 25–49; Nicholas, *Urban Europe*, pp. 138–43.

[93] Pirenne, "Stages," p. 513. Yet Pirenne's views were inconsistent. At least in the case of the Burgundian federated state as an ancestor of Belgium, Pirenne saw value in ending local municipal liberties. See the contribution by Jan Dumolyn in the present volume.

religious barriers on the one hand nor by the rational administration of a super-ordinate political association on the other."[94] Some medieval towns became cities, and the impulse for the transition was economic change. Although the increasing political centralization of Europe ended the legal particularism of the medieval city, its historic function, one acquired gradually between roughly 900 and 1200 and reaching its most complete development in the early sixteenth century, had been to develop a network of interlocking and interdependent markets against a background of a rule of law that fostered security of property and contract and developed accounting procedures and some legal principles that eventually were incorporated into the modern bureaucratic state.

Although Pirenne enjoyed good relations with German academics and was influenced strongly by the pioneering work of Gustav von Schmoller and Karl Lamprecht on medieval economic history, his experiences during the First World War caused him to turn against both German scholars and their scholar-ship.[95] Had he been more receptive to German work after 1918, he undoubtedly would have become familiar with most of the works bearing on the medieval city by which Weber is now best known, with the unfortunate exception of *The Protestant Ethic and the Spirit of Capitalism*. Weber's approach was essentially deductive. Even his paragraph organization shows him starting with general pat-terns, then in masterful comparative analysis building examples of and exceptions to them across continents and eras. Pirenne's work was inductive, building on his unequaled knowledge of the economic history of the Low Countries toward a general synthesis of history that never quite lost its local foundation. This paper has shown that Pirenne's work was more conceptually sophisticated than his crit-ics have realized and that the mature studies of Pirenne and Weber are comple-mentary, not contradictory, and are still vitally relevant for the understanding of mature medieval urbanization.

Bibliography

Abramowski, Günter. *Das Geschichtsbild Max Webers: Universalgeschichte am Leitfaden des okzidentalen Rationalisierungsprozesses*. Stuttgart: Ernst Klett, 1964.

Bachrach, Bernard S., and David Nicholas, eds. *Law, Custom, and the Social Fabric in Medi-eval Europe: Essays in Honor of Bryce Lyon*. Kalamazoo: Medieval Institute Publica-tions, 1990.

Hodges, Richard. *The Anglo-Saxon Achievement: Archaeology and the Beginnings of English Society*. Ithaca, NY: Cornell University Press, 1989.

———. *Dark Age Economics: The Origins of Towns and Trade, A.D. 600–1000*. New York: St. Martin's Press, 1982.

[94] Weber, *City*, p.106.

[95] Lyon, *Henri Pirenne*, pp. 63–64, 378–83.

Lachmann, Richard. *Capitalists in Spite of Themselves: Elite Conflict and Economic Transitions in Early Modern Europe*. Oxford: Oxford University Press, 2002.

Lyon, Bryce. *Henri Pirenne: A Biographical and Intellectual Study*. Ghent: E. Story-Scientia, 1974.

Masschaele, James. *Peasants, Merchants, and Markets: Inland Trade in Medieval England, 1150–1350*. New York: St. Martin's Press, 1997.

McCormick, Michael. "Complexity, Chronology and Context in the Early Medieval Economy." *Early Medieval Europe* 12 (2003): 307–23.

———. *Origins of the European Economy: Communications and Commerce, A.D. 300–900*. Cambridge: Cambridge University Press, 2001.

Nicholas, David. *The Growth of the Medieval City: From Late Antiquity to the Early Fourteenth Century*. London: Longman, 1997.

———. *The Later Medieval City*. London: Longman, 1997.

———. "Lords, Markets, and Communities: The Urban Revolution of the Twelfth Century." In *European Transformations: The Long Twelfth Century*, ed. Thomas F. X. Noble and John Van Engen, pp. 229–58. Notre Dame: University of Notre Dame Press, 2012.

———. "Structures du peuplement, fonctions urbaines et formation du capital dans la Flandre médiévale." *Annales: Économies, sociétés, civilisations* 33 (1978): 501–27.

———. *Urban Europe, 1100–1700*. Houndmills: Palgrave, 2003.

Pirenne, Henri. *Early Democracies in the Low Countries: Urban Society and Political Conflict in the Middle Ages and the Renaissance*. New York: Harper and Row, 1963. First published in English as *Belgian Democracy: Its Early History*. London: Longmans, Green, 1915. First published in French as *Les anciennes démocraties des Pays-Bas*. Paris: Ernest Flammario, 1910. Reprinted in *Les villes et les institutions urbaines*, 1:143–301.

———. *Economic and Social History of Medieval Europe*. New York: Harcourt, Brace, 1937.

———. *Medieval Cities: Their Origins and the Revival of Trade*. Princeton, NJ: Princeton University Press, 1925; repr. 1970.

———. "Northern Towns and Their Commerce." In *The Cambridge Medieval History*, ed. J. R. Tanner et al. Vol. 6, *Victory of the Papacy*, pp. 505–27 (Cambridge: University Press, 1929).

———. "L'origine des constitutions urbaines au Moyen Âge." *Revue historique* 57 (1895): 57–98, 293–97. Reprinted in *Les villes et les institutions urbaines*, 1:1–110.

———. "The Stages in the Social History of Capitalism." *American Historical Review* 19 (1914): 494–515.

Pirenne, Henri. *Les villes du Moyen Âge: Essai d'histoire économique et urbaine*. Brussels: M. Lamertin, 1927. Reprinted in Pirenne, Henri. *Les villes et les institutions urbaines*. 2 vols. (Paris: Alcan, 1939), 1:1–110.

———. *Les villes et les institutions urbaines*. 2nd ed. 2 vols. Brussels: Nouvelle société d'éditions, 1939.

Schluchter, Wolfgang. *Rationalism, Religion, and Domination: A Weberian Perspective*. Trans. Neil Solomon. Berkeley and Los Angeles: University of California Press, 1989.

Schulz, Knut. *Die Freiheit des Bürgers: Städtische Gesellschaft im Hoch- und Spätmittelalter*. Herausgegeben von Matthias Krüger. Darmstadt: Wissenschaftliche Buchgesellschaft, 2008.

Spufford, Peter. *Money and Its Use in Medieval Europe*. Cambridge: Cambridge University Press, 1988.

Swedberg, Richard. *Max Weber and the Idea of Economic Sociology*. Princeton, NJ: Princeton University Press, 1998.

Van Caenegem, R. C. "Henri Pirenne: Medievalist and Historian of Belgium." In *Law, History*, by van Caenegem, pp. 161–78.

———. "History and Experiment." In *Law, History*, by van Caenegem, pp. 1–13.

———. *Law, History, the Low Countries, and Europe*. London: Hambledon, 1994.

———. *Max Weber: Historicus en Socioloog*. Amsterdam: Koninklijke Academie van Wetenschappen, 1988.

Verhulst, Adriaan. *The Rise of Cities in North-West Europe*. Cambridge: Cambridge University Press, 1999.

Weber, Max. *The Agrarian Sociology of Ancient Civilizations*. Trans. R. I. Frank. London: Humanities Press, 1976.

———. *The City*. Ed. and trans. Don Martindale and Gertrud Neuwirth. New York: Free Press, 1958.

———. *Essays in Sociology*. Ed., trans., and intro. H. H. Gerth and C. Wright Mills. New York: Galaxy Book, 1958.

———. *General Economic History*. With a new intro. by Ira J. Cohen. Trans. Frank H. Knight. 1923. New Brunswick, NJ: Transaction, 1995.

———. *The Protestant Ethic and the Spirit of Capitalism*. Trans. Talcott Parsons, with a foreword by R. H. Tawney. New York: Charles Scribner's Sons, 1958.

———. *The Theory of Social and Economic Organization*. Ed. and intro. Talcott Parsons. Trans. A. M. Henderson and Talcott Parsons. New York: Free Press, 1947.

A Victorious State and Defeated Rebels? Historians' Views of Violence and Urban Revolts in Medieval Flanders

Jelle Haemers

> It is not difficult, however, to recognize that it [the Ghent revolt of
> 1449–53] was also a crisis in the eternal conflict between the past
> and the future; and even if the heroism of the Ghentenars commands
> respect, the cause for which they fought cannot be justified when
> one looks without prejudice at the conditions at whose cost political
> progress was achieved in the fifteenth century.
> (Pirenne, *Histoire de Belgique*, 2:362)

ALTHOUGH HENRI PIRENNE (1862–1935) SHOWED SYMPATHY for the Ghent
rebels who took up arms in 1449 against their prince, the Burgundian duke
Philip the Good, his final verdict is clear. The inhabitants of Ghent took arms to
defend their corporate liberties against a future which they could not prevent,
and their revolt was therefore useless, even self-destructive. The Burgundian
dynasty (from Philip the Bold until Charles the Bold, 1384–1477) was the dominant political power in the Low Countries. Enemies such as the French king
could not prevent the dukes from constructing an independent political union
in "the sensitive point of Europe," as Pirenne called the regions where Romance
and Germanic culture meet.[1] It also followed for Pirenne that the subjects of
the Burgundian dukes who fought to maintain privileges and political autonomy
were destined to lose, for no rebel could overcome the centralizing efforts of the
dukes of Burgundy. Pirenne saw the emergence of the so-called central state as an
inevitable and linear process. By assuming this teleological vision of the history of
his beloved country, Pirenne both legitimized the origins of the Belgian state and

---

[1] This is a point of view he shared with Johan Huizinga; see Lyon, "Henri Pirenne and Johan Huizinga"; Boone, "L'automne du Moyen Âge"; Tollebeek, "At the Crossroads."

condemned the revolts of cities that strove for autonomy. In Pirenne's view these revolts were ghosts of the past, without a future. The inhabitants of these cities (such as Ghent) were brave citizens (they still were "Belgians," of course), but their revolts were a regrettable waste of men, money, and means, for they were fighting a losing battle.

In his brilliant essay on medieval constitutionalism Bryce Lyon commented that historians always evaluate medieval politics "on lessons of their own national history."[2] This is certainly true of Henri Pirenne, whose publications influenced Bryce Lyon profoundly. In his biography of the Belgian master Lyon stated emphatically that Pirenne was a child of a "European age when nationalism was most rampant."[3] In writing *Histoire de Belgique* Pirenne clearly wanted to legitimize the Belgian state's existence.[4] He sought elements in the history of the Low Countries that would justify his contention that the existence of Belgium was a logical outcome of history. This point of view did not hinder Pirenne from conducting excellent research on medieval cities, but his writings not only legitimized the existence of Belgium they were also very biased toward urban rebellions (although Pirenne claimed that they were not). Pirenne's view of the medieval state and its formation process was strongly influenced by his opinions about the state in which he lived. Pirenne, of course, is not the only historian whom we can accuse of prejudices or rationalization after the fact. As Bryce Lyon suggested, many historians view the political events of the Middle Ages through the prism of the concerns and lessons of their own histories. In this article I argue that historians in the nineteenth and twentieth centuries who studied the political history of the Low Countries in general, and the urban revolts in the county of Flanders in particular, were strongly influenced by their views of state structure at that time. The personal political opinions of historians about the states in which they lived have always affected their evaluations of the state formation and urban revolts of the past.

In this article I am undertaking an in-depth study of the historiography of the Ghent revolt of 1449–53.[5] In this revolt social networks of members of the craft guilds in the town took up arms against fellow citizens who tried to concentrate political power in their own hands. The craft group wanted to protect their corporate privileges, while the town elite increasingly tried to limit the political participation of the craft guilds in civic affairs. In fifteenth-century Ghent

---

[2] Lyon, "Medieval Constitutionalism," p. 158.

[3] Lyon, *Henri Pirenne*, p. 143. Concerning Lyon's professional relations with Pirenne, see Bachrach and Nicholas, *Law, Custom*, pp. x–xiii.

[4] Dhondt, "Henri Pirenne."

[5] Preliminary versions of the arguments of this article are in Haemers, "De dominante staat"; and Haemers, *De Gentse opstand.*

the craft guilds had the right to elect two-thirds of the Ghent aldermen, which regulated the judicial, political, and economic affairs the city.[6] The other third were members of the urban elite, originating from the wealthy families of town (the so-called *poorters*). Due to their numerical majority in the city government, the craft guilds had the political power to obstruct the city from paying financial contributions to the duke. Philip the Good, however, wanted to strengthen his political grip on Ghent's politics and treasury by diminishing the political power of the craft guilds. Thus he allied with the *poorters*, who also wanted to increase their political power in town, to the detriment of the craft guilds. The alliance between the duke and the *poorters* would emerge victorious with the defeat of the Ghent rebels in 1453, after a four-year revolt. The duke's military victory may show that the seeds of absolutism were present in fifteenth-century Flanders, but the many subsequent revolts of the city demonstrate that his political opponents were far from excluded from political power and that the historical "victory" of the central state was not as inevitable as Pirenne claimed. A good example is the crisis of the 1480s, in which the urban elites of Ghent, Bruges, and Ypres jointly seized rule of the county from Maximilian of Austria, who then ruled the Low Countries by right of his wife, Mary of Burgundy.[7]

Most historians agree that political power in fifteenth-century Flanders was fairly balanced between the state, the nobility, and the wealthy citizens.[8] The following overview of the historiography of the Ghent revolt will show that this less teleological perspective on the political history of the county of Flanders is as influenced by contemporary political ideas as Pirenne's standpoint. It says more about the historians and the lessons they discovered in their national histories, as Lyon said, than about the revolt itself. I will therefore try to ascertain how and why this view influenced the writings of several generations of historians on the medieval revolts.

Romanticism and Revolt: "Dominance Crushes Heroism"

In 1839 Philippe Blommaert (1808–71) composed the first study of the Ghent revolt of 1449–53. In his *Causes de la guerre de la ville de Gand*, he jeered at the Burgundian dynasty because the dukes used French as the main language of politics and administration. Blommaert saw the Burgundian regime as a capricious tyranny that had brutally suppressed *Nederduits*, the dialect of Dutch that was still spoken in Flanders in the nineteenth century. The angry nobleman went even further by extending his accusations to the entire politics of the Burgundian dukes. In

---

[6] About Ghent's institutional structure, see Boone, *Gent en de Bourgondische hertogen*.
[7] About this revolt see Haemers, *For the Common Good*.
[8] Blockmans, "Voracious States"; Boone, "Dutch Revolt."

his final verdict on the Burgundian era he depicted the Valois house as a dynasty of dictators who were unfamiliar with the customs and morals of the Flemish people, their sense of independence, and everything that they cherished. Blommaert openly wondered, to give just one example, why Duke Philip the Good had deserved his nickname, because the history of his reign was "written with letters of blood."[9] In Blommaert's eyes the alleged tyranny of the dukes rightly aroused in the Flemish citizens a fundamental disgust at Burgundian domination. The dukes had destroyed the liberties of the citizens, ignored their traditions, violated their rights, and above all suppressed their language. They had violated the "national character" of their subjects and had "made us bastards in a country in which the inhabitants had always maintained their stamp of originality."[10] Political repression caused both the Dutch language and the Flemish community to be abandoned. Thus in Blommaert's view political resistance against such a regime, such as the Ghent revolt, was just and lawful.

The perspective of the erudite Blommaert on Burgundian history was not new. His discourse joined seamlessly the historiography of the Belgian state that was founded in 1830. Blommaert's publication coupled the two directions that Belgian historiography had taken in the first decade of the country's existence, for it both exuded an atmosphere of romanticism and studied the authenticity of local history.[11] Blommaert's article was published in the *Messager des sciences historiques de Belgique*, a review which stimulated Belgian patriotism by focusing on exciting moments of the history of the county of Flanders in general and its largest city, Ghent, in particular. In the 1830s the glorification of Flemish history amounted to a humble act of love for country, and the heightened attention that Blommaert paid to the revolt of one of the most rebellious cities of the Low Countries therefore occasions no surprise. His special concern for the language of the Ghent rebels and Flemish town dwellers can be deduced from his personal opinion about the French-speaking regime under which he lived. His mother tongue, Dutch, was not taught in Flemish schools nor used in administration, because the economic and political elite of the country was mainly French-speaking. To save his language from extinction, Blommaert already had written polemical pamphlets calling for the preservation of the Dutch language before his publication about the Ghent revolt. He and Constant Serrure (1805–72) had founded the Society of Flemish Bibliophiles (Maetschappij der Vlaamsche bibliophilen), which edited old medieval Dutch texts in order to encourage the study of the origins of their beloved language. For example, they

[9] Blommaert, "Causes de la guerre," p. 428.

[10] Blommaert, "Causes de la guerre," p. 432.

[11] Tollebeek, "Historical Representation," p. 344; Tollebeek, "De *Messager*."

edited jointly the *Kronyk van Vlaenderen*, one of the main sources for the Ghent revolt.[12]

Historiography is a powerful weapon for legitimizing existing political situations. The Belgian monarchy was not yet a decade old in 1839, and French occupation after the conquest of Napoleon was only twenty years in the past. The latent threat of a possible French annexation of Belgium in the 1830s was fed by the newly born myth of the "foreign occupations" of the young nation. This story claimed that the regions that made part of Belgium had been governed since the beginning of their history by foreign rulers such as the Romans, the Burgundian dukes, and the French.[13] The young country wanted to be politically independent, and therefore it stimulated historiography that accentuated the presumed "barbaric character" of past occupying forces, such as the Burgundian dynasty. Similar myths played a decisive role in the construction of a national identity in Belgium, as it had been growing since the 1780s.[14] Blommaert's publication about the Ghent revolt fit very well into the historiography of a period in which Belgian independence was a recent development. From this point of view, it is easy to understand that Blommaert saw the Ghent revolt as righteous resistance against the French-speaking dynasty.

Ten years later a second history of the Ghent revolt was written by Baron Joseph Kervyn de Lettenhove (1817–91). It used the *Diary of Ghent*, a new source about the Ghent revolt that had been edited in 1842 by the Belgian archivist Anton Schayes.[15] The Belgian state sponsored the edition of this manuscript, which had been handed over to the State Archives by French authorities after intensive diplomacy by the Belgian government. The diary, actually a chronicle with copies of documents of the Ghent government in the first year of the revolt, was kept in the Archives départementales du Nord in Lille after being confiscated from the Ghent city archives by Charles V in 1540. With publication of the edition of the manuscript, the interest of historians in the Ghent revolt increased further.

When writing his general overview of Flemish history,[16] Kervyn de Lettenhove dedicated a whole chapter to the Ghent revolt. The famous Romanticist, sometimes described as the "Belgian Michelet,"[17] largely echoed the

---

[12] Deschamps, "Blommaert"; Deprez, "Blommaert." Concerning Serrure, see Deprez, "Serrure." For the edition, see Blommaert and Serrure, *Kronyk van Vlaenderen*.

[13] Stengers, "Le mythe." See also Lambert, "De Guldensporenslag," p. 390.

[14] Verschaffel, *De hoed en de hond*, pp. 61–98 and 445–46; Vercauteren, *Cent ans d'histoire nationale*; specifically about the historiography of the Burgundian period, see Carlier, "Contribution à l'étude," and Jongkees, "Une génération d'historiens."

[15] On Schayes's edition of the *Dagboek der Gentsche Collatie*, see Fris, "Ontleding van drie Vlaamsche kronijken."

[16] Kervyn de Lettenhove, *Histoire de Flandre*.

[17] De Schryver, *Historiografie*, p. 317.

views of his predecessor, Philippe Blommaert. The supposed "Flemish national character" was again used to show disrespect toward the repressive Burgundian dynasty. At the end of the chapter the "glory of Flanders" was defeated by the bold Burgundian-French aggressor who had crushed the "national liberties" of the future Belgians. A contemporary poem on the Ghent Revolt by the Flemish poet Albrecht Rodenbach (1856–80), who was inspired by Kervyn's books, refers to this vision. In his "Sneyssens" (1878) he depicted the Ghent soldier Cornelis Seyssoone, who died in battle with Burgundian troops in 1452, with the Ghent standard still in his hands. The conclusion of the poet, "Dominance crushes heroism," strikingly describes the way in which romantic authors thought about the Ghent revolt.[18]

As had been true of Blommaert, Kervyn de Lettenhove's background, surroundings, and political beliefs can explain his animosity toward the Burgundian dynasty. The author was a prominent Catholic politician, becoming Interior Minister in the Catholic government of Belgium in 1870. Therefore, in contrast to Blommaert's article, Kervyn de Lettenhove's story concentrated more on the morals of the rebels than on the language they spoke. Because Kervyn de Lettenhove was favorably disposed toward the Flemish people, he tried to promote the formation of a Flemish, Catholic identity by the publication of his *Histoire de Flandre*.[19] He found an authentic Catholic morality in the medieval cities, which he contrasted to the splendor and moral misbehavior of the Burgundian dukes and other rulers of their time. This vision is wonderfully illustrated by the last sentence of his chapter on the Ghent revolt. Referring to the defeat of the Ghent rebels at Gavere and the occupation of Christian Constantinople by the Turks, he wrote: "The year 1453 is the saddest of the fifteenth century; it witnessed, at the two extremes of Europe, the triumph of force over enlightenment and civilization."[20]

Positivism: "The Triumph of the Centralizing System"

In the second half of the nineteenth century, historical writing slowly but surely became a science. The romantic "longing" of amateur historians and archaeologists was replaced by a less emotional approach toward historic reality. History was reshaped from an amateurish and nostalgic voyage of discovery in the past into professional and well-considered research. Henceforth scientific history was being written in universities by professional historians who claimed a superior

---

[18] "Overmacht verplettert heldenmoed": Rodenbach, *Eerste Gedichten*, p. 99. On Cornelis Seyssoone, see Haemers, "Seyssoone."

[19] De Schryver, "Kervyn de Lettenhove."

[20] Kervyn de Lettenhove, *Histoire de Flandre*, 4:497.

knowledge and better skills in interpreting historical documents. In these temples of science academic historians formed a community who approached history with a common method that was taught at the university in seminars. During these teaching sessions, professors and their students composed a research group in their laboratory filled with a growing number of edited sources. In short, the positivist research method was emerging.[21]

This method involved the belief that an empirical study of sources could discern "objective" facts about the past. Positivists believed that a critical and philological method of detailed scrutiny could enable them to abandon the subjectivity that had colored previous historiography. One of the pioneers of this new method was the German historian Leopold von Ranke (1795–1886), who sent his disciples throughout Western Europe. Ranke's ideas reached Belgium in the last decades of the nineteenth century, because his pupil Ernst Curtius (1814–96) taught the Belgian historian Godefroid Kurth (1847–1916), who had Paul Fredericq (1850–1920) and Henri Pirenne as his pupils in Liège. While Fredericq concentrated his research on the sixteenth-century Reformation (because he had converted to Protestantism in 1876), Henri Pirenne dedicated his scientific activities to the medieval history of his beloved country. Pirenne became one of the most renowned historians of Belgium, among other reasons because he was part of the first generation of educated social scientists in Belgium.[22]

"First, I want to insist on the formation of what can be called the civilization of Belgium." Establishing this thesis as fact was the main goal of his life's work, the *Histoire de Belgique* (1894–1932).[23] Pirenne discovered the nucleus of this civilization in the so-called *pax Belgica*, the eternally peaceful coexistence of different ethnic (in this case Romance and Germanic) groups within the geographical boundaries of what would become Belgium. Writing about the formation of the Burgundian state in the introduction to the second volume of *Histoire de Belgique*, Pirenne said: "It is not a historical coincidence, nor an arbitrary evolution, and seeing it as a brutal triumph of force over justice would display utter

---

[21] About the emergence of positivism in Belgium, see Lorenz, *De constructie van het verleden*, p. 250; De Schryver, *Historiografie*, p. 302; Tollebeek, *Fredericq en zonen*; Tollebeek, "Stormy Family."

[22] In 2008 Ghent University commemorated its former rector by a conference (organized by Marc Boone and Claire Billen) and an exhibition in the Ghent University Library. These events not only demonstrate the continuing popularity of Pirenne among his followers but also showed that some historical hypotheses of Pirenne (in particular his renowned *Mahomet et Charlemagne*) still are at the heart of historical debate. See also the articles in part 1 of the present volume.

[23] "Insister davantage sur la formation de ce qu'on pourrait appeler la civilisation de la Belgique": quoted in De Schryver, *Historiografie*, p. 366. For a scientific analysis of his work, see (among others): Dhondt, "Henri Pirenne"; Tollebeek, "'Au point sensible'"; and Carlier, "Contribution à l'étude."

misunderstanding."[24] Pirenne thus completely broke with his romantic predecessors by evaluating the actions of the Ghent rebels as a regrettable but logical outcome of the political transformations of the fifteenth century.[25] This standpoint legitimized the existence of the modern state, and in spite of their belief in objective science, positivist historians were less critical toward the political regimes in which they lived.[26]

As already stated, Pirenne wrote his masterpiece from the viewpoint of the triumphant central state. The *Histoire de Belgique* was an unalloyed winner's history of a nation whose identity already existed in the Middle Ages in spite of its territorial division. In contrast to the first decades of Belgium's history, the French were no longer a foreign threat in Pirenne's epoch, and therefore the Burgundian era was evaluated as a decisive and positive step toward the formation of a new nation in a remarkable setting. According to Pirenne the Belgian "common law" logically replaced the private "privileges" of the autonomous towns in the Low Countries during the late Middle Ages. Pirenne stated that the legal power of state structure therefore was more based on the emergence of a unified legal system than on military victories of the Burgundian dynasty, as the romantic amateur historians had claimed.[27] Pirenne described the duke of Burgundy as *conditor Belgii*, the founder of Belgium. The duke was one of the "most sympathetic figures of the fifteenth century," Pirenne said in his biography of the "Grand Duke of the West."[28] The contrast with the opinions of the Romantics could hardly be more profound.

Seen from this viewpoint, Pirenne evaluated the political resistance of the Ghent rebels of 1449–53 as a battle that was lost in advance. The above-mentioned passage, in which he sees the Ghentenars fighting against an inevitable future and the powerful state structure of the Burgundian dukes, demonstrates Pirenne's thesis that the Ghent rebels committed a breach of the so-called Belgian peace.

This argument was elaborated in depth by one of his pupils, Victor Fris (1877–1925), who dedicated his doctoral thesis to the Ghent revolt. Fris

---

[24] Pirenne, *Histoire de Belgique*, 2:345. See also Pirenne, "Formation and Constitution."

[25] In his survey of the Ghent revolt Richard Vaughan did not contest this point of view. Basing his research on the rebellion solely on the writings of Pirenne and Fris, Vaughan described the revolt as an "unnecessary and costly blunder," which was brought to a good end, thanks to strategic moves of a clever duke (*Philip the Good*, p. 333). On Vaughan's point of view, see Blockmans, "Van buitenaf bekeken."

[26] Iggers, *Historiography*, p. 5.

[27] In the eighteenth century Philip the Good was seen as "one of the most fortunate and powerful princes of Europe"; Verschaffel, *De hoed en de hond*, p. 339. In this century the Low Countries were ruled by the Habsburg dynasty, the successors of Philip the Good.

[28] Pirenne, *Histoire de Belgique*, 2:267; see also Pirenne, "Philippe de Bourgogne."

concluded in an early article that the Schayes edition of the *Diary of Ghent* that we discussed above was inadequate, because it had not followed scientific (i.e., positivist) edition rules.[29] After he had defended his PhD thesis in 1899 under Pirenne's supervision, the future Ghent city archivist reedited the *Diary of Ghent* and other main sources of the Ghent revolt.[30] In the *History of Ghent* that Fris wrote on the occasion of the Ghent World Exhibition of 1913, Pirenne seems to speak through the mouth of his pupil. Fris argued that the battle between cities and state "is unequal, and one can easily notice that the cities, which wallowed in egoism and only thought about their own interests, were fated to surrender."[31] He considered the fall of the Ghent rebels inevitable, and the blame was easily assigned. In the introduction to the edition of the *Dagboek van Gent*, Fris found an indisputable harbinger of the approaching victory of the "modern state structure" in the egoism and corruption of the Ghent aldermen. He considered their corrupt behavior an argument that urban autonomy was by its nature inefficient; the existence of privileges encouraged corruption. Moreover, instead of setting out a "wise policy" by which they could have united resistance against the duke, the venal Ghent politicians gave Philip the Good the opportunity to intervene in urban politics and to win the final battle of the revolt: "By only being concerned for themselves, the urban government can even be seen as accomplices of the duke."[32] Fris concluded that the political autonomy of Ghent was self-destructive, and therefore defending it was useless and even harmful to the city.

Typical of the historical vision of Pirenne, Fris, and other positivist historians is their close, yet naive reading of the sources. The quotation about the corruption of the Ghent aldermen, for example, is based on the propaganda of Philip the Good, who had wanted to discredit the privileges of Ghent by saying that their existence had fostered corruption in town. "Those who have money in town can afford justice," said Philip the Good in a letter of 1450.[33] According to the "sympathetic duke," whom Fris followed uncritically, the corruption of Ghent politicians preserved the autonomous regime in town. Thus the Ghent regime had to be replaced by a government in which people were judged only by "common law," and therefore the corporate privileges of the town had to be abandoned. The servile obedience of positivist historians to their sources has

---

[29] Fris, "Ontleding van drie Vlaamsche kronijken," pp. 164–67. On Fris's career, see Tollebeek, "De *Messager*," pp. 129–32; and Verhulst, "Fris, Victor."

[30] *Dagboek van Gent van 1447 tot 1470*; Fris, "Oorkonden betreffende"; Fris, "Nieuwe oorkonden."

[31] Fris, *Histoire de Gand*, p. 105.

[32] *Dagboek van Gent*, 1:56.

[33] *Dagboek van Gent*, 1:119.

been called "naïve realism," a paradigm that tolerates historical criticism concerning the edition of sources but not concerning their contents.[34] Sources are seen as a mirror of their time, and therefore positivists thought that they could be used as a true and valuable reflection of the period from which they originated. With this principle in his mind, Fris tried to reconstruct history from his ivory tower. Desiring to approach history as objectively as possible and considering himself a sincere and consistent scientist, he thought his positivist method would save him from subjectivity.

But a closer look at his work shows that Fris did not remain objective. For the paleographer not only criticized the corruption of the Ghent aldermen, but also the bribery and fraud of ducal councillors. Fris did not accuse the duke himself of corruption, because he again blindly believed the sources (letters of the Ghent rebels never charged the duke with brutality; they only blamed his advisors for "bad governance"). In the introduction to the *Diary of Ghent*, he accused ducal "accomplices" of plotting and machinations. Fris remarked that "no one can see the fall of the biggest Flemish city and its autonomy as the end of the regime of dishonesty for which we above blamed the aldermen and those around them, because the Burgundian administrators would even surpass these scheming activities."[35]

How can we explain Fris's prejudices? His personal background provides the answer. Fris was favorably disposed toward the Flemish struggle for the recognition of the Dutch language in Belgian administration in the beginning of the twentieth century, just as Blommaert and Kervyn de Lettenhove had been several decades before. Fris was a conspicuous supporter of the Belgian state, but he could not accept that some of its politicians governed the country without taking the grievances of the Flemish population into account. His personal vision of contemporary politics therefore seriously influenced his historical writings. Many of his articles were published in Flemish journals that promoted political opposition against the monopoly of the French language in Belgian administration, such as the *De Vlaamsche Gids* and the *Tijdschrift van het Willemsfonds*. In 1902 Fris's popular book about the Battle of the Golden Spurs was the spearhead of the commemoration of the victory of the Flemish militia over the French army in 1302.[36] Even in his work on the Ghent revolt, Fris saw heroic Flemish-speaking rebels at work. For example, when he described the valorous deeds of the Ghent soldier

---

[34] Lorenz, *De constructie van het verleden*, p. 23.

[35] *Dagboek van Gent*, 1:156.

[36] Fris, *De slag bij Kortrijk*. See also Tollebeek, "De cultus van 1302." The *Dagboek van Gent* was edited by the Maetschappij voor Vlaamsche bibliophilen, the historical society that was founded by Blommaert and Serrure; compare above and Prevenier, "Fris," p. 541.

Cornelis Sneyssens, he was inspired more by the poem of Albrecht Rodenbach than by the historical sources about the unfortunate Ghentenar. Sneyssens was a hero who had given his life for the Flemish cause.[37] The positivist historian therefore was led by subjective feelings and political ideas about the functioning of the state of which he was a subject. This can also explain why Fris's judgment of the Ghent craft guilds was less harsh than Pirenne's. The latter was not indifferent to the grievances of his Dutch-speaking compatriots in the first decades of the twentieth century, but he nevertheless opposed the plan to make Dutch the only language used in teaching at the University of Ghent and retired disillusioned when this happened in 1930.[38]

Modern Historiography: "The Lapse of Deliberation"

Our overview of romantic and positivist historiography has shown that contemporary state formation has strongly influenced the historiography of the Ghent revolt. I suggest that a similar tendency has persisted in the second half of the twentieth century. In the postwar decades several political developments transformed contemporary state structure, and therefore these trends also indirectly affected historical perception of the state and its opposition movements. In the 1960s and 1970s new viewpoints on the history of the state arose in Europe because the central state structure of nineteenth-century states was no longer seen as a teleological terminus in history.[39] Clearly influenced by the new developments in historical research noted above, but also building on the legacy of Pirenne, the Belgian historians Jan Dhondt and Walter Prevenier did new research on the origins of medieval state structure and its competing powers in the fourteenth and fifteenth centuries. By studying political assemblies of cities, representative institutions of subjects, and revolts of the powerless in society, Dhondt and Prevenier broke new ground in medieval historiography in Belgium.[40] In their view rational economic, political, and social arguments drove people to contest the emergence of a central state in the Low Countries. The tendency to study the history of individuals in particular and the "mob" in general can be traced back to the romantic era, but the growing attention of historians to the personal motives of historical personages when explaining their actions can be aligned with the so-called integrated or newer social history, which studies such topics as democratic values in the past, the history of informal politics, social networks, and women.[41] The "newer" history was influenced by actual

---

[37] Fris, *Histoire de Gand*, pp. 130–31, and Fris, "Seyssone," pp. 356–58.
[38] Lyon, *Henri Pirenne*, p. 349.
[39] Van den Eeckhout and Scholliers, "Social History," pp. 149–50.
[40] Prevenier, *De leden en staten van Vlaanderen*; Dhondt, *Les assemblées d'états*.
[41] Boone, "Zu einer integrierten Sozialgeschichte," pp. 78–94.

tendencies of democratization, popularization, and "feminization" of society. The scholarly attention paid to marginal social groups, and the "common man" in town had changed historians' perceptions on the rise of the modern state, and those on urban revolts. This new understanding of political protest was probably affected by the street protests of the 1960s and 1970s, when young students (and also scholars) demonstrated for political participation. Consequently, similar protest movements of the "mob" in late medieval Europe were widely studied, as for example by Eric Hobsbawm, George Rudé, Yves-Marie Bercé, and Philippe Mollat.[42]

Belgium also witnessed new studies of the late medieval rebellions. While studying representative institutions in medieval Flemish cities, Wim Blockmans, a pupil of Walter Prevenier at the University of Ghent, wrote the first postwar study of the Ghent revolt of 1449–53. Blockmans found the causes of the revolt in the centralizing efforts of Duke Philip the Good of Burgundy, who had refused political participation to his subjects. Against the wishes of the inhabitants of Ghent, the duke had wanted to strengthen the fiscal autonomy of the state apparatus. "Evidently," as Blockmans says, "protest arose against these measures."[43] In contrast to what Pirenne said, Blockmans held the duke responsible for the outbreak of the Ghent revolt. By establishing a central state in the Low Countries, the Burgundian dukes violated the privileges and common law of their subjects. Moreover, the political resistance of the Ghent rebels was "rightful," because they defended the basic political rights of the city.[44]

Political resistance only could be broken with military violence, which shows—following Blockmans's logic—that the duke of Burgundy acted against the will of the people. In contrast to positivist historiography, Blockmans thus no longer glorified the central state and its origins in his writings on medieval politics. Rebellious defense of privileges was seen as a lawful action of people with sophisticated political beliefs, who resisted the violations of privileges by state officers. In contrast to the positivist historians, Blockmans does not take a personal position in the political conflict between Ghent and its count, but he sees politics as a process of negotiation. If bargaining parties stop negotiating with each other, or violate each other's privileges, political conflict is the logical outcome. Blockmans therefore wrote that both parties (the court of the Burgundian duke and the Ghent inhabitants) bore responsibility for the conflict. When the Ghent regime elected radical leaders in 1451, for instance, Blockmans regretted that the rebels burned all bridges between the parties. Politics is about

[42] Hobsbawm, *Primitive Rebels*; Rudé, *Crowd in History*; Mollat and Wolff, *Ongles bleus*; Fourquin, *Les soulèvements populaires*; Bercé, *Révoltes*.

[43] Blockmans, *De volksvertegenwoordiging*, p. 356.

[44] Blockmans, *De volksvertegenwoordiging*, p. 376.

consultation, Blockmans argued, and revolts therefore were in his eyes "lapses of deliberation."[45]

Blockmans elaborated on these views on urban politics and state formation in a general research project on "the making of the modern state," which he directed jointly with Jean-Philippe Genet in the 1980s and 1990s.[46] This program advocated an interdisciplinary approach to history, which reflected another scientific tendency in postwar historiography. Henceforth, state formation in medieval and early modern Europe was studied with the help of political science, anthropology, and sociology. Theoretical insights from Michael Mann, Charles Tilly, Anthony Giddens, and others were used to show why the central state became the most important political power in early modern Europe, despite numerous political and military conflicts of state rulers with competing subjects, nobles, and cities.[47]

In a collection of essays edited by Blockmans and Charles Tilly, the rise of states was seen as a growing concentration of capital and coercive power in the hands of the fortunate few.[48] The accumulation of fiscal resources in order to wage war was seen as the driving force behind the formation of "national" states. A similar state formation process took place in the Low Countries, as several of Blockmans's detailed studies have shown.[49] Tilly elaborated on this viewpoint by comparing the state-making process with a remarkable metaphor, namely "organized crime."[50] He discovered, and many historians agree, that corruption was one of the "criminal" acts which the power holders of the medieval central state used to enhance their political influence within its boundaries. Using anthropological insights, Blockmans found signs of incipient state formation in corruption, patronage, and power brokerage.[51] He argued that along with military action and the use of coercive power, the formation of social networks among the urban elite was of vital importance for the emergence of the central state. Informal tactics, such as bribing officers and marrying into leading networks in the cities, helped the dukes of Burgundy to strengthen their grip indirectly on the urban elites of Flanders.

Blockmans's argument of course was inspired by findings of anthropologists, but we must not ignore his personal experience with contemporary state for-

[45] Blockmans, *De volksvertegenwoordiging*, p. 371.
[46] Genet, "La genèse"; Blockmans, "Les origines des états modernes."
[47] Tilly, *Formation of National States*; Giddens, *Constitution of Society*; Mann, "Autonomous Power." About state formation theory and its influence on historical writing, see Davies, "Medieval State," and Ertman, "State Formation."
[48] Tilly and Blockmans, *Cities and the Rise of States*.
[49] Summary in Blockmans, *History of Power*.
[50] Tilly, "Warmaking and Statemaking."
[51] Blockmans, "Patronage."

mation in Belgium. In a remarkable essay on Belgian political culture of the 1980s, he vented his spleen on corrupt politicians in his homeland, writing that "political life in Belgium seems so absurd as to be almost a hallucination."[52] On the cover of the offprint of this article that he offered his colleagues Marc Boone and Thérèse de Hemptinne, he revealingly wrote: "some old fury" (wat oude gramschap).[53] Among other things he worried in this article about the "formidable administrative problems which have been created by the system of patronage and brokerage" in Belgium, problems that would be "at the expense of debts on the shoulders of future generations."[54] It remains an open question if Blockmans's personal vision of the (dis)functioning of contemporary state structure is influenced by his work on the politics of the medieval state, or vice versa, but it still is remarkable that he sees similar processes at work in the medieval and contemporary state, of which some are evaluated as "politically incorrect," or even as "criminal"—as Tilly would have said.

Other pupils of Walter Prevenier also concentrated on the study of corruption and influence peddling in late medieval society and its impact on state formation. In his research on the Ghent revolt of 1449–53, Marc Boone exposed social networks between members of the Ghent elite and the councillors of Philip the Good. Boone considered brokerage and patronage to be the glue of these networks, as informal ties between the urban elite in Flanders and the Burgundian state administration helped the duke to enhance his political influence in town. Boone claims that political resistance of townspeople against these "dangerous liaisons" led to overt revolt against the state formation process in Ghent in 1449.[55] The framework of Boone's study therefore is closely connected to the approach of Blockmans and Tilly, but his study focused in particular on human behavior in politics. Using the method of prosopography, which investigates the biographies of individuals and groups in history, Boone tried to evaluate the personal role of individuals associated with particular groups in the making of the modern state. His analysis of social networks among the Ghent elite showed that the different special interests of members of the Ghent elite can explain why some parts of it chose to support the formation of the central state in Flanders. Corporate interests of the craft guilds, however, were more helpful in maintaining the social and political positions of guild leaders and craftsmen. According to Boone, the growing power of the Burgundian dukes and their allies in town clearly diminished the political influence of the craft guilds in urban affairs. Thus the different backgrounds of individuals explain why people chose to resist the emergence of

---

[52] Blockmans, "Political Culture," p. 219.
[53] To be found in their personal library.
[54] Blockmans, "Political Culture," p. 222.
[55] Boone, *Gent en de Bourgondische hertogen.*

the central state in the Low Countries. In Boone's eyes, rebels did not want to abolish the central state, but rather strove for a state apparatus that showed respect for privileges and political rights of self-conscious burghers. This new vision on urban revolts clearly fitted the tendency of the above mentioned "newer history" to reevaluate political protest in history.

Recent Historiography: Collective Action and Realms of Ritual

In the second half of the twentieth century historiography on urban revolts no longer had the purpose of legitimizing the emergence of the central state in late medieval Europe. It is therefore not a surprise that one of the most important theoreticians about state formation, Charles Tilly, also concentrated his research on opposition movements and collective action by subjects against the politics of courts and states.[56] In Tilly's "resource-mobilization" model, violence of urban rebels and collective claim-making were seen as means of communication by which grievances about urban politics were articulated by the powerless in society. As we shall see, these new insights strongly influenced recent historical studies of the Ghent revolt. A second tendency, the growing influence of spectacle and the importance of the use of all kinds of visual media in contemporary politics, also affected historical analysis of the revolts in the medieval Flemish cities. Sociological and anthropological studies of contemporary politics (such as the publications of Clifford Geertz) heightened historians' awareness of political ceremonies in the past.[57] Following these insights, Blockmans and Prevenier described the Burgundian state as a "theatre state" in which the dukes enhanced their power through the intensive use of rituals and ceremonial pomp.[58]

But it was Peter Arnade who fully elaborated on this anthropological point of view in his book about late medieval Ghent. He identifies himself as a late disciple of Johan Huizinga, who introduced hermeneutics into the historical analysis of medieval politics,[59] but in contrast to Huizinga, Arnade did not evaluate the late medieval era as the "autumn" of the Middle Ages. He considered the rituals of the Burgundian duke and the Ghent rebels a kind of social action by which they communicated with each other. Following Richard Trexler and Clifford Geertz, Arnade wrote that the ceremonial repertoire of the Burgundian theater-state was one of the main political foundations of ducal power.[60] He concluded that the

---

[56] Tilly, *From Mobilization to Revolution*; Tilly, "History, Sociology." See also the essay of Van der Linden, "Charles Tilly's Historical Sociology."

[57] Debord, *La société du spectacle*; Kertzer, *Ritual, Politics*; Geertz, *Negara*.

[58] Blockmans and Prevenier, *Promised Lands*.

[59] Arnade, *Realms of Ritual*. See also Arnade, "Crowds, Banners."

[60] Like Geertz, he made "dramaturgy an essential category of political analysis" (Arnade, *Realms of Ritual*, p. 5).

Ghent war opened and closed with ceremonies that complemented one another and demonstrated the central role that public ritual assumed in the conflict. These ceremonies (the speech that the duke gave at his formal entry into the city with the purpose of introducing a new tax in 1447, the humiliating submission of the rebel leaders after the Battle of Gavere in 1453) had the purpose of conquering symbolically the urban space in the city.[61] In Arnade's eyes, the Ghent revolt was not only a conflict between two parties with different political interests, but also a battle between two different realms of ritual.

A comparable insight is given by Elodie Lecuppre-Desjardin, who discovered self-conscious groups and corporate societies in the city that fought for recognition through the use of characteristic ceremonies.[62] According to this point of view, rebels had no intention of fighting against the emergence of a central state. By showing their presence and their political ideas in a ritualized and sophisticated manner, they merely wanted to preserve their particular interests in a changing society. This revalorization of collective violence brings the gestures, opinions, writings, social networks, factions, and even the cries and shouting of rebels back into the attention of historians, as numerous studies on urban revolts in the Low Countries demonstrate.[63] Following the studies of Boone and Blockmans on the one side, and those of Arnade and Lecuppre-Desjardin on the other, recent historiography therefore brings the existence of alternative nuclei of power in medieval society to our attention. Rebels and marginal groups in society did not manage to concentrate as much coercive power and financial means into their hands as the urban elite, but they nevertheless succeeded in maintaining alternative use of rituals and different ideas about the exertion of power.

Conclusion: Toward a New History of Violence?

This article has argued that the personal opinions of historians on contemporary state structures in particular, and on politics in general, significantly influenced their views of medieval state formation and urban revolts. Until 1950 a positive value judgment about the politics of the establishment corresponded to a remarkable positive opinion of medieval state power, and vice versa. Romantic pioneers discovered in the Ghent revolt a heroic fight for liberty of self-conscious craft guilds against an aggressive French-speaking oppressor. At the end of the

---

[61] Arnade, *Realms of Ritual*, p. 124.

[62] Lecuppre-Desjardin, *La ville des cérémonies*. See also Boone, "Urban Space."

[63] Boone, "'Armes, coursses'"; Prevenier, "Conscience et perception"; Dumolyn and Haemers, "Patterns of Urban Rebellion"; Haemers, *For the Common Good?*; Dumolyn, "Criers and Shouters"; Prak, "Corporate Politics." See also Cohn, *Lust for Liberty*; Haemers, "Factionalism"; Haemers and Lecuppre-Desjardin, "Conquérir et reconquérir"; Verbruggen, *Geweld in Vlaanderen*.

nineteenth century, however, when history had become science, nationalistic tendencies entailed a revaluation of centralist models of government in historical writing. Moreover, Belgian positivists legitimized the winner's history of the central state, while urban revolts of craft guilds were seen as futile fights against the inevitable rise of the state, as Pirenne says in the quotation in the beginning of this article. Inspired by actual political tendencies, such as an increasing democratization of society, postwar historians discovered corruption, informal networks, and the protection of particular interests at work in medieval politics. The reevaluation of street protest and political alternatives of established structures in anthropology, sociology, and political science has significantly influenced historical writings on urban revolts. In the historical studies of the recent decades, opposition movements against the emergence of central state power were reevaluated as valuable political alternatives to the emergent state in the Burgundian Low Countries.

In the 2000s historians have opted for a dynamic approach to medieval violence. The use of "legal" coercive power by state administration and the collective action of subjects are treated as complementary and dialectical phenomena. Historians now argue that both the violence of the state elite and the aggression of urban rebels had a communicative aspect, for example, through the intensive use of rituals and ceremonies. According to recent historiography, hostile factions and craft guilds still wanted to compromise during political conflicts, even during the most violent phases of revolts. The insights of contemporary historians are probably influenced by new forms of disorder, to which the twenty-first century is becoming accustomed, namely blind terror by belligerent groups which try to disturb social order with shocking violence. The perpetrators of this cruel type of violence are anonymous and do not want to compromise with their enemies. Governments do not know how to react, and their violent signals to the invisible threat mostly complicate the confrontation even more. The historical vision on medieval and other disorder inevitably is influenced by this vicious circle, and therefore it evolves, just as the violence itself, to an unknown future.

Bibliography

Arnade, Peter. "Crowds, Banners and the Market Place: Symbols of Defiance and Defeat during the Ghent War of 1452–1453." *Journal of Medieval and Renaissance Studies* 24 (1994): 471–97.

———. *Realms of Ritual: Burgundian Ceremony and Civic Life in Late Medieval Ghent.* Ithaca, NY: Cornell University Press, 1996.

Bachrach, Bernard S., and David Nicholas, eds. *Law, Custom, and the Social Fabric in Medieval Europe: Essays in Honor of Bryce Lyon.* Kalamazoo: Medieval Institute Publications, 1990.

Bercé, Yves-Marie. *Révoltes et révolutions dans l'Europe moderne (XVI*–XVIII* siècles).* Paris: Presses universitaires de France, 1980.

Blockmans, Wim. *De volksvertegenwoordiging in Vlaanderen in de overgang van Middeleeuwen naar Nieuwe Tijden (1384–1506)*. Brussels: Paleis der Academiën, 1978.

———. *A History of Power in Europe: Peoples, Markets, States*. Antwerp: Mercator Paribas, 1997.

———. "Les origines des états modernes en Europe, XIIIᵉ–XVIIIᵉ siècles: État de la question et perspectives." In *Visions sur le développement des états européens: Théories et historiographies de l'état moderne*, ed. Wim Blockmans and Jean-Philippe Genet, pp. 1–14. Rome: École française de Rome, 1993.

———. "Patronage, Brokerage and Corruption as Symptoms of Incipient State Formation in the Burgundian-Habsburg Netherlands." In *Klientelsysteme im Europa der Frühen Neuzeit*, ed. Anthony Mączak, pp. 117–26. Munich: R. Oldenbourg, 1988.

———. "Political Culture in Belgium." In *Modern Dutch Studies: Essays in Honour of Peter King, Professor of Modern Dutch Studies at the University of Hull on the Occasion of His Retirement*, ed. Michael Wintle and Paul Vincent, pp. 209–23. London: Athlone, 1988.

———. "Van buitenaf bekeken: Buitenlandse historici over staatsvorming in de Nederlanden van de veertiende tot de zestiende eeuw." *Bijdragen en Mededelingen betreffende de Geschiedenis der Nederlanden* 100 (1985): 600–604.

———. "Voracious States and Obstructing Cities: An Aspect of State Formation in Preindustrial Europe." In *Cities and the Rise of States*, ed. Tilly and Blockmans, pp. 218–50.

Blockmans, Wim, and Walter Prevenier. *The Promised Lands: The Low Countries under Burgundian Rule, 1369–1530*. Philadelphia: University of Pennsylvania Press, 1999.

Blommaert, Philippe. "Causes de la guerre des Gantois contre le duc de Bourgogne." *Messager des Sciences historiques de Belgique* (1839): 418–32.

Blommaert, Philippe, and Constant Serrure, eds. *Kronyk van Vlaenderen van 580 tot 1467*. 2 vols. Ghent: Maatschappy der Vlaamsche bibliophilen, 1839–40.

Boone, Marc. "'Armes, coursses, assemblees et commocions': Les gens de métiers et l'usage de la violence dans la société urbaine flamande à la fin du Moyen Âge." *Revue du Nord* 87 (2005): 1–33.

———. "L'automne du Moyen Âge: Johan Huizinga et Henri Pirenne ou 'plusieurs vérités pour la meme chose.'" In *Autour du XVᵉ siècle: Journée d'étude en l'honneur d'Alberto Varvaro*, ed. Paul Moreno and Giovanni Palumbo, pp. 27–51. Geneva: Droz, 2008.

———. "The Dutch Revolt and the Medieval Tradition of Urban Dissent." *Journal of Early Modern History* 11 (2007): 351–75.

———. *Gent en de Bourgondische hertogen, ca. 1384– ca. 1453: Een sociaal-politieke studie van een staatsvormingsproces*. Brussels: Paleis der Academiën, 1990.

———. "Urban Space and Political Conflict in Late Medieval Flanders." *Journal of Interdisciplinary History* 32 (2002): 621–40.

———. "Zu einer integrierten Sozialgeschichte der niederländischen Städte: Das Beispiel Gent und die burgundische Staatsbildung (14.–16. Jahrhundert)." *Rheinische Vierteljahrsblätter* 54 (1990): 78–94.

Carlier, Philippe. "Contribution à l'étude de l'unification bourguignonne dans l'historiographie nationale belge de 1830 à 1914." *Belgisch Tijdschrift voor Nieuwste Geschiedenis* 16 (1985): 1–12.

Cohn, Sam. *Lust for Liberty: The Politics of Social Revolt in Medieval Europe, 1200–1425*. Cambridge, MA: Harvard University Press, 2006.

Dagboek der Gentsche Collatie, bevattende een nauwkeurig verhael van de gebeurtenissen te Gent en elders in Vlaenderen, voorgevallen van de jaren 1446 tot 1515. Ed. Anton Schayes. Ghent: L. Hebbelynck, 1842.

Dagboek van Gent van 1447 tot 1470, met een vervolg van 1477 tot 1515. Ed. Victor Fris. 2 vols. Ghent: Annoot Braeckman, 1901–4.

Davies, Rees. "The Medieval State: The Tyranny of a Concept." *Journal of Historical Sociology* 16 (2003): 280–93.

De Schryver, Reginald. *Historiografie, vijfentwintig eeuwen geschiedschrijving van West-Europa.* Leuven: Universitaire Pers Leuven, 1997.

———. "Kervyn de Lettenhove (Baron Joseph C.M.B.)." In *Nieuwe Encyclopedie,* ed. De Schryver, 2:1710–11.

———, ed. *Nieuwe Encyclopedie van de Vlaamse Beweging.* 3 vols. Tielt: Lannoo, 1998.

Debord, Guy. *La société du spectacle.* Paris: Gallimard, 1992.

Deprez, An. "Blommaert (jonkheer Philip M.)." In *Nieuwe Encyclopedie,* ed. De Schryver, 1:515–16.

———. "Serrure (Constant P.)." In *Nieuwe Encyclopedie,* ed. De Schryver, 2:2734–35.

Deschamps, Jan. "Blommaert (jonkheer Philip Marie)." *Nationaal Biografisch Woordenboek* 2 (1966): 63–68.

Dhondt, Jan. *Les assemblées d'états en Belgique avant 1795.* Ghent: University of Ghent, 1965.

———. "Henri Pirenne: Historien des institutions urbaines." In *Machten en mensen: De belangrijkste studies van Jan Dhondt over de geschiedenis van de 19e en 20e eeuw,* by Jan Dhondt, pp. 63–119. Ghent: Jan Dhondt Stichting, 1976.

Dumolyn, Jan. "'Criers and Shouters': The Discourse on Radical Urban Rebels in Late Medieval Flanders." *Journal of Social History* 42 (2008): 111–35.

———. *De Brugse opstand, 1436–38.* Kortrijk: UGA, 1997.

Dumolyn, Jan, and Jelle Haemers. "Patterns of Urban Rebellion in Medieval Flanders." *Journal of Medieval History* 31 (2005): 369–93.

Ertman, Thomas. "State Formation and State Building in Europe." In *The Handbook of Political Sociology: States, Civil Societies, and Globalization,* ed. Thomas Janoski et al., pp. 367–83. New York: Cambridge University Press, 2005.

Fourquin, Guy. *Les soulèvements populaires au Moyen Âge.* Paris: Presses universitaires de France, 1972.

Fris, Victor. *De slag bij Kortrijk.* Ghent: Koninklijke Vlaamsche Academie voor Taal-en Letterkunde, 1902.

———. *Histoire de Gand.* Brussels: G. Van Oest, 1913.

———. "Nieuwe oorkonden betreffende den opstand van Gent tegen Philips de Goede." *Handelingen van de Maatschappij voor Geschiedenis en Oudheidkunde te Gent* 7 (1906–7): 179–220.

———. "Ontleding van drie Vlaamsche kronijken." *Handelingen van de Maatschappij voor Geschiedenis en Oudheidkunde te Gent* 3 (1901–2): 157–71.

———. "Oorkonden betreffende den opstand van Gent tegen Philips de Goede (1450–1453)." *Handelingen van de Maatschappij voor Geschiedenis en Oudheidkunde te Gent* 4 (1903): 55–146.

———. "Seyssone (Corneille)." *Biographie Nationale* 22 (1914–1920): 356–58.

Geertz, Clifford. *Negara: The Theatre State in Nineteenth-Century Bali.* Princeton, NJ: Princeton University Press, 1980.

Genet, Jean-Philippe. "La genèse de l'etat moderne: Les enjeux d'un programme de recherche." *Actes de la recherche en sciences sociales* 118 (1997): 3–18.

Giddens, Anthony. *The Constitution of Society: Outline of the Theory of Structuration.* Cambridge: Cambridge University Press, 1984.

Haemers, Jelle. "De dominante staat: De Gentse opstand (1449–1453) in de negentiende-en twintigste-eeuwse historiografie." *Bijdragen en Mededelingen betreffende de Geschiedenis der Nederlanden* 119 (2004): 39–61.

———. *De Gentse opstand (1449–1453): De strijd tussen netwerken om het stedelijke kapitaal.* Kortrijk: UGA, 2004.

———. "Factionalism and State Power in the Flemish Revolt (1477–1492)." *Journal of Social History* 42 (2009): 1009–39.

———. *For the Common Good: State Power and Urban Revolts in the Reign of Mary of Burgundy, 1477–1482.* Studies in European Urban History (1100–1800) 17. Turnhout: Brepols, 2009.

———. "Seyssoone (Cornelis)." *Nationaal Biografisch Woordenboek* 17 (2005): 574–77.

Haemers, Jelle, and Elodie Leuppre-Desjardin. "Conquérir et reconquérir l'espace urbain: Le triomphe de la collectivité sur l'individu dans le cadre de la révolte brugeoise de 1488." In *Voisinages, coexistences, appropriations: Groupes sociaux et territoires urbains du Moyen Âge au 16ᵉ siècle,* ed. Chloé Deligne and Claire Billen, Studies in European Urban History (1100–1800) 10, pp. 119–43. Turnhout: Brepols, 2007.

Hobsbawm, Eric. *Primitive Rebels: Studies in Archaic Forms of Social Movement in the 19th and 20th centuries.* New York: W. W. Norton, 1966.

Huizinga, Johan. *Herfsttij der middeleeuwen: Studie over levens- en gedachtenvormen der veertiende en vijftiende eeuw in Frankrijk en de Nederlanden.* Haarlem: Tjeenk-Willink, 1919.

Iggers, Georg. *Historiography in the Twentieth Century: From Scientific Objectivity to the Postmodern Challenge.* Hanover, NH: Wesleyan University Press, 1997.

Jongkees, Anton. "Une génération d'historiens devant le phénomène bourguignon." *Bijdragen en Mededelingen betreffende de Geschiedenis der Nederlanden* 88 (1973): 215–32.

Kertzer, David. *Ritual, Politics and Power.* New Haven, CT: Yale University Press, 1988.

Kervyn de Lettenhove, Joseph. *Histoire de Flandre.* 6 vols. Brussels: A. Vandale, 1847–50.

Lambert, Véronique. "De Guldensporenslag van fait-divers tot ankerpunt van de Vlaamse identiteit (1302–1838): De natievormende functionaliteit van historiografische mythen." *Bijdragen en Mededelingen betreffende de Geschiedenis der Nederlanden* 115 (2000): 365–91.

Lecuppre-Desjardin, Elodie. *La ville des cérémonies: Essai sur la communication symbolique dans les anciens Pays-Bas bourguignons.* Studies in European Urban History (1100–1800) 4. Turnhout: Brepols, 2004.

Lorenz, Chris. *De constructie van het verleden: Een inleiding in de theorie van de geschiedenis.* Amsterdam: Boom, 1998.

Lyon, Bryce. *Henri Pirenne: A Biographical and Intellectual Study.* Ghent: E. Story-Scientia, 1974.

———. "Henri Pirenne and Johan Huizinga in Search of Historical Truth: Two Different Approaches." In *Papers from the Second Interdisciplinary Conference on Netherlandic Studies,* ed. William Fletcher, pp. 3–16. New York: University Press of America, 1987.

———. "Medieval Constitutionalism: A Balance of Power." In *Album Helene Maud Cam:*

Studies Presented to the International Commission for the History of Representative and Parliamentary Institutions, XXIV, pp. 157–83. Louvain: Presses universitaires de Louvain, 1961.

Mann, Michael. "The Autonomous Power of the State: Its Origins, Mechanisms and Results." In *States in History*, ed. John Hall, pp. 109–36. Oxford: B. Blackwell, 1986.

Mollat, Michel, and Philippe Wolff. *Ongles bleus, Jacques et Ciompi: Les révolutions populaires en Europe aux XIVe et XVe siècles*. Paris: Calman-Lévy, 1970.

Pirenne, Henri. *Les anciennes démocraties des Pays-Bas*. Paris: E. Flammarion, 1910.

———. "The Formation and Constitution of the Burgundian State (Fifteenth and Sixteenth Centuries)." *American Historical Review* 14 (1909): 477–502.

———. *Histoire de Belgique*. Vol. 2, *Du commencement du XIVe siècle à la mort de Charles le Téméraire*. 3rd ed. Brussels: Maurice Lamertin, 1922.

———. "Philippe de Bourgogne (dit le Bon ou l'Asseuré)." *Biographie nationale* 17 (1903): 220–50.

Prak, Maarten. "Corporate Politics in the Low Countries: Guilds as Institutions, 14th to 18th Centuries." In *Craft Guilds in the Early Modern Low Countries: Work, Power and Representation*, ed. Maarten Prak et al., pp. 74–106. Aldershot: Ashgate, 2006.

Prevenier, Walter. "Conscience et perception de la condition sociale chez les gens du commun dans les anciens Pays-Bas des XIIIe et XIVe siècles." In *Le petit peuple dans l'Occident médiéval: Terminologies, perceptions, réalités*, ed. P. Boglioni, R. Delort, and Claude Gauvard, pp. 177–89. Paris: Publications de la Sorbonne, 2002.

———. *De leden en staten van Vlaanderen (1384–1405)*. Brussels: Paleis der Academiën, 1961.

———. "Fris (Victor)." In *Encyclopedie van de Vlaamse Beweging*, ed. Jozef Deleu et al., 1:541. 2 vols. Tielt: Lannoo, 1973.

Rodenbach, Albrecht. *Eerste Gedichten*. Roeselare: Den Wijngaert, 1878.

Rudé, George. *The Crowd in History, 1730–1848*. New York: Wiley, 1964.

Stengers, Jean. "Le mythe des dominations étrangères dans l'historiographie belge." *Revue belge de philologie et d'histoire* 59 (1981): 382–401.

Tilly, Charles. *The Formation of National States in Western Europe*. Princeton, NJ: Princeton University Press, 1975.

———. *From Mobilization to Revolution*. Reading: Addison-Wesley, 1978.

———. "History, Sociology and Dutch Collective Action." *Tijdschrift voor Sociale Geschiedenis* 15 (1989): 142–57.

———. "Warmaking and Statemaking as Organized Crime." In *Bringing the State Back In*, ed. Dieter Rueschemeyer, Theda Skocpol, and P. Evans, pp. 169–91. Cambridge: Cambridge University Press, 1985.

Tilly, Charles, and Wim Blockmans, eds. *Cities and the Rise of States in Europe, A.D. 1000 to 1800*. Boulder: Westview, 1994.

Tollebeek, Jo. "At the Crossroads of Nationalism: Huizinga, Pirenne and the Low Countries in Europe." *European History Review* 17 (2010): 187–215.

———. "De cultus van 1302: Twee eeuwen herinnering." In *1302: Feiten en mythen van de Guldensporenslag*, ed. Raoul Van Caenegem, pp. 194–239. Antwerp: Mercatorfonds, 2002.

———. "De *Messager* en de Maatschappij: Over geschiedbeschouwing te Gent (1870–1914)." *Handelingen van de Maatschappij voor Geschiedenis en Oudheidkunde te Gent* 52 (1998): 107–32.

————. *Fredericq en zonen: Een antropologie van de moderne geschiedwetenschap*. Leuven: Prometheus-Bert Bakker, 2008.

————. "Historical Representation and the Nation-State in Romantic Belgium (1830–1850)." *Journal of the History of Ideas* 59 (1998): 329–53.

————. "A Stormy Family: Paul Fredericq and the Formation of an Academic Historical Community in the Nineteenth Century." *Storia della storiografia* 53 (2008): 58–72.

Van Den Eeckhout, Patricia, and Peter Scholliers. "Social History in Belgium: Old Habits and New Perspectives." *Tijdschrift voor Sociale Geschiedenis* 23 (1997): 147–81.

Van der Linden, Marcel. "Charles Tilly's Historical Sociology." *International Review of Social History* 54 (2009): 237–74.

Vaughan, Richard. *Philip the Good: The Apogee of Burgundy*. London: Longman, 1970.

Verbruggen, Raf. *Geweld in Vlaanderen: Macht en onderdrukking in de Vlaamse steden tijdens de veertiende eeuw*. Bruges: Van de Wiele, 2005.

Vercauteren, Fernand. *Cent ans d'histoire nationale en Belgique*. Brussels: Renaissance du livre, 1959.

Verhulst, Adriaan. "Fris, Victor." *Nouvelle biographie nationale* 7 (2003): 142–43.

Verschaffel, Tom. *De hoed en de hond: Geschiedschrijving in de Zuidelijke Nederlanden (1715–1794)*. Hilversum: Verloren, 1998.

Henri Pirenne and Particularism in Late Medieval Flemish Cities: An Intellectual Genealogy

Jan Dumolyn

T HIS ARTICLE TRIES TO LAY BARE the intellectual genealogy of a marginalized element in the work of one of the founding fathers of the history of Belgium and of modern medieval history in general: the concept of particularism in the work of the great Belgian medievalist Henri Pirenne, who was, of course, the scholarly hero of Bryce Lyon. During his lifetime Pirenne was one of the most prominent historians in the world, and some of his theories and approaches remain influential to this day. *Particularism* is a somewhat awkward and ill-defined concept, but historians often use it and seem to take for granted that it actually has some explanatory power. In fact, particularism is a heavily ideologically charged term, and a closer look at the history of this concept is needed.

Since Pirenne greatly contributed to the popularity of "particularism" in his historical narrative on the later Middle Ages, I will study the use of the term and the ideological assumptions that support this concept, in the works of Pirenne himself, his predecessors, and his followers,[1] by means of a classic *begriffsgeschichtliche* (conceptual-historical) approach. Particularism will rear its head as a creation of Liberal, Marxist, Nationalist, and similar modernist universalistic readings of history, mostly in nineteenth-century Germany and France. In conclusion, we will see whether this singular concept, inspired by more recent scholarly approaches, deserves a full-fledged life of its own or should, on the contrary, be dismissed once and for all from the historian's repertory of concepts.

Many thanks to Jan Art, Marc Boone, Walter Prevenier, and Jo Tollebeek for their remarks and suggestions. An earlier version of this article appeared in Dutch in the *Belgisch Tijdschrift voor Filologie en Geschiedenis*, 2009.

[1] A first, partial step toward this has already been taken by Haemers, "De dominante staat," in which the question of particularism is taken up indirectly.

Burgundian state formation, especially the government of Philip the Good (1419–67), *conditor Belgii*, is of course the key moment in the Belgian Nationalist story Henri Pirenne outlined in his masterpiece, the *Histoire de Belgique*.[2] For Pirenne the unification of the Low Countries under the Burgundian-Habsburg house was the culmination of an inevitable evolution in which several regions that had shared a common culture and socioeconomic structures for centuries were at last united under the authority of one dynasty. The eventual separation between north and south was temporarily disregarded, which was the Dutch historian Pieter Geyl's (Pirenne's great opponent) main point of criticism of this analysis whose intent was to legitimize the eventual reconstruction of the Belgian union state—a failure according to many—in the nineteenth century.[3] Especially for the highly urbanized county of Flanders the father of Belgian historiography outlined a coherent picture of the political, judicial, and financial "centralization" carried out by the dukes, an analysis that was based on very little original study of source material from the Burgundian period. The great opponents of this almost inevitable reinforcement of princely power were the "particularistic" large cities of Ghent, Bruges, and to a lesser extent Ypres. The autonomous Flemish cities, which had once played such a progressive role as "old democracies,"[4] were now past their prime and merely constituted a stumbling block to a new era of unification of the modern state and princely absolutism. This narrative of the founding myth of the bourgeois and French-speaking Belgian state is one of the classics of legitimizing historiography of European Nationalism and even today has a very strong after-effect, the ever-growing centrifugal tendencies of present-day Belgium notwithstanding. Paradoxically, the urban historian Pirenne abandoned the urban perspective in order to pay homage to an inevitable state formation. Thus he created a permanent tension in historical research into the late medieval county of Flanders between, on the one hand, an often uncritical admiration of the cities' enormous economic, political, and cultural importance and on the other, the vigor of the Burgundian dukes, whose key political position between France and England and splendid court culture have aroused the interest of an ever-growing army of foreign historians.

Before I search for the intellectual roots of the concept of urban particularism, I must investigate how Pirenne interpreted it in his different writings. First, although particularism is intrinsically applicable to any localized group phenomenon, it had a chiefly urban character in Pirenne's work. In his rhetoric "municipal particularism" was reinforced by "the growing particularism of the guilds." Urban particularism had been "born from the very conditions of urban life" and had

---

[2] Pirenne, *Histoire de Belgique*.

[3] Geyl, *Geschiedenis*.

[4] Pirenne, *Les anciennes démocraties*.

already blossomed under the patrician governments of the Flemish cities. This occurred, therefore, before the victory over France in the Battle of Courtrai of 1302, another key moment in Belgian-Flemish history able to stand the test of time. Whereas the patrician class mainly defined its particularism on the basis of its interests in long-distance trade, the artisans did so by means of retail trade. This was Pirenne's view of "economic" particularism, by which he really meant "protectionism" and "conservatism."

He already was clearly describing the entire particularistic program of the late medieval large cities: subjecting the surrounding countryside and the smaller cities in their direct sphere of influence, armed raids against rural industry, rivalry between the trades, and the ideological importance of privileges and customary law.[5] All these elements tended to return regularly in the writings of the so-called Ghent historical school of medieval history, with representatives such as Hans Van Werveke, Walter Prevenier, Wim Blockmans, Marc Boone and their younger disciples and followers, including the undersigned author.[6] The "Ghent" research, which also spread to Leiden, Brussels, and Antwerp, among other universities, with regard to late medieval society in the county of Flanders is probably one of the most coherent examples of school formation in recent Belgian historiography. In this tradition, an initial reference to—or patricide of—Henri Pirenne has almost become a ritual obligation, whether one is discussing the history of the textile industry or interpreting an urban revolt. We shall see that in this historiographical tradition the concept of particularism has started to take on a life of its own.

In the eyes of the great Belgian historian, particularism was not limited to our part of the world. He saw "a more or less pronounced republican feeling" in all urban governments of Western Europe, by means of which he introduced a link between particularism and "republicanism" that he would discuss later in a different context. He saw this as a historically necessary development: both the economic particularism of the middle classes and their "social makeup" drove city dwellers to secure complete autonomy and become "a state within the state," whether their regime was patrician or "democratic." In France and England central power was stronger, while in Italy and Germany municipal autonomy was complete, and the Netherlands held a position between these extremes.[7]

It is, of course, not difficult to see a back projection of nineteenth-century political developments in this European comparison, but for now we will concentrate on the situation in Flanders, the richest and most important Burgundian principality and also the most politically volatile one. Pirenne had ambivalent feelings

---

[5] Pirenne, *Les villes*, 1:253.

[6] References are endless here, but the most classic statement of these ideas by an active historian is in Blockmans, V*olksvertegenwoordiging*.

[7] Pirenne, *Les villes*, p. 262.

toward the Flemish cities: they showed "heroism" in their battles but also a kind of exclusivism that weakened them. Yet the other two medieval estates, the clergy and the nobility, were equally particularistic in their own ways: "urban particularism had collided with other particularisms" and was unable to stop the inexorable rise of the territorial state.[8]

Moreover, in their battle against the cities the Burgundian princes clearly acted in the public interest: according to Pirenne they not only rallied the clergy, the nobility, and the farmers—which for the latter group is rather unlikely—but also and mainly "that class of new men," the bourgeois upstarts who, from the fifteenth century onward, were to guarantee the free expansion of capitalism.[9] Like *dei ex machina* these new, enterprising forces regularly appear in Pirennian Belgian history. They were also the people who sided with the trades against the patricians in 1302. When they supported the Burgundians and their "centralizing institutions," Pirenne thought that without realizing it they were paving the way for the unstoppable rise of the free market. In a world of social stability and balance between different social groups, time and again these *homines novi* were a dynamic factor, a catalyst in a teleological transformation process. They would, for instance, have the same function in the course of the Industrial Revolution in nineteenth-century Liège and Verviers, home of the Pirenne family of industrial capitalists.

The universal and modernizing historical function of the social, economic, and political forces that battled against reactionary particularism remained a constant element in Henri Pirenne's vision, even when he commented on contemporary events. He kept using the notion of particularism in a way that bordered on the obsessive. Once he had returned from the German prison camps where he had been interned during the First World War, he pursued his antiparticularism with imperturbable zeal. In his *La Belgique et la guerre mondiale* he also reproached Flemish activist collaborators for displaying a "provincial particularism" and called their behavior "more lamentable than shameful." He compared their boundless, naive trust in the good will of the German occupiers to the eighteenth-century Belgian revolutionary Van der Noot's belief in the promises of the Prussians during the Brabant Revolution of 1790, another key event in the Belgian narrative.[10]

It is striking that Pirenne resurrected the term *exclusivism* when he reproached the activists with reducing the people to their language and wanting to establish a "a narrowly Flemish civilization."[11] I do not wish to go here into his subsequent opposition to the University of Ghent turning Flemish, but Pirenne's

---

[8] Pirenne, *Les villes*, p. 264.

[9] Pirenne, *Les villes*, p. 266. See also Pirenne, "Les périodes," where a more elaborate argumentation can be found.

[10] Pirenne, *La Belgique*, p. 220.

[11] Pirenne, *La Belgique*, p. 225.

attitude toward Prussian-German ideas after the First World War would prove to be ironic in the light of his concept of particularism. It is common knowledge that after his imprisonment during the Great War, Pirenne broke off all contact with his German friends and colleagues.[12] French "civilization" had conquered German *Kultur*.

We will see, however, that the influence of the spectacular rise of German intellectual life in the nineteenth century was of fundamental importance to Pirenne's view of the opposition between centralization and particularism. Although the basis of his antiparticularism can be found in an undeniably French political centralism, this Jacobean range of ideas came trickling into his ideological vision in a roundabout way through Germany. In my hypothesis, the discourse that was developed during the unification of the German *Reich* in the nineteenth century determined Pirenne's narrative structure of the Burgundian centralization movement. The first catastrophe that the Belgian medievalist attributed to the destructive power of particularism was nothing less than the collapse and fragmentation of the Carolingian Empire. That development was the precursor of both the feudalization of Europe and the reaction to this, the eventual growth of the French and German states, that of the former from the late Middle Ages onwards, that of the latter not completed until the generation prior to Pirenne's own adult life. "Regional particularism" was responsible for the failed Carolingian project of state formation and was thus associated with the "irresistible pressure of feudalism," although additional causes such as the raids of the Normans, Saracens, Slavs, and Magyars, and personal intrigues within the Frankish dynasty could not be ignored either.[13]

Particularism then resurfaces in the urban development of Italy in the twelfth century, where the progress of urban economy corresponds to a policy of particularism that became "ever more confined and ferocious."[14] That was only a prologue: the fourteenth century was to become the real heyday of particularism. The apparent opposition between paying homage to the urban capitalist view as trailblazer for economic modernity on the one hand, and the "narrow" particularism of the same later medieval citizens which stood in the way of political unification on the other, was obviously indebted to French nineteenth-century historians and their ideas about the class struggle and the rise of the bourgeoisie. Pirenne's intellectual dependence in particular on the romantic Liberal Augustin Thierry, a champion of civic freedom and constitutional monarchy, is evident from their similar choices of words.

[12] See, among others, Schöttler, "Henri Pirenne." The classic biography of Pirenne of course remains Lyon, *Henri Pirenne*.

[13] Pirenne, *Histoire de l'Europe*, p. 78.

[14] Pirenne, *Histoire de l'Europe*, p. 230.

Thierry, of course, honored the "third estate" throughout the history of France, and therefore also medieval bourgeoisie. Nevertheless his view of medieval cities was not unequivocally positive. He considered the mind-set of the medieval burghers and their guilds "liberal, but narrow and immobile" and too much attached to local privileges. Improvement was on the way, however. Under the influence of new ideas, "more elevated and generous," since the thirteenth century, there was "a slow but sure march towards civic equality, national unity and administrative unity," typical of the French national character.[15]

The terminal point was, of course, French bourgeois politics during the Constituent Assembly and other revolutionary conclaves. This historical tradition, with an emphasis on constitutional and parliamentary achievements of the people, had its counterpart in English Whig history, but here the intellectual similarities to Pirenne's work are less obvious.[16] In any case, Pirenne resolutely dismissed the comparison between the Great Privilege of 1477 for the Netherlands and Magna Carta. This was too great an honor, so he said, for a charter that merely provided a restoration of provincial particularism.[17] The 1477 representation of the states ensured the victory of "medieval politics" over "modern politics."[18] Magna Carta is, of course, the starting point par excellence of the entire Whig historical tradition, and Pirenne presented his very own Continental version of Liberal modernization teleology. In his view, Parliament was not the center but rather the result of the sovereign's centralizing action. Pirenne gave credit to the monarchy for freeing France from "feudal particularism" and protecting the prospering cities. The centralizing institutions the French kings developed moreover served to protect the people against violence and extortion.[19]

The father of Belgian national historiography was not the first Belgian historian who made use of the concept of particularism.[20] A study of Philippe Carlier has shown that particularistic tendencies in Belgian history were especially condemned from the 1890s onwards, when patriotic awareness increased under the influence of external threats. Between 1890 and 1914 the general tendency was to pay homage to Philip the Good's attempts at centralization. Before Pirenne historians now long forgotten, such as Quoidbach and Boddaert, already were using the term *particularism*. Carlier is right to refer to a definition in Émile Littré's French dictionary, in an 1869 volume (three years after the Prussian-Austrian Battle of

---

[15] Thierry, *Recueil des monuments*, 1:lv–lvi.

[16] See Butterfield, *Whig Interpretation*.

[17] Pirenne, *Histoire de Belgique*, 3:10.

[18] Pirenne, *Histoire de Belgique*, 3:12.

[19] Pirenne, *Histoire de l'Europe*, p. 275.

[20] A general overview of nineteenth-century Belgian and Dutch historiography is given in many contributions by Jo Tollebeek; see, among other articles, "Historical Representation" and "Enthousiasme en evidentie."

Sadowa), in which particularism is defined as "the system of those Germans who want the states annexed to Prussia to remain independent and subjected to their own laws."[21]

Previously, historians such as Joseph Kervyn de Lettenhove and Paul Fredericq had spoken quite differently, blaming the Burgundians for being despots. Now, a new nationalistic historiography was supported by the discursive battle against a stigmatized particularism.[22] The general spread of this term was, as the definition in Littré's dictionary indicates, more German than French, although the first visible attestation of the concept in its present meaning was apparently in the *Mémoires secrets sur les règnes de Louis XIV et Louis XV* by the French court historiographer Charles Pinot Duclos (d. 1772), posthumously published in 1791.[23] It is curious to note here that the young Napoleon Bonaparte, who was in the habit of making notes in small notebooks while he read, wrote down two words from Duclos's work: "hobereau" and "particularisme."[24] Some decades earlier, Denis Diderot and Jean le Rond d'Alembert merely attributed to "particulariste" the theological meaning that awarded individual grace to the predestined.[25] Walther von Wartburg's *Französisches etymologisches Wörterbuch*, apart from that theological meaning, as it was formulated by Jacques-Bénigne Bossuet in 1689, for example, also lists the meaning of "selfishness, personal interest," which also features in Duclos in 1791, and from around 1868 provides an explanation of the "sentiment of a population which, contained within a state, claims a certain independence sentiment."[26] The *Dictionnaire français illustré et encyclopédie universelle*, edited by Dupiney de Vorepierre already interprets particularism as "a spirit of selfishness or exclusive spirit" but adds that this is "rarely used."[27] Further lexicographical research is necessary, but the chronology seems more or less clear: the concept of particularism used by Pirenne from the 1890s onward entered the French language in the 1870s via German.

This is also apparent from conceptual-historical research conducted by German scholars. In the monumental *Geschichtliche Grundbegriffe* Irmlinde Veit-Brause defines *particularism* as "the mentality and the political value concepts and programs of individual social or political groups that are founded on it, in a given political or social whole, which grants priority to the defense of independence, autonomy and the special interests of the individual parts over the interests of the

---

[21] Littré, *Dictionnaire*, s.v. "particularism."

[22] Carlier, "Contribution à l'étude," pp. 13–15.

[23] Duclos, *Mémoires secrets*, 2:48: "en France, où le particularisme l'emporte toujours sur l'intérêt général," in the context of a royal project to change the distribution of taxes in the kingdom in 1719.

[24] Chuquet, *La jeunesse de Napoléon*, 2:209.

[25] Diderot and d'Alembert. *Encyclopédi*, 24:321.

[26] Wartburg, *Französcher etymologisches Wörterbuch*, 7:677.

[27] Vorepierre and Dupiney, *Dictionnaire français*, 2:643.

whole, yet only rarely are prepared to proceed to actual dissolution (separatism)."[28] In the German states this concept found general acceptance between 1815 and 1848, clearly with a negative connotation as a reproach to the political powers that opposed the unification of Germany by appealing to justice, tradition, language, and "tribe."[29] Particularism was defined from the beginning as the opposite of such "modernizing" forces as centralizing, enlightened absolutist bureaucracy, civic liberty and equality, Liberalism, and natural law.[30]

The word *particularism* is derived from the late classical-medieval Latin adjective *particularis*, meaning "concerning one part." In itself it clearly refers to the Aristotelian doctrine that the Universal only expresses itself in what is specifically "Particular." In early nineteenth-century German dictionaries particularism is already called "complacency" (*Selbstgenügsamkeit*) and "selfishness" (*Selbstsucht*). It is probably a polemic neologism building on a constitutional terminology, in which *ius commune* opposed *ius particulare*. The political use of the term *particularism* should therefore be seen in the first place as judicial rhetoric, in which the weakness of "centralizing" imperial law was directly opposed to the stronger legislative traditions of the separate German principalities.

The nineteenth-century bourgeoisie in other words constructed a negative concept in order to contrast it with a revolutionary program of national unification. Hegel, for example, clearly subscribed to this viewpoint.[31] In 1844, German political economists such as Friedrich List talked about a "disorganizing particularism and individualism."[32] The influential historian Heinrich von Treitschke considered particularism to be the cause of the weak German position on an international and especially colonial level, and thus an obstacle to the necessary buildup and concentration of power that was, in his Hegelian vision, the responsibility of the state.[33] Treitschke, who began as a Liberal but in later life became more conservative and anti-Semitic, a statesman/politician, publicist and official historiographer of the Prussian-German state formation, was possibly the greatest champion of antiparticularism. In his pamphlet *Bundesstaat und Einheitsstaat* (1864), he took a merciless stand against the "small state particularism" that obstructed German unification, taking French political centralization as a shining example.[34] The most authoritarian champions of the construction of the modern state also used particularism for target

---

[28] Veit-Brause, "Partikularismus," p.735.

[29] Veit-Brause, "Partikularismus," p.735. See also White, "Regionalism and Particularism."

[30] Veit-Brause, "Partikularismus," p. 736.

[31] Veit-Brause, "Partikularismus," pp. 737–39.

[32] Veit-Brause, "Partikularismus," p. 745.

[33] Veit-Brause, "Partikularismus," pp. 756–57.

[34] Davis, *Political Thought*, pp. 47–52. See also Treitschke, *Bundesstaat und Einheitsstaat*; and Treitschke, *Deutsche Geschichte*.

practice. Bismarck even mentioned "parliamentary particularism."[35] It is more than likely that when Pirenne went to Germany to perfect his skills as a medievalist, he was strongly influenced by Treitschke's classic works and by the common contemporary circulation of this discourse in the young German state.

This political context of particularism was linked to an economic sense during Pirenne's student days. Gustav von Schmoller, the main representative of the German "historical school" in economics, whose lectures Pirenne attended during his stay in Germany, undeniably influenced his views on the socioeconomic development of Europe, as well as his economic definition of late medieval urban particularism in Flanders.[36] In Schmoller's *Grundriss der allgemeinen Volkswirtschaftslehre*, published from 1900 onwards, the German economist-historian speaks about the "strong urban patriotism" of the medieval cities, "together with their "egotism toward the outside world, through a certain exploitation of the countryside and often of the smaller neighboring towns" and "a narrow-minded total egotism that did not comprehend the great tasks of a new age." The solution par excellence was of course a "territorial state" and the "political-economic progress" that accompanied it.[37] In 1875, in one of his earliest works as a medievalist, Schmoller spoke of "the bare selfishness typical for that era" in describing Strasbourg's trade-dominated urban government, and he frequently reverted to this theme.[38] Almost the entire economic coloring that the Ghent historical school would subsequently give to Flemish urban particularism had thus been fixed by Schmoller.[39] The intellectual career of this term as a marginalized opposite of universal law, national political unification, and capitalist modernization had begun, and Pirenne became one of the main developers of the concept. The Liberal Belgian historian had an unexpected partner to reckon with, however, a thinker of modernity and progress who would prove much more influential than Pirenne has ever been.[40] I am, of course, talking about Karl Marx.

[35] Veit-Brause, "Partikularismus," p. 762.

[36] Lyon, *Henri Pirenne*, p. 63, speaks of Schmoller's "decisive influence" on Pirenne. Powicke, *Modern Historians*, pp. 97–98, was the first to point this out clearly.

[37] Schmoller, *Grundriss*, pp. 311–15. Note a polemic between Schmoller and Treitschke in Schmoller, *Über einige Grundfragen*.

[38] Schmoller, *Strassburg*, p. 41. A negative view concerning the politics of the craft guilds can also be found in Schmoller, *Die Strassburger*, p. 113.

[39] Another possible lead, the influence of Karl Lamprecht on Pirenne, was inconclusive. In Lamprecht's *Deutsche Geschichte*, pp. 3–4, and passim, he treats the conflicts between princes, nobility, and cities in a much more distant fashion than Pirenne, as a struggle between social groups, and without taking a stand. Violante, "Das Ende," p. 182, contrasts Lamprecht with Schmoller concerning the latter's "Staatszentralismus." Pirenne may also have been influenced by another academic Socialist whose work is preserved to this day in Pirenne's library: Sombart, *Der moderne Kapitalismus*, 1:332, 336–37.

[40] Violante, "Das Ende," p. 354; Dhondt, "Henri Pirenne," p. 127; see also the letter from Pirenne to Lamprecht that Dhondt cites where Pirenne discusses the "materialistic concept of history," printed in Lyon, "Letters," pp. 211–12.

Although François-Louis Ganshof often tried to minimize Marx's influence on Pirenne, Jan Dhondt, Walter Prevenier, Claire Billen, and Adriaan Verhulst have established in different ways how much Pirenne owed specifically to Hegel's work, but also to the latter's materialist counterpart.[41]

In a letter to his friend Friedrich Engels on June 7, 1864, the founder of modern Socialism contrasted "particularism" to "Teutonism" when he discussed the editorial line of an Augsburg newspaper.[42] This seems to be the first time that the theoreticians of "scientific socialism" adopted this loaded German political concept, although further research might clarify things. Marx's use of the concept of particularism is in itself unsurprising. After all, as opposed to many other Socialists, he was a great advocate of the unification of the national state in order to create the conditions for a speedy capitalist development and a subsequent proletarian revolution. Though Marx lived in exile for most of his life, on the run from the authoritarian Prussian state, he was one of the greatest supporters of Bismarck's unification policy.

Already in the *Communist Manifesto* he and Engels had explicitly opposed utopian Socialists who wanted a return to the guilds and other reactionary aspects of the feudal mode of production. It was therefore only logical that scientific Socialists strongly condemned every form of particularism. Although they do not seem to use this term explicitly at first, translators of Marx and Engels's earlier German works quietly inserted the term *particularism*. For example, in a French translation of the famous 1850 pamphlet *Address to the Communist League* we read: "In a country such as Germany, where so many vestiges of the Middle Ages have not yet disappeared and so much local and provincial particularism remains to be broken, we cannot tolerate under any circumstances that every village, town or province can set up a new obstacle to revolutionary activity, whose power can only emanate from the center."[43] Nevertheless the German original did not use the word *particularism* but the phrase "so much local and provincial obstinacy."[44] Later Marxists such as Kautsky, Trotsky, Rakovsky, Korsch, Gramsci, or Togliatti—or so a search in the Marxist Internet Archive teaches us—also used the concept of particularism as an extremely negative term, associated with the small-mindedness of feudal society.[45]

[41] Dhondt, "Henri Pirenne," p. 74; Ganshof, "Henri Pirenne"; Prevenier, "Henri Pirenne"; Billen, "L'économie"; Verhulst, "Conclusion."

[42] Marx and Engels, *Werke*, 41:536.

[43] Marx and Engels, *Adresse du Comité*, published as a pamphlet in 1850 and republished by Engels in 1875. Here a French translation was used: Marx, and Engels, *Oeuvres choisis*, p. 184.

[44] We are using Friederich Engels's publication in the new edition of the work *Enthüllungen über den Kommunisten-Prozeß zu Köln von Karl Marx*, cited here from Marx and Engels, *Werke*, 7:244–54.

[45] Marxist Internet Archive, http://www.marxists.org (accessed December 1, 2007).

Both Liberals and Marxists thus believed in centralization by the national state. In 1934 Franz Raab published an inaugural dissertation about the idea of progress in Schmoller's work, in which he pointed out the similarity between the latter's opinions and those of Hegel, Marx, Comte, Morgan, and Spencer.[46] Similarly, in her series of articles about Socialism and the national question, written in Polish, Rosa Luxemburg equally paid attention to so-called particularism. The typically Marxist point of view she held was that capitalism plays a progressive role in history by means of the centralization of the economic, legislative, administrative, judicial, and military domains within the territorial bourgeois state. During the Middle Ages, when the feudal mode of production predominated, social life was decentralized, which was characteristic of what Luxemburg called "natural economy" here.

From the end of the medieval era, a "revolution" in production and trade relationships, growth of industry and the money economy, and military transformations were to form the basis of centralizing absolutism. The sixteenth and seventeenth centuries saw a princely offensive against feudal particularism. After the heyday of centralism, however, this historic task of centralizing the state was to be taken over by the bourgeoisie, with the evident crystallization of this struggle in the French Revolution. The abolition of excises and of judicial and fiscal autonomy was the first accomplishment of the modern bourgeoisie in that Marxist story of progress.[47] Thus we find in different words exactly the same development scheme of a Liberal such as Pirenne, even if there is no direct intellectual dependence on the work of Luxemburg or an inspiration in the form of Schmoller's ideas and those of other German economic historians.

The polemic-political works of authors such as Luxemburg or Lenin—who also opposed particularism—only rarely contain references to the "bourgeois historiography" on which they were based. However, it seems likely that later Marxist authors were familiar with Pirenne's work. The main difference was, of course, that to Lenin or Luxemburg capitalist centralization was no more than the necessary pioneer of the Socialist society that was to come. According to Luxemburg, the Socialist movement had to be just as centralistic as the bourgeoisie and its state apparatus. She pointed out that German Social Democrats energetically fought particularism in southern Germany and Alsace, because every local autonomy was merely a cover for "noble or lower-middle-class reaction."[48]

Another necessary background element for this Marxist discourse is the polemic against utopian lower-middle-class anarchism with its "autonomist" and

---

[46] Raab, *Die Fortschrittsidee*, pp. 34, 40–41, 68–72.
[47] Luxemburg, *National Question*, pp. 187–88.
[48] Luxemburg, *National Question*, pp. 190–91.

"federalist" predilections that had been going on for half a century at the time and was most consistently worked out by Mikhaïl Bakunin, with whom Marx had already fought a paper war on Pan-Slavic federalism.[49] In the late nineteenth century, however, Marx's followers apparently did not apply the concept to the history of the Low Countries. We do not find it in the essay about "the class struggle in Flanders from 1336 to 1548" published by Marx's son-in-law Paul Lafargue in the Socialist paper L'Égalité in 1882. Lafargue does, however, mention the "cooperative aristocracy" of the Flemish cities, but it is a very weak text that leaves a sloppy and badly informed impression and as such had no intellectual influence on later historians.[50]

The Marxist tradition before the 1960s had little or no impact on the mainstream discourse of professional historians except for British Marxist historians such as Maurice Dobb and Rodney Hilton who, since the end of the Second World War, have examined the transition from feudalism to capitalism. In this debate as well, and especially in the works of the historically oriented American Marxist economist Paul Sweezy, Pirenne's ideas about urban economies rather than Marx's own have been influential.[51] Therefore we can easily argue that apart from the lasting influence of the works of nineteenth-century German historians and economists themselves, the oeuvre of the greatest Belgian medievalist has proven decisive in the spread of the term *particularism* as a target for all things economically and politically progressive. I am stating the obvious when I point out how authoritative Pirenne's view on the socioeconomic development of medieval Europe has been for a long time. Pirenne's theses have often still been indiscriminately adopted abroad.[52]

A random selection of the later use of *particularism* teaches us that the word is almost invariably negatively defined, but almost never clearly. Therefore, we have to derive the meaning of this term with its fundamentally negative connotation from the concepts or historical movements that are being contrasted with it. Historians studying German history have often used the concept of particularism. For example, in 1956 Lewis W. Spitz discussed the "importance [of particularism] to the major political events of the sixteenth century." What exactly particularism was, he could not say, but he was clearly negative about "the parochial preoccupations of the German princes," who apparently were unable to see the higher state interest.[53] Nevertheless, the implicit presupposition seems to be that persons or groups like to maintain power at a certain level, once they have attained it there.

---

[49] Luxemburg, *National Question*, p. 197, where Luxemburg quotes Marx.

[50] Originally published in *L'Égalité*, January 22 and 29, 1882, recently republished and translated in Belgium: Lafargue, *Les luttes*.

[51] Hilton, *Transition*, and primarily the contribution by Sweezy, "Critique," pp. 42–43.

[52] Harreld, "Urban Particularism."

[53] Spitz, "Particularism and Peace," p. 110.

Were the German sovereigns really "parochial" or did they simply have an intelligent policy of power vis-à-vis the larger European states? To ask the question is to answer it. The nineteenth-century idea of the nation-state remains the logical antipode of particularism, especially in German historiography. Volker Sellin considers "national consciousness" and "particularism" as "two opposite positions and programs" in nineteenth-century German history.[54] A century and a half after Treitschke, he still determines the fundamental paradigm about the history of his era. Sometimes "medieval particularism" also seems to imply other archaic aspects that constitute a stumbling block for modernity, for instance noble-feudal privileges such as the economic power the nobles still had over the weakened Polish cities of the eighteenth-century[55] or how particularism also caused the failing of modernity in "backward" Poland.

Particularism has become a part of the twentieth-century historian's lexicon of concepts. That it has never been clearly defined occasions little surprise, because historians until recently rarely took the trouble to define their concepts precisely. Even today that is often a difficulty. A selection from the numerous scholarly articles containing the concept of particularism confirms this. Sometimes the term was associated with related concepts, for instance in an article of 1979 by Judith Hook, who connects particularism to Siena's "republicanism." This republicanism is linked to the defense of *libertas* in the sense of privileges and thus in a slightly more positive sense is contrasted to the "imperialism" of the House of Habsburg.[56] It is certainly not exceptional to promote particularism to a central concept by giving it a place in the title of a work without any attempt whatsoever at conceptualizing it.[57] After all, it was clear to all what was meant by it, and the exact interpretation of the concept is implicitly derived from one or more dichotomic concept pairs.

What of the social scientists? They also seem to have yielded to the siren song of particularism. Anthropologists and sociologists sometimes describe particularism as "a mentality prevailing in collectivistic societies in which the standards for the way a person should be treated depend on the group to which the person belongs." It is thus contrasted to "universalism," a practice in "individualistic" societies where everyone is treated equally, regardless of the group to which one belongs. As such, universalism is a product of modernization processes.[58] The sociologist Antonio Mutti points out that "the term 'particularism' has a poor reputation in the classical theory of modernization. It refers to social closure as

---

[54] Sellin, "Coscienza nazionale," p. 497.
[55] Stone, "End of Medieval Particularism."
[56] Hook, "Habsburg Imperialism," p. 284.
[57] See, for example, Hibben, *Gouda in Revolt.*
[58] Mungiu-Pippidi, "Deconstructing Balkan Particularism," p. 50.

well as narrow and self-interested behaviour." Particularism is associated with traditional premodern societies.[59] Again, this sort of dichotomic thinking constitutes the essence of the Liberal modernization myth. Both sociologists quoted above, who are discussing "backward" areas such as the Balkans and southern Italy respectively, fit smoothly into this modernization discourse, albeit the neo-Durkheimian variant after Robert Putnam and Francis Fukuyama.[60] As is so often the case with this kind of study, they use quantitative approaches of immeasurable discursive constructions such as "social trust" in order to suggest "alternative policies" and stimulate modernity in areas in which neither capitalism nor communism has yet succeeded.

To Belgian and Dutch historiography, the concept of particularism and the logic derived from it have remained essential. In his preface to a study dating from 1946 about the defense of municipal liberties by the Catholics in the young state of Belgium, Henri Haag pleaded for a balance between the two "powers" he distinguished in national history. An "excessive centralization" would nip the people's spirit of liberty in the bud, but "a too extreme decentralization" would endanger Belgium itself.[61] The central binary opposition that Pirenne constructed in the historical development of the Belgian nation seems surprisingly relevant today, in the light of the stronger tensions between the communities since the 2007 federal election and might be recycled in polemic writing. Nor was our history's view of the Great Netherlands unaffected by Pirenne's central discursive opposition. After all, the Flemish particularistic cities found a predictable ally in Pieter Geyl, who reproached Pirenne with always casting these cities in a "bad role" of "backwardness, small-mindedness, indifference to any general interest." The Dutch historian pointed out that in his description of the risings against Maximilian of Austria, Pirenne omitted facts that put the ruler in a bad light, but that had been cited by earlier Belgian historians such as Kervyn de Lettenhove, Gachard, and Fris. The "tribal feeling" that he appears to sense in the Flemings is an altogether entirely different matter.[62]

Another supporter of the Great Netherlands idea, the Belgian Léon van der Essen, basically agreed with Pirenne when he wrote that the Burgundians were in favor of general welfare and against individual interests, for "common law" and against "the law of exception," for "natural freedom" and against "privilege."[63] His Liberal legalism prevailed. Even in 1982 Jongkees explicitly asked whether the 1477 rising deserved the term *particularistic*. He concluded that it did, because the monarchic state developed by Charles the Bold was partly dismantled by the

---

[59] Mutti, "Particularism and the Modernization Process," p. 579.

[60] Putnam, *Making Democracy Work*; Fukuyama, *Trust*.

[61] Haag, *Les droits de la cité*, p. 5.

[62] Geyl, *Noord en Zuid*, p. 132.

[63] Van Der Essen, *De historische gebondenheid*, p. 13.

Great Privilege and replaced by a union of autonomous countries, but also because the ancient liberties and customs of the regions were reinstated and significant powers were awarded to their representative institutions.[64] Jongkees therefore associates "particularism" with decentralization and the preservation of privileges, which does not seem surprising. It is striking, however, that he seems to consider a reinforcement of the powers of the representatives of the estates vis-à-vis the central authority particularistic as well.

Contemporary Ghent historians—and the present writer has also done this and therefore wishes to point the finger at no one—also keep using the term *particularism*, usually without any definition of what it means exactly. The examples are legion and could produce a long list of references. At times it is more thoughtfully approached, and there appears to be an evolution in the use of this concept. Marc Boone, for instance, in a comparison between Flemish and Breton particularism, states that "it is clear that there is particularism and particularism," meaning that local circumstances produce different forms of the phenomenon. He sees similarities between the viewpoints of Barthélémy-Amédée Pocquet du Haut-Jussé and Henri Pirenne, in which the "French" and "Belgian" "provinces" saw their common interest, thus matching the will of the majority of the population.[65] Particularism is implicitly defined here in its most common sense of a striving for political autonomy, and Boone states that Flemish particularism was more "urban" than Breton, which fits in with Pirenne's original point of view.[66] At the same time, in this and other publications, Boone points out the change of course in Belgian historians' evaluation of urban particularism, as well as the cost of sovereign centralization on a political, military, fiscal, and commercial level, the expenses of which were to be borne by the subjects.[67]

Today's discourse about the Flemish cities' particularism is rather ambivalent: sometimes it remains "narrow," but sometimes it is pointed out that Burgundian centralization was not such a philanthropic process after all. Elsewhere Boone associates the negative term *particularism* with the much more positive *pre-republicanism*, a term coined by Heinz Schilling, again based on urban liberties (in the sense of privileges) and corporatism.[68] As we have seen earlier, Pirenne had already associated corporatism with republicanism, but without pursuing the idea.

An entire meta-discourse could also be developed about the connotative value of the concept of privileges and especially about that of a concept such as

---

[64] Jongkees, "Particularisme hors de pair?," p. 31.

[65] Boone, "D'un particularisme à l'autre, " pp. 195–96, referring to Pocquet du Haut-Jussé, *Deux féodaux.*

[66] Boone, "D'un particularisme à l'autre," pp. 197–200.

[67] Boone, "D'un particularisme à l'autre," pp. 196–97.

[68] Boone, "Droit de bourgeoisie"; Schilling, "Gab es im späten Mittelalter."

corporatism, which also has had a very specific modern reception in the most authoritarian, fascist, and "class-collaborating" sense of the word. I will resist this temptation for now. And yet it seems that the interpretation of the concept *particularism* is becoming more balanced, less ideologically loaded, and more based on readings of discourse produced by medieval people themselves. In that sense it was mostly research done by Prevenier and Blockmans about the Burgundian era, with their emphasis on the tradition of popular representation and history from the bottom up, that constituted a turning point in the triumphant story of Burgundian centralization, which from now on is considered more like a "brutal process of power acquisition."[69] The historical sociologist Charles Tilly's view on early modern state formation, inspired by Weber and Marx, has played an important role here.[70] Nevertheless, Prevenier, Blockmans, and Boone have more often than not retained the concept of particularism, the concept thus holding them captive, however much they indicate "alternatives to monarchical centralization," urban pre-republicanism, and the like.[71]

After deconstruction it is time for a possible reconstruction of particularism. The last questions I must ask are therefore the following. First, is the use of the concept of particularism in any way legitimized by the political practices and discourses of the Flemish medieval townspeople themselves? And are there different concepts grounded in social theory that can describe better their economic, political, and ideological attitudes? I can only give some preliminary answers here, in an attempt to have particularism—a concept that has completely been marginalized by almost two centuries of modernization thinking— removed from obloquy and reconceptualized. A first conclusion is that *particularism* or related words were never used in medieval political discourse in the sense that has been reconstructed by later historians. There are only the philosophical and judicial derivations of the adjective *particularis* that I have pointed out.

In medieval theology particularism was already opposed to universalism, evidently in imitation of the Latin terminology into which Aristotelian terminology had been converted.[72] In this logic there were both the oppositions *universale— particulare* and *universale—individuale vel singulare*.[73] Even today German historians use the pair of philosophical concepts *Universalismus* and *Partikularismus*, for instance in their analysis of early Enlightenment thinking in the German states.[74]

---

[69] Marc Boone already proposed this in a postacademic college for teachers of history on November 22, 1989 (published in the form of a syllabus by what was then the Seminarie Vakdidactiek Geschiedenis).

[70] Tilly, *Formation of National States.*

[71] Blockmans, "Alternatives," and Boone and Prak, "Rulers, Patricians and Burghers."

[72] Wilpert, *Universalismus.*

[73] Auer, "Heilsuniversalismus," p. 1.

[74] Fink, "Universalismus."

A connection with the modern ideological use of the concept of particularism seems far off, except in the sense that nineteenth-century German historians were naturally also influenced by Hegel's triad of the Universal, the Particular, and the Individual.

It is also evident that many learned theological-political discussions in the Middle Ages concerned the so-called universal claims of power, especially when they involved papal or imperial authority. Much has been written about this "universalism" as a theoretical-philosophical tendency and its political implications,[75] and there is little need to expand on this already well known debate. Only the concept *universalis* in itself is important here. In the medieval period the term *universalis* was directly linked with the church. There supposedly was a tension between the universal church and the "ethnic particularism" of much medieval historiography. The latter term is in fact a historiographical reconstruction and does not seem to have been found in any of the sources.[76] Dante discerned political universalism in the Holy Roman Empire, but there is nothing in his discourse resembling "particularism."[77]

As has already been concluded in the *Grundbegriffe*, the opposite is in fact the case for the dichotomy *ius commune—ius particulare*, and it seems likely that the late eighteenth- or early nineteenth-century neologism "particularism" has its origins in this judicial concept. As stated in every legal-historical reference book, Roman law played an important role in the centralization of jurisdiction in late medieval and early modern states. The *ius commune* was not invoked until the *ius particulare* (also *lex specialis*), such as local privileges or the existing local common law, had failed or could not be invoked. Thus in the early modern German Empire we have *Partikularrecht*.[78] In the source material this concept was not found in German; even in an eighteenth-century judicial lexicon *ius particularia* (*sic*, a mistake for *iura particularia?*) was found as a collective term for different country and city rights, local customs and ordinances.[79]

In that sense, the concept *particularism* can be defended from a legal historical viewpoint, if it means lower courts holding on to their own liberties and common law and resisting interference by sovereign courts through an appeal or other forms of judicial redress, evocation, and the like. Concepts such as centralization and particularism in legal and institutional history are as carelessly used in historiography, but this is less problematic than the extension of these concepts to broader levels of society. In my opinion we are right to call this (judicial)

[75] Recently Tabacco and Arasse, *Universalismes*.
[76] Tugène, "Réflexions sur le particularisme," p. 138.
[77] Cheneval, "Quelques remarquest."
[78] Köbler, *Lexikon*, pp. 427–28.
[79] Oestmann, *Rechtsvielfalt vor Gericht*, pp. 119–20.

particularism.[80] In that sense contemporary judicial terminology legitimizes an expression such as "the particularism of the Flemish cities" when it concerned the tenacious defense of the judicial privileges of subordinate courts against the Burgundian centralization of the legal system[81] and the endless conflicts about powers.[82] These phenomena were characteristic of late medieval courts of law, but equally between cities themselves, between cities and cathedral chapters, between urban courts of law and courts in the countryside, and between religious and secular courts. Blockmans, however, also connects this Flemish judicial particularism to "a deeply rooted consciousness of identity."[83] There is conceptual vagueness here, although all authors seem to agree that the localist, regional, or corporative solidarity of the late Middle Ages formed a kind of collective identity that was much stronger than any sort of identification on a greater state level.

What about the political discourse that the Flemish cities produced for themselves? Research into this issue is still in its infancy.[84] In the contemporary political discourse of late medieval Flanders there is no explicit opposition between "centralization" and "particularism" or equivalent terms. Even the conceptual opposition that is the most closely connected to this dichotomy—the classic contradiction between the "common good" and its linguistic analogues and "singulier prouffit" (individual advantage)—does not seem to have been used in the context of a possibly perceived political conflict between the sovereign and the cities. This "singulier prouffit," as the corpus of ordnances by Philip the Good teaches us, is only invoked when it concerns individuals or groups of individuals, a local corporative group at most.[85]

Individual interest, as opposed to the common good, does have its place in judgments about individuals who act against the corporative spirit or specific trades that jeopardize the "common good" of a city. Apart from certain authors such as Marsilius of Padua, a vast majority of medieval thinkers subscribed to an entirely harmonious view of the social and political order:[86] in the case of the Low Countries, the stereotypical organic concept of the political body, with the duke of Burgundy as its head and the Four Members of Flanders, the representative assembly of the county, as its limbs.

---

[80] Cauchies, "Centralisation judiciaire."

[81] Boone, "De souverein baljuw."

[82] Lambrecht, "Centralisatie onder de Bourgondiërs."

[83] Blockmans, "Stadt, Region," p. 219.

[84] Dumolyn, "Privileges and Novelties"; and Dumolyn and Lecuppre-Desjardin, "Le bien commun."

[85] As is evinced by a statistical sample taken by Jonas Braekevelt (University of Gent), with our gratitude for this friendly gesture. A shared publication concerning the political discourse in these ordinances is in preparation.

[86] Black, "Harmony and Strife."

In all classic formulations of the medieval political order, as by John of Salisbury or Thomas Aquinas, this harmonious thinking is only disturbed by the unlawful prince, especially in the theory about the tyrant.[87] Feudal law, on the other hand, permits the *diffiducatio* or *ius resistendi* when there is a breach of the reciprocal contract stipulating the rights and duties of the liege lord and his liege subject. Objections by the Four Members of Flanders are formulated as charges against "novelties" (*nieuwicheden, novitates*), infringements of privileges and therefore as disturbances of the sociopolitical order, the justice safeguarded by God. A general impression of the dominant political discourse in the Flemish urban context shows, as is true of other parts of Europe, an emphasis on unity and cooperation, the spirit of the *commune, corpus, universitas, coniuratio,* or *institutio pacis.* A justification for centralization by the sovereign could possibly be found in the *reformacion* of the "bad customs" that proved to be "unreasonable," but here too we do not find a strong absolutist program.[88] The "urban" or "local" ideology, which was also held in rural districts in the county of Flanders, was corporative and harmonizing and emphasized a stable economic climate for which the sovereign was partly responsible. Boone and Prevenier have pointed out a quotation from the anonymous chronicler of the Ghent rising against Charles V who stated that Ghent tried to become "an independent town governed solely by its own laws, not subject to any prince or lord,"[89] but this is clearly only an accusation from the circles of the repression rather than a discourse that would have been produced by the people of Ghent themselves. The so-called political particularism as it has been constructed by twentieth-century medievalists, however, mostly fits in with a modernist ideology. That does not mean that we are taking up a fundamentally revisionist point of view here. I certainly do not intend to deny the many, often extremely sharp political and economic, fiscal, and financial conflicts between urban groups and the Burgundian sovereigns, for mainstream historiography about this era brings us all kinds of proof of that.

Thus within a broad historiographical and sociological discourse, particularism has been functioning for more than a century and a half as a marginalized opposite of everything that can be considered "progress" on a socioeconomic and political level, a barrier to the inevitable teleological progress of peoples. It remains a legitimate question, however, whether the concept of particularism with all its modernist connotations, is unsuitable for describing a certain medieval sociopolitical reality after all. This issue brings us back to the standard works

---

[87] See, among others, Nederman, "Duty to Kill."

[88] In the political thinking of Charles the Bold and his environment, there was a tendency toward this. However, see Blockmans, "Crisme de lèze majesté."

[89] "Une ville de commune et non subjecte à nul prince ne seigneur": Gachard, Relations *des Troubles,* p. 26; Boone and Prevenier, "De stadstaat-droom."

on political theory in the Middle Ages. Otto von Gierke, the founder of the modern study of medieval political thought with his *Deutsche Genossenschaftsrecht*, saw the *Genossenchaft*, or community, as a counterbalance to government and state (*Obrigkeit*). In Gierke's view, the *Genossenschaft* was a community of brotherhood, collectivism, and equality. He defended local autonomy and the freedom of association.[90]

Alongside the modernization thinking that dominates historiography and the social sciences, another intellectual tradition has remained, represented by authors such as the ethnologist Robert Redfield or the sociologist Robert Nisbet who, in line with Gierke and the German sociologist Ferdinand Tönnies, valorized the small communities against the centralizing violence of political-economic modernity.[91] It is pointless to distance oneself from one ideological reading of history as an inevitable progression toward rationality, enlightenment, bureaucratization, a free market, and state formation, and then go to the other extreme and idealize romantically the traditional "small communities," because interpersonal ties are supposedly stronger there, social networks are closer, and the total amount of "social capital" is therefore greater. That is only a reformulation of Tönnies's perspective, in which the "unity of will" of the *Gemeinschaft* strengthens internal cohesion by shared kinship networks, locations, and value systems. In this kind of harmonizing viewpoints, the numerous internal social and other oppositions within the idealized *communitas* are pushed into the background. That way we make no progress beyond the discussion between Marx and Proudhon or other utopian Socialists in the mid-nineteenth century. In my opinion, our attention should shift to systematic research into the discourse, practice, and solidarities within the medieval urban and other local communities.

By way of conclusion, I will indicate a few possible research perspectives that have been developed in recent years. A first approach is that of Peter Blickle and his strongly coherent oeuvre in relation to "communalism." According to Blickle, during the late Middle Ages a so-called *Kommunalisierungsprozeß* developed in Switzerland and other regions, whereby the local *Gemeinden*, urban or rural, were the main frameworks of social organization next to and separate from feudal power structures. They were characterized by "value systems" that highlighted concepts like peace, common interest, and judicial equality. These local communities supposedly had a crucial influence on the development of the modern state, rather than that they should be considered its opposite. However, this has not led to the development of a coherent political theory because communalism,

[90] Simon, *Germany in the Age of Bismarck*, p. 45.

[91] Tönnies, *Gemeinschaft und Gesellschaft*; Nisbet, *Quest for Community*; Redfield, *Little Community*.

as opposed to feudalism, absolutism, or capitalism, has never produced a dominant discourse since it was not a dominant social form.[92] Parallel to the communalist approach and in line with Gierke, one could also consider the medieval political communities in their "corporative" individuality as privileged communities since the communal movement of the eleventh and twelfth centuries. A specialist in the field of the communal revolution in northern France such as Alain Saint-Denis unsurprisingly associates the concept *urban identity* with the statutes and privileges shared by the citizens and their sworn association.[93] This socio-juridical viewpoint remains fundamental in the study of medieval communities, but new perspectives are also possible.

In a recent article the American specialist in late medieval urban history Martha Howell mainly emphasized the imagery and language by means of which cities exteriorized their identities, be it in visual arts, seals, by means of political theories based on urban privileges, or through ritual performances such as joyous entries or festivities. All these representations of urban identity had to be situated within a clear spatial framework.[94] Urban space was represented within a framework of privileged limits and clearly separate from the countryside, similar to the way in which they were *de facto* and *de iure* surrounded by city walls and had severe limitations on access to citizenship.[95]

Her approach fits in with the sociological study of the "communities of place" and with the fundamental work of the Norwegian anthropologist Fredrik Barth, who conducted research into the importance of "boundaries" in the social processes of inclusion, exclusion, and incorporation in ethnic communities.[96] In this socio-spatial sense the concept of particularism is therefore justifiable as well, and in this aspect Howell explicitly shares both Gierke's opinions and those of his contemporary Marx who considered a city as the locus of the production of goods and therefore as the antithesis of the feudal countryside. Weber and Pirenne, on the other hand, emphasized the medieval city's political and market autonomy, respectively.[97] Howell therefore considers the struggle between the state and the cities as a struggle for space, and this view is probably the most fertile one for further research that makes use of the most recent developments in social theory.

[92] Blickle, "Kommunalismus," p. 27. Blickle has empirically and theoretically supported his concept of communalism in many other contributions. The notion that there is no fundamental difference between communities in the city or in the countryside can also be found in Reynolds, *Kingdoms and Communities*.

[93] Saint-Denis, "L'apparition," p. 65.

[94] Howell, "Spaces," p. 3. This of course refers to Lefebvre, *La production de l'espace*.

[95] Howell, "Spaces," p. 5; compare Boone, "Droit de bourgeoisie."

[96] Barth, *Ethnic Groups*, pp. 9–10.

[97] Howell, "Spaces," p. 7, and Arnade, Howell, and Simons, "Fertile Spaces."

That there was political, judicial, and economic conflict between the late medieval Flemish cities and the Burgundian dukes is beyond dispute. That corporative solidarities, forms of urban political codetermination, spatial boundaries, and community-forming rituals and ceremonies[98] have established forms of urban identities in a dynamic way is equally clear. The question in what way these city-dwellers constructed those identities discursively and by means of other sign systems remains largely to be answered. Permanently situating this ideological production within an artificial opposition between "centralization" and "particularism" will, however, inevitably limit its scope of meaning. Medievalists therefore should reconstruct Flemish urban ideology with an open mind, and once and for all throw overboard the excess baggage of nineteenth-century progressive thinking.

Bibliography

Arnade, Peter, Martha Howell, and Walter Simons. "Fertile Spaces: The Productivity of Urban Space in Northern Europe." *Journal of Interdisciplinary History* 32 (2002): 515–48.

Auer, Johann. "Heilsuniversalismus und Praedestinationspartikularismus im Mittelalter." In *Universalismus und Partikularismus*, ed. Wilpert, pp. 1–19.

Barth, Fredrik, ed. *Ethnic Groups and Boundaries: The Social Organization of Culture Difference*. Bergen: Universitetsforlaget, 1970.

Billen, Claire. "L'économie dans les anciens Pays-Bas du XIIe au XVIe siècles: Conceptions pirenniennes et voies de recherches actuelles." In *La fortune historiographiques des thèses de Henri Pirenne*, ed. Raymond van Uytven and Adriaan E. Verhulst, pp. 61–86. Brussels: Archives et bibliothèques de Belgique, 1986.

Black, Anthony. "Harmony and Strife in Political Thought c. 1300–1500." In *Sozialer Wandel im Mittelalter: Wahrnehmungsformen, Erklärungsmuster, Regelungsmechanismen*, ed. Jürgen Miethke and Klaus Schreiner, pp. 355–64. Sigmaringen: Jan Thorbecke, 1994.

Blickle, Peter. "Kommunalismus: Begriffsbildung in heuristischer Absicht." In *Landgemeinde und Stadtgemeinde in Mitteleuropa: Ein struktureller Vergleich*, ed. Peter Blickle, pp. 5–38. Munich: Oldenburg, 1991.

Blockmans, Wim P. "Alternatives to Monarchial Centralisation: The Great Tradition of Revolt in Flanders and Brabant." In *Republiken und Republikanismus*, ed. Koenigsberger, pp. 145–54.

———. "Crisme de lèze majesté: Les idées politiques de Charles le Téméraire." In *Les Pays-Bas bourguignons, histoire et institutions: Mélanges André Uyttebrouck*, ed. Jean.-Marie Duvosquel et al., pp. 71–81. Brussels: Archives et bibliohèque de Belgique, 1996.

———. *De volksvertegenwoordiging in het graafschap Vlaanderen in de overgang van middeleeuwen naar nieuwe tijden*. Brussels: Paleis der Academiën, 1978.

———. "Stadt, Region und Staat: Ein Dreiecksverhältnis—Der Kasus der Niederlände im 15. Jahrhundert." In *Europa 1500: Integrationsprozesse im Widerstreit: Staaten, Regionen, Personenverbände, Christenheit*, ed. Ferdinand Seibt and Winfried Eberhard, pp. 211–26. Stuttgart: Klett-Cotta, 1987.

---

[98] See Lecuppre-Desjardin, *La ville des cérémonies*.

Boone, Marc. "De souverein baljuw van Vlaanderen: Breekijzer in het conflict tussen ste-
delijk particularisme en Bourgondische centralisatie." *Handelingen van het Genootschap
voor Geschiedenis* 126 (1989): 57–78.

———. "Droit de bourgeoisie et particularisme urbain dans la Flandre bourguignonne et
habsbourgeoise (1384–1585)." *Revue belge de philologie et d'histoire* 74 (1996): 707–26.

———. "D'un particularisme à l'autre: La Flandre et la Bretagne face à l'État centralisateur
(XIVᵉ–XVᵉ siècle)." In *La Bretagne, terre d'Europe*, ed. Jean Kervey and Daniel Tanguy,
pp. 192–204. Brest: Centre de recherche bretonne et celtique, 1992.

Boone, Marc, and Walter Prevenier. "De stadstaat-droom (veertiende en vijftiende eeuw)."
In *Gent: Apologie van een rebelse stad*, ed. Johan Decavele, pp. 81–105. Antwerp: Mercatorfonds, 1989.

Boone, Marc, and Maarten Prak. "Rulers, Patricians and Burghers: The Great and Little
Traditons of Urban Revolt in the Low Countries." In *A Miracle Mirrored: The Dutch
Republic in European Perspective*, ed. Karel Davids and Jan Lucassen, pp. 99–134. Cam-
bridge: Cambridge University Press, 1995.

Butterfield, Herbert. *The Whig Interpretation of History*. London: G. Bell and Sons, 1931.

Cantor, Norman F. *Inventing the Middle Ages*. New York: W. Morrow, 1991.

Carlier, Philippe. "Contribution à l'étude de l'unification bourguignonne dans l'historiographie nationale belge de 1830 à 1914." *Belgisch Tijdschrift voor Nieuwste Geschiedenis*
16 (1985): 1–24.

Cauchies, Jean-Marie. "Centralisation judiciaire et particularismes: les procédures de
recours en Hainaut au début des temps modernes." In *Hommages à la Wallonie.
Mélanges offerts à Maurice A. Arnould et Pierre Ruelle*, ed. Hervé Hasquin, pp. 45–64.
Brussels: Université libre de Bruxelles, 1981.

Cheneval, Francis. "Quelques remarques sur l'universalisme politique de Dante et de Kant."
Freiburger Zeitschrift für Philosophie und Theologie 42 (1995): 291–309.

Chuquet, Arthur. *La jeunesse de Napoléon*. Paris: A. Colin, 1899.

Culler, Jonathan. *On Deconstruction: Theory and Criticism after Structuralism*. London: Routledge & Kegal Paul, 1983.

Davis, Henry W. *The Political Thought of Heinrich von Treitschke*. London: C. Constable,
1914.

Derrida, Jacques. *De la grammatologie*. Paris: Éditions de Minuit, 1967.

De Vorepierre, Berter Dupiney. *Dictionnaire français illustré et encyclopédie universelle*. Paris:
Levy, 1876.

Diderot, Denis, and Jean le Rond d'Alembert. *Encyclopédie ou dictionnaire raisonné des sciences, des arts et des métiers par une société de gens de lettres*. Bern: Société typographique,
1780.

Dhondt, Jan. "Henri Pirenne, historien des institutions urbaines." In Jan Dhondt, *Machten
en Mensen*, pp. 63–121. Ghent: Jan Dhondt Stichting v.z.w, 1976.

Duclos, Charles P. *Mémoires secrets sur les règnes de Louis XIV et de Louis XV*. Paris: Buisson,
1791.

Fink, Gonthier-Louis. "Universalismus und Partikularismus in der deutschen Fru-
haufklärung." *Aufklärung* 10 (1998): 9–27.

Dumolyn, Jan. "Privileges and Novelties: The Political Discourse of the Flemish Cities
and Rural Districts in Their Negotiations with the Dukes of Burgundy (1384–1506)."
Urban History 35 (2008): 5–23.

Dumolyn, J., and Elodié Lecuppre-Desjardin. "Le bien commun en Flandré médiévale: La lutte discursive entre prince et sujets." In *De Bono Communi: The Discourse and Practice of the Common Good in the European City*, ed. E. Lecuppre-Desjardin and Anne-Laure Van Bruaene, pp. 253–66. Studies in European Urban History (1100–1800) 22. Turnhout: Brepols, 2010.

Fukuyama, Francis. *Trust*. New York: Free Press, 1995.

Gachard, Louis-Prosper, ed. *Relation des Troubles de Gand sous Charles-Quint*. Brussels: M. Hayez, 1846.

Ganshof, François-Louis. "Henri Pirenne and Economic History." *Economic History Review* 6 (1936): 179–85.

Geyl, Pieter. *Geschiedenis van de Nederlandse stam*. 6 vols. Amsterdam: Wereldbibliotheek, 1930–62.

————. *Noord en Zuid: Eenheid en tweeheid in de Lage Landen*. Utrecht-Antwerp: Het Spectrum, 1960.

Haag, Henri. *Les droits de la cité: Les catholiques-démocrates et la défense de nos franchises communales*. Brussels: Éditions universitaires, 1946.

Haemers, Jelle. "De dominante staat: De Gentse opstand (1449–1453) in de negentiende- en twintigste-eeuwse historiografie." *Bijdragen en Mededelingen betreffende de Geschiedenis der Nederlanden* 119 (2004): 39–62.

Harreld, Donald J. "Urban Particularism and State Centralization in the Revolt of Ghent, 1538–1540." *Proteus* 20 (2003): 39–44.

Hibben, Christopher C. *Gouda in Revolt: Particularism and Pacifism in the Revolt of the Netherlands, 1572–1588*. Utrecht: HES, 1983.

Hilton, Rodney, ed. *The Transition from Feudalism to Capitalism*. London: Verso, 1980.

Hook, Judith. "Habsburg Imperialism and Italian Particularism: The Case of Charles V and Siena." *European Studies Review* 9 (1979): 293–312.

Howell, Martha C. "The Spaces of Late Medieval Urbanity." In *Shaping Urban Identity in Late Medieval Europe*, ed. Marc Boone and Peter Stabel, pp. 65–87. Leuven: Garant, 2000.

Jongkees, Adriaan G. "Particularisme hors de pair? À propos de la genèse du Grand Privilège hollandais du 14 mars 1477." *Publications du Centre européen d'études Burgondo-Médianes* 22 (1982): 29–38.

Köbler, Gerhard. *Lexikon der europäischen Rechtsgeschichte*. Munich: C. H. Beck, 1997.

Koenigsberger, Helmut, ed. *Republiken und Republikanismus im Europa des frühen Neuzeit*. Munich: R. Oldenbourg, 1988.

Lafargue, Paul. *Les luttes de classes en Flandre, de 1336–1348 et de 1379–1385: De Klassenstrijd in Vlaanderen van 1336–1348 en van 1379–1385*. Brussels: Aden, 2003.

Lambrecht, Daniël. "Centralisatie onder de Bourgondiërs: Van Audiëntie naar Parlement van Mechelen." *Bijdragen voor de Geschiedenis der Nederlanden* 20 (1965–66): 83–109.

Lamprecht, Karl. *Deutsche Geschichte*. Berlin: Gärtner, 1906.

Lecuppre-Desjardin, Elodie. *La ville des cérémonies: Essai sur la communication politique dans les anciens Pays-Bas bourguignons*. Studies in European Urban History (1100–1800) 4. Turnhout: Brepols, 2004.

Lefebvre, Henri. *La production de l'espace*. Paris: Éditions Anthropos, 1974.

Luxemburg, Rosa. *The National Question: Selected Writings*. Ed. and intro. Horace B. Davis. New York: Monthly Review Press, 1976.

Littré, Émile Maximilien Paul. *Dictionnaire de la langue française*. 4 vols. Paris: Hachette, 1863–72.

Lyon, Bryce, ed. "The Letters of Henri Pirenne to Karl Lamprecht." *Bulletin de la Commission royale d'histoire* 132 (1966): 161–231.

Marx, Karl, and Friedrich Engels. *Adresse du Comité central à la ligue des communistes.* Pamphlet, 1850. http://www.marxists.org/francais/marx/works/1850/03/18500300.htm.

———. *Oeuvres choisis.* Moscow: Progress, 1976.

———. *Werke.* Berlin: Dietz, 1956–90.

Mijnhardt, Wijnand W. "The Dutch Republic as a Town." *Eighteenth-Century Studies* 31 (1998): 235–45.

Mungiu-Pippidi, Alina. "Deconstructing Balkan Particularism: The Ambiguous Social Capital of Southeastern Europe." *Southeast European and Black Sea Studies* 5 (2005): 49–68.

Mutti, Antonio. "Particularism and the Modernization Process in Southern Italy." *International Sociology* 15 (2000): 579–90.

Nederman, Cary J. "A Duty to Kill: John of Salisbury's Theory of Tyrannicide." *Review of Politics* 50 (1988): 365–89.

Nisbet, Robert A. *The Quest for Community: A Study in the Ethics of Order and Freedom.* New York: Oxford University Press, 1953.

Oestmann, Peter. *Rechtsvielfalt vor Gericht. Rechtsanwendung und Partikularrecht im Alten Reich.* Frankfurt a.M.: Klostermann, 2002.

Pirenne, Henri. *Les anciennes démocraties des Pays-Bas.* Paris: E. Flammarion, 1910.

———. *La Belgique et la guerre mondiale.* Paris: Presses universitaires de France, 1928.

———. *Histoire de Belgique.* 7 vols. Brussels: H. Lamertin, 1899–1932.

———. *Histoire de l'Europe: Des invasions au XVIe siècle.* Paris: F. Alcan, 1936.

———. *Les périodes de l'histoire sociale du capitalisme.* Brussels: Hayez, 1914.

———. *Les villes et les institutions urbaines.* Paris: Nouvelle société d'éditions, 1939.

Pocquet du Haut-Jussé, Barthélémy-Amédée. *Deux féodaux: Bourgogne et Bretagne (1363–1491).* Paris: Boivin, 1935.

Powicke, Frederick M. *Modern Historians and the Study of History.* London: Odhams, 1955.

Prevenier, Walter. "Henri Pirenne et les villes des anciens Pays-Bas au bas Moyen Âge (XIVe–XVe siècles)." In *La fortune historiographiques des thèses de Henri Pirenne*, ed. Raymond van Uytven and Adriaan E. Verhulst, pp. 27–50. Brussels: Archives et bibliothèques de Belgique, 1986.

Price, J. L. *Holland and the Dutch Republic in the Seventeenth Century: The Politics of Particularism.* Oxford: Clarendon Press, 1994.

Putnam, Robert. *Making Democracy Work.* Princeton, NJ: Princeton University Press, 1993.

Raab, Franz. *Die Fortschrittsidee bei Gustav von Schmoller.* Freiburg: T. Kehrer, 1934.

Redfield, Robert. *The Little Community: Viewpoints for the Study of a Human Whole.* Chicago: University of Chicago Press, 1956.

Reynolds, Susan. *Kingdoms and Communities in Western Europe, 900–1300.* Oxford: Clarendon Press, 1984.

Royle, Nicholas. "What Is Deconstruction?" In *Deconstruction: A User's Guide*, ed. Nicholas Royle, pp. 1–13. Houndmills: Palgrave, 2000.

Saint-Denis, Alain. "L'apparition d'une identité urbaine dans les villes de commune de France du Nord aux XIIe et XIIIe siècles." In *Shaping Urban Identity in Late Medieval Europe*, ed. Marc Boone and Peter Stabel, pp. 65–87. Leuven: Garant, 2000.

Schilling, Heinz. "Gab es im späten Mittelalter und zu Beginn der Neuzeit in Deutschland einen städtischen 'Republikanismus'? Zur politischen Kultur des alteuropäischen Stadtbürgertums." In *Republiken und Republikanismus*, ed. Koenigsberger, pp. 101–44.

Schmoller, Gustav von. *Grundriss der allgemeinen Volkswirtschaftslehre*. Munich: Duncker & Humblot, 1923.

———. *Strassburg zur Zeit der Zunftkämpfe und die Reform seiner Verfassung und Verwaltung im XV. Jahrhundert*. Strasbourg: Trübner, 1875.

———. *Die Strassburger Tücher- unde Weberzunft und das Deutsche Zunftwesen vom XIII.–XVII. Jahrhundert*. Strasbourg: Trübner, 1881.

———. *Über einige Grundfragen des Rechts und der Volkswirthschaft: Ein offenes Sendschreiben an Herrn Professor Dr. Heinrich von Treitschke*. Jena: F. Mauke, 1875.

Schöttler, Peter. "Henri Pirenne face à l'Allemagne de l'après-guerre ou la (re)naissance du comparatisme en histoire." In *Une guerre totale? La Belgique dans la Première Guerre mondiale: Nouvelles tendances de la recherche historique*, ed. Serge Jaumain et al., pp. 507–17. Brussels: Archives générales du royaume, 2005.

Sellin, Volker. "Coscienza nazionale e particolarismo nella Germania del XIX secolo." *Rivista storica italiana* 113/2 (2001): 497–518.

Simon, Walter M. *Germany in the Age of Bismarck*. London: George Allen and Unwin, 1968.

Sombart, Werner. *Der moderne Kapitalismus*. Munich: Duncker & Humblot, 1928.

Spitz, Lewis W. "Particularism and Peace: Augsburg, 1555." *Church History* 25 (1956): 110–26.

Stone, Daniel. "The End of Medieval Particularism: Polish Cities and the Diet, 1764–89." *Canadian Slavonic Papers* 20 (1978): 194–207.

Stoyle, Mark. "English 'Nationalism,' Celtic Particularism, and the English Civil War." *Historical Journal* 43, no. 4 (2000): 110–26.

Tabacco, Giorgio, and Daniel Arasse. *Universalismes et idéologies politiques: De l'Antiquité tardive à la Renaissance*. Paris: G. Monfort, 2001.

Thierry, Augustin. *Recueil des monuments inédits de l'histoire du Tiers état: Première série; chartes, coutumes, actes municipaux, statuts de corporations d'arts et métiers des villes et communes de France, région du Nord*. Paris: Firmin-Didot, 1850.

Tilly, Charles, ed. *The Formation of National States in Western Europe*. Princeton, NJ: Princeton University Press, 1975.

Tollebeek, Jo. "Enthousiasme en evidentie: De negentiende-eeuwse Belgisch-nationale geschiedschrijving." In *De IJkmeesters: Opstellen over de geschiedschrijving in Nederland en België*, ed. Jo Tollebeek, pp. 57–74. Amsterdam: B. Bakker, 1994.

———. "Historical Representation and the Nation-State in Romantic Belgium (1830–1850)." *Journal of the History of Ideas* 59 (1998): 329–53.

Tönnies, Ferdinand. *Gemeinschaft und Gesellschaft: Grundbegriffe der reinen Soziologie*. Darmstadt: Wissenschaftliche Buchgesellschaft, 1963.

Treitschke, Heinrich von. *Bundesstaat und Einheitsstaat*. In Heinrich von Treitschke, *Historische und politische Aufsätze vornehmlich zur neuesten deutschen Geschichte*, pp. 1–32. Leipzig: S. Hirzel, 1865.

———. *Deutsche Geschichte im neunzehnten Jahrhundert*. 5 vols. Leipzig: S. Hirzel, 1914–19.

Tugène, Georges. "Réflexions sur le particularisme et l'universalisme chez Bède." *Recherches augustiniennes* 17 (1982): 129–72.

Van Der Essen, Léon. "De historische gebondenheid der Nederlanden." *Nederlandsche Historiebladen* 1 (1938): 153–89.

Veit-Brause, Imlinde. "Partikularismus." In *Geschichtliche Grundbegriffe: Historisches Lexikon zur politisch-sozialen Sprache in Deutschland*, ed. Otto Brunner, Werner Conze, and Reinhard Koselleck, 4:735–66. 8 vols. in 9. Stuttgart: E. Klett, 1972–97.

Verhulst, Adriaan. "Conclusion: L'actualité de Pirenne." In *La fortune historiographiques des thèses de Henri Pirenne*, ed. Raymond van Uytven and Adriaan E. Verhulst, pp. 149–54. Brussels: Archives et bibliothèques de Belgique, 1986.

Violante, Cinzio. *Das Ende der 'groszen Illusion': Ein europäischer Historiker im Spannungsfeld von Krieg und Nachkriegszeit, Henri Pirenne (1914–1923)—Zu einer Neulesung der "Geschichte Europas."* Berlin: Duncker & Humblot, 2004.

Wartburg, Walter von. *Französischer Etymologisches Wörterbuch: Eine Darstellung des galloromanischen Sprachschatzes*. Basel: Sbinden, 1955.

White, Dan S. "Regionalism and Particularism." In *Imperial Germany: A Historiographical Companion*, ed. Roger Chickering, pp. 131–55. Westport, CT: Greenwood, 1996.

Wilpert, Paul, ed. *Universalismus und Partikularismus im Mittelalter*. Miscellanea Mediaevalia 5. Berlin: de Gruyter, 1968.

Part 2

Constitutional and Legal History: England and the Continent

Ending English Exceptionalism:
Bryce Lyon's Legacy for Constitutional and Legal Historians

Caroline Dunn

Tʜɪs ᴀʀᴛɪᴄʟᴇ's sᴜʙᴛɪᴛʟᴇ deliberately echoes Bryce Lyon's outstanding *Constitutional and Legal History of Medieval England*, but the direction that my research has taken, and the direction presented here, is more inspired by Lyon's prolific encouragement of scholars of English institutions to look beyond insularity toward comparative analyses. Lyon's appeal for broader focus is exemplified by his career, his cross-channel connections, and his numerous articles considering England within the broader European context, but it is encapsulated in his introduction to *Medieval Finance*, coauthored by his Belgian colleague Adriaan Verhulst, in which they write that although scholars of medieval religion, art, and urban development have emphasized unity, or at least similarities, among cultures of medieval Europe, "how different has been the approach of the historian when writing on medieval institutions. Here nationalism, chauvinism, and particularism rise to impose themselves as barriers."[1]

What follows is an attempt to remove some of these nationalist barriers. First, this chapter considers Bryce Lyon's important works on late medieval English history and his influence on contemporary scholars of law and government. Recent assessments of Magna Carta and the medieval institution known as "bastard feudalism" both testify to Lyon's impact. In tribute to Lyon's emphasis on European comparisons, the article then moves beyond England's shores to explore how knowledge of Continental legal systems enhances understanding of English common law attitudes toward abduction and adultery. I do not mean to argue that England did not have some unique qualities, nor did Bryce Lyon, for some parts of his *Constitutional and Legal History* follow traditional interpretations of

---

[1] Lyon and Verhulst, *Medieval Finance*, pp. 7–8.

English exceptionalism.[2] This tradition exists for a reason: there are institutional and especially legal differences between the English situation and Continental developments, but Lyon's career demonstrates his sensitivity and openness to the possibility that similarities as well as variations existed, an approach that has informed my own research as well as studies by more recent legal historians.[3]

Medieval English Constitutional Developments: Magna Carta and Bastard Feudalism

In February 2008 British Lord Chancellor and Secretary for Justice Jack Straw spoke at George Washington University about his proposal to establish a new Bill of Rights for the United Kingdom. Straw began his speech by linking Magna Carta to both British and American constitutions, but he was quick to adopt a less venerating tone, requesting his audience to "prick the illusion, that the *Magna Carta* was precipitated by the equivalent of thirteenth century civil rights campaigners."[4] Straw did not cite the origins of his views on Magna Carta, but in tempering the extreme reverence in which the charter is held he shares the perspective of that document that Bryce Lyon helped to promote, a moderated view that is now accepted by most academics and lawyers, but which is still filtering down to the general public. Early in his career Lyon called for legal scholars to reject the premise that Magna Carta promised and delivered democratic rights,[5] but the lure of the Magna Carta myth, reinvented by Coke and other seventeenth-century Parliamentarians and championed by American founders, remains strong among tabloid news pundits and indignant citizens composing letters to editors in both the United States and United Kingdom.

Lyon's subsequent advice, proffered in that same article, was more successful. He urged academics to turn away from the bright light of Magna Carta and research the wealth of English constitutional and legal history found in what he called "pile after pile of dull sources which record the uneventful progress of man in medieval England toward democracy and the rule of law."[6] The rise of cheap transatlantic travel has realized Lyon's dream of greater international cooperation researching English institutions and law, and scholars on both sides of the

---

[2] For example, Lyon wrote that fifteenth-century English common law was "completely insular" (*Constitutional and Legal History*, p. 436).

[3] Although many of England's scholars have been reluctant to turn eastward, impressive achievements toward comparative legal history have been made by Bryce Lyon's colleague Raoul C. van Caenegem. See, for example, his book *Judges, Legislators and Professors* and his articles collected in *Legal History*.

[4] Straw, "Modernizing the Magna Carta."

[5] Lyon, "Lawyer and Magna Carta."

[6] Lyon, "Lawyer and Magna Carta," p. 433.

Atlantic, as well as European, Antipodean, and Japanese scholars, have enriched our understanding by massive archival research.[7] This collaborative endeavor toward greater knowledge will only continue with the digitization projects now underway; some fruits of this effort can be seen at Robert Palmer's magnificent website hosted by the University of Houston.[8]

Lyon's desires for collaboration, cross-border scholarly conversations, and cultural comparisons further downplayed the alleged uniqueness and significance of Magna Carta as a sacred text delineating a special Anglo-American democratic birthright. He challenged the English-speaking world's celebration of the Great Charter by delving into the Belgian records, analyzing, among other charters, the Joyeuse Entrée concessions granted by Jeanne and Wenceslas of Brabant, and concluding that "England had no monopoly on constitutional precedents."[9] Not only did the Low Countries offer a similar, albeit later, example of legal privileges, but as Lyon pointed out, modern Belgians, like Anglo-American Enlightenment thinkers, developed their own mythology surrounding the meaning and central importance of these legal rights.[10]

Comparative analysis also characterizes Lyon's earliest book, *From Fief to Indenture: The Transition from Feudal to Non-feudal Contract in Western Europe*. This and his other studies of the money fief contributed to lively debates about bastard feudalism that raged through the latter half of the twentieth century, especially during the late 1980s and 1990s. More recent scholars have tended to emphasize that there is no sharp dividing line, but instead continuity, between the system of feudalism and what has become known as bastard feudalism, and Lyon's work on *fiefs-rentes* deeply informs this scholarship.[11] Although in England the money fief in the late twelfth and early thirteenth centuries may have been used only to recruit additional Continental forces during times of military crisis, and Lyon himself disavowed fifteenth-century indenture contracts as a form of feudalism, his thorough analyses of monetary contracts have

---

[7] For the call for transatlantic cooperation, see Lyon, "From Hengist and Horsa."

[8] The Anglo-American Legal Tradition: Documents from Medieval and Early Modern England from the National Archives in London, http://aalt.law.uh.edu/.

[9] Lyon, "Fact and Fiction," p. 101.

[10] Helmholz ("Magna Carta," p. 303) criticizes Lyon for displaying English insularity in his conclusions about Magna Carta, but he cites only Lyon's *Constitutional and Legal History* and neglects Lyon's more nuanced analyses elsewhere. More recently Magna Carta has been compared to Continental counterparts by Paul Hyams (*Rancor and Reconciliation*, pp. 162–63), who documents parallels to both older Germanic principles and Roman law.

[11] For this debate see in particular the exchanges between Coss, Carpenter, and Crouch in the journal *Past and Present* (nos. 125 and 131). See also Carpenter "Second Century," and Waugh, "Tenure to Contract."

provided genuinely important starting points for more recent inquiries into the field of crown-retainer relations.[12]

Bryce Lyon demonstrated his mastery of the aforementioned "pile after pile of dull sources" in his magisterial *Constitutional and Legal History of Medieval England*. This work should be used more by current scholars of administrative and legal history. Admittedly some aspects of this book have been supplanted by more recent scholarship, but it remains the best comprehensive guide to governance and law.[13] Finally Bryce Lyon, along with his wife, Mary, made it easier for scholars to access important Wardrobe Books. One reviewer called Lyon's introductory sections of William de Norwell's Wardrobe Book "a godsend to the uninitiated, for they constitute the best up-to-date short essay . . . ever written on medieval English administrative developments to the end of the fourteenth century."[14] In recent years this valuable edition has been used by scholars studying themes as diverse as Italian bankers financing the Hundred Years' War, pay and recruitment of English soldiers serving on the Continent, and the English sheriff at work.[15]

Approaching English Laws in a Comparative Context: Abduction and Adultery

Lyon's *Constitutional and Legal History of Medieval England* has been indispensable for illustrating how English governance, laws, and legal procedures worked and facilitated my research into the ravishment (rape or abduction) of medieval Englishwomen. Yet Lyon influenced my research beyond supplying technical details such as how suspects were arrested and bailed, how juries were summoned and gave their verdicts, and how the concept of trespass developed—all specific features unique to England or at least to the Anglo-Norman legal world. Yet it became clear in the course of my research into abduction that adultery, or the

---

[12] Church ("Rewards of Royal Service," p. 280) disagreed with Lyon that *fiefs-rentes* were given for typical feudal service, but in the same article he writes that "it is difficult not to conclude with Lyon that money fiefs were used primarily to retain men from the Continent who could provide John with additional forces during times of crisis" (p. 282). On Lyon's rejection of feudalism persisting into fifteenth-century contracts see Lyon, review of *Lord Hastings' Indentured Retainers*.

[13] Lyon has been criticized by Turner, for example, for accepting Brunner's pervasive thesis regarding the Norman introduction of the jury system ("Origins," p. 36). In some respects Lyon's synthesis has been superseded in governance by the Stanford University Press Governance of England series (Loyn, *Governance of Anglo-Saxon England*; Warren, *Governance of Norman and Angevin England*; Brown, *Governance of Late Medieval England*), but these works on the whole cover political and administration better than legal developments. One recent (2004) work relying on Lyon's *Constitutional and Legal History* is Kevin Shirley's *Secular Jurisdiction*.

[14] Cuttino, review of *The Wardrobe Book*.

[15] Hunt, "Dealings of the Bardi," p. 159; Ayton, "English Army," p. 237; Gorski, *Fourteenth-Century Sheriff*, p. 71.

phenomenon of consensually kidnapped wives, looms large in ravishment laws and ravishment prosecutions. Lyon's eagerness to compare English administration with Continental institutions offered an influential approach that opened my mind to the possibilities of cross-cultural connections between English concerns about adultery and secular prosecutions for adultery on the Continent.

Although most scholars of medieval English history since Maitland's time have conceded that English ecclesiastical law and jurisdiction fitted in with the wider policies and practices of Latin Christendom, the singularity of the English common law has been held more sacrosanct.[16] While there were variances between the English church's practices and secular laws and those apparent in Continental courts, I hope to persuade others to follow Lyon's lead and turn away from the abundant riches of medieval English records, at least on occasion, and research developments occurring on the other side of the channel. Not only are comparisons fruitful for the wider field of medieval European history, but for the unyielding English medievalist they offer fresh perspective and broader understanding of changes taking place in English laws and institutions. This universal approach is certainly required to understand secular prohibitions against what was deemed to be a moral sin of adultery, which in England first appear in the second statute of Westminster (1285), promulgated by the king known as the "English Justinian," Edward I.

Stolen Wives in Medieval England

Both the abduction of and adultery by wives are addressed in the Westminster statute. Since my research focused initially on abduction, I paid far more attention to the first and third clauses of chapter 34, which prohibited and punished kidnapping, than to the second clause restricting inheritance of adulterous wives, but all three excerpts are crucial to understanding English attitudes toward sexual crime and marriage.[17] The relevant clauses state:

> And of women carried away with the goods of their husbands, the king shall have suit for the goods so taken away.[18]

> And if a wife willingly leave her husband and go away and live with her adulterer, she shall be barred forever of the action to demand her dower

---

[16] Most scholars accept, however, that Bracton's thirteenth-century commentary was influenced by Roman law, especially by Azo's *Summa Codicis* and Justinian's *Institutes*. For example, see Thorne, "Henry de Bracton," pp. 78–80.

[17] See Post, "Ravishment of Women." The text and translation provided below are largely based on the texts provided by the Record Commission editors of the *Statutes of the Realm* (Luders et al., 1:87–88), but I am grateful to Dr. Paul Brand for sharing his revisions with me.

[18] "De mulieribus abductis cum bonis viri, habeat rex sectam de bonis sic asportatis."

that she ought to have of her husband's lands if she be convicted there-upon, except that her husband willingly, and without the coercion of the church, reconcile her and suffer her to cohabit with him; in which case she shall be restored to her action.[19]

He that carrieth a nun from her house, although she consent, shall be punished by three years' imprisonment, and shall make suitable satis-faction to the house from whence she was taken, and nevertheless shall make fine at the king's will.[20]

The three clauses occur separately, with no explicit links connecting them, but the anti-adultery act was deliberately, not carelessly, sandwiched between two abduction laws. The law condemning the theft of nuns, moreover, indicates that lawmakers acknowledged that "abducted" women sometimes departed will-ingly; nevertheless, the woman's consent did not vindicate the offender. Edward I's 1285 legislation reveals the conceptual link between abduction and adultery in late medieval England, and understanding this link helps the scholar appreciate why kidnapping prosecutions were so common in the fourteenth-century court of King's Bench. Hundreds, if not thousands, of men came to court to complain, based upon the terms of this statute, that their wives had been abducted from their households, but many of these cases should be interpreted as cuckolded husbands seeking to punish adulterous wives and their lovers for consensual departures.[21]

These English lawsuits—civil actions for the trespass of wife-theft—are unique. To my knowledge no other late medieval region offered comparable leg-islation or resulting civil lawsuits prosecuting the abduction of wives. Kidnapping was seemingly a problem in France, the Low Countries, and in parts of Italy, but laws and court cases are almost entirely concerned with the theft of marriageable

---

[19] "Et uxor, si sponte reliquerit virum suum et abierit et moretur cum adultero suo, amittat imper-petuum accionem petendi dotem suam que ei competere posset de tenementis viri, si super hoc con-vincatur, nisi vir suus sponte, et absque cohercione ecclesiastica, eam reconciliet et secum cohabitari permittat; in quo casu restituatur ei accio."

[20] "Qui monialem a domo sua abducat, licet monialis consenciat puniatur per prisonam trium anno-rum, et satisfaciat domui a qua abducta fuerit competenter, et nihilominus redimatur ad voluntatem regis."

[21] My investigation found 246 cases of wife theft in the King's Bench records, but my sample was limited to four counties (Bedfordshire, Devon, London/Middlesex, and Northumberland) and five-year sample periods at the beginning, middle, and end of relevant centuries (late thirteenth through late fifteenth centuries). Although I am not the first to emphasize that many prosecutions were prob-ably voluntary departures, I have, to my knowledge, completed the first systematic *longue durée* study of the ravishment records and am the first to chronicle the rise and fall of wife-theft prosecutions. On other discussions about consensual departure, see Baker, *Introduction to English Legal History*, pp. 518–20; Kelly, "Statutes of Rapes," pp. 398–400; and Walker, "Punishing Convicted Ravishers," p. 239.

daughters, rather than married wives.[22] Yet many of the English lawsuits that ostensibly punished kidnapping in fact disguise adultery and likely were interpreted that way by the lawyers, justices, juries, and scribes who were engaged in the English prosecution process.[23] Understanding this link enables scholars to situate the apparently unique English cases within a wider, pan-European process that increasingly punished adulterous wives in secular courts.

English lawmakers and jurists alike accepted that the adulterous wife was not entitled to receive her traditional widow's inheritance.[24] Not long into the reign of Edward II, when a widow named Alice sued for her dower, the opposition lawyer argued, "Dower she ought not to have, for she eloped from her husband and abode with her adulterer in such a county without being reconciled to her husband in his lifetime."[25] One of the five manuscript versions of this case sums up the point in rhyme: "Sponte virum mulier fugiens et adultera facta / Dote sua careat nisi sponsi sponte retracta."[26] But not all women departed willingly (or were depicted as having departed willingly). Instead, many cases appear to modern scholars as abductions. We see this link in a 1307 suit involving the (unnamed) widow of the baron of Greystoke. This woman tried to keep her widow's portion by portraying her departure from her husband's household as a violent kidnapping. Her attorney drew attention to the clause of the statute that stated that the misbehaving wife's departure must be of her own free will, claiming that in this instance the abductor, Simon, "came with force and arms and saddled horses and drove us off from [Robert]." The opposing attorney, however, argued that the widow must forfeit control over the land, emphasizing that she had now married her alleged abductor, had never reconciled with Robert during his lifetime, and that even if she had been kidnapped against her will, she was not required to

---

[22] Dean, "Fathers and Daughters," pp. 88–89, 92; Dean, "Secular Marriage," forthcoming; Greilsammer, "Rapts de séduction"; Ribordy, "Two Paths to Marriage," pp. 324, 330; Ribordy, *"Faire les nopces,"* pp. 19–23.

[23] This is true even for many of the suits that allege that the abduction took place "with force and arms" (*vi et armis* was a formulaic phrase in English civil records). See Milsom, "Trespass," pp. 203, 222–23.

[24] Paul Brand, analyzing forfeiture of dower pleas pursued during the reign of Edward I, uncovered eighty-five challenges to widows' dower initiated by litigants claiming that the widows had committed adultery. See his "'Deserving' and 'Undeserving' Wives," p. 9. The rule applied in urban custom as well as common law; thus Barbara Hanawalt ("Widow's Mite," p. 33) found cases in the London Hustings Court of Common Pleas in which widows were denied dower because they had committed adultery and failed to reconcile with their husbands. For further context, see Hanawalt's *Wealth of Wives*, esp. p. 102.

[25] "Dower ne deit ele avoir, par la reson qe ele se alopa de son baroun et demorra ove son advouter en tiel countee sanz estre reconsilie en la vie son baroun" (Maitland, *Year Books*, p. 145).

[26] Maitland, *Year Books*, p. 145. Whether the scribe authored the poem while copying this legal case or was merely repeating what he had heard said at the bench is unclear.

remain with him or to marry him after she was widowed. All this circumstantial evidence was narrated in support of the plaintiff's quest to obtain the widow's dower share.[27]

Most abduction references, however, appear in documents written when the husband was still alive. Since the English law of coverture prevented a spouse from prosecuting his wife, and hence cuckolds had no means to bar dower within their own lifetimes, husbands instead found the Westminster legislation useful for prosecuting and penalizing the lover for ravishment. An abduction lawsuit also offered the opportunity to make the wife's misbehavior known to the local community and royal justices. Because the widow's marriage portion was allocated after her husband's death, challenging her inheritance became the responsibility of the husband's nearest heirs, rather than the husband himself.[28] If the widow did not immediately acknowledge that she had lost her right to dower, her husband's kin, often a son or perhaps a stepson, initiated a legal challenge in the king's courts to prevent her from receiving it. Thus, although the cuckolded husband could neither bar his wife from dower nor prosecute her, he could use the royal legislation and civil law courts to publicize her adultery and put it on record for after his death.[29] Publicizing the desertion so that after his death his widow could not claim her dower may have allowed an abandoned husband some personal satisfaction, even if the lawsuit failed to result in a positive verdict and monetary restitution. In addition to gaining revenge, therefore, the husband secured his property for his children and prevented his remarrying wife and her spouse from controlling her one-third life interest in his patrimony.[30]

When we realize that English authorities were legislating against adultery and that husbands and communities initiated cases that were often prosecuting extramarital affairs rather than violent abduction, certain parallels between

---

[27] The case then went to a jury, and the report concludes without a recorded judgment. See Horwood, *Year Books*, 5:532–35. Brand also includes this case in his sample of dower forfeiture suits.

[28] The widow at common law was entitled to one-third of her husband's properties and to remain in the home (free bench) for forty days. Borough and manor customs sometimes differed from common law entitlements. Hence Londoners allowed a widow free bench for the rest of her life or until she remarried. See Barron, "Introduction," p. xvii.

[29] Once the law prohibiting wife theft was introduced into the common law corpus of trespass litigation, it became widely popular among abandoned husbands. Between 1287 and 1292 seven wives from my sampled counties were (allegedly) stolen, but in the following five-year sample period (1312–17) the number rose to twenty-nine civil pleas of ravishment. Despite the statute's assertion of the king's suit, lawsuits were most often brought as civil actions by aggrieved husbands, and moreover the king does not seem to have sued for the value of the goods taken. See Post, "Ravishment of Women," pp. 159–60.

[30] As Donahue argues (*Law, Marriage*, pp. 260, 379–80, 443, 558, 631), the type of case that a court appears to be prosecuting sometimes disguises another type of case entirely.

English and Continental developments become apparent. Both English kings and Italian cities, for example, introduced legislation that barred adulterous wives from receiving their traditional marriage portions (dower in England, dowry in Italy). In neither region were the statutes wholly original, for instead they borrowed from precedents found in Justinian's *Corpus iuris civilis*.[31] Prosecutions for wife theft in England are thus part of a broader European concern regulating female adultery and familial inheritance. In the following section I compare the situation in England with contemporary Continental legal systems that also borrowed from Roman legal ideas to regulate female adultery in both the secular ecclesiastical spheres of law.

Roman Legal Traditions

Roman law stipulated loss of property as one potential penalty for the convicted adulteress, who could also be killed by her husband, her father, or the state (depending on the era) with impunity.[32] Justinian's Novels, based on the precept of St. Paul, introduced the principle that an adulteress might be forgiven and reconciled to her husband. Justinian prescribed that the convicted adulteress should be placed in a monastery, but her husband could reclaim her within two years. If he did not, the offending wife was required to remain in the monastery, and her property would be divided among her children (if any) and the convent.[33]

Laws of the late Roman Empire deemed adultery to be a sexual sin but also a secular crime. Thus the rediscovery of the *Corpus iuris civilis* provided a framework for thirteenth-century secular authorities desiring to assert that a wife's sexual misbehavior fell under the purview of royal and municipal courts as well as under ecclesiastical jurisdiction. The principle of property forfeiture had made its way into English law by the late twelfth century, when the author of *Glanvill* asserted that "if a man's wife is separated from him during his lifetime because of some 'shameful act,' she cannot have any claim to dower."[34]

---

[31] The argument made here relies on original sources (statutes and court cases) for England, but upon secondary literature for developments elsewhere.

[32] Arjava, *Women and Law*, pp. 69, 193–200.

[33] Scott, *Civil Law*, 17:143–44, Novel 134.10 (556 CE); Reynolds, *Marriage*, p. 60. St. Paul writes in the First Epistle to the Corinthians that a departing woman should be reconciled to her husband (7:10–11).

[34] See Hall, *Treatise on the Laws and Customs*, p. 68. *Glanvill*'s term *turpitudinem*, which Hall translates as "a shameful act," does not necessarily refer to adultery, but that is the most likely interpretation. This evidence thus echoes Helmholz's arguments that English common law must not be viewed in a vacuum separated from canon and civil law traditions at work in Continental Europe. See Helmholz, "Roman Law," p. 245; Helmholz, *"Ius commune" in England*, pp. 3–15. See also Seipp, "Reception of Canon Law."

The origins of the 1285 legislation remain obscure but may relate to the presence of the Bolognese jurist Francis Accursius, son of the famous glossator, at the court of Edward I.[35] It is, however, no mere inference to argue that the English law requiring the fiscal punishment of the adulterous wife parallels developments also occurring in Continental Europe, where secular authorities added civil penalties for the offense of female adultery to earlier ecclesiastical penalties for the same offense.

Dowry Forfeiture in Italy

From at least the thirteenth century, Italian cities began to enact legislation against adultery and to prosecute the offense in their civil courts.[36] In particular the cities of Orvieto and Venice promulgated new statutes that reintroduced the principle of Roman law that granted the aggrieved husband the right to keep a misbehaving wife's dowry. Carol Lansing describes how authorities in Orvieto began to bring the offense of adultery into the secular courts during the late thirteenth century by prescribing a standard fine of two hundred libra for all convicted sexual offenses. She surmises that some husbands also directly accused their wives of adultery in order to receive control of their wives' dowries.[37] Most of the Italian municipal laws condemning adultery date to the fourteenth century, however, and in these years the penalty of dowry forfeiture was made more explicit.

Venetian laws and court records best document the practice of dowry forfeiture for convicted adulteresses.[38] Doge Jacopo Tiepolo promulgated statutes that followed the guidance of Roman law by prescribing that when couples separated after a wife's sexual misbehavior, the husband retained the right to keep her dowry. In contrast, the husband found guilty of adulterous activity was required only to pay maintenance to his separated spouse, although he did also forfeit control of her dowry.[39] It was not until the 1360s, however, that the laws on the statute

---

[35] Haskins, "Three English Documents," p. 87; Tierney, *Religion, Law,* p. 11.

[36] Although I focus here on forfeiture of property as a punishment, conviction for adultery sometimes also resulted in stricter penalties such as corporal punishment and even death. See Dean, "Secular Marriage," forthcoming.

[37] Lansing, "Gender and Civic Authority," pp. 45–48.

[38] On a similar punishment used in the cities of the papal states, see Esposito, "Adulterio," pp. 29–32, and for a wider Italian perspective, see Dean, "Secular Marriage," forthcoming, as well as his book *Crime and Justice,* pp. 138–40. A list of specific city statutes and commentaries upon the issue is available in Brundage, *Law, Sex,* pp. 521, 541.

[39] Guzzetti, "Separations," pp. 254–55. For a more complete view of separations in Venice, one should also turn to the church courts, in which Cecilia Cristellon found, in contrast to the English situation, many separations adjudicated by ecclesiastical officials. Cristellon, "I processi matrimoniali," pp. 103–4, and see in particular p. 110 for information about separations for adultery.

books were applied with any frequency; at that time adulterous wives began to be prosecuted in greater numbers along with their male lovers.[40]

Cuckolded husbands, as well as municipal authorities, instigated legal proceedings against offending wives, and Ruggiero suggests that some husbands initiated adultery allegations in order to obtain the forfeited marriage portion.[41] Furthermore, because the abandoned husband was allowed to retain the misbehaving wife's dowry, some of the adultery charges made in the Venetian courts, as in Orvieto, may have been falsely and thus opportunistically framed by husbands whose wives were suing for separation.[42] If the marriage was ending anyway, a husband might seek to hold on to the dowry through a false allegation that charged his wife with sexual impropriety.

Venetian law, like the 1285 second statute of Westminster, also suggested the potential for spousal reconciliation and stipulated that if the husband reconciled with his wife, her dowry would be restored. This similarity strongly suggests that English and Italian lawmakers were both referencing the same precept from Justinian's *Corpus* that allowed the husband to reconcile with his wife after her adultery and allowed restitution of the dowry if he formally received her back into his household.[43]

In both England and Italy during the thirteenth and fourteenth centuries, therefore, wives were increasingly prosecuted for adultery in the secular courts, and royal and municipal authorities in these disparate European communities revived the old Roman law that the misbehaving wife must forfeit her marriage portion to her husband (the Italian dowry) or to her husband's kin (English dower bypassed the unreconciled wife and property was directly inherited by the nearest heir). One significant regional difference was that the Venetian authorities required a judicial sentence officially proclaiming the wife's adultery, but no evidence for this procedure appears in either the ecclesiastical or the secular courts in England. There, those proclaiming that the widow deserved no dower because of her behavior provided no evidence other than *publica fama*; at least the legal

---

[40] During the same generation stricter penalties were given to their lovers, with the fine paid by the ravisher often equating the monetary value of the wife's forfeited dowry. The Black Death served as the tipping point, according to Guido Ruggiero, who argued that the epidemic linked immoral sexual behavior with the public well-being of the state, and authorities thus enacted more stringent punishments for sexual misbehavior. Ruggiero, *Boundaries of Eros*, pp. 52–55. Ruggiero (ibid., pp. 47–49) also documents a shift that occurred from the 1380s in the terminology used to depict the wife's part in the affair. The accusation against women increasingly shifted to the passive voice, for example stating that the wife "allowed herself to be known." I find it interesting that the rhetorical transformation occurred shortly after women were prosecuted in much greater numbers.

[41] Ruggiero, *Boundaries of Eros*, pp. 52–55.

[42] Ferraro, *Marriage Wars*, pp. 29, 129.

[43] Scott, *Civil Law*, 17:143–44, Novel 134.10; Guzzetti, "Separations," pp. 254–55.

documents remain silent on the matter. And if, as I have argued, abduction law-suits multiplied exponentially in fourteenth-century England because the cuck-olded husbands wished to make the affair a matter of public record, then *fama* was allowed to play a greater role in the English legal proceedings than in the Venetian cases. Legal process differed, but the principle of punishing the adulteress through property loss, using the secular courts, was initiated or revived in both regions.

French Customs and Iberian Laws

The thirteenth-century customs of Toulouse reveal the early revival of the Roman law tradition in some French regions. The custom prescribed dowry forfeiture for the misbehaving wife, and a particularly early court case, dating from 1176, depicts a cuckold requesting that his departed wife forfeit all claims to her or her husband's property.[44] Unlike England, which did not allow the living hus-band to document a wife's adultery or enact forfeiture in his lifetime, the Toulouse court found in favor of this twelfth-century husband. Although secular courts in the Midi retained the right to punish illicit sexuality, punishments were far from static. In the late thirteenth century, as the anonymous glossator of the Toulouse *Coutumes* describes, town customs more frequently prescribed public humiliation of both male and female adulterers, rather than dowry loss for the female, but by the fifteenth century both secular and ecclesiastical officials in the region pro-moted marital reconciliation.[45]

The customs of Beauvais and the late medieval laws of Spain and Portugal also document the similar trend that the matter of female adultery was brought into the royal courts during the thirteenth and fourteenth centuries, rather than remaining a moral offense governed by ecclesiastical authorities. Like the pun-ishment from later Toulouse, they did not require forfeiture of inheritance from adulterous wives. Nevertheless Beaumanoir's text reveals concern about property taken from the household of the departing woman and also notes how these goods should not necessarily be regarded as "stolen." Beaumanoir writes:

> [I]t often happens that men seduce other men's wives or daughters or nieces or women in their guardianship or care, and go off with them out of the area; and there are some who carry off (or have carried off by those who they run off with) whatever they can get or take from the houses which they leave. And when such cases arise and the seducers are sued, you should look very carefully at the manner of the theft and what moved the person seducing the woman to do it.[46]

[44] Mundy, *Men and Women*, pp. 126–27.

[45] Gilles, *Coutumes de Toulouse*, pp. 126–28; Carbasse, "Currant nudi," pp. 90–91; L'Engle, "Justice in the Margins," pp. 142–43; Otis-Cour, "*De jure novo*," pp. 366–80.

[46] Beaumanoir, *Coutumes de Beauvaisis*, p. 327.

The following sections of Beaumanoir's text then differentiate between the man who "takes nothing along with the woman except what she normally wears" and the man who "makes a bundle of [the husband's] property and carries if off with the woman."[47]

Along with two thirteenth-century Castilian codes (the *Fuero Juzgo* and the *Siete Partidas*) and a fourteenth-century royal law enacted by Alfonso IV of Portugal, Beaumanoir also accepted another punishment prescribed in Roman law before the time of Justinian: the right of a husband to kill his wife and her lover for the adultery.[48] Even if the illicit couple was not caught *in flagrante delicto*, the enraged husband would suffer no penalties for the death of one or both of the misbehaving individuals, as long as the circumstances were reasonably suspicious.[49] Augustus's *Lex Julia* had stipulated that the woman's father, not husband, was allowed to punish his daughter by killing her, and that the husband was only allowed to kill the lover; yet, later Roman laws extended the right of the husband to enact the death penalty for both lover and wife.[50] In parts of France and Iberia, therefore, the revival of Roman law took the form of punishment by death in the new secular laws, whereas in England and Italy authorities focused on disinheritance and the possibility of reconciliation in the husband's lifetime. Later French adultery cases, however, did follow Justinian's prescribed penalties for adultery. By the sixteenth century, women convicted of adultery suffered public whipping and were required to enter a convent for two years and forfeit their dowries to their husbands.[51] Similarly southern French and Spanish notarial formulae and contracts dating from the fifteenth century prescribe the pardon of a woman for adulterous behavior, and these pardons may be written evidence of the principle of reconciliation put into practice, for in these documents the husband renounces his right to employ secular or ecclesiastical law to punish his wife for adultery.[52] In these regions, as in England and Italy, as civil authorities became more involved in prosecuting the offense of adultery, they seem to have utilized their knowledge of

---

[47] Beaumanoir, *Coutumes de Beauvaisis*, p. 327.

[48] Otis-Cour ("*De jure novo*"), studying the fifteenth-century Toulousain, sees the right to kill the adulterous wife as a vestige of Germanic custom, rather than Roman law, and outlines how such killings became less acceptable as the church, following revived Roman law, became increasingly successful at reconciling spouses after adultery.

[49] Beaumanoir, *Coutumes de Beauvaisis*, pp. 330–31; Dillard, *Daughters of the Reconquest*, pp. 203–6; Mirrer, "'Unfaithful Wife,'" p. 146; Marques, *Daily Life*, p. 178. According to Mirrer ("'Unfaithful Wife,'" p. 154), the *Fuero Juzgo* followed seventh-century Visigothic precepts that mixed Roman laws with Germanic customs, while the *Siete Partidas* was designed by Alfonso X to centralize laws in the Castilian kingdom.

[50] Cantarella, "Homicides of Honor," pp. 234–35.

[51] Crawford, *European Sexualities*, p. 148; Carbasse, "Currant nudi," pp. 93–94.

[52] Otis-Cour, "*De jure novo*," pp. 374–77; Mirrer, "'Unfaithful Wife,'" p. 148.

the Roman laws to build their laws and punishments, although the specific penalties differed. Most importantly, secular officials claimed this authority, challenging or supplementing ecclesiastical jurisdiction, to punish female adultery.

Northern Europe

The northern regions of the Continent reveal similar secular concerns with prosecuting sexual offenses, rather than leaving them to the church courts, but in general they did not introduce the Roman law principle of inheritance loss for the convicted adulteress.[53] German resistance to foreign (Roman) legal traditions is well known.[54] Such resistance meant that they were far less eager to adopt laws from Justinian's *Corpus* than Italian cities and Iberian kings, but at the same time Germanic laws demonstrate the wider European trend of criminalizing and secularizing illicit sexuality.[55] It should be remembered when discussing laws of Germany and the Low Countries, however, that customs differed in cities across northern Europe, especially with regards to inheritance.[56]

The secular lawmakers studied by Walter Prevenier also increasingly deemed sexual offenses to be threats to public order, although they did not invoke Justinian's precedents. Elopement of a married woman, especially if some of her husband's property was taken away with her, was punished with banishment and usually financial compensation was required as well.[57] Unlike secular authorities elsewhere, however, municipal authorities in the Low Countries prosecuted men for the offense of adultery in greater numbers than women.[58] Mariann Naessens wonders whether this was because men were reluctant to publicize female adultery, as an affront to masculine honor, or whether men were seen as the greater offenders.[59] I suggest it is unlikely that sex ratios of those committing adultery were far differ-

---

[53] Nicholas, writing about practices of law and inheritance in Ghent, points out that "students of Roman law will note close correlations between the legal standing of women and children in Ghent and principles of classical jurisprudence. Yet these principles were as often honored in the breach as in the application." See Nicholas, *Domestic Life*, p. 4.

[54] Nicholas, *Northern Lands*, pp. 106, 156–57; Harrington, *Reordering Marriage*, p. 126; van Caenegem, *Judges, Legislators*, pp. 10, 44. For reception into the Burgundian state during the fifteenth and sixteenth centuries, see Blockmans and Prevenier, *Promised Lands*, pp. 117–20. Roman law was received earlier in southern Germany, however. See Nicholas, *Northern Lands*, p. 164.

[55] A trend also evident in Sweden; see Korpiola, "Rethinking Incest," and Korpiola, "Marriage Causes," forthcoming.

[56] Nicholas, *Domestic Life*, pp. 4, 190; Nicholas, *Northern Lands*, p. 158.

[57] Prevenier, "Violence against Women," 187. Also see Prevenier's contribution to the present volume.

[58] Otis-Cour ("*De jure novo*," pp. 380–90) argues that officials in Toulouse were also more concerned with male adultery by the fifteenth century.

[59] Naessens, "Judicial Authorities' Views," pp. 63–69.

ent in Flanders than elsewhere in Europe, though I concur with Naessens that in general cuckolds were unlikely to publicize their situation. In the Low Countries a man had no real incentive to make known his wife's adultery; whereas in England and in Italy husbands had financial and patrimonial reasons to do so.

A different type of inheritance system may explain the gender proportions of adultery prosecutions when comparing Flanders to England or Italy. Scholars studying marriage and separation have noted how judicial separations were far more common in the regions of northwestern Continental Europe than in England.[60] Separations occurred, but the English were more likely to separate informally, without intervention from, conflict with, or aid from ecclesiastical authorities.[61] Because the English separated themselves, no official record documented the marital dissolution, and a wife retained her right to dower unless her behavior was successfully questioned. The abduction lawsuits studied here thus provided a record of the informal separations stating that the wife had been taken or that she had departed. By contrast, in the Low Countries, although each spouse retained the individual property brought to the marriage, couples negotiated official separation agreements concerning the division of their communal property.[62] There was no need to publicize a wife's adultery, and a husband was not entitled to dowry forfeiture.[63] From a functional standpoint, civil authorities in the northern lands were content to wield wider powers in general, but differing inheritance traditions meant that they did not adopt the specific Roman law requiring dowry forfeiture from which secular authorities in England and Italy borrowed.

Conclusion

In 1963 Bryce Lyon published a call for scholars of English history to expand their scholarly horizons, writing that "to be meaningful in our shrinking world writing on English mediaeval history must increasingly portray England, not as an island apart, but as an integral member of a western European community."[64] Several years later he and Adriaan Verhulst satisfied that request in their collaboration on

[60] See Vleeschouwers–Van Melkebeek, "Separation and Marital Property," forthcoming, and Donahue, *Law, Marriage*, pp. 266–70, 558–61, 609–12. Sometimes these separation agreements were confirmed by municipal authorities; for examples see Nicholas, *Domestic Life*, pp. 34–35. Nicholas also points out however, that, as in England, some couples likely separated themselves informally.

[61] Helmholz, *Marriage Litigation*, pp. 59, 74–76; Vleeschouwers–Van Melkebeek, "Self-Divorce," pp. 85–86.

[62] Harrington, *Reordering Marriage*, p. 123.

[63] Alternatively, husbands may have publicized their wives' departures in other ways. Thus in Ghent both husbands and wives could make it known by proclamation in the parish church that they were no longer accepting responsibility for their spouses' debts. See Nicholas, *Domestic Life*, p. 78.

[64] Lyon, "From Hengist and Horsa," p. 422.

Medieval Finance. In this work Lyon and Verhulst went beyond arguing that only common heritage or borrowed influence made for the similarities in fiscal systems of England, Flanders, and France; instead "degree of political power, economic resources, and local need, whether in England or on the Continent, governed what rulers and their administrators did or could do with their institutions."[65]

Similarly, in western Europe during the late Middle Ages it was not merely the revival of Roman law that led England and Italian cities to adopt legislation to punish adulterous wives in the secular sphere with loss of marriage portion. Instead, it was shared concerns about this adulterous behavior, concerns shared by authorities in regions including France, Iberia, and the northern lands, that led them all to modify and introduce secular laws, even if only two regions specifically borrowed the principle of dowry forfeiture promulgated by Justinian. Moreover, those borrowing from Roman traditions did not adopt all Roman law principles, but only those that provided them with means to deal with what they wanted. These concerns about marital stability, and also about the link between marriage and property, were shared but handled differently.

Roman civil law provided English and Italian authorities with the opportunity to bring matrimonial disputes into the secular courts rather than leaving them entirely under ecclesiastical jurisdiction. Sexual impropriety could not be left exclusively to the church courts because its consequences affected the landed and movable property that so concerned the secular authorities. Certainly there were differences between England and Continental Europe, and within Continental cultures, but I hope that this preliminary survey of a similar attitude toward governing sexual impropriety through secular law serves to celebrate and propagate Lyon's desire for collaborative effort and comparisons.

Bibliography

Akehurst, F. R. P., ed. and trans. *The Coutumes de Beauvaisis of Philippe de Beaumanoir.* Philadelphia: University of Pennsylvania Press, 1992.

Arjava, Antti. *Women and Law in Late Antiquity.* Oxford: Oxford University Press, 1998.

Ayton, Andrew. "The English Army at Crécy." In *The Battle of Crécy, 1346,* ed. Andrew Ayton and Philip Preston, pp. 159–251. Woodbridge: Boydell, 2005.

Baker, John H. *An Introduction to English Legal History.* 4th ed. London: Butterworths, 2002.

Barron, Caroline M. "Introduction: The Widow's World in Later Medieval London." In *Medieval London Widows,* ed. Caroline M. Barron and Anne F. Sutton, pp. xiii–xxxiv. London: Hambledon, 1994.

Blockmans, Wim, and Walter Prevenier. *The Promised Lands: The Low Countries under Burgundian Rule, 1369–1530.* Ed. Edward Peters. Trans. Elizabeth Fackelman. Philadelphia: University of Pennsylvania Press, 1999.

---

[65] Lyon and Verhulst, *Medieval Finance,* pp. 96–97.

Brand, Paul. "'Deserving' and 'Undeserving' Wives: Earning and Forfeiting Dower in Medieval England." *Journal of Legal History* 22 (2001): 1–36.

Brown, A. L. *The Governance of Late Medieval England, 1272–1461.* Stanford: Stanford University Press, 1989.

Brundage, James. *Law, Sex, and Christian Society in Medieval Europe.* Chicago: University of Chicago Press, 1987.

Cantarella, Eva. "Homicides of Honor: The Development of Italian Adultery Law over Two Millenia." In *The Family in Italy from Antiquity to the Present*, ed. David I. Kertzer and Richard P. Saller, pp. 229–46. New Haven, CT: Yale University Press, 1991.

Carbasse, Jean-Marie. "Currant nudi: La répression de la adultère dans le Midi médiévale." In *Droit, histoire et sexualité*, ed. Jacques Poumarède and Jean-Pierre Royer, pp. 83–102. Paris: L'espace juridique, 1987.

Carpenter, David A. "Bastard Feudalism Revised." *Past and Present* 131 (1991): 177–89.

———. "The Second Century of English Feudalism." *Past and Present* 168 (2000): 30–71.

Church, S. D. "The Rewards of Royal Service in the Household of King John: A Dissenting Opinion." *English Historical Review* 110 (1995): 277–302.

Coss, Peter. "Bastard Feudalism Revised." *Past and Present* 125 (1989): 27–64.

Crawford, Katherine. *European Sexualities, 1400–1800.* New York: Cambridge University Press, 2007.

Cristellon, Cecilia. "I processi matrimoniali veneziani (1420–1545)." In *I tribunali del matrimonio (secolo XV–XVIII)*, ed. Silvana Seidel Menchi and Diego Quaglioni, pp. 101–22. Bologna: Il Mulino, 2006.

Crouch, David. "Bastard Feudalism Revised." *Past and Present* 131 (1991): 165–77.

Cuttino, George P. Review of *The Wardrobe Book of William de Norwell, 12 July 1338 to 27 May*, by Mary Lyon, Bryce Lyon, and Henry S. Lucas. *American Historical Review* 90 (1985): 118.

Dean, Trevor. *Crime and Justice in Late Medieval Italy.* Cambridge: Cambridge University Press, 2007.

———. "Fathers and Daughters: Marriage Laws and Marriage Disputes in Bologna and Italy, 1200–1500." In *Marriage in Italy*, ed. Dean and Lowe, pp. 85–106.

———. "Secular Marriage Laws in Late-Medieval Italy." In *Regional Variations*, ed. Korpiola, forthcoming.

Dean, Trevor, and K. J. P. Lowe, eds. *Marriage in Italy, 1300–1650.* Cambridge: Cambridge University Press, 1998.

Dillard, Heath. *Daughters of the Reconquest: Women in Castilian Town Society, 1100–1300.* Cambridge: Cambridge University Press, 1984.

Donahue, Charles. *Law, Marriage, and Society in the Later Middle Ages: Arguments about Marriage in Five Courts.* Cambridge: Cambridge University Press, 2008.

Esposito, Anna. "Adulterio, concubinato, bigamia: Testimonianze dalla normative statutaria dello Stato pontificio (secoli XIII–XVI)." In *Trasgressioni: Seduzione, concubinato, adulterio, bigamia (XIV–XVIII secolo)*, ed. Silvana Seidel Menchi and Diego Quaglioni, pp. 21–42. Bologna: Il Mulino, 2004.

Ferraro, Joanne M. *Marriage Wars in Late Renaissance Venice.* Oxford: Oxford University Press, 2001.

Gilles, Henri, ed. and trans. *Les coutumes de Toulouse (1286) et leur Premier Commentaire.* Toulouse: Recueil de l'Académie de législation, 1969.

Gorski, Richard. *The Fourteenth-Century Sheriff: English Local Administration in the Late Middle Ages.* Rochester, NY: Boydell, 2003.

Greilsammer, Myriam. "Rapts de séduction et rapts violents en Flandre et en Brabant à la fin du Moyen Âge." *Legal History Review* 56 (1998): 49–84.

Guzzetti, Linda. "Separations and Separated Couples in Fourteenth-Century Venice." In *Marriage in Italy*, ed. Dean and Lowe, pp. 249–74.

Hall, G. D. G., ed. and trans. *The Treatise on the Laws and Customs of the Realm of England Commonly Called Glanvill (Tractatus de legibus et consuetidinibus regni Anglie qui Glanvilla vocatur)*. London: Nelson, 1965.

Hanawalt, Barbara. *The Wealth of Wives: Women, Law, and Economy in Late Medieval London*. Oxford: Oxford University Press, 2007.

———. "The Widow's Mite: Provisions for Medieval London Widows." In *Upon My Husband's Death: Widows in the Literature & Histories of Medieval Europe*, ed. Louise Mirrer, pp. 21–46. Ann Arbor: University of Michigan Press, 1992.

Hanawalt, Barbara A., and David Wallace, eds. *Medieval Crime and Social Control*. Minneapolis: University of Minnesota Press, 1999.

Harrington, Joel F. *Reordering Marriage and Society in Reformation Germany*. Cambridge: Cambridge University Press, 1995.

Haskins, George L. "Three English Documents Relating to Accursius (Francis). " *Law Quarterly Review* 54 (1938): 87–94.

Helmholz, Richard H. *The "ius commune" in England: Four Studies*. Oxford: Oxford University Press, 2001.

———. "Magna Carta and the *ius commune*." *University of Chicago Law Review* 66 (1999): 297–371.

———. *Marriage Litigation in Medieval England*. London: Cambridge University Press, 1974.

———. "The Roman Law of Guardianship in England, 1300–1600." *Tulane Law Review* 52 (1978): 22–57. Reprinted in *Canon Law and the Law of England*, pp. 211–24. London: Hambledon, 1999.

Horwood, Alfred J., ed. and trans. *Year Books of the Reign of Edward the First*. Rolls Series 31. 5 vols. London: Longman, 1863–79.

Hunt, Edwin S. "A New Look at the Dealings of the Bardi and Peruzzi with Edward III." *Journal of Economic History* 50 (1990): 149–62.

Hyams, Paul. *Rancor and Reconciliation in Medieval England*. Ithaca, NY: Cornell University Press, 2003.

Kelly, Henry Ansgar. "Statutes of Rapes and Alleged Ravishers of Wives: A Context for the Charges against Thomas Malory, Knight." Ch. 9 in *Inquisitions and Other Trial Procedures in the Medieval West*. Aldershot: Ashgate, 2001.

Korpiola, Mia. "Marriage Causes in Late Medieval Sweden." In *Regional Variations*, ed. Korpiola, forthcoming.

———, ed. *Regional Variations of Matrimonial Law and Custom in Europe, 1150–1650*. Leiden: Brill, forthcoming.

———. "Rethinking Incest and Heinous Sexual Crime: Changing Boundaries of Secular and Ecclesiastical Jurisdiction in Late Medieval Sweden." In *Boundaries of the Law: Geography, Gender and Jurisdiction in Medieval and Early Modern Europe*, ed. Anthony Musson, pp. 102–17. Aldershot: Ashgate, 2005.

Lansing, Carol. "Gender and Civic Authority: Sexual Control in a Medieval Italian Town." *Journal of Social History* 31 (1997): 33–59.

L'Engle, Susan. "Justice in the Margins: Punishment in Medieval Toulouse." *Viator* 33 (2002): 133–65.

Loyn, Henry Royston. *The Governance of Anglo-Saxon England, 500–1087*. Stanford: Stanford University Press, 1984.

Luders, A., et al., eds. *Statutes of the Realm*. 11 vols. London: Record Commission, 1810–28.

Lyon, Bryce D. *A Constitutional and Legal History of Medieval England*. 2nd ed. New York: W. W. Norton, 1980.

———. "Fact and Fiction in English and Belgian Constitutional Law." *Medievalia et Humanistica* 10 (1956): 82–101.

———. "From Hengist and Horsa to Edward of Caernarvon: Recent Writing on English History." In *Changing Views on British History: Essays on Historical Writing Since 1939*, ed. Elizabeth C. Furber, pp. 1–57. Cambridge, MA: Harvard University Press, 1966.

———. "The Lawyer and Magna Carta." *Rocky Mountain Law Review* 23 (1951): 416–33.

———. Review of *Lord Hastings' Indentured Retainers*, by W. H. Dunham. *Speculum* 32 (1957): 558.

Lyon, Bryce D., and Adriaan Verhulst. *Medieval Finance: A Comparison of Financial Institutions in Northwestern Europe*. Rijksuniversiteit te Gent: Werken uitgegeven door de Faculteit van de Letteren en Wijsbegeerte 143. Bruges: De Tempel; Providence, RI: Brown University Press, 1967.

Lyon, Mary, Bryce Lyon, and Henry S. Lucas, eds., with the collaboration of Jean de Sturler. *The Wardrobe Book of William de Norwell: 12 July 1338 to 27 May 1340*. Brussels: Palais des Académies, 1983.

Maitland, F. W., ed. *Year Books of Edward II: 2 and 3 Edward II (1308–1309 and 1309–1310)*. Selden Society 19. London: B. Quairitch, 1904.

Marques, Antonio Henrique de Oliveira. *Daily Life in Portugal in the Late Middle Ages*. Trans. S. S. Wyatt. Madison: University of Wisconsin Press, 1971.

Milsom, S. F. C. "Trespass from Henry III to Edward III." *Law Quarterly Review* 74 (1958): 195–224, 407–36, 561–90.

Mirrer, Louise. "The 'Unfaithful Wife' in Medieval Spanish Literature and Law." In *Medieval Crime*, ed. Hanawalt and Wallace, pp. 143–55.

Mundy, John Hine. *Men and Women at Toulouse in the Age of the Cathars*. Toronto: Pontifical Institute of Mediaeval Studies, 1990.

Naessens, Mariann. "Judicial Authorities' Views of Women's Roles in Late Medieval Flanders." In *The Texture of Society: Medieval Women in the Southern Low Countries*, ed. Ellen E. Kittell and Mary A. Suydam, pp. 51–78. New York: Palgrave Macmillan, 2004.

Nicholas, David. *The Domestic Life of a Medieval City: Women, Children, and the Family in Fourteenth-Century Ghent*. Lincoln: University of Nebraska Press, 1985.

———. *The Northern Lands: Germanic Europe, c. 1270–c. 1500*. Malden, MA: Wiley-Blackwell, 2009.

Otis-Cour, Leah. "*De jure novo*: Dealing with Adultery in the Fifteenth-Century Toulousain." *Speculum* 84 (2009): 347–92.

Post, John B. "Ravishment of Women and the Statute of Westminster." In *Legal Records and the Historian: Papers Presented to the Cambridge Legal History Conference*, ed. J. H. Baker, pp. 150–64. London: Swift, 1978.

Prevenier, Walter. "Violence against Women in Fifteenth Century France and the Burgundian State." In *Medieval Crime*, ed. Hanawalt and Wallace, pp. 186–203.

Reynolds, Philip Lyndon. *Marriage in the Western Church: The Christianization of Marriage during the Patristic and Early Medieval Periods*. Leiden: Brill, 2001.

Ribordy, Geneviève. *"Faire les nopces": Le mariage de la noblesse française (1375–1475)*. Studies and Texts 146. Toronto: Pontifical Institute of Mediaeval Studies, 2004.

———. "The Two Paths to Marriage: The Preliminaries of Noble Marriage in Late Medieval France." *Journal of Family History* 26 (2001): 323–36.

Ruggiero, Guido. *The Boundaries of Eros: Sex Crime and Sexuality in Renaissance Venice*. Oxford: Oxford University Press, 1985.

Scott, Samuel Parsons, ed. and trans. *The Civil Law: Including the Twelve Tables, the Institutes of Gaius, the Rules of Ulpian, the Opinions of Paulus, the Enactments of Justinian, and the Constitutions of Leo*. 17 vols. Cincinnati: Central Trust, 1932.

Seipp, David J. "The Reception of Canon Law and Civil Law in the Common Law Courts before 1600." *Oxford Journal of Legal Studies* 13 (1993): 388–420.

Shirley, Kevin. *The Secular Jurisdiction of Monasteries in Anglo-Norman and Angevin England*. Woodbridge: Boydell, 2004.

Straw, Jack. "Modernizing the Magna Carta." Speech delivered at George Washington University. February 13, 2008. http://www.justice.gov.uk/news/sp130208a.htm.

Thorne, Samuel E. "Henry de Bracton, 1268–1968." Ch. 7 in *Essays in English Legal History*, pp. 75–92. London: Hambledon, 1985.

Tierney, Brian. *Religion, Law, and the Growth of Constitutional Thought, 1150–1650*. Cambridge: Cambridge University Press, 1982.

Turner, Ralph V. "The Origins of the Medieval English Jury: Frankish, English, or Scandinavian." In *Judges, Administrators and the Common Law in Angevin England*. London: Hambledon, 1994.

Van Caenegem, Raoul C. *Judges, Legislators and Professors: Chapters in European Legal History*. Cambridge: Cambridge University Press, 1993.

———. *Legal History: A European Perspective*. London: Hambledon, 1991.

Vleeschouwers–Van Melkebeek, Monique. "Self-Divorce in Fifteenth-Century Flanders: The Consistory Court Accounts of the Diocese of Tournai." *Legal History Review* 68 (2000): 83–98.

———. "Separation and Marital Property." In *Regional Variations*, ed. Korpiola, forthcoming.

Walker, Sue Sheridan. "Punishing Convicted Ravishers: Statutory Strictures and Actual Practice in Thirteenth- and Fourteenth-Century England." *Journal of Medieval History* 13 (1987): 237–50.

Warren, Wilfred L. *The Governance of Norman and Angevin England, 1086–1272*. Stanford: Stanford University Press, 1987.

Waugh, Scott L. "Tenure to Contract: Lordship and Clientage in Thirteenth-Century England." *English Historical Review* 101 (1986): 811–39.

The Good Parliament of 1376:
Commons, *Communes*, and "Common Profit" in Fourteenth-Century English Politics

W. Mark Ormrod

T HE PARLIAMENT that opened at Westminster in April 1376 has long been recognized as a defining moment in English constitutional history. The session broke old records and set new precedents. It was one of the longest-lived parliaments to date; it delivered more common petitions than any previous assembly; it was the first time that the Commons selected one of its number to act as a speaker; and, most famously, it established a new procedure—parliamentary impeachment—as a means of forcing the public trial and punishment of agents of the Crown.[1] Within a short time the parliament became celebrated as a moment when the polity made outspoken criticism of Edward III's government and forced through a great purge of the courtiers and financiers who were seen to have hobbled the regime of a once great and now feeble king.

It is generally accepted that the events of 1376 were responsible for creating a new public interest in the business of Parliament and prompted the development of unofficial narratives of parliamentary assemblies circulated in the form of political "pamphlets." Clementine Oliver has recently demonstrated the applicability of that term both to the Anglo-Norman account of the Good Parliament in the *Anonimalle Chronicle* of St. Mary's Abbey, York, and to Thomas Fovent's highly developed Latin commentary on the Wonderful and Merciless Parliaments of 1386 and 1388.[2] Oliver has also stressed the radicalism of such texts and the

Earlier versions of this study were delivered at the University of California at Los Angeles and the University of Rochester. I am very grateful to the participants in those seminars for their comments, and especially to Gwilym Dodd, Matthew Giancarlo, Barbara Gribling, Christopher Guyol, and Clementine Oliver for their insightful comments on earlier drafts.

[1] The standard work on the parliament of 1376 is Holmes, *Good Parliament*.

[2] Tout, *Collected Papers*, 2:173–90; Oliver, "First Political Pamphlet?"; Oliver, "New Light." See also Don C. Skemer's contribution to the present volume.

striking manner in which they represent Parliament as the principal bulwark of good governance. The tone therefore fits neatly with the reformist agenda that Kathryn Kerby-Fulton and Steven Justice have identified in later fourteenth-century bureaucratic culture and associate with contemporary interest in that great medieval textbook of parliamentary procedure, the *Modus tenendi parliamentum*.[3] In these contexts, the bold actions of the Commons in the Good Parliament can, indeed, be said to have set new standards in public life and new expectations of Parliament as a force for positive change.

This optimistic view was not, however, shared by all. Thomas Walsingham's account of the Good Parliament, written a decade or so after the event but informed by the recollections of one of its members, Sir Thomas Hoo, certainly extolled the bravery of the Commons in their stand against faction and corruption. But Walsingham was also sharply aware of the affront to traditional authority represented in the assembly and saw the Commons' actions as legitimate only because of the blatant unreasonableness of the Crown's chief representative, John of Gaunt.[4] The undoing of so many of the acts of 1376 by Gaunt in the so-called Bad Parliament of 1377 called seriously into question the ability of Parliament to enshrine political constraints to which the Crown was resistant. In the B-text of *Piers Plowman*, written in 1377, William Langland adapted an existing fable of the belling of the cat to reflect the hopelessness that had overwhelmed the reformist agenda. When a "rat of renown" (Peter de la Mare, speaker in the Good Parliament) argues the case for putting a bell on the cat (John of Gaunt) so that they can better know his actions and avoid his threats, a mouse "that had good sense" (perhaps Thomas Hungerford, speaker in the Bad Parliament) launches a disillusioned counterproposal, remarking that it would be better for the rats and mice to let the cat continue its depredations against another group, the rabbits, than to attract his attention and thus turn him against their own kind.[5]

Above all, the appropriation of the reformist agenda by the rebels in the Peasants' Revolt of 1381 forced the elite to reconsider the wisdom and legitimacy of political opposition. Well into the reign of Richard II, the parliamentary Commons continued to espouse some of the issues raised both in 1376 and

---

[3] Kerby-Fulton and Justice, "Reformist Intellectual Culture"; see also Dodd, "Changing Perspectives." Kerby-Fulton and Justice argue that the *Modus* cannot have been composed until ca. 1375. I favor the arguments for composition in the early 1320s; in the present context it is sufficient to emphasize that the circulation of manuscripts of the *Modus* undoubtedly increased significantly in the last quarter of the fourteenth century. See Pronay and Taylor, *Parliamentary Texts*, pp. 13–63.

[4] Walsingham, *St Albans Chronicle*, pp. 2–53.

[5] Langland, *Piers Plowman*, pp. 6–8 (Prologue, lines 146–208); Gross, "Langland's Rats"; Dodd, "Parliament Full of Rats?"

in 1381.[6] But Langland famously recast his representation of Parliament in the C-text of *Piers Plowman*, written shortly after the events of 1381, to eliminate any suggestion that the Commons had a rightful share in the king's sovereignty.[7] Finally, the anonymous Middle English poem *Richard the Redeless* (ca. 1400) turned disillusionment into bitter satire. The knights of the shires and the representatives of the towns, far from being the champions of good governance, are cast as a bunch of self-servers, king's friends and trimmers who fail to deliver a single effective proposal that might benefit the commons of the land.[8] Within a quarter-century of the Good Parliament, we are forced to concede, some elements of political society had begun to identify Parliament not as the essential agency of reform but as an inert institution that could itself seriously impede the application of principles of good governance.

This emphasis on the fragility and brevity of the Good Parliament's political achievements has driven much of the modern assessment of the assembly's place in constitutional history. Stubbs, Tout, and their pupils stressed not just the striking unanimity of purpose among the Commons in 1376 but also the support that their agenda received among the Lords, and thus emphasized what they saw as the contingent nature of de la Mare's success. For a long time in the twentieth century it was fashionable to discuss Parliament in terms of two rival groups, a "court party" led by John of Gaunt and a "popular party" that adopted the Black Prince, and subsequently the earl of March, as its figurehead.[9] New approaches to bastard feudalism after the 1930s overturned the assumption that the Commons were only capable of following where the Lords led or that Gaunt's demolition of the acts of the Good Parliament in 1377 was simply effected by "packing" the Commons in the Bad Parliament. Nevertheless, while general accounts of the crisis of 1376 produced since the 1950s tended to credit the Commons with a greater sense of independence, historians such as J. S. Roskell and Anthony Tuck continued to argue that the outspoken attack on the government of Edward III was only possible because the knights and burgesses thought they could expect a sympathetic response in high places.[10] It follows in this interpretation that, once Gaunt had restored a semblance of unity within court and council over the winter of 1376/77, the commitment

---

[6] Lewis, "Re-election to Parliament"; Ormrod, "Peasants' Revolt," p. 23; Dodd, "Parliament Full of Rats?" pp. 46–47.

[7] Baldwin, *Theme of Government*, pp. 50–51.

[8] Barr, *"Piers Plowman" Tradition*, pp. 130–33 (passus 4).

[9] Stubbs, *Constitutional History*, 2:448–55; Tout, *Chapters*, 3:290–307.

[10] Richardson, "John of Gaunt"; Walker, *Lancastrian Affinity*, pp. 237–40; McKisack, *Fourteenth Century*, pp. 387–93; Harriss, "Formation of Parliament," pp. 56–59; Roskell, *Commons*, pp. 119–20; Tuck, *Crown and Nobility*, pp. 145–48.

to reform faltered and failed. The Good Parliament, therefore, tends to stand simply as an unfortunate "blip," proof of the comfortingly functionalist notion that medieval English politics was only ever successful when it was consensual and cooperative.[11] In the new kind of constitutional history that Bryce Lyon so brilliantly championed, the older tradition of the "constitution" as the accretion of rights wrung from the Crown at moments of high political crisis—in 1215, 1258, 1297, 1327, 1376, 1399, and so on—therefore yields to a new emphasis on underlying structural and cultural continuities and on the long processes of organic evolution that determined the medieval English legal and political experience.[12]

This article takes a different approach from those set out above. Rather than judging the impact of the Good Parliament on the constitution, it frames the assembly in relation to the temporary but powerful sense of political unity and independence established among the Commons in 1376. It explores the activities and rhetoric of the Commons and their supporters and considers the "revolutionary" nature of the associations and actions that they undertook, whether these proved short-term aberrations or long-term gains. In so doing, it contends that the remnants of Whiggishness and the still pervasive liberal-empirical tradition of Anglo-American scholarship have conspired seriously to underplay the self-consciously "revolutionary" element that can be discerned in this great moment of constitutional crisis. The *longue durée* may provide the ultimate test of whether a crisis genuinely transformed the political landscape; but it is through the application of micro-history that we can best capture the mixture of excitement, panic, confusion, rumor, and counter-rumor that so often conditioned the attitudes of contemporary political culture.

The *Anonimalle Chronicle* includes two striking episodes from the early stages of the Good Parliament that help to demonstrate the ways in which the Commons of 1376 challenged the traditional restrictions set upon their power. The first is the account of the "charge" delivered by the chancellor at the opening session:

> Sir John Knyvet, the chancellor, demanded on behalf of the king from the knights and burgesses and all the Commons of the counties, by their allegiance, and on pain of forfeiture, that if any matter required to be redressed or amended in the same kingdom, or if the said kingdom was badly ruled and governed or ingenuously counselled, that they, by their good advice and counsel, should ordain a remedy [*qils ordinerent remedy*] as far as they were able as to how the kingdom might be more profitably governed to the honor of the king and the profit of the

---

[11] Ormrod, *Reign of Edward III*, pp. 37–38; Saul, *Richard II*, pp. 20–21.

[12] Lyon, *Constitutional and Legal History*.

kingdom [*coment la roialme purroit plus profitablement ester governe al honour le roy et profite al roialme*].[13]

Knyvet is hardly likely to have intended the Commons to believe that they were empowered to act as a legislative body in their own right, and the request that they "ordain a remedy" (which finds direct parallel in the official account of Knyvet's speech in the parliament roll) is perfectly compatible with the traditional role of the Commons as supplicants for, and assenters to, remedial legislation offered by the Crown in the form of statutes.[14]

It is a sign of the failure of so much of the business of 1376 that Edward III's government actually refused to issue any statutes at the end of this parliament. On the other hand, the Crown did acknowledge that several of the assembly's acts—the impeachments of the courtiers, the sanctions against Alice Perrers, the confirmation of the Calais staple, and in particular the appointment of the continual council—had the secondary status of formal ordinances.[15] It is therefore particularly noteworthy that the *Anonimalle* account repeatedly appropriates the language of "ordaining" to the Commons, not only in Knyvet's speech but throughout its account of the ensuing assembly. In asking Gaunt to name a group of the Lords to cooperate with the Commons in drawing up their proposals for reform, for example, de la Mare goes close to assuming the role of legislator: "When [the Lords' committee] have heard and seen our counsel, we will declare our purpose and ordinance to you [*nous declaroms a vous nostre purpose et ordinaunce*]."[16] Such assertiveness, even if only imagined, indicates the belief of political society that the Commons of 1376 had been authorized, at a moment of supreme political crisis, to determine for themselves the course that ought to be adopted for the reform of the realm.

The second vivid moment captured by the *Anonimalle Chronicle* has been largely suppressed from modern accounts of the political crisis, but is central to the present study's emphasis on the extraordinary status assumed by the Commons in 1376:

> The chapter house of the abbey of Westminster was assigned to the knights and Commons, in which they could deliberate privately with-

---

[13] Galbraith, *Anonimalle Chronicle*, p. 80; Taylor, *English Historical Literature*, pp. 301–2 (adapted). All translations from the *Anonimalle Chronicle* are based on Taylor's translation in *English Historical Literature*.

[14] Brand et al., *Parliament Rolls of Medieval England* (hereafter cited as *PROME*, by volume and page number from this edition), 5:295; Pronay and Taylor, *Parliamentary Texts*, pp. 77, 89–90; Wilkinson, *Studies*, pp. 82–107; Brown, "Parliament," pp. 126–29.

[15] *PROME*, 5:298–99, 313, 315; *Calendar of Close Rolls*, pp. 441–42; *Calendar of Patent Rolls*, p. 75.

[16] Galbraith, *Anonimalle Chronicle*, p. 84. See also the comments of Tout, *Chapters*, 3:297.

out being disturbed or being bothered by others. And on the said second day all the knights and Commons aforesaid gathered and went into the chapter house and sat around [*en viroune*], each close to the other, and they began to talk of the substance of the causes of parliament, saying that it would be good at the beginning to be sworn each to the other [*destre iurrez chescune a autre*] to hold counsel as to what was spoken and ordained among them, and loyally to treat and ordain for the profit of the kingdom [*treter et ordiner pur profit de la roialme*] without concealing anything; and to this they all unanimously assented and took an oath to be loyal one to the other [*et firent bone serement pur ester loialles chescune a autre*]. And then one of them said, "If any of us knows of anything to say for the profit of the king and kingdom [*pur profit del roy et roialme*] he should lay his knowledge before us.[17]

The emphasis placed here on the distinct character and unanimity of the Commons is very striking. As Matthew Giancarlo has recently emphasized, the environment enhanced the message: by seating themselves on the ring of stone benches set around the octagonal chapter house, the Commons configured themselves not in factions or "parties" facing each other across the floor of a debating chamber but as an unbroken circle of allies in the common cause of reform.[18]

The most important element in this second episode, however, is undoubtedly the oath to act collectively "for the profit of the kingdom." There is no evidence to indicate that the parliamentary Commons had ever previously turned themselves into such a sworn league. Insofar as their action had historical precedent, it was to be found in the "commune of England" (*le commun de Engleterre*) formed a century earlier, in 1258, by the baronial opposition to Henry III.[19] Michael Clanchy has resisted older interpretations that linked this "commune" with indigenous traditions of legitimate association bound up in the term *commonalty*, and instead argues for the "conspiratorial" nature of the association, whose precedents "were in revolutions in continental towns in the twelfth century rather than in the common folk of England."[20]

After 1258 English politics had usually eschewed this radical political form, tending to revert to the tradition that a representative "community of the realm" had the legitimate right to negotiate with the king on behalf of the kingdom. The adoption, by the 1330s, of the Anglo-French word *commune* to denote the parliamentary Commons is a striking example of the way that meanings could

---

[17] Galbraith, *Anonimalle Chronicle*, pp. 80–81.

[18] Giancarlo, *Parliament and Literature*, pp. 69–73. The Commons' deliberations in 1376 took so long that the floor coverings at their end in the chapter house were entirely worn out: Lyon, *Constitutional and Legal History*, p. 543.

[19] Treharne and Saunders, *Documents*, pp. 100–103.

[20] Clanchy, *England and Its Rulers*, pp. 16–17 (p. 17); see also pp. 190–203.

shift from the revolutionary to the quotidian.[21] Under exceptional circumstances, however, "commune" could retain its meaning of a sworn confederacy.[22] In January 1327, the supporters of Queen Isabella and the future Edward III (including several men sitting in Parliament as elected members) took a common oath to work for the overthrow of Edward II; and in the parliament that reconvened after the declaration of the abdication, the Commons petitioned, although unsuccessfully, that oaths should be taken in the county courts binding the community of the realm to the revolutionary enterprise thus begun.[23]

It is likely that the idea of the Commons in Parliament formally constituting themselves as a commune still had the power to shock fifty years later, partly because it marked such a striking downward appropriation of baronial political tactics, but principally because it could very readily be interpreted as an act of sedition or revolution.[24] If the episode has a basis in truth, it may well have reflected the considerable tensions, rather than the natural unity, that actually existed among the two hundred or so men gathered in the chapter house; the oath could be seen as the coercive instrument by which the demagogues disciplined more conservative elements into active complicity with their cause. Nevertheless, it also potentially transformed the knights and burgesses from mere supplicants for royal grace into a full-fledged conspiracy. The Commons were, in effect, employing a strategy that social scientists call "usurpationary closure," freeing themselves from the constitutional restrictions on their role and claiming the moral right to be involved fully and actively in the course of policy.[25]

An expansive reading of the collective oath might also see it as helping to determine the ways in which the Commons' leaders subsequently went about communicating their grievances and demands to the Crown. Under normal circumstances the Lords and Commons did not gather in plenary meetings except to observe the opening ceremonies of Parliament and to hear the announcement of grants of taxation and the Crown's responses to the common petitions on the last day of formal session. It is important to appreciate that the usual procedure employed to allow discussion between Lords and Commons—intercommuning—

[21] Prestwich, *English Politics*, pp. 129–45; Ormrod, "Agenda for Legislation"; Reynolds, *Kingdoms and Communities*, pp. 250–331.

[22] See also the active and explicit deployment of the theme of the *commune* in the French provincial leagues of 1314–15: Brown, "Reform and Resistance"; Reynolds, *Kingdoms and Communities*, pp. 285–88.

[23] Thomas, *Calendar of Plea and Memoranda Rolls*, pp. 11–14; *PROME*, 4:6, 9, 21, 35; Clarke, *Medieval Representation*, pp. 181–83; Valente, "Deposition and Abdication," pp. 858–59.

[24] Harding, "Origins."

[25] Rigby, *English Society*, pp. 1–14.

was only consultative and that the delegates who attended such meetings were not authorized to make binding decisions.[26] This explains the particular concern expressed by Peter de la Mare that all the Commons should be allowed to accompany him when he went before John of Gaunt and the Lords to request assistance in drawing up proposals for reform.[27] The Commons' insistence that they be treated as a formally constituted collectivity may also account, in turn, for the duke of Lancaster's outburst at this point, as expressed by Walsingham: "What are those degenerate knights of the hedgerows plotting? Do they think they are kings or the chief men of this land, and where do they get such pride and arrogance?"[28] The social merges here with the procedural to emphasize the novelty and (from Gaunt's point of view) temerity of the Commons' challenge. De la Mare and his advisers surely well understood that there were few clear precedents either for the process they had forced through or, indeed, for the demands they were about to make. In such uncharted waters, their one element of security was the binding nature of the commune to which they and their fellows had all subscribed.

The formative influence of the sworn oaths on the Commons' subsequent development of a coherent political agenda can be tracked at a number of levels. Three broad initiatives stand out: de la Mare's successive speeches before Gaunt and the Lords in the opening weeks of the parliament (May 12–24) about fiscal policy, during which William Latimer, Richard Lyons, and Alice Perrers were identified as targets of public wrath and the removal of evil counselors was made a condition of the Commons' further cooperation; the specific request for the appointment of a continual council of nine bishops, earls, and barons to take general charge of royal government (May 24), subsequently accepted (after May 26) by the king; and the common petitions, which may have been submitted as early as May 24 but did not receive their final answers until as late as July 10.[29] In all three respects the Commons stretched the bounds of normative political practice. The episode in the *Anonimalle Chronicle* in which de la Mare upbraided Lancaster for breaking a (nonexistent) statute guaranteeing the stability of the wool staple at Calais, and his insistence, on written authority, that "what was done in parliament by statute could not be undone without parliament," are well-known scenes in the political drama of 1376.[30] Recently, Gwilym Dodd has also emphasized that one reason why the schedule of common petitions submitted to the Crown in 1376 was so long was that de la Mare and his fellows had made particularly active use of the newfound practice of "avowing" or

[26] Edwards, *Second Century*, pp. 1–16. Edwards also stresses the highly unusual situation in 1376.

[27] Galbraith, *Anonimalle Chronicle*, pp. 83–84; Giancarlo, *Parliament and Literature*, pp. 55–56.

[28] Walsingham, *St Albans Chronicle*, pp. 10–11.

[29] *PROME*, 5:290–92.

[30] Galbraith, *Anonimalle Chronicle*, pp. 85–86, 182–83.

adopting private petitions and incorporating them into the Commons' own political agenda.[31]

In what follows, I examine three specific elements of the Commons' wider program—the debate over taxation, the impeachment of the financiers, and the disgrace of Alice Perrers—before going on to make some more general points about their appropriation of the principle of "common profit" to give special moral force to their political campaign.

The Good Parliament was asked to make two separate grants of taxation: to renew indirect taxation in the form of the *maltolt*, or wool subsidy; and to authorize a direct tax in the standard form of a fifteenth and tenth. The Commons conceded on the former point but, in a notable act of resistance, resolutely declined to allow further direct taxes.[32] The best justifications for their stance lay in the state of truce that had obtained since the treaty of Bruges of 1375.[33] But the formal statement of the Commons' position does not engage with this, preferring instead to concentrate on the economic plight of the realm and to hold out the prospect of assistance at some undefined moment in the future when the people might once more be able to afford it.[34] This may suggest the influence of the chancery clerk assigned to assist the Commons in drawing up their schedules of taxation, who may have felt it better to avoid complicated legal arguments over whether a state of emergency did or did not obtain in the summer of 1376.

Whatever the case, the refusal was a very considerable blow to the Crown's financial stability and political authority. During the years of victory in the 1340s and 1350s, Edward III had successfully used the doctrine of necessity to argue the case for taxation in times of truce as well as of active military operations.[35] Now, quite suddenly, all those achievements were called into question by the insistence of de la Mare and his fellows that the country could no longer afford the extravagance of further military engagement with the French. In this way, the Commons of 1376 revealed their determination to engage at a new and much higher level in determining financial and diplomatic policy and helped set the parameters for vigorous debate in subsequent reigns as to the occasions and conditions under which Parliament could be obliged to authorize taxation.[36]

[31] Dodd, *Justice and Grace*, pp. 148–51.

[32] *PROME*, 5:297–98; Galbraith, *Anonimalle Chronicle*, p. 80. Knyvet also reportedly requested a tenth from the clergy; although this would have to have been remitted to the convocations of Canterbury and York, the clergy, as so often, followed Parliament's lead and in this case granted no direct subsidy.

[33] *PROME*, 5:294.

[34] *PROME*, 5:297–98. This set a precedent for subsequent appeals of poverty by the Commons: *PROME*, 6:294–95, 315.

[35] Harriss, *King*, pp. 313–75; Ormrod, *Reign of Edward III*, pp. 65, 77–80.

[36] Harriss, "Theory and Practice."

Impeachment was already a recognizable procedure in the common law courts by the mid-fourteenth century, allowing a charge brought collectively by a group of accusers to be taken up and pursued in the name of the king.[37] What was new in 1376 was the application of those principles to judicial process in Parliament, with the Commons making the initial charges and the Lords sitting as judges on the cases. Recent scholarship tends to stress that the process adopted in 1376 was impromptu and thus downplays the Commons' attempt to arrogate the right to make ministers of the Crown publicly accountable for their actions.[38] But Edward III's representatives obviously regarded the Commons' ability to press charges against the courtiers as a deeply ominous development impinging directly on the king's right to regulate his household and government as he thought fit.[39]

All three main sources for the Good Parliament—the *Anonimalle Chronicle*, Walsingham, and the parliament roll—make it clear that de la Mare repeatedly insisted that the accusations made against the courtiers and financiers represented a collective charge on which the Commons were all agreed and in which they were all fully implicated.[40] Nor were the Commons mere passive spectators to the trials that ensued before the Lords. They probably brought the charges against Lord Neville, Adam Bury, and others at a later stage than those against Latimer and Lyons, aiming both to play on the success of the first wave of impeachments and to bring further pressure to bear on the Lords to impose the appropriate penalties on the principal offenders.[41] The Commons also requested that all articles of impeachment brought in the assembly that had initially failed for lack of evidence should be put to special inquiry, and attempted to prevent disgraced ministers from being readmitted to the king's council so as to prevent them from tyrannizing those responsible for their original impeachment.[42] All of this suggests a clear and persistent strategy that drew inspiration from the common oath sworn at the start of the assembly.

The third area of activity in which the Commons of 1376 can be seen to have employed "revolutionary" or "usurpatory" techniques is in their campaign against Alice Perrers. Perrers was closely associated with Lyons and others of the London mercantile community who acted as brokers for royal loans and was, therefore,

---

[37] The key works in the older debate about the procedural elements of impeachment are Clarke, *Fourteenth Century Studies*, pp. 242–71; Plucknett, "Origin of Impeachment"; Wilkinson, *Studies*, pp. 82–99; Bellamy, "Appeal and Impeachment."

[38] Lambrick, "Impeachment"; Prestwich, *Three Edwards*, p. 290; Ormrod, *Reign of Edward III*, p. 36; Waugh, *England*, pp. 225–26.

[39] Edwards, "'Justice' in Early English Parliaments," pp. 292–93.

[40] Galbraith, *Anonimalle Chronicle*, pp. 84–92; Walsingham, *St Albans Chronicle*, pp. 8–19; *PROME*, 5:299–307.

[41] *PROME*, 5:291–92, 307–14; Given-Wilson, *Royal Household*, pp. 146–53.

[42] *PROME*, 5:321, 374.

implicated in the Commons' first wave of allegations in the Good Parliament.[43] More particularly, she was accused of taking money directly from the king's coffers for her own advancement and of manipulating the judicial system; the imputation was that her well-known personal portfolio of real estate was being enlarged by the misappropriation of public funds and by her blatantly unscrupulous pursuit of claims to legal title in the courts.[44]

It is important to note that Perrers was not subjected to the same judicial processes as her male counterparts. Gaunt attempted to take preemptive action against the scandal that might result from the cross-questioning of the king's mistress and instead persuaded his infirm father to promise that Alice would be banished from his presence and never again admitted to royal company.[45] Later in the assembly, however, as the parliament roll makes clear, the Commons returned to demonize Perrers, forcing through a remarkable ordinance: "Because a complaint was made to the king that some women have pursued various business and disputes in the king's courts by way of maintenance, bribing and influencing the parties, which thing displeases the king; the king forbids any woman to do it, and especially Alice Perrers, on penalty of whatever the said Alice can forfeit and of being banished from the realm."[46] This piece of blatant misogyny, though framed in the general, was clearly aimed at a specific target; it is interesting that the failure of the Bad Parliament to overturn the 1376 ordinance formally meant that when Alice Perrers was once again exposed to public wrath in the first parliament of Richard II, she was actually condemned and deprived of all her lands and moveable property on the basis of this legislation.[47] That the Crown was constrained to accept and enforce such a crude piece of legislation provides a particularly striking example of the Commons' assertion of the power to ordain remedies for the ill repute of the court and the good governance of the country during the political crisis in the Good Parliament.

It is the appropriation of the notion of "common profit" by the Commons of 1376 that perhaps best emphasizes the scope and ambition of the wider reform project they espoused. Chancellor Knyvet's charge "that the kingdom might be more *profitably* governed to the honor of the king and the *profit* of the kingdom" echoes throughout the *Anonimalle Chronicle*'s account of the Good Parliament in

---

[43] Galbraith, *Anonimalle Chronicle*, pp. 87, 89. See also the obvious reference to Perrers in the sermon preached by the bishop of Rochester on May 18: Holmes, *Good Parliament*, pp. 103–4.

[44] Walsingham, *St Albans Chronicle*, pp. 42–47; Bothwell, "Management of Position"; Ormrod, "Trials of Alice Perrers."

[45] Galbraith, *Anonimalle Chronicle*, pp. 91–92.

[46] *PROME*, 5:313.

[47] *PROME*, 6:26–32; Given-Wilson, *Royal Household*, pp. 142–45; Giancarlo, "*Piers Plowman*," pp. 135–74; Ormrod, "Trials of Alice Perrers," pp. 375–81.

repeated references to the Commons' discussion of how they and the Lords might act "loyally and profitably" for the "profit of the kingdom."[48] "Common profit" (Anglo-Norman *commune profit*; Middle English *commune profyt*) was the normal vernacular rendering of the Latin *bonum commune*, "common good."[49] Long established as a fundamental philosophical and legal concept, *bonum commune* was deeply rooted in the political discourse of the English Crown, which repeatedly claimed its actions, both in general legislation and in specific grants of rights and privileges, to be undertaken (as it put it in letters patent of 1376) for the "common profit of our people" (*commune commodum populi nostri*).[50]

Surprisingly little was made of the principle by baronial rebels and critics during the later thirteenth and early fourteenth centuries, probably because so much attention in the political crises of Edward I and II's reigns was focused on the more immediate issue of consent.[51] Indeed, the parliament rolls suggest that the rhetoric of common profit was still largely controlled by the Crown in the middle of the fourteenth century.[52] In 1346, for example, the Commons were told by the king's representatives that they should "put forward any petition which could turn to the common profit."[53] The chancery clerks responsible for compiling the schedules of common petitions may well have played a part in teaching the Commons how to use such language: from as early as 1327 we find the phrase "for the common profit" inserted into the standard formulae used by these clerks in the opening clauses of the common petitions.[54] Before the early 1370s, however, the phrase remains unusual even in those contexts, and is only very rarely found embedded in the main texts of common petitions.[55] If there was an obvious argument that the representative element in Parliament was particularly well qualified to determine what constituted "common profit," there is remarkably little to show for it in what is left to us of the Commons' early discourses.

In the Good Parliament, however, all this changed.[56] Just as the *Anonimalle Chronicle* concentrates on the Commons as the arbiters of what might constitute the "profit of the kingdom," so too do all the uses of "common profit" on the parliament roll for 1376 occur in relation to the Commons' own program. "Common profit" occurs no fewer than thirteen times in the common petitions

---

[48] Galbraith, *Anonimalle Chronicle*, pp. 80–92.

[49] Peck, *Kingship*; Wallace, *Chaucerian Polity*; Robertson, "Common Language."

[50] *PROME*, 5:406–7; Harding, *Medieval Law*, pp. 141–42.

[51] Kempshall, *Common Good*, p. 254n70.

[52] *PROME*, 4:461; 5:46, 62, 81, 93, 185.

[53] *PROME*, 4:393.

[54] *PROME*, 4:15, 29, 311, 393, 414.

[55] *PROME*, 4:394, 397, 454; 5:21, 85, 211, 224, 243.

[56] See also the recent discussion by Harriss, *Shaping the Nation*, pp. 441–44.

of 1376. Even given the fact that there are more such petitions in this than any other parliament roll of the later Middle Ages, the concentration is unparalleled. It is applied in a whole series of contexts, from the abolition of the controversial charter for the town of Yarmouth to public fishing rights on the river Brent, from the enforcement of Edward I's mortmain legislation to the proposed campaign against alien religious and foreign spies, and from concerns over the rights of urban corporations to the benefits that were to be had from the current impeachments of evil counselors.[57] In all cases, furthermore, the phrase is located within the substantive text of the petitions rather than in their opening flourishes. This makes more credible an argument that common profit was an integral part of the (Middle English) vocabulary of *viva voce* debate among the Commons out of which the written (Anglo-Norman) text of their petitions sprang.[58] Even if the clerk of the Commons was complicit with de la Mare and his fellows and sought to enhance the petitions by appropriating a rhetoric whose reverberations he understood rather better than did the Commons, it still can be remarked that 1376 represented a radical departure from the norm: in the surviving common petitions of the three preceding parliaments of 1371, 1372, and 1373, for example, there is but a single instance of the use of "common profit."[59] It seems plausible, then, that the Commons and their clerical assistants conspired in 1376, in a new and self-conscious manner, to adopt a language of power and persuasion that added considerable moral force to their remedies for the better governance of the kingdom.

The story of the adoption of "common profit" into the discourse of the Commons in 1376 has some obvious and revealing parallels in a wide range of legal and literary texts of the later fourteenth century. Recent analyses of the rhetoric of "clamor" in the parliament rolls and *Piers Plowman* has demonstrated that a theme often deployed in a political context to represent unanimity and purposefulness could also, in the unsettled social context of the 1370s and 1380s, denote partisan politics, factionalism, and anarchy.[60] In the same vein, it is hard to escape the conclusion that "common profit" was often most keenly asserted in defense of policies that actually promoted sectional interests. The bitter factional infighting among the civic elite of London in the late 1370s was played out in a blatantly hypocritical competition for the moral high ground of the common good.[61] Much

---

[57] *PROME*, 5:318, 322, 324, 334, 337–40, 344, 374, 384.

[58] For the likelihood that most of the debates of the Good Parliament were conducted in English, see Ormrod, "Use of English."

[59] *PROME*, 5:243; Rayner, "Forms and Machinery," pp. 225–27; Ormrod, "On—and Off—the Record," p. 47.

[60] Steiner, "Commonalty"; Ormrod, "Murmur."

[61] Lindenbaum, "London Texts," pp. 286–93; Turner, *Chaucerian Conflict*, pp. 8–55.

more disturbingly, the demographic and economic effects of the Black Death, which came into particularly sharp focus during the 1370s, called seriously into question the notion that the parliamentary Commons had any interest in working for the welfare of the lower orders.[62]

In this latter respect it is especially striking that six of the thirteen usages of "common profit" in the common petitions of 1376 occur in the Commons' extended complaints about idlers, vagrants, and beggars and their far-reaching demands for additional legislation that would, if adopted by the Crown, have severely jeopardized both the economic well-being and the legal rights of the labor force.[63] If their claims to act as a sworn commune had added a revolutionary element to the program of the Commons in 1376, their view of the proper functioning of society remained resolutely traditional, not to say reactionary. Such attitudes contributed directly to the attempts by the leaders of the Peasants' Revolt to claim that they, rather than the representative element in Parliament, stood for the "true commons" (*trew communes*) of the land.[64] The resulting collapse of consensus is strikingly represented in Chaucer's *Parliament of Fowls*, written in the mid-1380s, which argues that no social group is sufficiently disinterested and altruistic to act as arbiters of *commune profyte*. In its strongly implied criticism of the elite's failure to adopt an appropriately inclusive and functionalist notion of common profit,[65] the *Parliament of Fowls* may be said to be just as much an expression of disillusionment over the failure of the Good Parliament as it was an attack on the presumption of the lower orders in the Peasants' Revolt.

If an analysis of the theme of common profit in the common petitions of 1376 serves to emphasize the general social conservatism of the Commons' program in the Good Parliament, this need not undermine the political radicalism they also espoused and the notable excitement and apprehension evoked by their sworn commune. Thomas of Walsingham provides a unique detail that vividly captures the nervousness of political society about the revolutionary implications of the Commons' stance:

> At this time there was a knight called Richard [Stury] who was a very close friend of the king and ever hungry for high office. . . . He had been made an intermediary [*referendarius*] by the king so that the king's wishes might be made known to the knights and their wishes to the king. However, he was bribed, so it is believed, and went out of his

---

[62] Palmer, *English Law*, pp. 14–27; Fryde, *Peasants and Landlords*, pp. 29–53.

[63] *PROME*, 5:337–40; Dobson, *Peasants' Revolt*, pp. 72–74.

[64] Galbraith, *Anonimalle Chronicle*, p. 139; Dobson, *Peasants' Revolt*, p. 130; Watts, "Public or Plebs."

[65] Benson, *Riverside Chaucer*, pp. 383–94; Aers, "*Vox populi*," pp. 439–51; Steiner, "Commonalty," p. 221.

way to misrepresent what the knights were doing and saying: he told the king that they were taking steps to depose him and to do with him as they had previously done with his father, and that he must oppose them immediately, before they obtained the strong support of the common people and could succeed in carrying out their wishes. The king, being most trustful of him, was alarmed by what he said, for his feelings towards the knights were not as they had once been. . . . In the end, however, after the matter had been looked into closely, and the truth was only with difficulty discovered, that [Stury] was a liar and sower of discord, the king removed him from his council.[66]

The well-timed disgrace of Richard Stury derives some support from other sources and has been accepted, at least in spirit, into modern accounts of the Good Parliament. But the most remarkable element in the story—the allegation that the Commons intended to depose Edward III on the direct precedent of his father's forced abdication in 1327—has at the same time been almost completely eliminated from the received narrative.[67] This is hardly surprising in light of the strong sense of loyalty expressed by the Commons of 1376 to the person of the decrepit but still venerable king; Walsingham's own motive in introducing the story seems merely to have been to expose the malice and hypocrisy of those whom he believed to have invented it. If, however, we treat the passage as more generally indicative both of parliamentary action and of public reaction in the summer of 1376, then it may illustrate usefully some of the wider concerns raised by the Commons' usurpation of normal political process.

Walsingham's account of Stury's malevolent intervention seems likely to be rooted in the succession crisis that broke out with the death of the Black Prince during the Good Parliament, and over which the chronicler certainly took a keen interest: in another flight of fancy, Walsingham actually accused Gaunt of plotting to poison his nephew Richard of Bordeaux and disinherit the descendants of Lionel of Clarence in order to have the throne for himself.[68] We know that the Commons discussed the question of the succession in 1376, for the parliament roll includes their request that the young Richard be brought into Parliament and formally created Prince of Wales.[69] In this context, it seems possible that some (lost) accounts of the Good Parliament circulating in its immediate aftermath may have spread a rumor that the Commons had wished not merely to guarantee the line of succession but also artificially to speed up the transfer of power from the old king to his new heir. If the author of the

[66] Walsingham, *St Albans Chronicle*, pp. 30–31. See also Walsingham's allegation that Stury had attempted to turn the Black Prince against the Commons: ibid., pp. 34–35.

[67] Holmes, *Good Parliament*, p. 106; Given-Wilson, *Royal Household*, pp. 148–49.

[68] Walsingham, *St Albans Chronicle*, pp. 38–41; Bennett, "Edward III's Entail."

[69] *PROME*, 5:315.

Anonimalle Chronicle was aware of such stories, he might also have been aware of its treasonous implications and wisely let it drop it from his apologia for Peter de la Mare. In the minds of conservative commentators, however, the very fact that the Commons had taken a sworn oath of confederacy at the beginning of that same parliament could have stimulated the false idea that they had intended nothing less than the deposition of Edward III. The last time that a sworn league had been constituted at the national level was for the overthrow of Edward II's regime in the winter of 1326/27. There were at least some political observers in late fourteenth-century England who recognized all too readily the historical parallels of the sworn commune of 1376.

Since the eighteenth and nineteenth centuries the history of the Good Parliament has been readily accommodated into a comfortable, liberal tradition about the inexorable rise of the democratic element in English politics from Simon de Montfort to Oliver Cromwell. This study has suggested that, while the actions of the 1376 parliament were certainly appreciated and openly celebrated in their own time, late fourteenth-century political culture remained distinctly ambivalent over the implications of some of those actions. The self-conscious appropriation of the language of "common profit" in the rhetoric and reportage of the Good Parliament may have created its own momentum, driving understandings of the aims of the Commons far beyond the conservative instincts of many of its members and provoking much more vexed speculation as to revolutionary means and ends. Such a position helps, in turn, to explain the passivity and fatalism demonstrated by the polity to the systematic reversal of the reform program over the winter of 1376/77. If, as this article has suggested, the Commons of 1376 self-consciously appropriated the revolutionary mantle of the *communes* of 1258 and 1327, then the Good Parliament ought to find a genuine place not just in accounts of the rise of parliamentary democracy but also, and just as importantly, in the history of English radicalism.

Bibliography

Aers, David. "*Vox populi* and the Literature of 1381." In *Cambridge History*, ed. Wallace, pp. 432–53.

Baldwin, Anna P. *The Theme of Government in "Piers Plowman."* Cambridge: D. S. Brewer, 1981.

Barr, Helen, ed. *The "Piers Plowman" Tradition.* London: J. M. Dent, 1993.

Bellamy, J. G. "Appeal and Impeachment in the Good Parliament." *Bulletin of the Institute of Historical Research* 39 (1966): 35–46.

Bennett, Michael J. "Edward III's Entail and the Succession to the Crown, 1376–1471." *English Historical Review* 113 (1998): 580–609.

Benson, Larry, gen. ed. *The Riverside Chaucer*, 3rd ed. Boston: Houghton Mifflin, 1987; repr. Oxford: Oxford University Press, 1988.

Bothwell, James. "The Management of Position: Alice Perrers, Edward III, and the Creation of a Landed Estate, 1362–1377." *Journal of Medieval History* 24 (1998): 31–51.

Brand, P., A. Curry, C. Given-Wilson, R. E. Horrox, G. Martin, W. M. Ormrod, and J. R. S. Phillips, eds. *The Parliament Rolls of Medieval England*. 16 vols. Woodbridge: Boydell and Brewer, 2005 [*PROME*].

Brown, A. L. "Parliament, c. 1377–1422." In *English Parliament*, ed. Davies and Denton, pp. 109–40.

Brown, Elizabeth A. R. "Reform and Resistance to Royal Authority in Fourteenth-Century France: The Leagues of 1314–1315." *Parliaments, Estates and Representation* 1 (1981): 109–37.

Calendar of Close Rolls Preserved in the Public Record Office, Edward III, 1374–77. London: His Majesty's Stationery Office, 1913.

Calendar of Patent Rolls Preserved in the Public Record Office, Richard II, 1377–81. London: Her Majesty's Stationery Office, 1896.

Clanchy, M. T. *England and Its Rulers, 1066–1272*. 2nd ed. Oxford: Blackwell, 1998.

Clarke, M. V. *Fourteenth Century Studies*. Oxford: Clarendon Press, 1937.

———. *Medieval Representation and Consent*. London: Longmans, 1936.

Davies, R. G., and J. H. Denton, eds. *The English Parliament in the Middle Ages*. Manchester: Manchester University Press, 1984.

Dobson, R. B., ed. *The Peasants' Revolt of 1381*. 2nd ed. London: Macmillan, 1983.

Dodd, Gwilym. "Changing Perspectives: Parliament, Poetry and the 'Civil Service' under Richard II and Henry IV." *Parliamentary History* 25 (2006): 299–322.

———. *Justice and Grace: Private Petitioning and the English Parliament in the Later Middle Ages*. Oxford: Oxford University Press, 2007.

———. "A Parliament Full of Rats? *Piers Plowman* and the Good Parliament of 1376." *Historical Research* 79 (2006): 21–49.

Edwards, J. Goronwy. "'Justice' in Early English Parliaments." In *Historical Studies of the English Parliament*, ed. E. B. Fryde and Edward Miller, 1:279–97. 2 vols. Cambridge: Cambridge University Press, 1970.

———. *The Second Century of the English Parliament*. Oxford: Clarendon Press, 1979.

Fryde, E. B. *Peasants and Landlords in Later Medieval England*. Stroud: Alan Sutton, 1996.

Galbraith, V. H., ed. *The Anonimalle Chronicle, 1333–1381*. Manchester: Manchester University Press, 1927.

Giancarlo, Matthew. *Parliament and Literature in Late Medieval England*. Cambridge: Cambridge University Press, 2007.

———. "*Piers Plowman*, Parliament, and the Public Voice." *Yearbook of Langland Studies* 17 (2003): 135–74.

Given-Wilson, Chris. *The Royal Household and the King's Affinity: Service, Politics and Finance in England, 1360–1413*. New Haven, CT: Yale University Press, 1986.

Gross, Anthony. "Langland's Rats: A Moralist's View of Parliament." *Parliamentary History* 9 (1990): 286–301.

Harding, Alan. *Medieval Law and the Foundations of the State*. Oxford: Oxford University Press, 2002.

———. "The Origins of the Crime of Conspiracy." *Transactions of the Royal Historical Society*, 5th ser., 33 (1983): 89–108.

Harriss, Gerald L. "The Formation of Parliament, 1272–1377." In *English Parliament*, ed. Davies and Denton, pp. 29–60.

———. *King, Parliament and Public Finance in Medieval England to 1369*. Oxford: Clarendon Press, 1975.

———. *Shaping the Nation: England, 1360–1461*. Oxford: Clarendon Press, 2005.

———. "Theory and Practice in Royal Taxation: Some Observations." *English Historical Review* 97 (1982): 811–19.

Holmes, George. *The Good Parliament*. Oxford: Clarendon Press, 1975.

Kempshall, M. S. *The Common Good in Late Medieval Political Thought*. Oxford: Clarendon Press, 1999.

Kerby-Fulton, Kathryn, and Steven Justice. "Reformist Intellectual Culture in the English and Irish Civil Service: The *Modus tenendi parliamentum* and Its Literary Relations." *Traditio* 53 (1998): 149–202.

Lambrick, Gabrielle. "The Impeachment of the Abbot of Abingdon in 1368." *English Historical Review* 82 (1967): 250–76.

Langland, William. *The Vision of Piers Plowman*, ed. A. V. C. Schmidt. London: J. M. Dent, 1978.

Lewis, N. B. "Re-election to Parliament in the Reign of Richard II." *English Historical Review* 48 (1933): 364–94.

Lindenbaum, Sheila. "London Texts and Literate Practice." In *Cambridge History*, ed. Wallace, pp. 284–309.

Lyon, Bryce D. *A Constitutional and Legal History of Medieval England*. 2nd ed. New York: W. W. Norton, 1980.

McKisack, May. *The Fourteenth Century*. Oxford: Clarendon Press, 1959.

Oliver, Clementine. "The First Political Pamphlet? The Unsolved Case of the Anonymous Account of the Good Parliament." *Viator* 38 (2007): 251–68.

———. "New Light on the Life and Manuscripts of a Political Pamphleteer: Thomas Fovent." *Historical Research* 83 (2010): 60–68.

Ormrod, W. Mark. "Agenda for Legislation, 1322–c. 1340." *English Historical Review* 105 (1990): 1–33.

———. "Murmur, Clamour and Noise: Voicing Complaint and Remedy in Petitions to the English Crown, *c*. 1300–*c*. 1460." In *Medieval Petitions: Grace and Grievance*, ed. W. Mark Ormrod, Gwilym Dodd, and Anthony Musson, pp. 135–55. York: York Medieval Press, 2009.

———. "On—and Off—the Record: The Rolls of Parliament, 1337–1377." *Parliamentary History* 23 (2004): 39–56.

———. "The Peasants' Revolt and the Government of England." *Journal of British Studies* 29 (1990): 1–30.

———. *The Reign of Edward III: Crown and Political Society in England, 1327–1377*. New Haven, CT: Yale University Press, 1990.

———. "The Trials of Alice Perrers." *Speculum* 83 (2008): 366–96.

———. "The Use of English: Language, Law, and Political Culture in Fourteenth-Century England." *Speculum* 78 (2003): 750–87.

Palmer, R. C. *English Law in the Age of the Black Death, 1348–1381*. Chapel Hill: University of North Carolina Press, 1993.

Peck, Russell A. *Kingship and Common Profit in Gower's "Confessio Amantis."* Carbondale: Southern Illinois University Press, 1978.

Plucknett, T. F. T. "The Origin of Impeachment." *Transactions of the Royal Historical Society*, 4th ser., 24 (1942): 47–71.

Prestwich, Michael. *English Politics in the Thirteenth Century*. Basingstoke: Macmillan, 1990.
———. *The Three Edwards*. London: Weidenfeld and Nicolson, 1980.
Pronay, Nicholas, and John Taylor, eds. *Parliamentary Texts of the Later Middle Ages*. Oxford: Clarendon Press, 1980.
Rayner, Doris. "The Forms and Machinery of the 'Commune Petition' in the Fourteenth Century." *English Historical Review* 56 (1941): 198–233, 549–70.
Reynolds, Susan. *Kingdoms and Communities in Western Europe, 900–1300*. 2nd ed. Oxford: Clarendon Press, 1997.
Richardson, H. G. "John of Gaunt and the Parliamentary Representation of Lancashire." *Bulletin of the John Rylands Library* 22 (1938): 175–222.
Rigby, S. H. *English Society in the Later Middle Ages: Class, Status and Gender*. Basingstoke: Macmillan, 1995.
Robertson, Kellie. "Common Language and Common Profit." In *The Postcolonial Middle Ages*, ed. Jeffrey Jerome Cohen, pp. 209–28. Basingstoke: Palgrave Macmillan, 2000.
Roskell, J. S. *The Commons and Their Speakers in English Parliaments*. Manchester: Manchester University Press, 1965.
Saul, Nigel. *Richard II*. New Haven, CT: Yale University Press, 1997.
Steiner, Emily. "Commonalty and Literary Form in the 1370s and 1380s." *New Medieval Literatures* 6 (2003): 199–221.
Stubbs, William. *The Constitutional History of Medieval England*. 3rd ed. 3 vols. Oxford: Clarendon Press, 1887.
Taylor, John. *English Historical Literature in the Fourteenth Century*. Oxford: Clarendon Press, 1987.
Thomas, A. H., ed. *Calendar of Plea and Memoranda Rolls of the City of London, 1323–1364*. Cambridge: Cambridge University Press, 1926.
Tout, Thomas Frederick. *Chapters in the Administrative History of Mediaeval England*. 6 vols. Manchester: Manchester University Press, 1920–33.
———. *The Collected Papers of Thomas Frederick Tout*. 3 vols. Manchester: Manchester University Press, 1932–34.
Treharne, R. E., and I. J. Saunders, eds. *Documents of the Baronial Movement of Reform and Rebellion, 1258–1267*. Oxford: Clarendon Press, 1973.
Tuck, Anthony. *Crown and Nobility: England, 1272–1461*. 2nd ed. Oxford: Blackwell, 1999.
Turner, Marion. *Chaucerian Conflict: Languages of Antagonism in Late Fourteenth-Century London*. Oxford: Clarendon Press, 2007.
Valente, Claire. "The Deposition and Abdication of Edward II." *English Historical Review* 113 (1998): 852–81.
Walker, Simon. *The Lancastrian Affinity, 1361–1399*. Oxford: Clarendon Press, 1990.
Wallace, David, ed. *The Cambridge History of Medieval English Literature*. Cambridge: Cambridge University Press, 1999.
———. *Chaucerian Polity: Absolutist Lineages and Associational Forms in England and Italy*. Stanford: Stanford University Press, 1997.
Walsingham, Thomas. *The St Albans Chronicle: The "Chronica maiora" of Thomas of Walsingham*. Vol. 1, *1376–1394*. Ed. and trans. John Taylor, Wendy R. Childs, and Leslie Watkiss. Oxford: Clarendon Press, 2003.
Watts, John. "Public or Plebs: The Changing Meaning of 'The Commons,' 1381–1529." In *Power and Identity in the Middle Ages: Essays in Memory of Rees Davies*, ed. Huw Pryce and John Watts, pp. 242–60. Oxford: Clarendon Press, 2007.

Waugh, Scott L. *England in the Reign of Edward III*. Cambridge: Cambridge University Press, 1991.

Wilkinson, Bertie. *Studies in the Constitutional History of the Thirteenth and Fourteenth Centuries*. 2nd ed. Manchester: Manchester University Press, 1952.

Constitutional Discourse in Illuminated English Law Books

Anthony Musson

CONSTITUTIONAL HISTORY is normally studied with regard to texts: the documents that preserve and safeguard rights, privileges, gains, and concessions and cumulatively form a legal and constitutional "canon." Moving away from the traditional text-based approach, this essay provides a fresh analysis of the key constitutional themes by employing visual sources as a means of recovering and reevaluating contemporary discourse. Accordingly, on the basis of illuminations in statute books, charters, and legal treatises, this study articulates attitudes toward justice and good governance, toward the perceived qualities of kingship (and queenship), the exercise of the royal prerogative of grace and the king's relationship with Parliament. It considers the reality behind the images and evaluates how far they differ from conventional textual and contextual interpretations. It also assesses the extent to which the images reveal a coherent and instructive picture not only of the responsibilities of the Crown, but also the expectations of the ruled, especially those who commissioned, owned, and used the legal volumes and themselves had a stake in the system.

Illuminated Law Books as Sources

Vernacular literature of this type is not normally thought of as containing illumination owing to its technical content and utilitarian nature. The volumes that survive are bespoke collections that were copied and assembled in both regular quarto and smaller, pocket-sized volumes.[1] While there is not necessarily a uniformity or set pattern to the material contained in the volumes, their organization and content

The research for this essay was funded by the British Academy.
[1] Skemer, "From Archives"; Skemer, "Reading the Law," pp. 113–15.

can be similar.[2] They frequently start with collections of English statutes (either the *statuta antiqua*[3] or the *nova statuta*,[4] occasionally both) and then include common-law treatises, some lengthy (such as Bracton or Britton), some shorter (such as Fet Asaver, Judicium Essoniorum, Hengham Parva, and Hengham Magna). Volumes sometimes include or comprise precedents on pleading (such as *Brevia placitata* or *Novae narrationes*) and/or registers of writs.

Legal historians have understandably been more concerned with the substantive content of the textual material of the volumes than their visual import,[5] but there has been some interest in the wider legal context. Michael Clanchy, for example, has drawn attention to the use of visual representation in the transition from a memorial to a documentary culture[6] and Baker has examined the images in a number of law books for what they can tell us about lawyers and the development of legal costume in the later Middle Ages.[7] Art historians, too, have highlighted the significance of legal manuscripts in the wider study of English Gothic illumination, but they have tended to concentrate on the texts of Roman and canon law, rather than those pertaining to the English common law.[8] Special studies of illuminated English texts have been made by art historians (such as Michael Camille, Adelaide Bennett, and M. A. Michael), who have provided detailed and illuminating discussions of the art and its immediate context.[9] They have tended to concentrate their analysis on individual volumes,[10] however, so to date there has been no systematic study of the images in English law books, nor an attempt to explore the wider significance of their iconography within a legal and political context.

A major hurdle in trying to evaluate the continuum of ideas portrayed in the images is the dearth of information concerning the provenance of the books.

---

[2] Skemer, "Sir William Breton's Book," pp. 27–28. Skemer provides the contents and organizational scheme for Breton's statute collection (pp. 38–42), which can be compared with the structure of Anthony Bek's volume as set out in Bennett, "Anthony Bek's Copy," pp. 18–21.

[3] Magna Carta (1215, 1225, or 1297 version) and statutes from the reigns of Henry III, Edward I, and Edward II (including ordinances and pseudo-statutes that have not been precisely dated).

[4] Depending upon when the volume was compiled, they usually comprised statutes from the reign of Edward III through to Richard II, Henry IV, or Henry VI. Later volumes included statutes of Edward IV, Richard III, and Henry VII.

[5] Richardson and Sayles, "Early Statutes"; Plucknett, *Early English Legal Literature*; Ramsay, "Law," p. 284; Baker, "Books of the Common Law," p. 422.

[6] Clanchy, *From Memory*. For a comparison of different sizes of statute books and an illuminated page, see ibid., plates 16–18.

[7] Baker, "History"; Baker, *Order of Serjeants*, pp. 67–75.

[8] See Sandler, *Gothic Manuscripts*; Scott, *Later Gothic Manuscripts*. For discussion of illuminated Roman civil law and canon law texts see L'Engle and Gibbs, *Illuminating the Law*.

[9] Bennett, "Anthony Bek's Copy," pp. 3–7; Michael, "Manuscript Wedding Gift"; Camille, "At the Edge."

[10] Notably volumes of extraordinary artistic merit which are now in the United States.

Little is known about the identities of those who compiled them or carried out the illustrations. Much legal business was concentrated in London and Westminster and it may be surmised that legal volumes were produced in the cosmopolitan London workshops by scribes and artists located there. We should not assume, though, that all legal books were the product of London workshops, since the various cathedral cities and the scholarly milieu of Oxford and Cambridge also provided an environment for the production of illuminated texts. Moreover, it should be remembered that for much of the early fourteenth century the central courts and other organs of government were centered on York rather than the capital. Legal volumes with illuminated initials could well have been produced to order for the judges, lawyers, and officials serving in a variety of locations outside of London.[11]

Connections between groups of artists working on legal manuscripts have been established by art historians through analysis of idiosyncratic stylistic traits appearing in the various genres of manuscript on which the illuminators worked.[12] Similarities have been noted in the art of a number of mid- to late fifteenth-century books of statutes,[13] though the linkage has normally been made only within the "exceptionally handsome copies of collections of statutes"[14] by virtue of the lavish and detailed illumination. With the exception of British Library, MS Harley 926, which has been attributed to the De Bois master, who is known to have illuminated books of hours,[15] the artistic context of the smaller, more sparsely pictured fourteenth-century volumes is understandably obscure.

The extent of the commissioning patron's or donor's influence on the imagery is another area that demands consideration. Research carried out in this field has revealed that the grantee of a charter usually commissioned and paid for its illumination.[16] Similarly, psalters and books of hours could be elaborately illuminated, their images providing a social and political commentary at the request of the commissioning patron.[17] Although contracts linking scribe and artist to a particular patron have not survived, it is likely that the same situation pertained for illuminated law books as for these forms, thereby making the resulting volume intrinsically personal to its original owner. Even if some of them were copied to a standard, preordained programmatic scheme approved in advance (of which

---

[11] Michael, "Oxford, Cambridge and London"; Ormrod, "Competing Capitals."

[12] Camille, "Visualising in the Vernacular," pp. 101, 104; Michael, "Manuscript Wedding Gift," pp. 585–86; Binski and Panayotova, *Cambridge Illuminations*, pp. 283–84.

[13] Scott, "Late Fifteenth-Century," pp. 102–5.

[14] Ramsay, "Law," p. 284.

[15] Smith, *Art, Identity and Devotion*, p. 28n71.

[16] Danbury, "English and French Artistic Propaganda," pp. 76–77, 80.

[17] Camille, *Mirror in Parchment*; Sandler, "Political Imagery."

there is some evidence amongst the *nova statuta* group),[18] there was still scope for modification of detail and format. Indeed, systematic comparative study of the law books reveals that deviations from the familiar and the standard can be found among the surviving corpus of volumes. The variety is particularly evident in the illustration for Magna Carta, but also holds true for some of the portraits of the sovereign delineating the various *nova statuta*.[19] The image, therefore, was the product of the commissioning patron's instructions intermingled with the illuminator's interpretation of these instructions.

The extent to which the end product conformed to the commissioning patron's expectations is not ascertainable, but the finished work was essentially the product of various mental impulses: a cocktail of imagination, perceptions, factual knowledge, aspirations, and ideals. As such it represents both a personal and (where there was collaboration in the production or multiple ownership) a collective form of engagement in political/legal cogitation and commentary. We should also bear in mind that artistic conventions could affect the choice of image and the format of the miniature. Indeed, the researcher has to be alive to the possible infusion of style and content from other genres, especially borrowings from Roman and canon law illuminated programs as well as those of Bibles, psalters, chronicles, and volumes of romance literature.[20]

Law books (with or without illumination) were essentially privately produced for a relatively small market and, given their modest size, usually destined for individual readers.[21] Clients were not just lawyers, but a whole range of "consumers" of legal literature, among whom were public officials, lay landowners, merchants, estate stewards, ecclesiastical institutions, and urban corporations.[22] We know that people sometimes borrowed each other's statute books,[23] and they may have compared the images between books. The extent to which such activity took place and how widely the import of illuminated volumes traveled beyond what was a comparatively small circle of users is difficult to discern.[24] Again, the information we do have about who owned or commissioned them tends to be in connection with the most lavish and elaborate "presentation" copies, rather than the smaller utility grade, practitioner copies, although these are occasionally inscribed

---

[18] Scott, "Late Fifteenth-Century," pp. 102–5.

[19] For analysis of the latter see below.

[20] For example, the scene of jousting knights reflecting a Roman law maxim in a copy of the English Bracton treatise (see below).

[21] The most elaborate and lavish versions (some of which are large in size) were no doubt intended to reflect the status and probity of the patron.

[22] Musson, *Medieval Law*, pp. 122–23.

[23] Bodleian Douce 132, fol. 82v (for example, the prior of Drax).

[24] Occasionally illuminated books were stolen from their owners and distributed elsewhere.

with words indicating ownership.[25] This knowledge is vital in assessing the extent to which the images can be thought to contain meaning and convey ideas or messages. The fact that Edward III was the intended recipient of a splendidly illustrated volume,[26] that Anthony Bek, bishop of Durham commissioned one,[27] and that Thomas Pygot, a serjeant-at-law, was the original owner of another,[28] provides valuable insight into the intentions behind particular iconographic programs and enables a more nuanced evaluation of their wider impact and significance to constitutional historians.

Justice and Good Governance

Royal image is employed to enhance the leading constitutional document, Magna Carta. Regarded by contemporaries as the touchstone of good governance and the exercise of right justice, a text of the Great Charter usually prefaces *statuta antiqua*.[29] Medieval people were familiar with royal images and understood their associated symbolism both in an ecclesiastical context (symbolizing God or biblical monarchs) and in the secular world (serving as an icon of royal government).[30] The illuminated initial at the opening employs the image of an enthroned king looking and/or pointing toward the start of the written text.[31] Comparatively few volumes, however, contain versions of the text appropriate to its promulgation in the reigns of John or Henry III.[32] The majority of surviving legal collections in fact use Edward I's 1297 confirmation, defined by the king in the illuminated initial *E* (appropriate for the beginning 'Edwardus Rex . . .'). The king should be viewed in conjunction with the written text: his gesture (the raised index finger or sword) not only serves as a directional device for the reader, but can be regarded as underlining the importance of the text and/or endorsing its authority.[33] A graphic instance of this can be seen in an Exchequer memoranda roll of 1300, which unusually has the marginal figure of a bearded and crowned Edward I pointing to a request that the barons of the Exchequer should observe the clauses of Magna Carta.[34]

[25] For example, some reveal names: Gille (BL Hargrave 274); Coleridge (BL Harley 947). The owners of these volumes, however, have not been definitively linked to a particular "consumer" group.

[26] Harvard 12.

[27] Scheide 30.

[28] Bodleian Hatton 10.

[29] Some volumes of *nova statuta* also lead with Magna Carta before going on to the statutes of Edward III's reign (for example, Bodleian Hatton 10; Merton 297B).

[30] Kauffmann, *Biblical Imagery*; Watts, "Looking for the State," pp. 245, 264–65.

[31] For example: Bodleian Rawl. C 454, fol. 19r; CUL DD. 15.12, fol. 9r; St. John's A.7, fol. 1r.

[32] For example: BL Add. 62534, fol. 1r (John); BL Add. 71713, fol. 8r; BL Add. 62534, fol. 6r (Henry III).

[33] L'Engle and Gibbs, *Illuminating the Law*, pp. 77, 80–82; Hibbitts, "Making Motions," pp. 56–57.

[34] NA E 368/72 m. 12 (reproduced in Prestwich, *Edward I*, plate 20, in between pp. 330 and 331).

The formal iconic qualities and rigidity of the kingly figure offer *gravitas* to the portrayal in the initial and to the statute book as a whole. The picture is emblematic of royal judicial authority. It is *his* law (royal law) that is enshrined in these acts and given effect through *his* person (and likewise the apparatus of justice he controls).[35] In this there are clear parallels with royal charters issued to individuals and institutions, the design of which was intended to convey in visual terms the charter's authority or legal effect.[36] The significance of the portrait of the king at the opening of *nova statuta* collections or in other legal texts lies similarly in the fact that he is the embodiment and executor of both law and justice. An image of the originating fount of justice was clearly felt to be a significant symbol as well as a reminder of his jurisdictional power.[37]

In some illustrations Magna Carta (or the volume of statutes) is specifically depicted as a book with a green cover (or as a parchment document with a green seal) and is demonstrably being presented or raised aloft by an archbishop, with judges and lords in attendance (see figure 1).[38] The symbolism associated with the physical appearance of the volume is significant. First, the color is probably not immaterial, for green, notably the green wax of Exchequer bureaucracy, has connotations of the exercise of royal authority.[39] Indeed, a number of clauses in Magna Carta deal with matters of finance and judicial procedure.[40] Moreover, portrayal in medieval art of the presentation of a sealed document normally indicates that the document has a performative aspect and here may symbolize its oral proclamation.[41] This iconographic motif has its basis in reality as Magna Carta was read out in every county court four times a year by royal decree. Statutes were also proclaimed orally not just in the county courts, but in marketplaces and other public

---

[35] Clanchy, *From Memory*, p. 311, similarly makes the point that the Great Seal "was a portentous object which gave weight, physically and symbolically, to the king's most solemn grants. . . . Its wax impression was a visible sign of the king's will."

[36] Clanchy, *From Memory*, p. 292. The initial *E* of Edward III's grant of privileges to the University of Oxford in 1375, for example, depicts the elderly king, scepter in one hand, handing the charter to the chancellor of the University (Oxford University Archives A.1, fol. 17r.), while another initial *E*, this time of an *inspeximus* (confirmation copy) from Edward III to Richard of Arundel (son of Edmund, lately earl of Arundel) shows the young king giving a charter complete with green seal to a young man kneeling (BL Harley Charter 83.C.13; the green seal pictured is similar to the one attached to the surviving charter).

[37] See below in relation to specific legal treatises.

[38] For example: BL Hargrave 274, fol. 204v; BL Harley 926, fol. 9r; BL Lansdowne 1174, fol. 3r; Bodleian Douce 35, fol. 25r.

[39] Clanchy, *From Memory*, p. 317.

[40] Holt, *Magna Carta*, pp. 317–37.

[41] Seals themselves carried symbolic power and authority as well as helping "to bridge the gap between the literate and the non-literate" (Clanchy, *From Memory*, pp. 308, 314–17).

Figure 1. Edward I confirms Magna Carta. Oxford, Bodleian Library, MS Douce 35, fol. 25r.

spaces within the county.[42] In 1279, the archbishop of Canterbury ordained that copies of Magna Carta should be affixed to church doors, where they could be seen by all comers.[43] Public awareness of its dissemination and its significance can also be seen in its citation in litigation and petitions, even those from disaffected villeins to their manorial lords.[44] The images, therefore, underline the charter (and statute book) both as a physical entity and as having a continuing psychological impact.

---

[42] Luders, et al., *Statutes of the Realm*, 1:136; Maddicott, "County Community," pp. 32, 34–35; Doig, "Political Propaganda," pp. 259–60.

[43] Clanchy, *From Memory*, p. 265. Edward I ordered their removal not long after (Prestwich, *Edward I*, p. 251).

[44] Musson, *Medieval Law*, pp. 250–52; Nichols, "Early Fourteenth Century," pp. 300–307.

The format of the opening initial would also have overtones in a wider context. The illuminator or his patron may have been inspired to employ existing familiar conventions in a new context, for in some ways the scene in this opening illustration is an iconographical construct: it is reminiscent of (or a variation on) the "presentation," a common motif at the preface to volumes commissioned by or dedicated to a royal or lordly patron. The seated patron is shown being handed and graciously accepting the book in question, whether it is a chronicle, romance, or treatise.[45] Indeed, this is precisely the format of the final miniature in one late fourteenth-century volume of statutes, which depicts a kneeling cleric presenting a book to Richard II (seated on a crenellated throne).[46] There is a more constitutional precedent for this presentational scene, too, in volumes of canon and Roman civil law: the introductory miniature to the Fitzwilliam Museum's Decretales shows the text's compiler presenting it to Pope Gregory IX,[47] while in the Durham Cathedral Codex the product of the lawyers' and jurists' codification is being received by Emperor Justinian.[48] In these scenes there is an implication that the pope and the emperor, respectively, by accepting the volume of laws are approving and certifying the authenticity of the texts being given to them.[49] In one volume the king even appears (from his pointing gesture and the scribbling scribe) to be dictating the law.[50]

The observer may query, however, whether the book represents something promulgated by the English king as just lawgiver (supported by the great men deployed alongside him), or in fact signifies royal concessions and a guarantee of royal behavior won by the people (represented by those who are pictured holding it or gathered near it). Royal confirmation of the laws of the realm was expected of a monarch at his coronation and Magna Carta itself was confirmed by kings on numerous occasions from its first issue in 1215 onwards. Yet, a straightforward transference of the concept of the king as lawgiver, certifying the authenticity of texts, as in the Justinian and papal models, does not sit well with the historical context.

The king may appear to be endorsing Magna Carta (as drawn up by the assembled archbishops, magnates, and judges), but there is an element of ambiguity

[45] For example: BL Burney 169, fol. 11r; BL Harley 4431, fol. 53r; BL Royal 16.G.v, fol. 6r; Christ Church 92, fol. 8v; Alexander, "Painting and Manuscript Illumination." The supposed presentation scene is sometimes ambiguous. The miniature in Hoccleve's *Regement of Princes* (BL Arundel 38, fol. 37r), for example, which has been taken to show the author giving a copy of the work to the future Henry V (then Prince of Wales), may in fact be Henry V presenting the book to John Mowbray.

[46] St. John's, A.7, fol. 133.

[47] Fitwilliam McClean 136, fol. 1r; reproduced in L'Engle and Gibbs, *Illuminating the Law*, p. 83.

[48] Durham Cathedral C.I.6, fol. 3r; reproduced in L'Engle and Gibbs, *Illuminating the Law*, p. 84.

[49] L'Engle and Gibbs, *Illuminating the Law*, pp. 82–85.

[50] BL MS Royal 10 D ix, fol. 6r.

underlying the scene for those whose reading of it is informed by their knowledge of the past, since in the case of Magna Carta, quite unlike Justinian or the Decretals, its issue (and subsequent reissues) was coincident with and a product of acute constitutional crisis.[51] Contemporary responses to the representation may have varied according to how Magna Carta itself was understood by the different sections of medieval society and how it came to be reinterpreted over time. For some contemporaries it may have symbolized restraint on the potential arbitrariness of royal power, for others, a "constitution" that litigants could point to in an endeavor to uphold legal rights and justify complaints.[52] The image depicted in the *statuta antiqua*, therefore, rather than being limited to a single, immutable reading is considerably more complex.

Kingship

The monarch's constitutional position and his royal obligations are highlighted in a number of different miniatures. A coronation scene depicted in an image accompanying Magna Carta focuses attention on the king's oath, taken during the ceremony, to uphold the laws and customs of the realm.[53] In the picture, the king is being crowned by two archbishops and receiving from them a parchment document with a green seal (presumably meant to symbolize Magna Carta).[54] Building on the discourse outlined in the previous section, the image implies recognition of the principle that the king was obliged to rule in accordance with the laws. It also represents a desire to highlight Magna Carta as the touchstone of the relationship between the king and his people. An archbishop presenting or holding up Magna Carta juxtaposed with the text of the charter (as depicted in several initials) could thus operate as a symbol of a compact between the king and his people and provide a potent reminder that the king was not above the law.[55] His personal relationship with the law (to the extent that he even meditates upon it, or has it at his fingertips) is implied in another initial that shows the king with a book (the book of statutes?) lying open on a desk positioned just in front of his throne.[56] This image of the king musing on the law is ambiguous, though, and highly contentious if taken in conjunction with the deposition articles against Richard II, which accused him of claiming he alone could change and establish laws in the kingdom

[51] Holt, *Magna Carta*; Prestwich, *Edward I*, pp. 426–30.

[52] Maddicott, "Magna Carta," pp. 46–64; Thompson, *Magna Carta*.

[53] Richardson, "English Coronation Oath."

[54] BL Harley 926, fol. 9r.

[55] See Bracton, *De legibus*, 2:10: "The king has a superior, namely God. And also the law by which he is made king."

[56] Yale G.St.11, fol. 55r.

and that "his laws were in his mouth . . . [and] in his breast" (echoing a Roman law maxim inimical to English law).[57]

The king's constitutional duty toward his subjects, enshrined in notions of kingship, is also captured in the iconography of certain manuscripts of the influential treatise attributed to Henry de Bracton, *De legibus et consuetudinibus regni Angliae* (On the Laws and Customs of England). Although many of the surviving copies of Bracton are unadorned,[58] some do contain royal images, at least on their opening page.[59] Indeed, these pictures go beyond the conventional initial of an enthroned king and encapsulate (through the iconography) a significant Roman law maxim, "graced with arms, armed with laws," which is incorporated in the opening section of the English treatise. In one copy, at the bottom of the page, underneath the text the king is portrayed seated with a sword held aloft in his right hand. In his left hand he is holding up an open book (the treatise?) while two knights in armor on horseback engage in combat with lances, duly observed by three coifed individuals (lawyers), one of whom is gesticulating.[60] The action in the scene directly reflects the opening words of the Bracton treatise: "To rule well requires two things, arms and laws, that by them both times of war and of peace may rightly be ordered. For each stands in need of the other, that the achievement of arms be conserved [by the laws], the laws themselves preserved by the support of arms."[61]

This depiction has a direct if slightly less dramatic counterpart in the miniature contained in another copy of the Bracton treatise, one in which, significantly, the king himself is portrayed fulfilling the requirements of the maxim. Straddling the margin between the two columns seated on a bench-like throne, the crowned king awards (with his right hand) a sword to six mailed knights (wearing blue, green, and red surcoats), while at the same time presenting (with his left hand) a document bearing a white seal to a corresponding number of lawyers (see figure 2).[62] It is interesting that at least two copies of Bracton have received special illumination since (unlike the statute collections) the treatise is more of a

---

[57] Strachey, *Rotuli parliamentorum*, 3:418–19.

[58] For example, Bodleian Rawl. C 159, BL Harley 653, and BL Stowe 380. Merton 320 has gilt and colored initials for the titles of the various books on the contents page (fol. 1r) and some red and gold brackets around the text at the beginning (fol. 5r); but apart from a dragon drawn in red ink in the margin (fol. 7r) there are no miniatures. Cambridge Trinity O.9.24, fol. 5v, has a pen drawing of a hooded man with long fingers pointing toward the opening of the text.

[59] For example, Yale G.B.72, no. 2, fol. 1r.

[60] Bodleian Rawl. C 160, fol. 1r.

[61] Bracton, *De legibus*, 2:19: "In rege qui recte regit necessaria sunt duo haec, arma videlicet et leges, quibus utrumque tempus bellorum et pacis recte possit gubernari. Utrumque enim istorum alterius indiget auxilio, quo tam res militaris possit esse in tuto, quam ipsae leges armorum podio sint servatae."

[62] BL Add. 11353, fol. 9r. The martial theme is continued in the right hand margin, where a herald blows a trumpet, and at the bottom of the page, where various hybrids engage in combat.

Figure 2. "Armed with Laws." © The British Library Board, London, BL MS Add. 11353, fol. 9r.

specialist practitioner text and suggests that lawyers themselves were instrumental in the choice of illustration. They would probably have been aware that the image has parallels with a scene that is depicted at the beginning of canon and Roman law texts: the delegation of temporal and spiritual powers from the divine ruler to earthly secular and religious leaders.[63]

The king's judicial responsibilities are further pictured in some of the practitioner texts that provide forms and precedents for pleading, especially the *Nova narrationes* and registers of writs. The monarch is explicitly shown in some of their opening miniatures hearing the pleas of plaintiffs and petitioners through the mediation of lawyers, while in others he receives plaints from the litigants directly in person.[64] The fact that this same image is replaced with a judge in similar texts underlines not simply the delegation of judicial power, but also the notion of interchangeability: that royal judges are notionally holding sessions in the king's presence (*coram Rege*) and that he, in turn, is acting on behalf of a higher authority, God.[65]

The presence of the judges in the pictures also serves as a reminder that while the king gave his assent to and formally promulgated statutes, much of the legislation contained in the *statuta antiqua* volumes was in fact common law and judge-made case law that was being incorporated into a statutory framework. This fact was made plain by Chief Justice Ralph Hengham when in 1305 he cautioned legal counsel, saying: "Do not gloss the statute. We know it better than you, for we made it."[66] Lawyers owning or commissioning statute books may themselves have felt a slight tension between portrayals of the king as lawgiver (which effectively

---

[63] L'Engle and Gibbs, *Illuminating the Law*, pp. 92, 126, 132 (pl. 5k).

[64] For example: CUL F.6.5; Lambeth 564, fol. 5r; Lambeth 429, fol. 163r; BL Lansdowne 652, fol. 231r.

[65] For example: BL Harley 947, fol. 107r.

[66] Horwood, *Year Books*, 5:82.

likened English legislation to the decrees of emperor and pope set down in the essentially fixed bodies of Roman and canon law) in the light of the role of the judge, whose particular interpretation of legislation and personal decision-making in court gave life to the law.[67]

As the preceding discussion has indicated, the pictures employed in legal texts are not simply illustrating aspects of kingship, law, and justice, but in their juxtaposition of different representational elements insinuate a range of possible meanings thereby manipulating the reader's response to the image. While the subject matter of the majority of miniatures conventionally directs attention toward the king and is employed in such as way as to underline his role as the source of legal authority and the head of the body politic,[68] the images in the statute books are sometimes unexpected and may carry criticism of the monarch or the prevailing constitutional framework. Sometimes they may be shocking, such as a figure baring his bottom in the *bas-de-page* scene of an early fourteenth-century version of Magna Carta (see figure 3).[69] Yet their inclusion and relationship to the program of legislation may ultimately serve to underline the overriding importance of good governance and highlight the qualities required of a just king. It is unlikely for example that the original owner of Bodleian Library, MS Hatton 10 (a serjeant-at-law) was merely poking fun at the establishment. For although the king is wholly absent from the Magna Carta initial in this volume and has been replaced by someone who resembles a jester or court fool,[70] there are iconographic and literary contexts that resonate with this imagery and may serve to explain it.[71] The fool figure has a bird on his arm and his legs are either side of the bar of the initial letter as if riding it, which has parallels with depictions of the trickster known as Marculf, who is sometimes shown riding a goat with an owl or hawk on his arm.[72] The latter is familiar in literary contexts from the *Dialogue between Solomon and Marculf.* This literary association is afforded a visual reality in a copy of Bede's *History*, where a mounted Solomon is shown beckoning to Marculf, whose response is to mock the king in a profane and grotesque manner (in similar fashion to the figure in the *bas-de-pas* scene of Magna Carta mentioned above).[73]

---

[67] Plucknett, *Legislation*, pp. 72–73; Ramsay, "Law," pp. 282–83.

[68] For example, Bodleian Rawl. C 456, fol. 25r; Rawl. C 454, fol. 19r; CUL DD.15.12, fol. 9r.

[69] BL Lansdowne 1174, fol. 3r.

[70] Bodleian Hatton 10, fol. 43r.

[71] Stevens and Paxon, "Fool," pp. 48–79; Gifford, "Iconographical Notes."

[72] Marculf appears in the Pierpont Morgan Register of Writs and is also depicted variously in the Smithfield Decretals, the Ormesby Psalter, and a misericord in Worcester Cathedral: Camille, "At the Edge," pp. 6–13; Camille, *Image on the Edge*, p. 26 (fig. 15); Alexander and Binski, *Age of Chivalry*, p. 433 (cat. no. 536).

[73] Cambridge Trinity R.7.3, fol. 1r; BL Lansdowne 1174, fol. 3r.

Figure 3. Edward I confirms Magna Carta. © The British Library Board. London, BL, MS Lansdowne 1174, fol. 3r.

The prevalence of this conceit makes it likely that it would not be stretching medieval interpretation too far to suggest that a meaningful correspondence is intended between the substitution of the jester for the normal king in MS Hatton 10. Since a fool is quite literally without reason, the king's absence can be interpreted as a lack of rationality. As Magna Carta's provisions are infused with the requirement for reasonableness, the inherent irrationality highlighted by the image may thus be read as a clever visual pun that in turn signals the deeply held notion that the king ought to rule in accord with reason.

While invocation of Magna Carta brought Kings John, Henry, and Edward I to heel, the consequences of royal failure to be guided by reason and rule justly eventually led to the depositions of Edward II, Richard II, and Henry VI. To what extent was this constitutional breach reflected in the world of the illuminated law volumes? The need to uphold the coronation oath and laws of the realm is featured retrospectively in the confirmations of Magna Carta,[74] but in the case of late thirteenth- or early fourteenth-century volumes the constitutional crisis leading to the reissue of Magna Carta in 1297 and 1300 was then still, for some, within living memory, as too, were the events leading to Edward II's deposition. This gave the images contemporary political resonance and because of the provenance of at least one particular book, the opportunity to influence future constitutional affairs. The book in question (now MS 12 in the Harvard Law Library) is believed to have been a present from Philippa of Hainault to Prince Edward on the occasion of their betrothal in 1326.[75] The initial E of Edward I's confirmation of Magna Carta in this volume comprises a double scene (one above the middle bar of the letter and one below it): the upper picture, a king seated on a throne, holding a book in his left hand, supported by archbishops and laymen, may represent the original issuing of Magna Carta under John; the lower picture is similar in composition, but presumably depicts its reissue under Edward I, itself the outcome of another bout of constitutional debate.[76] The image cannot have been formulated without regard to recent political events and was given greater clarity of meaning by Edward II's deposition in 1327. It would, therefore, have held particular significance not just for contemporaries who had lived through the constitutional upheaval, but for the new king himself, whose very position as monarch lay in the hands of the archbishops, magnates, and judges portrayed alongside the king.

---

[74] The images accompanying the text were usually formulated at some distance from the events that gave rise to those documents. Indeed, the earliest surviving statute books are late thirteenth century. Merton 297B, fol. 69v, and St. John's A.7, fol. 1r, which have illuminated versions of Magna Carta from John's and Henry's reign, are of fifteenth-century origin.

[75] Michael, "Manuscript Wedding Gift," pp. 586, 589.

[76] Harvard 12, fol. 2r; Michael, "Manuscript Wedding Gift," p. 598 and fig. 38. Unfortunately in the upper portion the king's face has been rubbed and is virtually obliterated.

Usually royal documents perpetuated a fiction of the king's legal capacity and were issued in his name in spite of the reality arising from his minority or mental disorder. The true nature of power in such situations (irrespective of the constitutional niceties and legal fictions) is not normally revealed in the illuminations. In at least two examples of the initial corresponding to the opening statute of Edward III's reign (traditionally the statute condemning the Despensers), however, rather than conveniently ignoring the reality, an historical perspective is implied and the problem of the Regency and who wielded power during the minority is raised. The young Edward III is flanked by clerics and lords (his natural councillors); but unusually, the lord nearest to the throne (and wearing a gold chain) is pointing to himself or appears to be speaking, which may suggest he has assumed or been accorded some precedence.[77] It is unlikely that it is the patron or owner of the volume identifying himself, since in such cases he would be portrayed kneeling.[78] Since there was no lay chancellor at this time, he may well be identifying himself as the leading magnate of the day. Two contenders fit the bill: Henry of Lancaster, the heir of Earl Thomas (executed in 1322) or Roger Mortimer, earl of March, who with Queen Isabella was one of the beneficiaries of the deposition and the male power behind the throne during their brief regime. The question as to who he represents would seem to rest on the reader's knowledge of history and his particular perspective. Since both volumes in which this individual lord arises were illuminated in the fifteenth century, Roger Mortimer may be considered a valid choice from the point of view of historical hindsight. Henry of Lancaster, however, was president of the regency council at the time of Edward III's accession and might provide a more "constitutional" reading of the image. In any event the image significantly undermines the normal portrayal of Edward III in post-1330 guise (see figure 4).

All *nova statuta* collections have a royal image at the start of each reign, but their imagery does not seem to provide any overt commentary on the reign as a whole. The constitutional positions of Richard II and Henry IV, given the former's deposition and the latter's usurpation, are not questioned. One fifteenth-century miniature, this time accompanying the statutes of Henry VI, does have a topical slant and represents an historical reality, but rather than illustrating the problems of the reign or detracting from the king's regality, it in fact portrays the king's enhanced constitutional role arising from the dual monarchy. Henry is seated on a red canopied throne, dressed in a blue robe edged with fur and a green fur-trimmed hat, holding a crown in each hand (the one in his right hand is smaller than the other) with two scepters in his lap. The symbolism relates to

---

[77] BL Hargrave 274, fol. 50r; BL Cotton Nero C.i, fol. 44r.
[78] Scott, "*Caveat Lector,*" p. 22.

Figure 4. Edward III and lords. © The British Library Board. London, BL, MS Hargrave 274, fol. 50r.

the French and English Crowns, officially united in his person for the first time following his coronation in Rouen in 1431. In case the viewer was in any doubt, there is an accompanying speech bubble which has the phrase "vivere pacifice mihi sit: et unique corone."[79] The illuminator or his patron has used the opportunity provided by the kingly representation to move beyond the obvious imagery and make a particular constitutional statement, one wholly in keeping with the role of the king as endorsing the authority of the law.

Queenship

The constitutional duties and obligations of the medieval queen consort have been highlighted through recent studies of queenship,[80] though the legal role of the royal consort within the monarchy has not as yet been clearly defined by scholars,

[79] Merton 297B, fol. 331r.
[80] Parsons, *Eleanor of Castille*; Laynesmith, *Last Medieval Queens*; Collete, *Performing Polity*.

nor are queens normally represented alongside the king in English legal texts. However, in the same collection that substitutes a judge for a king, the miniature accompanying the opening initial *E* (Edward) to the writ of right in a register of writs, rather than showing the king in authoritative pose as expected, depicts the Blessed Virgin Mary (dressed in a light blue mantle) seated on a bench-like throne with the Christ child (dressed in red) standing next to her on the edge of the throne.[81] At first blush it may appear that the artist has confused the subject matter of his commission in employing a devotional image of the Virgin instead of the normal picture of a king or judge. Yet there may be a rationale underlying the choice of image. Iconographic correspondence was a device used by artists to invoke parallels between the images of religious and secular persons usually in order to emphasize their authority or imply divine association. Substitution of a representation of the Virgin Mary, the Queen of Heaven, for the more accustomed picture of an enthroned king may be intended to reflect and underline not just the status and regality of the heavenly queen, but also that of her earthly counterpart (see figure 5).

The image is appropriate, if surprising, for the opening initial of a Register of Writs given the primacy accorded royal writs within the legal system and the common law's link with divine order.[82] It also makes sense internally since the text of the accompanying writ is directed to the bailiff of the honor of Peveril (in the High Peak, Derbyshire), which was under the personal control of the queen consort. Since the text of the writ refers specifically to Queen Isabella, a direct correspondence with the Virgin Mary may well have been intended by the artists. It would be significant, too, if the image of the Virgin and the Christ child were intended to correspond to Isabella and the young Prince Edward (Edward III). Depending upon the date of the volume, the queen/mother and prince/child combination in the image might thus be felt to represent her political ambitions (and thus a challenge to the existing regime) or provide a visual reflection of her de facto position as queen regent during the minority of her son, the new king.[83]

[81] BL Harley 947, fol. 170r.

[82] The Christ child's right hand is raised in blessing, while his left points toward the opening of the text. Moreover, Mary has one arm around her son, while the other rests on her belly, perhaps signifying that in theological terms she has given birth to the Word of God. While it is not known to what extent fourteenth- or fifteenth-century lawyers equated God's Word with the common law, it was certainly a widely held notion during the sixteenth century. See Raffield, *Images and Cultures*, pp. 1–2, 15.

[83] The volume comes from the early fourteenth century, but no precise date has so far been accorded it. The writ of right refers to Isabella as queen consort, though the king's style in it does not reveal whether it is issued in the name of Edward II or his son. The following writ is one addressed to the bailiff of Thomas, earl of Lancaster, which might suggest a date prior to the earl's death in 1322. On the other hand, the compiler may have wanted to memorialize Thomas of Lancaster by inserting his name in the writ.

Figure 5. Virgin and Child. © The British Library Board. London, BL, MS Harley 947, fol. 170r.

Recent studies of queenship have highlighted the queen's quasi-constitutional role as intercessor, mediating with her husband or son, on behalf of subjects in circumstances or situations that required the king's grace.[84] This relationship may be hinted at in a statute book miniature that has a woman interloper in the bottom left-hand corner,[85] but is more graphically depicted in the Shrewsbury royal charter, which shows Anne of Bohemia interceding on behalf of the citizens of Shrewsbury, kneeling before Richard II.[86] Queen Anne, herself, was

[84] Parsons, "Queen's Intercession"; Parsons, "Intercessory Patronage."
[85] CUL FF.3.1, fol. 77r.
[86] Saul, *Richard II*, plate 15.

particularly cast in this mold of intercessor in popular and literary imagination and again reflected the Virgin's dual role as Heavenly Queen and Madonna of Mercy, interceding on behalf of human souls for God's grace.[87] The latter role is afforded significance in the iconography of the charter marking Henry VI's foundation of King's College, Cambridge, where she is being carried up to heaven and presumably mediating with the Almighty on behalf of the king.[88]

Parliament

If the king as lawgiver were the intended representation in the *statuta antiqua*, the volumes of *nova statuta*, which in their latest versions cover laws of the reigns of kings from Edward III to Henry VII,[89] mark a shift of emphasis in the picturing of royal legislative authority, reflecting the participatory nature of governance and underlining the fact that legislation was not simply a decree of the sovereign. Instead of the king as the sole figure on a simple bench-like throne, or with a few additional figures with whom he is interacting (as is the case in the thirteenth and fourteenth-century miniatures), the initials by fifteenth-century artists usually show him enthroned in the center with bishops on his right and lords to his left, in a stylized recognition of the king's natural allies and supporters in government.[90] In one volume, the pictures for the opening statutes of the reigns of Edward IV, Richard III, and Henry VII, significantly differ from the norm in showing ordinary people, some of them kneeling and gesturing, approaching a wooden bar in front of the king and the lords.[91] This image may be intended to represent subjects who have come in person to petition the grace of the king in sessions of Parliament and seek redress of grievances in what was by then a well-established practice (see figure 6).[92]

In another reading, the addition of commoners to the standard court scene suggests that it symbolizes the three complementary and mutually supportive estates—the Lords Spiritual, Lords Temporal, and Commons—who according to

---

[87] Strohm, *Hochon's Arrow*, pp. 106–9. The Virgin can also be found in representations of the Last Judgment in illuminated manuscripts and wall paintings in churches.

[88] King's College Archives KC/18. See below for further discussion.

[89] A few early volumes of *nova statuta* cover only the reigns of Edward III and Richard II and so do not venture into the fifteenth century.

[90] Scott, "Late Fifteenth-Century," pp. 102–5.

[91] BL Add. 15728, fols. 222v, 232v, 265v. This manuscript is not mentioned as being identified by Dr. Hunt or listed amongst the eight images included in his collection, though it may be referred to obliquely in the final sentence: "Dr Hunt would have been pleased to learn that the known corpus of *nova statuta* of this type had been expanded to include ten copies, with four or five other copies related but made in a somewhat different format" (Scott, "Late Fifteenth-Century," p. 102).

[92] For discussion of this phenomenon see Dodd, *Justice and Grace*, and Ormrod, Dodd, and Musson, *Medieval Petitions*.

Figure 6. Edward IV with lords and Commons. © The British Library Board. London, BL, MS Add. 15728, fol. 232v.

the speech made by Chancellor Robert Stillington, bishop of Bath and Wells, in the parliament of 1467 are understood to carry out their political functions under the guiding hand and watchful eye of the king.[93] Significantly the king (Edward IV) does not carry a sword or scepter in this miniature (his unencumbered hands are across his chest), and his eyes are directed not toward the opening words of the text, but toward the bishop nearest to him on his right, who judging by the bishop's hand gestures appears to be speaking. This may be an acknowledgment of the role of Bishop Stillington and of the chancellor, who usually made the speech commencing parliament and in outlining the issues to be considered and measures to be taken embodied the voice of the king. It was he also who presided over the court of chancery, hearing petitions and redressing grievances, and thus performed an important role on behalf of the king.[94]

[93] Strachey, *Rotuli parliamentorum*, 5:622–23.
[94] Haskett, "Conscience."

The scene may appear to focus on the king and lords (both spiritual and temporal), who are physically separated by the wooden bar, but the presence of the commons should not be overlooked. Their determination to be heard and have their views taken seriously is suggested in the actions of the man singled out in the picture, who appears to be addressing the king. In an acknowledgment of another constitutional phenomenon, he may well represent not just a random petitioner addressing the king, but the Speaker of the Commons, regarded from 1376 as their official mouthpiece.[95] Indeed the imagery formally recognizes the Commons as a constituent part of Parliament. Their political prominence and role in parliamentary business is also recognized in the iconography of the King's College foundation charter. The charter's artwork encapsulates both private petitioning and the parliamentary process: it shows King Henry VI, kneeling at a prayer desk holding the charter and offering up a prayer (in a scroll) to St. Nicholas (one of the patrons of the College). He in turn is interceding with the Virgin (the other patron), who is being carried up to heaven, presumably to offer to mediate to the Almighty on the king's behalf. As with the presentation of common petitions (often the basis for parliamentary legislation), the royal prayer is endorsed by representatives of the Commons, whose scroll reads "Prient les communes," and above them members of the Lords add "Et nous le prioms auxi."

The prominence accorded the Commons in these two fifteenth-century legal texts contrasts with volumes of a similar date that concentrate solely on the Lords. Moreover, the introduction of this imagery appears to suggest that the Commons were only newly prominent in Parliament in the fifteenth century, which goes against the historical reality. Indeed, the seeming reluctance to associate them with the legislation of the fourteenth and fifteenth centuries not only neglects their significance in terms of parliamentary business but also suggests that the illuminators or commissioners of these volumes were essentially conservative in their outlook or their constitutional models lagged behind.[96] The deliberate association of legislation with the lords temporal and spiritual thus flies in the face of more "political" or polemical fourteenth-century texts such as the *Modus tenendi parliamentum*, which had long emphasized the importance of the participation of the Commons in government.[97]

Conclusion

This essay has demonstrated that the pictures contained in English law books are more than simply illustrative. They are given relevance and contemporary

[95] Holmes, *Good Parliament*; Roskell, *Commons*. See also Mark Ormrod's contribution to the present volume.

[96] For consideration of the changing meaning of "Commons" over time, see Watts, "Public or Plebs."

[97] Maddicott, *English Parliament*, pp. 364–66; Dodd, *Justice and Grace*, pp. 130–31.

resonance by the fact that the subject matter of the pictures is by and large related to the texts they introduce, documents such as Magna Carta, the statutes promulgated during the reigns of specific late medieval monarchs, or treatises that explain the derivation of the power of the monarch or reveal the substance and operation of the law. In many instances the images may have been intended by the artist or his commissioning patron to reflect the nature of royal judicial power and authority and thus complement the text. The inclusion of the kingly image, prevalent in many miniatures, was not, however, a deliberate piece of royal-inspired propaganda, but an acknowledgment of the king's role as legislator and fount of justice. Interestingly, the images usually maintain a fiction of constitutional continuity and unbroken legal tradition, untarnished by the personality deficiencies of the various monarchs depicted and unflustered by the political realities and disputes that in some cases underlay the legislation they serenely presided over.

While the written text may often be a straightforward statement of the law, the images accompanying Magna Carta and other statutes are sometimes complex, contain ambiguities, and can be interpreted in several ways. Indeed, for contemporaries, the pictures would operate on numerous levels, activating thought patterns and articulating ideological positions.[98] Unlike the original constitutional texts, very few of the copies are contemporary with the events they are purporting to portray. It is this flexibility of interpretation, depending upon the image's date and context, and sometimes lagging behind or flying in the face of the "political" reading, that makes these pictures remarkable.

The images can introduce elements that are antiauthoritarian and subversive, hinting at royal shortcomings or providing warnings for the legal and political communities. Where the artist does not reproduce the standard or orthodox image, or introduces elements of a subversive nature, we can discern an authorial hand at work inviting critique of the status quo. Indeed, it is in the enhancement or distortion of the standard image that it is possible to discern historical, theological, philosophical, and political commentary on the nature of royal power. This realization is of added significance when the provenance of the volume can be determined and is someone we know was closely connected to the establishment (even the king himself). In this way the potentiality of the images in English law books to convey an alternative constitutional discourse whose import was meant to be deciphered by leading courtiers, judges, and royal officials is a key phenomenon articulated in this essay. What we do not know is the extent to which the images were recognized and shared across the spectrum of owners and users. It would be misleading to imply that the illuminated books of common law texts and statutes taken en masse offer a natural and coherent constitutional discourse,

---

[98] Camille, "Language of Images," p. 33; Lewis, *Reading Images*, pp. xxi–xxii.

although there is clearly some degree of overlap in the intended illustrations and meaning. Nevertheless, individually and as a group they provide both an alternative and complementary perspective to pure texts and offer remarkable insight into perceptions of the theory and practice of law and governance.

Bibliography

Manuscripts

Cambridge, Cambridge University Library [CUL], MSS DD. 15.12, F.6.5, FF.3.1.
Cambridge, Fitzwilliam Museum, MS McClean 136.
Cambridge, King's College, King's College Archives, KC/18.
Cambridge, St. John's College, MS A.7.
Cambridge, Trinity College, MSS O.7.27, O.9.24, R.7.3.
Cambridge, MA, Harvard Law Library, MS 12.
Durham, Durham Cathedral, Chapter Library, MS C.I.6.
London, British Library [BL], MSS Additional 11353, 15728, 62534, 71713; MS Arundel 38; MS Burney 169; MS Cotton Nero C.i; MS Hargrave 274; MSS Harley 653, 926, 947, 4431; MS Harley Charter 83.C.13; MSS Landsdowne 652, 1174; MS Royal 16.G.v.; MS Stowe 380.
London, Lambeth Palace Library, MSS 429, 564.
London, The National Archives [NA], E 368/72.
New Haven, Yale Law Library, MSS G.B.72, no. 2; G.St.11.
Oxford, Bodleian Library, MSS Douce 35, 132; Hatton 10; MSS Rawlinson C 159, C 160, C 454, C 456, C 612B.
Oxford, Christ Church College, MS 92.
Oxford, Merton College, MSS 297B, 320.
Oxford, Oxford University Archives, A.1.
Princeton, Scheide Library, MS 30.

Published Sources and Literature

Alexander, Jonathan J. G. "Painting and Manuscript Illumination for Royal Patrons in the Later Middle Ages." In *English Court Culture in the Later Middle Ages*, ed. V. J. Scattergood and J. W. Sherborne, pp. 141–62. London: Duckworth, 1983.
Alexander, Jonathan J. G., and Paul Binski. *The Age of Chivalry: Art in Plantagenet England, 1200–1400*. London: Royal Academy of Arts, 1987.
Baker, John. "The Books of the Common Law." In *The Cambridge History of the Book in Britain, 1400–1557*, ed. Lotte Hellinga and J. B. Trapp, pp. 411–32. Cambridge: Cambridge University Press, 1999.
———. "A History of English Judges' Robes." *Costume* 12 (1978): 27–39.
———. *The Order of Serjeants at Law*. Selden Society, Supplementary Series, 5. London: Selden Society, 1984.
Bennett, Adelaide. "Anthony Bek's Copy of *Statuta Angliae*." In *England in the Fourteenth Century*. Proceedings of the 1985 Harlaxton Symposium, ed. W. Mark Ormrod, pp. 1–27. Woodbridge: Boydell, 1986.
Binski, Paul, and Stella Panayotova, eds. *The Cambridge Illuminations: Ten Centuries of Book Production in the Medieval West*. London: Harvey Miller, 2005.

Bracton, Henry de. *De legibus et consuetudinibus regni Angliae*. Ed. G. E. Woodbine. Trans. S. E. Thorne. 4 vols. Cambridge, MA: Belknap, 1968–77.

Camille, Michael. "At the Edge of the Law: An Illustrated Register of Writs in the Pierpont Morgan Library." In *England in the Fourteenth Century*. Proceedings of the 1991 Harlaxton Symposium, ed. Nicholas Rogers, pp. 1–14. Stamford: Paul Watkins, 1993.

———. *Image on the Edge: The Margins of Medieval Art*. London: Reaktion, 1992.

———. "The Language of Images in Medieval England, 1200–1400." In *The Age of Chivalry*, ed. Alexander and Binski, pp. 33–40.

———. *Mirror in Parchment: The Luttrell Psalter and the Making of Medieval England*. London: Reaktion Books, 1998.

———. "Visualising in the Vernacular: A New Cycle of Early Fourteenth-Century Bible Illustrations." *Burlington Magazine* 130 (1988): 97–106.

Clanchy, Michael. *From Memory to Written Record: England, 1066–1307*. 2nd ed. Oxford: Blackwell, 1993.

Collete, Carolyn P. *Performing Polity: Women and Agency in the Anglo-French Tradition, 1385–1620*. Medieval Women: Texts and Contexts 15. Turnhout: Brepols, 2005.

Danbury, Elizabeth. "English and French Artistic Propaganda during the Period of the Hundred Years' War: Some Evidence from Royal Charters." In *Power, Culture and Religion in France, c.1350–1550*, ed. Christopher Allmand, pp. 73–97. Woodbridge: Boydell, 1989.

Dodd, Gwilym. *Justice and Grace: Private Petitioning and the English Parliament in the Late Middle Ages*. Oxford: Oxford University Press, 2007.

Doig, J. A. "Political Propaganda and Royal Proclamations in Late Medieval England." *Historical Research* 71 (1998): 253–80.

Gifford, D. J. "Iconographical Notes towards a Definition of the Medieval Fool." In *The Fool and the Trickster*, ed. Paul V. A. Williams, pp. 18–35. Cambridge: D. S. Brewer, 1979.

Haskett, Timothy. "Conscience, Justice and Authority in the Late-Medieval English Court of Chancery." In *Expectations of the Law in the Middle Ages*, ed. Anthony Musson, pp. 151–64. Woodbridge: Boydell, 2001.

Hibbitts, Bernard J. "Making Motions: The Embodiment of Law in Gesture." *Journal of Contemporary Legal Issues* 6 (1995): 50–81.

Holmes, George. *The Good Parliament*. Oxford: Clarendon Press, 1975.

Holt, James. *Magna Carta*. 2nd ed. Cambridge: Cambridge University Press, 1992.

Horwood, Alfred J., ed. and trans. *Year Books of the Reign of Edward the First*. Rolls Series 31. 5 vols. London: Longman, 1863–79.

Kauffmann, Michael. *Biblical Imagery in Medieval England, 700–1550*. London: David Brown, 2003.

Laynesmith, J. L. *The Last Medieval Queens: English Queenship, 1445–1503*. Oxford: Oxford University Press, 2004.

L'Engle, Susan, and Robert Gibbs, eds. *Illuminating the Law: Medieval Legal Manuscripts in Cambridge Collections*. London: Harvey Miller, 2001.

Lewis, Suzanne. *Reading Images: Narrative Discourse and Reception in the Thirteenth Century Illuminated Apocalypse*. Cambridge: Cambridge University Press, 1995.

Luders, A., et al., eds. *Statutes of the Realm*. 11 vols. London: Record Commission, 1810–28.

Maddicott, John. "The County Community and the Making of Public Opinion in Fourteenth Century England." *Transactions of the Royal Historical Society*, 5th ser., 18 (1978): 27–43.

———. "Magna Carta and the Local Community, 1215–1259." *Past and Present* 102 (1984): 25–65.

———. *The Origins of the English Parliament, 924–1327* (Oxford: Oxford University Press, 2010).

Michael, M. A. "A Manuscript Wedding Gift from Philippa of Hainault to Edward III." *Burlington Magazine* 127 (1985): 582–98.

———. "Oxford, Cambridge and London: Towards a Theory for 'Grouping' Gothic Manuscripts." *Burlington Magazine* 130 (1988): 107–15.

Musson, Anthony. *Medieval Law in Context: The Growth of Legal Consciousness from Magna Carta to the Peasants' Revolt.* Manchester: Manchester University Press, 2001.

Nichols, J. F. "An Early Fourteenth Century Petition from the Tenants of Bocking to Their Manorial Lord." *Economic History Review*, 1st ser., 2 (1929–30): 300–307.

Ormrod, W. Mark. "Competing Capitals? York and London in the Fourteenth Century." In *Courts and Regions in Medieval Europe*, ed. S. Rees Jones, R. Marks, and A. J. Minnis, pp. 79–98. York: York Medieval Press, 2000.

Ormrod, W. Mark, Gwilym Dodd, and Anthony Musson, eds. *Medieval Petitions: Grace and Grievance.* York: York Medieval Press, 2009.

Parsons, John Carmi. *Eleanor of Castille: Queen and Society in Thirteenth-Century England.* New York: Palgrave, 1997.

———. "The Intercessory Patronage of Queens Margaret and Isabella of France." In *Thirteenth Century England VI*, ed. M. Prestwich and R. Britnell, pp. 145–56. Woodbridge, Boydell, 1997.

———. "The Queen's Intercession in Thirteenth-Century England." In *The Power of the Weak: Studies on Medieval Women*, ed. J. Carpenter and S. B. Maclean, pp. 147–77. Urbana: University of Illinois Press, 1995.

Plucknett, Theodore F. T. *Early English Legal Literature.* Cambridge: Cambridge University Press, 1958.

———. *Legislation of Edward I.* Oxford: Clarendon Press, 1949.

Prestwich, Michael. *Edward I.* New Haven, CT: Yale University Press, 1988.

Raffield, Paul. *Images and Cultures of Law in Early Modern England: Justice and Political Power, 1558–1660.* Cambridge: Cambridge University Press, 2004.

Ramsay, Nigel. "Law." In *The Cambridge History of the Book in Britain: 1100–1400*, ed. Nigel Morgan and R. M. Thomson, pp. 250–89. Cambridge: Cambridge University Press, 2008.

Richardson, H. G. "The English Coronation Oath." *Speculum* 24 (1949): 43–75.

Richardson, H. G., and G. O. Sayles. "The Early Statutes." *Law Quarterly Review* 50 (1934): 201–23, 540–71.

Roskell, J. S. *The Commons and Their Speakers in English Parliaments.* Manchester: Manchester University Press, 1965.

Sandler, Lucy Freeman. *Gothic Manuscripts, 1285–1385.* A Survey of Manuscripts Illustrated in the British Isles 5. London: Harvey Miller, 1986.

———. "Political Imagery in the Bohun Manuscripts." In *English Manuscript Studies, 1100–1700.* Vol. 10, *Decoration and Illustration in Medieval English Manuscripts*, ed. A. S. G. Edwards, pp. 114–53. London: British Library, 2002.

Saul, Nigel. *Richard II.* New Haven, CT: Yale University Press, 1997.

Scott, Kathleen L. "*Caveat Lector:* Ownership and Standardization in the Illustration of Fifteenth-Century English Manuscripts." In *English Manuscript Studies, 1100–1700.* Vol. 1, ed. Peter Beal and Jeremy Griffiths, pp. 19–63. London: Basil Blackwell, 1989.

———. "A Late Fifteenth-Century Group of *Nova Statuta* Manuscripts." In *Manuscripts at Oxford: R. W. Hunt Memorial Exhibition*, ed. A. C. de la Mare and B. C. Barker-Benfield, pp. 102–5. Oxford: Bodleian Library, 1980.

———. *Later Gothic Manuscripts, 1390–1490*. A Survey of Manuscripts Illuminated in the British Isles 6. London: Harvey Miller, 1996.

Skemer, Don C. "From Archives to the Book Trade: Private Statute Rolls in England, 1285–1307." *Journal of the Society of Archivists* 16 (1995): 193–206.

———. "Reading the Law: Statute Books and the Private Transmission of Legal Knowledge in Late Medieval England." In *Learning the Law: Teaching and the Transmission of English Law, 1150–1900*, ed. Jonathan A. Bush and Alain Wijfells, pp. 113–31. London: Hambledon, 1999.

———. "Sir William Breton's Book: Production of *Statuta Angliae* in the Late Thirteenth Century." In *English Manuscript Studies, 1100–1700*. Vol. 7, ed. Peter Beal and Jeremy Griffiths, pp. 11–37. London: British Library, 1998.

Smith, Kathryn A. *Art, Identity and Devotion in Fourteenth-Century England: Three Women and Their Books of Hours*. London: British Library, 2003.

Stevens, Martin, and James Paxon. "The Fool in the Wakefield Plays." *Studies in Iconography* 13 (1989–90): 48–79.

Strachey, John, ed. *Rotuli parliamentorum: Ut et petitiones et placita in Parliamento tempore Edwardi R.I. (Edwardi II., Edwardi III., Ricardi II., Henrici IV., V., VI., Henrici VII., 1278–1503)*. 6 vols. London: n.p., 1767–77.

Strohm, Paul. *Hochon's Arrow: The Social Imagination of Fourteenth Century Texts*. Princeton, NJ: Princeton University Press, 1992.

Thompson, Faith. *The First Century of Magna Carta*. Minneapolis: University of Minnesota, 1925.

Watts, John. "Looking for the State in Later Medieval England." In *Heraldry, Pageantry and Social Display in Medieval England*, ed. Peter Coss and Maurice Keen, pp. 243–67. Woodbridge: Boydell, 2002.

———. "Public or Plebs: The Changing Meaning of 'the Commons,' 1381–1549." In *Power and Identity in the Middle Ages: Essays in Memory of Rees Davies*, ed. Huw Pryce and John Watts, pp. 242–60. Oxford: Oxford University Press, 2007.

"No more but hang and drawe": Politics and Magic in the Execution of Sir Robert Tresilian, 1388

Don C. Skemer

T HE CHARGES OF HIGH TREASON that the Lords Appellant brought in 1387 against Sir Robert Tresilian, lord chief justice of King's Bench, and other royal officials and councilors, followed by their trial and conviction by the Merciless Parliament in 1388, were significant events in the troubled reign of Richard II (r. 1377–99). Students of English constitutional history have viewed the prosecution of Tresilian and the others as politically motivated and vindictive, in some cases verging on judicial murder. But the crisis did make Parliament temporarily the center of baronial opposition to the concentration of royal power and thus serves as a milestone on the long path to parliamentary sovereignty. "However transitory their victory," Bryce Lyon argued, "the Lords Appellant with the support of other lords and the commons had struck a hard blow at the royal prerogative. The actions of the Merciless Parliament made Parliament the ultimate legal arbiter of the realm and attributed to it supreme political authority."[1] The present article focuses on details of Tresilian's public execution as narrated by Thomas Favent [Fovent] (d. 1404) in his nearly contemporary chronicle of the Merciless Parliament, in which he suggests that the lord chief justice had been involved in necromancy or ritual magic based on the use of amulets. Tresilian was a Cornwall native and Oxford-educated lawyer, who became a king's serjeant-at-law in 1376 under Edward III (r. 1327–77) and rose rapidly under Richard II to become a justice of King's Bench in May 1378 and its chief justice in June 1381.[2] In this capacity, he presided over the

---

[1] Lyon, *Constitutional and Legal History*, p. 503.

[2] Sainty, *Judges of England*, pp. 37n6, 158, 541; Leland, "Sir Robert Tresilian," concludes that Tresilian "may have been ruthless in his interpretation of the law for private and political ends, but as one of the principal intellectual architects of the 'high' doctrine of royal prerogative, he had a lasting if often unfortunate influence" (p. 319).

treason trials and executions of John Ball and other rebel leaders in 1381–82 for their roles in the Peasants' Revolt.[3] Tresilian again loyally represented the young king's interests against Parliament in the constitutional crisis that began in 1386, when Lord Chancellor Michael de la Pole was impeached and a commission of regency was appointed. In August 1387 Tresilian persuaded or compelled other justices in councils at Shrewsbury and Nottingham to support royal prerogative and declare the king's opponents traitors for setting up the commission. Tresilian's role in these councils and his reputation for financial self-aggrandizement would make him an obvious target for the Lords Appellant.[4]

On November 17, 1387, the Lords Appellant appealed Tresilian and four other prominent royal supporters of high treason and demanded that the king call Parliament to consider the charges. After Richard II's supporters failed in battle on December 19 at Radcot Bridge, the king agreed to a treason trial before the next parliament, where Tresilian and the others were ostensibly to enjoy the benefits of impartiality. Yet Parliament would prove to be anything but impartial. Fearing the worst, Tresilian went into hiding during the Michaelmas 1387 term, after being appealed of treason, and by January 1388 he had been replaced as lord chief justice by Walter Clopton. On January 4 the constable of Gloucester Castle was ordered to receive Tresilian, though his whereabouts were unknown, and Sir Nicholas Brembre, former lord mayor of London.[5]

Chroniclers provide vivid but widely differing accounts of Tresilian's three months in hiding, methods of disguise, and subsequent capture on February 19, 1388. Favent records that Tresilian had been hiding in a house adjacent to Westminster Hall, where Parliament had been meeting since the beginning of the month, and that when Tresilian was taken into custody he appeared more like a pilgrim or beggar than chief justice of the realm. The chronicler Jean Froissart (ca. 1337–ca. 1405) added that Tresilian had tried to pass himself off first as a poor traveling merchant and later as a Kentish peasant, traveling to Westminster in order to file complaints against men of the archbishop of Canterbury.[6]

---

[3] Oman, *Great Revolt*, pp. 87–89; Tout, *Chapters*, 3:376–77; McKisack, *Fourteenth Century*, p. 419.

[4] Saul, *Richard II*, pp. 183–84; Stubbs, *Constitutional History*, 2:495–99; Holdsworth, *History of English Law*, 3:560; Zane, "Year Book of Richard II," pp. 441–42; Thornley and Plucknett, *Year Books of Richard II*, p. ix. Article 2 of thirty-three articles against Richard II in 1399 related to the questions to the judges at Shrewsbury in 1387, though the king was held accountable. See Carlson, *Deposition of Richard II*, pp. 30–31.

[5] Hardy, *Syllabus*, 2:514.

[6] Favent, *Historia*, p. 17; Davies, "Some Notes," p. 558; Knighton, *Chronicle*; Froissart, *Chronicle*, 5:26–27 (ch. 92). Froissart perhaps introduced the reference to the archbishop of Canterbury as a reminder of the Peasants' Revolt, when Simon Theobald or Simon of Sudbury (d. 1381), archbishop of Canterbury, was murdered.

Convening on February 3, 1388, the Merciless Parliament condemned Tresilian in articles of impeachment as a "false justice" and sentenced him in absentia to be drawn and hanged, along with Alexander Neville, archbishop of York; Robert de Vere, duke of Ireland; Michael de la Pole, earl of Suffolk; and Sir Nicholas Brembre.[7] Tresilian was apprehended during the parliamentary proceedings against Brembre. The Issue Rolls record that a certain William Forest received a ten-pound reward for finding Tresilian.[8] The *Westminster Chronicle* claims that the Lord Appellant Thomas of Woodstock (1355–97), duke of Gloucester, the youngest son of Edward III, arrested Tresilian within the precincts of Westminster Abbey. Perhaps with the assistance of John de Cobham (d. 1408), Thomas of Woodstock had Tresilian taken by force to the Wool House, also within the precincts, where his claims of religious sanctuary were denied because he had already been condemned for treason. He was then taken to Parliament, which confirmed the earlier sentence of death and forfeiture against him. He did not respond when asked to explain any mitigating circumstances in the intervening period since his original sentence. Responsibility for carrying out the sentence was assigned to one of the Lords Appellant, Thomas de Mowbray, earl of Nottingham, who was to be assisted by Sir Nicholas Exton, lord mayor of London, and by the sheriffs and aldermen.[9]

On the same day Tresilian was first taken to the Tower of London and from there to the gallows at Tyburn on a horse-drawn hurdle or sledge, past crowds of jeering Londoners.[10] Favent suggests that he was accompanied by his Franciscan confessor.[11] Chroniclers described the physical form of the gallows as *furcae*, which

---

[7] Strachey, *Rotuli parliamentorum*, 3:229–38; Hector and Harvey, *Westminster Chronicle*, pp. 240–68.

[8] Sayles, *Select Cases*, p. xi, n3.

[9] Hector and Harvey, *Westminster Chronicle*, pp. 311–13, 324–27. Saul, *Death, Art, and Memory*, p. 23n66; Davies, "Richard II," p. 91; Sharpe, *London and the Kingdom*, p. 239. Sir Nicholas Exton, who had been lord mayor of London in 1386–87, remained in this post until the election of Sir Nicholas Twyford (d. 1390) in October 1388.

[10] Geoffrey Chaucer (ca. 1343–1400) described such a scene in the "Man of Law's Tale," written in the 1390s (Benson, *Riverside Chaucer*, pp. xxiii–xxiv). Benson notes that Chaucer had worked with Tresilian and two other officials executed during the Merciless Parliament. "Whether or not Chaucer saw them moving through the London streets to their deaths, he described such a scene memorably in 'The Man of Law's Tale' (II.645–50)" (Benson, *Riverside Chaucer*, p. xx). Tyburn, then a village in the parish of St. Marylebone, served as a place of execution from the twelfth to eighteenth centuries. The gallows were located near present-day London's Marble Arch. Strachey, *Rotuli parliamentorum*, 3:238: "Et q' la dite Execution serroit faite par le Mareschall d'Engleterre, prise a lui eide & force de Maire, Viscountes, & Aldermaunes de Loundres; Et ensi feust faites mesme le jour"; see also Hector and Harvey, *Westminster Chronicle*, pp. 282–83. The word *drawing* refers to Tresilian having been drawn to the gallows by horse, rather than "drawing" in the sense of being dismembered (as when someone was hanged, drawn, and quartered), a cruel refinement in execution of death sentences for high treason, as at the execution of John Ball; see Campbell, *Black's Law Dictionary*, p. 716.

[11] Favent, *Historia*, p. 18.

is consistent with the form of gallows most often depicted in English illuminated manuscripts of the twelfth to fourteenth centuries. Hanged men are depicted fully clothed, shirtless, and wearing only breeches or a loincloth, or even completely naked. Condemned men might be stripped as part of the humiliation of public execution. Executioners might even claim their clothing. For a man to be hanged, he could have been turned off the sledge or cart that had transported him to the gallows, or he could have been made to climb a ladder, which was then removed.[12]

Tresilian seems to have arrived at Tyburn fully clothed, if we can trust Favent's account; for after being beaten with clubs and sticks to make him climb the ladder up to the hangman's noose, Tresilian supposedly said, "So long as I do wear certain things [*aliqua*] upon me, I shall not die."[13] The condemned man was referring to textual amulets, almost certainly parchment, worn on his body, a widespread practice in the medieval world. Amulets believed to offer general protection were most commonly worn around the neck, so that they were concealed under clothing and positioned directly over the heart, which in medieval thinking was the gateway to the soul. One may well wonder why Tresilian would have foolishly volunteered his concealed source of magical protection to the executioner. If Tresilian had arrived shirtless, it would have been obvious to all that he was wearing amulets in a leather pouch or fabric sack dangling by its drawstring over his heart. Or if he had arrived fully clothed, one could imagine the earl marshal ordering his clothes removed. But Favent reports only the hangman's immediate reaction to Tresilian's boast, which was to have the condemned man stripped naked.[14] Once the amulets were found and removed, Tresilian was summarily hanged, and his throat was cut for good measure. The next day his

---

[12] Pictorial representations in manuscripts show the hangman's rope and noose suspended from a horizontal pole or crossbeam, supported from each side by a forked upright post. This may be seen in pictorial representations accessible through the database of the Index of Christian Art, at http:// ica.princeton.edu. A group of eight thieves hanged on the gallows (*furcae*) are shown stripped to the waist in a ca. 1130 manuscript *Vita Sancti Edmundi* (Morgan M.736, fol. 19v). Hanged men are shown in all states of dress or undress in two English illuminated psalters dating from the first third of the thirteenth century (Staatsbibliothek clm. 835, fols. 14v, 30v, 110r; Trinity B.11.4, fols. 7r, 11v). There are two hanging scenes in ink-and-wash drawings in Queen Mary's Psalter, produced in London, ca. 1310–20 (BL Royal 2.B.vii, fols. 61v, 206r). In one, two sons of Saul and five sons of Michal are shown stripped to the waist; in the other, Ebbo the Thief is depicted fully clothed. All of the hanged men had their arms bound behind their backs. Finally, sculpture in the arch spandrels of the Chapter House of Salisbury Cathedral, ca. 1280–1300, shows a hanged man wearing only short trousers. In general, see Bartlett, *Hanged Man*, ch. 5 ("Death by Hanging"), pp. 42–52. Bartlett has suggested that "the hanged man's clothes were a perquisite of whoever performed the hanging" (p. 43).

[13] Favent, *Historia*, p. 18: "Dummodo aliqua feram circa me, mori non possum."

[14] In the rituals of medieval public executions, transportation on a hurdle, stripping, and hanging were also appropriate for a common criminal. Cohen, "Symbols of Culpability," p. 410.

wife claimed the body, which was interred in the Chapel of St. Francis at Christ Church, Grey Friars of London.[15]

Favent implies that Tresilian's amulets were based on demonic magic or necromancy. They were comprised of *experimenta* and *signa* painted in the manner of astrological signs or talismanic seals, a painted head of a devil, and the names of many evil demons.[16] Whether the executioner had acted alone or under the direction of the earl marshal, clearly there was a belief that these magical devices could offer Tresilian powerful protection against execution or any other form of sudden death. Favent's reference to magic devices has been interpreted in different ways, but generally as amulets of some sort. Scholars have used the incident to show royal courtiers dabbling in magic and astrology, and as evidence of witchcraft, demon worship, and necromancy.[17] For the purpose of this discussion, textual amulets (a term that I use in preference to talismans and charms) were brief apotropaic texts written on separate sheets, rolls, and scraps of parchment or paper of varying dimensions, and then worn around the neck or placed elsewhere on the body for personal protection against demons, disease, and sudden death.

Favent was either referring to a small group of parchment amulets or to a single multipurpose amulet comprised of separate sections. In late medieval England the component texts of a multipart amulet might be called *brevia*. By *experimenta*, Favent probably meant textual amulets of the sort that included pseudo-Solomonic rituals and seals essential to invoke or summon powerful angels and helpful demons by name to the aid of the bearer.[18] Pseudo-Solomonic texts influenced by Hellenistic and Jewish magic began to circulate in the West after the twelfth century. Christianity and Solomonic magic coalesced in handbooks that influenced textual amulets, including magical seals and figures. Textual amulets resulting from a union of traditions combined Christian prayers and

---

[15] Kingsford, *Grey Friars*, pp. 96, 143; "Register of Sepulchral Inscriptions Existing temp. Hen. VIII in the Church of the Grey Friars, London," in Madden, *Collectanea topographica et genealogica*, 5:289. Ironically, the chronicler Thomas Favent ("dominus Thomas Favent capilanus [*sic*]") was later interred nearby in the same chapel; see Kingsford, "Wills."

[16] Favent, *Historia*, p. 18: "Mox spoliarunt eum et inuenerunt certa experimenta et certa signa depicta in eisdem ad modum carecterum celi; et unum caput demonis depictum, et plura nomina demonum inscripta fuerunt, quibus ablates, nudus suspensus est."

[17] Ewen, *Witchcraft*, pp. 34–35. Kittredge, *Witchcraft*, pp. 54–55; Russell, *Withcraft*, p. 209; Kieckhefer, *European Witch Trials*, pp. 116–17; Carey, *Courting Disaster*, pp. 105–6; Skemer, *Binding Words*, pp. 194–99.

[18] The word *experimentum* could signify magical operations (as in alchemical experiments) guided by manuscript texts of natural magic or collections of *secreta philosophorum*. It could also refer to a magical charm or recipe, or to a diagnostic procedure. Concerning the meaning of the word *experimentum*, see Roy, "Household Encyclopedia," pp. 63–65. Latham, *Revised Medieval Latin*, p. 179, offers a conjectural definition of the word *experimentum*: "(?) amulet c. 1390."

invocations of divine names, along with magic circles, seals, and figures incorporating bands of formulaic text, astrological signs, strange *characteres* (magical script or symbols), and names of powerful spirits and angels.

If Favent's account of Tresilian's execution can be trusted, we may wonder who had identified the textual amulets and described their elements. The hangman, though very likely unlettered, could still have identified magic seals and figures by shape. Favent's reference to signs painted on charms might suggest that they were in red and would thus stand out boldly. But the hangman might not have known the difference between the angelic and demonic names that filled pseudo-Solomonic texts and the transliterated Hebrew and Greek divine names of amulets in the common tradition. Favent does not mention the presence of parliamentary, judicial, or public officials, who would have been literate and thus able to read the amulets, though the executioner clearly had unnamed helpers who beat and later stripped Tresilian. Perhaps Favent's most damning detail was the painted head of a demon. This could have been something as harmless as the seal of an angel or symbols of a day of the week over which that angel had power, as illustrated in some manuscripts of the pseudo-Solomonic *Sworn Book of Honorius*; or something far more sinister, such as the portraits of demons that can be found in later handbooks of black magic, which a fourteenth-century observer would not hesitate to view as necromancy.[19]

Curiously, English chronicles of the late fourteenth and fifteenth centuries do not use Favent's *Historia*.[20] Instead, without any reference to amulets or magic, they merely record that Tresilian was drawn to Tyburn gallows and hanged. This is as much as we learn in the chronicles of the Monk of Evesham and Henry Knighton, the register of Henry de Wakefield, the *Westminster Chronicle*, the *Cronica tripartita* (ca. 1400) of John Gower, the *Chronica maiora* of Thomas Walsingham; and an anonymous chronicle for the years 1377–1461. A few chroniclers even disagree on the mode of execution. Adam de Usk (ca. 1352–1430), who used the Evesham

---

[19] The *Liber juratus Honorii*, falsely attributed to Honorius of Thebes or Pope Honorius III (1216–27), is one of the leading texts of ritual and ceremonial magic. The text may date from the second half of the thirteenth century but was certainly used in the fourteenth century to guide magicians through highly structured sequences of purifications, suffumigations, conjurations, mystical prayers, and rituals using magic circles and seals to attain a beatific vision of God, knowledge of things, and material benefits such as protection against fire and evil spirits. Hedegård, *Liber iuratus*, pp. 30–40, 67–71, 130. For portraits of demons in *Le véritable dragon rouge*, which purports to date from 1522 but is probably from the nineteenth century, see Seligmann, *Magic and the Occult*, p. 203, fig. 84.

[20] Although there is one other extant manuscript, as we shall see, the chronicle hardly circulated. Walsingham, *St Albans Chronicle*, p. xcvi n134: "The important description by Favent may never have circulated in the Middle Ages." Gransden, *Historical Writing*, pp. 185, 485. Under the impression that no medieval copy survives, Gransden suggests: "Possibly early copies were deliberately destroyed during Richard II's tyranny in 1397, or the work may have been intended for very limited circulation" (p. 185n161).

chronicle or a source common to both, writes that Tresilian was beheaded. Jean Froissart also indicates beheading but adds that Tresilian was thereafter hanged on a gibbet. A miniature in a ca. 1475 Flemish illuminated manuscript of Froissart's *Chroniques* shows a fully clothed Tresilian about to be decapitated by an executioner's sword, while three officials calmly observe the proceedings. Of course, beheading was not the appropriate form of execution for a convicted traitor like Tresilian, who was not of noble birth.[21] Reference to Tresilian's amulets is also absent from later literary accounts, such as "The Fall of Robert Tresilian, Chief Justice of England" by the Elizabethan poet George Ferrers (ca. 1500–1579), written as the first part of *The Mirror for Magistrates* (1559). In Ferrers's work Tresilian and the others posthumously confessed grave misdeeds and admit to having so perverted law to suit royal interests and power that for them (like their victims) the result was "no more but hang and drawe."[22] Reference to necromancy was unnecessary in Ferrers's emphasis on baronial resistance to royal abuse of power.[23]

Fortunately, a nearly contemporary English manuscript offers additional evidence about Tresilian's execution. The Cistercian monk John Northwood, perhaps from the Coventry area, kept his devotional miscellany from 1386 to 1410 at the Cistercian abbey of the Blessed Virgin Mary at Bordesley, nearly 120 miles northwest of London.[24] The monastery was not well connected politically,

[21] Davies, "Some Notes," p. 558. Hector and Harvey, *Westminster Chronicle*, pp. 312–13. Walsingham, *St Albans Chronicle*, pp. 850–51. The *Westminster Chronicle* supplemented Ranulph Higden's *Polychronicon* and was formerly attributed to John Malvern (d. ca. 1414), a monk of Worcester. Chrimes and Brown, *Select Documents*, p. 143; Gower, *Complete Works*, 4:318; Riley, *Thomae Walsingham*, 2:173; Hearne, *Historia vitae*, p. 101; Stow, *Historia vitae*, p. 117; Marx, *English Chronicle*, p. 155; Thompson, *Chronicon Adae de Usk*, p. 6: "et alios quam plures decapitarunt"; Given-Wilson, *Chronicle of Adam Usk*, p. 12; Galloway, "Politics of Pity," pp. 87–89. The Flemish miniature is in BnF fr. 2645, fol. 238v; it is reproduced on the cover of Oliver, *Parliament and Political Pamphleteering*.

[22] Haslewood, *Mirror for Magistrates*, 2:13–21; Campbell, *Mirror for Magistrates*, pp. 73–80. Ferrers was a Tudor lawyer, poet, and translator of the Magna Carta, who as a member of the House of Commons in 1542 became embroiled in a legal dispute about the privilege of freedom from arrest.

[23] However, later struggles between the Crown and Parliament did lead to a revival of Favent's chronicle. Political opponents of Charles I (r. 1625–49) printed a crude English translation of the chronicle as a political pamphlet (1641), while scribal copies of the original Latin manuscript in the Bodleian Library also circulated from that time. Concerning the circulation of printed pamphlets of an English translation during Parliament's struggle with Charles I, see Tout, "English Parliament," p. 311. Manuscript copies of the seventeenth century include NLS 2703; BL Add. 48102A, B [Yelverton 111], fols. 36r–38v; and BL Add. 48172 [Yelverton 183], fols. 119r–128v.

[24] BL Add. 37787, fols. 175v–176r. This is one of only three extant Bordesley manuscripts listed in Ker, *Medieval Libraries*, p. 11. For descriptions of BL Add. 37787, see Baugh, *Worcestershire Miscellany*, and the British Library Manuscripts Catalogue (http://www.bl.uk/catalogues/manuscripts/HITS0001.ASP?VPath=html/35022.htm&Search='bordesley'&Highlight=T). Established in 1138, Bordesley Abbey was located in the West Midlands town of Redditch, in what is now the county of Hereford-Worcester, and had more than thirty monks in the fourteenth century.

though Thomas de Beauchamp, one of the Lords Appellant, was a grandson of Guy de Beauchamp (1278–1315), tenth earl of Warwick, who had donated some forty-two manuscripts to Bordesley Abbey in 1305 and was interred in a chapel near the altar.[25] Northwood suggests that Tresilian's hanging could proceed only after an otherwise efficacious textual amulet had been removed from his body. Northwood's reference comes in connection with a Middle English version of the multipurpose Heavenly Letter, one of the most ancient and enduring medieval amuletic texts, originating in the apocryphal letter from Christ to King Abgar V of Edessa. In Northwood's version, Pope Leo III (r. 795–816) is remembered as giving to Charlemagne a list of more than a hundred divine names in Latin, beginning "Hec sunt nomina dei patris omnipotentis. Messias † Sother † Emanuel † Sabaoth † Adonay." The powerful names are interspersed with crosses, in alternating red and blue ink, and are followed by the apotropaic opening verse in the Gospel of St. John ("In principio erat verbum"), which had been a standard element in textual amulets since the early Christian centuries. Northwood's Middle English version of the Heavenly Letter offers a broad promise of divine protection to Christians who wore the amulet with the names of God on their bodies:

> [A]lle þes holy namys of alle myȝtty god, seynt leo þe pope of Rome wrote to Kyng Charulse & sayde, who so berit þis letter wyth hym he þar not drede hym of hys enmy to be ouercome, & he schal not be dampned ne wyth findys be cumberyd, ne wyth sekenes day ne nyght be takyn, ne with oust schryfte due, ne in no nede schal myssare, ne in no batel to be ouercome, ne in fire be brende, ne in water be drownde, ne of wykkyd enmy by þe way be assaylyd, ne be smieton with yondur ne layte. And for sothe in þis wryting ar to names ho so nemyth hem þat day he schal not dye þey he were hongud on a tre. And þis was prouyd by syr Robard tresylyan.[26]

Northwood goes on to recommend laying this *wryt* (a Middle English word that could refer to an amulet) on the body to cure sickness or guarantee successful childbirth.[27]

---

[25] Blaess, "L'Abbaye de Bordesley"; Benham, *English Literature*, pp. 441–44; Woodward, *History of Bordesley Abbey*, p. 75.

[26] BL Add. 37787, fols. 175v–176r.

[27] In BL Add. 37787, Northwood also included other amuletic uses of text, such as prayers to be recited and worn on the body, an amuletic text or verbal charm against toothache, and a version of the common narrative charm about Christ coming upon a feverish St. Peter at the Jerusalem Gate (fols. 174v–180r). Instructions recommend writing out this narrative charm as a fever amulet and wearing it on the body ("quicumque hoc scriptum super se portauerit"). For a discussion of Northwood and his manuscript, see Baugh, *Worcestershire Miscellany*, pp. 14–23. Concerning the Heavenly Letter in English textual amulets, see Bühler, "Prayers and Charms," pp. 270–78.

Like the hangman in Favent's chronicle, the Cistercian monk believed that powerful words worn on the body had magical efficacy, though divine protection from death by hanging was not among the Heavenly Letter's standard promises in either Latin or English versions, such as the one quoted by Reginald Scot (1538?–99) in his treatise *The Discoverie of Witchcraft* (1584).[28] It would not have been surprising for Tresilian to wear one or more textual amulets containing standard Christian elements such as the Heavenly Letter, though surveys of Tresilian's property, pursuant to the parliamentary judgment of forfeiture, did not identify anything of a magical nature.[29] References to condemned men wearing amulets cannot be dismissed as a literary motif or trope, though medieval miracle tales about saints intervening to save the lives of men on the gallows were not uncommon, and there were associations in popular culture between hanged bodies and magic.[30] Northwood was surely referring to what he believed was a recent event that offered proof of the magical efficacy of the Heavenly Letter and divine names. Such a textual amulet could have been obtained from a cleric, who (like Northwood) retained copies of amuletic texts so that he could dispense magic in written form. Perhaps Tresilian obtained amulets from his unnamed Franciscan confessor, who was probably associated with Grey Friars of London. But Northwood's notion of the amulets protecting Tresilian is quite different from Favent's.

It is possible that Northwood was using a contemporary political pamphlet or other written source, no longer extant.[31] But oral communication was a more

---

[28] Scot, *Discoverie of Witchcraft*, p. 187 (bk. 12, ch. 9).

[29] An inquest into Tresilian's landholdings and possessions in 1388 at Salden, Buckinghamshire, mentions an illuminated psalter. *Calendar of the Close Rolls*, 3:627: "a book called a 'Salter' illuminated with gilt letters price 100*s*." However, this is the only reference to his ownership of manuscripts. No reference can be found in the Patent Rolls and Close Rolls relative to the commissions appointed in 1388 to investigate Tresilian's property.

[30] Concerning such miracle tales about Thomas de Cantilupe (ca. 1218–82), bishop of Hereford, and other saints who intervened at hangings, see Bartlett, *Hanged Man*, pp. 49–50; Bull, *Miracles of Our Lady*, pp. 111–12. For medieval and later uses of hanged bodies and associated materials (e.g., pieces of the gallows and hangman's rope) in black magic and as amulets, see Cohen, *Crossroads of Justice*, pp. 136–37; Veenstra, *Magic and Divination*, p. 66; Hand, "Hangman," pp. 324–25; Opie and Tatem, *Dictionary of Superstitions*, pp. 172, 189.

[31] An Anglo-Norman pamphlet about the Merciless Parliament survives textually as part of the *Westminster Chronicle*. Clarke, "Forfeitures and Treason," pp. 73–74: "More valuable [than Favent], because less biased, is the French pamphlet preserved in the Chronicle of Westminster, probably also written for immediate circulation." The Anglo-Norman additions to the *Westminster Chronicle* include the appeals of treason, articles of impeachment, "process" of parliament, petitions, and oaths at the conclusion of the Merciless Parliament, February 3–June 3, 1388. See Hector and Harvey, *Westminster Chronicle*, pp. xliv–xlv, 236–307. The Monk of Westminster used the French pamphlet in codex format. At one point, the chronicle (pp. 258–59) refers to a place in the text "five folios back" ("come desuit est escript en le cynk' foyll").

likely source. This could take the form of everything from a reliable eyewitness account to vicious gossip. Richard II's strife-ridden reign saw a proliferation of political news, false rumors, and personal attacks, most intensely in London at the time of the Merciless Parliament. For example, the Mercers' Petition (1388) and other parliamentary petitions by London craft guilds offered support to the Lords Appellant through a litany of complaints and accusations of treason against Sir Nicholas Brembre.[32] During the 1380s London's mayor and magistrates occasionally prosecuted people for making false statements in private and spreading malicious rumors.[33] In 1379 and 1389 Richard II reissued the *scandalum magnatum* statute of 1275 against slanderous reports, and in 1387 he forbade hostile speech and dissemination of "evel or dishoneste" reports about the king, queen, and royal courtiers.[34]

Yet rumors did not subside after the king regained power. Richard Maidstone (d. 1396) decried the evils of the Wicked Tongue in *Concordia*, his poem about the reconciliation of the king and London in 1392.[35] In 1395, Philippe de Mezières (ca. 1327–1405) noted in his *Epistre au Roi Richart* that rumors about Richard II reached France.[36] The anonymous author of *Mum and the Sothsegger*, a Middle English poem written around 1402–9, observed that courtiers, peers, prelates, and others could spread false rumors from London faster than a man on horseback. Such rumors could circulate orally by gossip and idle talk, and in writing, such as a political pamphlet (*copie*), filled with inaccurate news accounts, that might find its way into the author's "bag of books."[37] *Mum and the Sothsegger* may have been recalling the proliferation of rumors in 1402, especially among Franciscan friars, that the late king was living in Scotland and planning a return to England in order to regain his throne.[38]

---

[32] Scase, *Literature and Complaint*, pp. 67–71; Turner, *Chaucerian Conflict*, p. 28. See also Rosenthal, *Telling Tales*, pp. 47–49; Davies, "Richard II," p. 86. Tout, *Chapters*, 4:56–57.

[33] Riley, *Memorials of London*, pp. 454, 462–63, 504–6, 518–19.

[34] Hanrahan, "Defamation," pp. 259–76 (esp. pp. 267–68); Riley, *Memorials of London*, p. 500 (Corporation of London, Letter-Book H).

[35] Maidstone, *Concordia*, p. 50, verses 21–22: "Namque tuum regem, sponsum dominumque tuumque, / Quem tibi sustulerat Perfida Lingua, capis."

[36] Mezières, *Letter to King Richard II*, p. 107. Mezières's metaphorical reference to rumors related to medicinal remedies that physicians had ostensibly prescribed for Richard II.

[37] Day and Steele, *Mum and the Sothsegger*, pp. 67–68; Dean, *Richard the Redeless*, pp. 124–25. The first part of *Mum and the Sothsegger*, probably by the same author, is sometimes referred to as *Richard the Redeless*. The text concerns the reign of Richard II and deposition in 1399. See Dodd, "Changing Perspectives," p. 315–16; Scattergood, "Remembering Richard II," p. 225.

[38] Rumors of the "false Richard" threatened to undermine the reign of Henry IV (1399–1413) and thus led to several treason cases that year before King's Bench. Thornley, "Treason by Words," pp. 560–61; Sayles, *Select Cases*, pp. 126–28.

Considering such evidence, one may assume that clerics traveling from London could have easily returned with news and rumors of the Merciless Parliament, which were then spread locally by word of mouth to trusted friends or total strangers. Most of the English episcopate attended the Merciless Parliament and were recognized as peers, though they did not participate in the parliamentary trial. The lords' spiritual and clerical assistants could have been eyewitnesses and possible conduits of political news and rumors. The city of Worcester was a likely hub of information for Northwood, since Bordesley Abbey lay only twenty-five miles to the northeast, within the diocese. In the fourteenth century the abbots of Bordesley made professions of obedience to the bishops of Worcester and received benediction.[39] Henry de Wakefield, who had served as bishop of Worcester since 1375, attended the Merciless Parliament, as did all but four English bishops.[40] As we have seen, he noted Tresilian's execution in a register, though without mentioning amulets. Redditch was located about nineteen miles north of the Benedictine monastery of Evesham, whose anonymous monk-chronicler made comments similar to those of the bishop of Wakefield. Bordesley Abbey also had relations with the Augustinians at Studley, Benedictines at Alcester, Cistercians at Stoneleigh and Malvern, and other religious communities.[41] Northwood clearly had several possible sources of such information.

It is important to remember that Northwood kept his devotional miscellany for himself, without ulterior motive, and did not intend it for dissemination. By contrast, Favent clearly was trying to demonize Tresilian by associating him with a brand of magic or necromancy that his intended audience, or more likely a particular ecclesiastical patron, would have found suspect or inappropriate. Favent was emphasizing that Tresilian relied on black magic, not on divine grace, and he satirically contrasted Tresilian's public execution at Tyburn with Christ's crucifixion at Calvary.[42] Reliance on amulets summoning demons, ostensibly offering him an iron-clad guarantee of bodily protection—at least until they had been removed—was viewed as being inconsistent with a Christian's faith in the divine power freely dispensed by God. In addition, Tresilian's use of disguises to avoid capture made it possible for him to cross social boundaries and infect the common folk with demonic magic. Tresilian's flight from justice was perhaps reminiscent of John Ball's seven years earlier, prior to his trial and condemnation before the King's Bench, with Tresilian himself presiding as lord chief justice. In the wake of the Peasants' Revolt, with its own brand of anticlericalism, Favent might have

---

[39] Woodward, *History of Bordesley Abbey*, p. 75.

[40] Davies, "Episcopate," pp. 659–93 (esp. pp. 669–70).

[41] Woodward, *History of Bordesley Abbey*, pp. 26–28. Concerning the abbey, its precincts, and outlying possessions, see Willis-Bund and Page, *Victoria History*, 2:151–54.

[42] Galloway, "Politics of Pity," p. 84; Butterfield, *Chaucer and the City*, p. 46.

been suggesting that the common folk could be easily infected with dangerous ritual practices.

Thomas Favent wrote his chronicle, probably shortly after the Merciless Parliament, with direct and intimate knowledge of contemporary political events, though he almost certainly invented or embellished some of the details. Thomas Frederick Tout and May McKisack suggested that he was probably a Wiltshire native and a clerk in the diocese of Salisbury and may have written his anti-royalist chronicle while serving as a clerk or chaplain for one of the Lords Appellant. Tout described Favent's chronicle as "a political pamphlet, written in Latin, and therefore addressed to clerical and educated circles, and aiming at glorifying rather than apologizing for the work of the Lords Appellant."[43] This had been the prevailing interpretation until Clementine Oliver identified Favent with a person of the same name who served between 1391 and 1394 as collector of tunnage and poundage in the port of London. In this capacity, if not before, Oliver argues, Favent grew hostile to the city's wealthy merchant class and especially to Sir Nicholas Brembre, who was lord mayor of London in 1377 and 1383–85. Local politics turned Favent, probably living in London by 1388 and an eyewitness to events, into an independent political pamphleteer, who penned his *Historia* to celebrate the Merciless Parliament's recent triumph and wrote for other reform-minded London civil servants.[44]

Oliver's view has been challenged by Gwilym Dodd, who notes that Favent enjoyed the favor of John Waltham (d. 1395), a close ally of the Lords Appellant and especially Richard FitzAlan, earl of Arundel.[45] Waltham was in attendance when the Lords Appellant appealed Tresilian and four others of treason in November 1387.[46] It was through the influence of the Lords Appellant that Waltham became bishop of Salisbury in 1388. Richard II had Waltham removed as Keeper of the Privy Seal in 1389 because of his association with the Lords Appellant. But Waltham was such a capable administrator that he was on his way back to royal favor within a year and was appointed lord high treasurer in 1391. In the early 1390s Waltham as bishop appointed Favent to several benefices in the diocese of Salisbury, and as royal treasurer he

---

[43] Tout, "English Parliament," pp. 310–12. See also Tout, "Literature and Learning," p. 380; and McKisack's edition of Favent, *Historia*, p. vi; Davies, "Episcopate," p. 670. See also Clarke, "Forfeitures and Treason," p. 74; Chrimes and Brown, *Select Documents*, p. 140; Taylor, *English Historical Literature*, p. 207; and Gransden, *Historical Writing*, p. 185.

[44] Oliver, "Political Pamphleteer," pp. 167–98; Oliver, "New Light." Favent's will (1404) confirms that the chronicler and the custom's officer were the same person; see Oliver, "New Light," p. 67. See also Oliver, *Parliament and Political Pamphleteering*, pp. 56–83.

[45] Dodd, "Changing Perspectives," pp. 299–322, esp. p. 314n63.

[46] Hector and Harvey, *Westminster Chronicle*, p. 238.

nominated Favent to be a London customs collector.[47] Favent's likely association with Waltham may help explain the chronicle's intense partisanship, though a prelate like Waltham would have understood that Tresilian's amulets, if really tainted with necromancy, were transgressions under canon law, not the common law.[48]

In addition, Favent wrote in an elegant, rhetorical, and florid Latin prose, consistent with the principles of *dictamen* and administrative curial style.[49] A less formal mode of expression in Latin or Anglo-Norman would have been more suitable for a political pamphlet written to reach many people. The Mercers' Petition and other parliamentary petitions by London craft guilds against Sir Nicholas Brembre were in Middle English and Anglo-Norman. Wendy Scase has recently suggested that the petitions might have been "published," in the sense of being posted, possibly in the Guildhall or Westminster Hall, to support the Lords Appellant.[50] By contrast, Favent's polished Latin chronicle was composed soon after the Merciless Parliament ended in June 1388 and was long thought to survive in a single manuscript at the Bodleian Library, which would not suggest a political pamphlet that achieved wide dissemination.[51] It is a scribal copy on a five-membrane parchment roll (355.6 × 28.3 cm) of the late fourteenth or early fifteenth century. Its illuminated borders and initials are at a higher level of physical presentation, appropriate for a brief chronicle, like many genealogical chronicle rolls, made for a wealthy patron. Possibly copied from this manuscript is a second manuscript of Favent's chronicle, recently rediscovered in an American private

[47] Timmins, *Register*, p. 76, no. 522; p. 133, no. 973. Concerning Waltham's career and 1388 appointment as bishop, see Timmins, *Register*, pp. ix–x, xix–xx; Saul, *Richard II*, p. 251; Hector and Harvey, *Westminster Chronicle*, p. 334n1; Tuck, "Cambridge Parliament," p. 231; Tout, *Chapters*, 3:430, 442–43, 461–62.

[48] Relatively few cases of magic, witchcraft, and sorcery were being prosecuted in English royal courts or in ecclesiastical courts at the diocesan, deanery, or other jurisdictions. Such cases became more common in the fifteenth century, along with politically motivated accusations of necromancy. Pollock and Maitland, *History of English Law*, 2:554–55; Ewen, *Witchcraft and Demonism*, pp. 33–38. Richard Kieckhefer's chronological survey of witch trials shows their infrequency before the fifteenth century; Kieckhefer, *European Witch Trials*, p. 11.

[49] Catto, "Written English," p. 45; Burnley, "Curial Prose," pp. 593–614 (esp. pp. 595–97); Gransden, *Historical Writing*, pp. 185–86.

[50] Scase, *Literature and Complaint*, pp. 71–72, pls. 1–3. Scase notes "the presence of a small hole in the centre of the top margin of each petition might be evidence that they were in fact displayed."

[51] Bodleian Misc. 2963; Bodley Rolls 9. The Bodley Roll's early provenance is unknown. It was acquired around 1607, according to Madan, *Summary Catalogue*, 2.1:557. On the year of acquisition, Bruce Barker-Benfield notes in an email of 9 July 2008 to the author: "Perhaps it might be more accurate to say that the roll was formally accessioned in 1607 or later, not after 1612." Unfortunately, there is no reference to the roll or how it was acquired in Wheeler, *Letters of Sir Thomas Bodley*.

collection, written on a five-membrane parchment roll in the second quarter of the fifteenth century.[52]

Favent's detail about Tresilian's amulet use at the gallows was probably related to the opinions of the Lords Appellants, including their leader Thomas of Woodstock, duke of Gloucester, who had come to be lord high constable of England as a result of his marriage to the daughter of Humphrey de Bohun, earl of Northampton (d. 1372), in whose family the office had been hereditary. In this capacity, Thomas was responsible for tournaments and presided over the High Court of Chivalry (also known as the Earl Marshal's Court). It had grown in prominence since the 1340s and came to have an expanded judicial scope since the 1370s, beyond its original focus on questions relating to military matters and heraldry.[53] The court operated under Roman law (like the Court of Admiralty) and could adjudicate cases through hearings and the examination of witnesses, documents, and physical evidence, as in the celebrated law-of-arms case of *Scrope v. Grosvenor*, 1385–90.[54] But the court could also turn to trial by combat, even though it had long before fallen into disfavor under common law,[55] to resolve appeals of treason and other cases in which the appellant and defendant were unable to prove their cases by witnesses brought before the lord high constable and earl marshal. Judicial duels were fought in the lists, enclosed areas surrounded by wooden fences or barriers of upright posts with two horizontal rails.[56]

[52] Oliver, "New Light," pp. 61–63, fig. 1. The roll measures approximately 274.3 × 30.5 cm. and has a sixteenth-century title on the dorse: "Succincta de facinoribus Alexandri Nevyle, archiepiscopi Eboracensis, Roberti de Vere ducis Hibernie, Michaelis de la Pole comitis Sulfocie, cancellarii Anglie, Roberti Tresylian, capitalis justiciarii, et Nicholai Brembre, militis, consiliariorum intimorum Ricardi II Regis et de eorum poenis historia." The manuscript was in the libraries of the British antiquarians Craven Ord (1786–1836), vicar of St. Mary-de-Wigtoft, Lincolnshire; and Sir Thomas Phillipps (1792–1872), of Middle Hill, Worcestershire (Phillipps no. 4115 [1050]). Ord had acquired many of his manuscripts from the antiquarian Thomas Martin (1696/97–1771), of Thetford, Suffolk. In 1830 Ord's manuscripts were auctioned by Richard Harding Evans in London. A brief description of the manuscript is found in Munby, *Phillipps Manuscripts*, p. 59. On June 29, 1936, at a Phillipps sale at Sotheby's, London, Howard L. Goodhart purchased the roll for Phyllis Goodhart Gordan.

[53] A suspicion grew that Richard II steered treason cases to the High Court of Chivalry for adjudication, as we see in Parliament's accusations against Richard II in 1399. See Carlson, *Deposition of Richard II*, pp. 47–48.

[54] The dispute between Sir Richard Scrope (ca. 1387–1403) and Sir Robert Grosvenor concerned the right to bear the heraldic shield "azure, a bend or." In general, see Nicolas, *Controversy*. Chaucer was one of some 450 people giving depositions. Richard II took an active interest in the case and rendered judgment on May 27, 1390, in favor of Scrope. Rosenthal, *Telling Tales*, pp. 63–94; Patterson, *Chaucer*, p. 180.

[55] Pollock and Maitland, *History of English Law*, 2:632–34; Kaye, *Placita corone*, pp. xvii, xxvii, xxxi–xxxii; Grazebrook, *Earl Marshal's Court*, p. 5.

[56] For medieval depictions of lists, see Arthur and Dillon, "On a MS. Collection," pl. 6 (facing p. 37); Crapelet, *Cérémonies des gages*, pls. 4–11. The miniatures are reproduced lithographically from BnF fr. 2258.

The lord high constable exercised his responsibility for the High Court of Chivalry in conjunction with the earl marshal, and interestingly both men used their titles in the articles of appeal against Tresilian and the others.[57] As we have already seen, the Merciless Parliament made the earl marshal responsible for carrying out Tresilian's death sentence. M. V. Clarke suggested that the parliamentary appeals of treason may have originated in the civil law procedures in the Court of Chivalry. In her view, "the appellants manipulated procedure according to circumstances, readily giving up their appeal to the Constable's court when they understood that Parliament was better suited for their purpose." Recent scholarship has argued against Clarke's suggestion that appeals of treason had been borrowed from civil procedures under the Court of Chivalry. The rolls of Parliament show that the Lords Appellant consulted justices, sergeants, and "autres Sages du Ley du Roialme" about various legal traditions but concluded that neither common nor civil law were appropriate for appealing Tresilian and the others in Parliament. The Lords Appellant opted for trial under parliamentary law.[58]

Yet the Court of Chivalry remained on the minds of the Lords Appellant and their victims. When Sir Nicholas Brembre was brought before the Merciless Parliament to respond to the charge of high treason, he asked to prove his innocence in a judicial duel under the Court of Chivalry—in Favent's words, "infra limites pugnaturos." The Lords Appellant and their supporters were more than eager to engage Brembre in wager of battle and signaled this by throwing down their gages at the feet of Richard II, who was in attendance. But Parliament denied Brembre the right to trial by battle as a knight, only possible if there had been no witnesses. Indeed, Tresilian's capture and execution on February 19 interrupted the steady stream of London witnesses testifying against Brembre and thus delayed the conclusion of his trial and execution at Tyburn a day later.[59]

The High Court of Chivalry probably informed the attitudes and actions of the lord high constable and earl marshal, if not the other Lords Appellant, through the customs and procedures articulated in the *L'Ordonnance d'Angleterre pour le camp à l'outrance, ou gaige de bataille*. Thomas of Woodstock's goal was to regulate the proper conduct of trials by battle, as Philip IV (r. 1285–1314) of France had

---

[57] Hector and Harvey, *Westminster Chronicle*, p. 237n3: "Gloucester's style of constable and Nottingham's of marshal may mean that the Appellants at one time hoped for a hearing in the court of chivalry."

[58] Clarke, "Forfeitures and Treason," pp. 84–86 (p. 85). Strachey, *Rotuli parliamentorum*, 3:236; Saul, *Richard II*, p. 192; Rogers, "Parliamentary Appeals," pp. 95–124; McKisack, *Fourteenth Century*, p. 455n1; Plucknett, "State Trials," pp. 168–69.

[59] Favent, *Historia*, p. 16; Hector and Harvey, *Westminster Chronicle*, pp. 282–83. Favent incorrectly records the date of this confrontation as 12 February 1388, the first day of Shrovetide, though that date would have been Ash Wednesday. Parliament Rolls give the correct date, February 17.

done earlier through the *Droite ordonnance de gaige de bataille* (1306).[60] But the English *Ordonnance* also drew upon the court's unwritten rules and on Thomas of Woodstock's two decades of experience as lord high constable. He offered the *petit livret* in Anglo-Norman to Richard II; the text was translated into a Middle English version in the fifteenth century. Among the problems addressed in both the English and French *Ordonnances* was that of combatants—the appellant and defendant, or their champions—wearing powerful amulets and engaging in other magical practices that could allow guilty men to triumph in single-combat judicial duels. Magic could allow them to evade divine justice and death in cases of treason and other serious crimes. Patricia J. Eberle has concluded that Thomas of Woodstock completed his Anglo-Norman text around 1386 and that Richard II, in whose presence judicial duels would often take place, approved it not long afterward.[61] Also arguing for this dating of the *Ordonnance* are descriptions by Chaucer in the "Knight's Tale" and the "General Prologue" to the *Canterbury Tales*.[62] In short, the *Ordonnance* was probably in force at the time of the Merciless Parliament and thus provides some insight into the views of at least two of the Lords Appellant.

Thomas of Woodstock's *Ordonnance* proscribed combatants using magic, including amulets worn on their bodies, beneath their armor, to give themselves unfair advantage. The proscription applied to the appellant or defendant who fought judicial duels or the champions who fought for them. The lord high constable was to have the earl marshal make the appellant, referred to formulaically as "A. de K.," swear on a missal that he was properly armed and possessed (here quoting the Middle English version),

> "oonly in God and thi body" and possessed "ne stone of vertue, ne herbe of vertue, ne charme, ne experiment, ne carocte, ne othir inchauntment by the, ne for thee, by the which thou trustest the þe to ovircome the foreseide C. de B. [the defendant] thyne adversarie, that shall come ayenst the within theise listes this day in his defence; ne that thou trustith in noon othir thyng, but oonly in God and thi body, and on thy rightfull quarell, so helpe the God and theise halowes [i.e., relics]."

[60] *Ordonnances*, 1:435–41; Clephan, *Tournament*, pp. 151–52, 179 (appendix E: "Ashmolean MSS. relating to Judicial Duels").

[61] This dating is based on a manuscript miscellany (BL Cotton Nero D.vi) made for Richard II that includes copies of the *Ordonnance* and the king's 1386 letter of appointment for Thomas Mowbray to be the earl marshal. Eberle, "Richard II," pp. 237–39. Among the early manuscripts of the *Ordonnance* is one found in a miscellany belonging to the family of the earl marshal.

[62] The poet describes tournaments and judicial duels to be consistent with contemporary norms, including the practices prescribed in the *Ordonnance*. Lester, "Chaucer's Knight," pp. 460–68. Concerning the dating of the "Knight's Tale," see Benson, *Riverside Chaucer*, pp. xxix, 5–7. Benson consigns the "Knight's Tale" to 1380–87 and the "General Prologue" to 1388–92.

Then the earl marshal would ask the defendant to make the same oath.[63] The proscribed magic includes charms and *experimenta*, in the sense of textual amulets;
characteres, probably magical script; and other enchantments or sources of magical power, which could have included Solomonic seals.[64] With respect to appeals
of treason and other cases resolved by judicial duel in the Court of Chivalry, the
Ordonnance stipulates that the lord high constable should first disarm any vanquished combatant who escaped death in the judicial duel and then turn him over
to the earl marshal, who was responsible for having the condemned drawn by
horse to the "place of justice" and beheaded or hanged.[65] Surely, it was no accident
that the Merciless Parliament made the earl marshal responsible for Tresilian's
execution, where the act of stripping the condemned man of amulets and other
magical devices took the place of disarming the defeated combatant in the lists.

Thomas of Woodstock's *Ordonnance* was clearly responding to perceived
abuses in judicial duels, which had grown out of knightly efforts at self-defense.
For centuries, English knights and soldiers had worn amulets into battle under
their armor almost as magical shields to provide an added layer of protection, in
addition to receiving blessing in liturgical ceremonies, seeking divine protection
by ecclesiastical blessing of their swords, or by having their swords and shields
inscribed with Christ's name or other divine names and liturgical formulas.
Chronicles provide accounts of Crusaders armed with textual amulets for protection. References to knightly use of amulets are also found in vernacular literature
aimed at lay readers and audiences who already believed in the magical efficacy
of powerful words and symbols to protect the bearer against all enemies and prevent sudden death, whether in battle or elsewhere. We find such a reference in
John Gower's *Confessio amantis*, a work commissioned by Richard II around 1386
and completed in 1390–93.[66] In *Sir Gawain and the Green Knight*, an anonymous
Middle English romance of the late fourteenth century, the Lady of the Castle

[63] Thomas of Woodstock, "Order of Battle," p. 317. For another version of the Middle English text,
see Arthur and Dillon, "On a MS. Collection," appendix B, pp. 61–66 (p. 64).

[64] In the 1306 *Ordonnance* that served as a model, the appellant and defendant were to kneel and
take oaths on the Gospels and a crucifix. Trusting only in God, the two combatants were to swear that
they were not wearing textual amulets or using other sources of magic either on themselves or their
horses (*Ordonnances*, 1:440). See *Cérémonies des gages*, pls. 7–8. Godefroid, *Dictionnaire*, 2:77, defines
charrois as "sortilège, charme, enchantement."

[65] Thomas of Woodstock, "Order of Battle," p. 324. Arthur and Dillon, "On a MS. Collection," p. 66.

[66] Gower, *Complete Works*, 3:44–45; 3:274 (*Confessio amantis*, bk. 5, lines 3578–92; *Confessio amantis*, bk. 7, lines 1567–69). In the tale of Jason and Medea, based in part on Gower's reworking of the
ancient Greek story, the Greek princess and sorceress Medea prepares Jason, leader of the Argonauts,
for combat by giving him a textual amulet (*charme* or *carecte*) and an arsenal of other *materia magica*,
which he was supposed to carry along on his legendary quest to capture the Golden Fleece from the
king of Colchis. Gower's Medea taught Jason to "read" the text, in the sense of teaching him how to
recognize talismanic seals and articulate powerful names that he had already committed to memory.

gives Sir Gawain a green silk girdle to wear as protection against all harm, including the Green Knight's axe.[67]

References to amulets were not uncommon in Ricardian literature, which enjoyed courtly readership and occasionally royal patronage, just as magical devices made regular appearances in the older romances preferred by aristocratic book owners and readers.[68] However, authors often qualified references to magic with the reminder that one should not trust practices guaranteeing protection, healing, or success in love without divine intervention. Chaucer expressed this sentiment in the seven deadly sins section of the "Parson's Tale." Chaucer upheld God's role in allowing textual amulets and verbal charms to work on occasion: "Charmes for woundes or maladie of men or of beestes, if they taken any effect, it may be peraventure that God suffereth it, for folk sholden yeve the moore feith and reverence to his name."[69] Similar sentiments were expressed by Thomas Usk (ca. 1354–88), who knew Chaucer as an author and public administrator, and was condemned to death by the Merciless Parliament because of his association with Sir Nicholas Brembre. In the *Testament of Love*, a prose allegory written in 1384–85, Usk expressed his disapproval of men who did not serve God, but instead engaged in love magic by means of textual amulets, magical enchantments, and conjuring "the spirits of the air."[70] Nonetheless, even when Ricardian authors questioned the propriety of Christians using textual amulets, they did not deny their magical efficacy.

A belief that amulets worked informs Thomas of Woodstock's rejection of amulets and other forms of magic in judicial duels. God was supposed to protect the combatant who was in the right, but powerful amulets could enable the guilty party to win and thus subvert justice. Wager of battle was the equivalent of judicial ordeal as a means of determining a person's guilt or innocence through divine judgment. The *Ordonnance*'s proscription of amulets was designed to prevent unfairness due to combatants employing magical devices to gain victory. This had been a problem at least since the reign of Edward III. In 1355, for example, Robert Wyvill (1330–75), bishop of Salisbury, brought a writ of right in the Court of Common Pleas against William of Montacute (1328–97), second earl of Salisbury, over ownership of Sherborne (or Salisbury) Castle, Dorset. The earl offered to settle the question of ownership by wager of battle. The bishop and earl designated champions—Robert (or Richard) Shawel and Nicholas D.—to fight for them in the judicial duel. Bishop Wyvill asked for prayers and masses in the archdeanery of Berkshire for his champion's success in battle. When the time for combat came, Henry Green and other justices had the two combatants stripped, only to discover

[67] Hardman, "Gawain's Practice," pp. 247–67; Takamiya, "Gawain's Green Girdle," pp. 75–79.

[68] Saul, *Richard II*, pp. 358–65; Bennett, "Court of Richard II," pp. 3–20.

[69] Benson, *Riverside Chaucer*, p. 308, line 606; Pollard et al., *Works of Geoffrey Chaucer*, p. 288, line 606.

[70] Usk, *Testament of Love*, p. 326 (1.9.27–29), p. 240nn26–29. Bressie, "Date," pp. 17–29.

that the bishop's champion was concealing several prayer rolls and amulets in his coat. The judges postponed the duel because they believed these magical devices could alter its outcome. The case was soon settled when the bishop gave the earl 2,500 marks, the earl defaulted, and the bishop officially recovered the castle.[71]

By the beginning of Richard II's reign it was probably not unusual for combatants in judicial duels to be asked to swear that they were not wearing magical devices for protection. Thomas of Walsingham refers to such an oath being made in 1380 at Westminster by Sir John Annesley and Sir Thomas Catterton, in a case brought before the High Court of Chivalry about ownership of a castle in Normandy said to have been surrendered by Catterton to the French. Annesley had appealed Catterton of treason and offered battle, thus making the court under Woodstock the appropriate venue. But before the combatants faced each other in a judicial duel, they had to swear that they were not aware of any magical art, nor were they wearing any magical device ("genus experimenti") by means of which a wicked man might be able to triumph over his enemies.[72] This case certainly suggests that the High Court of Chivalry followed a set of orally transmitted rules before the *Ordonnance*.

Favent's account should be considered against this background. He may have been aware of the stipulations of the *Ordonnance*, as was Chaucer. The reference to Tresilian employing the magical arts to cheat justice would have had particular resonance with Thomas of Woodstock and Thomas de Mowbray because of their association with the High Court of Chivalry. After all, they were the appellants in the cases before the Merciless Parliament, and Mowbray (as earl marshal) was responsible for Tresilian's death sentence being carried out, just as he would have been in the Court of Chivalry for conducting the vanquished combatant to the place of execution. Moreover, Favent would have been inclined to embellish details about Tresilian's execution to cast him in an unfavorable light.

The accusation of practicing necromancy was often raised against powerful but unpopular courtiers, such as Edward III's ambitious royal mistress, Alice Perrers (ca. 1348–1400), who survived judicial condemnation and continued to be denigrated by chroniclers and poets during Richard II's reign.[73] Thomas

---

[71] Brooke, Fitzherbert, and Statham, *Les reports del cases*, "2: anno xxix Edwardi III," p. 12. An English translation of the law report is provided in Kite, *Monumental Brasses*, pp. 15–19. Shawel is depicted on a brass monument at Salisbury Cathedral (Kite, *Monumental Brasses*, pl. 1).

[72] Walsingham, *St Albans Chronicle*, pp. cix, 358n433, 360–61. For a discussion, see Bellamy, "Sir John de Annesley," pp. 94–105; Squibb, *High Court*, p. 24.

[73] Thomas Walsingham, who considered Alice Perrers no more than a harlot, relates that she ensnared the aged king with assistance from a Dominican, who had used wax effigies of the king and his mistress, as well as rings of forgetfulness, magical incantations, and herbs. Walsingham, *St Albans Chronicle*, pp. cix, 46–48. Concerning charges of magical practices, see Riley, *Thomae Walsingham*, 1:327. For Alice Perrers's life and literary connections, see Ormrod, "Who Was Alice Perrers?," pp. 219–29; Ormrod, "Trials," pp. 366–96; Ormrod, *Reign of Edward III*, pp. 34, 36.

Walsingham and contemporary chroniclers such as Adam of Usk, who like Favent were supporters of the Lords Appellants, were unsympathetic to Richard II's court, seen as tainted by an interest in astrology, divination, and geomancy. In these chronicles, filled with anecdotes and gossip unflattering to the Royalist cause, astrology is treated as synonymous with sorcery.[74] One might dismiss Favent's account of the execution as just another accusation against courtiers dabbling in magic. But Northwood's reference suggests that Favent's account was more than pure fabrication. Perhaps he put a negative "spin" on a firsthand account or political rumor that Tresilian wore textual amulets to escape death for high treason, just as other people armed themselves with amulets before judicial duels.

In fact, textual amulets were widely used in the medieval west, often with support of local clerics. People of all social classes shared a fundamental belief in the magical efficacy of powerful words worn on the body. Physical evidence from the thirteenth to fifteenth centuries sheds light on the changing mix of scriptural quotations, names of God, common prayers, liturgical formulas, Christian legends and apocrypha, narrative charms, and magical seals or sigils that were used in amulets to protect the wearer against sudden death, mortal danger, evil spirits, and human affliction. While theologians and canon lawyers might decry the use of textual amulets as idolatry, clerics and others who were sufficiently literate willingly produced them for Christians of all social levels. Most amulets fall under the rubric of "white magic." Only textual and visual elements related to aggressive magic and demon worship were likely to raise the ire of the Church, especially when they claimed to guarantee people supernatural protection without God's grace.[75] Textual amulets were very common in late medieval spirituality, especially from the time of the Black Plague. Keith Thomas and Eamon Duffy have noted the persistent use of amulets in England from the late Middle Ages through the Reformation.[76]

The textual elements in Tresilian's amulets, as described by Favent and Northwood, may seem very different—one suggesting black magic, the other common Christian magic. Brief versions of the Heavenly Letter had circulated in Anglo-Saxon England and after the Norman Conquest as the

---

[74] Carey, *Courting Disaster*, pp. 93–94. For an assessment of astrology and divination at the royal court of Richard II, see pp. 93–116; see also Mead, "Geoffrey Chaucer's *Treatise*," p. 985. Indeed, Richard II owned manuscripts related to the magical arts; Eberle, "Richard II," pp. 241–44. Patterson, *Chaucer*, p. 217: "After Richard's deposition in 1399, it was reported in Parliament that a king's clerk named Maudeleyn was found with a scroll belonging to Richard on which were written magic incantations." Given-Wilson, *Royal Household*, p. 181.

[75] For a general survey, see Skemer, *Binding Words*.

[76] Thomas, *Religion*, esp. chs. 7–9; and Duffy, *Stripping of the Altars*, esp. chs. 7–8. Their approach has tended to exaggerate the differences between church-sanctioned religion and peasant folk beliefs. For a summary of this approach and its shortcomings, see Pounds, *History of the English Church*, pp. 326–27. See also Swanson, *Indulgences*.

Epistola salvatoris.[77] England was not exceptional in this regard. Textual amulets proliferated in the medieval west and left a train of extant artifacts beginning in the thirteenth century. Physical evidence is confirmed and contextualized by vernacular literature (particularly chronicles, *chansons de geste*, and other types of courtly literature) and other sources. The two strains of textual amulets were not incompatible. By Tresilian's time it was not unusual to combine older, traditional Christian textual elements, often including a version of the Heavenly Letter and divine names in series having numerological significance, with newer Christian traditions of magic influenced by pseudo-Solomonic *grimoires*, such as the *Key of Solomon* (*Clavicula Salomonis*). For example, a surviving multipurpose mid-thirteenth-century manuscript from Canterbury mixes a dense eight-column array of standard amuletic texts firmly rooted in Christian tradition and ritual practice, such as scriptural quotations, common prayers, varying lists of divine names (many derived from Hebrew and Greek), invocation of Christ and the saints, and versions of the Heavenly Letter, with pseudo-Solomonic elements circulating in the West, such as demonic conjurations, magic seals and figures, *characteres*, and *experimenta*. The Canterbury amulet includes a version of the Heavenly Letter and references to a variant version of the Abgar Legend in which Pope Leo III gave the Heavenly Letter to Charlemagne—as with Northwood—for divine protection in battle and against sudden death.[78]

In conclusion, Tresilian may have worn a version of the Heavenly Letter to the gallows. Such a relatively innocuous textual amulet, offering divine protection, night and day, against a wide range of dangers and causes of sudden death, was so commonplace in the fourteenth century that it should never have led to an accusation of necromancy or witchcraft. Even the young king, who subscribed to the *Ordonnance*'s ban against amulets despite his penchant for the magical arts, would have found it difficult to disagree on this point. In the highly charged political atmosphere of the Merciless Parliament and its aftermath, Favent most likely embellished reports of Tresilian's use of amulets for the benefit of his patron, the bishop of Salisbury, and the bishop's allies, the Lords Appellant, particularly Gloucester and Mowbray—the lord high constable and earl marshal—for whom the use of textual amulets had been a long-standing problem that undermined the course of justice in the High Court of Chivalry.

---

[77] Concerning the *Epistola salvatoris* in Anglo-Saxon England, see Biggs, Hill, and Szarmach, *Sources*, p. 38; Cain, *Sacred Words*, pp. 168–69.

[78] Cathedral Library Add. 23. For a brief description, see Ker, *Medieval Manuscripts*, 2:306–7. Skemer, *Binding Words*, pp. 199–212 (discussion), pp. 285–304 (transcription of text), pp. 200–201, figs. 5–6 (photographs of recto and verso).

Bibliography

Manuscripts

Cambridge, Trinity College Library, MS B.11.4.
Canterbury Cathedral Library, MS Add. 23.
Edinburgh, National Library of Scotland [NLS], MS 2703.
London, British Library [BL], MSS Add. 37787, Add. 48102A, B [Yelverton 111], Add.
    48172 [Yelverton 183]; MS Royal 2.B.vii.
Munich, Bayerische Staatsbibliothek, clm. 835.
New York, Morgan Library and Museum, MS M.736.
Oxford, Bodleian Library, MS Bodley Rolls 9; MS Misc. 2963.
Paris, Bibliothèque nationale de France [BnF], MSS fr. 2258, fr. 2645.

Published Sources and Literature

Arthur, Harold, and Viscount Dillon. "On a MS. Collection of Ordinances of Chivalry of
    the Fifteenth Century, Belonging to Lord Hastings." *Archaeologia: or Miscellaneous
    Tracts Relating to Antiquity* 57, 2nd ser., 7 (1902): 29–70.
Baker, J. H. *The Order of Sarjeants at Law.* Selden Society, Supplementary Series, 5. London:
    Selden Society, 1984.
Bartlett, Robert. *The Hanged Man: A Story of Miracle, Memory, and Colonialism in the Middle
    Ages.* Princeton, NJ: Princeton University Press, 2004.
Baugh, Nita Scudder, ed. *A Worcestershire Miscellany, Compiled by John Northwood, c. 1400.
    Edited from British Museum MS. Add. 37,787.* Philadelphia: Bryn Mawr College, 1956.
Bellamy, J. G. "Sir John de Annesley and the Chandos Inheritance." *Nottingham Medieval
    Studies* 10 (1966): 94–105.
Benham, Allen Rogers. *English Literature from Widsith to the Death of Chaucer: A Source
    Book.* New Haven, CT: Yale University Press, 1916.
Bennett, Michael J. "The Court of Richard II and the Promotion of Literature." In *Chaucer's
    England: Literature in Historical Context,* ed. Barbara A. Hanawalt, pp. 3–20. Minne-
    apolis: University of Minnesota Press, 1992.
Benson, Larry, gen. ed. *The Riverside Chaucer.* 3rd ed. Boston: Houghton Mifflin, 1987.
Biggs, Frederick M., Thomas D. Hill, and Paul E. Szarmach, eds. *Sources of Anglo-Saxon
    Literary Culture: A Trial Version.* Binghamton, NY: Center for Medieval and Early
    Renaissance Studies, 1990.
Black, Henry Campbell. *Black's Law Dictionary.* 6th ed. St. Paul, MN: West Publishing,
    1990.
Blaess, Madeleine. "L'Abbaye de Bordesley et les livres de Guy de Beauchamp." *Romania*
    78 (1957): 511–18.
Bressie, Ramona. "The Date of Thomas Usk's *Testament of Love.*" *Modern Philology* 26
    (1928): 17–29.
Brooke, Robert, Anthony Fitzherbert, and Nicolas Statham, eds. *Les reports del cases en ley
    que furent argues en le temps de le tres haut et puissant prince roy Edward le Tierce.* Lon-
    don: Printed by George Sawbridge, William Rawlins, and Samuel Roycroft, 1679.
Bühler, Curt F. "Prayers and Charms in Certain Middle English Scrolls." *Speculum* 39
    (1964): 270–78.
Bull, Marcus. *The Miracles of Our Lady of Rocamadour.* Woodbridge: Boydell, 1999.

Bumley, J. D. "Curial Prose in England." *Speculum* 61 (1986): 593–614.

Cain, Christopher M. "Sacred Words, Anglo-Saxon Piety, and the Origins of the *Epistola salvatoris* in London, British Library, Royal 2.A.xx." *Journal of English and Germanic Philology* 108 (2009): 168–89.

Calendar of the Close Rolls Preserved in the Public Record Office: Richard II. 6 vols. London: Her Majesty's Stationery Office, 1914–27.

Campbell, Lily B, ed. *The Mirror for Magistrates: Edited from Original Texts in the Huntington Library.* Cambridge: Cambridge University Press, 1938.

Carey, Hilary M. *Courting Disaster: Astrology at the English Court and University in the Later Middle Ages.* Houndsmills: Macmillan, 1992.

Carlson, David R. *The Deposition of Richard II: The Record and Process of the Renunciation and Deposition of Richard II (1399).* Toronto Medieval Latin Texts 29. Toronto: Pontifical Institute of Mediaeval Studies, 2008.

Catto, Jeremy. "Written English: The Making of thc Language 1370–1400." *Past and Present* 179 (2003): 24–59.

Chrimes, S. B., and A. L. Brown. *Select Documents of English Constitutional History: 1307–1485.* London: Adam and Charles Black, 1961.

Clarke, M. V. "Forfeitures and Treason in 1388." *Transactions of the Royal Historical Society*, 4th ser., 14 (1931): 73–74.

Clephan, R. Coltman. *The Tournament: Its Periods and Phases.* London: Methuen, 1919; repr. New York, Frederick Ungar, 1967.

Cohen, Esther. *The Crossroads of Justice: Law and Culture in Late Medieval France.* Leiden: Brill, 1993.

———. "Symbols of Culpability and the Universal Language of Justice: The Ritual of Public Executions in Late Medieval Europe." *History of European Ideas* 11 (1989): 407–16.

Crapelet, Georges Adrient, ed. *Cérémonies des gages de bataille, selon l'ordonnance de roi Philippe-le-bel, représentées en onze planches.* Collection des anciens monuments de l'histoire et de la langue française 7. Paris: Crapelet, 1830.

Davies, Richard G. "The Episcopate and the Political Crisis in England of 1386–1388." *Speculum* 51 (1976): 659–93.

———. "Richard II and the Church." In *Richard II*, ed. Goodman and Gillespie, pp. 83–106.

———. "Some Notes from the Register of Henry de Wakefield, Bishop of Worcester, on the Political Crisis of 1386–1388." *English Historical Review* 86, no. 340 (1971): 547–58.

Day, Mabel, and Robert Steele, eds. *Mum and the Sothsegger: Edited from the Manuscripts Camb. Univ. Ll iv. 14 and Brit. Mus. Add. 41666.* Early English Text Society, Original Series, 199. London: Published for the Early English Text Society by Humphrey Milford, Oxford University Press, 1936.

Dean, James M., ed. *Richard the Redeless and Mum and the Sothsegger.* TEAMS Middle English Texts Series. Kalamazoo: Medieval Institute Publications, 2000.

Dodd, Gwilym. "Changing Perspectives: Parliament, Poetry and the 'Civil Service' under Richard II and Henry IV." *Parliamentary History* 25 (2006): 299–322.

Duffy, Eamon. *The Stripping of the Altars: Traditional Religion in England, c. 1400–1580.* New Haven, CT: Yale University Press, 1992.

Eberle, Patricia J. "Richard II and the Literary Arts." In *Richard II*, ed. Goodman and Gillespie, pp. 231–54.

Ewen, C. L'Estrange. *Witchcraft and Demonism: A Concise Account Derived from Sworn Depositions and Confessions Obtained in the Courts of England and Wales.* London: Heath Cranton, 1933.

Favent, Thomas. *Historia siue narracio de modo et forma mirabilis parliamenti apud Westmonasterium anno domini millesimo CCCLXXXVI regni vero Regis Ricardi Secundi post conquestum anno decimo, per Thomam Fauent clericum indictata.* Ed. May McKisack. Camden Miscellany 14; Camden Society, 3rd ser., 37. London: Camden Society, 1926.

Froissart, Jean. *The Chronicle of Froissart, Translated out of French by Sir John Bourchier Lord Berners, annis 1523–25.* Tudor Translations 31. London: David Nutt, 1902.

Galloway, Andrew. "The Politics of Pity in Gower's *Confessio amantis.*" In *The Letter of the Law: Legal Practice and Literary Production in Medieval England,* ed. Emily Steiner and Candace Barrington, pp. 67–104. Ithaca, NY: Cornell University Press, 2002.

Given-Wilson, Chris. *The Chronicle of Adam Usk, 1377–1421.* Oxford: Clarendon Press, 1997.

———. *The Royal Household and the King's Affinity: Service, Politics, and Finance in England, 1360–1413.* New Haven, CT: Yale University Press, 1986.

Godefroid, Frédéric. *Dictionnaire de l'ancienne langue française et de tous ses dialectes du IXe au XVe siècle.* 10 vols. Paris: F. Vieweg, 1881–1902.

Goodman, Anthony, and James L. Gillespie, eds. *Richard II: The Art of Kingship.* Oxford: Clarendon Press, 1999.

Gower, John. *The Complete Works of John Gower.* Ed. G. C. Macaulay. 4 vols. Oxford: Clarendon Press, 1899–1902.

Gransden, Antonia. *Historical Writing in England.* London: Routledge and Kegan Paul, 1982.

Grazebrook, George. *The Earl Marshal's Court in England: Its History, Procedure and Powers: Comprising also an Account of the Heralds' Visitations and the Penalties Incurred by Neglecting to Conform to Their Demands.* Liverpool: Thomas Brakell, 1895.

Hand, Wayland D. "Hangman, the Gallows, and the Dead Man's Hand in American Folk Medicine." In *Medieval Literature and Folklore Studies: Essays in Honor of Francis Lee Utley,* ed. Jerome Mandel and Bruce A. Rosenberg, pp. 323–30. New Brunswick, NJ: Rutgers University Press, 1970.

Hanrahan, Michael. "Defamation as Political Contest during the Reign of Richard II." *Medium Aevum* 72 (2003): 259–76.

Hardman, Phillipa. "Gawain's Practice of Piety in Sir Gawain and the Green Knight." *Medium Aevum* 68, no. 2 (1999): 247–65.

Hardy, Thomas Duffus. *Syllabus of the Documents Relating to England and Other Kingdoms Contained in the Collection Known as "Rymer's Foedera."* 3 vols. London: Longmans, Green, 1869–85.

Haslewood, Joseph, ed. *Mirror for Magistrates.* 2 vols. London: Printed for Lackington, Allen, 1815.

Hearne, Thomas, ed. *Historia vitae et regni Ricardi II Angliae regis, a monacho quodam de Evesham consignata.* Oxford: E Theatro Sheldoniano, 1739.

Hector, L. C., and Barbara F. Harvey, eds. *The Westminster Chronicle, 1381–1394.* Oxford Medieval Texts. Oxford: Clarendon Press, 1982.

Hedegård, Gösta, ed. *Liber iuratus Honorii: A Critical Edition of the Latin Version of the Sworn Book of Honorius.* Acta Universitatis Stockholmiensis, Studia Latina Stockholmiensia 48. Stockholm: Institutionen för klassiska språk, 2002.

Higden, Ranulf. *Polychronicon Ranulphi Higden monachi Cestrensis*. Ed. Joseph Rawson Lumby and Churchill Babington. Rolls Series 41. 9 Vols. London: Longmans, Green, 1865–86.

Holdsworth, William S. *A History of English Law*. 12 vols. London: Methuen, 1903–38.

Kaye, J. M., ed. *Placita corone or La Corone pledee devant justices*. Selden Society 4. London: Selden Society, 1966.

Keen, Maurice. "The Jurisdiction and Origins of the Constable's Court." In *War and Government in the Middle Ages*, ed. John Gillingham and J. C. Holt, pp. 159–69. Totowa, NJ: Barnes & Noble Books, 1984.

———. *Nobles, Knights, and Men-at-Arms in the Middle Ages*. London: Hambledon, 1996.

———. "Treason Trials under the Law of Arms." In *Transactions of the Royal Historical Society*, 5th ser., 12 (1962): 85–103.

Ker, N. R., ed. *Medieval Libraries of Great Britain: A List of Surviving Books*. 2nd ed. London: Offices of the Royal Historical Society, 1964.

Ker, N. R., et al. *Medieval Manuscripts in British Libraries*. 5 vols. Oxford: Oxford University Press, 1969–2002.

Kieckhefer, Richard. *European Witch Trials: Their Foundations in Popular and Learned Culture, 1300–1500*. Berkeley and Los Angeles: University of California Press, 1976.

Kingsford, Charles Lethbridge. *The Grey Friars of London: Their History, with the Register of Their Convent and an Appendix of Documents*. Aberdeen: Aberdeen University Press, 1915.

———. "Wills Relating to Grey Friars, London: 1374–1430." *Additional Material for the History of the Grey Friars, London* 79–91 (1922). British History Online. http://www.british-history.ac.uk/source.

Kite, Edward. *The Monumental Brasses of Wiltshire*. Oxford: John Henry and James Parker, 1860.

Kittredge, George Lyman. *Witchcraft in Old and New England*. Cambridge, MA: Harvard University Press, 1929.

Knighton, Henry. *Knighton's Chronicle, 1337–1396*. Ed. G. H. Martin. Oxford Medieval Texts. Oxford: Clarendon Press, 1995.

Latham, R. E. *Revised Medieval Latin Word-List*. London: Published for the British Academy by the Oxford University Press, 1965.

Leland, John L. "Sir Robert Tresilian (d. 1388)." In *Oxford Dictionary of National Biography*, 55: 317–19. 60 vols. Oxford: Oxford University Press, 2004–8.

Lester, G. A. "Chaucer's Knight and the Medieval Tournament." *Neophilologus* 66 (1982): 460–68.

Lyon, Bryce. *A Constitutional and Legal History of Medieval England*. 2nd ed. New York: W. W. Norton, 1980.

Madan, Falconer, et al. *A Summary Catalogue of Western Manuscripts in the Bodleian Library at Oxford*. 7 vols. in 8. Oxford: Clarendon Press, 1895–1953.

Madden, Frederick, Bulkeley Bandinel, John Gough Nichols, eds. *Collectanea topographica et genealogica*. 8 vols. London: John Bowyer Nichols and Son for the Society of Antiquaries, 1834–43.

Maidstone, Richard. *Concordia: The Reconciliation of Richard II with London*. Ed. David R. Carlson. Verse translation by A. G. Rigg. TEAMS, Middle English Texts Series. Kalamazoo: Medieval Institute Publications, 2003.

Marx, William, ed. *An English Chronicle, 1377–1461: A New Edition. Edited from Alberst-*

wyth, National Library of Wales MS 21068 and Oxford, Bodleian Library MS Lyell 34. Medieval Chronicles 3. Woodbridge: Boydell and Brewer, 2003.

McKisack, May. *The Fourteenth Century, 1307–1399.* Oxford: Clarendon Press, 1959.

Mead, Jenna. "Geoffrey Chaucer's *Treatise on the Astrolabe." Literature Compass* 3 (2006): 973–91.

Mézières, Philippe de. *Letter to King Richard II: A Plea Made in 1395 for Peace between England and France.* Ed. G. W. Coopland. Liverpool: Liverpool University Press, 1975.

Munby, A. N. L., ed. *The Phillipps Manuscripts: Catalogus librorum manuscriptorum in Bibliotheca D. Thomae Phillipps, Bt., Impressum typis Medio-Montanis, 1837–1871.* London: Orskey-Johnson, 2001.

Neilson, George. *Trial by Combat.* New York: Macmillan, 1891.

Nicolas, Nicholas Harris, ed. *Controversy between Sir Richard Scrope and Sir Robert Grosvenor in the Court of Chivalry.* London: Samuel Bentley, 1832.

Oliver, Clementine. "New Light on the Life and Manuscripts of a Political Pamphleteer: Thomas Fovent." *Historical Research* 83 (2010): 60–68.

———. *Parliament and Political Pamphleteering in Fourteenth-Century England.* Woodbridge: York Medieval Press, 2010.

———. "A Political Pamphleteer in Late Medieval England: Thomas Fovent, Geoffrey Chaucer, Thomas Usk, and the Merciless Parliament of 1388." *New Medieval Literatures* 6 (2003): 167–98.

Oman, C. W. C. *The Great Revolt of 1381.* New York: Greenwood, 1969.

Opie, Iona, and Moira Tatem, eds. *A Dictionary of Superstitions.* Oxford: Oxford University Press, 1989.

Ordonnances des roys de France. 21 vols. Paris: Imprimerie royale, 1723–1849.

Ormrod, W. M. *The Reign of Edward III: Crown and Political Society in England, 1327–1377.* New Haven, CT: Yale University Press, 1990.

———. "The Trials of Alice Perrers." *Speculum* 83 (2008): 366–96.

———. "Who Was Alice Perrers?" *Chaucer Review* 40 (2006): 219–29.

Patterson, Lee. *Chaucer and the Subject of History.* Madison: University of Wisconsin Press, 1991.

Plucknett, T. F. T. "State Trials under Richard II." *Transactions of the Royal Historical Society,* 5th ser., 2 (1952): 159–72.

Pollard, Alfred, et al., eds. *The Works of Geoffrey Chaucer.* The Globe Edition. London: Macmillan, 1965.

Pollock, Frederick, and Frederic William Maitland. *The History of English Law before the Time of Edward I.* 2nd ed. 2 vols. Cambridge: Cambridge University Press, 1968.

Pounds, N. J. G. *A History of the English Church: The Culture of Religion from Augustine to Victoria.* Cambridge: Cambridge University Press, 2000.

Riley, Henry Thomas, ed. *Memorials of London and London Life, in the XIIIth, XIVth, and XVth Centuries.* London: Longmans, Green, 1868.

———, ed. *Thomae Walsingham, quondam Monachi S. Albani, Historia Anglicana.* Rolls Series 28. London: Her Majesty's Stationery Office, 1863.

Rogers, Alan. "Parliamentary Appeals of Treason in the Reign of Richard II." *American Journal of Legal History* 8 (1964): 95–124.

Rosenthal, Joel T. *Telling Tales: Sources and Narration in Late Medieval England.* University Park: Pennsylvania State University Press, 2003.

Roy, Bruno. "The Household Encyclopedia as Magic Kit: Medieval Popular Interests in Pranks and Illusions." *Journal of Popular Culture* 14 (1980): 60–69.

Russell, Jeffrey Burton. *Witchcraft in the Middle Ages*. Ithaca, NY: Cornell University Press, 1972.

Sainty, John. *The Judges of England, 1272–1990: A List of Judges of the Superior Courts*, Selden Society, Supplementary Series, 10. London: Selden Society, 1993.

Saul, Nigel. *Death, Art, and Memory in Medieval England: The Cobham Family and Their Monuments, 1300–1500*. Oxford: Oxford University Press, 2001.

———. *Richard II*. New Haven, CT: Yale University Press, 1997.

Sayles, G. O., ed. *Select Cases in the Court of King's Bench under Richard II, Henry IV and Henry V*. Selden Society 87. London: Bernard Quaritch, 1971.

Scase, Wendy. *Literature and Complaint in England, 1272–1553*. Oxford: Oxford University Press, 2007.

Scattergood, John. "Remembering Richard II: John Gower's *Cronica Tripartita*, *Richard the Redeles*, and *Mum and the Sothsegger*." Ch. 12 in *The Lost Tradition: Essays on Middle English Alliterative Poetry*, pp. 200–25. Dublin: Four Courts, 2000.

Scot, Reginald. *The Discoverie of Witchcraft*. Ed. Brinsley Nicholson. Totowa, NJ: Rowman and Littlefield, 1973.

Seligmann, Kurt. *The History of Magic and the Occult*. New York: Gramercy Books, 1997.

Sharpe, Reginald R. *London and the Kingdom: A History Derived Mainly from the Archives at Guildhall in the Custody of the Corporation of the City of London*. 3 vols. London: Longmans, Green, 1894–95.

Skemer, Don C. *Binding Words: Textual Amulets in the Middle Ages*. University Park: Pennsylvania State University Press, 2006.

Squibb, George D. *The High Court of Chivalry: A Study of the Civil Law in England*. Oxford: Clarendon Press, 1959.

Stow, George B., Jr., ed. *Historia vitae et regni Ricardi secundi*. Philadelphia: University of Pennsylvania Press, 1977.

Strachey, John, ed. *Rotuli parliamentorum: Ut et petitiones et placita in Parliamento tempore Edwardi R.I. (Edwardi II., Edwardi III., Ricardi II., Henrici IV., V., VI., Henrici VII., 1278–1503)*. 6 vols. London: n.p., 1767–77.

Stubbs, William. *Constitutional History of England*. 3rd ed. 3 vols. Oxford: Clarendon Press, 1883.

Swanson, R. N. *Indulgences in Late Medieval England: Passports to Paradise?* Cambridge: Cambridge University Press, 2007.

Takamiya, Toskiyuki. "Gawain's Green Girdle as a Medieval Talisman." In *Chaucer to Shakespeare: Essays in Honour of Shinsuke Ando*, ed. Toskiyuki Takamiya and Richard Beadle, pp. 75–79. Woodbridge: D. S. Brewer, 1992.

Taylor, John. *English Historical Literature in the Fourteenth Century*. Oxford: Oxford University Press, 1987.

Thomas, Keith. *Religion and the Decline of Magic*. New York: Oxford University Press, 1997.

Thompson, Edward Maunde, ed. *Chronicon Adae de Usk, A.D. 1377–1404*. London: John Murray, 1876.

Thornley, Isobel D. "Treason by Words in the Fifteenth Century." *English Historical Review* 32, no. 128 (1917): 556–61.

Thornley, Isobel D., and T. F. T. Plucknett, eds. *Year Books of Richard II: 11 Richard II, 1387–1388*. Year Books Series. London: Spottiswoode, Ballantyne, 1937.

Timmins, T. C. B., ed. *The Register of John Waltham, Bishop of Salisbury*. Canterbury and York Society 80. Woodbridge: Boydell, 1994.

Tout, T. F. *Chapters in the Administrative History of Mediaeval England: The Wardrobe, the Chamber and the Small Seals*. 6 vols. Manchester: Manchester University Press, 1920–33.

———. "The English Parliament and Public Opinion, 1376–88." In *Historical Studies of the English Parliament*, ed. E. B. Fryde and Edward Miller, 1:298–315. 2 vols. Cambridge: Cambridge University Press, 1970.

———. "Literature and Learning in the English Civil Service of the Fourteenth Century." *Speculum* 4 (1929): 365–89.

Tuck, J. A. "The Cambridge Parliament, 1388." *English Historical Review* 84, no. 331 (1969): 225–43.

Turner, Marion. *Chaucerian Conflict: Languages of Antagonism in Late Fourteenth-Century London*. New York: Oxford University Press, 2007.

Twiss, Travers, ed. *Monumenta juridica: The Black Book of the Admiralty*. Rolls Series 55. 4 vols. London: Longman, Trübner, 1871.

Usk, Thomas. *Testament of Love*. Ed. Gary W. Shawyer. Based on the edition by John F. Leyerle. Toronto: University of Toronto Press, 2002.

Veenstra, Jan R. *Magic and Divination at the Courts of Burgundy and France: Text and Contest of Laurens Pignon's "Contre les devineurs" (1411)*. Leiden: Brill, 1998.

Walsingham, Thomas. *The St Albans Chronicle: The "Chronica maiora" of Thomas of Walsingham*. Vol. 1, *1376–1394*. Ed. and trans. John Taylor, Wendy R. Childs, and Leslie Watkiss. Oxford: Clarendon Press, 2003.

Wheeler, G. W., ed. *Letters of Sir Thomas Bodley to Thomas James, First Keeper of the Bodleian Library*. Oxford: Clarendon Press, 1926.

Willis-Bund, John William, and William Page, eds. *The Victoria History of the County of Worcester*. 5 vols. Westminster: Archibald Constable; London: St. Catherine Press, 1901–26; vol. 2 repr. Dawsons of Pall Mall, 1971.

Woodward, J. M. *The History of Bordesley Abbey, in the Valley of the Arrow, near Redditch, Worcestershire*. London: J. H. and J. Parker, 1866.

Zane, John M. "A Year Book of Richard II." *Michigan Law Review* 13 (1915): 439–65.

Military Industrial Production in Thirteenth-Century England: The Case of the Crossbow Bolt

David S. Bachrach

T HE FOCUS OF THIS STUDY is on the production and acquisition by the English government of ammunition for the many thousands of crossbows used by royal troops from the reign of Richard I (1189–99) to that of Edward I (1272–1307).[1] Over this long century, the English government devoted considerable resources to producing and purchasing millions of crossbow quarrels of a variety of types. The regular employment of crossbowmen in the royal armed forces meant that the government had to have available a steady stream of ammunition supplies. This led kings from Richard to Edward I to maintain ammunition production facilities on a regular footing in peacetime as well as during periods of overt military operations. In periods of intense military activity, however, the royal government found it necessary to supplement production from its own facilities with purchases on the private market.

Sources

Due in no small part to Bryce Lyon's extensive publications, the legal and administrative sources for thirteenth- and early fourteenth-century England are

When I began working on the administrative history of England, Bryce Lyon's works provided the crucial grounding in the sources that helped me to navigate the tremendous volume and variety of texts collected at the National Archives in London that make this field so rewarding. One of the very first works of medieval history that I read, encouraged by one of Lyon's former students, was *From Fief to Indenture*. But I owe an even deeper debt of gratitude to Professor Lyon for stimulating my very interest in this fascinating field. I am, therefore, doubly grateful for the opportunity to participate in this memorial volume honoring Bryce Lyon.

[1] Regarding the important role of crossbows in English warfare from the late twelfth through the early fourteenth century, see Bachrach: "Origins of the English Crossbow," "Crossbow Makers," "Royal Arms Makers," "Crossbows for the King," "Crossbows for the King (Part Two)."

accessible to scholars.[2] The basic source for administrative history of the royal government during the twelfth century consists of the Pipe Rolls, which are the records of the biannual audits of the accounts of sheriffs at the Exchequer.[3] The reign of King John witnesses the survival of the Patent Rolls and Close Rolls.[4] The Patent and Close Rolls are supplemented in King John's reign by *misae* accounts, which deal with the king's daily expenses; the *praestita* roll, which records money given as advanced payments to individuals, usually for military purposes, and by the Norman Rolls, which were preserved in the Tower of London and record some of the king's military expenses in Normandy.[5] Finally, during the first six years of John's reign, a subset of the Close Rolls, identified by scholars as Liberate Rolls, were kept separately by royal clerks.[6]

The Pipe Rolls, Close Rolls, and Patent Rolls survive in a more or less full sequence for the reigns of Henry III and Edward I, although the years 1216–21 and 1233–36 have extensive lacunae.[7] *Liberate* documents continued to be enrolled with letters close until 1226, when royal clerks began to enroll them separately. In addition to these major collections of documents kept by the clerks of Chancery and Exchequer, tens of thousands of individual administrative texts, including letters, memoranda, writs, reports, and receipts, most of which are still unedited, also survive from the reigns of Henry III and Edward I.[8] These texts were issued by a wide range of royal officials and individuals who had dealings with the royal government. During the reign of Edward I, in particular, these documents provide invaluable insight into the exceptionally large production and purchase of crossbow quarrels by the royal government.

---

[2] Lyon, *Constitutional and Legal History*, provides an essential introduction to the numerous corpora of administrative documents that shed light on the actions of the royal government from King John onward. Similarly, Lyon, Lyon, and Sturler, *Wardrobe Book of William de Norwell*, and Lyon and Lyon, *Wardrobe Book of 1296–1297*, have helped illuminate the value of the voluminous wardrobe accounts for numerous aspects of administrative history, including military affairs.

[3] The Pipe Rolls for the reigns of Henry II, Richard I, and John have been edited separately by the Pipe Roll Society. Each roll is cited individually. For a valuable introduction to the Pipe Rolls, see Lyon, *Constitutional and Legal History*, pp. 257–65.

[4] The basic published collections are *Rotuli litterarum patentium* and *Rotuli litterarum clausarum*.

[5] The *misae* accounts and *praestita* rolls are recorded in *Rotuli de liberate ac de misis*. For the Norman rolls, see *Rotuli Normannie*.

[6] For a useful introduction to the development of the Liberate Rolls, see *Rotuli de liberate*, pp. iii–xv.

[7] Several of the Pipe Rolls from Henry III's reign have been edited by the Pipe Roll Society. The majority of the Pipe Rolls for the reigns of Henry III and Edward I, however, have not been edited. These are cited by their catalogue numbers in the National Archives at Kew Gardens (formerly the Public Record Office). Editions of the close roll texts for the reign of Henry III appear in *Close Rolls, 1227–1272* (hereafter *CR*). Calendars of the Close Rolls for the reign of Edward I appear in *Calendar of Close Rolls, 1272–1307* (hereafter *CCR*).

[8] They are cited below according to their catalogue number at the National Archives (hereafter NA).

The Reigns of Richard and John (1189–1216)

It is not until the reign of King John that we have evidence for the royal government's involvement in crossbow production in England.[9] By contrast, the production of ammunition for crossbows significantly antedates John's successful effort to transplant a crossbow industry across the channel in 1203–4. By Richard I's reign at the latest, the royal government already had spent considerable sums purchasing, producing, and stockpiling crossbow quarrels for use in the king's military and naval campaigns. In 1192, for example, the pipe roll entry for London and Middlesex records that the sheriffs of London were stockpiling *quarellae*, along with other war materiel, including stone-throwing engines (*petrariae*), stones, and shields at the Tower of London, which was one of England's main magazines.[10] Two years later, in 1194, the pipe roll account for Hampshire and Winchester notes the expenditure of funds by the sheriff on iron to be used for the production of quarrel heads.[11] In 1196, the sheriff of Shropshire was credited four shillings in the pipe roll for his purchase of *quarellae*.[12]

During King John's reign the Pipe Rolls record a significant increase both in the sums spent by the government to produce quarrels in royal workshops and on the purchase of this ammunition from private sources. The pipe roll account in 1200, for example, records that Reginald Cornhill, the sheriff of Kent, spent fifty shillings for 5,000 quarrels.[13] After the opening of the earliest royal crossbow workshops, first in Nottingham and five other centers during the summer of 1204, the Pipe Rolls show an even more dramatic rise in the quantity of quarrels obtained by the government.[14] In 1207, the royal officials administering the bishopric of Lincoln for King John are credited in the pipe roll with spending in excess of £70 to purchase 92,000 crossbow bolts as well as chests and barrels in which to store them.[15] That same year the sheriff of Nottingham spent an additional £5 for about 7,000 quarrels.[16] The Pipe Rolls record a second major series of expenditures on crossbow bolts in 1211. The royal keepers of the bishopric of

---

[9] Bachrach, "Origins of the English Crossbow."

[10] *Pipe Roll, 1191 and 1192*, p. 158.

[11] *Pipe Roll, 1194*, p. 212: "et pro ferro ad fabricandas quarellas ad opus R."

[12] *Chancery Roll, 1196*, p. 42.

[13] *Pipe Roll, 1200*, p. 209.

[14] Regarding the establishment of these production facilities in England, see Bachrach, "Origins of the English Crossbow."

[15] *Pipe Roll, 1207*, p. 14. The see of Lincoln was vacant in 1207 following the death of Bishop Walter of Coutances.

[16] *Pipe Roll, 1207*, p. 114. The next year the royal officials overseeing the vacant see of Lincoln purchased an additional 42,000 quarrels for use in the garrisons in the Poitou, and at Winchester Castle. See *Rotuli litterarum clausarum*, 1:100 (hereafter *RLC*).

Durham purchased just under 86,000 quarrels that year.[17] The sheriff of Yorkshire purchased 40,000 quarrels.[18] The royal officer Brian de L'Isle spent in excess of £21 on 32,000 crossbow bolts.[19] Finally, John Fitzhugh purchased 34,500 quarrels for the Crown, for a grand total of just under 200,000 bolts.[20]

Purchases of this magnitude continue to characterize royal arms acquisitions up through King John's failed French expedition of 1214. The pipe roll for 1212 records purchases of 140,000 quarrels by the royal officials overseeing the vacant see of Durham, as well as by Bishop Mauger of Worcester and by the sheriff of Derbyshire.[21] In addition to these large purchases of ready-to-use quarrels, John Fitzhugh was credited for the expenses he incurred to have 28,000 bolt heads fitted with shafts and feathers.[22] The pipe roll for 1213 is lost, but the evidence from 1214 indicates that the large-scale purchases of quarrels continued up to the eve of King John's final Continental campaign. The sheriff of Gloucestershire, for example, purchased 45,000 quarrels in 1214.[23] Brian de L'Isle, now serving as the constable of Knaresburgh Castle in Yorkshire's West Riding, purchased an additional 15,000 crossbow bolts. Moreover, he sent a shipment of 30,000 bolts to Portsmouth to be transported to the English fleet gathering there for the invasion of France.[24] Finally, William Saint John, the sheriff of Southampton, added a further 10,000 quarrels to the royal stockpiles.[25]

Even without accounting for the undoubtedly large number of quarrels purchased in 1213, the four years before King John's final Continental campaign saw the acquisition of approximately half a million quarrels on the private market.[26] Of

---

[17] *Pipe Roll, 1211*, p. 39.

[18] *Pipe Roll, 1211*, p. 43.

[19] *Pipe Roll, 1211*, p. 88.

[20] *Pipe Roll, 1211*, pp. 108, 111.

[21] *Pipe Roll, 1212*, pp. 47, 61, 169. The bishopric of Durham was without a prelate following the death in 1208 of Philip of Poitou, who was not replaced until 1217.

[22] *Pipe Roll, 1211*, p. 44.

[23] *Pipe Roll, 1214*, p. 55.

[24] *Pipe Roll, 1214*, p. 67. Alan was originally ordered to produce as many quarrels as possible in a writ issued by the Chancery on 23 May 1214. See *RLC*, 1:206: "Dei gratia etc. dilecto sibi Alano de S. Georgio (sic) constabulario de Gnaresburgh salutem. Mandamus vobis quod fieri faciatis omnes quarellos quos poteritis et eos mitti usque Portsmouth, retentis ad garnesturam castri de Gnaresburgh uno millario is opus fuerit. Et custum quod in opere et in cariagum posueritis vobis faciemus computari." A similar order was sent the same day to Reginald Cornhill, one of King John's chief procurement officers. See *RLC*, 1:206.

[25] *Pipe Roll, 1214*, p. 126.

[26] Some indication of royal expenditures on crossbow bolts in 1213 can be gleaned from a letter issued by the Chancery to the Exchequer authorizing the barons to credit Brian de L'Isle the expenses he incurred for purchasing 10,000 quarrels and transporting them from Knaresburgh Castle, where he served as constable, to Portsmouth. See *RLC*, 1:148.

course, this number must be seen as a minimum figure. Not only are all records for 1213 lost, but a great majority of the pertinent documents produced by the royal Chancery and Exchequer also have not survived. As we shall see, the surviving administrative records of this type from the reigns of Henry III and Edward I also refer to the purchases of very substantial numbers of quarrels by the Crown.

The purchase by royal officials of large numbers of quarrels from private producers was complemented in John's reign by the regular output of crossbow bolts from royal workshops. The latter can be understood as operating in conjunction with the crossbow workshops established by John in the period 1203–12.[27] At least three fletchers, Denis, Philip, and Thomas, who specialized in the fabrication of crossbow quarrels, as contrasted with fletchers making arrows, can be identified in King John's service.[28] In addition to these three men, the pipe roll of 1214 records the service of unnamed smiths who produced iron heads for crossbow bolts for the royal government during John's reign.[29]

The evidence from the Pipe Rolls makes clear that John's government maintained workshops for the production of crossbow quarrels, with a major center at the Tower of London. In addition, the royal government supplemented the supplies of quarrels available from its own workshops with the purchase of this ammunition on the private market. Indeed, as noted above, many of these purchases were in excess of 10,000 bolts, and it is clear that government obtained many hundreds of thousands, if not millions of quarrels, from private manufacturers.

The Reign of King Henry III (1216–72)

Henry III's government continued the policies of King John regarding both the production and purchase of quarrels. The much larger corpus of surviving administrative documents in the period after 1216, however, permits a far more detailed understanding of royal efforts both to purchase crossbow bolts on the private market as well as to maintain and even expand royal workshops that specialized in the production of ammunition. Before the spring of 1221, as noted above, the royal government already had in place a major production facility for crossbow bolts at the Tower of London. A letter from the Chancery on May 25, 1221, instructed the officers of the Exchequer to disburse £10 to a royal officer named Alex of Dorset

[27] Bachrach, "Origins of the English Crossbow."

[28] *Pipe Roll, 1199*, p. 132; *Pipe Roll, 1211*, p. 171; and *RLC*, 1:2, respectively.

[29] *Pipe Roll, 1214*, p. 136. In this case William Saint John, the sheriff of Southampton, noted above, was credited with the expenses he incurred for transporting the smiths from Winchester to Portsmouth. The original order to dispatch the smiths was issued on May 23, 1214, by Bishop Peter des Roches of Winchester. He wrote to the sheriff of Southampton to instruct him to find transportation for the smiths serving there along with their wives, children, and tools, as well as the quarrels they had produced, and to send them to Portsmouth. See *RLC*, 1:205.

to pay the wages of the smiths and crossbow makers producing *quarelli* and *balistae* at the Tower.[30] A second royal production facility was in full operation no later than 1222. The pipe roll for this year records that the sheriff of Gloucestershire and the constable of St. Briavels Castle paid the wages of the smith William Malemort, his two assistants (*garciones*), and a fletcher named William, who were all engaged in producing crossbow bolts for the Crown in a workshop located in the forest of Dean.[31] In addition to paying the wages of the two Williams and their assistants, the sheriff and constable also purchased iron, coal, a forge, bellows, and hammers for use in the workshop.[32]

The surviving administrative records suggest that the two workshops at the Tower of London and the forest of Dean produced a sufficient quantity of crossbow bolts for peacetime needs. In periods of intense conflict, however, the royal government sought additional quarrels from private makers. The royal response to the siege of Bedford Castle in 1224 exemplifies this pattern.[33] On June 20, 1224, the Chancery issued an order to the sheriff of London requiring that he send a large quantity of military supplies to the royal forces encamped outside Bedford Castle. Of particular importance in this context, the sheriff was ordered to send as many quarrels as he could.[34] The text emphasizes that the sheriff was to send these supplies *sub omni festinacione*, indicating that the war materiel was to be taken out of current stocks stored in the magazines.

That same day, however, the Chancery sent a second order to the sheriff of London ordering him to find five or six smiths (*fabri*) to work nonstop, literally day and night (*de die et nocte*), to produce as many quarrels as possible for use at the siege of Bedford Castle.[35] Within eight days, that is by June 28, 1224, the sheriff of London was able to acquire an additional 3,000 quarrels, which he then sent to Bedford.[36] However, even the additional supplies of crossbow bolts sent from London proved insufficient, and the government sought further shipments of ammunition. On July 23, 1224, the Chancery issued orders to the bailiffs of Northampton to mobilize all smiths in town who knew how to make quarrels to

[30] *RLC*, 1:460.

[31] *Pipe Roll, 1222*, p. 39.

[32] *Pipe Roll, 1222*, p. 39. Concerning the role of St. Briavels Castle and the forest of Dean as an important arsenal during the reign of Edward I, see Hart, *Royal Forest*.

[33] For a detailed discussion of the logistical efforts undertaken by the royal government during the siege, see Amt, "Besieging Bedford."

[34] *RLC*, 1:605: "Mandamus vobis sicut nos diligitis sub omni festinacione qua poteritis ad nos mittatis usque Bedeford duas carectatas vel tres de cordis et xx funas ad mangonellos et petrarias et targias et quarellos quotquot poteritis."

[35] *RLC*, 1:605.

[36] *RLC*, 1:608.

produce 4,000 of them as quickly as possible.[37] Further orders were issued the next day to the royal bailiffs of Oxford, as well as to the sheriffs of London, requiring that they have the local smiths produce 6,000 and 10,000 quarrels respectively.[38] It should be noted that this was the second lot of crossbow bolts required from the sheriffs of London in the space of a month.

The pattern of quarrel production and purchases established by the royal government during the early 1220s remained the norm for the rest of Henry III's reign. Henry's government employed no fewer than thirteen master smiths and fletchers in royal workshops between 1225 and 1272, and several of these men, including William Malemort, employed teams of assistants.[39] Perhaps the best known of these men was William Malemort's brother, John, who began working with William in 1225, and subsequently supervised his own workshop at the forest of Dean from 1230 until at least 1278, during the reign of Edward I.[40] The Tower of London also continued to house a major production facility through the end of Henry III's reign, although the smiths and fletchers there served for much shorter terms of service than John Malemort.[41] In addition to these major facilities, Henry III's government established at least one subsidiary production center for crossbow quarrels in 1261 at Dover Castle under the direction of a smith named Adam.[42]

The annual output of the two major production centers at the forest of Dean and the Tower of London reached 50,000 quarrels by 1229. On November 18 of that year, the Chancery issued orders to the bailiff of St. Briavels Castle, located in the forest of Dean, to increase the pay of William Malemort, his brother, John, and William the Fletcher on condition that they raise their daily level of production

---

[37] *RLC*, 1:613: "mandamus vobis quod . . . visis litteris tam die quam de nocte fieri faciatis per omnes fabros ville Northampton qui in arte fabricanti quarellos sunt instructi, quatuor milia quarellorum." A letter issued by the Chancery on August 19, 1224, to the constable of the castle at Northampton required him to store at his castle 900 of the 4,000 quarrels, which were produced by the smiths of the city. See *RLC*, 1:617.

[38] *RLC*, 1:638.

[39] I intend to write a prosopographical study of all arms makers who served during the reign of Henry III, including the smiths, fletchers, crossbow makers, and artillery builders. Concerning the arms makers employed by the royal government during the reign of King John, see Bachrach, "Royal Arms Makers."

[40] *RLC*, 2:54; and *CCR*, 1:438. John Malemort's career has been studied by Webb, "John Malemort."

[41] At least six master smiths can be identified serving as quarrel makers at the Tower of London between 1225 and 1273. They are Thomas, Roger, Ogerus, Henry, Alan, and Richard. For Thomas see *RLC*, 2:45, 55, 58, 68, 84, 115, 140, 143, and *Calendar of Liberate Rolls* (hereafter *CLR*), 1:5, 15, 24, 32, 39, 43–44; for Roger see E372/76, fol. 8v, and *CLR*, 4:376, 401; for Ogerus see E372/77, fol. 12r, and *CLR*, 1:203; for Henry see *CR*, 11:205–6 and *CLR*, 5:3, 7, 70–71, 112; for Alan see *CR*, 11:205–6, and *CLR*, 5:119, 144, 220, 221, 224, 253, 282; and for Richard see *CLR*, 6:24, 32.

[42] *CLR*, 5:53.

to 200 from 100 quarrels.[43] Other surviving letters in the Liberate Rolls make clear that the Malemort brothers, William the Fletcher, and their assistants were expected to work on average five days a week, that is 250 days, to produce a total of 50,000 quarrels per year.[44] In 1230, however, William Malemort left royal service, and John Malemort's daily production quota was reduced to 100 quarrels a day, where it remained until the end of Henry III's reign.[45] This level of output likely was matched by the royal production facility at the Tower of London, although the surviving records do not indicate how many quarrels the master smiths and fletchers working there were supposed to produce on a daily basis.

This substantial output of crossbow bolts from the production facilities at the Tower of London and the forest of Dean was deemed sufficient by the royal government for peacetime conditions. During Henry III's many military actions on the Continent, and in Wales, and in civil wars in England, however, the government found it prudent to continue to supplement its normal supplies of quarrels with purchases from private manufacturers. For example, before undertaking the Welsh campaign of 1228, the royal government first ordered substantial additional stocks of quarrels. On July 15, 1227, Chancery issued orders to the sheriff of Cumberland to have the smiths in his shire produce 100,000 quarrels at the cost of the royal government.[46] In February of the same year Stephen de Lucy, the royal official administering the vacant see of Durham, was ordered to have suitable smiths in the bishopric produce as many quarrels as possible at royal cost.[47] In the end, this royal officer succeeded in acquiring no fewer than 25,000 bolts for the central government.[48] The Welsh campaign of 1242 saw similar preparations. The constable of Windsor Castle purchased 50,000 iron heads for crossbow bolts from local smiths, and on August 27, 1242, the Chancery issued an order to the royal bailiffs of Windsor to provide shafts and feathers for them.[49]

In one final example, following the defeat of the baronial forces at Evesham (August 4, 1265), Henry III and his son Edward spent much of the next two years hunting down and defeating isolated pockets of rebel resistance. The most important of these centers was the castle of Kenilworth, which fell in December 1266,

---

[43] *CLR*, 1:157–58.

[44] See *CR*, 8:96–97; and *CLR*, 4:373.

[45] See *CLR*, 1:181–82, 103–4, 228, 240, 263, 320, 381–82, 468; *CLR*, 2:77–78, 175; *CLR*, 3:41, 119, 204, 229, 357; *CLR*, 4:45, 151, 226, 373; and *CLR*, 5:192. The one exception to this pattern was in December 1257, when the royal government asked John Malemort to double his production from 25,000 to 50,000 quarrels for use in the king's Welsh campaign. See *CLR*, 3:415.

[46] *CLR*, 1:44.

[47] *CLR*, 1:19. This order was repeated on September 21, 1228. See *CR*, 1:81.

[48] *CLR*, 1:164.

[49] *CLR*, 2:146.

although scattered resistance continued into 1267.[50] In order to conduct these military operations the royal government first sought to increase production at its own facilities. In July 1266 John Malemort was asked to produce an additional 6,000 quarrels above his normal quota.[51] But this proved insufficient. The royal government therefore ordered the sheriffs of the City of London to have the local smiths produce 20,000 quarrels, of which 13,200 were produced and shipped to the king's forces.[52] In March 1267, the government sought an additional 50,000 quarrels from the sheriffs of London and 30,000 from the bailiffs of Colchester, which were supposed to be produced by local smiths.[53]

During Henry III's reign the government established its main production centers for quarrels at the forest of Dean and the Tower of London. The annual output of these two facilities was 25,000 quarrels each, although in times of crisis output at these centers was doubled. This regular production was supplemented in wartime by very large purchases of quarrels on the private market. Given the consistently large production of quarrels by royal workshops over half a century and the continuing effort by the government to purchase quarrels on the private market, it seems clear that Henry III's logistics officers obtained many millions of quarrels.

The Reign of Edward I (1272–1307)

The early years of King Edward's reign saw the continued production of quarrels at the traditional workshops located in the Tower of London and the forest of Dean. John Malemort produced quarrels for the government at St. Briavels Castle located in the forest of Dean, until at least 1278.[54] The production staff at the Tower of London in 1273 and 1274 included a smith named Henry and two fletchers named Hugh and Peter.[55]

Nevertheless, the surviving evidence indicates that Edward's government made a decision at some point in the 1270s both to decentralize its production facilities and perhaps to rely more heavily on private producers to supply quarrels. John Malemort, the chief of the production facility at St. Briavels Castle, probably died at this time, having been in royal service for nearly four decades, for he does not appear in the royal records after 1278. He evidently was not replaced. Yet the constables of St. Briavels Castle continued to have responsibility for the large-scale production of crossbow bolts, at least sporadically, throughout Edward I's reign. Evidence for the production of quarrels at the Tower of London becomes

[50] Prestwich, *Edward I*, pp. 51–59.
[51] *CLR*, 5:221–22.
[52] *CLR*, 5:230, 263.
[53] *CLR*, 5:264, 276.
[54] *CCR*, 1:438.
[55] NA C 62/49, fol. 5r; and NA C62/50, fols. 2r, 6r, and 15r.

scarce in the surviving administrative documents after 1274, although some master smiths and fletchers can still be identified working there. Thus, for example, in 1294 the smith John of Northampton and the carpenter Robert de Colbroke were authorized in a writ of *liberate* to receive their daily wages of ninepence and fourpence, respectively, for producing quarrels at the Tower.[56]

Instead of centralizing quarrel production in two government workshops, which was the norm through most of Henry III's reign, Edward's government appears to have hired smiths and carpenters to produce crossbow bolts in the same places where crossbows were now being made, namely in the royal castles of Wales, Scotland, and the marches. This decentralization had the benefit of lowering transportation costs for the finished products. In 1294, for example, Reginald de Grey, the commander of the royal army in Wales, employed a smith at Chester Castle to make quarrels for his troops as they prepared to deal with Welsh rebels. The smith was accompanied in his work by an *attiliator* who was repairing the crossbows of Reginald de Grey's troops.[57]

King Edward's wars in Scotland and the consolidation of his conquests saw the establishment of several centers for the production of quarrels there. The liberate roll for 1298 records, for example, that John Kirkeby, the sheriff of Northumberland, paid the wages of fletchers who completed 2,415 quarrels at Newcastle.[58] The sheriff also paid the wages of two smiths who repaired 10,000 old bolt heads so that they could be reused.[59] The English garrison town of Berwick also served as a major center for the production of quarrels for use by royal garrisons in Scotland. A garrison roster for Berwick Castle, issued in 1300, indicates that the specialists on staff there included a crossbow maker and two smiths.[60]

The significant level of quarrel production achieved at Berwick is indicated by several surviving administrative documents. In 1298, for example, the account of John Burdon, the constable of Berwick Castle, includes expenses for the production of 4,300 quarrels designed for "two-foot" crossbows.[61] A memorandum issued in September 1302 records that Richard de Bremesgrave, the chief logistics officer at Berwick, transported large quantities of food as well as crossbows and 5,000 quarrels from his magazine to the garrison at Selkirk Castle.[62] A memorandum issued two years later in May 1304 by Walter Bedewind recorded that he had received 23,000

[56] NA C62/71, fol. 2r.

[57] NA C62/75, fol. 6r. The payment to Reginald de Grey for his expenses was recorded in the liberate roll for 1298.

[58] NA C62/74, fol. 5r.

[59] NA C62/74, fol. 5r.

[60] NA E101/8/24.

[61] NA E101/7/6. Regarding the types of crossbows deployed by the royal government during Edward I's reign, see Bachrach, "Crossbows for the King (Part Two)."

[62] NA E101/9/30, no. 14.

quarrels from Richard de Bremesgrave for the garrison at Stirling Castle. A further memorandum, issued in August of 1304, recorded that the ship captain Robert, the son of Walter, carried a further load of "quarellos pro balistis preparatos apud dictum Berwick" to Stirling Castle.[63] Other surviving documents from the English officers in Scotland indicate that the garrisons at Roxburgh and Dumfries Castles also had smiths and fletchers on staff to produce quarrels in each of these fortresses in 1303.[64]

As had been true during Henry III's reign, however, Edward I's government also found it necessary to supplement the regular supply of quarrels from its own workshops with purchases from private producers. The bulk of these purchases by the Crown came during royal military campaigns. The Welsh campaigns of 1277, 1282–84, 1287, and 1294–95 all saw exceptionally large purchases of crossbow bolts. A writ to the Exchequer issued on June 23, 1277, for example, ordered the clerks there to credit the account of Robert, a royal treasury official, for almost £70 that he had spent on the production of 100,000 quarrels, and a further £7 for the costs involved in transporting 77,000 of these quarrels to the fortresses of Chester and Montgomery.[65] Earlier that year, on March 12, the king had issued orders to the royal steward, Ralph of Sandwich, to have 200,000 quarrels produced at St. Briavels Castle, the site of the major workshop earlier overseen by John Malemort.[66]

The Welsh campaigns of 1282–84 saw even larger purchases of quarrels by the royal government. The chief logistics officer for the royal army in Wales, a clerk named Ralph, recorded in his *compotus* that in 1283 he had received and subsequently distributed to garrisons and troops in Wales 164,000 completed quarrels and an additional 18,750 iron heads. This included in excess of 80,000 quarrels and heads shipped into England from Gascony.[67] In January and May 1283 additional purchases of crossbow bolts numbering 90,000 and 30,000 respectively were shipped by Peter de la Mare, constable of Bristol Castle, and Grimbald Pauncefoot, constable of St. Briavels, to the royal garrisons at Chester, Carmarthen, and Rothelan.[68] In December 1284, King Edward ordered Peter de la Mare to purchase a further 200,000 quarrels for use by the royal garrisons in Wales.[69]

---

[63] NA C47/22/9, nos.70 and 71.

[64] NA E101/9/30, no. 25, and E101/14/1. The second of these documents, which is not dated, notes that James Dalilegh, one of the chief royal logistics officers for the Scottish war, sent glue *pro quarellis* to the castle at Bonfres. James was appointed receiver at Stirling in 1300. Concerning James Dalilegh's career in Scotland, see Prestwich, *War, Politics and Finance*, pp. 122, 136, 165.

[65] NA C62/54, fol. 2r.

[66] *CCR*, 1:373.

[67] NA E101/4/6/1. On April 14, 1282 Edward I ordered a royal official in London named Gregory Rokesleye to purchase 4,000 quarrels for use on the king's ships preparing to set sail for Wales. See *CCR*, 1:153.

[68] NA C62/59, fols. 8r and 6r.

[69] *CCR*, 1:308.

Purchases of quarrels on a similar scale marked the Welsh campaigns of 1287 and 1294–95. On November 25, 1287, for example, a writ of *liberate* was issued to the Exchequer authorizing the payment of £120 to Thomas, the sheriff of Canterbury, for the purchase and shipment of just under 150,000 quarrels to the royal garrison at Carmarthen.[70] Similarly, in 1296 John Botetourt, the constable of St. Briavels, was authorized to receive almost £130 for the purchase and production of 146,000 quarrels to be stored at the magazine at Corfe Castle and for the royal garrisons in Wales. This sum also included the costs of producing 312 chests that were used to carry these quarrels and an additional 150,000 bolts that were transported to the royal arms depot at Bristol Castle. Thus, roughly 1,000 crossbow bolts were carried in each chest.[71] Edward's Gascon campaigns also saw large-scale purchases of crossbow bolts. In a turnabout from the state of affairs in 1283, the royal government now shipped quarrels produced in England to the Continent. A *rotulus* drawn up in 1298 recorded the purchase of quarrels from five separate private workshops in England in July and August of that year. The document records the purchase of 88,200 quarrel heads at a cost of just under £50.[72]

If we turn our attention to Edward I's Scottish campaigns (1296–1307), the surviving administrative records suggest that the government relied more heavily on its own workshops than on the purchase of quarrels from private makers. The only year in which we see the acquisition of very large numbers of quarrels on the private market is 1298. In that year Thomas of Suffolk and Adam Fuleham, the sheriffs of London, purchased 104,000 crossbow bolts for use in Scotland, including 72,000 for "one-foot" weapons, 24,000 for "two-foot" weapons, and 8,000 for crossbows equipped with a winch (*turnus*).[73] The royal government made an additional purchase of 100,000 bolts in 1298, but for use in Wales. Nicholas Fermbaud, the constable of Bristol Castle, was issued orders on December 18 of that year to send 100,000 quarrels to the royal fortress at Caernarvon, from where they would be sent to the castles at Conway, Beaumarais, Harlech, and Criccieth under the direction of John de Havering, the justiciar of North Wales.[74]

The documents make clear that the royal government purchased well in excess of one million crossbow bolts for use in Edward I's Welsh and Scottish wars. Yet, this is only a fraction, perhaps even a small fraction, of the total number of quarrels produced for the royal government in the thirty-five years between

[70] NA C62/64, fol. 1r. In 1290 Peter de la Mare sent an additional 19,000 quarrels and forty crossbows to the garrison in Carmarthen. See NA C62/66, fol. 5r.

[71] NA C62/73, fol. 5r.

[72] NA E101/5/15.

[73] NA C62/74, fol. 6r. Regarding the types of crossbows used in the armies of Edward I, see Bachrach, "Crossbows for the King (Part Two)."

[74] NA E101/6/4.

1272 and 1307. The surviving administrative records, although numerous, are only a small percentage of the original volume of documents that dealt with military logistics. As a result, it is almost certain that many records dealing with the purchase of quarrels have been lost. In addition, the numbers of crossbow bolts discussed here does not include the normal production from the royal facilities in workshops at Chester, Berwick, Roxburgh, Dumfries, and perhaps other centers as well. As we have seen, the facility at Berwick alone was capable of producing many thousands of quarrels in a short time. Indeed, the royal government apparently relied largely on its own workshops in Scotland to produce quarrels for the forces stationed there. Thus, the crossbow bolts acquired by the royal government during King Edward's reign should probably be numbered in the many millions.

Conclusion

Although the surviving administrative documents from the reigns of John, Henry III, and Edward I are only a fraction of the original output produced by the royal government, they nevertheless illustrate the clear and continuing commitment of the Crown to produce and acquire staggering quantities of quarrels from the late twelfth through the early fourteenth century. The royal government churned out tens of thousands of quarrels every year in its own workshops. In periods of war the government purchased many hundreds of thousands more to supplement existing stockpiles. If one can measure the significance attached by government officials to particular policies by the resources they devote to them, then we can be reasonably sure that for well over a century the royal government of England attached considerable importance to securing large supplies of crossbow quarrels for its troops.

Bibliography

Amt, Emilie. "Besieging Bedford: Military Logistics in 1224." *Journal of Medieval Military History* 1 (2002): 101–24.

Bachrach, David S. "The Crossbow Makers of England, 1204–72." *Nottingham Medieval Studies* 47 (2003): 168–97.

———. "Crossbows for the King: Some Observations on the Development of the Crossbow during the Reigns of King John and Henry III of England, 1204–72." *Technology and Culture* 45 (2004): 102–19.

———. "Crossbows for the King (Part Two): The Crossbow during the Reign of Edward I of England (1272–1307)." *Technology and Culture* 47 (2006): 81–90.

———. "The Origins of the English Crossbow Industry." *Journal of Medieval Military History* 2 (2003): 73–87.

———. "The Royal Arms Makers of England 1199–1216: A Prosopographical Survey." *Medieval Prosopography* 25 (2008): 49–75.

Calendar of Close Rolls Preserved in the Public Record Office, 1272–1307. 5 vols. London: Royal Stationary Office, 1900–1908.

Calendar of Liberate Rolls Preserved in the Public Record Office 1226–1272. 6 vols. London: Royal Stationary Office, 1916.

Close Rolls Preserved in the Public Record Office, 1227–1272. 13 vols. London: Royal Stationary Office, 1902–38.

The Chancery Roll for the Eighth Year of the Reign of King Richard the First Michaelmas 1196. Ed. Doris M. Stenton. Pipe Roll 42. London: Pipe Roll Society, 1930.

The Great Roll of the Pipe for the First Year of the Reign of King John Michaelmas 1199. Ed. Doris M. Stenton. London: Pipe Roll Society, 1933.

The Great Roll of the Pipe for the Fourteenth Year of the Reign of King John Michaelmas 1212. Ed. Patricia M. Barnes. Pipe Roll 58. London: Pipe Roll Society, 1955.

The Great Roll of the Pipe for the Ninth Year of the Reign of King John Michaelmas 1207. Ed. A. Mary Kirkus. Pipe Roll 53. London: Pipe Roll Society, 1946.

The Great Roll of the Pipe for the Second Year of the Reign of King John Michaelmas 1200. Ed. Doris M. Stenton. Pipe Roll 46. London: Pipe Roll Society, 1934.

The Great Roll of the Pipe for the Sixth Year of the Reign of King Henry III Michaelmas 1222. London: Pipe Roll Society, 1999.

The Great Roll of the Pipe for the Sixth Year of the Reign of King Richard the First Michaelmas 1194. Ed. Doris M. Stenton. Pipe Roll 40. London: Pipe Roll Society, 1928.

The Great Roll of the Pipe for the Sixteenth Year of the Reign of King John Michaelmas 1214. Ed. Patricia M. Barnes. Pipe Roll 60. London: Pipe Roll Society, 1962.

The Great Roll of the Pipe for the Third and Fourth Years of the Reign of King Richard the First Michaelmas 1191 and Michaelmas 1192. Ed. Doris M. Stenton. Pipe Roll 37–38. London: Pipe Roll Society, 1926.

The Great Roll of the Pipe for the Thirteenth Year of the Reign of King John Michaelmas 1211. Ed. Doris M. Stenton. Pipe Roll 57. London: Pipe Roll Society, 1953.

Hart, Cyril E. *Royal Forest: A History of Dean's Woods as Producers of Timber*. Oxford: Clarendon Press, 1966.

Lyon, Bryce D. *A Constitutional and Legal History of Medieval England*. 2nd ed. New York: W. W. Norton, 1980.

Lyon, Bryce, and Mary Lyon, eds. *The Wardrobe Book of 1296–1297: A Financial and Logistical Record of Edward I's 1297 Autumn Campaign in Flanders against Philip IV of France*. Brussels: Commission Royale d'histoire, 2004.

Lyon, Mary, Bryce Lyon, and Henry S. Lucas, with the collaboration of Jean de Sturler, eds. *The Wardrobe Book of William de Norwell, 12 July 1338 to 27 May 1340*. Brussels: Commission Royale d'histoire, 1983.

Prestwich, Michael. *Edward I*. 2nd ed. New Haven, CT: Yale University Press, 1997.

———. *War, Politics and Finance under Edward I*. Totowa, NJ: Rowman and Littlefield, 1972.

Rotuli de liberate ac de misis et praestitis, regnante Johanne. Ed. Thomas D. Hardy. London: G. Eyre and A. Spottiswoode, 1844.

Rotuli litterarum clausarum in turri Londonensi asservati, 1204–1227. Ed. Thomas D. Hardy. 2 vols. London: G. Eyre and A. Spottiswoode, 1833–34.

Rotuli litterarum patentium in turri Londinensi asservati. Ed. Thomas D. Hardy. London: G. Eyre and A. Spottiswoode, 1835.

Rotuli Normannie in turri Londinensi asservati, Johanne et Henrico quinto Angliae regibus. Ed. Thomas D. Hardy. London: G. Eyre and A. Spottiswoode, 1835.

Webb, Alf. "John Malemort—King's Quarreler: The King's 'Great Arsenal,' St. Briavels and the Royal Forest of Dean." *Society of Archer Antiquaries* 31 (1988): 40–46 and 32 (1989): 52–58.

Part 3

The Low Countries and Economic History

The Notions of Honor and Adultery in the Fifteenth-Century Burgundian Netherlands

Walter Prevenier

T HE ANTHROPOLOGIST Julian Pitt-Rivers described "honor" in 1965 as a universal concept, common to diverse individuals, societies, and civiliza-tions.[1] Honor may well be a universal concept: it is fundamentally colored by typical cultures, periods, social, and gender groups. David Gilmore discovered that fascinating similarities in the concept of honor could be found in various societies that border on the Mediterranean.[2] For him it is clear that in that world honor is a male attribute: the reputation of men before their peers depends largely upon the sexual behavior of the women in their family.[3] But this anthropological the-sis has, at least for early modern Spain, been disputed by the historian Scott K. Taylor, who claims that men's honor did not depend exclusively upon the sexual reputation of female kin but also revolved around competence in craft or office, credit-worthiness and debt relationships, and performance in the rough-and-tumble rites of male sociability.[4] Yet the geographical specificity still seems to be a valuable argument. That consideration was the core of Pierre Bourdieu's study of the notion of honor (the *nif*) in the North-African Kabyle society.[5] A more recent case is the fascinating thesis of a different culture of honor in the North and the South of the United States by Richard Nisbett and Dov Cohen, who were convinced that the genesis of the typical Southern honor culture should

---

[1] Pitt-Rivers, "Honour and Social Status," p. 21.

[2] Gilmore, *Honor and Shame*, p.16.

[3] Gilmore, *Honor and Shame*, pp. 3–4.

[4] Taylor, *Honor and Violence*.

[5] Bourdieu, "From the 'Rules' of Honour," pp. 10–15. One of the specific themes is the obligation of family members to defend the honor of each member against all outsiders.

be linked to the presence there of a herding economy.[6] In conclusion, the key notions seem to be culture, geography, economy, and sociability.

Both the urban and the courtly culture in the Burgundian Netherlands cultivated strong networks with cities and courts abroad that may have been responsible for a typical cosmopolitan society, permissive on ethical issues such as adultery, prostitution, and other forms of illicit sex. This tolerance may have been the background for a specific notion of honor.[7] Cosmopolitanism was certainly setting the tone in places with many foreign merchants, artists, and members of the fifteenth-century ducal court, patricians of Brussels and Mechelen,[8] as well as in economic centers such as Bruges, with a large presence of international businessmen and clergymen, mostly male singles, and so the obvious market for local prostitutes.[9]

Dishonor for the Duped Husband

A first fact about adultery in the Burgundian Netherlands is the perception of this action as a source of profound humiliation and extreme dishonor for the duped husband. Contemporaries considered the male victim to be obsessed by the shame of being incapable of exacting aggressive revenge on his spouse's lover. If vengeance took the form of homicide, for which the perpetrator could be sentenced to death, or to perpetual banishment, the uncontrollable outburst of anger, the so called *chaude colle*, was often used as a successful argument to introduce a pardon application at the administration of the duke of Burgundy for "honor killing," in line with the tradition at the French royal court.[10] *Chaude colle* may often have been more a ritualized and codified cliché than a tool of clever defense lawyers. A workable cliché, however, easily becomes a social reality. Princes, public opinion, and court judges of the fifteenth century in the Low Countries, as in France, exhibited an unmistakable understanding and clear empathy for the violent behavior of the duped individual.[11] Sympathy for the perpetrator was conditioned, however, by at least four variables for the weightiness of dishonor and the potential granting of pardon. I illustrate the thesis by quoting from four letters of remission.

The first consideration that could ease significantly the request of the duped husband for pardon was the fact that the adultery could be qualified as a public scandal. One such case is that of Jacot Barcueille in July 1455:

---

[6] Nisbett and Cohen, *Culture of Honor*, pp. 5–9, 82–93.

[7] Vertovec and Cohen, *Conceiving Cosmopolitanism*, pp. 1–14, 211–17.

[8] On Mechelen as a "cosmopolitan" place in the fifteenth century, see Prevenier, "Mechelen circa 1500."

[9] On the density of prostitution in Bruges in the fifteenth century (1 girl per 312 inhabitants, or 1 per 78 adult males), see Dupont, *Maagdenverleidsters*, pp. 84–87.

[10] Davis, *Fiction in the Archives*, pp. 36–76, esp. p. 37; Gauvard, *"De grâce espécial,"* pp. 448–56, 705–52.

[11] A similar clemency for aggression by dishonored husbands was present in the region of Toulouse: Otis-Cour, *"De jure novo,"* pp. 357–59.

[It is said that] the supplicant forbade the forenamed Estevenin from frequenting his house ... and also from approaching his wife; ... coming back home at night, he found the forenamed Estevenin ... in his house, with his wife ... and found out that they slept with each other ... so that the forenamed supplicant was seized by rage and assaulted the forenamed Estevenin, and injured him with a knife, so thoroughly that Estevenin died. Estevenin was a man of bad conduct, who boasted about [his success with] women ... he bragged many times that he had had sexual intercourse with the wife of the supplicant [Jacot]."[12]

Dishonesty was much stronger if a close friend of the husband committed the adultery, because then a second infraction, treason, came on the table. A letter of pardon of 1438 tells us that Ywain Voet and his friend Jean were like "brothers" to each other, often eating and drinking together. But Jean took profit of the unconcern and the naiveté of his friend by having sexual intercourse with his spouse over four years. In the end, Jean abducted the woman, taking most of Ywain's moveable property with them. In great anger Ywain killed his friend, fled Flanders, asked and got pardon.[13] The remission letter contrasted the honesty of Ywain and his candor toward his friend with the dishonesty of Jean.[14]

A third reason for clemency in the pardon procedure was the additional shame caused by the birth of an illegitimate child. In 1438 Jehanette, wife of Pierre Monié of Cuiseaux, had a huge number of adulterous affairs, "day and night, in various suspicious situations, with people of doubtful reputation." By one of them, the knight Estienne Raton, she conceived a female bastard. Jehanette continued

[12] AdN, B 1686, fols. 39v–40r: "ledit suppliant, le lundi es festes de Pentecouste dairenierement passé, estoit retourné de dehors ladite ville de Mortan de nuyt en son hostel, bien tard, il trouva ledit Estevenin, qui estoit en sondit hostel avec sadite femme. Et oy qu'ilz se acorderent ensemble de couchier l'ung avec l'autre, telement que ledit suppliant, estant moult desplaisant, de chaude colle couru sus audit Estevenin, et le navra telement d'ung costel en son visage que icellui Estevenin dechus la mesme nuyt et termina vie par mort.... Estevenin estoit vanteur de femmes, et homme de dissolue et mauvaise vie et gouvernement, et qu'il s'estoit par plusieurs fois vanté en divers lieux qu'il avoit eu habilitacion charnelle avec la femme d'icellui suppliant."

[13] AdN B 1682, fols. 34r–v (edited in Petit-Dutaillis, *Documents nouveaux*, pp. 14–15): "Yeulvain Voet, chevaucheur de notre escuierie, aiant amour, congnoissance et grant affinité a ung appelé maistre Jehan, lors messaigier dudit Neufport, et auquel ledit suppliant se confioit moult, et estoient souvent buvans et mengans ensemble, et avec lui avoit compaignie fraternelle comme a son frere.... Pendant laquelle societe et communicacion ledit maistre Jehan, meu de mauvaise et dampnable voulente, et duquel ledit suppliant ne se doubtoit en riens, ... se acointa de la femme dudit suppliant, telement qu'il en fist sa voulente. Et non content de ce, mais en acroissant le blasme et honte dudit suppliant, environ a IIII ans, esleva et emmena sadicte femme, et avec elle emporta pluseurs de ses biens meubles."

[14] AdN B 1682, fols. 34r–v: "esmeu de couraige, lui souvenant et remembrant de la bonne amour et fraternelle compaigyne ... la grant desloiaulté, honte, blasme, dommaige et deshonneur que maistre Jehan, en rendant mal pour bien, faicte lui avait."

her "reprehensible and damaging life," and "the adulteries got worse the longer they went on, in Lyon, from city to city, as far as Avignon. . . . Some of Pierre Monié's friends were so displeased by the great dishonor he suffered from the bad conduct of his spouse that they spied on her and killed her." When after some time both Jehanette and these friends had died, some enemies of Monié filed a complaint against him with the bailiff of Châlons for murder. Expecting a death sentence, Monié requested and obtained pardon from Duke Philip the Good on grounds of the dishonor, shame, and blame that the late Jehanette had caused.[15]

A fourth consideration explaining the toleration of murder or homicide when committed out of passion is the additional use of verbal violence at the expense of the duped husband and the presence of gossip by neighbors in the village or the urban parish. These actions of the local community turned the adultery case into a more global social drama. Pierre de Scelewe, a poor innkeeper of Langemark, became aware in 1458 of the frequent sexual intercourse of his neighbor Christian Le Cloot with Pierre's wife. The public scandal was enhanced since Le Cloot had publicly and painfully insulted Scelewe in his own inn, by calling him impotent. The weight of "public rumor," "several reports by various persons," and his own "true presumptions" became unbearable for Scelewe, and he killed the lover. The double humiliation, and consequently the damage to reputation, was mentioned in the letter of grace: first, the doubt about his virility, and secondly, the fact that Le Cloot had laughed loudly when his friends warned him of violence from Scelewe if he did not stop his adulterous behavior. At the end of the remission letter one sentence refers to the dialectical interaction between rumors and perception: "Because of the rumors the supplicant absorbed in his imagination that the adultery of his wife was real."[16]

[15] AdN B 1682, fols. 11v–12v: "Jehanette, fille de feu Jehan Boudot, seduitte et temptee de l'ennemi, depuis ledit mariaige consommé, commensa a converser jour et nuit en divers et suspectz lieux, avec gens de mauvaise vie et conversacion, en adulterant avec eulx, et telement qu'elle eut une fille bastarde de messire Estienne Raton, chevalier. . . . ladite Jehanette, en continuant sa mauvaise et dampnable vye et adultier de mal en pis, s'en ala a Lion, et de la de bonne ville en bonne ville, jusques en Avignon, ou elle persevera tousjours . . . aucuns amis et bien vueillant dudit suppliant, qui estoient desplaisans du grant deshonneur qu'il souffroit pour le petit gouvernement de ladite femme, l'espierent, et en ladite bergerie tuerent icelle femme . . . ledit suppliant a des haynneux qui se sont vantez de lui porter mal et de deposer a sa charge . . . eu regart au grant deshonneur, honte, vitupere et blasme que ladite feue Jehanette par sa mauvaise et detestable vye lui faisoit, . . . remettons et pardonnons."

[16] AdN B 1688, fol. 3v (edited in Petit-Dutaillis, *Documents nouveaux*, pp. 23–25): "poursuivoit sa femme pour avoir compaignie charnelle avec elle, et que la renommee et fame commune estoit en ladicte parroisse que congneue l'avoit charnellement et que, aux semblans et manieres que ledit Christian tenoit vers sa femme, il prinst en son ymagination et courage que vray estoit. . . . avoient pluseurs foiz blasmé et dit que mal faisoit de suivir la femme, et que mal lui en vendroit, mais toujours [Christian le Cloot] s'en mocquoit, disant que il congnoissoit bien ledit suppliant, et que riens ne lui mefferoit."

Although in most pardon letters the seducing lover got all the blame for the seduction, rather than the spouse,[17] the last sentence of the last remission letter shows that the female side of adultery was also a source of dishonor. In 1413 the bailiff of Beveren delivered Eleinne, wife of Jacques Martin, the formal document written by the aldermen of the village of Kieldrecht, in Flanders, by which she was banished from Kieldrecht for one year, because she had an adulterous relationship with Clais Lammyn. The aldermen considered her action as scandalous and dishonoring, defining it as a "repudiation" of the husband, and as "behaving unworthily to stay in her domicile." At the same time the bailiff restored the husband to honor, at the request of "several good people," who were convinced that the spouse would come back to him.[18]

The Honor of the Family

As soon as we turn to the connection between various forms of illicit sex and family honor, we enter a different world. Adultery can be a dishonor for the husband, but also for the rest of the family. This is more specifically the case if the adultery happened at the initiative of the spouse and resulted in an adulterous child. Then the shame and disgrace were not limited to the wife and the husband, but also concerned the other, legitimate children and the extended family. A fictional text, the *Ménagier de Paris*, written around 1393, gives the exemplum of a woman confessing in her dying hour to her husband that one of her three children is not his. But before she can specify which one, the husband interrupts and asks her not to reveal the child's identity, because he wants to continue to love all his children with equal intensity. The story reveals the love of a father for a child who is not his biological offspring. But the text also insisted that one other argument was on the table here: the care of the father to protect the dying mother and the rest of the family against vile and continuous rumors in the neighborhood about the misconduct of the mother.[19] That is why the *Ménagier* suggested a strategic discretion on adultery both by the cuckolded husband and the adulterous spouse.[20] The

---

[17] Otis-Cour, "'De jure novo,'" pp. 359 and 371: in twenty-seven of thirty cases of crimes of passion the lover is the victim.

[18] AgR, Chambre des Comptes, 6886 (account of the bailiff of Beveren): "de Eleinne, femme Jacque Martins, laquelle estoit banni par la loy de Kieldrecht ung an, en aiant title de non estre digne en la ville pour ce qu'elle demoura en le maisme ville avuec ung nommé Clais Lammyn, en deboutant son mari. Lui rendu la ville, a la priere de pluseurs bones gens, veu qu'elle s'en garderoit doresenavant."

[19] Pichon, *Le ménagier*, pp. 177–85: "Jamais plus ne le dictes, ne nommez à moy ne à autre lequel c'est de vos enfans, car je les vueil aimer autant l'un que l'autre si également que en vostre vie ne après vostre mort vous ne soiez blasmée, car en vostre blasme aroie-je honte, et vos enfans mesmes et autres par eulx, c'est assavoir nos parens, en recevroient vilain et perpétuel reproche. Si vous en taisiez."

[20] Otis-Cour, "'De jure novo,'" p. 354n29.

Ménagier's anecdote may be fiction, but it probably reflects contemporary perceptions of honor faithfully.

Indeed, "reality is often stranger than fiction." In Ghent in 1450 Pieter
de Wilde had been in a legal marriage for years with Lysbette Scheerms and
took care, as any father would, of the "material support" of their two children,
providing clothing, shoes, and school tuition. Suddenly Lysbette contacted the
local priest, confessed, and swore that both her children were the result of her
adulterous adventures with two different biological fathers, a Franciscan friar and
Berthelmeeus Valke, burgher of Ghent. Pieter de Wilde did not know anything
about this adultery, and said that "he supported the children as if he were the
father." Since there was no doubt about the adultery between Berthelmeeus and
Lysbette, and Lysbette swore that her lover was the father, the aldermen of Ghent
decided that Berthelmeeus should pay Pieter a fine of three pounds groat in addition to the costs of clothes, shoes, and school tuition.[21] The customs and laws of
the city allowed the child, as soon as it reached the adult age of eighteen (or, in
some cases, twenty-one), to choose the biological or the social father as his legal
father. It is clear that illegitimate children could belong to the family of the biological father, although not living with him and his household, in Flanders[22] as
well as in Italy.[23] In 1422 the aldermen of Bruges entrusted Pieter Menin, the
biological father of the bastard children he fathered on a single mother, with their
support, "as a good father ought to do," although the children lived with their
mother.[24] It is clear that the Ghent and the Bruges aldermen considered the protection of bastards, widows, and orphans as a core responsibility.[25] In the fifteenth
century they also exerted considerable effort to force runaway husbands to provide
support to their spouses in difficult conditions such as divorce or separation "in
bed and board."[26]

In the early middle ages the honor of the family was a more "dramatic"
issue: "honor killings" by kin of the adulterous spouse who had brought dishonor
on the family did happen in those days. But from the Carolingian period on,
the church strongly opposed using female adultery as an argument justifying her
offended husband in repudiating her and remarrying. This rejection by the church
was explicitly confirmed in many juridical texts of twelfth-century canon law on

---

[21] Stadsarchief Gent, series 301, section 41, vol. 1, fols. 8r–v: text of trial before the aldermen of
Ghent, September 10, 1450.

[22] Carlier, *Kinderen van de minne?*, pp. 221–62.

[23] Kuehn, "Honor and Conflict."

[24] Stadsarchief Brugge, section 208, O.L.V. Zestendeel, reg. 3, fol. 215 (March 13, 1422): "in also
varren als hij zijner voorseide kinderen doet ende houdt ghelijc een goed vadere sculdich es van doene."

[25] Danneel, *Weduwen en wezen*, pp. 23–130, 423–24.

[26] Vander Linden, "Vorzienicheit van goede."

the indissolubility of marriage. The ecclesiastical discourse on adultery and other sexual transgressions contrasted with the views of the secular public authorities, which continued to favor the "patriarchal" discourse and the option of repudiation of the adulterous spouse, with the interests of the well-to-do families and their patrimonies in their minds.[27]

This very specific background explains why the use of the argument of family (dis-) honor was in many circumstances fundamentally window dressing for material, rather than ethical, motives. The fifteenth-century public discourses on family honor do not express a moral statement. The ordinance of Duke Philip of Burgundy in 1438 against rape, abduction, and seduction of women in Flanders has not a single word on the honor or on the moral and physical identity of the raped young women, but a long discourse on the risks for upper-class family patrimonies of abductions and unwanted marriages.[28] In some specific dramatic conditions, however, altruistic arguments emerged, with a genuine concern for the family honor. In 1480 Jacob de Pottere was found guilty, essentially on the basis of rumors, of raping several girls. He was put to the rack, tortured, and after "confessing" was sentenced to death. That happened after many attempts by members of his family to prevent worse. Jacob's parents paid for twenty-six days of prison time in order to give the bailiff a chance to delay the judgment, hoping to obtain pardon in the meantime. The action was not effective, probably because this family was not influential enough, did not pay enough, or did not use the right technique.[29] Pottere was hanged, and this was followed by a second, ecclesiastical sanction: the impossibility "of burying the corpse of Jacobus de Pottere in sacred ground publicly, after he had been condemned to death by lay judges for his indecent conduct." Thus his family had to pay a second time, twelve pounds now, to the ecclesiastical court to get its permission to bury him in consecrated ground.[30] The two actions can be explained by family solidarity and parental love, but also by the risk of a long-standing double shame: for the alleged rape and for a humiliating burial.[31]

---

[27] Otis-Cour, "'De jure novo,'" pp. 349–52.

[28] AdN B 1682, fols. 7r–v (edited in Gheldolf, *Coutumes*, 1:623–25): "remédier à ce que les facteurs et coulpables de telz énormes cas et crimes soient pugniz capitalment, ou mis hors loy . . . les violences de pucelles et autres femmes . . . par convoitise d'avoir leurs chevances, dont maulx et inconvéniens irréparables se sont ensuivis."

[29] AgR Chambre des Comptes, 14461, fol. 41v (account of the bailiff of Waas, May–July 1480): "pour ce que ledit bailli fist ung peu de delay a lui fere justice en esperant de obtenir grace, ce que faire ne se povoit."

[30] Vleeschouwers–Van Melkebeek, *Compotus sigilliferi*, 2:1128, no. 15610: "pro gratia sepeliendi in terra sancta cadaver Jacobi de Pottere publice per laicales justiciarios propter sua demerita morte puniti, solutum: 12 lb."

[31] Vleeschouwers–Van Melkebeek, "Het parochiale leven," p. 50.

Honor in Professional Life

If we turn from families to the public sphere of professional life, we find more critical discourses on the dishonoring effects of adultery and illicit sex. In the few surviving fifteenth-century judgments promulgated by the guild deans of Ghent, honor was a crucial element when the behavior of one of the guild's members was being judged.[32] Various connotations of the notion of honor were used in guild regulations. First and foremost was the concept of honor stemming from professional pride, including control of quantity and quality of production. Secondly, honor involved showing respect for the authority of the guild deans: a text of 1426 prohibited the use of "ungracious words" about the guild's ordinances, which were considered "an assault against (the honor of) the whole community of the deans."[33] Thirdly, honor in strictly personal affairs was demanded. Sexual behavior and the family life of guild members were closely scrutinized. In 1402 the dean of the Ghent fruit sellers forbade a young woman, who was the concubine and also the professional employee of a fruit seller, to bring fruit onto the marketplace. In 1448 the dean of the wine weighers in Ghent hesitated to allow the matriculation in the craft of a master's son, because rumors held that he was the fruit of an adulterous adventure of his mother; the dean only agreed to a temporary membership, pending the verdict about his legitimate birth of the episcopal court of Tournai. In 1450 the dean of the grocers opposed the reception in the guild of Beatrice de Wilde, even though she was the daughter of a grocer, because she cohabited with a certain Christophe Vanden Hove, against the will of her extended family. Beatrice appealed to the general board of the small businesses. They displayed more tolerance and accepted the young woman, on condition, however, that she correct her situation by a formal marriage. In 1457 Jacob de Paermentier was pardoned by the duke of Burgundy after he had been banished by the aldermen of Bruges for publicly insulting the deans of the crafts of the city, as they were gathered on the Burg square in order to render a public report of their policy.[34]

In fact, this professional pride was a crucial component of the collective identity of a city, the body politic to which a majority of the people referred when defining their position in society. All citizens enjoyed the so-called freedoms, but that implied collective responsibility, a strong sense of rights and duties, and hence a strong drive to model the behavior of city-dwellers, obliging them to reflect in their private life the honor of the collectivity. This was expressed through a common responsibility for the well-being of the community: paying taxes, serving in

---

[32] Boone, "Les gens de métier."

[33] Stadsarchief Gent, series 156, section 1, fol. 79r: "quade woorden . . . dat zouden de dekene ghemeenlic nemen als up haren persoen ghedaen."

[34] AdN B 1687, fol. 19r.

the city's militia, and exemplifying an honorable way of life. The latter implied close control by public authorities and intervention even in the private matters of citizens.

Collective Systems of Public Social Control

Apart from control by the guild structures, other collective systems of public social control of honorable conduct were operative. The most important was that by the parish priest and the local synod of honorable burghers that worked as a watchdog and a moral commission. All kinds of "immoral" behavior, from concubinage to adultery, from clandestine marriages to insulting a cleric, were denounced to the local priest by convinced moralists and shocked citizens, but also by jealous or rancorous neighbors.[35] The accusations were subsequently brought to the ecclesiastical court in Tournai or Cambrai.[36] Until the fourteenth century the episcopal courts assessed in most cases spiritual penances, such as excommunication, but thereafter the sanctions became fiscal. These fines were adjusted to the social status of the sinners.

Apart from this ecclesiastical defamation system, the aldermen of Ghent in 1423 established a public office where burghers could present their complaints, called *vérités générales*, comparable to the Onestà that had functioned in Florence since 1378.[37] We should not forget that local priests also acted *motu proprio* to safeguard the principles of canon law and protect the sacraments, especially marriage, which was a fundamental cornerstone of the church and of civil society. This ecclesiastical system had also a civil effect: it helped to prevent the marriage of a respected citizen with a morally or socially unreliable individual, with a criminal or a jobless person, and finally it prevented breaches in social order and political stability.

The Extreme Dishonor of Sodomy

One type of illicit sex was the subject of extreme disapproval and dishonor: sodomy. There was no more effective way for an individual to lose honor and life and dishonor his family than to be involved in the "sin and enormity of sodomy." There was no more radical means of destroying a person's reputation and honor than the accusation of sodomy. Cynical and perfidious games with

---

[35] A lot of rumors were probably false, such as the case of a man accused of sodomy in the castellany of Ghent in 1469–70: AgR, Chambre des Comptes, 14159, fol. 2v: "certains tesmoings qui savoyent a parler du dit Jehan et de son dit fait; il fu mis a torture et examinacion, neantmoins riens ne confessa."

[36] Lambrecht, *De parochiale synode*, pp. 11–17.

[37] Chojnacki, *Women and Men*, pp. 29–32.

this argument were used for interpersonal family conflicts. In 1473 Jehanne Sey, who "entertained an immense hatred" for her husband, tried to bring about his condemnation to death by accusing him falsely of sodomy; instead, the aldermen of Bruges sentenced her to humiliating exposure on the wheel for two days for bringing a false accusation.[38]

Also in 1473 Katerine van der Leene in Bruges accused her husband, the merchant Jean van de Leene, of sodomy, for which the penalty was burning at the stake.[39] Jean was imprisoned, but the aldermen of Bruges must have had doubts regarding the fairness of the accusation. They subjected the spouse to a rigid interrogation, in which the woman weakened the charges and admitted that her claim was caused by hate, that she had spoken these words "in the heat of anger because of the harmful words that her aforesaid husband was hurling daily at her, as common report holds." The husband had, indeed, proclaimed in the past that his wife should be burned at the stake. We should note the perspicacity of the Bruges bailiff as he exposed the cruel games of both partners, aiming to kill each other's social honor: "through malice and great hatred and envy . . . and to destroy the spouse totally."[40]

That statement included two connotations of "killing," physical and moral. It is certainly true that accusations before the courts, based on the concept of honor, were often more tactical discourse or fraud than reality. Scott K. Taylor found similar attitudes in Spain's Golden Age: he concluded that appealing to honor was a rhetorical strategy and that insults, gestures, and violence were all part of a varied repertoire that allowed both men and women to decide how to dispute issues of truth and reputation. It was not a rigid noble code that led inexorably to violence, but instead a flexible rhetorical instrument employed by everyday men and women.[41]

---

[38] AgR, Chambre des Comptes, 13780, fol. 20r: "accusa son dit mary du pechié de sodomie pour ce qu'elle l'avoit en grant hayne, cuidant par ce faire prendre par justice deshonnestement la vie de son dit mary."

[39] Boone, "State Power"; in Italy sodomy was likewise called the "abominable vice": Chojnacki, *Women and Men*, p. 33.

[40] AgR, Chambre des Comptes, 13780, fol. 40r: "elle soupçonnait son mari du peché et enhorme cas de sodomie . . . proclame qu'il était digne . . . d'estre brulez a une estaque. . . . Et apres qu'elle estoit tout au long oye pardevant la justice, a l'encontre de son dit mary, sur les dites parolles et charges elle se refebly desdites charges, confessant que tout ce de quoy elle avoit chergé son dit mary, elle avoit dit par grand courouch, non pensant ne sachant le grant mal qui estoit es dis parolles, et a l'occasion qu'elle ne pooit vivre en paix avec lui, et que lui meismes avoit paravant dit qu'elle estoit digne d'estre brulee a une estaque . . . qu'elle avoit dit les dites parolles a chaut sang, a l'occasion des injurieuses parolles que ledit son mary usoit journelement sur elle, comme la commune renommee estoit . . . par malice et grande haynne et envye qu'elle avoit et portoit sur le dit son mary, et pour destruire totalement son dit mari."

[41] Taylor, *Honor and Violence*.

Perception and Repression of Adultery
by Civil and Ecclesiastical Authorities

A second, very different, perception of medieval adultery was also widespread in medieval works of fiction. From Chaucer to Boccaccio, from the fourteenth-century Flemish farces in theater to the frivolous fifteenth-century stories of Duke Philip the Good's *Cent nouvelles nouvelles*, duped husbands are systematically represented as naive and pitiable dunces who are duped by their adulterous spouses and their intelligent and clever lovers. The general irony of fiction had a perfect counterpart in real life of the fifteenth-century Netherlands.

The medieval church condemned adultery as a form of illicit sex, because it betrayed the marriage vows and entailed the risk of illegitimate children.[42] Urban authorities such as those of Aardenburg in the fourteenth century, Ghent at the end of the fifteenth century, and Ypres in the sixteenth century were considering adultery as a source of social disorder that should be punished by imprisonment or banishment.[43] The mainstream lifestyle of all social classes in the fifteenth-century Low Countries, however, shows that adulterous sex was considered as a rather trivial behavior, more a source of ironic remarks than of scandal.[44] So many ordinary citizens, villagers, and even parish priests committed concubinage, adultery, fornication, and other illicit sex that it did not cause significant dishonor. At worst, if they were denounced to the competent ecclesiastical courts, they were forced to pay a small fine, adjusted to the social status of the sinner, to the episcopal "official" for this "minor" offense, so small that it did not prevent them from repeating the action as soon as possible.

The fine for a *defloratio*, with or without pregnancy, varied between twelve and twenty-five days' wages of an unskilled worker. Restricted but suggestive research on the prosecution of sexual offenses in ten villages of the Deinze area of Flanders between 1446 and 1481 reveals an average of 5.2 cases a year. Even more revealing is the demographic comparison: the percentage of inhabitants accused and convicted of sexual offenses varied from village to village in this area, between 1.6 to 7.1 percent annually, so that in some villages up to 40 percent of the population had a chance to come in touch with the episcopal court at least once in a lifetime.[45] The

---

[42] Brundage, "Sex and Canon Law," p. 42.

[43] Aardenburg penalized adultery with a fine of ten pounds and one year of banishment (Vorsterman van Oyen, *Rechtsbronnen der stad Aardenburg*, art. 121, p. 110). Ghent decreed in 1491 that adultery was punishable by two weeks' imprisonment on water and bread (Gheldolf, *Coutumes*, 1:672, no. 1). Ypres in 1535 penalized with banishment any man who did not repudiate his adulterous wife (Gilliodts–van Severen, *Coutume*, no. 1, p. 489).

[44] Nicholas, *Domestic Life*, p. 168, mentions the general acceptance of concubinage in fourteenth-century Flanders.

[45] Prevenier, Huys, and Dupont, "Misdaad en straf.," pp. 238–40.

variety of levels can be ascribed to different levels of efficiency or willingness of the local priest to bring the cases to court. In the accounts of the official of the bishop of Tournai for the year 1474–75 no fewer than 227 moral transgressions in the towns and villages of this bishopric were entered, all providing no more than small financial sanctions. And that is only the tip of the iceberg. Most "sinners" probably escaped punishment entirely.

A second explanation for the high level of tolerance and candor toward adultery and all other illicit sex, at least in the absence of violence, might be the presence of an impressively frivolous role model in the upper classes of Burgundian society. The members of the court and the urban elites attached no stigma to extra-marital sex. The frivolous sexual behavior of the ducal family, high-level noblemen, bishops, and patricians is a symptom of an open-minded attitude on ethical issues, such as adultery and bastardy, in the fifteenth-century Low Countries, which have been rightly called "a bastard-prone subsociety."[46] In Bruges 9 percent of all registered successions of minor children concerned bastards. The elites attached no moral condemnation to entertaining mistresses or producing bastard children. It was part of a snobbish way of life that rather conferred high status instead of dishonorable reputation. Duke Philip the Good was proud of his twenty-six bastards and thirty-three mistresses. So was John of Burgundy, bishop of Cambrai, illegitimate son of John the Fearless and Agnes de Croy, imitating his natural brother by boasting twenty-two illegitimate children of his own. Jean de Heinsberg, bishop of Liège, was even more productive, with sixty-five bastards, but he barely outdid Duke John II of Clèves, who had sixty-three.[47] Their social status was never in danger. Their social game involved total immunity and invulnerability. Producing illegitimate offspring was a statement of the nearly total social control of the powerful. They were not afraid at all of the few critical voices. One lonely Breton Carmelite was courageous enough in 1428 to criticize the adulterous and frivolous behavior of the dukes and the Flemish clerics.[48] Apart from him, only foreign visitors, such as the Czech Leo von Rozmital in 1465–67[49] and the Spaniard Pero Tafur in 1438,[50] were scandalized by the respect shown toward ducal bastards at the court of Burgundy.

A third reason for the lack of an effective repression by the church, aside from the financial sanctions that had replaced the spiritual penalties, is that many of the clergy, who were responsible for enforcing the transgressions of the moral boundaries, lacked the slightest moral authority because of their own

[46] Carlier, *Kinderen*, pp. 91–133, esp. pp. 129–33.
[47] Bergé, "Les bâtards"; Carlier, *Kinderen*, pp. 251–54.
[48] Prevenier and Blockmans, *Burgundian Netherlands*, p. 149.
[49] Letts, *Travels*, pp. 4, 39–40.
[50] Letts, *Bruges*, p. 202.

irresponsible behavior. Year after year numerous parish priests appear in the accounts of the bishops for the same sexual actions as their parishioners, from concubinage to visits to brothels.[51] In 61 of the 157 villages (38.8 percent) of the bishopric of Tournai (1474–75) in which the episcopal notary mentioned moral transgressions, the local parish priest was involved.[52] In theory, clergymen had no access to sexual activities. The celibacy rule, decreed by Pope Nicholas II in 1059 and firmly established by the First Lateran Council in 1123, was considered an impracticable behavior by many clergymen.

One can understand why parish priests had no desire to denounce adultery cases in their parish to their bishop if they themselves were involved in concubinage.[53] The bishop too did not want to impose a harsher sanction than a fine. He preferred a symbolic warning, keeping the priest in charge of his parish. In 1480, the parish priest of Tielt, Vincent Andries, was accused of no less than four misdeeds. First, he had encouraged several women to oppose a marriage in his parish, so that he could then share a part of the fines with them. Second, he had blessed a marriage without calling the banns for the third time. Third, he had questionable contacts with a married woman and had stolen a substantial part of her husband's property. Fourth, he had sexual congress with a nun in the local hospital. All of these scandalous activities were conducted publicly, which left the ecclesiastical court no choice other than to intervene.[54]

But as long as the dissolute behavior of the clergymen remained discreet, they could expect considerable tolerance from the bishop. In many cases a sinning priest also got a compassionate reaction and sympathy from his parishioners. In 1444, the parish priest of the village of Blankenberge, Symoen de Grispeere, had been accused of misconduct at the ecclesiastical court, but Joos van Halewijn, the local lord of Uutkerke, mediated successfully with the episcopal judge by using the argument that the priest was an honorable man, "of good repute and well loved by his parishioners." Yet the nobleman ended his plea by saying, "I trust that the deed is neither as serious nor horrible as what you have been told." This language suggests some disquieting underlying reality, for the lord succeeded in convincing the local dignitaries to withdraw their complaint.[55] Another aspect of this

---

[51] In 1461–62 a priest gave hospitality in his house to several prostitutes, which certainly caused a scandal (account of the episcopal court of Tournai: AdN, 14.G.93, fol. 75r). In January 1480 Andries Neut, priest of St. Michael in Ghent, had sex with a nun in a public bordello, which means that it was a public scandal, making repression by an ecclesiastical court unavoidable (account of the episcopal court of Tournai: AdN, 14.G.98, fol. 85v).

[52] AdN 14.G.96.

[53] Vleeschouwers–Van Melkebeek, "Het parochiale leven," pp. 38–39, 46–47, 54–56.

[54] Vleeschouwers–Van Melkebeek, "Het parochiale leven," pp. 51, 53.

[55] Rijksarchief Gent, Fonds Bisdom, B 3295, fol. 22r.

problem is the ease with which the duke of Burgundy legitimized priests who were themselves illegitimate children, a condition that posed several handicaps for their ecclesiastical career. In March 1439 Philip the Good unhesitatingly delivered to Willem de Voghelare, parish priest in the village of Wachtebeke and bastard son of another priest, a letter of legitimation that qualified the priest as "an honorable man," despite "the defect of his birth."[56]

We should not forget, however, two forms of hypocrisy embedded in the concept of honor in clerical behavior. First, on what was meant by "public scandal," in 1454 the town of Breda introduced a fine for priests, but only if they engaged in sexual behavior within a radius of two miles of their own homes.[57] Secondly, there was a double standard regarding priests' concubines. They were generally considered prostitutes, although they were not. If we learn about a women involved in adultery or concubinage with a priest, disapproval was generally reserved for the concubine but did not apply to the priest. In 1459 Anthoine de Bavichove met a young man, Omaer de Vos, who wanted to marry the former concubine of a priest. Anthoine warned him not to marry her, if he wanted to keep his honor.[58] A similar double standard also existed when no priest was involved. When a woman dishonored her husband by living with a lover, she could be banished from her village, as "not respectable." But for a parish priest to keep one or more concubines and even visit brothels was not prejudicial for his reputation or his priestly function, and it certainly entailed no risk that he would lose the sympathy of most of his parishioners. Often hypocrisy was involved, such as by calling the concubine a maid or by limiting the scandal of illicit sex to a perimeter of two miles around the parish.

In adultery cases discrimination based on gender lines is much more general than in those involving priests' concubines. David Nicholas discovered that loss of chastity was a handicap for marriage in fourteenth-century Ghent.[59] In a play entitled *Mirror of Love*, written in Brussels between 1480 and 1500, the rhetorician Colijn van Rijssele described the impossibility of marriage, because of social distinction, between Dirk de Hollander, the rich son in a merchant's

---

[56] AdN B 1682, fol. 42v: "Guillaume de Voghelare, prestre, cure de Wachtebeke, filz bastart de feu sire Jehan de Voghelare, prestre, et engendré ou corps de feue Catherine sBallius pour lors non mariés, lequel Guillaume est homme honeste, nous ledit deffault de sa nativité abolissons."

[57] Bezemer, *Oude rechtsbronnen*, pp. 56–57.

[58] AdN B 1690, fol. 5v (edited in Champion, *Les cent nouvelles nouvelles*, p. xcii): "Ledit suppliant [Anthoine de Bavinchove] trouva en son chemin ung josne compaignon nommé Omaer de Vos, lequel venoit de Therouenne avec une femme que l'en disoit estre concubine d'ung prestre, et pource qu'il entendit que icellui Omaer avoit entencion de prandre en mariage icelle femme, il eut pitié de lui et pour garder son honneur et eviter cette alliance le fit monter derriere lui et en lui blamant icelle aliance, l'amena en la maison d'une sienne tante."

[59] Nicholas, *Domestic Life*, p. 65.

family of Middelburg, and Katherine s'Heermertens, a poor seamstress in that city, although they were madly in love. One friend of the young woman proposed that she drop the idea of marriage and be satisfied by becoming the mistress of the rich businessman. Katherine vigorously rejected the suggestion, because she (and not the man) would lose her honor and any hope for a future marriage by this. For wealthy ladies the price of adultery was not dishonor. If they lost virginity by such an affair, they still had their patrimonies to offer.[60]

Four Crucial Components of the Concept of Honor

In concluding this summary, we should recognize that the corpus of violations of individual and collective honor reveals a typical paradox in the perceptions, judgments, and sanctions of adultery and other forms of illicit sex: in some cases contemporaries show tolerance, in others rigidity. This variety of perceptions does not mean that the notion of "honor" was meaningless in the "promiscuous" fifteenth century. But it is a concept different from ours, a box filled with different components. We can distinguish at least four conditions and four contexts.

The dominant attitude is an overwhelming clemency toward adultery as part of a social game, which can be linked to the cosmopolitan conditions of the Low Countries. The tolerance for bastards was not limited to the Court of Burgundy and the social elites. For most citizens no shame was attached to admitting an illegitimate child to their family and their neighborhood. Because of this open-mindedness there was no reason for the biological father not to provide moral and material care publicly to his illegitimate children. Negative reactions only appeared if the father gave more affection and patrimony to the bastards than to his legitimate offspring, as was the case with Arnold van den Boembeke in 1458.[61]

The opposite discourse, inflexible hostility toward adultery, was present in the ideological framework of the guild authorities and can be decoded as a deep concern for the "honor" of the guild at large. Guild masters considered concubinage by guild members an assault on the reputation of the global guild's community. Reliability was a key notion and a strategy for the credibility of the profession, for the confidence in the high quality of the luxury they produced. In the ideology of their economic universe the ruthless laws of commercial competition and respectability never allowed an unfair price, never a fake product. In that logic blameless professional and also moral conduct by guild members was crucial. Throughout the period the distinction between natural and legal birth

[60] Immink, *De Spiegel*, verses 1402–3, 2774, 4911–12.

[61] AgR, Chartes du sceau de l'audience, no. 455: "icelui Arnould aians plus d'amour et affection a iceulx deux enfans illegitimes qu'auxdit autres ses vrais hoirs et heritiers"; more comments in Carlier, *Kinderen*, p. 234.

of guild members' children was a matter of great concern. The guild authorities are clearly convinced that private morality had a direct impact on the collective honor of the group. The underlying philosophy was the interdependence of social respectability and the global credibility of the guild as a production unit and an export business.

Rigidity toward sexual "violence," including abduction, rape, and even seduction, was more strategic and hypocritical than genuine. For the urban patrician upper class safeguarding the family honor may be decoded as the protection of the patrimonies of the well-to-do families. The ducal decree of 1438 was explicitly published at the demand of the aldermen of Ghent, who represented the wealthy families of the city. It aimed to eliminate abduction and seduction as dishonorable ways to gain an advantageous marriage with a wealthier partner. The measure was a perfect combination of the social peace agenda of the prince and the property protection ambition of the social elites. In this analysis of family honor there was no respect for the individual free will of their own daughters, if it involved taking the wild side by following the lover-seducer for an informal or clandestine alliance without parental consent. The girl then lost all her property rights, including her future inheritance, "as if she were dead." Only if the girl left her seducer and was prepared to marry a candidate of her parents' choice could she recover part of her property and future inheritance.[62] The Burgundian Netherlands presented a coexistence of two powers, central and urban, sometimes in conflict on political and economic matters, but always close for cultural issues and lifestyle. They also had common interests in the maintenance of social peace, a concept that mostly implied social immobility.

The third discourse on adultery as an important offense causing fundamental dishonor appears in the letters of remission of the dukes of Burgundy. In many letters the perpetrator of a passionate murder gets a pardon easily, because adultery and concubinage were considered fundamental offenses against the honor of a duped husband. Even the "progressive" Flemish society was so fundamentally patriarchal that a wife's adultery could be considered a real damage to male identity and a social stigma.[63] This disgrace was thought to justify a crime as horrible as killing the spouse's lover and to deserve the indulgence of the courts, at least if there was no clear premeditation.[64]

How should we explain this moralizing discourse, which is totally in contrast with the general social tolerance for adultery? Exaggerating the argument of dishonor of a deceived husband is of course an effective topos in the procedure of

---

[62] Gheldolf, *Coutumes*, 1:623–25.
[63] Carlier, "Paternity," pp. 239–42.
[64] Davis, *Fiction in the Archives*, pp. 36–37.

legitimization of pardon and presents the appearance of a meaningless cliché and of a purely rhetorical instrument. I am convinced, however, that these compassionate stories hide an underlying statement that is an instrumental social and political discourse. In absence of pardon the person committing a murder out of passion would be executed, or banished for life, or kept in jail. The grace procedure, on the contrary, brings him back into society. I refer here to a recent publication in which I develop the thesis that in the fifteenth century princely pardon was, at least in a certain number of cases, an instrument of social cohesion for all parties concerned, both for the family of the murder victim and for the perpetrator and his family.[65]

The annulment of guilt was normally the result of a negotiation before the court by which the consent of the aggrieved party was requested and certain compensations awarded to the victims. The "social" advantage of such a settlement was the possibility of social reintegration of the pardoned killer and probably also the recovery of the perpetrator's family life. I take my strongest argument in favor of the thesis on social cohesion and reconciliation from the numerous signs of concern by the civil authorities in the late medieval Low Countries to ensure a normal family life for children born out of wedlock. It is well known that the dukes of Burgundy not only produced many illegitimate children, but also took all possible initiatives to secure the best possible material conditions for their bastards and their mothers and to favor their careers in political, administrative, and ecclesiastical offices.

Urban authorities also eliminated most of the social handicaps and discriminations of illegitimate children and simultaneously tried to maintain the original family life of the adulterer. In fourteenth-century Ghent bastards' fathers were expected to take care of them legally and morally.[66] Such a discourse was very typical for the mid-fifteenth century, when Ghent was confronted with a lot of unwanted pregnancies and unmarried mothers, caused by the actions of certain "golden youth," the sons of wealthy bourgeois families. In 1451 Gherem Borluut, a member of one well-known Ghent family, deflowered and so dishonored Lysbeth van der Steene, but he could or would not marry her because of the difference in their social ranks. The aldermen forced him to pay a substantial sum for her trouble and for her lying-in, and for the rest of her life an annuity of ten shillings groat, a sum that would be transferred to the bastard should the mother misbehave.[67] A similar arrangement was imposed in 1435 on Jan de Heere, a married inhabitant of Waasmunster. After siring two illegitimate children on the unmarried Katheline

---

[65] The argument of "social cohesion" is also put forward for the area of Toulouse in the fifteenth century: Otis-Cour, "'De jure novo,'" pp. 358, 367; Prevenier, "The Two Faces," pp. 179–80.

[66] Nicholas, *Domestic Life*, pp. 163–72.

[67] Stadsarchief Gent, series 301, section 41, vol. 1, fol. 99r.

Marien Jansdochter, he was forced by the court of the Council of Flanders to buy a house for the mother and to secure an annuity for the children's support in the form of a yearly amount of rye.[68]

It is clear that the Ghent aldermen had a subtle understanding of adultery as a normal human behavior. They preferred compassionate social care and the reconstruction of mainstream family life to rigid morality. We should not forget that, at least within a specific sociocultural context, there has been a long tradition of tolerance and acceptance of adultery all over Europe. In the twelfth century many troubadours, especially Chrétien de Troyes, celebrated courtly love as essentially extramarital[69] and adultery as true love.[70] Their romance is seldom married love, but rather *adultère courtois*.[71] I observe here a fascinating parallel to the tolerance on adultery by medieval canonists, such as Baldus de Ubaldis, who allowed women to have extramarital sex if they were afraid of violence from their husbands.[72] This statement inspired Leah Otis-Cour to conclude that "the late-medieval Church clearly preferred the charity of the New Testament to the rigor of the Old Testament law, which had prescribed stoning of the adulterous wife."[73]

Bibliography

Archival Sources

Brussels, Archives générales du Royaume [AgR], Chambre des Comptes, 6886, 13780, 14461, 14159; Chartes du sceau de l'audience, no. 455.
Lille, Archives départementales du Nord [AdN], 14.G.93, 14.G.96, 14.G.98; B 1682, B 1686, B 1687, B 1688, B 1690.
Rijksarchief Gent, Fonds Bisdom, B 3295; Raad van Vlaanderen, no. 7510.
Stadsarchief Brugge, section 208, O.L.V. Zestendeel, reg. 3.
Stadsarchief Gent, series 156, section 1; series 301, section 41.

Published Sources and Literature

Bergé, Marcel. "Les bâtards de la maison de Bourgogne." *L'intermédiaire des généalogistes* 60 (1955): 316–408.
Bezemer, Willem. *Oude rechtsbronnen der stad Breda.* The Hague: Nijhoff, 1892.
Boone, Marc. "Les gens de métier à l'époque corporative à Gand et les litiges professionnels (1350–1450)." In *Individual, Corporate and Judicial Status in European Cities*, ed. Marc Boone and Maarten Prak, pp. 23–47. Leuven: Garant, 1996.

---

[68] Rijksarchief Gent, Raad van Vlaanderen, no. 7510, fols. 89v–90r.

[69] Doody, *True Story*, p. 187; Howell, "From Land to Love," p. 229.

[70] McCracken, *Romance of Adultery*, pp. 18–19, 52, 63, 84, 103–7.

[71] The expression "courtly adultery" was coined by Christiane Marchello-Nizia: see Marchello-Nizia, "Amour courtois," esp. p. 969.

[72] Brundage, *Law, Sex and Christian Society*, p. 520.

[73] Otis-Cour, "'De jure novo,'" pp. 350–52.

Boone, Marc. "State Power and Illicit Sexuality: The Persecution of Sodomy in Late Medieval Bruges." *Journal of Medieval History* 22 (1996): 135–53.

Bourdieu, Pierre. "From the 'Rules' of Honour to the Sense of Honour." In *Outline of a Theory of Practice (Esquisse d'une théorie de la pratique)*, trans. Richard Nice, pp. 10–15. Cambridge: Cambridge University Press, 1977.

Brundage, James A. *Law, Sex and Christian Society in Medieval Europe.* Chicago: University of Chicago Press, 1987.

———. "Sex and Canon Law." In *Handbook of Medieval Sexuality*, ed. Vern L. Bullough and James A. Brundage, pp. 33–50. New York: Garland, 1996.

Carlier, Myriam. *Kinderen van de minne? Bastaarden in het vijftiende-eeuwse Vlaanderen.* Brussels: Koninklijke Vlaamse Academie van België, 2001.

———. "Paternity in Late Medieval Flanders." In *Secretum Scriptorum: Liber alumnorum Walter Prevenier*, ed. Wim Blockmans, Marc Boone, and Thérèse de Hemptinne, pp. 235–58. Leuven: Garant, 1999.

Champion, Pierre, ed. *Les cent nouvelles nouvelles.* Paris: E. Droz, 1928.

Chojnacki, Stanley. *Women and Men in Renaissance Venice.* Baltimore: Johns Hopkins University Press, 2000.

Danneel, Marianne. *Weduwen en wezen in het Laat-middeleeuwse Gent.* Leuven: Garant, 1995.

Davis, Natalie Zemon. *Fiction in the Archives: Pardon Tales and Their Tellers in Sixteenth-Century France.* Stanford: Stanford University Press, 1987.

Doody, Margaret A. *The True Story of the Novel.* New Brunswick, NJ: Rutgers University Press, 1996.

Dupont, Guy. *Maagdenverleidsters, hoeren en speculanten: Prostitutie in Brugge tijdens de Bourgondische periode (1385–1515).* Bruges: Vlaamse Historische Studies, 1996.

Gauvard, Claude. *"De grâce espécial": Crime, état et société en France à la fin du Moyen Âge.* Paris: Publications de la Sorbonne, 1991.

Gheldolf, A. E., ed. *Coutumes de la ville de Gand.* Brussels: Commission royale pour la publication des anciennes lois et ordonnances de la Belgique, 1868.

Gilliodts–van Severen, Louis, ed. *Coutume de la ville d'Ypres.* Brussels: Commission royale pour la publication des anciennes lois et ordonnances de la Belgique, 1908.

Gilmore, David D. *Honor and Shame and the Unity of the Mediterranean.* Washington, DC: American Anthropological Association, 1987.

Howell, Martha. "From Land to Love: Commerce and Marriage in Northern Europe during the Late Middle Ages." *Jaarboek van Middeleeuwse Geschiedenis* 10 (2007): 216–53.

Immink, Margaretha Wilhelmina, ed. *De Spiegel der Minnen door Colijn van Rijssele.* Utrecht: Oosthoek, 1913.

Kuehn, Thomas J. "Honor and Conflict in a Fifteenth-Century Florentine Family." In *Law, Family and Woman*, ed. Thomas J. Kuehn, pp. 129–42. Chicago: University of Chicago Press, 1991.

Lambrecht, Daniel. *De parochiale synode in het oude bisdom Doornik, 11de eeuw–1559.* Brussels: Koninklijke Vlaamse Academie van België, 1984.

Letts, Malcolm H. I., ed. *Bruges and Its Past.* Bruges: C. Beyaert, 1924.

———, ed. *The Travels of Leo of Rozmital through Germany, Flanders, England, Spain, Portugal and Italy, 1465–1467.* Cambridge: Cambridge University Press, 1957.

Marchello-Nizia, Christiane. "Amour courtois, société masculine et figures de pouvoir." *Annales: Économies, sociétés, civilisations* 36 (1981): 969–82.

McCracken, Peggy. *The Romance of Adultery: Queenship and Sexual Transgression in Old French Literature*. Philadelphia: University of Pennsylvania Press, 1998.

Nicholas, David. *The Domestic Life of a Medieval City: Women, Children, and the Family in Fourteenth-Century Ghent*. Lincoln: University of Nebraska Press, 1985.

Nisbett, Richard G., and Dov Cohen. *Culture of Honor: The Psychology of Violence in the South*. Boulder: Westview, 1996.

Otis-Cour, Leah. "'*De jure novo*': Dealing with Adultery in the Fifteenth-Century Toulousain." *Speculum* 84 (2009): 347–92.

Petit-Dutaillis, Charles. *Documents nouveaux sur les moeurs populaires et le droit de vengeance dans les Pays-Bas au XVe siècle: Lettres de rémission de Philippe le Bon*. Paris: Honoré Champion, 1908.

Pichon, Jérôme, ed. *Le ménagier de Paris: Traité composé vers 1393 par un bourgeois Parisien*. Lille: Régis Lehoucq, 1992.

Pitt-Rivers, Julian. "Honour and Social Status." In *Honour and Shame: The Values of Mediterranean Society*, ed. Jean G. Péristiany, pp. 21–77. London: Weidenfeld and Nicolson, 1965.

Prevenier, Walter. "Mechelen circa 1500: A Cosmopolitan Biotope for Social Elites and Non-conformists." In *Women of Distinction: Margaret of York, Margaret of Austria*, ed. Dagmar Eichberger, pp. 31–41. Turnhout: Brepols, 2005.

———. "The Two Faces of Pardon Jurisdiction in the Burgundian Netherlands: A Royal Road to Social Cohesion and an Effectual Instrument of Princely Clientelism." In *Power and Persuasion: Essays on the Art of State Building in Honour of W. P. Blockmans*, ed. Peter Hoppenbrouwers, Antheun Janse, and Robert Stein, pp. 177–95. Turnhout: Brepols, 2010.

Prevenier, Walter, and Willem P. Blockmans. *The Burgundian Netherlands*. Cambridge: Cambridge University Press, 1985.

Prevenier, Walter, Paul Huys, and Guy Dupont. "Misdaad en straf." In *Geschiedenis van Deinze, deel 3, Het platteland en de dorpen van Deinze*, ed. Walter Prevenier et al., pp. 225–48. Deinze: Stad Deinze en Kring voor Geschiedenis en Kunst van Deinze, 2007.

Taylor, Scott K. *Honor and Violence in Golden Age Spain*. New Haven, CT: Yale University Press, 2008.

Vander Linden, Florence. "Vorzienicheit van goede: Uitkering tot levensonderhoud aan gehuwde vrouwen in noodsituaties in het laatmiddeleeuwse Gent." *Handelingen der Maatschappij voor Geschiedenis en Oudheidkunde te Gent* 62 (2008): 81–120.

Vertovec, Steven, and Robin Cohen, eds. *Conceiving Cosmopolitanism: Theory, Context and Practice*. Oxford: Oxford University Press, 2002.

Vleeschouwers–Van Melkebeek, Monique. *Compotus sigilliferi curie Tornacensis: Rekeningen van de officialiteit van Doornik (1429–1481)*. Brussels: Koninklijke Commissie voor Geschiedenis, 1995.

———. "Het parochiale leven in het oude bisdom Doornik tijdens de late middeleeuwen." In *Ter overwinning van een historische drempelvrees: De historicus en juridische bronnen*, ed. Serge Dauchy, pp. 31–59. Iuris scripta historica 7. Brussels: Koninklijke Academie voor Wetenschappen van België, 1994.

Vorsterman van Oyen, G. A. *Rechtsbronnen der stad Aardenburg*. The Hague: Werken der Vereeniging tot uitgave der bronnen van het oude vaderlandsche recht, 1892.

The Case of the Disappearing Mintmaster

James M. Murray

A N IDLER or sturdy beggar on the St. Veerle square of Ghent might have seen an unusual sight on a late July day in 1357. No, it was not a procession issuing from the count's church there, or a beheading, for St. Veerle's was the city's place of execution as well. Rather, it was the alderman Goessin Mulaerd at the head of a band of Ghentenars on their way toward the count's castle on a critical errand. Reports had reached the Ghent business world of the flight of the count's Florentine mintmaster, Bardet of Malpilys, and this well-dressed band was castle-bound, perhaps at the trotting, barely seemly pace of those who have lost a lot of money and fear they may lose more. In the castle they were met by Jan Bernard, the count's guardian of the currency, who conducted the group to Malpilys's strongbox, unlocked it, and extracted moneybags and other unspecified goods. Then immediately, aldermen being present as well as Bernard, money and goods were distributed to Malpilys's creditors as partial payment of debts owed them.[1]

The Ghent magistrates in a letter to the count justified impounding and dispersing the mintmaster's assets as a necessary measure to prevent a greater financial emergency than had already occurred. But in so doing they ran the risk of incurring the count's anger because they had violated his property and sovereignty. Indeed, Count Louis of Male came in person to Ghent to lodge a complaint against the Ghent aldermen because, as he bluntly stated, "[T]hey had no right nor business there, for the castle resided under our lordship and

---

[1] This narrative is based on two letters issued by the Ghent aldermen, dated August 5 and 7, 1357. Both appear in Limburg-Stirum, *Cartulaire*, 1:567–68. The standard work on Ghent for this period is Nicholas, *Metamorphosis*.

knowledge."[2] The Ghent aldermen soon issued an apology to Louis, citing the emergency and exceptional circumstances as well as the role of his official Jan Bernard in the affair and assuring him that this constituted neither a precedent nor predictor of future actions.[3]

Cases of fleeing mintmasters are not unknown in the long history of medieval minting, and this incident was cited and discussed long ago by the leading historian of the monetary and legal history of the fourteenth-century counts of Flanders.[4] Yet the case has never been analyzed for what it shows about the financial system of which the mint was a part. Specifically, what were the roles of the mintmaster, his customers, and the count in the functioning and near foundering of that system? And finally, how was the crisis resolved?[5] The story and its ending might sound eerily familiar in our panicky, recession-bound world.

What our sturdy beggar may have witnessed resembles an old-fashioned "run on the bank" quite like the one portrayed by the director Frank Capra in *It's a Wonderful Life*. There, of course, rumor led to crowd action, headed off by the heroic Jimmy Stewart distributing ready cash to cover customers' short-term needs without forcing the "bank" into liquidation. In the Ghent case the actual flight of the mintmaster led to a similar chain of events in which a portion of Malpilys's obligations was covered by distributing what he had left behind in his strongbox. Or did it? In other words, is the resemblance between the twenty-first and fourteenth centuries more apparent than real? After all, Malpilys was not a "banker" but the chief official of the count's mint at Ghent: a government official then? But Mulaerd and his men insisted they were on a mission to seize the assets of a private, not a public, figure, who just happened to have his place of business in the imposing hulk of the count's castle. What is the truth of the matter?

There was no scarcer commodity in medieval northern Europe than sympathy for Italian merchant/bankers like Malpilys. They were notoriously disliked in England, for example, where they were simultaneously "bankers to the king" for

---

[2] Limburg-Stirum, *Cartulaire*, 1:567–68: "Om dwelke miin here zeer gram was, tract te Ghent ende calengierde scepenen ende alle deghone die in ziin castel ghetruct waren, want zy int casteel gheen recht noch kennesse hadden noch hebben, maer behoort toe mins heren herlichede ende te miins heren kennesse."

[3] This is quite disingenuous as later events were to show, for relations between Ghent and the count steadily worsened in the 1360s and 1370s, leading to civil war in 1382; for this see Nicholas, *Metamorphosis*, p. 299n18; also see ch. 1.

[4] Two years later, in fact, the Lucchese mintmaster, Henri de Lestrigo, fled leaving behind considerable debts as well; see Bigwood, *Le régime juridique*, 1: 229–31, esp. p. 232. Alan Stahl describes a similar case in Venice in 1381 in which the mintmaster also left behind a considerable quantity of silver in his strongbox; see Stahl, *Zecca*, p. 73.

[5] Besides Bigwood, see also Murray, *Bruges*, pp. 250–51.

all three Edwards and convenient scapegoats for unpopular royal policies.[6] That being said, Malpilys seems to deserve at least some pity for landing in an impossible position that was not entirely of his own making. He was not, it seems, a representative of one of the large merchant/banking houses of Florence; thus he may have simply been working for his own account, using his position as mintmaster as part of his entrepreneurial ventures in the Low Countries. He was, after all, only an "accidental" official; since the count of Flanders probably "sold" the office to the highest bidder, Malpilys may have simply been both unskillful in bidding and unlucky in his boss, Count Louis of Male.[7]

It might be useful to visit the business economics of tax farming for a moment, for in effect with his successful bid to become mintmaster, Malpilys added the governmental enterprise of purchasing bullion and striking gold and silver coins to his business portfolio. Medieval and early modern governments routinely auctioned off their prerogatives to collect taxes in return for either a lump-sum payment or a steady cash stream. Modern economists have always dismissed this arrangement as backward, arguing that it was an always inefficient stopgap solution to the lack of skilled personnel and adequate bureaucracy.[8] This is a presentist and shortsighted view of things, however, which obscures the very real benefits for both sides. As mintmaster, Malpilys gave Count Louis what amounted to a line of credit advanced upon expectation of collecting the coinage fee (seigniorage) that was levied on every coin struck at the mint. Louis then simply directed creditors to obtain payment in Ghent from Malpilys, who in effect gave ready money in return for a debit entry in his ledger for the mint. In the surviving account roll covering payments made from December 1356 to July 1357, Malpilys covered the count's expenses for marriage gifts, fees for his confessor and surgeon, and payments made to his admiral and fleet involved in the siege of Antwerp. There are even expenses charged to his account for charity given to a "poor man" and disguised interest payments given to money changers who loaned the count money.[9]

The use of Italians as government officials was already a long-established tradition in Flanders by the 1350s. Countess Margaret (1244–78) was probably the first ruler to engage Italian firms in government finance. She was followed by her son Guy of Dampierre (1278–1305), whose favorites came from Florence and

---

[6] In this way, Italians were analogous to Jews in serving as fronts for what in effect was royal taxation. Spufford, *Power and Profit*, pp. 12–59.

[7] Inquiries of experts in Florentine economic history have not resulted in the identification of Malpilys. It is not even clear what the proper form of his name was.

[8] Kiser, "Markets and Hierarchies."

[9] Brussels, Algemeen Rijksarchief, MS Rekenkamer, Rolrekening 796 (hereafter ARAB 796), as described by Nélis, *Chambre des comptes*, p. 45.

Siena, with members of the Siennese Buonsignori serving as comital receivers.[10] In the early fourteenth century many prominent Florentine companies served the Flemish counts, including the Bardi and Peruzzi, as well as the Alberti and Frescobaldi. As the fortunes of the "super-companies" waned after 1340, more individual merchants stepped into comital service, working apparently on their own account. Malpilys was one of these, but unlike him, most of his confreres were natives of Lucca.[11]

Scandals and malfeasance also antedated Malpilys's flight from financial responsibility. Italians serving as comital and royal receivers in particular occasioned troubles, such as the infamous Guidi brothers, who served France's Philip the Fair (1285–1314); the Fini brothers of Siena served as comital receivers, and Thomas was even made a "special" receiver and entrusted with expanded powers of government by count Robert of Béthune (1305–22) before falling into scandal and disgrace. Bartholomeo Fini was arrested and executed for his "crimes."[12] Mintmasters were of course a full step below receivers on the scale of significance, yet this position too came generally to be filled by Italians by the fourteenth century. This had not always been the case in Flanders, however, for in the thirteenth century the practice was to link the feudal grant of money changer with the office of mintmaster, thus making explicit the changers' duty to oversee and sustain the county's coinage.[13] After 1300, following the example of the kings of France and Avignon popes, the counts of Flanders and dukes of Brabant usually appointed Italians as their mintmasters.[14]

We have seen that Malpilys's franchise allowed him to purchase bullion for a price stipulated by the count and produce both gold and silver coins at the Ghent mint, reserving the customary tax for himself. Knowledge and experience were critical in the business calculation made by Malpilys, balancing an estimate of the quantity of coins he could produce quarterly and what the count's demand for liquidity might be. In any event, Malpilys badly misjudged things, as the audit of July 27, 1357—after his disappearance—showed: receipts were 31,563 pounds parisis, and outlays amounted to just over 37,240 pounds parisis. In other words, the count was able to overdraw his account by 5,677 pounds in the nine months covered by the account. There was also some irregularity in the recording of

---

[10] Bigwood, *Le régime juridique*, 1:183.

[11] Bigwood, *Le régime juridique*, 1:185–89; the Lucchese community of Bruges flourished in the fourteenth century; see Roover, "La communauté de Lucquois"; for merchants of Lucca in general, see the important collection of Blomquist, *Merchant Families*.

[12] Bigwood, *Le régime juridique*, 1:202–6; on the Guidi brothers, see Strayer, "Italian Bankers."

[13] Murray, *Bruges*, p. 150.

[14] Bigwood, *Le régime juridique*, 1:222–26.

payments owed creditors, as the comital auditors included in that figure expenses for which "Bardet had no itemized bill."[15]

Yet we would be wrong to underestimate the allure of the office of mintmaster to a foreign merchant: it offered access to the most important circles of finance in one of the wealthiest areas of northern Europe, as well as possible customers within the comital family and Flemish aristocracy. A generation later the Lucchese merchant Dino Rapondi demonstrated the possibilities of such service to the ruler of Flanders, becoming an important financier to both the count and the cities of Bruges and Ghent while successfully marketing fine silks and other luxury goods to the duke of Burgundy and his entourage.[16] Some of the losses incurred by Malpilys may simply have been the sort of "pay to play" required of all merchants who sought the patronage of the prince.[17]

That being said, however, there was a tremendous premium on insider knowledge in the medieval system of tax farming. A good example is the farming of urban excise taxes that by the fourteenth century had become the major source of tax revenue for towns and cities in the Low Countries.[18] In Bruges the right to collect the consumption tax on wine, beer, and mead was auctioned quarterly to a revolving set of the same wealthy brokers, money changers, and other rich merchants who took turns in the office of city treasurer charged with holding the auctions. This variant of "crony capitalism" gave an edge to members of the inner core of city financiers who had a good idea of what the receipts from the tax were likely to be and thus were able to tailor their bids accordingly.[19] In the case of the count's mint, the vast majority of his mintmasters had been merchants from Lucca, making Malpilys a rare exception to that rule. Lack of insider knowledge and experience may have affected severely the soundness of his decision-making.

Another potential obstacle might have been the count's practice of appointing alongside the mintmaster a "Guardian of the Coinage," who often was a money changer and thus native of one of the major Flemish cities. The Jan

---

[15] ARAB 796, membrane 6: "Che sont les parties desquelles Bardet na nulle cedule." The word used here is the French form of the Latin *cedula*, usually a small piece of rolled-up paper or parchment upon which a bill or other accounting entry would be written. It is unclear why these expenses were not attested to in this way, but the thirty-nine items that follow are mostly payments for goods and services consumed by the count's and countess's households. Chronic overdrafts by sovereign rulers were nothing new, as the case of Edward I of England and the Ricciardi of Lucca shows. The Ricciardi farmed the wool customs from 1272 to 1294, allowing Edward I a line of credit, which he exceeded annually by an amount equal to the income of the tax. See Bell, Brooks, and Moore, "Credit Crunch."

[16] Lambert, *City*.

[17] Hunt and Murray, *Medieval Business*, pp. 114–22.

[18] Van Uytven, "Stages of Decline," pp. 263–66.

[19] Murray, *Bruges*, pp. 115–16, and the works cited therein.

Bernard who opened Malpilys's strongbox after escorting the mob into the castle was apparently an exception to this rule, but his near contemporary, Bernard Priem, had been a money changer in Bruges in the 1350s.[20] His role seems duplicitous, given that he was the count's official yet allowed an act that clearly angered his lord and could have endangered his job. The most likely explanation was hostility and jealousy within the mint, at least between the mintmaster and guardian, which clearly contributed to the events of July 1357. Perhaps a prosopographical study along the lines of what has been done for the Venetian mint might document the complex personnel politics in the context of Louis of Male's rapacious use of the coinage as a tool for enhancing his income.[21] Tensions and jealousies were abundant between Louis and his subjects throughout his long reign, which ended in a vastly destructive civil war, and it is unlikely that his officials and servants entirely escaped such forces.[22]

I have left for last the essential question: Did the count's mint function as a bank by the mid-fourteenth century? In one sense this is a "question mal posée" because we risk anachronism in even using the word *bank*. No medieval institution was housed in a grand building or had well-defined deposit or credit creating functions. Yet if we narrow the definition to what banks do—accepting deposits, making payments and loans, creating in effect bank money—then a good case can be made that Malpilys's failure was a true bank failure.[23] One key is in the two descriptions of what happened that July. The one of August 7, written by the Ghent aldermen, reports that Malpilys had received considerable sums from many citizens of the city "to sustain and support the coinage" but had fled without fulfilling his obligation to "make payments" to said citizens.[24] This is the very language of medieval banking, to "receive and make payments"; and if we accept that numerous Ghentenars were depending on a stipulated payment, the subsequent "soft storming" of the count's castle makes perfect sense.[25] As the aldermen state, their actions were taken to "prevent worse consequences," which suggests a credit network dependent on the liquidity that either disbursement of ready coin from the mint or book transfers provided. If those were to freeze suddenly, then

[20] On Priem, see Bigwood, *Le régime juridique*, 1:228. In the 1360s the Bruges changer Clais Rapesaert was guardian; see Murray, *Bruges*, p. 314.

[21] Stahl, "Prosopography."

[22] On the Ghent war, see Nicholas, *Medieval Flanders*, pp. 227–31.

[23] Raymond de Roover did mention the possibility that "medieval mints sometimes performed functions of a central bank" without pursuing that idea further (*Money*, p. 234).

[24] The original language is "omme de munte te voldoene ende te sustinerne" and that Bardet had "niet ghenouch doende den vorseide poortren ten daghe van haren paiementen." Texts are from Limburg-Stirum, *Cartulaire*, 1:567–68.

[25] On this terminology, see Murray, *Bruges*, pp. 154–55.

a domino effect of credit calls and panic selling could ensue. Such effects would have fully justified the aldermen's fears of "worse" to come.[26] Fortunately, we have additional evidence of the wide range of financial services provided by the mints of Flanders. The surviving account books of the Bruges money changer Collard de Marke provide conclusive evidence that the Ghent mint functioned as a bank in Marke's exchange business. First, money changers were obliged by law and personal oath to deliver bullion and noncurrent coinage to the count's mint for reissue.[27] In effect, changers were often required to wait the interval between delivery of their bullion and the disbursement of new coin. Quite naturally, one assumes, this arrangement came to function as a deposit banking system, and we see by the mid-1360s that Marke was using it as such. He kept a separate register, which does not survive, for bullion deliveries that he made to the mint. But enough references were carried over to his general register for us to observe him drawing on his balance in Ghent to pay business partners and customers via book transfers, as well as furthering his bullion business that he maintained with partners from Hainault.[28]

A picture of the operation of the network emerges mosaic-like from the general registers, in the absence of Marke's account of the mint (*papier de la monnoie* or *billon*). The mechanism for credit/debit transactions with the mint was a running account kept in the name of the Ghent mintmaster, precisely the same method used in payment/credit relations with other money changers and hostelers in Bruges and elsewhere.[29] In most, but not all, of these accounts, the holder(s) is/are called "li mestre(s) de le monnoie," indicating the public nature of this business relationship.[30] One complication is that two associates of the Interminelli, Jehan Jourdain of Lucca and Tumas Sarlande, also held accounts with Marke and seem to have served as deputies for mint business, at least insofar as the surviving

---

[26] The language of the documents is quite explicit about this: (August 7, 1357) "omme twelke [Bardet's failure to cover payments] scepenen van der keure in Ghend in dien tyt, Goossin Mulaerd ende sine gesellen, bi groten ende nerensten vervolghe van den vorseide poortren ende die hem aenclevende waren, omme beters wille ende om meerre grief te scuwene"; (August 5, 1357) "So dat scepenen ende de goede liede van Ghent minen here supplierden dat hyt hem vergheven wilde, want zyt ghedaen hadden te goeder trauwen ende om argher te bevelne" (Limburg-Stirum, *Cartulaire*, 1:567–68).

[27] For money changers in general, see Murray, *Bruges*, pp. 148–58, and on France, see Bompaire, "Compétences et pratiques."

[28] For the Marke registers, see Murray, "Merchant Account Books"; these are kept in the City Archives of Bruges (hereafter SAB).

[29] See Murray, *Bruges*, pp. 249–51, on money changers as regional bankers.

[30] The title occurs at the heading of two accounts, on SAB, Marke, register 1, fol. 213r, "li mestres de le monnoie Andrughe et Jehan Terminiel," which is correct in their joint holding of the office; and SAB, Marke, register 3, fol. 277v, "le mestre de le monnoie," here indicating Jehan alone, who indeed was sole mintmaster at Ghent from 1367 to 1370. See Bigwood, *Le régime juridique*, 1:233.

accounts show.[31] Other accounts are given only under the name of the mintmaster himself. This suggests the usual intermixture of "public" and "private" business in the financial operations of late medieval Europe.

Marke's business involves the Ghent mint in several ways. First, he used his mint account to make payments to clients who may have been involved in the trade in cloth that Marke organized from Bruges.[32] Second was his trade in bullion, much of it coming from agents in Hainault, who sometimes sent it directly to the Ghent mint rather than to Marke in Bruges.[33] And third are twin indications of the changer/hosteler exchange network that is well attested to in Bruges and left tantalizing hints of other links with the mint as nodal point. For example, in Marke's fourth ledger, the account of "Jehan Terminiel," records that the Leuven hosteler, Roulof Rabone, deposited to his account at the mint more than 395 pounds *groot* worth of silver. As customary, this is indicated as a debit to Interminelli's account. It was discharged three weeks later when a messenger arrived from Jehan Jourdain with the money.[34] Marke also had dealings with a Ghent hosteler, Zegher van Love, revolving around mint business.[35] By 1369, Marke's business interests in Ghent were such that they required the presence of his son, Collart, to oversee them. Thus even without specific evidence as to the nature of these business transactions, it is clear that Ghent and its mint played a part in all branches of Marke's business activities. But was this true for other money changers?

We know from the 1357 affair that money changers from both Bruges and Ieper were also account holders at the Ghent mint. These accounts were for delivery of bullion and were denominated in gold coins. Historians have interpreted this as simply an obligation from the mintmaster for delivery of physical coins in return for bullion. The Marke accounts show, however, that such obligations could be assigned to third parties via book transfers at the mint, which makes it very likely

[31] Jourdain at least had a business relationship attested to in comital documents; Bigwood, *Le régime juridique*, 1:233. Sarlande is a shadowier figure, although he, too, acted as Interminelli's agent in 1369 (SAB, Marke, register 4, fol. 3v). In Jourdain's account in SAB, Marke, register 5, fol. 170r, Marke notes that Jourdain owes him for "plusieurs parties de billon" delivered presumably to the mint, amounting to the considerable sum of 301 pounds *groot*. In the account of Jehan Interminelli (SAB, Marke, register 4, fol. 69v) Jourdain is the agent of a large transfer of money (300 pounds *groot*) credited to Interminelli on February 15, 1369. The pound parisis was an older money of account still used in the mid-fourteenth century as well as the current pound *groot* Flemish. The relationship of the currencies was 12:1, where 1 pence *groot* equaled 1 shilling parisis.

[32] This is the likeliest explanation for the account activity of Renier Campion, whose account runs through three ledgers and who was apparently living in Ghent from ca. 1367 to 1369: SAB, Marke, register 3, fols. 159r, 209r, 254v; 4, fols. 12r, 18v; 5, fol. 258r.

[33] An example is Thiery Brochons and Jehan Hanart (SAB, Marke, register 5, fol. 308v) "pour plusieurs parties de billon qui furent livrees a Gant," and Murray, *Bruges*, pp. 256, 297.

[34] SAB, Marke, register 4, fol. 69v.

[35] I discuss this more fully in Murray, *Bruges*, p. 252.

that other changers used their balances in a similar fashion. In effect, the comital mint was the center of its own credit/payment network over and above its role as the count's private bank. The fact that, judging from the 1357 documents, Ghent merchants and select foreign merchants had similar accounts hints at broader dependent credit networks than anyone has hitherto suspected. One might even suspect the origins of regional and long-distance payment/credit networks in the operations of Italian merchants in the employ of the Flemish count. I confess that this is a possibility I missed in my earlier work on banking and credit in Bruges.[36]

Conclusion

The French word *dénouement* means literally "untangling," and it is an appropriate description to apply to the solution of what the historian Georges Bigwood called this "fatuous affair."[37] To restore confidence in the financial system, the count brought in two trusted Lucchese merchants, one to take over the striking of gold coins at Ghent, and the other to strike the silver coinage. It was the first of these, Perceval du Porche, who was charged with clearing up the mess left by Malpilys, and his solution is instructive. All those left with unpaid account balances at the mint were paid a third of what was owed them and were granted a discount of half the seigniorage charge for any future bullion deliveries until the outstanding sum was paid. Ghent merchant creditors required further assurances, and Perceval and Jan Bernard stood as personal guarantors for a "considerable sum of deniers" in order to quiet the Ghentenars. As his reimbursement Perceval received two pennies on each marc of gold *mouton* coins struck in Ghent.[38] In effect, creditors were forced to be content with a little cash and long-term promissory notes. The fears of the Ghentenars could only be assuaged by a display of massive liquidity.

All this brings home the truth of what Walter Bagehot wrote in the *Economist* around 1850: "The problem of managing a panic must not be thought of as mainly a 'banking' problem. It is primarily a mercantile one. All merchants are under liabilities. . . . In other words, all merchants are dependent on borrowing money."[39] As the case of the disappearing mintmaster shows, this was as true in the fourteenth as in the nineteenth century.

Bibliography

Bagehot, Walter. *Lombard Street: A Description of the Money Market*. Homewood, IL: Richard D. Irwin, 1962.

[36] It is ironic that just such a connection was discussed in the earliest works on national banking, notably Bagehot, *Lombard Street*, pp. 38–39, who echoes Adam Smith's *Wealth of Nations*, bk. 4, ch. 3.

[37] Bigwood, *Le régime juridique*, p. 231.

[38] Bigwood, *Le régime juridique*, pp. 230–31.

[39] Bagehot, *Lombard Street*, p. 25.

Bell, Adrian R., Chris Brooks, and Tony Moore. "The Credit Crunch of 1294: Causes, Consequences and the Aftermath." May 13, 2009. http://www.voxeu.org/index. php?q=node /3563.

Bigwood, Georges. *Le régime juridique et économique du commerce de l'argent dans la Belgique du Moyen Âge.* 2 vols. Brussels: Académie royale de Belgique, 1921–22.

Blomquist, Thomas. *Merchant Families, Banking and Money in Medieval Lucca.* Aldershot: Ashgate, 2005.

Bompaire, Marc. "Compétences et pratiques de calcul dans les livres de changeurs francais XIVᵉ–XVᵉ siècles)." In *Écrire, Compter, Mesurer: Vers une histoire des rationalités pratiques,* ed. Natacha Coquery, Francois Menant, and Florence Weber, pp. 143–62. Paris: Presses de l'école normale supérieure, 2006.

Hunt, Edwin S., and James M. Murray. *A History of Business in Medieval Europe, 1200–1550.* New York: Cambridge University Press, 1999.

Kiser, Edgar. "Markets and Hierarchies in Early Modern Tax Systems: A Principal-Agent Analysis." *Politics and Society* 22 (1994): 284–315.

Lambert, Bart. *The City, the Duke and Their Banker: The Rapondi Family and the Formation of the Burgundian State (1384–1430).* Studies in European Urban History (1100–1800) 7. Turnhout: Brepols, 2006.

Limburg-Stirum, T., ed. *Cartulaire de Louis de Male, comte de Flandre de 1348 à 1358.* 2 vols. Bruges: Louis de Planck, 1898–1901.

Murray, James M. *Bruges, Cradle of Capitalism, 1280–1390.* Cambridge: Cambridge University Press, 2005.

———. "Merchant Account Books in Fourteenth-Century Flanders." In *Kopet Uns Werk by Tyden: Beiträge zur hansischen und preussischen Geschichte; Festschrift für Walter Stark zum 75. Geburtstag,* ed. N. Jörn, D. Kattinger, and H. Wernicke, pp. 27–31. Schwerin: Helms, 1999.

Nélis, H. *Chambre des comptes de Flandre et de Brabant: Inventaire des comptes en rouleaux.* Brussels: Goemaere, 1914.

Nicholas, David. *Medieval Flanders.* London: Longman, 1992.

———. *The Metamorphosis of a Medieval City: Ghent in the Age of the Arteveldes, 1302–1390.* Lincoln: University of Nebraska Press, 1989.

Roover, Raymond de. "La communauté de Lucquois." *Annales de la Société d'émulation de Bruges* 86 (1949): 23–89.

———. *Money, Banking and Credit in Mediaeval Bruges.* Cambridge, MA: Medieval Academy of America, 1948.

Spufford, Peter. *Power and Profit: The Merchant in Medieval Europe.* London: Thames & Hudson, 2002.

Stahl, Alan. "A Prosopography of Medieval Venetian Officials." *Medieval Prosopography* 21 (2000): 41–131.

———. *Zecca: The Mint of Venice in the Middle Ages.* Baltimore: Johns Hopkins University Press, 2000.

Strayer, Joseph. "Italian Bankers and Philip the Fair." Ch. 15 in *Medieval Statecraft and the Perspectives of History: Essays,* pp. 239–47. Princeton, NJ: Princeton University Press, 1971.

Van Uytven, Raymond. "Stages of Decline: Late Medieval Bruges." In *Peasants & Townsmen in Medieval Europe: Studia in Honorem Adriaan Verhulst,* ed. Jean-Marie Duvosquel and Erik Thoen, pp. 259–69. Ghent: Snoeck-Ducaju and Son, 1995.

Work, Business, and Investments: Economic Networks in a Fifteenth-Century City

Marci Sortor

IN THE PAST TWO DECADES the economic history of the Middle Ages has taken important strides, and in a direction rather different from that taken a generation or so ago by Raymond de Roover, Roberto Lopez, and Armando Sapori. Examples of this new direction include Edwin Hunt's study of the Peruzzi company of Florence, which tests key assumptions about how the great Italian merchant companies went about their business. Examining the other end of the business spectrum is Richard Marshall's work on the local merchants of Prato and the day-to-day practices of retailers.[1] Recently, Kathryn Reyerson and James Murray in their very different ways have significantly deepened our understanding of the infrastructure of services that made long-distance commerce "scalable," allowing for the growth of international trade to late medieval and early modern levels. Both Reyerson and Murray explore the logistics of international trade and the functions essential to supporting large-scale international commerce, including legal services, transportation, housing, information, and financial services. Murray frames his discussion of this infrastructure in fourteenth-century Bruges in terms of "nodes" where services and the people who provided them clustered along key points in international merchants' networks. Reyerson's study of business in Montpellier and its region reveals significant interconnection among services supporting commerce, including transporters and hostellers who could ensure the arrival of goods at their final destination without the direct supervision of the

Bernard Bachrach, James Murray, and David Nicholas helped improve this paper with their excellent editorial remarks. I also thank Walter Prevenier for his comments on an earlier version of this paper, delivered at the 2009 International Congress of Medieval Studies, Kalamazoo, Michigan.

[1] Hunt, *Medieval Super-Companies*; Marshall, *Local Merchants*. See also Hunt and Murray, *History of Business*.

merchant. Exploring the networks of services through which information, credit, and goods flowed underscores not simply the logistics of doing business. These studies reveal the inherently social nature of business and of making money.[2]

In this study I shall explore further the social aspects of moneymaking, focusing not on business practices but rather on the social and economic networks that helped urban residents make a living in a variety of ways. By the early fifteenth century, Saint-Omer was no longer an international entrepôt but had found new prosperity as a regional center of some importance, helping to integrate the economies of Picardy, Artois, and the Low Countries.[3] I will use an unusual source for exploring its residents' social and economic networks: the accounts of Saint-Omer's treasurers (the Comptes des Argentiers). In the first half of the fifteenth century the *argentiers* often were recruited from the commune's ruling council, the *échevins*. Individuals of financial substance and acumen, the *argentiers* were responsible for keeping track of the city's expenditures and revenues, regularly reporting on the commune's financial status, and producing the accounts used in this study. Perhaps as added insurance that they would perform their tasks honestly and competently, they were expected to use their own resources to advance money to the city when revenues fell short.[4]

The Comptes des Argentiers provide a glimpse of Saint-Omer's society through the particular lens of municipal finances. Through the accounts, we learn about individuals' economic behaviors and relationships as these intersected with the business of governing the town and protecting its various interests (and those of its citizens). The Comptes make record of people paying rents on houses, shops, market stalls, fields, pastures, and open spaces, and paying fees and fines. They list the names of the purchasers of municipal annuities and the right to farm the city's various excise taxes, and devote page after page to the detailed lists of payments to those who invested in the public debt. In the section devoted to the commune's expenses, the accounts record the payment of pensions for dozens of municipal servants and officials, wages for laborers, and payment for services ranging from legal representation at the Parlement of Paris to dog catching (and disposal).[5] The

---

[2] Reyerson, *Art of the Deal*; Murray, *Bruges*; Murray, "Of Nodes and Networks," pp. 2–4. See also Reyerson, *Business*. Reyerson discusses the shifts in the study of medieval commerce in *Art of the Deal*, pp. 1–3; see also Sortor, "Business of Business."

[3] Sortor, "Saint-Omer," pp. 1483–99.

[4] Archives municipales (hereafter Archives), Comptes des Argentiers, 1415/16, 1416/17; d'Hermansaart, "Les Argentiers," pp. 274–86, 300, 314–17. The detail and coverage of Saint-Omer's Comptes des Argentiers compare favorably to the various municipal accounts described by Walter Prevenier in "Quelques aspects," pp. 140–44.

[5] For example, the city paid Tanne Cots, the widow of Lamin Lamesins, for his work catching and destroying six hundred dogs (at 2 d. par. per dog: "pour pieche"): MS Comptes des Argentiers, 1415/16, fol. 101r.

Comptes record expenses for the seemingly endless work of repairing municipal properties of all sorts: pipes and fountains, buildings, walls, gates and locks, waterways and roads. They make note of the purchase of delicacies like heron for the tables of the powerful *échevins* and their guests, and the cost of the final meals of prisoners destined for the gibbet. They record the purchase of workaday items, such as wax and parchment, rope, and bricks. Even the costs linked to the account books themselves—from the purchase and lining of the paper to the binding of the books—find their way into the Comptes des Argentiers.

Every entry records an economic exchange between the city and an individual, sometimes several people. In instances where two or more individuals appear in an entry, or where an individual appears in two or more contexts in the accounts, we have an opportunity to reconstruct a variety of economic relationships. Understandably, the Comptes shed light on only a portion of the economic activities taking place in Saint-Omer. Most money changed hands without making a stop in the city's coffers and therefore left no record in the accounts. Nevertheless, this source presents information about a broad cross-section of economic activities and the kinds of relationships that made them possible. The following pages will explore the economic networks of three people from different walks of life: a money changer, a taverner, and a hard-working handyman with a boat.

A few explanatory comments may be useful for the reader. First, several currencies common in the Low Countries and northern France circulated in Saint-Omer. The *argentiers* translated the value of these currencies into a money of account, the *livre parisis*. Second, Saint-Omer's fiscal year began at Easter. This paper will identify the fiscal year in hyphenated form (e.g., 1415/16). Dating of individual transactions will follow this notation unless the *argentiers*' clerk indicated the day or month when they took place. Third, following many, multistranded connections of even a few individuals strains the narrative form. For this reason, this preliminary exploration of the economic networks of the residents of Saint-Omer focuses on just two years: 1415/16 and 1416/17. To further simplify these complicated narratives, I have included among the case studies two individuals whose life stories and economic interests overlapped. I have also provided a visual depiction of the profitable relations of these two individuals. The third case study does not need this kind of visual depiction. Fourth, and last, spelling of names was not standardized in the Middle Ages. It is common to see variant spellings for the same name even in a single entry. This paper uses the most common variant of each name. I have resisted modernizing names (e.g., "Bouloignge" is not modernized to "Boulogne"), but have inserted punctuation and accent marks wherever these seem necessary.

Demoiselle Peronne le Grise

Our first case study involves the economic network of demoiselle Peronne le Grise, whom the account book of 1416/17 identifies in an entry regarding rent for a house and shop on Saint-Omer's Exchange. Hers was a network that linked her to business partners Catheline de Wissoc and Jehan Pollart, and through them to Robert Bachelier, a young clerk serving in the finance side of the municipal government, and his wife, Maroie. It also connected Peronne to the Saquespée family: Jaques, Jehan, Agnes, and Betrix, and through Betrix to a wealthy and influential family involved in money changing.

Peronne le Grise was far from exceptional in making her way into Saint-Omer's accounts. Records of women's moneymaking and spending activities are abundant in the Comptes. They reflect the kinds of economic behaviors typical for a northern European town in the later Middle Ages. Women appear in the Comptes des Argentiers as employers and employees, and as owners of property, fishing boats, and mills. They paid fines to the commune when they were caught breaking the city's laws and commercial regulations, and sometimes they ended up in prison. Women fulfilled their deceased husbands' obligations by delivering goods, collecting payments, paying rents, and maintaining membership in the city's prestigious merchant guild (usually, but not always, for their underage sons).[6] In the accounts we see a small slice of their commercial activities. Only women, for example, sold *toilles* (linen textiles) at Saint-Omer. Others were involved in the production and sale of inexpensive cloth (*draps deskirez*) and women's items (*keuvrechefs*) and in retail cloth sales. The accounts occasionally record women renting stalls in other trades' halls as well.[7] It was as investors in annuities offered by the city, however, that women appear most frequently in the Comptes.

Saint-Omer sold annuity-like instruments called *rentes viagères* (or *rentes à vie*, and *rentes à deux vies*) to fund its public debt. These *rentes*, or annuities, were an

[6] One widow appears in both 1415/16 and 1416/17 in her own capacity and acting for no one else: the widow of Willem du Taillich continued to pay for membership in Saint-Omer's Hanse. Unlike other widows making these payments, she was not listed as paying with or for her husband's heirs (MS Comptes des Argentiers, 1415/16, fol. 22r; 1416/17, fol. 35r).

[7] For example, in 1416, the widow of Jehan le Mol rented a stall in the "halle des boulangers," the widow of Thomas le Commele rented a stall in the "halle des wantiers," the wife of Jehan le Honelt paid fees on the retail sale of cloth, Jaquemine le Barsilhauwere and the wife of Robert d'Amman rented stalls along with other sellers of "draps deskirez," and the wife of Ancret Baignat paid for a "demy estal" (half stall) in the mercers' hall (the account emphasizes that the only items she sold there were "keuvrekefs"): MS Comptes des Argentiers, 1415/16, fol. 9v; 1416/17, fols. 10r–11v. Women's entrepreneurial activities in fourteenth-century Ghent were numerous and varied; Nicholas, *Domestic Life*, pp. 70–106. For women's entrepreneurial activities in the Low Countries and Germany see Howell, *Women, Production*, pp. 87–94, 152–58. Howell also notes the presence of women drapers in early modern Diksmuide, a town not far from Saint-Omer ("Women's Work," p. 208).

important part of the finances of cities in northwestern Europe during the Middle Ages. They were a means of raising substantial revenues and they also figured significantly in cities' annual expenditures.[8] In the early fifteenth century, Saint-Omer paid 11 percent annually on the purchase price of annuities bought for one life, and 10 percent on those purchased for two lives.[9] These were investments for the well off; the smallest purchase recorded in 1416/17 was £171 par., although there is evidence of a few that must have sold a few years earlier for around £110 par. (see the annuity payments collected by Jaque and Jehan Saquespée, below). Of the women whose names are recorded in Saint-Omer's account books, those who invested heavily in these annuities tended to have the most dense economic networks. Women investing in these annuities often did so in partnership with husbands, children, and other relatives and friends. These fellow investors shared annuity payments or sometimes belonged to groups of individuals who purchased separate annuities (and subsequently received annual payments) on the same day. Women also appear in large numbers paying rent for shops, market stalls, warehouses, fields, and residential property. The women who rented houses, cellars, and shops in the most important commercial districts—the Grant Markiet, the Vieux Markiet, and the "Cange" (Exchange)—almost always did so with their husbands or were identified as widows. Nine women and twenty-one men were identified as renting or having recently rented these commercial properties in 1415–17, and demoiselle Peronne le Grise was among them.[10]

Peronne le Grise shared a life tenure in a house and shop on the Exchange with the demoiselle Catheline de Wissoc and Catheline's husband

---

[8] See the excellent discussion of the history of *rentes* and their role in urban finance from the thirteenth to the fifteenth century in northwestern Europe, in Munro, "Medieval Origins," pp. 518–33. Nicholas likens *rentes* to bond issues (*Metamorphosis*, pp. 213–23). See also Galvin, "Credit and Parochial Charity," pp. 141–42.

[9] For example, in 1416/17 an entry recorded the receipt of the purchase price of an annuity paying, for the duration of the lives of the two holders, at a rate of "10d. the denier." Fisherman Jehan de Honelt paid £200 for an annuity paying £20 par. for the duration of his life and that of his wife Willemine Svincs: "De Jehan de Honelt poissonier de mer qui a accate a prendre sur ledite ville xx livres parisis aux vies de lui et de Willemine Svincs se femme a x d. le denier . . . iic livres" (Comptes des Argentiers, 1416/17, fol. 29r).

[10] A tenth, the wife of Willem Bladque, was not included with him as the renter of three shops on the Exchange, but she did pay *hallage* for a place in the "halle des toilles" (Comptes des Argentiers, 1415/16, fols. 6r–7r; 1416/17, fol. 8 r–v). These properties represent only a portion of what the commune controlled in the three districts. Some rents were due every three years or paid in installments over just a few years. Others took the form of a one-time payment. For example, in 1415/16 the commune collected a single rent payment for a three-year tenure of the *Pot Lavoir*, and Jehan Lambert (who appears in this study's second case study) paid one of three £9 10s. par. installments for a life tenure of a shop previously controlled by Lusse, widow of Pasquin Lambert (Comptes des Argentiers, 1415/17, fols. 6r, 7r).

Jehan Pollart. Peronne's business with Catheline and Jehan on the Exchange was very likely money changing. Women's involvement in money changing in Flanders and particularly in Bruges was first noted by Raymond de Roover in the 1940s and has recently been discussed thoroughly by James Murray.[11] By the fourteenth century, money changers performed a number of financial services in Flanders, including money transfers and deposit banking.[12] Saint-Omer's Exchange was exclusively the location of money changers in the fourteenth century.[13] By the first decades of the fifteenth, at least one goldsmith was located there as well, an occupation well suited for proximity to those charged with, among other things, assessing the precious metal content of the coins they received.[14]

We encounter Peronne le Grise and her partners in the year that they transferred their rights to the property to Jaque Saquespée, who paid the city £6 par. "for a house and shop . . . that the said Jaque holds for the duration of the lives of Jehan Pollart, his wife demoiselle Catheline [de Wissoc], and demoiselle Peronne le Grise, daughter of the deceased Baudin le Gris, and presently wife of Tassart d'Averhoud" (see figure 1).[15] The account stipulates that Peronne was "ad present" the wife of Tassart d'Averhoud. This qualification of her "present" marital status indicates that Tassart was not her first husband. Moreover, Tassart did not share Peronne's claim to the house and shop, an unusual arrangement, judging from similar entries in the Comptes. It was also unusual for a married woman, let alone one married at least once previously, to be identified in relation to her deceased father, but Peronne was. In Bruges, money changing was a family business into which some men married,[16] but there is no indication that Peronne's husband participated in the business. Tassart d'Averhoud's economic activities, if he was active at that time, left no record in the accounts for these two years. He did have financial expertise, however, and was sufficiently prominent to have served for a short while many years earlier as a *juré* in the municipal government. *Jurés* were the city's financial officers, charged with overseeing the commune's revenues and

---

[11] Roover, *Money, Banking*, pp. 171–74; Murray, *Bruges*, pp. 155–77.

[12] Murray, *Bruges*, p. 122.

[13] Derville, *Saint-Omer des origines*, p. 237.

[14] In 1416/17, the goldsmith Renaut le Vacque paid the commune 102s. 10d. par. for three shops on the Exchange adjoining the mercers' hall: "De Renaut le Vacque orfevre pour iii escoppes . . . ou cange joignant le porte de le halle des merchiers . . . cii s. x d." (Comptes des Argentiers, 1416/17, fol. 8v). It is not clear whether the mercers' hall was located on or adjacent to the Exchange.

[15] "De Jaque Saquespee pour une maison et escoppe qui soloit tenir Pierre Lomme estans ou cange que ledit Jaque tient les vies durans de Jehan Pollart et de demoiselle Catheline se femme et demoiselle Peronne fille de feu Baudin le Gris ad present femme Tassart dAverhoud . . . vi livres par" (Comptes des Argentiers, 1416/17, fol. 8r). Catheline is identified as Catheline de Wissoc in a later entry (fol. 42v).

[16] Murray, *Bruges*, pp. 171–77.

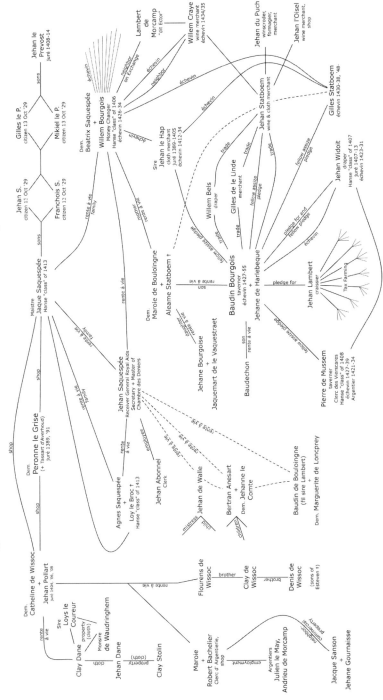

Figure 1. Economic Networks of Peronne le Grise and Baudin Bourgois, 1415 and 1416

expenditures.[17] Peronne's business partner, Jehan Pollart, demonstrated similar financial credentials with his own relatively short stint as *juré* some two decades after Tassart's service.[18] A number of individuals advanced from the office of *juré* to membership in the commune's ruling council, the *échevinage*, but this was not the case for either Jehan Pollart or Tassart d'Averhoud.

In addition to their money-changing business, Peronne's partners Catheline de Wissoc and Jehan Pollart invested in annuities (*rentes viagères*) sold by the city. Catheline and her husband Jehan received each year on two different dates annuity payments totaling £52 10s. par. These payments represented initial purchases amounting to the substantial sum of £525 par. Every September 11, Catheline and Jehan each received £15 par. on individually held annuities, and seven days later they collected another £22 10s. par. on a jointly held annuity.[19] Three other people joined Catheline de Wissoc and Jehan Pollart in receiving payments on September 11. Flourens de Wissoc, son of Estevene, was undoubtedly related to Catheline. The Wissocs were a large extended family occupying positions in the communal government through much of the fourteenth and fifteenth centuries. Flourens collected £30 par., roughly the equivalent of a year's employment for an unskilled laborer.[20] Neither he nor his two brothers served in a high-level government position as *échevin* or *juré*.[21] The account books make no more mention of Flourens in 1415/16 and 1416/17, so we will turn our attention briefly to the other investors in the September 11 annuity: Robert Bachelier and his wife, Maroie.

Robert Bachelier and Maroie received roughly half the amount paid to Flourens or to Catheline de Wissoc and her husband Jehan Pollart that day. Robert and Maroie each received an annuity payment of £7 par. As clerk of the *argenterie* in 1416/17, Robert Bachelier was charged with collecting and recording rent and other payments for the city's treasurers, the *argentiers*. His pension as clerk was £24 par., roughly two-thirds that paid to the *argentiers* for their services. In 1416/17, Robert's income from his clerical duties doubled. In that year, the

[17] Tassart d'Averhoud served as one of twelve *jurés pour le commune* in 1389 and 1391. *Jurés* were charged with oversight "sur les revenues et mises de la ville," as quoted in Justin de Pas, "Listes des membres," pp. 16, 43. Saint-Omer boasted among its citizens and residents the lady and later the seigneur of Averhoud, but I cannot establish a connection with Tassart.

[18] Jehan Pollart served as a *juré* in 1404/05, 1406/07, and 1408/09 (Pas, "Listes des membres," pp. 48–49).

[19] Comptes des Argentiers, 1415/16, fol. 39r; 1416/17, fol. 42v.

[20] The city paid manual laborers 2s. 6d. par. per day. Assuming full employment for 250 days results in an annual income of about £31 par.

[21] Flourens de Wissoc had two brothers, Denis and Clay. Denis collected an annuity payment of £20 par. on May 13 each year. Denis de Wissoc also paid for a stall in Saint-Omer's tanners' hall (Comptes des Argentiers, 1416/17, fols. 10r, 40v, 162v). Their father, Estevene, deceased by 1416/17, also did not appear in the registers of the *échevins* and *jurés*.

city paid him an additional £24 6s. 2d. par. for especially onerous duties involving extra travel and work ("grant vacation et travail"). The additional compensation was broken down into two payments: £14 for receiving rents on houses, market halls, and stalls (*hallages* and *estalages*) and fees for membership in Saint-Omer's Hanse, and £12 for writing out receipts, certifications, and quittances for all work done for the city.[22] The account books also record that Robert Bachelier purchased the 4.5 *rasières* of wheat that Nicaise Pigache paid as rent to the city. In 1415/16 Robert paid 27 sols *monnaie courant* per *rasière*; in 1416/17 he paid 26s./r.[23] Most payments in kind to the city were nominal, such as a single capon. In contrast, Pigache's payment was substantial, and something that the commune would want to monetize. Robert's purchase of Pigache's payment did just that, in a transaction that mingled his public role as clerk with his private interests.

Another source of income for Robert Bachelier was the business he ran from the shop that he rented in the Grant Marquiet, a prime business location. Perhaps it was his wife Maroie who ran the shop while Robert was traveling about collecting payments on behalf of the city.[24] Robert and Maroie were probably a young couple when we first encounter them in the account books, financially comfortable and able to take advantage of the opportunities presented by Robert's official activities. Robert, who proved himself so useful to the commune in 1416/17, continued to provide essential services over the following decades. He eventually advanced to the office of clerk for the Cambre du Conseil, and in 1436 enjoyed an annual pension of £40.[25] Let us return once more to Peronne le Grise and explore another group of relationships stemming from her partnership with Catheline de Wissoc and Jehan Pollart. In 1416/17, Master Jaque Saquespée took over paying the £6 par. rent and presumably also took over the usufruct of the property for the duration of the lives of Peronne, Catheline, and Jehan.[26] Jaque Saquespée was then probably relatively early in his career; in 1415/16 he made the third of what would be ten annual 40s. par. installments in the purchase of a membership in Saint-Omer's prestigious merchant guild, the Hanse.[27] Membership in the Hanse

---

[22] Comptes des Argentiers, 1416/17, fol. 115v.

[23] Comptes des Argentiers, 1415/16, fol. 8r; 1416/17, fol. 9v. Robert's acquisition would have supported a household of six to eight people. A *rasière* was roughly the equivalent of 442.8 liters. See Tits-Dieuaide, *Formation des prix*, p. 263; and Aymard, *Venise*, p.17.

[24] However, Maroie was not listed as having tenure in the shop. Robert paid an annual rent of 24s. for the shop. The neighboring shop was rented by the married couple Jaque Sanson and Jehane Gournaise (Comptes des Argentiers, 1415/16, fol. 6v; 1416/17, fol. 8r).

[25] As excerpted in d'Hermansart, "Argentiers," pp. 393–94.

[26] See n. 15, above.

[27] The price of membership in the Hanse amounted to £20 par., spread out over ten annual payments. The installments could be completed by a man's widow and heirs (Comptes des Argentiers, 1415/16, fol. 22r).

indicates that Jaque was involved in long-distance commerce. In the two years covered by this study, however, there is no mention in the account books of Jaque supplying the city with goods or of other commercial activity (which, in the latter case, could mean simply that he was fortunate in not needing the city's help to extricate him from a conflict). Fourteen years later, in 1429, Jaque Saquespée's two sons enrolled as citizens of Saint-Omer alongside the two sons of Jehan le Prevost. All four boys were under the age of twenty-one when they enrolled, and so this youthful network undoubtedly was formed around their fathers' shared economic interests. Indeed, Jehan le Prevost was also involved in finance, having served as a *juré* on at least four occasions.[28]

We gain a further glimpse into Jaque Saquespée's profitable relations in 1415/16 and 1416/17, in the section of the Comptes des Argentiers devoted to the commune's payments to annuity holders. Receiving annuity payments together with Jaque each May 16 and November 26 were his brother, *maistre* Jehan Saquespée, and Agnes and Betrix Saquespée.[29] All of these individuals (or their spouses) were involved in the money business. Each year on May 16, Jaque Saquespée collected a modest payment of £11 10s. on the lives of himself and his brother Jehan. Like Jaque, Jehan Saquespée was involved in the handling and transfer of money. Jehan worked in public finance as both the receiver general of the royal taxes called *aides* for the counties of Artois, the Boullenois, and Saint-Pol, and as the secretary and master of the Chambre des Deniers, positions he would continue to hold for at least the next twenty years. Assisted by his clerk Jehan Abonnel, he received £1,339 6s. 4d. par. for the king's share of the *aides* at Saint-Omer in 1416/17.[30] Every November 26, Jaque also collected an annuity payment along with Agnes and Betrix Saquespée. Each collected £10 par. on that day. Agnes's husband Loys le Broc had joined the Hanse the same year as Jaque, but by 1415 he was dead. The absence of any mention of Agnes in

---

[28] Archives BB.59.16. All four boys claimed the right to enroll by virtue of their fathers' *bourgeois* status. As sons of citizens (*filii*), they had the right to enroll as citizens without paying the entry fee until their twenty-first birthday. After that point they were required to enroll as *extranei* and pay a fee of 10s. par. (see Sortor, "Measure of Success," p. 175 and n. 46). Unfortunately only a handful of the citizen lists that include the enrollment of *filii* (the sons of citizens) survive. Jehan le Prevost served as *juré* in 1408/09, 1410/11, 1412/13, and 1414/15 (Pas, "Listes des membres," pp. 49–51). Registers of the *jurés* from 1415/16 to 1479 are no longer extant.

[29] Jaque received £11 10s. par. on May 16 and £10 on November 26 (Comptes des Argentiers, 1415/16, fol. 40r; 1416/17, fols. 46v, 48r).

[30] The funds were transported to the treasury at Arras by Jaquemart Coutay, Baudin Boutry, and Jaquemart de Jeury, *sergens des aides du roy* (Comptes des Argentiers, 1415/16, fol. 47r; 1416/17, fols. 49r, 164r). A short excerpt from the Comptes of 1435/36 shows that Jehan was still serving in this capacity in 1435 (d'Hermansart, "Argentiers," pp. 384–85).

the 1416/17 account book leads to the conclusion that she did not long survive her husband.[31]

The other Saquespée to collect an annuity payment with Jaque each November 26 was Betrix, wife of Willem Bourgois (var.: Borgois). Betrix Saquespée and Willem Bourgois enjoyed a joint life tenure in the Cherf Volant, a high-rent house and money-changing business (*cange*) on the Exchange. Their next-door neighbors were a future *échevin* and a member of a prominent family that dominated city government for years.[32] In 1415/16 Willem Bourgois paid the final installment of his membership fee for the merchant guild. The account book for 1416/17 uniquely identified him as the "money changer of this city," an expression suggesting an official relationship between Willem and the communal government. He served Saint-Omer in the capacity of money changer on a number of occasions, valuing orphans' goods and converting them into currency for investment until the children reached majority.[33] In 1416/17, he traveled to Lille and Tournai to settle Saint-Omer's obligations with people there who had invested in annuities (*rentes à vie)*. He was charged with the task of renegotiating the city's annual payments, the value of which had been adversely affected by recent currency devaluations, and arranging for the transfer of funds to investors.[34] Baudin and Betrix's network extended even further, to their neighbors and his Hanse "class," and to his association with members of the *échevinage*. These, however, take us far from Peronne le Grise and her partners in that house and shop on the Exchange.

The Comptes des Argentiers for 1415/16 and 1416/17 say little directly about Peronne le Grise. We know who her father and husband were, have a very

---

[31] Loys le Broc died between 1413/14 and 1415/16, when the accounts show Agnes Saquespée and Loys Broc's heirs paying for "the third year" of his Hanse membership. There is no mention in the accounts of the repurchase of Agnes's annuity by the city.

[32] "Item le maison et cange qui tient Willem Bourgois ou cange qui le dit Willem doit tenir les vies de lui et demiselle [Betrix] Saquespee se femme" (Comptes des Argentiers, 1415/16, fol. 12r). Willem Craye and Lambert Morcamp (going by the name of Ector) rented houses next to Willem and Betrix's (Comptes des Argentiers, 1415/16, fol. 131v). Willem Cray (var.: Craie) served in the *échevinage* from 1434/35 to 1448/49. Lambert Morcamp "dit" Ector belonged to a family frequently represented in Saint-Omer's government for two centuries (see Pas, "Listes des membres," pp. 29–92). Lambert did not serve as *échevin* or *juré*, although he did serve as *sergeant à berghe* during the two years of this study.

[33] Willem Bourgois valued and purchased varieties of coins and silver vessels that comprised the orphans' inheritance. The resulting sum was entered as a receipt for the commune. Two *échevins* served as the *advoez d'orphelines*, charged with administering orphans' inheritance. The accounts describe the city delivering funds to a third orphan, upon reaching majority, "by the hand" of Willem Bourgois (Comptes des Argentiers, 1416/17, fols. 26r, 132v, 171r).

[34] Comptes des Argentiers, 1415/16, fols. 22r, 102v; 1416/17, fol. 56r, 111r. In 1420 Duke Philip the Good dismissed cases regarding the value of annuity payments resulting from the devaluation of the currency (see d'Hermansart, "Argentiers," p. 307).

good idea of her business, and can conclude that in 1416 she retired from the business of money changing. Nevertheless, we can learn a good deal about the network of business, property, and familial interests to which she belonged. From the perspective of just these two years in the account books, twelve individuals in the money business were connected to Peronne le Grise. Family, place, and professional connections overlapped in this network formed by economic interest. Overwhelmingly, those connections involved the business of money changing and public finance.

Baudin Bourgois

In addition to Willem Bourgois's relationships with the Saquespée family, a single *rente à vie* linked him and his wife Betrix to seven other members of the Bourgois family, including his sister Jehane, brother Baudin, and their respective spouses and children. They were linked in this investment through the matriarch of the family, the demoiselle Maroie de Bouloigne. Maroie de Bouloignge had been widowed at least twice. The account books identify her as the widow of Aleame Statboem, her most recent husband. An earlier union had produced Jehane, Baudin, and Willem Bourgois.[35] For our second case study, let us turn to Baudin Bourgois and briefly explore what the account books of 1415/16 and 1416/17 reveal about his connections. By 1416, Baudin had a legitimate male heir (who was also named as a recipient of an annuity payment), apparently the only member of the next generation of the Bourgois family at that time.

Baudin Bourgois is identified as a taverner in the account books. He was engaged in the retail trade in wine and in speculation on Saint-Omer's wine excise. Among his clients was the communal government itself; the Comptes des Argentiers make record of his reimbursement for wine provided for various official functions. By the fourteenth century, taverners belonged to the "urban elite," with connections to Saint-Omer's great merchant families.[36] Together, Baudin Bourgois and his brother Willem represented two of three institutions that, according to Murray, "functioned as one" in commercial centers in Flanders: money changers, taverners, and hostellers.[37] Baudin was also involved in regional and perhaps long-distance trade. In 1415/16 he was among four merchants whose merchandise was seized at Bruges. The seizure was collateral damage stemming from a ban on the export of grain from Artois during a time of poor harvests. Cities in west Flanders were sufficiently dependent upon Saint-Omer for supplies of French grain that they would retaliate against any grain export bans by seizing

---

[35] Comptes des Argentiers, 1415/16, fol. 43r; 1416/17, fol. 164r.
[36] Derville, *Saint-Omer des origines*, p. 177.
[37] Murray, "Of Nodes and Networks."

its merchants' goods and banning the export of dairy products, eggs, poultry, and livestock south into France via Saint-Omer.[38]

According to the account books, the goods that Baudin Bourgois and the other Saint-Omer merchants lost in 1415/16 were fine cloth (*draps*) and "other merchandise." Considering one of the members of that unhappy group of merchants, the "other merchandise" may have included wine; Jehan Statboem was involved in long-distance commerce in wine. He shipped wine through the town of Peronne, where in 1414/15 he ran afoul of the collector of the road tax (*pavage*). In 1415/16 the account books also chart his travels through Dunkerque, where he was arrested on account of a local resident's dispute with Saint-Omer regarding annuity payments in arrears. The following year Jehan Statboem again had difficulty with his wine shipments, this time at the nearby village of Watten, as he brought Rhine wine either in or out of Saint-Omer.[39] Despite these difficulties, Statboem apparently prospered. His relationship with Baudin Bourgois extended beyond their commercial interest in wine and their bad luck in Bruges. They were related by marriage through Baudin's mother, Maroie de Bouloignge, the widow of Aleame Statboem. We cannot know whether Baudin had fond memories of his stepfather Aleame, let alone whether he considered Jehan Statboem a member of his family. There is no question, however, that theirs was a relationship based in some measure on profit and, later in their lives, power.

In addition to their commercial connections, Baudin Bourgois and Jehan Statboem were members of a partnership farming Saint-Omer's excise tax on wine. During both years covered in this study, Baudin speculated on the wine excise. As was the case in many cities, the tax was probably awarded to the highest bidder, who then paid Saint-Omer the agreed-upon price in monthly installments. The commune required that the tax farmer supply guarantors (pledges) who committed

[38] Sortor, "Yperleet Affair," pp. 1093–96; Derville, *Histoire de Saint-Omer*, p. 611. The king of France imposed a grain export ban in 1415; in 1416/17 Saint-Omer sought an exemption from the duke and argued that mutual dependence imposed undue hardship on both sides of the border. Bruges, Ghent, and Ypres also petitioned for a lifting of the prohibition. In 1433 and 1439 Bruges imposed retaliatory export bans on the export of foodstuffs to Saint-Omer by several Flemish towns (see Archives BB.61.10, BB.216.6b, BB.216.11, BB.216.12; Comptes des Argentiers, 1416/17, fols. 56v, 61v; Tits-Dieuaide, *Formation des prix*, p. 148).

[39] The growing division between the French monarchy and the duke of Burgundy in this decade inclined tax collectors in towns like Peronne to ignore Saint-Omer's long-established commercial and tax privileges through much of Artois and Picardy and to classify its trade as foreign rather than French. The case with Peronne was still underway in 1415/16. The monastic lord of Watten, a village located just a few miles from Saint-Omer and along one of the waterways that Saint-Omer's merchants often used, frequently contested Saint-Omer's rights to keep the route unobstructed and for its citizens to travel on it free from any taxation (Comptes des Argentiers, 1415/16, fols. 55r, 56r–v, 61v–62v; 1416/17, fol. 112r).

themselves to pay the sum in case the farmer defaulted. The exact number of guarantors depended on the amount bid and the resources of the bidder and the people serving as pledges.[40] In fifteenth-century Saint-Omer, each guarantor was potentially liable for the entire amount of the tax farm price, a fact explicitly noted in the Comptes at the end of every list of pledges with the phrase "et cascun pour le tout."[41] Bringing in roughly £2,500 annually, the wine excise was one of Saint-Omer's most significant sources of revenue.[42] At this level of liability, guarantors were partners with the tax farmer in a speculative enterprise. Indeed, one of the account books refers to the men serving as guarantors for the farmer of the wine excise as his *consors*.[43] In the two years examined for this study, there were a number of instances where the tax farmer in one year appeared as a pledge for the same excise in the next, and vice versa. For example, Jaque de Bares (var.: Jaque de le Barre) was a pledge for Jehan Lambert in the farm of the leather excise in 1415/16 and was the farm's purchaser in 1416/17. Jehan Lambert was also the farmer of the excise on meat in 1415/16, and Jehan Parisis was his pledge. In 1416/17, they exchanged roles.[44]

People farming these indirect taxes on consumption often chose to speculate on what they knew best. For example, the excise on grain used for baking was controlled by bakers in 1415/16 and 1416/17.[45] Similarly, many persons involved in farming the excises on the sale and measurement of cloth had a connection to the manufacture, regulation, or sale of textiles. People also tended to speculate on excises on related goods. For example, individuals might move from speculating on the tax on grain one year to the beer excise the next. However, judging from the two years covered by the study, the various trades did not normally monopolize the collection of taxes on their products.[46] Rather, a core of individuals seem to

[40] A handful of taxes—or perhaps their farmers—did not seem to require pledges. These included the *cauchie* and *fouich* (road tax), for which sire Nichole de Wissoc paid £550 in 1415/16 and Simon Kendale paid £450 in 1416/17, and the right of *issue* (collected on property of residents leaving the city): Comptes des Argentiers, 1415/16, fol. 14r; 1416/17, fol. 15r).

[41] In fourteenth-century Lucca, guarantors could limit their liability; Meek, "Public Policy," pp. 51–53.

[42] Only the beer excise farm came close to generating the revenue that the wine excise did. In 1415/16 the farm revenues from the *assize de cervoise* was £2,916. It fell sharply to £2,100 the following year (Comptes des Argentiers, 1415/16, fol. 29r; 1416/17, fol. 31r).

[43] Comptes des Argentiers, 1416/17, fols. 26v, 172v. See also Meek, "Public Policy," pp. 56–58.

[44] Comptes des Argentiers, 1415/16, fols. 31r–32v; 1416/17, fol. 29r–30v.

[45] The excise on grain for baking was farmed both years by Jehan Lemps and Jehan Staes. Thomas Voye, Clay le Wette, and Robert le Clut served as pledges one or both years. These men were part of a larger group that paid for stalls in the bakers' hall (Comptes des Argentiers, 1415/16, fols. 8r, 29r; 1416/17, fols. 10r, 31r).

[46] In fourteenth-century Ghent, "tax farmers were usually, though not invariably, syndicates of wealthy brokers who specialized in the types of goods coming under the tax that they farmed" (Nicholas, "Governance" p. 243). In early fourteenth-century Siena, guilds occasionally would control the farming of assizes taxing their products, but only for short periods (see Bowsky, *Finances*, p. 149).

have been more or less deeply involved in this kind of speculation. Counting every position listed in the account books—farmers plus pledges—results in ninety-two "positions," of which sixty-two were held by those who participated in tax farming more than once.[47] Several were involved in three or more of these partnerships, with two individuals involved in six and one person involved in ten deals either as the purchaser of record or as a pledge (see the appendix below). For those tax farmers involved in several excises at once, their specialization seems to have been tax farming itself rather than a particular category of goods.

Baudin Bourgois's involvement in speculation on the wine excise conforms to these general patterns in tax farming at Saint-Omer. As a taverner, he knew the trade in wine well, as did his fellow pledges, the wine merchant Jehan Statboem and Pierre de Mussem, another taverner. Jehan Statboem served as pledge with Baudin in 1416/17 and Pierre served both years. Joining these three professionals in the retail and wholesale wine business were Gilles Statboem (acting as pledge in 1415/16), cloth merchants Jehan le Hap (acting as pledge in 1416/17) and Jehan Widoit (farmer of the excise in 1415/16 and pledge in 1416/17), and wax and candle merchant Jehan Lambert. Jehan Lambert belonged to that small group of men who speculated extensively in Saint-Omer's taxes. He farmed the excise on beer as well as that on wine, and partnered as a pledge in four other tax farms (cloth measuring, cloth, butchered meat, weights, and sea fish) in 1416/17.

The connection of tax farming at Saint-Omer to money changing is not definitive. Money changers were heavily involved in tax farming in Bruges in the fourteenth century.[48] Their ability to move large amounts of money and their relationships with merchants and the city government suited them for tax farming. I cannot yet verify if this was the case for early fifteenth-century Saint-Omer, but the participation of Baudin Bourgois, whose brother Willem was a money changer, is suggestive. Some of Baudin's partners in farming the wine excise also seem to have had networks involving the money business. Jehan Lambert rented property on the Exchange, an indication of involvement in money changing. And Baudin's fellow pledge, the taverner Pierre de Mussem, later served as an *argentier*.[49]

Baudin Bourgois's economic relationships, as reflected in the accounts for 1415/16 and 1416/17, concentrated heavily on the wine trade. They were also

[47] Forty-nine individuals farmed the assizes and other taxes in 1415/16 and 1416/17, either as the tax farmer of record or as a pledge. Almost three-fifths of these appeared just once during this period.

[48] Roover, "Les comptes communaux," p. 92; Murray, *Bruges*, p. 161, 173. Until the mid-fourteenth century pledges for tax farmers at Siena were exclusively bankers; see Bowsky, *Finances*, p. 125.

[49] For the duties of *argentiers*, see above, n. 4. Pierre de Mussem served as *argentier* between 1421 and 1434 (d'Hermansaart, "Argentiers," pp. 314–17). Jehan Statboem also seems to have provided financial services in the case of the delivery of £378 *monnaie courant* representing the inheritance of Malin and Grielle, orphans of Danel du Wez, to the *argentiers* in 1416/17 (Comptes des Argentiers, fols. 26r, 172r). For Jehan Lambert, see above, n. 10.

overlapping: fellow speculators in the wine excise participated in regional or long-distance commerce with Baudin; relatives invested in the public debt with him. We get a hint of the later successes of Baudin Bourgois and his brother Willem from the registers of *échevins*, the commune's executive body. Beginning in the mid-1420s, both men served as *échevins*, alternating with each other.[50] Baudin served in office a very long time, well into the 1450s. His brother Willem's name disappears from the register in 1434, but for at least a decade there was a continuous representation of the Bourgois family on the commune's ruling council. And, alongside the Bourgois brothers, served four of the six men who once partnered with Baudin in the wine assize: Gilles Statboem, Pierre de Mussem, Jehan le Hap, and Jehan Widoit.[51]

Pierre le Tammacre

The last case study takes us from the shops on the Exchange and the investment circles of the wealthy to the waterways on which many people in and around Saint-Omer made their living. One of those people was Pierre le Tammacre. Perhaps better than the other two examples, Pierre's story helps delineate what can and cannot be known about the relationships recorded in Saint-Omer's municipal account books. Pierre le Tammacre's name was recorded ten times in the two years covered by the Comptes des Argentiers: seven times in 1415/16 and three in 1416/17. Few others appear so many times in the period of this study, and most of these were influential, wealthy men engaged in a variety of economic activities. In contrast, the range of activities and relationships in which we see Pierre engaged was limited. Despite the number of times that his name appears in the account books, all indications are that he was a humble man who earned his bread doing back-breaking work. The account book entries describe him variously: as a boat owner (*navieur*), a boat owner's servant (*varlet de navieur*), and as a laborer (*ouvrieur*). However, he was not without a network of economic relationships that helped him earn his bread in Saint-Omer.

The city's records link Pierre le Tammacre to fifty-seven people. Although abundant, the connections that the account books record for Pierre are of just two

[50] Willem Bourgois served as *échevin* in 1426/27, 1428/29, 1432/33, and 1434/35; Baudin served regularly every other year from 1427/28 to 1455/56. Individuals were eligible to serve as *échevins* and *jurés* only in alternate years (see Pas, "Listes des membres," pp. 54–63).

[51] Jehan Widoit served as *juré* from 1407 to 1413. The register of *jurés* after this date is missing, and when we next see Widoit it is as an *échevin* in 1423–31. Pierre de Mussem served from 1427 to 1439 and Gilles Statboem from 1430 to 1438 (Jehan Statboem was not listed in the extant records as either a *juré* or an *échevin*). Jehan le Hap was a senior member of the group, having served as a *juré* 1389–1405, and then after a hiatus returning to serve as *échevin* 1412–34 (see Pas, "Listes des membres," pp. 43–57).

sorts: those related to fishing or fish selling, and work on public projects. We first encounter his name in the section of the Comptes des Argentiers recording the city's expenditures stemming from a five-week visit by the duke of Burgundy in 1415/16. Pierre was one of twenty *varlets de navieurs* who helped provision the ducal household with fish. The four boat owners employing them were the widow of Guerart le Hepple, who provided two boats for the task, and Willem le Wert, Baudin le Bloc, and Simon Smerheuze, each of whom supplied a single vessel. Baudin le Bloc and Simon Smerheuze are identified elsewhere in the accounts as shipwrights.[52] Baudin le Bloc and Willem le Wert appear elsewhere in the accounts, paying rent for houses in "le Petit Ghierquin," a neighborhood close to one of the city's main ports and the home of many boat owners and shipwrights.[53] Unfortunately, the account book does not specify for which of the four boat owners—or with which of the other servants—Pierre worked. He was not among the suppliers of foodstuffs the following year, when the duke again visited Saint-Omer.

In addition to this single entry regarding the provisioning of the ducal household, Pierre le Tammacre's name appeared in the account book's section regarding expenditures on several public projects related to the city's waterways. Saint-Omer's waterways varied from small, shallow routes providing access to neighboring communities and market gardens to a river deep enough to bring in ships from the coast.[54] Given the low elevation of this region, Saint-Omer waged a constant battle against silt. The city also was vigilant regarding obstacles placed in or across the water routes. Take, for example, the low bridge at Watten, which halted merchants like Jehan Statboem as they moved their merchandise to and from the sea or along the main inland waterways that linked Saint-Omer to the cities of west Flanders. Forced to unload their boats before proceeding, the city's residents could be taxed (in violation of its privileges).[55] Even the humble work of clearing routes of muck and obstacles could be an act of defense of the city's rights. Thus, for example, an entry in the 1415/16 account book explains the payment of 60 sols par.: "To Jehan le Bloc, Clay Diers, Pierre le Tammacre, Jehan Maillart, Pierre Fierlebeen, et Jehan Benedit, each of the six for four days at 2 sols 4 deniers, for having destroyed and removed the [fishing] weirs recently built in the city's Great River between Vieux

[52] Comptes des Argentiers, 1415/16, fols. 103r, 159v. In the first half of the fifteenth century, the duke of Burgundy, as the count of Artois, was Saint-Omer's most direct though not its ultimate lord.

[53] Comptes des Argentiers, 1415/16, fol. 2r; 1416/17, fols. 2v– 3r. The Petit Ghierquin was located outside of the city walls, a short walk from the Haut Pont.

[54] Within Saint-Omer's walls was a canal deep and wide enough to accommodate ships of four to six tons; see Derville, *Histoire de Saint-Omer*, p. 37.

[55] Sortor, "Ieperleet Affair," pp. 1077–78; Comptes des Argentiers (1425/26); Archives BB.204.4 (1424), BB.204.1–.2 (1425), 204.3–.6 and 203.21–22 (1427), 203.14 (1427–35), 204.3 (1429); Blockmans, *Handelingen van de leden*, pp. 283–84, 330, 338, and 353–57, nos. 234–36, 278, 287, and 301–2.

Moustier and Gravelines [Saint-Omer's seaport], and then destroying all of the other weirs in the public waterways around the city, as these weirs infringed on the city's rights and liberties. For this [work], 60 sols. par."[56]

Beginning in mid-March and continuing through September, the work of clearing and repairing Saint-Omer's waterways took place. Teams of men inspected the waterways in their boats, breaking and removing fishing weirs and illegal structures, dredging, clearing out plants and fishing lines in and along their banks, and then transporting and spreading the soil on the city's pastures and paths.[57] Nearly three thousand boatloads of soil were taken out of the canals and rivers and moved elsewhere in one project alone. A different category of men—shipwrights and well-to-do fishermen (*poissoniers*)—conducted boat tours of the routes for Saint-Omer's *échevins* and other officials.[58]

In 1415/16 and 1416/17 maintenance of the waterways was overseen by the city's "maistre maresquier," Andrieu Smekart. During that time, Andrieu Smekart employed fifty-three men. Pierre le Tammacre worked on several projects along-side thirty-four other workers, in teams ranging from two to twelve. There was a good deal of overlap in team membership. Sixteen individuals worked on two or more projects with Pierre. Also appearing in Pierre's work teams was another man with the distinctive Le Tammacre name and eleven other men who had family members working on projects for Andrieu Smekart (including Tassart and Climent Smekart). In addition to demolishing obstacles, transporting silt in their boats, and helping improve adjacent pastures, Pierre le Tammacre and another team member, Jehan Maillart, appear once in the 1415/16 account book using their boats to transport materials to a road project.[59] Not surprisingly given the nature of their work, a few individuals with whom Pierre worked seem to have had connections with those supplying fish to the ducal household in 1415/16. In one case, the link is indisputable. Guerart le Heple (var.: Hesple) worked on a team

---

[56] "A Jehan le Bloc, Clay Diers, Pierre le Tammacre, Jehan Maillart, Pierre Fierlebeen, et Jehan Benedit sont eux vi pour cascun iiii jours ii s. vi d. pour jour cascun pour avoir rompu et oste tous les les wers qui de nouvel estoient fait en le grant riviere de le ville en allant entre le Vieux Moustier et Gravelines et enseuit avoir rompre tous les autres werpes qui estoient fais es autres communes reivieres entour de icelle ville lesquelx wers y estoient en empechant les franchises et libertes de le ville. Pour ce ici lx s par." (Comptes des Argentiers, 1415/16, fol. 137r).

[57] Depending on the local geology, artificial waterways and those modified by human beings tended to silt in. Weirs for ponding water for fish ponds, mills, or locks presented obstructions to water traffic, and could lead to silting as well as flooding upstream (Blair, "Transport and Canal-Building," pp. 262–71). See also Rippon, "Waterways," pp. 224–26.

[58] They moved 2,828 boatloads of soil (*neifs*) at 34s. par./100 (Comptes des Argentiers, 1415/16, fols. 137r–140r; 1416/17, fols. 111r–v, 154r–155v). *Poissoniers* included fish farmers raising fish in ponds, a profitable business according to Desportes, *Reims et les Rémois*, p. 360.

[59] Comptes des Argentiers, 1415/16, fol. 123v.

with Pierre in 1415/16. The connection with the widow of Guerart le Heple, boat owner and provisioner of fish to the ducal household that same year, is certain but its exact nature (as son, nephew, or ill-fated husband) is unclear.

Pierre le Tammacre earned the typical wage paid by the city to unskilled laborers: 2s. 6d. par. per day. At times this was supplemented by compensation for the use of his boat (*neif*), for which he received another 4d. per day. By comparison, a skilled craftsman working for the city received a daily wage of 3s. 6d. par.[60] In 1415/16 Pierre worked more than twenty-eight days (the number of days for one project was not specified) and earned £4 8s. 4d. par. In 1416/17 he worked a good deal less for the city (thirteen days) and earned just £1. We only see evidence of Pierre's work, of course, as it appears as an expense in the city's account books for these two years. His work clearing and dredging the waterways in and around the city was seasonal. How was he employed when he was not working on public projects for Andrieu Smekart? Probably doing much the same sort of thing: hard manual work, most (if not all) of it linked to the waterways around the city, and much (but not all) of it using his boat. He probably did some fishing. As a boat owner he may also have worked transporting merchandise, particularly in the busy winter season when the canals and rivers were full.[61] If Pierre did work transporting goods, he may have subcontracted his services to a larger shipper.[62]

Conclusion

What preliminary observations can be drawn from the information that the account books of 1415/16 and 1416/17 provide about moneymaking networks in the fifteenth century? The stories that the Comptes tell about Pierre le Tammacre, Baudin Bourgois, and Peronne le Grise point to three tentative conclusions. First, complexity matters. The strongest, and potentially most profitable, networks were made up not simply by the number of economic connections but also by the density of interconnections. Compare, for instance, the networks of Pierre le Tammacre with those of Baudin Bourgois and Peronne le Grise. The boatman's connections were abundant; few others appearing in the account books in these two years had so many. Significantly, Pierre's many connections were almost entirely of the same sort: work on the public projects. Furthermore, in all but one case, Pierre

---

[60] In one case a mason's *varlet* earned just 20d. per day (Comptes des Argentiers, 1416/17, fol. 135r).

[61] Nearby Ypres, for example, taxed traffic on its main waterway only between November and March or April (Smet, "Le compte"). In more shallow waterways around Ypres, shippers were required to operate their boats at half capacity during summer months (Busshe, "L'Yperleet," p. 200). Water traffic, particularly along the major routes in this area, however, took place year round; see Sortor "Ieperleet Affair," p. 1073, and Algemeen Rijksarchief, Trésor de Flandre 588.1 (ca. 1416) and 588.3 (1416).

[62] For a case in which a shipper subcontracted transportation to another, see Sortor, "Ieperleet Affair," p. 1074; Archives BB. 201.4 (1390–92).

le Tammacre's connections go no further than the work teams themselves. Most of the people whose names are recorded alongside Pierre's in the account books appear only in the section pertaining to work on the waterways. Their stories, as they are recorded in the Comptes, end there. Indeed, Pierre's single appearance selling fish distinguishes him among his cohort. Compare this truncated network with those of Peronne le Grise and Baudin Bourgois. Their profitable relationships were multiple, various, and multistranded. For Baudin, and also for the husbands of Peronne and her partner Catheline, these connections went beyond work and investments to include influence and power. The significance of the complexity of economic networks is reminiscent of the importance of interconnected relations among Saint-Omer's immigrants. Those who thrived often had multistranded connections based on family, location of origin, and economic interest.[63]

Second, the wealthier and more influential the members of an economic network were, the more women belonged to it. Compare Pierre le Tammacre's masculine connections (with a single possible link to Guerart le Heple's widow) to the networks of Peronne le Grise and Baudin Bourgois. It is also instructive that we see most women, and women in more than one economic capacity, among those involved in finance. Did Pierre's familial and social network include women? It most certainly did. Pierre's work for Andrieu Smekart dredging canals and hauling mud was men's work, so opportunities for discovering the women in Pierre's network are limited. Yet, this fact in itself is significant. As they are revealed by the Comptes des Argentiers, the relationships by and through which Pierre earned his living were completely masculine.

Third, much as their rural counterparts, city dwellers in the later Middle Ages tended to diversify their economic activities within a particular scope of expertise. Pierre le Tammacre and Baudin Bourgois were engaged in a variety of moneymaking activities. Pierre fished, worked on the public projects, and at times transported materials for the projects. In the two years covered by this study, Baudin's moneymaking activities included selling wine retail, engaging in regional and perhaps long-distance commerce, investing in the public debt, and speculating on the city's tax revenues. Although the two men pursued very different economic paths, in both cases their diverse enterprises drew on a common theme of expertise and resources. Pierre had his boat and his knowledge of the rivers and canals around Saint-Omer. Baudin had his knowledge of wine and its trade, and his familiarity (through his family and its connections) with public finance. The potential for Baudin to form and capitalize on networks linked to his activities was clearly greater than for Pierre, judging from the kinds of connections that we see for each.

[63] Sortor, "Measure of Success," pp. 181–83.

In comparison to Pierre le Tammacre and Baudin Bourgois, the only activity in which we see Peronne le Grise in these two years is her involvement in the money changer's shop. Overall, women appear in the account books engaged in a more narrow range of activities than do men. Also, their names are recorded in the accounts less frequently than those of men of the same social position. (Take, for example, Agnes and Betrix Saquespée, whose names appear in a number of contexts in the Comptes, but less often than do those of Jehan Saquespée or Betrix's husband Willem Bourgois.) However, the network of Peronne le Grise reveals a pattern of activities defined by expertise and resources that is similar to those of Pierre le Tammacre and Baudin Bourgois. Peronne's network was extensive and varied, and focused one way or another on the business of money. It begins with her business partnership with Catheline de Wissoc and Jehan Pollart in a shop on the Exchange. The network continues through the partners' financial connection to Jaques Saquespée and through Jaques and Betrix Saquespée to a prominent and powerful money changer, Willem Bourgois. Catheline de Wissoc, Jehan and Jaque Saquespée, and Peronne le Grise were also connected to others in the money business: to those who collected and managed royal and ducal tax monies and to others who served as municipal finance officers as *clercs*, *argentiers*, and *jurés*. Among the various economic activities and interests that defined her network of profitable relations, it is remarkable how many people, particularly within two steps from Peronne, were occupied with the business of tracking, recording, receiving, dispensing, valuing, and transferring money.

Clearly, the kinds of networks that Pierre le Tammacre, Peronne le Grise, and Baudin Bourgois could draw on and their potential for engaging in money-making opportunities were defined by gender, wealth, and family. Our glimpse of their experiences suggests the importance of relationships: numerous, multistranded, grounded in expertise and economic interest, and often though not always connected to and through family.

Bibliography

Primary Sources

Archives municipales de Saint-Omer [Archives], MSS Comptes des Argentiers (1415/16, 1416/17, 1424/25), BB.59.16, BB.61.10, BB.204.4, BB.204.1–.2, BB.204.3–.6, BB. 203.21–22, BB.203.14, BB.204.3, BB. 216.6b, 216.11.

Brussels, Algemeen Rijksarchief/Archives générales du Royaume, MSS Trésor de Flandre, 588.1 (ca. 1416) and 588.3 (1416).

Blockmans, Willem P., ed. *Handelingen van de leden en van de staten van Vlaanderen: Regering van Filips de Goede (10 september 1419–15 juni 1467); Excerpten uit de rekeningen van de Vlaamse steden en kasselrijen en van de vorstelijk ambtenaren*. Part 1, *Tot de onderwerping van Brugge (4 maart 1438)*. Brussels: Paleis der Academiën, 1990.

Secondary Sources

Aymard, M. *Venise, Raguse et le commerce du blé pendant la seconde moitié du XVIe siècle*. Paris: SEVPEN, 1966.

Blair, John. "Transport and Canal-Building on the Upper Thames, 1000–1300." In *Waterways*, ed. Blair, pp. 254–86.

———, ed. *Waterways and Canal-Building in Medieval England*. Oxford: Oxford University Press, 2007.

Bowsky, W. M. *The Finances of the Commune of Siena, 1287–1355*. Oxford: Clarendon Press, 1970.

Busshe, Emile vanden. "L'Yperleet." *La Flandre* 13 (1882): 177–246.

Derville, Alain. *Saint-Omer des origines au début du XIVe siècle*. Lille: Presses universitaires de Lille, 1995.

Derville, Alain, et al., eds. *Histoire de Saint-Omer*. Lille: Presses universitaires de Lille, 1981.

Desportes, Pierre. *Reims et les Rémois aux XIIIe et XIVe siècles*. Paris: A. et J. Picard, 1979.

Finances et comptabilités urbaines du XIIIe au XVIe siècle: Actes du colloque internationale de Blankenberge du 6–9 septembre 1962, pp. 31–67. Brussels: Pro Civitate, 1964.

Galvin, Michael. "Credit and Parochial Charity in Fifteenth-Century Bruges." *Journal of Medieval History* 28 (2002): 131–54.

Glénisson, Jean, and Charles Higounet. "Remarques sur les comptes et sur l'administration financière des villes françaises entre Loire et Pyrénées (XIV–XVIe siècles)." In *Finances et comptabilités*, pp. 31–67.

Greve, Anke. "Hôteliers et marchands de la Hanse à Bruges aux XIVe et XVe siècles." In *Les Marchands*, ed. Vandewalle, pp. 99–104.

d'Hermansart, Pagart. "Les Argentiers de la ville de Saint-Omer: Rentiers, les clercs de l'argenterie." *Société des antiquaires de la Morinie* 27 (1901–2): 265–468.

Howell, Martha C. *Women, Production, and Patriarchy in Late Medieval Cities*. Chicago: University of Chicago Press, 1986.

———. "Women's Work in the New and Light Draperies of the Low Countries." In *The New Draperies in the Low Countries and England, 1300–1800*, ed. N. B. Harte, pp. 197–216. Oxford: Oxford University Press, 1997.

Hunt Edwin S. *The Medieval Super-Companies: A Study of the Peruzzi Company of Florence*. Cambridge: Cambridge University Press, 1994.

Hunt, Edwin S., and James M. Murray. *A History of Business in Medieval Europe, 1200–1550*. Cambridge: Cambridge University Press, 1999.

Marshall, Richard K. *The Local Merchants of Prato: Small Entrepreneurs in the Late Medieval Economy*. Baltimore: Johns Hopkins University Press, 1999.

Meek, Christine. "Public Policy and Private Profit: Tax Farming in Fourteenth-Century Lucca." In *The "Other Tuscany": Essays in the History of Lucca, Pisa, and Siena during the Thirteenth, Fourteenth, and Fifteenth Centuries*, ed. Thomas Blomquist and Maureen Mazzaoui, pp. 41–82. Kalamazoo: Medieval Institute Publications, 1994.

Mertens, Jacques. "Un réseau commercial européen: Hildebrand Veckinchusen à Bruges." In *Les Marchands*, ed. Vandewalle, pp. 112–20.

Molho, Anthony. *Florentine Public Finances in the Early Renaissance, 1400–1430*. Cambridge, MA: Harvard University Press, 1971.

Munro, John. "The Medieval Origins of the Financial Revolution: Usury, Rentes, and Negotiability." *International History Review* 25 (2003): 505–62.

Murray, James M. *Bruges, Cradle of Capitalism, 1280–1390*. Cambridge: Cambridge University Press, 2005.

———. "Of Nodes and Networks: Bruges and the Infrastructure of Trade in Fourteenth-Century Europe." In *International Trade in the Low Countries (14th–16th Centuries): Merchants, Organisation, Infrastructure*, ed. Peter Stabel, Bruno Blondé, and Anke Greve, pp. 1–14. Leuven: Garant, 2000.

Nicholas, David. *The Domestic Life of a Medieval City: Women, Children, and the Family in Fourteenth-Century Ghent*. Lincoln: University of Nebraska Press, 1985.

———. "The Governance of Fourteenth-Century Ghent: The Theory and Practice of Public Administration." In *Law, Custom, and the Social Fabric in Medieval Europe: Essays in Honor of Bryce Lyon*, ed. Bernard S. Bachrach and David Nicholas, pp. 235–60. Kalamazoo: Medieval Institute Publications, 1990.

———. *The Metamorphosis of a Medieval City: Ghent in the Age of the Arteveldes, 1302–1390*. Lincoln: University of Nebraska Press, 1987.

Pas, Justin de. "Listes des membres de l'échevinage de Saint-Omer 1144–1790." *Memoires de le société des antiquaires de la Morinie* 28 (1906–7): 1–565.

Prevenier, Walter. "Quelques aspects des comptes communaux en Flandre au Moyen Âge." In *Finances et comptabilités*, pp. 111–45.

Reyerson, Kathryn. *The Art of the Deal: Intermediaries of Trade in Medieval Montpellier*. Leiden: Brill, 2002.

———. *Business, Banking and Finance in Medieval Montpellier*. Toronto: Pontifical Institute of Mediaeval Studies, 1985.

Rippon, Stephen. "Waterways and Water Transport on Reclaimed Coastal Marshlands: The Somerset Levels and Beyond." In *Waterways*, ed. Blair, pp. 207–27.

Roover, Raymond de. "Les comptes communaux et la comptabilité communale à Bruges au XIVe siècle." In *Finances et comptabilités*, pp. 86–102.

———. *Money, Banking, and Credit in Mediaeval Bruges: Italian Merchant-Bankers, Lombards and Money-Changers; A Study in the Origins of Banking*. Cambridge, MA: Mediaeval Academy of America, 1948.

Smet, A. de. "Le compte de la navigation entre Bruges, Nieuport, et Ypres (1395–1404)." *Annales de la Société d'émulation de Bruges* 72 (1930): 174–80.

Sortor, Marci. "The Business of Business in the Middle Ages." *Journal of Urban History* 34 (2008): 712–17.

———. "The Ieperleet Affair." *Speculum* 73 (1998): 1068–1100.

———. "The Measure of Success: Evidence for Immigrant Networks in the Southern Low Countries, Saint-Omer 1413–1455." *Journal of Family History* 30 (2005): 164–90.

———. "Saint-Omer and Its Textile Trades in the Late Middle Ages: A Contribution to the Proto-Industrialization Debate." *American Historical Review* 98 (1993): 1475–99.

Tits-Dieuaide, Marie-Jeanne. *La formation des prix céréaliers en Brabant et en Flandre au XVe siècle*. Brussels: Editions de l'Université de Bruxelles, 1975.

Vandewalle, André, ed. *Les Marchands de la Hanse et la banque des Médicis*. Bruges: Stichting Kunstboek, 2002.

Appendix
Tax Farmers and Pledges at Saint-Omer 1415/16 and 1416/17

	1415/16	1416/17
Road taxes	**sire Nicole de Wissoc** Tassart de Thiennes and illegible v^c l livres parisis	**Simon Kendale** Willem de le Hofstede, Tassart de Thiennes iiii^c l livres x s.
Cloth measurement	**Jehan Gornay** Pierre le . . . et Mahieu Copillon *(Copillan)* xlvii livres iii s. monnaie royale	**Mahieu de Kerscamp** Jehan Lambert xlix livres xvj s. viij d.
Issue	**Henry de Halettes** iii^c livres parisis	**Henry de Halettes** iiii^c livres
Draps (le caltre)	**sire Nicole de Wissoc**	**Tassart de Thiennes** No pledges vi^c lxxi livres xi s. iii d.
Wine	**Jehan Widoit** Baudin Bourgois, Gilles Statboem et Pierre de Mussem v^m iiii^c xvi livres xii s	**Jehan Lambert** sire Jehan le Hap, Jehan Widoit, Jehan Statboem, Baudin Bourgois, Pierre de Mussem vi^m v^c livres
Grain		**Jehan Robbes le jovene** Baudin le Pap le jovene, Pierre de Rexpoude, Leurens Couders, Jaque des Bares vi^c xx livres
Illegible (1415/16)	**Jaque de le Bar** Jehan Knapgoet et Tassart de Thienes	
Beer	**Baudin le Pap le jovene** Gilles le Hogge, Leurens Couders, Jaquemart Couders, Jaque des Bares, Henry Dune, Simon Litelbond, Lambert Vinchent, Hue Pietavaine, et Jehan le Pap fil Baudin, ii^m ix^c xvi livres	**Jehan Lambert** sire Loy le Coureur, Baudin le Fevre ii^m c livres

Purchaser of Cense in bold, pledges in plain font

Appendix *(continued)*

	1415/16	1416/17
"Bakers' wheat"	**Jehan Lemps** Jehan Staes, Thomas Voye, et Clay le Wette ii^c iiii^{xx} xii livres	**Jehan Lemps** Robert le Clut, Jehan Staes, Thomas Voye iii^c xxxvi livres
Draps and Sayes	**sire Nicole de Wissoc** Jehan Sturpe	**Jehan Knapgoet** Tassart de Thiennes, Jehan Lambert mil iii^c lxxi livres xix s. iii d.
Dyeing	**Thomas de Volcrincove** Pierre de Rexpoude c xli livres xiii s	**Thomas de Volcrincove** Pierre de le Rexpoude, Jehan de Noyon cxliiij livres iiii s.
Tanned leather, cordovan, bazane	**Jehan Lambert** Jehan Knapgoet, Jaques de Bares ii^c iiii^{xx} v livres	**Jaque des Bares** Gilles le Hoghe, Tassart de Nieles ii^c lii livres vii s.
Meat	**Jehan Lambert** Jehan Parisis c iii livres	**Jehan Parisis** Jehan Lambert ciii livres
Wood	**Jehan Lambert** Henry de Halettes, Clay Stolin, Enguerran le Sauvage ii^c lxvii livres xvi s.	**Jehan le Sauvage** Willem Gamel, Henry de Halettes iii^c vi livres xviii s. ob.
Pois et Gratterie	**Pierre Voye** Jaque des Bares, Jehan Knapgoet, Tassart de Thiennes ix^c liii livres xvi s.	**Enguerran le Sauvage** Jehan Lambert, Jehan LOste mil xxx livres
Sea fish	**Gilles le Gay** Willem Musebecque, Pierre Coquillon ii^c lvii livres x s.	**Jehan L'Oste** Jehan Lambert, Colart le Fevre ii^c xx livres

Coinage Debasements in Burgundian Flanders, 1384–1482: Monetary or Fiscal Policies?

John H. A. Munro

Coinage Debasements in Late Medieval Europe

C OINAGE DEBASEMENTS were one of the most prominent and most harmful features of the later medieval and early modern European economies, though they can also be found in the ancient and earlier medieval worlds. In the later medieval era, the first monarch to undertake large-scale aggressive debasements was Philip IV of France (r. 1285–1314), in 1295, thereby inciting a two-century-long "guerre monétaire."[1] The subsequent Burgundian rulers of the Low Countries (r. 1384–1482), which included the French royal fief of Flanders, were among the most active and avid practitioners of this "dark art." Debasement was a policy that the eminent French philosopher Nicolas Oresme, bishop of Lisieux, chaplain and counselor of King Charles V (r. 1364–80), had thoroughly condemned—unless undertaken with public approval—on the eve of the Burgundian era, in his famous *Treatise on Coins* (*De origine, natura, jure et mutationibus monetarum*).[2] The first Valois duke of Burgundy, Philip the Bold (r. 1384–1404), son of King John II of France and younger brother of King Charles VI (r. 1380–1422), was certainly well aware of Oresme's strong views on debasements.

Nevertheless, the rationale, nature, forms, and economic and social consequences of medieval and early modern coinage debasements remain very

---

[1] Serres, *Le variations monétaires*; Girard, "La guerre des monnaies"; Graus, "La crise monétaire"; Grunzweig, "Les incidences internationales"; Cipolla, "Currency Depreciation"; Cazelles, "Quelques reflexions."

[2] The tract is also known as *De moneta*, written ca. 1355; see Johnson, *"De moneta."* On Oresme see also Spufford, *Money and Its Use*, pp. 295–304; Bridrey, *La théorie de la monnaie*; and the discussion below.

contentious issues in an ongoing vexatious debate. Two central issues must be resolved. First, were coinage debasements pursued principally as monetary policies or as fiscal policies? Second, whatever the rationale, were the consequences beneficial or harmful to the economies and societies of this era?

Two eminent economists, Thomas Sargent and François Velde, in a much-praised monograph on *The Big Problem of Small Change* (2002), have recently set forth a compelling view that is substantially different from Oresme's hostile verdict. They contend that most medieval and early modern coinage debasements were rational and public-spirited monetary policies undertaken to remedy the chronic, pervasive shortages of "small change," or petty coins.[3] "Small change," as they rightly contend, was generally a "big problem" for premodern Europe, for these were the coins, and the only coins, that the poor, most of the peasantry and laboring classes, and the substantial majority of the population used to purchase food, drink, and other basic necessities.[4]

In support of their arguments, Sargent and Velde cite conclusions from an important article of Debra Glassman and Angela Redish: namely, that "the motive for most debasements was to maintain adequate supplies of coins, not to raise government revenues."[5] While Glassman and Redish analyzed the monetary problems of only early modern Europe, many historians of later-medieval Europe have similarly contended that coinage debasements had often been a necessary remedy for the periodic deflationary "bullion famines" and thus general monetary scarcities of this era.[6]

---

[3] Sargent and Velde, *Big Problem*, pp. 5, 7–8, 10, 40, 152, 187, 261, 321, 324, and esp. p. 161: "We interpret many of these debasements as having been designed to cure shortages of small change, not primarily to gather seigniorage."

[4] A basic fault in their book, however, is the failure to define such terms as "small coins" and "full-bodied coins." For most medieval economic historians, small or petty coins were those that were a fraction of the silver penny, such as the English half-pence and farthings, and the Flemish mites (*mijten*), but even pennies also became, after centuries of debasement, such "small change" (e.g., in later medieval France, Italy, Castile).

[5] The quotation is from Sargent and Velde, *Big Problem*, p. 261n1. See Glassman and Redish, "Currency Depreciation." Their thesis is, however, more complex: that coin shortages or disappearances were due to periodic undervaluations of especially silver coins (in relation to gold), primarily the result of wear and tear, clipping, counterfeiting, and "bimetallism," and thus that "depreciation [debasement] was frequently a response to undervaluation, rather than a trade policy or a means to raise revenue or reduce government debt" (pp. 75, 95). Their thesis does not, in these terms, differ from my explanations for defensive coinage debasement, as explained below.

[6] For this debate, see Munro, *Bullion Flows and Monetary Policies*; Munro, "Wage-Stickiness"; Miskimin, *Economy of Early Renaissance Europe*, pp. 25–32, 132–50; Miskimin, "Money and Money Movements"; Day, *Medieval Market*; Spufford, *Money and Its Use*, pp. 339–62; and the sources cited in n.1, above. Note that these views differ from those of Sargent and Velde, which concern only shortages of "small change."

Medieval Coinages, Moneys of Account, and Debasements

Whatever the rationale for late medieval coinage debasements, any answers to questions about their possible roles as monetary or fiscal policies must begin with an examination of the technology of minting and coinage alterations, which in turn requires a firm understanding of the relationship between coined money and moneys of account. The money-of-account system of Burgundian Flanders, the *pond groot* Flemish, and the prevailing systems used in medieval and early modern western Europe, were all based on one devised by Charlemagne's government between 790 and 802, in which 1 pound weight of fine silver was valued at 1 *libra* or pound of money of account, consisting of 20 shillings (s.), each of which contained 12 pence (d.), so that 1 pound = 240d.[7] One pence in money of account was always equal or tied to the currently circulating silver penny, whatever its current fineness and weight. That original link between the pound weight of silver and the pound money of account was severed forever by subsequent coinage debasements, over many centuries.

In the simplest terms, a *physical* debasement means the reduction of the quantity of precious metal (silver or gold) contained in the currently circulating coins of a given face value, and thus also in the related unit of money of account: the penny, the shilling, and the pound. Such physical reductions in the precious metal of the coin itself took place either by reducing the weight of the coin itself or by diminishing its precious metal fineness by adding proportionately more base metal—usually copper—or, most commonly, by both methods combined.[8] The consequence was to increase the number of coins with a given face value (the penny or the shilling) minted from a pound or *marc* weight (244.753 g) of commercially fine silver.[9]

---

[7] According to Fournial, *Histoire monétaire*, pp. 24–27, the weight of the Carolingian pound was 489.6 grams; and that is the accepted weight for the later livre (pound) of Paris. Until 1201, when Venice struck its matapan, the penny was the largest silver coin struck in western Europe. See Spufford, *Money and Its Use*, pp. 226–27.

[8] In France and the Low Countries the fineness of silver coins was reckoned in terms of commercially fine silver, known as *argent le roy*, which was 23/24 or 95.833 percent pure, with 4.167 percent copper alloy. *Argent le roy* was reckoned in terms of 12 deniers, each of which contained 24 grains, and thus 288 grains in total (see tables 1 and 3). The fineness of gold coins was reckoned everywhere in terms of carats, so that fine gold coins had 24 carats (which, however, were probably 23.875 carats = 99.479 percent pure gold, with 0.53 percent copper: the actual fineness of Florentine florins, Venetian ducats, and English nobles). Gold coins were commonly alloyed with both silver and copper. Thus the Burgundian gold florin, from 1466, contained 19 carats of gold, 4 carats of silver, and only 1 carat of copper.

[9] The mint weight used in France and the Low Countries was the *marc de Troyes* = one half of the French pound, or *livre de Paris* = 244.7529 grams (see nn. 7–8, above). The *marc* contained 8 *onces*, each of which contained 24 deniers, each of which in turn contained 24 grains, for a total of 4608 grains to the *marc*. The medieval English mint weight was the Tower pound, with 12 ounces, each containing 20 dwt (penny-weight), each of which contained 32 grains, for a total of 7680 grains = 5400 Troy grains = 11.25 Troy ounces = 349.9144 grams. In 1525 it was superseded by the Troy pound, also of 12 ounces, with 20 dwt to the ounce and 24 grains to the dwt, for a total of 5760 grains = 373.242 grams. See Munro, "Maze"; Munro, "Money and Coinage"; and especially Tye, *Early World Coins*, pp. 128–41, 163–66.

That meant as well a corresponding increase in the nominal money-of-account value of that pound or *marc* of silver, known as the *traite*, as can be seen in tables 1 and 3, below.

Another form of coinage debasement, which normally applied only to gold coins and to more full-bodied, high-valued silver coins, was to increase their official exchange rates, or nominal money-of-account values. It must be clearly understood that gold values, and thus exchange rates, were always expressed in terms of the silver-based money of account that had been established for that particular jurisdiction or territory. Such increases in official coinage values were necessary to maintain the former value relationships of these high-valued coins, if they were not similarly debased in fineness and/or weight, with the debased silver penny and other fractional coins.

That can be best understood by relating the market values of gold and silver coins, when, in this era, the typical bimetallic mint ratio for these two metals was about 11:1 or 12:1. A debasement of just one of the two coinages—say, the silver coinage—would have altered the bimetallic mint ratio to favor silver and thus to "disfavor" gold, simply because that debasement would have increased the relative money-of-account value of the new silver coins. To some extent a small change in the bimetallic ratio may have been undertaken to favor one of the two metals and thus to encourage a greater influx of that metal into the prince's mint. But too drastic an alteration of the mint-ratio in favor of one metal (e.g., silver) would have led to the outflow of the other metal (gold). To prevent that exodus, the prince would have had to raise the official exchange rate or money-of-account value of the gold coins, or debase the gold coins as well, by the physical means just discussed.[10]

The reasons why monetary transactions were almost invariably conducted in coin, even debased coin, rather than in bullion (or ingots), is fundamental to comprehending the nature and rationale for debasements in medieval and early modern Europe. First, almost everywhere it was illegal to trade or to make transactions in bullion. For the law in most medieval countries or principalities stipulated that all precious metals deemed to be bullion (*billon*)—excluding metals for licensed goldsmiths—had to be surrendered to the prince's mint for coinage.[11] Secondly, even if it had been legal to make transactions in bullion, doing so would

[10] The same set of changes were also required for full-bodied, high-value silver coins, if they were left unchanged during a debasement of lower-value coins. See table 1.

[11] The modern English term *billon* is commonly defined as a base or petty coin, one in which silver constitutes less than half of the metallic content, and thus copper (base metal) accounts for over half. The medieval term—*billon, billoen, billio*—meant instead "bullion": any precious metal, including demonetized coinage, domestic and foreign, that was legally required to be surrendered to the prince's mint for coinage. It excluded precious metals in jewelry, plate, objets d'art, dress, and raw materials legitimately acquired by jewelers and goldsmiths for their crafts. See Munro, "Billon—Billoen—Billio."

not have been economically feasible in terms of the required transaction costs: the cost of weighing the bullion, assaying it for fineness, and determining its market or exchange value. Gold and silver coins were generally worth more than their intrinsic bullion costs simply because they were a fully recognized legal tender—with the ruler's stamp of authorization or approval.

Official, legal tender coins were thus a cost-saving medium of exchange. That savings on transaction costs constituted an *agio*, or premium, that legal tender coins thereby commanded over their intrinsic bullion values. Merchants paid for that premium in their mintage fees, which were deducted from the total value of the coins produced from their bullion.[12] As long as this *agio* that coins thereby commanded over bullion was at least equal to the sum of the mintage fees, merchants would have continued to deliver bullion to the mints. Conversely, whenever domestic coins lost that *agio*, merchants would no longer have delivered bullion to the prince's mint and would most likely have either hoarded or exported that bullion to some foreign mint.[13] Usually those precious metals so exported were sold to a foreign prince's mint as bullion and converted into his debased coins, provided that the aggregate value of those coins, so converted from the bullion, commanded a higher purchasing power there than in the country from which the original coins (or bullion) had been exported.

The objectives of any coinage debasement—whether undertaken by fineness, weight, or value, or some combination thereof—were twofold. The first was to increase the number of coins of any given coin denomination that could be struck from a pound weight or *marc* of fine metal delivered to the mint and thus to increase the aggregate money-of-account value of the total coinage struck from bullion so delivered (the *traite* value). Such increases in both the number and the money-of-account values of coins so struck can also be seen in tables 1 and 3. The second objective was to induce a much greater influx of precious metals into the ruler's mint: from both domestic and foreign bullion, including demonetized coins.[14]

Burgundian Coinage Debasements as Monetary Policies: The Debate about the Late Medieval "Bullion Famines," Deflation, and Their Resolution

The foregoing analysis of the mechanics and economics of medieval coinage debasements certainly seems to provide good prima facie grounds for contending that they were indeed undertaken as monetary policies specifically to remedy periodic or even chronic coin scarcities during the well-known "bullion famines" of

---

[12] For the economics of these mintage fees—brassage and seigniorage—see below, pp. 331–32, and table 1.

[13] For reasons why coins would lose that *agio*, see below, pp. 322, 328.

[14] See n. 11, above.

late medieval western Europe. Earlier in my academic career I had cavalierly dismissed any notions of so-called bullion famines or any general problems of monetary scarcities, contending that inadequate supplies of bullion delivered to a prince's mint constituted a situation very different from any general scarcity of coinage in any regional economy and had to be explained by deficient mint policies.[15]

Since then, however, my research convinced me that much of western Europe, and especially the Low Countries and England, did indeed experience severe monetary scarcities, if not precisely full-fledged bullion famines, with attendant problems of severe deflation, especially in two periods: from ca. 1375 to ca. 1415 and from ca. 1440 to ca. 1470.[16] Furthermore, my research on Burgundian monetary history also convinced me that there were good prima facie grounds for contending that the late medieval Low Countries experienced a chronic and severe shortage of petty coins: for the Burgundian mint accounts show that rarely was more than 1 percent of the bullion received minted into these petty coins, known as *monnaies noires* (because they were largely copper).[17]

The evidence for such monetary scarcities can be found in the drastic declines in mint outputs—often verging on a complete cessation of new coinages—and of deflations that prevailed in northwestern Europe during these two periods (see figs. 1–4). Several of my publications since then have been devoted to this theme, in particular to demonstrating the seriously negative economic consequences of deflation, that is, of a serious, continuous, sustained fall in the price level. I also contended that the late medieval bullion famine era came to an end in the 1470s, after low commodity prices (i.e., deflation) had provided the economic motivation or profit incentive for the two technological innovations that resolved this monetary problem: by increasing the purchasing power of silver. Those innovations, in both civil engineering (water pumps) and chemical engineering (the *Seigerhütten* process), made possible the south German silver-copper mining boom, which in turn quintupled Europe's supply of mined silver from the 1460s to the 1540s (though much was exported).[18] From the 1550s, Europe began receiving even larger influxes of silver from the new Spanish American colonies.[19]

Neither coinage debasements nor any reputed advances in late medieval banking and finance had ever played an effective role in combating the periodic

---

[15] For such views, which I no longer endorse, see Munro, *Wool, Cloth and Gold*, esp. pp. 11–41.

[16] Munro, "Mint Policies"; Munro, "Bullion Flows and Monetary Contraction"; Munro, "Mint Outputs"; Munro, "Monnayage"; Munro, "Deflation"; Munro, *Bullion Flows and Monetary Policies*; Munro, "Wage-Stickiness"; Munro, "Monetary Origins"; Munro, "Before and After."

[17] Munro, "Deflation," in particular table 3, p. 396.

[18] Munro, "Central European Mining Boom"; Munro, "Monetary Origins."

[19] Munro, "Money, Prices, Wages"; Hamilton, *American Treasure*.

late medieval monetary scarcities and deflation.[20] Nor have I ever been able to find any evidence, in the vast documentation now available for Burgundian Flanders, that its rulers ever undertook coinage debasements as monetary policies specifically to pursue any such reflationary monetary objectives, with one minor, indeed trivial, exception.

On August 31, 1457, during the worst phase of the mid-century bullion famine, the Burgundian monetary authorities instructed the Bruges mintmaster to strike a greater number of *monnaies noires*, called *courtes* or double mites (= 1/12th of a penny *groot*), from the alloyed *marc*: 240 per *marc* instead of the previously stipulated number (or *taille*), 216. Two perspectives may be offered on the resulting mint outputs for the quinquennium 1456–60. On the one hand, only 51.302 kg of fine silver were minted—compared to 112 times as much in 1426–30: 5,724.645 kg. On the other hand, 11.4 percent of the fine silver struck in the Flemish mints in the later 1450s (none from October 1458 to June 1466) was coined into mites—and that high percentage may be compared to a typical percentage, as previously noted, of about 1 percent of such silver coined in mites during the rest of the Burgundian era.[21]

Late Medieval "Bullionism" and Defensive Motives for Coinage Debasements

Although late medieval mint and monetary policies in northwestern Europe were otherwise unrelated to current problems of monetary scarcities and deflation, they must be understood in the context of this era's bullionist philosophies. "Bullionism"—producing the medieval roots of early modern mercantilism— refers to all those government policies and measures designed to increase the influx of precious metals into the ruler's lands, and more specifically into his mints, and also related policies designed to prevent the export of precious metals except legal-tender coins.[22] Late medieval bullionist policies may be attributed not just to a ruler's mint-profit motives, but also to the strong, almost universal conviction

---

[20] See Munro, "Bullionism"; Munro, "Patterns of Trade"; Munro, "English 'Backwardness,'"; Munro, "Wage-Stickiness."

[21] These *courtes* had a fineness of 12 grains silver = 4.17 percent *argent le roy*. See Deschamps de Pas, "Histoire monétaire," pp. 123–24, and Munro, "Deflation," in particular table 3, p. 396. This exception is nowhere mentioned in Sargent and Velde, *Big Problem*.

[22] See Munro, *Wool, Cloth and Gold*, pp. 11–41; Munro, "Bullionism"; Munro, "Bullion Flows and Monetary Contraction." Medieval and early modern England was an exception. From 1364 to 1663 Parliament banned the export of all English legal tender coins. See statute 38, Edwardi III, stat. 1, cap. 2 (Jan. 1364), in Tomlins, *Statutes of the Realm*, 1:383, and Rymer, *Foedera*, 3.2:728; and statute 15, Carolus II, cap. 7 (May 1663), in Tomlins, *Statutes of the Realm*, 5:452, sec. 9. See also Munro, "Bullionism," pp. 187–205, 216–39.

that the wealth, prosperity, and power of a realm fundamentally depended upon its stock of precious metals.

Those bullionist policies obviously also became an integral feature of medieval mint policies, especially those designed both to protect the realm against foreign debasements and to permit the prince to engage in defensive coinage debasements. Thus, if the monetary policies practiced by so many late medieval princes may be viewed as aggressive, their victims would have been not only their own subjects but also residents of neighboring principalities. As in any form of warfare, victims of these late medieval *guerres monétaires* would have instinctively sought to defend themselves; and if the best defense is offense, many princes did so by engaging in retaliatory debasements and related bullionist measures.

In pursuing debasements and related bullionist policies, the Burgundian dukes, along with most medieval princes, banned not only the export of precious metals but also the import of foreign coins, especially silver coins. Such foreign coins, so demonetized (denied the status of legal tender), were declared or deemed to be bullion (*billon*) and thus had to be surrendered to the prince's mints.[23] What these rulers clearly perceived, correctly, was the operation of what is called "Gresham's Law": in essence, that cheap money—debased or counterfeit and thus bad money—drives out dearer coins, in the form of better-quality, higher-silver or higher-gold content coins.[24]

Though without specific references to Gresham's Law, Peter Spufford has contended that periodic coinage debasements, instead of alleviating coin scarcities, too often acted only to exacerbate hoarding, with negative consequences for the economy.[25] Gresham's Law assumes that the good coin that is driven out by the influx of debased foreign coins or by the circulation of domestic debased coins is either hoarded, converted into plate, or exported.[26] Indeed, with continuous competitive medieval debasements, much coin and bullion were exported to gain a higher value from foreign mints engaged in aggressive debasements. One can also readily appreciate that virtually all late medieval bullionist policies must be blamed, along with warfare and its consequences, for seriously impeding and diminishing the circulation of precious metals in the European economy. As I have contended elsewhere, late medieval monetary contractions or the periodic bullion famines

[23] See n. 11, above.

[24] See Munro, "Gresham's Law"; Munro, *Wool, Cloth and Gold*, pp. 11–41; and nn. 30, 38, below. This law is attributed to Sir Thomas Gresham (1519–79), a merchant-banker and royal agent in Antwerp and financial advisor to Queen Elizabeth I; he was also the founder of the Royal Exchange in London (1565). But he did not formulate the law as such, and it was well known centuries before.

[25] Spufford, *Money and Its Use*, p. 347: "Fear of debasements, and the instability of money, made men happier to keep their silver in the form of plate, in addition to the desire for ostentation."

[26] See nn. 24, above, 30 and 38 below.

were more the consequence of reduced monetary flows than of reduced monetary stocks, including supposed outflows of bullion in trade with the East.[27]

Clearly, therefore, a common motive for late medieval debasements was purely defensive: to protect a prince's realm and his mints from the economic as well as purely monetary damages inflicted by an influx of debased foreign coins. That was an all the more serious problem when those foreign influxes contained fraudulent or counterfeit imitations of that prince's own coins and thus with a smaller precious metal content. A related problem was the circulation of coins, domestic and foreign, that had been fraudulently clipped or otherwise subjected to a diminution of their precious metal contents.

The same consequences, however, could also have been produced by simple wear and tear of the coins over time, since both silver and gold are soft metals, even when alloyed with copper as a necessary hardening agent.[28] When such clipping, wear and tear, or other diminutions in the precious-metal content of so many coins in current circulation had led to the market's elimination of the *agio*, or premium, that coins commanded over bullion, then, as noted earlier, bullion would have ceased to flow into the prince's mints.[29] That would have forced the prince to engage in a defensive debasement that reduced the silver contents of the penny and related coins to the level of the silver found in the currently circulating coinage. Such a debasement would have restored the *agio* of coinage over bullion and thereby also renewed an influx of bullion into the prince's mints.[30]

Finally, if many medieval debasements were indeed merely defensive, many of those coinage alterations can be understood properly only as reactions to aggressive debasements in neighboring realms.

Burgundian Coinage Debasements:
Aggressive Motives for Fiscal Policies to Finance Warfare

Almost all late medieval mint ordinances, certainly those from France and the Low Countries, include virtual renditions of Gresham's Law, and citations of these

---

[27] See Munro, *Bullion Flows and Monetary Policies*; Munro, "Patterns of Trade"; Munro, "Wage-Stickiness."

[28] See Patterson, "Silver Stocks"; and Mayhew, "Numismatic Evidence." Feavearyear, *Pound Sterling*, pp. 1–45, argues that most English debasements, before those of Henry VIII, were undertaken for such defensive reasons; but medieval England was a monetary anomaly. See nn. 30 and 64, below.

[29] For the concept of coinage *agio*, or its premium in value over bullion, see above, pp. 318, 328.

[30] On this, see Feavearyear, *Pound Sterling*, pp. 1–45. For early modern Europe, see very similar arguments in Glassman and Redish, "Currency Depreciation." For the importance of both coinage "wear and tear" and Gresham's Law in Henry VIII's defensive debasement of 1526, see Munro, "Monetary Policies of Henry VIII," pp. 437–50.

very adverse circumstances, to justify defensive motives for the prince's coinage debasements.[31] Obviously it was better to appear to be the victim than the victimizer. Only in England, however, and there only in 1351 and 1411, can coinage debasements be judged to have been purely defensive; the next one, Edward IV's debasement of 1464, was only partly defensive and certainly much more aggressive.[32] Virtually all debasements in late medieval France and the Low Countries, where the evidence can be weighed carefully, were essentially aggressive in nature even when retaliatory.

In brief, the fundamental aggressive motive to explain so many late medieval coinage debasements was a lust for mint profits. That concept may be difficult to understand in today's world, but in medieval and early modern Europe mints were operated with a goal of producing profits. The term *seigniorage* is still used for the same purpose: to indicate a source of government revenue from printing money.[33] In medieval and early modern Europe, those profits came from the revenues that most (if not all) governments of this era earned by virtue of their rigid monopoly on coinage in their own states or principalities.

If, however, the primary motive for most aggressive debasements was such profit-seeking, what lay behind that princely demand for seigniorage revenues? In my view, the rationale for such debasements, and the real justification from the prince's point of view, was the need for readily available and elastic revenues to finance both warfare and defense. Medieval princes were rarely able to increase their ordinary incomes in the short run, and securing additional revenues from taxes, *aides*, loans, or grants from town assemblies, estates, or other legislative assemblies was difficult and usually involved unwelcome concessions.

The mint and the coinage, however, were the prince's exclusive prerogative, even though that prerogative was sometimes challenged.[34] Often late medieval

---

[31] See Munro, *Wool, Cloth and Gold*, pp. 28, 33, 35n24, 40, 44n6, 49, 58n54, 60, 74n33, 87n58, 101n20, 150n76, 161n19, 169.

[32] Feavearyear, *Pound Sterling*, pp. 15–45; Munro, *Wool, Cloth and Gold*, chs. 1–6.

[33] Investopedia Dictionary, http://www.investopedia.com/dictionary (accessed August 2011): "Seigniorage may be counted as revenue for a government when the money that is created is worth more than it costs to produce it. This revenue is often used by governments to finance a portion of their expenditures without having to collect taxes. If, for example, it costs the U.S. government $0.05 to produce a $1 bill, the seigniorage is $0.95, or the difference between the two amounts."

[34] In England, after Edward III's very minor, defensive debasement in 1351, the 1352 parliament, by its Statute of Purveyors, decreed that the coinage "shall never be worsened, neither in weight nor in fineness (*aloi*)," without its consent. The Crown did observe that parliamentary statute for over a century, until Edward IV's debasement of 1464. Tomlins, *Statutes of the Realm*, 1:322 (stat. 25, Edwardi III, stat. 5, cap. 13). See Munro, *Wool, Cloth, and Gold*, pp. 35, 159–63; Mayhew, "Monetary Background," pp. 62–73. See below for Flanders, in 1418 and 1433, on pp. 334–35; and Spufford, "Coinage"; Spufford, *Monetary Problems*, pp. 1–46.

mints did produce very large seigniorage revenues, as Hans Van Werveke has demonstrated, for example, for the reign of Flanders' Count Louis de Male (r. 1346–84).[35] Few would doubt that such fiscal motives had a strong priority in the coinage debasements of Philip IV and all of his royal successors in fourteenth- and fifteenth-century France. Certainly the aforementioned French philosopher and royal advisor Nicholas Oresme had no such doubts, as stated in his treatise *De moneta* (ca. 1355): "I am of the opinion that the main and final cause why the prince pretends to the power of altering the coinage is the profit or gain that he can get from it; [for] it would otherwise be vain to make so many and so great changes."[36]

The Mechanics and Economics of Profit-Seeking Coinage Debasements

Both the mechanics and economics of debasement as a fiscal policy to earn seigniorage revenues can be seen clearly in table 3, below. It compares the coinage of the Flemish double *groot*, as struck from June 1418 to October 1428, with the new, debased coinage of November 1428. The official exchange value of this coin remained 2d. *groot*, but its pure silver content had been reduced from 1.725 grams to 1.522 grams, for a loss of 0.203 grams, or 11.77 percent of its former (1418) fine silver content. That diminution in silver content had been achieved by reducing both the fineness and the weight of the double *groot*: the former, from 50.00 percent fineness (6 deniers *argent le roy*) or 47.92 percent purity, to 42.59 percent purity (5 deniers 8 grains); the latter from a weight of 1.800 grams (68 cut to the *marc de Troyes*) to 1.588 grams (68.5 to the *marc*). The number of double *groot* coins cut from a *marc de Troyes* of commercially fine silver (*argent le roy*) rose from 136 to 154.125 coins; and thus the change in *traite* or money-of-account value of that *marc* rose from 22s. 8d. (i.e., 136 × 2d.) to 25s. 8d. 6 mites.[37] The consequences can be seen in table 4.

[35] Van Werveke, "De economische"; Van Werveke, "Currency Manipulation."

[36] Johnson, *"De Moneta,"* p. 24: "Videtur michi quod principalis et finalis causa propter quam princeps sibi vult assumere potestatem mutandi monetas, est emolumentum vel lucrum quod inde potest habere; aliter enim frustra faceret tot mutanciones et tantas."

[37] Note, in table 3, that the reduction in the coin's silver content, by 11.77 percent, resulted in a 13.33 percent increase in the value of the *traite per marc de Troyes* of commercially fine silver. Thus, the number of double *groot* coins struck from that *marc* in November 1428, namely 154.125, is 13.33 percent greater than the 136 double *groot* coins struck from the same *marc* from June 1418 to October 1428: that is, a difference of 18.125 double *groot* coins = 36.25d. or 3s. 0d. 6 mites. Note also that this difference in the total number of coins struck from the fine silver *marc* exactly equals the difference between the two *traite* values for the *marc*: 25s. 8d. 6 mites by the November 1428 mint indenture, compared to a sum of 22s. 8d., for the previous coinage, of June 1418. This relationship between debasement and the increase in *traite* values is in accordance with the ΔT (*traite*) = $[1/(1 - x)] - 1$, relating changes involving reciprocals. Its importance is discussed below, pp. 328–31. For definitions of the monetary terms, see nn. 8–9, above.

The Merchants' Gains from Late Medieval Coinage Debasements

For any debasement to succeed, and to induce a much larger influx of bullion into the prince's mints, the mint had to offer merchants who delivered bullion a real gain, or a better price for their bullion (including previous and demonetized domestic coin issues) than that offered by any competing mints. The merchants' actual gains depended on the fulfillment of three conditions. First, the merchants had to receive a greater number of coins, with the same face value, than they had previously received, and a higher value, in terms of goods and gold, than they would have received from any other mint. Secondly, the public, including other merchants, had to accept the newly debased coins at the same nominal or face value, by *tale* (discussed below). The third condition was that these new coins had to retain their purchasing power, at least in terms of goods and services within the domestic economy, within the "short run"—in time for the merchants to spend their new coins.

Comparing the number and the money-of-account values of the double *groot* coins that merchants received for their bullion in June 1418 with those received after the debasement of November 1428, as indicated in table 3, we find that in June 1428 they received, per *marc* of commercially fine silver, 127 double *groot* coins worth 21s. 2d. *groot* (93.38 percent of the bullion delivered); and in November 1428, 144 double *groot* coins, now worth 24s. 0d. *groot* (93.43 percent of the bullion delivered). Their purely *nominal* gain of the extra 17 coins (or 34d.: or 2s. 10d. *groot*) was 13.38 percent. Thus the mint ordinance fulfilled the first of our conditions.

The second condition is the most complex of the three. Why would the public have accepted these newly debased coins at face value, when they contained less fine silver than before? This is a very important question, because several economists have recently put forward two contrary propositions, to prove, in effect, that medieval debasements could not have worked, despite the evidence that debasements were so commonly practiced, and for several centuries. The critics' first argument is that the general populace would not have accepted such newly debased coins at face value, but only at a proportionally lesser or discounted value, that is, in proportion to the amount of silver contained in the immediately preceding coin issue. Such discounting would thus have denied those merchants who converted bullion into debased coins any real gains. In effect, these critics are contending that Gresham's Law did not apply to medieval coinages, and that it is therefore a modern fallacy.[38]

---

[38] See Rolnick and Weber, "Gresham's Law"; Rolnick, Velde, and Weber, "Debasement Puzzle"; Sargent and Smith, "Coinage Debasements"; and Velde, Weber, and Wright, " Model of Commodity Money." A much more nuanced, highly modified view appears in Sargent and Velde, "Big Problem," and especially in the more recent Sargent and Velde, *Big Problem of Small Change* (2002). See an attack on their earlier views in Selgin, "Salvaging Gresham's Law." For even earlier views, influencing Rolnick and Weber, see Miskimin, "Enforcement of Gresham's Law"; and Miskimin, "Money, the Law, and Legal Tender." For my own views, see Munro, "Gresham's Law" (and n. 24, above).

In part that view can be rejected on the various grounds cited earlier to explain why domestic commerce was always transacted in legal tender coins rather than in bullion.[39]

Medieval Hammered Coinages:
Problems of Detecting Changes in Weight and Fineness

An even more compelling argument to explain the general acceptance of even debased legal tender coins at face value can be found in the technology of medieval mints for what is known as "hammered" coinages. In striking silver coins from thin alloyed sheets of metal with the required proportions of silver and copper, the mintmaster's employees first cut out circular disks, known as blanks. The mintmaster or his trained deputy then placed each blank on the anvil-like lower coin dye. He then used a hammer to strike the upper coin-dye placed above the blank, thereby implanting the obverse and reverse stamps with the appropriate symbols or emblems of the prince on each side of the coin. The employees then used shears to trim the disks, which had been flattened and extended by this hammering, into approximately round disks. As a consequence, coins so struck were never exactly the same in size, shape, and weight. Indeed, coin weights were never specified by any measure other than the *taille*: that is, the number cut from the alloyed *marc*, with a tolerance or *remède* of the number of coins (plus or minus), permitted to be struck from each *marc*.

Thus most individuals handling separate and individual coins were never able to tell whether differences between the weights of coins of a given denomination were purely the accidental results of these techniques or the result of fraud, including counterfeiting. From a comparison of the two mint ordinances, we can well understand that the very minute changes in weight would have been very difficult to detect, even for those very few money specialists, usually just money changers and bankers, who were equipped with accurate scales. They in turn might have required sets of perhaps fifty to one hundred coins to detect differences on such scales. Needless to say, most retail merchants, let alone individual customers, would not have been so equipped to undertake such costly tests.

Detecting changes in the coin's fineness was even more difficult, especially when the changes were as small as those indicated in table 3, for the Flemish debasement of November 1428. For, again only money changers and bankers would likely have been equipped with the required device for such testing, known as touchstones: instruments on which coins were rubbed to produce color comparisons, as a gauge of the fineness, or the mixture of silver and

---

[39] See above, pp. 317–18.

copper alloy. Under the best of circumstances, they were very crude measuring devices that were rarely accurate within 5 or even 10 percent.[40] The only certain way to detect and measure changes in silver content after a debasement was by melting the coins, in order to separate the silver from the copper. No merchant, of course, could have afforded to take such drastic measures, though mint officials sometimes did so. Even differences in the stamp on the obverse and reverse sides, if observed, would not have been an indication of the actual changes in value, since such changes took place with changes in princes and mintmasters, without debasements.

Indeed, contrary to some erroneous views in the economic history literature, most people—whether merchants, tradesmen, artisans, laborers, or peasants—almost always accepted coins by *tale*—that is, by number, at face value, without ever weighing, assaying, or otherwise testing them.[41] Indeed, as contended earlier, coins with the prince's official stamp certifying their value circulated with a premium value or *agio* over the comparable value of the bullion contents precisely because their ability to do so provided significant savings on transaction costs, vital for all trades. To be sure, in foreign trade transactions, some wealthy merchants, particularly Italians or Hanseatic Germans, might have tested gold coins in large-value transactions, because the transaction costs of doing so were relatively lower, while the potential costs of fraud were much higher. But very few, if any, would have done so for low value silver coins circulating in domestic trade.

Even if some persons had done so, and discovered deficiencies in the silver content, how and when would they have discounted the value of, say, a penny coin? Consider the fact that in 1300, the Flemish silver penny *groot*, with 11 deniers 12 grains *argent le roy* (95.83 percent fine = 91.84 percent pure), contained 3.794 grams pure silver. But in 1384, when the Burgundian era commenced, its fineness had been reduced to just 6 deniers *argent le roy* (50.00 percent fine), and it contained only 1.173 grams pure silver, only 30.92 percent as much as in 1300 (table 1). Over those years, would its exchange value have been discounted to just one-third of a penny *groot*? Of course not: the 1384 *groot* still circulated at the same nominal value of 1d., just as it had done in 1300.[42] Nevertheless, if confidence in the coin-

[40] Grierson, *Numismatics*, pp. 100–111, 150–55; Grierson, "Medieval Numismatics," pp. 124–34; Grierson, "Coin Wear"; Grierson, "Weight and Coinage"; Girard, "Guerre des monnaies"; Fournial, *Histoire monétaire*, pp. 9–38.

[41] See pp. 317–18, above. But Sargent and Velde, *Big Problem*, pp. 16–19, 22, 75, did conclude subsequently that commercial transactions using coin were generally conducted by *tale*, rather than by weight.

[42] If the debasement reduced the silver content by exactly 10 percent, then by the formula given in n. 37 for changes in the *traite* values—ΔT (*traite*) = $[1/(1 - x)] - 1$—the requisite discount, by this approach, would have been 11.11 percent. Such a discount could not have been achieved and translated into any practical money-of-account.

age in general did wane, especially with increased supplies of counterfeit coins, merchants and tradesmen would finally have resorted to discounting the entire coinage: by raising their prices and thus eliminating, as suggested earlier, the *agio* on coinage, with negative consequences for the prince's mint outputs (see p. 318).

Did Inflation Eliminate the Potential Gains from Debasements?

The second and seemingly compelling objection or counterargument from the critics is that the consequent and quickly ensuing inflation would have eliminated any possible gains from the debasement.

Let us first consider the statistical evidence on coinage debasements, mint outputs, and prices trends in Burgundian Flanders, presented in figures 1–4. That evidence provides convincing proof that these periodic coinage debasements did indeed increase the Flemish coined money supply, and that such increases did lead to some periodic inflations. The pure silver content of the Flemish penny *groot* had fallen even more, during the century-long Burgundian era: from the aforesaid 1.173 grams in 1384 to 0.522 grams in 1482, a loss of 0.651 grams = 55.49 percent of its 1384 content (table 1). During this same era the Flemish Consumer Price Index (base 1451–75 = 100) rose from 122.185 to 193.932, an increase of 71.75 = 58.72 percent (fig. 4).[43] Those figures seem comparable.

But these statistics are misleading in several ways. In the first place, a comparison of diminutions in metal content with rises in prices, in this fashion, is statistically false, since we are dealing with reciprocals. The following is the formula needed to compare the consequence of a reduction of the coin's silver contents with the expected rise in the money-of-account value of a *marc* weight of commercially fine silver (244.753 g)—that is, its *traite* value:[44] ΔT (*traite*) = $[1/(1 - x)] - 1$, in which x represents the percentage reduction of the fine silver content of the penny and the corresponding pence in money of account, and ΔT represents the consequent change in the money-of-account value of a *marc* of fine silver after the coinage debasement. By this formula a 10 percent reduction in the fine silver content of the penny would have produced an 11.11 percent rise in the nominal value of the new coined *marc* of silver and thus a potential increase of 11.11 percent in the coined money supply.

---

[43] For the construction of the Flemish Consumer Price Index, see Munro, "Wage-Stickiness," table 1, p. 231, and Munro, "Builders' Wages," esp. table 1, pp. 1048–49.

[44] For definitions of fineness and weight in terms of the *marc de Troyes*, see nn. 8–9, above. The computation of the *traite* or money-of-account value of a *marc* of commercially fine silver simply involves the calculation of the number of coins of a given denomination struck from the *alloyed marc* (i.e., with the copper added)—a number known as the *taille per marc*—and then a multiplication of that number by the official value of the coin itself; and finally that sum is divided by the fineness of the alloy (as a percentage of purity). Thus the *Traite* = (*taille* * face value)/percentage fineness.

By the crude, simplistic Quantity Theory of Money, that should also have been the rate of inflation. In Flanders, however, the expected rate of inflation over the century 1384–1482, resulting from a 55.47 percent reduction in the penny's silver content, should have been 124.57 percent, by this formula—instead of the far more modest 58.72 percent rise in prices that did occur.[45] While this snapshot is useful for purely heuristic purposes, the real statistical tests would have to be undertaken by measuring the year to year changes in the domestic price index, following each coinage debasement.

The historical lesson is clearly demonstrated in table 2, which relates changes in the Flemish silver coinages to changes in the price level, for each year from 1380 to 1482. Coinage debasements, and consequent increases in money supplies, never produced correspondingly proportional inflations. There are five possible reasons why inflations were never directly and predictably related to coinage debasements. First, coinage debasements rarely succeeded in reminting the entire domestic coined money supply, even if the financial terms should have compelled merchants to surrender all their own current coins to the mint. But many would have chosen to retain their higher-weight specimens, knowing that their higher bullion content would later fetch a higher market value. Second, even if a silver debasement was also designed to attract other sources of bullion, especially from neighboring lands, the expected monetary loss would have been in some outflow of the other metal, gold, for reasons noted earlier. Third, coins did not account for the entire money supply. We must therefore also take account of changes in credit instruments and the supply of credit, a subject that I have considered in several other publications.[46]

Fourth, consider the logic of the modernized Quantity Theory of Money, whose basic formula is M.V = P.y. Any inflationary consequences—that is, a rise in P (Consumer Price Index or CPI)—from an increase in the money supply (M) may have been offset by a decrease in the income velocity of money (V) and/or by an increase in y: net national product (NNP) and income (NNI). The more useful version of the quantity theory is the Cambridge Cash Balances equation: M = k.P.y, in which k is the reciprocal of V, that is, k = 1/V and V = 1/k. The symbol or variable k represents that percentage share of net national income that the public chooses to hold in cash balances, rather than profitably investing those funds or spending them. The reasons for holding cash balances are known collectively as *liquidity preference*, involving a mixture of transaction, precautionary, and speculative motives. According to Keynesian economics, an increase in the money supply without any changes in liquidity preference would have led to a fall in interest rates, which in turn would have led to an increase in k (cash

---

[45] See table 1, below, and the mathematical relationships indicated in nn. 37, 42, and 44, above.

[46] See pp. 319–20 and nn. 20 and 22, above.

balances held). That is the equivalent to a reduction in V, the income velocity of money.

Fifth, perhaps the most important factor was simply the failure of coinage debasements (along with credit instruments) to counteract or fully offset the prevailing deflationary consequences of long-term, widespread monetary scarcities: the prevalent bullion famines noted earlier. One obvious reason why they failed to do so is that coinage debasements were almost always periodic or episodic and thus relatively short-term, as well as being merely regional in their impact. Furthermore, four series of coinage debasements in Burgundian and then Habsburg Flanders were followed by the exact monetary opposite: a coinage *renforcement* or a restoration (usually only partial) and strengthening of the coinage, adding more silver: in 1384, 1389–90, 1433–35, and 1492–93. By necessarily contracting the money supply, in reminting debased coins into necessarily fewer but stronger coins, these *renforcements* themselves had severely deflationary consequences that are readily apparent in figure 4.[47]

We may offer three more specific observations about the inflationary consequences of coinage debasements. First, when price changes did take place following debasements, they did not do so immediately, but relatively slowly, since some time was necessary for the increased number of coins to enter and become part of the coinage circulation. That observation applies also to the previously enunciated proposition: that wholesalers and retailers would ultimately have reacted to a debasement only by raising their prices. Their success in doing so, however, still depended upon the increased circulation of the new coins.

Second, the extent of any subsequent rise in prices was far from being uniform. The price changes for individual commodities depended on both their supply and demand elasticities; and the latter must also be seen in terms of both the price- and income-elasticities of demand.[48] Provided, therefore, that the merchants spent those double *groot* coins quickly enough after receiving their newly debased coins, and spent them on the right selection of goods and services, before prices rose, they would certainly have realized a genuine net *real* gain.

Third, we may observe further that money changers and merchants who gained from delivering bullion to the mints and from quickly spending their increased number of coins benefited from what is now known in economics as asymmetric information: that they were privy to the knowledge of the mint changes that remained unknown, for some time, to the general public.[49] But

---

[47] See table 1.

[48] See above, pp. 327–28; table 2 and figure 4. See also, in support of these views, the evidence cited in Munro, "Monetary Contraction"; Munro, "Mint Outputs"; Munro, "Deflation"; Munro, "Wage-Stickiness"; Munro, "Money, Prices, Wages"; Munro, "Monetary Origins"; Munro, "Before and After."

[49] See Gandal and Sussman, "Asymmetric Information." Note that in 2001, George Akerlof, Michael Spence, and Joseph Stiglitz won the Nobel Prize in Economics for their analyses of markets with asymmetric information.

inevitably such information was disseminated to most of the general public. That information, combined with the increased number of coins in circulation, would have led to some inflation, and thus to some loss, though rarely a total loss, of the net gains from a debasement.

The Mintage Fees: Brassage and Seigniorage

As noted earlier, the mint retained from the bullion supplied a small proportion, usually under 10 percent (table 1), for the stipulated mintage fees, which comprised two items: the brassage, for the mintmaster; and the seigniorage, for the prince. The brassage fee can be readily understood: it cost money to make money. Obviously, the mintmaster had to be compensated for his production expenses: the copper alloy added, the labor costs of production, the capital costs of his tools (hammers, dyes, furnaces, forges, melting pots, shears), and the administrative costs of operating the mint.[50] Those costs were normally modest, except for the petty coinage, the *monnaies noires*, with high copper contents. In accordance with the Flemish mint ordinance of June 1418, the mintmaster retained 7 of the 136 double *groot* coins struck (table 3). That amounted to 1s. 2d. *groot* or 5.15 percent of the bullion delivered. But the mint ordinance for the debasement of November 1428 awarded the mintmaster a miniscule increase of just 1/8 double *groot* = a quarter-*groot*, or just 6 mites. In fact, his share of the total bullion received fell from 5.15 percent to 4.62 percent, an amount that likely was insufficient to cover his increased costs for labor and copper alloy. So much for the view that mintmasters had instigated most debasements for their own profit.

The other mintage fee was seigniorage: the tax that the prince imposed on minting coins, as a fixed percentage of the bullion delivered to his mint, by virtue, as noted earlier, of his official monopoly on coinage within his realm. Counterfeiting was, of course, a very serious violation of the prince's monopoly on coinage and indeed of his sovereignty, and it was usually treated therefore as a capital crime.[51] Clearly, at least in proportional terms, the agent who realized the greatest gain was the prince; in this case Duke Philip the Good. In his 1428 Flemish debasement, his seigniorage tax was increased from 2 double *groot* coins (4d.) to 3 such coins (6d.), a 50 percent rise, increasing his share of the bullion delivered to the mint from 1.47 percent to 1.95 percent (table 3).

Indeed, the single best test for whether a coinage debasement was aggressive, motivated by profit seeking, or merely defensive is whether the prince increased his

---

[50] Since the mint was the property of the prince, he was responsible for the capital and maintenance costs of the mint buildings, but not of the mintmaster's equipment.

[51] See Munro, "Profits of Counterfeiting"; Munro, "Maze."

seigniorage rate.[52] If the debasement had been designed to remedy deficiencies in the coin supply, why would the prince have raised his seigniorage rate? We should consider especially the fact that the higher the seigniorage rate, the lower would have been the mint price for merchants, thus reducing their incentive to bring bullion to that particular prince's mint, in competition with other mints. Calculating the most effective increase in rates was indeed a skilled art.

The prince's increased mint profits were based on two factors: the increase in the seigniorage rate itself, and the debasement's success in increasing the Flemish mint output, subject to the constraints on total mintage fees just noted. As table 4 demonstrates, Duke Philip's 1428 debasement was very successful indeed: from 1428 to 1429, it increased the quantity of silver bullion struck by 1475.68 percent (from 1,078.65 kg to 16,996.01 kg); the current value coinage output, in pounds *groot* Flemish, by 1666.02 percent (from £5,267.28 to £93,021.38 *groot*); and the seigniorage revenues by 1554.47 percent (from £123 to £2,035 *groot* Flemish). As this table also indicates, coinage debasements were subject to rapidly diminishing returns, a condition that often forced princes, as just noted, to engage in subsequent debasements. In this case, however, Duke Philip the Good instead chose, if in response to pressure from the Flemish towns, to reform the Flemish coinage and impose a monetary unification on his Low Countries's domains, in 1433–35.[53]

Debasements and Warfare in the Burgundian Low Countries

Of course, it would be an enormous and tedious task to demonstrate that each of the numerous Flemish coinage debasements was undertaken primarily for such fiscal motives, specifically to finance warfare and defense. Only the major wars need to be cited here.[54] First, under Duke Philip the Bold (r. 1384–1404): the second Van Artevelde or Ghent rebellion (aided by English intervention), from 1379 to 1385; and the Guelders war of 1388. Under Duke John the Fearless (r. 1404–19): the Burgundian-Armagnac civil wars (1411–19), culminating in Duke John's murder at Montereau. His son and successor Philip the Good (r. 1419–67) immediately defied the French dauphin Charles (later Charles VII), by contracting a military alliance with England, whose king, Henry V, had achieved such a major victory over the French at Agincourt in 1415. From 1424 to 1428, during his wars with Charles, Philip also became involved in the Hoek/Kabeljauw civil

[52] See table 1. Note the increase in the seigniorage rates with all the major debasements and their reductions with a return to stronger and stable coinages. For changes in seigniorage charge under Henry VIII (r. 1509–47), for these reasons, see Munro, "Monetary Policies," pp. 442–56, and table 1: part 3, pp. 461–63; table 2: part 3, pp. 470–75.

[53] See p. 334 and nn. 60–61, below.

[54] See Vaughan, *Philip the Bold*; Vaughan, *John the Fearless*; Vaughan, *Philip the Good*; Vaughan, *Charles the Bold*; Calmette, *Golden Age*; Nicholas, *Medieval Flanders*, pp. 317–99.

war in Holland-Zeeland, which also embroiled him in conflict with England, and ended with Burgundian acquisition of these imperial counties. Duke Philip subsequently complained to his subjects how costly these wars were:

> You also well know how, during a lull in the war in France, I had to wage a burdensome and murderous war against the English [Humphrey, duke of Gloucester] in my lands of Holland, Zeeland and Friesland in order to protect Flanders. . . . This war . . . had cost me, besides all the heavy expenses that I incurred throughout this period in the French war, over a million gold *saluts*, which at first I was extremely ill-prepared to find.[55]

The troubled Anglo-Burgundian military alliance finally ended in 1435 with Duke Philip's volte-face, in making peace with Charles VII by the Treaty of Arras, which then led to the Anglo-Burgundian war of 1436–39, complicated by the separate Dutch-Wendish wars of 1438–41.[56] Then, relative peace, and an absence of coinage debasements, ensued over the next two decades, until Philip's son Charles the Bold (r. 1467–77) renewed the Burgundian conflicts with Louis XI's France. That struggle began with the rebel League of the Common Weal in 1465–66, before Charles became duke. That in turn led to Charles's suppression of the French-sponsored revolt of Liège in 1468; his abortive invasion of Normandy in 1471; and then his wars with imperial Alsace, Lorraine, and the Swiss, all allies of Louis XI, culminating in the Burgundian defeat and Charles's death at the hands of the Swiss, at Nancy in 1477. In that year, his daughter Mary married the Habsburg archduke Maximilian (d. 1519). Her accidental death in March 1482 and Maximilian's succession led to protracted civil wars in Flanders and to even more horrendous coinage debasements, ending only in 1492–93. These events are all beyond the scope of this study.[57]

Some Brief Conclusions: Debasements Were Generally More Harmful than Beneficial

We may conclude that late medieval coinage debasements, at least those examined in Burgundian Flanders, were generally more harmful than beneficial. They failed to provide any long-term remedy for the combined problems of chronic monetary

[55] Speech before the deans of Ghent's craft guilds in January 1447, cited (and translated) by Vaughan, *Philip the Good*, pp. 307–8, quoted from the Flemish texts in *Dagboek van Gent*, 1:57–68.

[56] See the sources cited in n. 54, above, and also Munro, "Economic Aspect"; and Munro, *Wool, Cloth, and Gold*, pp. 65–126.

[57] Duchess Mary, unlike her father Charles but following her grandfather's admonition to maintain "la bonne monnoie," had opposed further debasements. The debasement of July 18, 1482, was thus undertaken by the widower Maximilian (see table 1). See Spufford, *Money*, p. 313. See also nn. 62, 64, below.

scarcity and deflation. Indeed, as stressed earlier as a crucial point in this study, the Burgundian rulers always ended their rounds of debasements with severely deflationary *renforcements*. Secondly, as also observed earlier, the combination of coinage debasements and related bullionist measures generally served only to aggravate monetary scarcities by impeding bullion flows and coinage circulations and also by encouraging hoarding. Third, to the extent that debasements did lead to some degree of inflation, that inflation reduced real incomes, since wages normally lagged behind prices, and thus provided an additional tax burden on the entire population.[58] Fourth, debasements injured creditors by reducing the real values of their investment returns and repayments; and in that respect, they damaged Flemish international commercial relations.

Finally, coinage alterations sometimes caused social unrest: understandably so, when, as just emphasized, money wages usually lagged behind debasement-induced rises in consumer prices. But, somewhat paradoxically, the opposite monetary policy, a coinage *renforcement* (strengthening), was the more likely cause of unrest, especially industrial strikes, when Burgundian or civic leaders imposed sudden wage cuts—reductions in nominal money wages—as a necessary component of monetary reform. Yet such unrest, the product of "money illusions," proved to be socially unjustified, because those reforms always led to a deflation in which the fall in consumer prices was greater than the nominal wage cuts, so that real wages actually rose (as they did in the 1390s, 1440s, and 1490s).[59]

Finally, the view that coinage debasements had been undertaken to remedy severe coin shortages, and thus to benefit the public, is contradicted by Flemish public demands, as put forth by the Four Members (*vier leden*: Ghent, Ypres, Bruges, Franc de Bruges), and also by the Burgundian Estates-General, which regarded debasements as a cure worse than the disease. After two of Philip the Good's debasements, Flanders' Four Members forced Philip not to undertake any further coinage alterations for specified periods: in 1418–19, for fifteen years;[60] and in 1433, for another twenty years.[61] Philip, however, broke his first promise, chiefly

---

[58] See Munro, "Usury Doctrine"; Munro, "Wage-Stickiness."

[59] See Munro, "Gold, Guilds, and Government"; Munro, "Wage-Stickiness"; Munro, "Builders' Wages"; and the publications by Van Werveke cited in n. 35, above.

[60] See Munro, *Wool, Cloth and Gold*, pp. 74–76, and p. 75n34 in particular. The most important study on this issue is Spufford, "Coinage." In March 1418 the Four Members of Flanders (*vier leden*) had in fact requested no changes for the next forty years, that "dese munte sal ghedeurch zijn zonder angheven ofte veranderen xl jaer"; but that period was reduced to fifteen years in the final ordinance, in Algemeen Rijksarchief, Rekenkamer, reg. no. 1158, fol. 7v. When Philip became count in his own name in 1419, the Four Members required him to repeat this promise; Gilliodts–Van Severen, *Cartulaire*, 1:526, no. 630. See above, n. 51.

[61] Munro, *Wool, Cloth and Gold*, pp. 101–3; Spufford, "Coinage," pp. 63–88; Van Dusye and Busscher, *Archives de la ville de Gand*, no. 552, p. 192: charter of January 18, 1434.

by engaging in debasements in his recently acquired and neighboring provinces of Namur, Holland-Zeeland, and Brabant, but also once in Flanders itself, at Ghent, in November 1428 (table 3). Yet he did keep his second promise (at least for silver) for more than thirty years, up to the final year of his reign, in 1466–67. In that year Philip resumed his long-dormant practice of debasements of both coinages, partly in reaction to the debasements of King Edward IV of England, in 1464–65.[62] But Philip's debasements were mild compared to those of his successors, Duke Charles the Bold and Archduke Maximilian, from 1467 to 1492, especially in the 1480s.[63]

In viewing the monetary history of late medieval western Europe, no one would contend that the Burgundian Low Countries were unique. Most, if not all, countries and principalities practiced very similar monetary policies, with the same observable links between warfare, coinage debasements, and seigniorage profits.[64] What does makes this study unique for this era is the documentation for those policies and their economic consequences: the fact that only the Burgundian Low Countries provide such complete archival evidence, especially in the exceptionally detailed mint accounts—with details for each coin denomination issued, brassage, seigniorage, total outs in both fine metal struck and money-account values of coin issued—reports of monetary officials, consumer prices, industrial data, to permit us to measure the causes, processes, and consequences of these monetary policies.[65]

[62] Edward IV reduced the silver contents of the sterling penny by 20.00 percent and the gold contents of the English noble by 25.93 percent, thus altering the mint-ratio in favor of gold. Duke Philip (d. June 15, 1467) reduced the silver content of the penny *groot* by 13.57 percent in May 1466 and his son, Duke Charles, did so by another 3.77 percent in October 1467. The value of gold coins and the gold *traite* rose from £15 0s. 0d. in 1454 to £15 18s. 4d. in October 1467, with an overall change in the mint ratio favoring silver. See the details in Munro, *Wool, Cloth, and Gold*, pp. 160–77, appendices B–K, pp. 190–211; Mayhew, "Monetary Background'; and n. 34, above.

[63] See p. 333 and nn. 57, 62, above.

[64] See n. 1, above. For the principal offenders, see Spufford, *Money and Its Use*, ch. 13, "The Scourge of Debasement," pp. 289–318, esp. table 5, p. 295, and graph 3 (on twelve currencies, 1252–1500), pp. 296–99. The two principal exceptions were England before Henry VIII's "Great Debasement" of 1542–52 and Spain (Castile), from 1497 to 1686. See n. 65, below. See also Mayhew, "Monetary Background," pp. 62–73; Munro, "Monetary Policies of Henry VIII," pp. 423–76; Ulloa, "Castilian Seigniorage," pp. 459–79; Motomura, "Best and Worst of Currencies," pp. 104–27; Motomura, "New Data," pp. 331–37; and the next note.

[65] See the tables and their sources, and the list of my publications in the bibliography, below. While similar documentation and archival sources can also be found for late medieval England, there are some significant differences: in particular, the Tower Mint accounts do not provide detailed evidence on coin denominations, brassage, and seigniorage. The more important difference is that, apart from Edward IV's monetary changes of 1464–65, which came after a half-century of monetary stability, England was one of the few exceptions in not otherwise pursuing the debasement monetary polices, as indicated in nn. 62, 64, above.

Table 1. The Flemish Silver Coinages: from 1300 to 1482

Table 1 A. The Flemish Silver Groot: Silver Contents and Values of a Kilogram of Silver 1300–1482

Silver Groot: Constant Nominal Value of 1d Groot Flemish

Date	Fineness in Argent-le-Roy in deniers	Fineness in Argent-le-Roy in grains	Fineness as a Percentage	Taille to Marc de Troyes	Grams Pure Silver in the Groot	Percentage Change of Silver in the d groot	Traite of Marc de Troyes in Shillings	Value of 1 kg Pure Silver in £ groot	Index 1351 = 100.00
1300-04-02	11	11.50	95.660%	59.133	3.7944		5.1513	1.0981	50.73
1331-08-08	10	12.00	87.500%	57.000	3.6006	-5.11%	5.4286	1.1572	53.46
1332-03-13	10	6.00	85.417%	57.500	3.4843	-3.23%	5.6098	1.1958	55.25
1335-05	10	6.00	85.417%	57.500	3.4843	0.00%	5.6098	1.1958	55.25
1337-05-25	9	0.00	75.000%	60.500	2.9077	-16.55%	6.7222	1.4330	66.20
1343-04-16	8	0.00	66.667%	66.000	2.3692	-18.52%	8.2500	1.7587	81.25
1344-01	8	0.00	66.667%	66.000	2.3692	0.00%	8.2500	1.7587	81.25
1344-08	8	0.00	66.667%	66.000	2.3692	0.00%	8.2500	1.7587	81.25
1345-09	8	0.00	66.667%	66.000	2.3692	0.00%	8.2500	1.7587	81.25
1346-01-20	7	16.00	63.889%	66.000	2.2705	-4.17%	8.6087	1.8351	84.78
1346-08	7	16.00	63.889%	66.000	2.2705	0.00%	8.6087	1.8351	84.78
1346-11-24	6	23.50	58.160%	66.000	2.0669	-8.97%	9.4567	2.0159	93.13
1351-05-28	6	12.00	54.167%	66.000	1.9250	-6.87%	10.1538	2.1645	100.00
1351-07	6	12.00	54.167%	66.000	1.9250	0.00%	10.1538	2.1645	100.00
1353-09-7	6	8.00	52.778%	67.500	1.8340	-4.73%	10.6579	2.2719	104.96
1354-12-20	6	4.00	51.389%	69.000	1.7469	-4.75%	11.1892	2.3852	110.20
1359-10-22	6	0.00	50.000%	70.000	1.6754	-4.09%	11.6667	2.4870	114.90
1361-12-04	6	0.00	50.000%	72.000	1.6289	-2.78%	12.0000	2.5580	118.18
1363-12-01	6	0.00	50.000%	78.000	1.5036	-7.69%	13.0000	2.7712	128.03

1365-04-12	8	0.00	66.667%	114.000	1.3717	-8.77%	14.2500	3.0377	140.34
1368-01-21	7	12.00	62.500%	114.000	1.2859	-6.25%	15.2000	3.2402	149.70
1369-04-21	7	4.00	59.722%	114.000	1.2288	-4.44%	15.9070	3.3909	156.66
1369-09-22	6	0.00	50.000%	100.000	1.1728	-4.56%	16.6667	3.5528	164.14
1373-06-18	6	12.00	54.167%	114.000	1.1145	-4.97%	17.5385	3.7387	172.73
1380-01-30	6	0.00	50.000%	116.000	1.0110	-9.28%	19.3333	4.1213	190.40
1383-09-12	5	18.00	47.917%	116.000	0.9689	-4.17%	20.1739	4.3005	198.68
1384-09-10	6	0.00	50.000%	100.000	1.1728	21.04%	16.6667	3.5528	164.14
1386-04-18	5	8.00	44.444%	102.000	1.0220	-12.85%	19.1250	4.0769	188.35
1386-10-29	5	6.00	43.750%	102.000	1.0061	-1.56%	19.4286	4.1416	191.34
1387-04-03	5	4.00	43.056%	119.000	0.8486	-15.65%	23.0323	4.9098	226.83
1388-10-01	4	20.00	40.278%	121.000	0.7808	-8.00%	25.0345	5.3366	246.55
1389-12-20	5	0.00	41.667%	96.000	1.0180	30.39%	19.2000	4.0929	189.09
1391-01-24	5	0.00	41.667%	97.000	1.0075	-1.03%	19.4000	4.1355	191.06
1393-06-20	5	0.00	41.667%	96.000	1.0180	1.04%	19.2000	4.0929	189.09
1407-04-30	5	0.00	41.667%	88.500	1.1043	8.47%	17.7000	3.7731	174.32
1407-07-07	5	0.00	41.667%	96.000	1.0180	-7.81%	19.2000	4.0929	189.09
1409-08-17	5	0.00	41.667%	82.667	1.1822	16.13%	16.5333	3.5244	162.83
1411-11	5	0.00	41.667%	82.667	1.1822	0.00%	16.5333	3.5244	162.83
1416-12-06	4	4.00	34.722%	85.000	0.9581	-18.95%	20.4000	4.3487	200.91
1418-06-12	5	0.00	41.667%	115.000	0.8498	-11.30%	23.0000	4.9029	226.52
1428-11-07	4	12.00	37.500%	117.500	0.7486	-11.91%	26.1111	5.5661	257.15
1433-10-12	6	0.00	50.000%	144.000	0.8144	8.80%	24.0000	5.1161	236.36
1464-08	6	0.00	50.000%	144.000	0.8144	0.00%	24.0000	5.1161	236.36
1466-05-23	5	0.00	41.667%	139.000	0.7031	-13.67%	27.8000	5.9261	273.79
1467-10-13	4	12.00	37.500%	130.000	0.6766	-3.77%	28.8889	6.1582	284.51
1474-12-10	4	0.00	33.333%	131.000	0.5968	-11.79%	32.7500	6.9813	322.54
1477-09-20	3	12.00	29.167%	131.000	0.5222	-12.50%	37.4286	7.9786	368.61
1482-07	3	3.00	26.042%	131.000	0.4663	-10.71%	41.9200	8.9361	412.85

Sources: See Sources for Tables and Figures

Table 1 B. Alterations of the Flemish Silver Coinages: 1384–1482
with Bullion Prices, Seigniorage and Brassage Fees

Date and names of the silver coins Double Groot Single Groot	Value in d. groot	Fineness Percent Argent-le-Roy	Percent Purity	Weight Taille	Weight in Grams	Grams Pure Silver	Traite of marc AR £ gr	Bullion Price £ gr	Seigniorage £ gr	Brassage £ gr
1384-07-16										
Double Groot	2.000	50.00%	0.4792	50.00	4.8951	2.3455	0.8333	0.7167	0.05000	0.06667
Groot	1.000	50.00%	0.4792	100.00	2.4475	1.1728	0.8333	0.7167	0.05000	0.06667
1386-10-29										
Double Groot	2.000	50.00%	0.4792	57.00	4.2939	2.0575	0.9500	0.8833	0.01042	0.05625
Groot	1.000	44.44%	0.4259	102.00	2.3995	1.0220	0.9563	0.8833	0.01667	0.05625
1387-04-03										
Double Groot	2.000	43.06%	0.4126	59.50	4.1135	1.6973	1.1517	1.0375	0.03507	0.07917
Groot	1.000	43.06%	0.4126	119.00	2.0567	0.8486	1.1517	1.0375	0.03507	0.07917
1388-10-01										
Double Groot	2.000	40.28%	0.3860	60.50	4.0455	1.5615	1.2566	1.1000	0.03333	0.12326
Groot	1.000	40.28%	0.3860	121.00	2.0228	0.7808	1.2566	1.1000	0.03333	0.12326
1389-12-20										
Double Groot	2.000	50.00%	0.4792	57.00	4.2939	2.0575	0.9500	0.8500	0.01667	0.08333
Groot	1.000	41.67%	0.3993	96.00	2.5495	1.0180	0.9600	0.8500	0.01667	0.09332

1391-01-24									
Double Groot	2.000	50.00%	0.4792	57.50	4.2566	2.0396	0.9583	0.8583	0.01667	0.08333
1393-08-24									
Double Groot	2.000	50.00%	0.4792	57.00	4.2939	2.0575	0.9500	0.8750	0.01667	0.05833
Groot	1.000	41.67%	0.3993	96.00	2.5495	1.0180	0.9600	0.8750	0.01667	0.06832
1409-08-17									
Double Groot	2.000	50.00%	0.4792	49.00	4.9950	2.3934	0.8167	0.7583	0.00833	0.05000
Groot	1.000	41.67%	0.3993	82.67	2.9607	1.1822	0.8266	0.7583	0.00833	0.05998
1416-12-06									
Double Groot	2.000	41.67%	0.3993	50.00	4.8951	1.9546	1.0000	0.8625	0.06667	0.07083
Groot	1.000	34.72%	0.3328	85.00	2.8794	0.9581	1.0208	0.8625	0.06667	0.09167
1418-06-12									
Double Groot	2.000	50.00%	0.4792	68.00	3.5993	1.7247	1.1333	1.0583	0.01667	0.05833
Groot	1.000	41.67%	0.3993	115.00	2.1283	0.8498	1.1500	1.0583	0.01667	0.07500
1428-11-07									
Double Groot	2.000	44.44%	0.4259	68.50	3.5730	1.5218	1.2840	1.2000	0.02500	0.05903
Groot	1.000	37.50%	0.3594	117.50	2.0830	0.7486	1.3056	1.2000	0.02917	0.07639
1433-10-12									
Double Groot	2.000	50.00%	0.4792	72.00	3.3993	1.6289	1.2000	1.1375	0.00833	0.05417
Groot	1.000	50.00%	0.4792	144.00	1.6997	0.8144	1.2000	1.1375	0.00833	0.05417

Table 1 B (continued)

Date and names of the silver coins	Value in d. groot	Fineness Percent Argent-le-Roy	Percent Purity	Weight Taille	Weight in Grams	Grams Pure Silver	Traite of marc AR £ gr	Bullion Price £ gr	Seigniorage £ gr	Brassage £ gr
1466-05-23										
Double Patard Double Groot	4.000	95.83%	0.9184	79.50	3.0787	2.8274	1.3826	1.3375	0.00625	0.03885
Double Groot or Patard	2.000	50.00%	0.4792	82.50	2.9667	1.4215	1.3750	1.3167	0.00625	0.05208
Groot	1.000	41.67%	0.3993	139.00	1.7608	0.7031	1.3893	1.3167	0.00625	0.06641
1467-10-13										
Double Patard Double Groot	4.000	91.67%	0.8785	77.50	3.1581	2.7743	1.4091	1.3667	0.00625	0.03617
Double Groot or Patard	2.000	50.00%	0.4792	84.50	2.8965	1.3879	1.4083	1.3500	0.00625	0.05208
Groot	1.000	37.50%	0.3594	130.00	1.8827	0.6766	1.4444	1.3458	0.00625	0.09236
1474-10-27										
Double Patard Double Groot	4.000	83.33%	0.7986	80.00	3.0594	2.4433	1.6000	1.5333	0.02500	0.04167
or Patard	2.000	41.67%	0.3993	80.00	3.0594	1.2216	1.6000	1.5167	0.02500	0.05833
Groot	1.000	33.33%	0.3194	131.00	1.8683	0.5968	1.6375	1.5167	0.02500	0.09583
1477-12-20										
Double Patard Double Groot	4.500	83.33%	0.7986	80.00	3.0594	2.4433	1.8000	1.7333	0.02500	0.04167
or Patard	2.250	41.67%	0.3993	80.00	3.0594	1.2216	1.8000	1.7167	0.02500	0.05833
Groot	1.000	29.17%	0.2795	131.00	1.8683	0.5222	1.8714	1.7167	0.02500	0.12969

1482-07-18									
Double Patard	5.000	83.33%	0.7986	80.00	3.0594	2.4433	2.0000	1.9406	0.01354	0.04583
Double Groot or Patard	2.500	41.67%	0.3993	80.00	3.0594	1.2216	2.0000	1.9198	0.01354	0.06667

Date and names of the silver coins	Total Mint Charges £ gr	SUM BP+MC = Traite £ gr	Seigniorage as % of Traite	Brassage as % of Traite	Bullion Price as % of Traite	Percent Change in Silver Content	Percent Change in the Traite
1384-07-16							
Double Groot	0.1167	0.8333	6.00%	8.00%	86.00%		
Groot	0.1167	0.8333	6.00%	8.00%	86.00%		
1386-10-29							
Double Groot	0.0667	0.9500	1.10%	5.92%	92.98%	-12.28%	14.00%
Groot	0.0729	0.9563	1.74%	5.88%	92.37%	-12.85%	14.75%
1387-04-03							
Double Groot	0.1142	1.1517	3.04%	6.87%	90.08%	-17.51%	21.24%
Groot	0.1142	1.1517	3.04%	6.87%	90.08%	-16.96%	20.44%
1388-10-01							
Double Groot	0.1566	1.2566	2.65%	9.81%	87.54%	-8.00%	9.10%
Groot	0.1566	1.2566	2.65%	9.81%	87.54%	-8.00%	9.10%
1389-12-20							
Double Groot	0.1000	0.9500	1.75%	8.77%	89.47%	31.76%	-24.40%
Groot	0.1100	0.9600	1.74%	9.72%	88.54%	30.39%	-23.60%

Table 1 B (continued)

Date and names of the silver coins	Total Mint Charges £ gr	SUM BP+MC = Traite £ gr	Seigniorage as % of Traite	Brassage as % of Traite	Bullion Price as % of Traite	Percent Change in Silver Content	Percent Change in the Traite
1391-01-24							
Double Groot	0.1000	0.9583	1.74%	8.70%	89.57%	-0.87%	0.88%
Groot	0.1100	0.9600	1.74%	9.72%	88.54%	0.00%	0.00%
1393-08-24							
Double Groot	0.0750	0.9500	1.75%	6.14%	92.11%	0.88%	-0.87%
Groot	0.0850	0.9600	1.74%	7.12%	91.15%	0.00%	0.00%
1409-08-17							
Double Groot	0.0583	0.8167	1.02%	6.12%	92.86%	16.33%	-14.04%
Groot	0.0683	0.8266	1.01%	7.26%	91.74%	16.13%	-13.89%
1416-12-06							
Double Groot	0.1375	1.0000	6.67%	7.08%	86.25%	-18.33%	22.45%
Groot	0.1583	1.0208	6.53%	8.98%	84.49%	-18.95%	23.49%
1418-06-12							
Double Groot	0.0750	1.1333	1.47%	5.15%	93.38%	-11.76%	13.33%
Groot	0.0917	1.1500	1.45%	6.52%	92.03%	-11.30%	12.65%
1428-11-07							
Double Groot	0.0840	1.2840	1.95%	4.60%	93.46%	-11.76%	13.30%
Groot	0.1056	1.3056	2.23%	5.85%	91.91%	-11.91%	13.53%

1433-10-12							
Double Groot	0.0625	1.2000	0.69%	4.51%	94.79%	7.03%	-6.54%
Groot	0.0625	1.2000	0.69%	4.51%	94.79%	8.80%	-8.09%
1466-05-23							
Double Patard	0.0451	1.3826	0.45%	2.81%	96.74%		14.58%
Double Groot or Patard	0.0583	1.3750	0.45%	3.79%	95.76%	-12.73%	15.78%
Groot	0.0727	1.3893	0.45%	4.78%	94.77%	-13.67%	
1467-10-13							
Double Patard	0.0424	1.4091	0.44%	2.57%	96.99%	-1.88%	1.92%
Double Groot or Patard	0.0583	1.4083	0.44%	3.70%	95.86%	-2.37%	2.42%
Groot	0.0986	1.4444	0.43%	6.39%	93.17%	-3.77%	3.97%
1474-10-27							
Double Patard	0.0667	1.6000	1.56%	2.60%	95.83%	-11.93%	13.55%
Double Groot or Patard	0.0833	1.6000	1.56%	3.65%	94.79%	-11.98%	13.61%
Groot	0.1208	1.6375	1.53%	5.85%	92.62%	-11.79%	13.37%
1477-12-20							
Double Patard	0.0667	1.8000	1.39%	2.31%	96.30%	0.00%	12.50%
Double Groot or Patard	0.0833	1.8000	1.39%	3.24%	95.37%	0.00%	12.50%
Groot	0.1547	1.8714	1.34%	6.93%	91.73%	-12.50%	14.28%
1482-07-18							
Double Patard	0.0594	2.0000	0.68%	2.29%	97.03%	0.00%	11.11%
Double Groot or Patard	0.0802	2.0000	0.68%	3.33%	95.99%	0.00%	11.11%
Groot	0.1760	2.0958	0.65%	7.75%	91.60%	-10.71%	12.00%

Table 2. Flemish Silver Coinage Changes and Price Changes, 1380–1482

Relationship between Coinage Debasement and the Money-of-Account Value of a Kilogram of Pure Silver, in Coin

$\Delta T \text{ (traite)} = [1/(1 - x)] - 1 \times x$ = percentage change in silver contents of 1d groot

Flemish Price Index: Mean of 1451–75 = 100 = 126.295 d groot Flemish

Date of coinage change	Year 1 Jan–31 Dec	Silver grams in 1d groot	% change in silver	Traite of Silver Marc AR in shillings groot	Value of 1 kg Pure Silver in £ groot 1 d groot	% change in value	Value of Flemish Basket in d groot Flemish	Flemish Price Index from 1350	% change
1380-1-30	1380	1.0110	-9.28%	19.333	4.121	10.23%	134.373	106.396	-0.46%
	1381	1.0110	0.00%	19.333	4.121	0.00%	133.718	105.878	-0.49%
	1382	1.0110	0.00%	19.333	4.121	0.00%	145.040	114.843	8.47%
1383-9-12	1383	0.9689	-4.17%	20.174	4.300	4.35%	143.218	113.400	-1.26%
1384-9-10	1384	1.1728	21.04%	16.667	3.553	-17.39%	154.314	122.185	7.75%
	1385	1.1728	0.00%	16.667	3.553	0.00%	176.381	139.658	14.30%
1386-4-18	1386	1.0220	-12.85%	19.125	4.077	14.75%	167.336	132.496	-5.13%
1386-10-29	1386	1.0061	-1.56%	19.429	4.142	1.59%	167.336	132.496	0.00%
1387-4-3	1387	0.8486	-15.65%	23.032	4.910	18.55%	169.142	133.926	1.08%
1388-10-1	1388	0.7808	-8.00%	25.035	5.337	8.69%	132.960	105.278	-21.39%
1389-12-20	1389	1.0180	30.39%	19.200	4.093	-23.31%	153.323	121.401	15.32%
	1390	1.0180	0.00%	19.200	4.093	0.00%	164.806	130.493	7.49%
1391-1-24	1391	1.0075	-1.03%	19.400	4.135	1.04%	134.037	106.130	-18.67%
	1392	1.0075	0.00%	19.400	4.135	0.00%	113.614	89.959	-15.24%
1393-6-20	1393	1.0180	1.04%	19.200	4.093	-1.03%	99.657	78.908	-12.28%
	1394	1.0180	0.00%	19.200	4.093	0.00%	110.844	87.766	11.23%
	1395	1.0180	0.00%	19.200	4.093	0.00%	100.768	79.788	-9.09%
	1396	1.0180	0.00%	19.200	4.093	0.00%	105.820	83.788	5.01%
	1397	1.0180	0.00%	19.200	4.093	0.00%	128.543	101.780	21.47%
	1398	1.0180	0.00%	19.200	4.093	0.00%	117.823	93.292	-8.34%

Date	Year								
	1399	1.0180	0.00%	19.200	4.093	0.00%	104.026	**82.368**	-11.71%
	1400	1.0180	0.00%	19.200	4.093	0.00%	110.824	**87.751**	6.54%
	1401	1.0180	0.00%	19.200	4.093	0.00%	113.341	**89.743**	2.27%
	1402	1.0180	0.00%	19.200	4.093	0.00%	116.456	**92.209**	2.75%
	1403	1.0180	0.00%	19.200	4.093	0.00%	122.507	**97.001**	5.20%
	1404	1.0180	0.00%	19.200	4.093	0.00%	102.946	**81.512**	-15.97%
	1405	1.0180	0.00%	19.200	4.093	0.00%	103.799	**82.188**	0.83%
	1406	1.0180	0.00%	19.200	4.093	0.00%	105.226	**83.318**	1.37%
1407-4-30	1407	1.1043	8.47%	19.200	4.093	0.00%	124.277	**98.402**	18.10%
1407-7-7	1407	1.0180	-7.81%	19.200	4.093	0.00%	124.277	**98.402**	0.00%
1409-8-17	1408	1.1822	16.13%	16.533	3.524	-13.89%	133.170	**105.444**	7.16%
	1409	1.1822	0.00%	16.533	3.524	0.00%	166.534	**131.861**	25.05%
	1410	1.1822	0.00%	16.533	3.524	0.00%	135.488	**107.279**	-18.64%
	1411	1.1822	0.00%	16.533	3.524	0.00%	100.492	**79.569**	-25.83%
	1412	1.1822	0.00%	16.533	3.524	0.00%	114.743	**90.853**	14.18%
	1413	1.1822	0.00%	16.533	3.524	0.00%	126.848	**100.438**	10.55%
	1414	1.1822	0.00%	16.533	3.524	0.00%	124.889	**98.887**	-1.54%
	1415	1.1822	0.00%	16.533	3.524	0.00%	134.880	**106.798**	8.00%
1416-12-6	1416	0.9581	-18.95%	20.400	4.349	23.39%	150.185	**118.916**	11.35%
	1417	0.9581	0.00%	20.400	4.349	0.00%	168.555	**133.461**	12.23%
1418-6-12	1418	0.8498	-11.30%	23.000	4.903	12.75%	116.493	**92.239**	-30.89%
	1419	0.8498	0.00%	23.000	4.903	0.00%	118.932	**94.170**	2.09%
	1420	0.8498	0.00%	23.000	4.903	0.00%	123.917	**98.118**	4.19%
	1421	0.8498	0.00%	23.000	4.903	0.00%	135.816	**107.538**	9.60%
	1422	0.8498	0.00%	23.000	4.903	0.00%	141.966	**112.408**	4.53%
	1423	0.8498	0.00%	23.000	4.903	0.00%	130.379	**103.234**	-8.16%
	1424	0.8498	0.00%	23.000	4.903	0.00%	149.826	**118.632**	14.92%
	1425	0.8498	0.00%	23.000	4.903	0.00%	150.416	**119.099**	0.39%
	1426	0.8498	0.00%	23.000	4.903	0.00%	135.544	**107.323**	-9.89%
	1427	0.8498	0.00%	23.000	4.903	0.00%	146.895	**116.311**	8.37%

Table 2 (*continued*)

Date of coinage change	Year 1 Jan–31 Dec	Silver grams in 1d groot	% change in silver	Traite of Silver Marc AR in shillings groot	Value of 1 kg Pure Silver in £ groot 1 d groot	% change in value	Value of Flemish Basket in d groot Flemish	Flemish Price Index from 1350	% change
1428-11-7	1428	0.7486	-11.91%	26.111	5.566	13.53%	141.851	112.317	-3.43%
	1429	0.7486	0.00%	26.111	5.566	0.00%	160.475	127.064	13.13%
	1430	0.7486	0.00%	26.111	5.566	0.00%	158.941	125.849	-0.96%
	1431	0.7486	0.00%	26.111	5.566	0.00%	155.796	123.359	-1.98%
	1432	0.7486	0.00%	26.111	5.566	0.00%	147.576	116.851	-5.28%
1433-10-12	1433	0.8144	8.80%	24.000	5.116	-8.09%	175.816	139.210	19.14%
	1434	0.8144	0.00%	24.000	5.116	0.00%	164.300	130.092	-6.55%
	1435	0.8144	0.00%	24.000	5.116	0.00%	136.456	108.046	-16.95%
	1436	0.8144	0.00%	24.000	5.116	0.00%	122.225	96.777	-10.43%
	1437	0.8144	0.00%	24.000	5.116	0.00%	140.259	111.057	14.76%
	1438	0.8144	0.00%	24.000	5.116	0.00%	234.974	186.052	67.53%
	1439	0.8144	0.00%	24.000	5.116	0.00%	241.337	191.090	2.71%
	1440	0.8144	0.00%	24.000	5.116	0.00%	146.317	115.854	-39.37%
	1441	0.8144	0.00%	24.000	5.116	0.00%	156.040	123.552	6.65%
	1442	0.8144	0.00%	24.000	5.116	0.00%	136.240	107.875	-12.69%
	1443	0.8144	0.00%	24.000	5.116	0.00%	178.214	141.109	30.81%
	1444	0.8144	0.00%	24.000	5.116	0.00%	126.467	100.136	-29.04%
	1445	0.8144	0.00%	24.000	5.116	0.00%	119.790	94.850	-5.28%
	1446	0.8144	0.00%	24.000	5.116	0.00%	144.775	114.632	20.86%
	1447	0.8144	0.00%	24.000	5.116	0.00%	160.241	126.879	10.68%
	1448	0.8144	0.00%	24.000	5.116	0.00%	142.056	112.479	-11.35%
	1449	0.8144	0.00%	24.000	5.116	0.00%	118.072	93.490	-16.88%
	1450	0.8144	0.00%	24.000	5.116	0.00%	129.378	102.441	9.57%
	1451	0.8144	0.00%	24.000	5.116	0.00%	124.475	98.559	-3.79%

Year	Event								
1452		0.8144	0.00%	24.000	5.116	0.00%	121.500	**96.203**	-2.39%
1453		0.8144	0.00%	24.000	5.116	0.00%	136.156	**107.808**	12.06%
1454		0.8144	0.00%	24.000	5.116	0.00%	133.161	**105.437**	-2.20%
1455		0.8144	0.00%	24.000	5.116	0.00%	121.880	**96.505**	-8.47%
1456		0.8144	0.00%	24.000	5.116	0.00%	149.444	**118.330**	22.62%
1457		0.8144	0.00%	24.000	5.116	0.00%	164.206	**130.018**	9.88%
1458		0.8144	0.00%	24.000	5.116	0.00%	150.723	**119.342**	-8.21%
1459		0.8144	0.00%	24.000	5.116	0.00%	132.542	**104.947**	-12.06%
1460		0.8144	0.00%	24.000	5.116	0.00%	147.310	**116.640**	11.14%
1461		0.8144	0.00%	24.000	5.116	0.00%	125.656	**99.494**	-14.70%
1462		0.8144	0.00%	24.000	5.116	0.00%	121.121	**95.903**	-3.61%
1463		0.8144	0.00%	24.000	5.116	0.00%	103.168	**81.688**	-14.82%
1464		0.8144	0.00%	24.000	5.116	0.00%	98.413	**77.923**	-4.61%
1465	1466-5-23	0.7031	-13.67%	27.800	5.926	15.83%	111.793	**88.518**	13.60%
1466		0.7031	0.00%	27.800	5.926	0.00%	121.154	**95.930**	8.37%
1467	1467-10-13	0.6766	-3.77%	32.750	6.158	3.92%	129.006	**102.146**	6.48%
1468		0.6766	0.00%	37.429	6.158	0.00%	121.436	**96.153**	-5.87%
1469		0.6766	0.00%	37.429	6.158	0.00%	121.243	**96.000**	-0.16%
1470		0.6766	0.00%	37.429	6.158	0.00%	116.661	**92.372**	-3.78%
1471		0.6766	0.00%	37.429	6.158	0.00%	125.794	**99.604**	7.83%
1472		0.6766	0.00%	37.429	6.158	0.00%	120.760	**95.617**	-4.00%
1473		0.6766	0.00%	37.429	6.158	0.00%	104.770	**82.957**	-13.24%
1474		0.6766	0.00%	37.429	6.158	0.00%	136.661	**108.208**	30.44%
1475	1474-12-10	0.5968	-11.79%	32.750	6.981	13.37%	118.337	**93.699**	-13.41%
1476		0.5968	0.00%	32.750	6.981	0.00%	116.659	**92.370**	-1.42%
1477	1477-9-20	0.5222	-12.50%	37.429	7.979	14.29%	124.747	**98.775**	6.93%
1478		0.5222	0.00%	37.429	7.979	0.00%	164.072	**129.911**	31.52%
1479		0.5222	0.00%	37.429	7.979	0.00%	188.593	**149.327**	14.95%
1480		0.5222	0.00%	37.429	7.979	0.00%	146.097	**115.679**	-22.53%
1481		0.5222	0.00%	37.429	7.979	0.00%	174.173	**137.910**	19.22%
1482	1482-7	0.4663	-10.71%	41.920	8.936	12.00%	244.926	**193.932**	40.62%

Table 3. Flemish Coinage Debasement: The Flemish Mint Ordinances of June 1418 and November 1428

Double Groot (Gros)	June 1418	November 1428
Value in money-of-account [a]	2d *groot* [or *gros* Flemish]	2d *groot* [or *gros* Flemish]
Fineness [b] in *argent-le-roy* (AR)	6 deniers AR = 50.0% fine = 47.92% pure	5 deniers 8 grains AR = 44.44% fine = 42.59% pure
Weight (Taille) [c] in grams	68 cut to the marc = 3.599 grams	68.5 cut to the marc = 3.573 grams
Fine silver content AR in g.	1.800 g.	1.588 g.
Pure silver content in g.	1.725 g.	1.522 g.
Traite per *marc* [d] *argent-le-roy*	68.0 x 2d = 136d = 22s 8d 6/12 0.5 5.333/12	68.5 x 2d = 137d = 25s 8d 6 mites 0.444

Division of the Traite Value per marc argent-le-roy	June 1418			November 1428		
	Value in groot Flemish	Number of coins	Percentage of the traite	Value in groot Flemish	Number of coins	Percentage of the traite
Brassage	1s 2d	7	5.15%	1s 2d 6m	7 1/8	4.62%
Seigniorage	4d	2	1.47%	6d 0m	3	1.95%
Total Mint Charges (of the above)	1s 6d	9	6.62%	1s 8d 6m	10 1/8	6.57%
Mint Price: for merchants' bullion	21s 2d	127	93.38%	24s 0d 0m	144	93.43%
Traite per Marc argent-le-roy	22s 8d	136	100.00%	25s 8d 6m	154 1/8	100.00%

[a] Values in money-of-account: 1 penny or 1d groot = 24 mites = 12d or 1s parisis
12d groot = 1s (sou, sol, schelling); 1 livre or pond (£1 pound) = 20 shillings = 240d (pence)

[b] Fineness: reckoned out of 12 deniers argent-le-roy, with 24 grains per denier: 23/24 or 95.833% pure

[c] Weight: reckoned in terms of the taille or number cut from the marc de Troyes of 8 onces: 244.753 g.

[d] Traite per marc: official value of coinage struck per marc argent le roy: T = taille * face value/fineness
fineness: (Fineness/12 deniers Argent-le-Roy)

Table 4. The Flemish Silver Coinage Debasement of November 1428 and its Aftermath

Year	Mint Outputs in Marcs argent le roy*	Mint Outputs Kilograms of pure silver	Percentage Change	Output in £ groot Flemish	Percentage Change	Seigniorage in £ groot Flemish	Percentage Change
1428	4,598.700	1,078.647		5,267.280		123	
1429	72,460.700	16,996.010	1475.68%	93,021.380	1666.02%	2,035	1554.47%
1430	34,992.400	8,207.638	-51.71%	45,065.400	-51.55%	1,316	-35.33%
1431	5,595.200	1,312.381	-84.01%	7,240.240	-83.93%	283	-78.50%
1432	104.300	24.464	-98.14%	135.140	-98.13%	55	-80.57%

* *Marc argent-le-roy* = 244.7529 grams commercially fine silver, at 23/24 or 95.833% purity, with 4.167% copper.

Figure 1. The Mint Outputs of England and Flanders
(Burgundian Low Countries: from 1420)

Gold and Silver Coinage Outputs expressed in terms of the value of a constant pound sterling (English value: 1351–1411), in quinquennial means, from 1346–50 to 1496–1500
Sources: see Sources for Tables and Figures

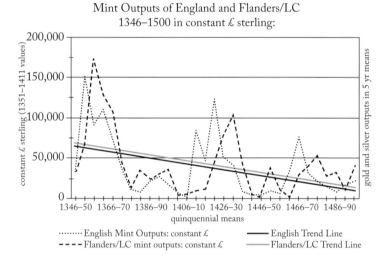

Mint Outputs of England and Flanders/LC
1346–1500 in constant £ sterling:

Figure 2. The Gold and Silver Mint Outputs of Flanders and Brabant,
in Current Pounds Groot of Flanders,
in Quinquennial Means, from 1336–40 to 1496–1500

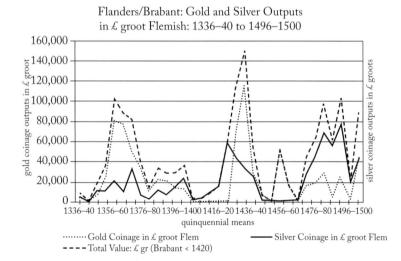

Flanders/Brabant: Gold and Silver Outputs
in £ groot Flemish: 1336–40 to 1496–1500

Figure 3. Flemish Commodity Price Indexes and the Composite Flemish
Price Index, in Quinquennial Means, from 1346–50 to 1496–1500,
with the Index Base: Mean of 1451–75 = 100

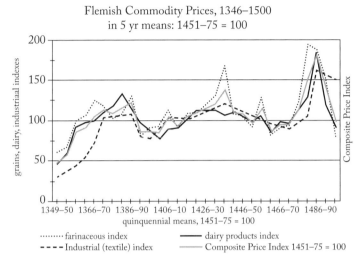

Flemish Commodity Prices, 1346–1500
in 5 yr means: 1451–75 = 100

Figure 4. The Relationship between Coinage Outputs and Prices
in Flanders and the Burgundian Low Countries,
in Quinquennial Means: from 1351–55 to 1496–1500

The value, in current pounds groot Flemish, of the combined gold and silver mint outputs
of Flanders (and the Burgundian Low Countries, from 1420) and the Flemish Composite
Price Index (base: mean of 1451–75 = 100)

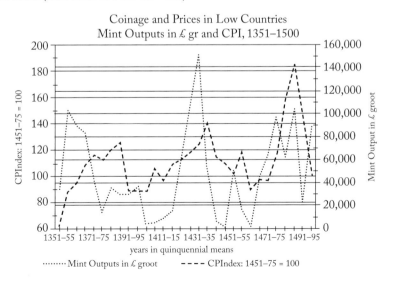

Coinage and Prices in Low Countries
Mint Outputs in £ gr and CPI, 1351–1500

Sources for Tables and Figures

Mint Outputs and Monetary Ordinances: 1350–1500 (Tables 1, 2, and 4)

See the archival and other sources (published documents) cited in John H. Munro, *Wool, Cloth and Gold: The Struggle for Bullion in Anglo-Burgundian Trade, 1340–1478,* Centre d'histoire économique et sociale (Brussels: Editions de l'Université de Bruxelles; Toronto: University of Toronto Press, 1973), appendix, tables B–K, pp. 190–213.

John H. Munro, "Wage-Stickiness, Monetary Changes, and Real Incomes in Late-Medieval England and the Low Countries, 1300–1500: Did Money Matter?" *Research in Economic History* 21 (2003): 185–297.

Prices and the Flemish Price Index (Table 3)

Stadsarchief Gent, Stadsrekeningen, 1350–51 to 1499–1500.

Charles Verlinden et al., eds., *Documents pour l'histoire des prix et des salaires en Flandre et en Brabant/Dokumenten voor de geschiedenis van prijzen en lonen in Vlaanderen en Brabant,* 4 vols. (Bruges: De Tempel, 1959–65).

John H. Munro, "Wage-Stickiness, Monetary Changes, and Real Incomes in Late-Medieval England and the Low Countries, 1300–1500: Did Money Matter?" *Research in Economic History* 21 (2003): 185–297.

John H. Munro, "Builders' Wages in Southern England and the Southern Low Countries, 1346–1500: A Comparative Study of Trends in and Levels of Real Incomes," in *L'Edilizia prima della rivoluzione industriale, secc. XIII–XVIII,* ed. Simonetta Cavaciocchi, Atti delle "Settimana di studi" e altri convegni 36 (Florence: Le Monnier, 2005), pp. 1013–76.

Prices and the English Price Index (Figures 1–4)

E. H. Phelps Brown and Sheila V. Hopkins, "Seven Centuries of the Prices of Consumables, Compared with Builders' Wage Rates," *Economica* 23, no. 92 (1956): 296–314. Reprinted in *Essays in Economic History,* ed. E. M. Carus-Wilson, 3 vols. (London: Edward Arnold, 1954–62), 2:168–78, 179–96; and in *Perspective of Wages and Prices,* by E. H. Phelps Brown and Sheila V. Hopkins (London: Methuen, 1981), pp. 13–39 (with price indexes not in the original).

Bibliography

Archival Sources

Belgium, Algemeen Rijksachief, Rekenkamer, register no. 1158.

Published Sources

Note: for all of the following publications that have been reprinted in Ashgate's Variorum Reprint series, Ashgate has presented them with the original pagination, while indicating each reprint by Roman numerals (as indicated in the following list).

Bigwood, Georges. *Le régime juridique et économique du commerce de l'argent dans la Belgique du Moyen Âge.* Academie royale de Belgique, Classe des lettres 14. 2 vols. Brussels: Académie royale de Belgique, 1921–22.

Bordo, Michael. "Moncy, Deflation, and Seigniorage in the Fifteenth Century." *Journal of Monetary Economics* 18 (1986): 337–46.

Borrelli de Serres, Léon Louis. *Les variations monétaires sous Philippe le Bel.* Chalon-sur-Saône: E. Bertrand, 1902.

Bowden, Peter. *The Wool Trade in Tudor and Stuart England.* London: Macmillan, 1962.

Boyer-Xambeu, Marie-Thérèse, Ghislain Deleplace, and Lucien Gillard. *Private Money and Public Currencies: The 16th Century Challenge.* London: M. E. Sharpe, 1994. First published as *Monnaie privée et pouvoir des princes: L'économie des relations monétaire à la Renaissance.* Trans. Azizeh Azodi. Paris: CNRS, 1986.

Bridrey, Émile. *La théorie de la monnaie au XIVe siècle: Nicole Oresme; Étude d'histoire des doctrines et des faits économiques.* Paris: Girard et Brière, 1906.

Calmette, Joseph. *The Golden Age of Burgundy: The Magnificent Dukes and Their Courts.* Trans. Doreen Weightman. New York: W. W. Norton, 1963. First published as *Les grands ducs de Bourgogne.* Paris: Albin Michel, 1949.

Cazelles, Raymond. "Quelques reflexions à propos des mutations monétaires de la monnaie royale française (1295–1360)." *Le Moyen Âge* 72 (1966): 83–105, 251–78.

Chalon, Renier. *Recherches sur les monnaies des comtes de Hainaut.* Brussels: Libraire scientifique et littéraire, 1848.

Cipolla, Carlo M. "Currency Depreciation in Medieval Europe." *Economic History Review,* 2nd ser., 15 (1963): 413–33. Reprinted [with minor alterations] in *Change in Medieval Society: Europe North of the Alps, 1050–1500,* ed. Sylvia Thrupp, pp. 227–36. New York: Appleton-Century-Crofts, 1964. Reprinted Toronto: University of Toronto Press, 1988.

Cross, Harry E. "South American Bullion Production and Export, 1550–1750." In *Precious Metals,* ed. Richards, pp. 397–423.

Dagboek van Gent van 1447 tot 1470, met een vervolg van 1477 tot 1515. Ed. Victor Fris. 2 vols. Ghent: Annoot Braeckman, 1901–4.

Day, John. "Colonialisme monétaire en Méditerranée au Moyen Âge." In *Actes du IIe colloque internationale d'histoire: Economies méditerranéennes: Équilibres et intercommunications, XIIIe–XIXe siècles,* pp. 305–19. Athens: Centre de recherches néohelléniques, 1985. Reprinted in translation as "Monetary Colonialism in the Medieval Mediterranean." In *Medieval Market Economy,* by Day, pp. 116–28.

———. "'Crise du Féodalisme' et conjoncture des prix à la fin du Moyen Âge." *Annales: Économies, sociétés, civilisations* 34 (1979): 305–18. Reprinted in translation as "Late

Medieval Price Movements and the 'Crisis of Feudalism.'" In *Medieval Market Economy*, by Day, pp. 90–107.

———, ed. *Études d'histoire monétaire, XIIᵉ–XIXᵉ siècles.* Lille: Université de Paris, 1984.

———. "The Fisher Equation and Medieval Monetary History." In *Problems of Medieval Coinage in the Iberian Area*, ed. Mario Gomes Marques, pp. 139–46. Santarém: Instituto Politécnico de Santarém, 1984. Reprinted in *Medieval Market Economy*, by Day, pp. 108–17.

———. *The Medieval Market Economy.* Oxford: Basil Blackwell, 1987.

———. "The Question of Monetary Contraction in Late Medieval Europe." In *Coinage and Monetary Circulation in the Baltic Area, c. 1350–c. 1500*, ed. Jørgen Steen Jensen. Special issue, *Nordisk Numismatisk Årsskrift: Nordic Numismatic Journal* (1981): 12–29. Reprinted in *Medieval Market Economy*, by Day, pp. 55–71.

Day, John, and Huguette Bertand. "Les frappes de monnaies en France et en Europe aux XIVᵉ–XVᵉ siècles." In *Rythmes de la production monétaire, de l'Antiquité à nos jours*, ed. Georges Depeyrot, Tony Hackens, and Ghislaine Moucharte, pp. 537–77. Ottignies: Université de Louvain-la-Neuve, 1987.

Deschamps de Pas, Louis. "Essai sur l'histoire monétaire des comtes de Flandre de la Maison de Bourgogne et description de leurs monnaies d'or et d'argent: Charles le Téméraire (1467–1477)." *Revue numismatique*, n.s., 7 (1862): 351–65.

———. "Essai sur l'histoire monétaire des comtes de Flandre de la Maison de Bourgogne et description de leurs monnaies d'or et d'argent: Jean Sans-Peur (1405–1419)." *Revue numismatique*, n.s., 6 (1861): 211–37.

———. "Essai sur l'histoire monétaire des comtes de Flandre de la Maison de Bourgogne et description de leurs monnaies d'or et d'argent: Marie (1477–1481)." *Revue numismatique*, n.s., 7 (1862): 460–80.

———. "Essai sur l'histoire monétaire des comtes de Flandre de la Maison de Bourgogne et description de leurs monnaies d'or et d'argent: Philippe le Bon (1419–1467); Première partie." *Revue numismatique*, n.s., 6 (1861): 458–78.

———. "Essai sur l'histoire monétaire des comtes de Flandre de la Maison de Bourgogne et description de leurs monnaies d'or et d'argent: Philippe le Bon (1419–1467); Suite." *Revue numismatique*, n.s., 7 (1862): 117–43.

———. "Essai sur l'histoire monétaire des comtes de Flandre de la Maison de Bourgogne et description de leurs monnaies d'or et d'argent: Philippe le Hardi (1384–1404)." *Revue numismatique*, n.s., 6 (1861): 106–39.

———. "Histoire monétaire des comtes de la Flandre de la maison d'Autriche et classement de leurs monnaies (1482–1556): Philippe-le-Beau (1482–1506)." *Revue numismatique*, n.s., 14 (1869–70): 86–114, 243–66, 319–34, 419–40; 15 (1874–77): 80–104, 151–63.

———. "Supplement à l'essai sur l'histoire monétaire des comtes de Flandre de la Maison de Bourgogne." *Revue numismatique*, n.s., 11 (1866): 172–219.

Feavearyear, Albert. *The Pound Sterling: A History of English Money.* 2nd ed. Revised E. V. Morgan. Oxford: Clarendon Press, 1963.

Fournial, Etienne. *Histoire monétaire de l'Occident médiéval.* Paris: F. Nathan, 1970.

Gaillard, Victor, ed. *Recherches sur les monnaies des comtes de Flandre.* Vol. 2, *Sous les règnes de Louis de Crécy et de Louis de Male.* Ghent: H. Hoste, 1856.

Gandal, Neil, and Nathan Sussman. "Asymmetric Information and Commodity Money: Tickling the Tolerance in Medieval France." *Journal of Money Credit and Banking* 29 (1997): 440–57.

Gilliodts–Van Severen, Louis, ed. *Cartulaire de l'ancienne estaple de Bruges*. 2 vols. Bruges: Louis de Plancke, 1904.

Girard, Albert. "La guerre des monnaies." *Revue de synthèse* 19 (1940–45): 83–101. Reissued as *Synthèse historique* 60 (1940–45): 83–101.

Glassman, Debra, and Angela Redish. "Currency Depreciation in Early Modern England and France." *Explorations in Economic History* 25 (1988): 75–97.

Graus, F. "La crise monétaire du XIVᵉ siècles." *Revue belge de philologie et d'histoire* 29 (1951): 445–54.

Grierson, Philip. "Coin Wear and the Frequency Table." *Numismatic Chronicle*, 7th ser., 3 (1963): i–xvi. Reprinted in *Later Medieval Numismatics*, by Grierson, no. XIX, pp. i–xvi.

———. *Later Medieval Numismatics (11th–16th Centuries): Selected Studies*. London: Variorum Reprints, 1979.

———. "Medieval Numismatics." In *Medieval Studies: An Introduction*, ed. James Powell, pp. 103–36. Syracuse: Syracuse University Press, 1976. Reprinted in *Later Medieval Numismatics*, by Grierson, no. I, pp. 103–36.

———. *Numismatics*. Oxford: Oxford University Press, 1975.

———. "Weight and Coinage." *Numismatic Chronicle*, 7th ser., 4 (1964): iii–xvii. Reprinted in *Later Medieval Numismatics*, by Grierson, no. XX, pp. iii–xvii.

Grunzweig, A. "Les incidences internationales des mutations monétaires de Philippe le Bel." *Le Moyen Âge* 59 (1953): 117–72.

Hamilton, Earl. *American Treasure and the Price Revolution in Spain, 1501–1650*. Cambridge, MA: Harvard University Press, 1934; Reprinted New York: Octagon Books, 1965.

———. *War and Prices in Spain, 1651–1800*. Cambridge, MA: Harvard University Press, 1947.

Johnson, Charles, ed. *The "De moneta" of Nicholas Oresme and English Mint Documents*. London: Thomas Nelson and Sons, 1956.

Landry, Adolphe. *Essai économique sur les mutations des monnaies dans l'ancienne France de Philippe le Bel à Charles VII*. Paris: Honoré Champion, 1910. Reprinted 1969.

Laurent, Henri. "Crise monétaire et difficultés économiques en Flandre aux XIVᵉ et XVᵉ siècles." *Annales d'histoire économique et sociale* 5 (1933): 156–60.

Lopez, Robert. *The Shape of Medieval Monetary History*. London: Variorum Reprints, 1986.

Lopez, Robert S., Harry A. Miskimin, and A. L. Udovitch. "England to Egypt, 1350–1500: Long-Term Trends and Long-Distance Trade." In *Studies in the Economic History of the Middle East: From the Rise of Islam to the Present Day*, ed. M. A. Cook, pp. 93–128. London: Oxford University Press, 1978. Reprinted in *Cash, Credit, and Crisis*, by Miskimin, no. VIII, 93–128.

Mayhew, Nicholas. "Numismatic Evidence and Falling Prices in the Fourteenth Century." *Economic History Review*, 2nd ser., 27 (1974): 1–15.

Miskimin, Harry. *Cash, Credit, and Crisis in Europe, 1300–1600*. London: Variorum Reprints, 1989.

———. *The Economy of Early Renaissance Europe, 1300–1460*. Englewood Cliffs, NJ: Prentice-Hall, 1969. Reprinted Cambridge: Cambridge University Press, 1977.

———. "The Enforcement of Gresham's Law." In *Credito, banche e investimenti, secoli XIII–XX: Atti della quarta Settimana di Studio (Prato, 14–21 aprile 1972)*, ed. Anna Vannani Marx, pp. 147–61. Florence: Le Monnier, 1985. Reprinted in *Cash, Credit, and Crisis in Europe*, by Miskimin, no. IX, pp. 147–61.

————. "Le problème de l'argent au Moyen Âge." *Annales: Économies, sociétés, civilisiations* 17 (1962): 1125–30. Reprinted in *Cash, Credit and Crisis*, by Miskimin, no. IV, pp. 1125–30.

————. "L'or, l'argent, et la guerre dans la France médiévale." *Annales: Économies, sociétés, civilisations* 40 (1985): 171–84. Reprinted in *Cash, Credit and Crisis*, by Miskimin, no. XII, pp. 171–84.

————. "Monetary Movements and Market Structures: Forces for Contraction in 14th and 15th Century England." *Journal of Economic History* 24 (1964): 470–90. Reprinted in *Cash, Credit, and Crisis*, by Miskimin, no. VII, pp. 470–90.

————. "Money, the Law, and Legal Tender." In *Rythmes de la production monétaire, de l'Antiquité à nos jours: Actes du Colloque international Paris, 10–12 janvier 1986*, ed. Georges Depeyrot and Tony Haeckens, pp. 697–705. Numismatica Lovaniensia 7 Louvain-la-Neuve: Séminaire de numismatique Marcel Hoc, 1987. Reprinted in *Cash, Credit, and Crisis*, by Miskimin, no. X, pp. 697–705.

————. "Money and Money Movements in France and England at the End of the Middle Ages." In *Precious Metals*, ed. Richards, pp. 79–96. Reprinted in *Cash, Credit, and Crisis*, by Miskimin, no. XI, pp. 79-96.

————. *Money and Power in Fifteenth-Century France.* New Haven, CT: Yale University Press, 1984.

————. *Money, Prices, and Foreign Exchange in Fourteenth-Century France.* New Haven, CT: Yale University Press, 1963.

Motomura, Akira. "The Best and Worst of Currencies: Seigniorage and Currency Policy in Spain, 1597–1650." *Journal of Economic History* 54 (1994): 104–27.

————. "New Data on Minting, Seigniorage, and the Money Supply in Spain (Castile), 1597–1643." *Explorations in Economic History* 34 (1997): 331–67.

Mueller, Reinhold. "Guerra monetaria tra Venezia e Milano nel quattrocento." In *La zecca di Milano: Atti del Convegno internazionale di studio Milano, 9–14 maggio 1983*, ed. Giovanni Gorini, pp. 341–55. Milan: Società numismatica italiana, 1984.

Munro, John H. "An Aspect of Medieval Public Finance: The Profits of Counterfeiting in the Fifteenth-Century Low Countries." *Revue belge de numismatique et de sigillographie* 118 (1972): 127–48. Reprinted in *Bullion Flows and Monetary Policies*, by Munro, no. II, pp. 127–48.

————. "Before and After the Black Death: Money, Prices, and Wages in Fourteenth-Century England." In *New Approaches to the History of Late Medieval and Early Modern Europe: Selected Proceedings of Two International Conferences at the Royal Danish Academy of Sciences and Letters in Copenhagen in 1997 and 1999*, ed. Troels Dahlerup and Per Ingesman, pp. 335–64. Copenhagen: Royal Danish Academy of Sciences and Letters, 2009.

————. "Billon—Billoen—Billio: From Bullion to Base Coinage." *Revue belge de philologie et d'histoire* 52 (1974): 293–305. Reprinted in *Bullion Flows and Monetary Policies*, by Munro, no. III, pp. 293–305.

————. "Builders' Wages in Southern England and the Southern Low Countries, 1346–1500: A Comparative Study of Trends in and Levels of Real Incomes." In *L'edilizia prima della rivoluzione industriale, secc. XIII–XVIII*, ed. Simonetta Cavaciocchi, pp. 1013–76. Atti delle "Settimana di studi" e altri convegni 36. Florence: Le Monnier, 2005.

————. "Bullion Flows and Monetary Contraction in Late-Medieval England and the

Low Countries." In *Precious Metals*, ed. Richards, pp. 97–158. Reprinted in *Bullion Flows and Monetary Policies*, by Munro, no. VI, pp. 97–158.

———. *Bullion Flows and Monetary Policies in England and the Low Countries, 1350–1500*. Variorum Collected Studies Series 355. Aldershot: Ashgate, 1992.

———. "Bullionism and the Bill of Exchange in England, 1272–1663: A Study in Monetary Management and Popular Prejudice." In *The Dawn of Modern Banking*, ed. Center for Medieval and Renaissance Studies, University of California, pp. 169–239. New Haven, CT: Yale University Press, 1979. Reprinted in *Bullion Flows*, by Munro, no. IV, pp. 169–239.

———. "The Central European Mining Boom, Mint Outputs, and Prices in the Low Countries and England, 1450–1550." In *Money, Coins, and Commerce: Essays in the Monetary History of Asia and Europe (From Antiquity to Modern Times)*, ed. Eddy H. G. Van Cauwenberghe, pp. 119–83. Leuven: Leuven University Press, 1991.

———. "The Coinages and Monetary Policies of Henry VIII (r. 1509–47)." In *The Collected Works of Erasmus: The Correspondence of Erasmus*. Vol. 14, *Letters 1926 to 2081, A.D. 1528*, trans and ed. Charles Fantazzi and James Estes, pp. 423–76. Toronto: University of Toronto Press, 2011.

———. "Deflation and the Petty Coinage Problem in the Late-Medieval Economy: The Case of Flanders, 1334–1484." *Explorations in Economic History* 25 (1988): 387–423. Reprinted in *Bullion Flows and Monetary Policies*, by Munro, no. VIII, pp. 387–423.

———. "An Economic Aspect of the Collapse of the Anglo-Burgundian Alliance, 1428–1442." *English Historical Review* 85 (1970): 225–44. Reprinted in *Bullion Flows and Monetary Policies*, by Munro, no. I, pp. 225–44.

———. "English 'Backwardness' and Financial Innovations in Commerce with the Low Countries, 14th to 16th Centuries." In *International Trade in the Low Countries (14th–16th Centuries): Merchants, Organisation, Infrastructure*, ed Peter Stabel, Bruno Blondé, and Anke Greve, pp. 105–67. Leuven-Apeldoorn: Garant, 2000.

———. "Gold, Guilds, and Government: The Impact of Monetary and Labour Policies on the Flemish Cloth Industry, 1390–1435." *Jaarboek voor middeleeuwse geschiedenis* 5 (2002): 153–205.

———. "Gresham's Law." In *The Oxford Encyclopedia of Economic History*, ed. Joek Mokyr et al., 2:480–81. 5 vols. Oxford: Oxford University Press, 2003.

———. "A Maze of Medieval Monetary Metrology: Determining Mint Weights in Flanders, France and England from the Economics of Counterfeiting, 1388–1469." *Journal of European Economic History* 29 (2000): 173–99.

———. "Mint Outputs, Money, and Prices in Late-Medieval England and the Low Countries." In *Münzprägung, Geldumlauf und Wechselkurse (Minting, Monetary Circulation and Exchange Rates)*, ed. Eddy Van Cauwenberghe and Fritz Irsigler, pp. 31–122. Trierer Historische Forschungen 7: Akten des 8th International Economic History Congress, Section C-7, Budapest 1982. Trier: Trier University Press, 1984.

———. "Mint Policies, Ratios, and Outputs in England and the Low Countries, 1335–1420: Some Reflections on New Data." *Numismatic Chronicle* 141 (1981): 71–116. [Formerly listed as 8th ser., 1]. Reprinted in *Bullion Flows and Monetary Policies*, by Munro, no. V, pp. 71–116.

———. "Monetary Contraction and Industrial Change in the Late-Medieval Low Countries, 1335–1500." In *Coinage in the Low Countries (800–1500): The Third Oxford Symposium on Coinage and Monetary History*, ed. Nicholas J. Mayhew, pp. 95–162.

British Archeological Reports, International Series, 54. Oxford: British Archaeological Reports, 1979.

———. "The Monetary Origins of the 'Price Revolution': South German Silver Mining, Merchant-Banking, and Venetian Commerce, 1470–1540." In *Global Connections and Monetary History, 1470–1800*, ed. Dennis Flynn, Arturo Giráldez, and Richard von Glahn, pp. 1–34. Brookfield, VT: Ashgate, 2003.

———. "Money and Coinage of the Age of Erasmus: An Historical and Analytical Glossary with Particular Reference to France, the Low Countries, England, the Rhineland and Italy." In *The Collected Works of Erasmus: The Correspondence of Erasmus*. Vol. 1, *Letters 1 to 151, A.D. 1484–1500*, ed. Roger Mynors, Douglas Thomson, and Wallace Ferguson, pp. 311–48. Toronto: University of Toronto Press, 1974.

———. "Money, Prices, Wages, and 'Profit Inflation' in Spain, the Southern Netherlands, and England during the Price Revolution Era: ca. 1520–ca. 1650." *História e economia: Revista interdisciplinar* 4 (2008): 13–71.

———. "Monnayage, monnaies de compte, et mutations monétaires au Brabant à la fin du Moyen Âge." In *Études d'histoire monétaire, XIIe–XIXe siècles*, ed. John Day, pp. 263–94. Lille: Presses universitaires de Lille, 1984. Reprinted in *Bullion Flows and Monetary Policies*, by Munro, no. VII, pp. 2653–94.

———. "Patterns of Trade, Money, and Credit." In *Handbook of European History in the Later Middle Ages, Renaissance and Reformation, 1400–1600*. Vol. 1, *Structures and Assertions*, ed. James Tracy, Thomas Brady Jr., and Heiko Oberman, pp. 147–95. Leiden: Brill, 1994.

———. "The Usury Doctrine and Urban Public Finances in Late-Medieval Flanders (1220–1550): *Rentes* (Annuities), Excise Taxes, and Income Transfers from the Poor to the Rich." In *La fiscalità nell'economia Europea, secc. XIII–XVIII (Fiscal Systems in the European Economy from the 13th to the 18th Centuries)*, ed. Simonetta Cavaciocchi, pp. 973–1026. Florence: Firenze University Press, 2008.

———. "Wage-Stickiness, Monetary Changes, and Real Incomes in Late-Medieval England and the Low Countries, 1300–1500: Did Money Matter?" *Research in Economic History* 21 (2003): 185–297.

———. *Wool, Cloth and Gold: The Struggle for Bullion in Anglo-Burgundian Trade, 1340–1478*. Centre d'histoire économique et sociale. Brussels: Editions de l'Université de Bruxelles, 1973.

Nicholas, David. *Medieval Flanders*. London: Longman, 1992.

Patterson, C. C. "Silver Stocks and Losses in Ancient and Medieval Times." *Economic History Review*, 2nd ser., 25 (1972): 205–35.

Phelps Brown, E. H., and Sheila V. Hopkins. *A Perspective of Wages and Prices*. London: Methuen, 1981.

———. "Seven Centuries of the Prices of Consumables, Compared with Builders' Wage Rates." *Economica* 23, no. 92 (1956): 296–314. Reprinted in *Essays in Economic History*, ed. E. M. Carus-Wilson, 2:168–78, 179–96. 3 vols. London: Edward Arnold, 1954–62; and in *Perspective of Wages and Prices*, by Phelps Brown and Hopkins, pp. 13–39 (with price indexes not in the original).

Richards, John F., ed. *Precious Metals in the Later Medieval and Early Modern Worlds*. Durham, NC: Carolina Academic Press, 1983.

Rolnick, Arthur J., and Warren E. Weber. "Gresham's Law or Gresham's Fallacy." *Journal of Political Economy* 94 (1986): 185–99.

Rolnick, Arthur J., François R. Velde, and Warren E. Weber. "The Debasement Puzzle: An Essay on Medieval Monetary History." *Journal of Economic History* 56 (1996): 789–808.

Rotuli parliamentorum ut et petitiones et placita in Parliamento. 6 vols. London, 1767–77.

Rymer, Thomas, ed. *Foedera, conventiones, literae, et cujuscunque generis acta publica.* 12 vols. London, 1709–12. Reprinted London: Public Record Office, 1816–69.

Sargent, Thomas, and Bruce D. Smith. "Coinage Debasements and Gresham's Laws." *Economic Theory* 10 (1997): 197–226.

Sargent, Thomas J., and François R. Velde. "The Big Problem of Small Change." *Journal of Money, Credit, and Banking* 31 (1999): 137–61.

———. *The Big Problem of Small Change.* Princeton, NJ: Princeton University Press, 2002.

Selgin, George. "Salvaging Gresham's Law: The Good, the Bad, and the Illegal." *Journal of Money, Credit, and Banking* 28 (1996): 637–49.

Spufford, Peter. "Coinage, Taxation, and the Estates General of the Burgundian Netherlands." *Anciens pays et assemblées d'états (Standen en Landen)* 40 (1966): 63–88.

———. *Monetary Problems and Policies in the Burgundian Netherlands, 1433–1496.* Leiden: Brill, 1970.

———. *Money and Its Use in Medieval Europe.* Cambridge: Cambridge University Press, 1988.

Sussman, Nathan. "Debasements, Royal Revenues, and Inflation in France during the Hundred Years' War, 1415–1422." *Journal of Economic History* 53 (1993): 44–70.

———. "The Late-Medieval Bullion Famine Reconsidered." *Journal of Economic History* 58 (1998): 126–54.

Sussman, Nathan, and Joseph Zeira. "Commodity Money Inflation: Theory and Evidence from France in 1350–1430." *Journal of Monetary Economics* 50 (2003): 1769–93.

TePaske, John T. "New World Silver, Castile and the Philippines, 1590–1800." In *Precious Metals*, ed. Richards, pp. 425–45.

Tomlins, T. E., et al., eds. *The Statutes of the Realm.* 6 vols. London: Record Commission, 1810–22.

Tye, Robert. *Early World Coins and Early Weight Standards.* York: Early World Coins, 2009.

Ulloa, Modesto. "Castilian Seigniorage and Coinage in the Reign of Philip II." *Journal of European Economic History* 4 (1975): 459–79.

Van der Wee, Herman. "Monetary Policy in the Duchy of Brabant, Late Middle Ages to Early Modern Times." In *Het geld zoekt zien weg: Van Lanschot-Lectures over acht eeuwen geldwezen, bankieren en kapitaalbeweging in de Midden-Nederlanden,* ed. H. Van den Eerenbeemt. 's-Hertogenbosch: F. van Lanschot Bankiers, 1987. Special issue, *Bijdgragen tot de geschiedenis van het Zuiden van Nederland* (1987): 37–58. Reprinted in *The Low Countries in the Early Modern World,* by Herman Van der Wee, pp. 167–82. London: Variorum, 1993.

Van Dusye, Prudent, and Edmond de Busscher, eds. *Inventaire analytique des chartes et documents appartenant aux archives de la ville de Gand.* Ghent: Annoot-Braeckman, 1867.

Van Werveke, Hans. "Currency Manipulation in the Middle Ages: The Case of Louis de Male, Count of Flanders." *Transactions of the Royal Historical Society,* 4th ser., 31 (1949): 115–27. Reprinted in *Miscellanea mediaevalia,* by Van Werveke, pp. 255–67.

———. "De economische en sociale gevolgen van de muntpolitiek der graven van Vlaanderen (1337–1433)." *Annales de la Société d'émulation de Bruges* 74 (1931): 1–15. Reprinted in *Miscellanea mediaevalia,* by Van Werveke, pp. 243–55.

———. *Miscellanea mediaevalia: Verspreide opstellen over economische en sociale geschiedenis van de middeleewuen.* Ghent: E. Story-Scientia, 1968.

Vaughan, Richard. *Charles the Bold: The Last Valois Duke of Burgundy.* London: Longmans, Green, 1973.

———. *John the Fearless: The Growth of Burgundian Power.* London: Longmans, Green, 1966.

———. *Philip the Bold: The Formation of the Burgundian State.* London: Longmans, Green, 1962.

———. *Philip the Good: The Apogee of Burgundy.* London: Longmans, Green, 1970.

Velde, François R., Warren E. Weber, and Randall Wright. "A Model of Commodity Money, with Applications to Gresham's Law and the Debasement Puzzle." *Review of Economic Dynamics* 2 (1999): 291–333.

Verlinden, Charles, et al., eds. *Documents pour l'histoire des prix et des salaires en Flandre et en Brabant/Dokumenten voor de geschiedenis van prijzen en lonen in Vlaanderen en Brabant.* 4 vols. Bruges: De Tempel, 1959–65.

Contributors

Bernard S. Bachrach, Professor of History at the University of Minnesota, Minneapolis, earned his AB degree at Queens College, CUNY, in history and classical languages and his MA and PhD degrees at the University of California, Berkeley, in medieval history with supporting fields in Roman history, archaeology, and art history. He was elected a Fellow of the Medieval Academy of America in 1985 and is a co-founder of the Haskins Society and of the American Society for Medieval Military History (*De re Militari*). He is co-founder and co-editor of the journal *Medieval Prosopography* and founder and editor emeritus of the *Journal of Medieval Military History*. Among his almost four hundred publications are eighteen books, mostly on early medieval military history. His monographs include *Merovingian Military Organization 481–751* (1972), *A History of the Alans in the West* (1973), *Early Medieval Jewish Policy in Western Europe* (1977), *Fulk Nerra—the Neo Roman Consul* (1993), *The Anatomy of a Little War* (1994), *Early Carolinglian Warfare* (2002), and *The Mystic Mind* (2004) co-authored with Dr. Jerome Kroll.

David S. Bachrach is Associate Professor of medieval history at the University of New Hampshire. His research focuses on the military and institutional history of thirteenth-century England and on the institutional, military, and economic history of the German kingdom in the tenth and eleventh centuries. His publications include *Religion and the Conduct of War c. 300–c. 1215* (2003) and (with Bernard S. Bachrach) *The "Gesta Tancredi" of Ralph of Caen: A History of the Normans on the First Crusade* (2005).

Jan Dumolyn is a lecturer in medieval history in the Department of History at Ghent University, where he is also vice-president of the Einhard Research

Institute for Medieval Studies. His fields of interest include the social, political, and cultural history of the late medieval county of Flanders and the city of Bruges in particular, and the interdisciplinary relationship of medieval history and the social sciences. He is the author of three monographs: *De Brugse opstand van 1436–1438* (1997), *De Raad van Vlaanderen en de Rekenkamer van Rijsel* (2002), and *Staatsvorming en vorstelijke ambtenaren in het graafschap Vlaanderen (1419–1477)* (2003). He has also published over fifty scholarly articles in journals including *The Journal of Interdisciplinary History*, *The Journal of Medieval History*, *Urban History*, *History*, *The Journal of the Historical Association*, *The Journal of Social History*, *Revue Historique*, *Revue du Nord*, and *Le Moyen Age*.

Caroline Dunn is Assistant Professor of History at Clemson University, where she teaches courses in medieval social and political history. She earned her doctorate from Fordham University in New York, where, under the supervision of Maryanne Kowaleski, she completed a thesis entitled *Damsels in Distress or Partners in Crime? The Abduction of Women in Medieval England*. The Northeastern Association of Graduate Schools awarded her their 2009 doctoral dissertation award for that work, which she is now revising into a monograph that will consider rape, abduction, and adultery in medieval England. Her article "Forfeiting the Marriage Portion: Punishing Female Adultery in the Secular Courts of England and Italy" is forthcoming in *Regional Variations of Matrimonial Law and Custom in Europe, 1150–1600*, edited by Mia Korpiola.

Jelle Haemers is postdoctoral research fellow at the department of Medieval History at the Ghent University and collaborator on the IAP project "City and Society in the Low Countries, 1100–1800" (Federal Science Policy of Belgium). His main fields of research are the social history of medieval politics and the urban history of the Low Countries. He is the editor (with Céline Van Hoorebeeck and Hanno Wijsman) of *Entre la ville, la noblesse et l'Etat: Philippe de Clèves (1456–1528), homme politique et bibliophile* (2007) and author of *De Gentse opstand (1449–1453): De strijd tussen rivaliserende netwerken om het stedelijke hapitaal* (2004), and *For the Common Good: State Power and Urban Revolts in the Reign of Mary of Burgundy, 1477–1482* (2009).

John H. A. Munro received his BA from the University of British Columbia and his MA and PhD, both in history, from Yale University. In 1964 he returned to the University of British Columbia with a joint appointment in the Departments of History and Economics. In 1968 he joined the Department of Economics at the University of Toronto. Although he was subjected to mandatory retirement in 2003, he continues to be active in teaching (at Toronto), archival research, conferences, and publications. His research interests focus on monetary, financial, industrial (textiles), and labor history in the later medieval Low Countries and England. His major publications are *Wool, Cloth and Gold: The Struggle for Bullion in Anglo-Burgundian Trade, ca. 1340–1478* (1973), *Bullion Flows and Monetary Policies in England and the Low Countries, 1350–1500* (1992), and *Textiles, Towns, and Trade: Essays in the Economic History of Late-Medieval England and the Low Countries* (1994). He has also published ninety-two journal articles and essays. He is a Foreign Member of the Koninklijke Vlaamse Academie van België voor Wetenschappen en Kunsten (Royal Flemish Academy of Belgium for Science and the Arts).

James M. Murray is Professor of History and director of the Medieval Institute at Western Michigan University. After study at the University of Ghent, he finished his PhD under Robert Lerner at Northwestern University and spent more than two decades on the faculty of the University of Cincinnati. He has written on urban and economic history, especially that of Bruges in the late Middle Ages. His monograph on that subject is *Bruges, Cradle of Capitalism, 1280–1390*, which was issued in paperback by Cambridge University Press in 2009. He has also written on the history of medieval business, notaries and documents, and the history of finance. His work has been supported by grants from the Belgian-American Educational Foundation, the American Council of Learned Societies, the Fulbright program, and the National Endowment for the Humanities.

Anthony Musson is Professor of Legal History and co-director of the Institute for Legal History Research at the University of Exeter. He studied at King's College, Cambridge and is a Barrister of the Middle Temple. From 2003 to 2006 he was Visiting Senior Research Fellow at the Institute of Advanced Legal Studies, University of London. He has published several books on the administration of justice, notably *Public Order and Law Enforcement* (1996), (with Mark Ormrod) *The Evolution of English Justice* (1999), and *Medieval Law in Context* (2001). His recent research projects have explored visual representations of law and justice (funded by the British Academy) and the private lives of medieval and early Tudor lawyers (funded by the Economic and Social Research Council, United Kingdom). His latest book, (with Edward Powell) *Crime, Law and Society in the Later Middle Ages* (2009), provides translations and commentary on texts drawn from the abundant unpublished medieval legal records.

David Nicholas is Kathryn and Calhoun Lemon Professor Emeritus of History at Clemson University. After beginning his career, under Bryce Lyon's inspiration, as a historian of the Flemish cities in the fourteenth century, he has more recently studied broader patterns of comparative urbanization, law, and institutions. Professor Nicholas has written numerous book chapters and articles in such journals as *The American Historical Review, The English Historical Review, Revue Belge de Philologie et d'Histoire, Past and Present,* and *Annales. Économies. Sociétés. Civilisations.* He is the author or editor of sixteen books, including *Town and Countryside: Social, Economic, and Political Tensions in Fourteenth-Century Flanders* (1971), *The Domestic Life of a Medieval City: Women, Children, and the Family in Fourteenth-Century Ghent* (1985), *The Metamorphosis of a Medieval City: Ghent in the Age of the Arteveldes, 1302–1390* (1987), *Medieval Flanders* (1992), *The Growth of the Medieval City: From Late Antiquity to the Early Fourteenth Century* (1997), *The Later Medieval City 1300–1500* (1997), *Urban Europe, 1100–1700* (2003), and *The Northern Lands: Germanic Europe, c. 1270–c. 1500* (2009).

W. Mark Ormrod has been Professor of Medieval History at the University of York since 1995. Educated at the universities of London and Oxford, he is a specialist in later medieval English government, politics, and political culture. He is the author of *The Reign of Edward III: Crown and Political Society in England, 1327–1377* (1990), *Political Life in Medieval England, 1300–1450* (1995), (with Anthony Musson) *The Evolution of English Justice: Law, Politics and Society in the Fourteenth Century* (1999), and *Edward III* (2011) for the Yale University Press "English Monarchs" series. He edited the 1337–77 section of the Scholarly Digital Edition of *The Parliament Rolls of Medieval England* (2005) and directed the major project to calendar and digitize the contents of the "Ancient Petitions" in the National Archives, London. A regular contributor to leading journals, he has edited numerous essay collections, most recently (with Gwilym Dodd and Anthony Musson) *Medieval Petitions: Grace and Grievance* (2009). He is currently writing a book on English state finance in the period of the Hundred Years' War.

Walter Prevenier studied at the University of Ghent and did postgraduate work at the École des Chartes and the Law School of the Sorbonne (Canon Law) at Paris. He was Professor of History at the University of Ghent and Brussels from 1965 to 1999 and is now Professor Emeritus. He has been Visiting Professor at the Universities of Utrecht, California at Berkeley, Rutgers, Philadelphia, Columbia, William and Mary, Princeton, and UCLA. His early works concerned representative institutions in late medieval Flanders and paleography and diplomatics. More recently he has specialized in the social and cultural history of the Burgundian Netherlands, historiography, and the methodology of history and the social sciences. In addition to countless scholarly articles and text editions of the transactions of the Four Members of Flanders and charters of the Flemish counts, he has published (with W. Blockmans) *The Burgundian Netherlands* (1985), (with W.

Blockmans) *The Promised Lands: The Low Countries under Burgundian Rule, 1369–1530* (1999), and (with Martha Howell) *From Reliable Sources: An Introduction to Historical Methods* (2001).

Jeff Rider is a professor of Romance Languages and Literatures and Medieval Studies at Wesleyan University. His work focuses on the history and literature of northern Europe from the eleventh through the thirteenth centuries. He is the editor of Galbert of Bruges's *De multro, traditione et occisione gloriosi Karoli comitis Flandriarum*, Corpus Christianorum, Continuatio Medievalis 131 (1994) and Walter of Thérouanne's *"Vita Karoli comitis Flandri" et "Vita domni Ioannis Morinensis episcopi,"* Corpus Christianorum, Continuatio Medievalis 217 (2006). His publications include *God's Scribe: The Historiographical Art of Galbert of Bruges* (2001) and *Galbert of Bruges and the Historiography of Medieval Flanders* (2009), which he co-edited with Alan V. Murray. He is currently at work on English translations of Galbert of Bruges's *De multro, traditione et occisione gloriosi Karoli comitis Flandriarum* and Walter of Thérouanne's *Vita Karoli comitis Flandrie*. His work has been aided by grants from the National Endowment for the Humanities, the Fulbright Commission, the American Philosophical Society, and the Rotary Foundation.

Don C. Skemer has been Curator of Manuscripts in the Department of Rare Books and Special Collections, Princeton University Library, since 1991. He is the author of *Binding Words: Textual Amulets in the Middle Ages*, Magic in History (2006) and many articles in scholarly journals and annuals, such as *Viator*, *Miscellanea Marciana*, *Gutenberg Jahrbuch*, *Bibliofilía*, *Traditio*, *Scrittura e civiltà*, *Scriptorium*, *Gazette du livre médiéval*, *English Manuscript Studies*, *Historical Research*, *Journal of the Society of Archivists*, *Revue belge de philologie et d'histoire*, and the *Princeton University Library Chronicle*. He is a contributor to *Greek Manuscripts at Princeton, Sixth-Nineteenth Century: A Descriptive Catalogue* (Princeton University Department of Art and Archeology and the Program in Hellenic Studies, in association with Princeton University Press, 2009) and editor of *Medieval and Renaissance Manuscripts in the Princeton University Library* (2 volumes, forthcoming). He received his PhD in medieval history from Brown University, where he studied with Bryce Lyon, and holds an MLS from Columbia University. His particular research interests are the history of the medieval book, manuscript studies, and magic.

Marci Sortor is Provost and Dean of the College of St. Olaf College. Prior to taking up the position of provost at St. Olaf in 2011, she served as Professor of History and Vice-President for Institutional Planning at Grinnell College. She has written on immigration, proto-industrialization and the market networks of cities in fourteenth- and fifteenth-century Flanders and northern France. Her publications include "The Business of Business in the Middle Ages," *Journal of Urban History* 34:4 (2008); "The Measure of Success: Evidence for Immigrant Networks in the Southern Low Countries, Saint-Omer 1413-1455," *Journal of Family History* 30:2 (2005); "The Ieperleet Affair," *Speculum* 73:4 (1998); "Saint-Omer and Its Textile Trades in the Late Middle Ages: A Contribution to the Proto-Industrialization Debate," *American Historical Review* 98:4 (1993); and she co-edited with Stanley Chodorow the fourth and fifth editions of *The Other Side of Western Civilization*, vol. 1 (Harcourt Brace).

R. C. Van Caenegem studied law and history at the University of Ghent under the supervision of F. L. Ganshof, becoming doctor in both disciplines in 1951 and 1953 respectively. He also studied at the Law Faculty in Paris and the London School of Economics, where T. F. T. Plucknett supervised his research. He was Professor of both medieval and legal history at Ghent until his retirement in 1992. His books include works on the general history of England and on the birth of the common law, on the history of European private and public law, and on the sources of medieval history. His editions of documents include volumes on royal writs and lawsuits in England through the period of Richard I in the Selden Society Publications, and of Flemish appeals to the Parlement of Paris (1320–1453) through the Commission of Ancient Laws and Ordinances of Belgium. His work has been translated into several European and Asian languages. He is a fellow of several academies and lectured in numerous universities in Europe, America, and Australia, including three visiting professorships at the University of Cambridge and Harvard University. He received honorary degrees from the Universities of Tübingen, Leuven, and Paris.

Index

Typeset in 10/13 Adobe Caslon Pro
Composed by Tom Krol
Manufactured by Thomson-Shore, Inc.

Medieval Institute Publications
College of Arts and Sciences
Western Michigan University
1903 W. Michigan Avenue
Kalamazoo, MI 49008-5432
http://www.wmich.edu/medieval/mip

 WESTERN MICHIGAN UNIVERSITY